AIDA Europe Research Series on Insurance Law and Regulation

Volume 9

The AIDA Europe Research Series on Insurance Law and Regulation is the first book series of its kind and area of specialization. It comprises volumes on topics researched and written with an international, comparative or European perspective.

The regulatory response to the financial crisis in 2008 has pushed towards the adoption of transnational principles and rules also in the field of insurance by encouraging the convergence of national regulations to common regulatory framework. The need for a common legal language emerges to fully understand the process of transnational convergence in place and its impact on national legislation. On the other hand, persisting national peculiarities must be examined in the light of the transnational convergence of rules and concepts. Moreover, new risks, business practices and customers' issues are emerging worldwide, so requiring increasingly global responses.

The scope of the series is to bring together academics, practitioners and policy makers in order to exchange views and approaches to the topics concerned, which are based on the new transnational dimension of insurance law, business and regulation. All contributions are peer reviewed.

Katarzyna Malinowska • Dorota Maśniak
Editors

Managing Environmental Risks through Insurance

Legal and Economic Aspects

Springer

Editors
Katarzyna Malinowska
College of Law
Kozminski University
Warsaw, Poland

Dorota Maśniak
University of Gdansk
Gdańsk, Poland

ISSN 2662-1770 ISSN 2662-1789 (electronic)
AIDA Europe Research Series on Insurance Law and Regulation
ISBN 978-3-031-47601-3 ISBN 978-3-031-47602-0 (eBook)
https://doi.org/10.1007/978-3-031-47602-0

This Springer imprint is published by the registered company Springer Nature Switzerland AG
The registered company address is: Gewerbestrasse 11, 6330 Cham, Switzerland

Paper in this product is recyclable.

Contents

Law and Environment. Prevention, Control, Responsibility

Zdzisław Brodecki

Abstract The future of our planet depends primarily on technological and technical security in the IT and AI sectors. Awareness of the transition from cultural life (parallel civilisations, Life 2.0) to technological life (global civilisation, Life 3.0) is still negligible. Those who have struck out to be aware of the present are necessarily alone in their views. The state of collective unconsciousness results in a lack of appropriate response to all kinds of dangers that threaten humanity. Today, the idea of 'Sustainable Development' is in the spotlight. Sustainable development is shaping environmental consciousness with a significant impact on ethics, politics and law. At the core of this noble idea is the 'Golden Rule', which for centuries has committed to a balance between ethical values (humanity and justice) and praxeological values (efficiency as a synthesis of lawfulness and rationality) in the context of technology, governance and law. What seems urgent today is, taking the above into account, the need to create a system of effective international control. The power of the law also depends on the responsibility incumbent on the individual or collective. In environmental protection, preventive liability is leading the way, permeating the international responsibility of states and civil, criminal and administrative, tortfeasors' liability. The low level of legal culture means that it is still not appreciated in the practice of international, regional and national relations. In the real world, what counts above all is compensation liability, the effectiveness of which is ensured by insurance and public compensation funds. They ensure that risks are spread across a wide variety of actors and that the game is played in many arenas. The objective of the chapter is to present the idea of the evolution of the civilisation in the context of the rules of law, technology and their impact on environment and human future in that context. It begins with the dawn of the civilisation, goes through the first industrial revolution, the second scientific and technological revolution and finally reaches the analysis of the third—information revolution.

Z. Brodecki (✉)
University of Business and Administration in Gdynia, Gdynia, Poland

Gdynia, Poland
e-mail: katarzynamalinowska@kozminski.edu.pl

K. Malinowska, D. Maśniak (eds.), *Managing Environmental Risks through Insurance*, AIDA Europe Research Series on Insurance Law and Regulation 9,
https://doi.org/10.1007/978-3-031-47602-0_1

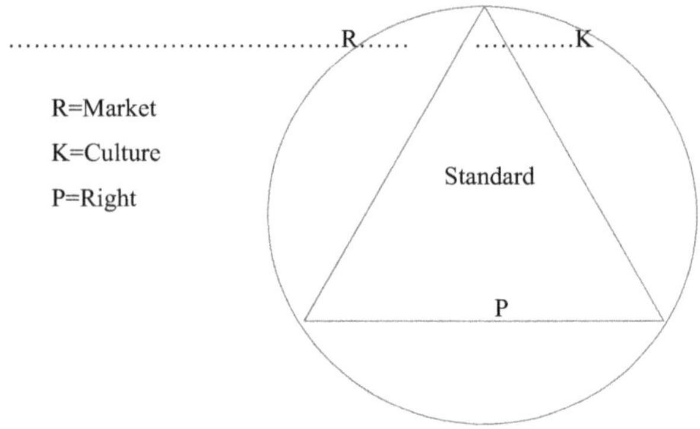

Fig. 1 The rule of law (source: author)

1 Preliminary Assumptions: First, Civilisation

Ten thousand years on, we are witnessing a breakthrough of civilisation on an unprecedented scale. Its first manifestations could be seen as early as the beginning of the twentieth century during the European conflict, the origins of which lay in the unconscious of people and nations.[1] 2D Q Awareness of the transition from cultural life (parallel civilisations, Life 2.0) to technological life (global civilisation, Life 3.0)[2] is still negligible. Those who have struck out to be aware of the present are necessarily alone in their views. The state of collective unconsciousness results in a lack of appropriate response to all kinds of dangers that threaten humanity. The governments of most countries still think in terms of the 'here and now'.

The slogan 'Law and Development', deeply rooted in the consciousness of the reformers of the global legal and economic order, is still relevant. In the first phase of the development of this doctrine, economic strategies predominated. Nowadays, increasing importance is attached to the 'rule of law', to instrumental *thinking* and rights *thinking*. The contemporary version of *The Rule of Law* does not so much serve development as it is at its core! Moving from opposition to mainstream consideration requires looking at law through the lens of the market (economics, management) and culture (anthropology, sociology and psychology). Through this perspective, the letter of the law becomes the norm (see Fig. 1).

Today, the idea of 'Sustainable Development' is in the spotlight. Sustainable development is shaping environmental consciousness with a significant impact on ethics, politics and law.[3] At the core of this noble idea is the 'Golden Rule', which for centuries has committed to a balance between ethical values (humanity and justice) and praxeological values (efficiency as a synthesis of lawfulness and rationality) in the context of technology, governance and law. This thought is illustrated

[1] Jung (2017), pp. 43–58.

[2] Tegmark (2019), pp. 37–70.

[3] See Pyć (2006), passim.

Table 1 Matrix of the code of the legal culture (source: author)

	Humanitarianism	Effectiveness	Justice
Technology	Personality algorithms and neural networks	Rationality and efficiency of the computer programme	Judgement
Management	The limits of creativity	Security	Distribution of common property
Law	Procedural dignity	Procedural rationality	Procedural fairness

by the 'mother frame' of the legal culture code, with security at its centre. Table 1 is a version of it adapted to the 'era of artificial intelligence':

Since contemporary environmental challenges have a global dimension, it is necessary to make skilful use of the research methods of comparative legal cultures when working on a sustainable development strategy. These methods focus on the analysis of the structure of legal systems (*comparative nomoscopy*), and the development of law (*comparative nomogenetics*).[4] Behind these methods is a metaphysics of jurisprudence, a feature of which is reasoning 'from law to philosophy' (in the *common law* system) or 'from philosophy to law' (in the European continental system). Thanks to this metaphysics, there is an opportunity to create a '*Droit commune de l'humanite*', the subject of which is the unity of man and the environment (a traditional approach, typical especially of Eastern philosophy) and the 'brain-computer interface' (an innovative approach, closely linked to the digitalisation and autonomisation of public life).

At the dawn of a new era in the history of humanity, we observe synergies in the context of civilisation (forms of dialogue in the spirit of universalism), capabilities (situations in which states limit their sovereignty based on the principle of *pacta sunt servanda* and act in good faith) and '*Legal-Tech*' (IT, AI). The tendency to merge legal cultures under the influence of automated expert systems is rarely appreciated. The development of legal engineering (combining law and IT into a single entity, i.e. *Ius-Net*) will certainly lead to the enrichment of codes and other laws of cyberspace with artificial intelligence, i.e. a 'synergistic mind'. It is already worth appreciating the virtues of the theory of an integrated legal order, which includes binary code (a way for computers to understand the language of humans) and source code (a way for humans to understand the language of computers). This theory is symbolised by the pyramid.

At the top in the hierarchy of sources of an integrated legal order the PRINCIPLES must be placed. They lay at the foundation of the *ius gentium* and today have the character of *ius cogens*. They are the ones that determine the axiology of modern law and the recognition of so-called failed states as those that do not adhere to the 'general principles recognised by civilised nations'.

The overshadowing of the RULE is the result of the declining validity of international agreements that bind only 'States Parties'. Moreover, questioning that

[4]Brodecki (2010), pp. 15–24.

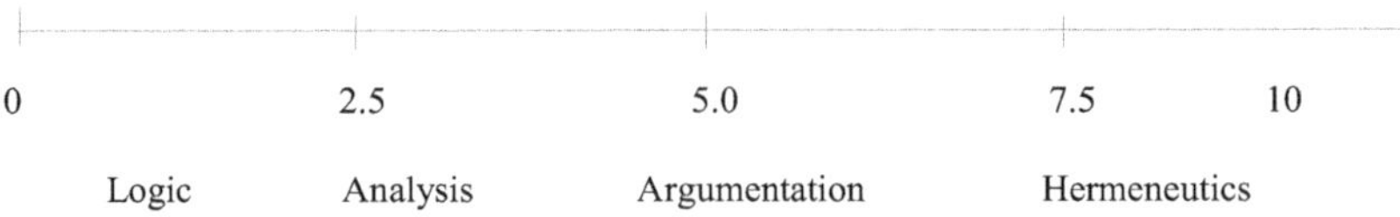

Fig. 2 Legal intelligence (source: author)

they also bind individuals bursts international law from within and thus ruins the international legal order, turning it into an '*order without law*', a 'force of law' into a 'law of force'.

In contemporary international relations, we are witnessing a renaissance of POLITICS in its ancient sense. At its core is '*The Rule of Conduct*', behind which are various types of codes of conduct (technological and protective standards). The term '*soft law*' is used in the literature. It has acquired a right of citizenship despite being in fact rather '*hard*' because of the powers and procedures involved in its enactment and application.

The foundation of the pyramid of an integrated legal order consists of PRECEDENTS. This is because they create the principles that determine the precedence of a particular legal order over individuals. It is difficult to imagine a rational law for the protection of individuals and environmental law without the primacy of international law over the law of integration of states (including EU law) and the national law of member states and, moreover, third countries, and without what is hidden behind the formula of *direct effect*.

The answer to the questions about the essence of law (what is law) and the source of knowledge about law (how law is learned) depends on the methods of researching legal phenomena. In the research practice of jurisprudence, we are confronted with a multiplicity of research methods of law and legal phenomena. In my reflections, I advocate a sequence of research according to the order: logic - > analysis - > argumentation - > hermeneutics.[5] According to this sequence, I assess the degree of legal intelligence. In a simplified and symbolic version, this degree is shown by a scale from 0 to 10 (see Fig. 2).

The logic-linguistic method in jurisprudence is characteristic of classical legal dogmatics, which attaches great importance to the analysis of legal texts. This method differs significantly from the methods of linguistic analysis used in the other human sciences. For this reason, it is subject to criticism among those who combat legal positivism and expose the error of formalism. The degree of legal intelligence behind so-called textology is the lowest.

Analytic jurisprudence is identified with analytical *jurisprudence,* which can be viewed through the metaphysics of the *jurisprudence* of international, supranational (such as the CJEU and ECtHR) and national courts (constitutional courts, supreme courts and others). This method of reasoning enriches legal logic with a semantic

---

[5] See Stelmach and Brożek (2004), passim.

'analysis' of terms and concepts found in legal language. It is therefore characterised by a slightly higher degree of legal intelligence.

Argumentation is an important element of legal discourse, which reveals its qualities when solving a 'difficult case' or designing changes to the law under the influence of a specific event. The literature highlights the qualities of legal reasoning used in legal proceedings—such as *argumentum a simili, argumentum a contrario, argumentum a forfiori, argumentum ab exemplo* and other arguments demonstrating the validity of a certain thesis by pointing out the lack of validity of the opposite thesis. Slightly different qualities of legal reasoning become apparent in the debate on law reform inspired by events such as the Titanic disaster. This is when the critical current of *jurisprudence*, assessing the real value of law and proposing necessary changes to the law (*critical jurisprudence*), the sociological current of *jurisprudence,* showing the links between law and social phenomena (*sociological jurisprudence*) and the economic current of jurisprudence, examining the influence of law on economic development, including private property (*economic jurisprudence*), are of crucial importance. Mastery of the art of argumentation demonstrates an even higher degree of intelligence on the part of the lawyer.

Hermeneutics derives from historiosophy, which studies law in development (*historical jurisprudence*). Its contemporary version draws on the thought of Radbruch (the concept of statutory lawlessness), Fuller (the concept of the intrinsic morality of law) and Dworkin (the division of law into principles, rules and standards). It assumes the development of jurisprudence along a spiral, as expressed by the 'hermeneutic circle'. Understanding the new version of the famous 'thesis-synthesis' requires extraordinary legal intelligence.

2 The First Industrial Revolution: The Beauty of Machines

The machine is an artificial construction that has fascinated people since the dawn of time, from primitive inventions to the triumph of the cog. Bacon proved to be a prophet of modern science, treating 'science as a technique', deriving his knowledge from the practice of craftsmanship. The English jurist, politician and philosopher argued in the *Novum Organum* that scientists must ask existential questions and focus on experiments. The method of induction he recommended was valued in Britain during the first industrial revolution. This revolution made its presence felt a little later on the Continent, where Perronet founded the *École des Ponts et Chaussées*—a forge of engineering education and Comte made the French school of engineering famous around the world, believing that through science and art, humanity would gain ultimate dominion over biology and cosmology. Only artists and poets were able to see how, beneath the icy patina of the transformations taking place, violent passions and destructive feelings loomed. Their reactions to 'industrial accidents' dampened the enthusiasm of the promoters of industrialisation, while at the same time drawing attention to the need to combat them in the spheres of prevention, control and responsibility.

The symbol of the first industrial revolution became the locomotive: 'beautiful' (because of its usefulness) and at the same time 'terrible' (because it caused damage to individuals and the environment). Historians of technology, science and education have begun to call for a new assessment of our enchantment with uncontrolled technical development. Their reflections on the 'religion of technology'[6] contributed to the creation of technological (and, in time, protective) standards, recommended initially by national institutions (and later also by international and regional organisations). They made their presence felt above all in the field of transport safety: rail, road, air and maritime.

In the initial phase of the industry's development, it was not possible to establish a system of effective control of hazardous activities. The control exercised by national institutions was one-sided even in the case of observation and monitoring of international obligations by diplomatic missions and consular offices. The control of obligations assumed by states or imposed on defeated states can only be spoken of once international and regional organisations have been equipped with supranational control powers. The most effective control appears to be that carried out by persons independent of states—experts or international officers. Their reports containing recommendations addressed to the controlled entity contribute to strengthening mutual trust and the international order. This type of control first made its presence felt in the field of communication security.

Industrial accidents have left their mark on civil, criminal and administrative liability. In civil law, there has been an increase in the importance of claims to implement the duty to prevent damage (preventive measures to protect non-pecuniary personal rights and rights in rem, as well as preventive measures for tort liability) and the duty to compensate for damage (based on the principle of risk). In criminal law, offences in the form of 'bringing about the danger of a catastrophe' have emerged. And in administrative law, the monetary penalty for 'gross' violations of the law has 'blossomed', prompting this type of sanction due to the fact that many areas of social and economic life have developed as a result of technological progress.

The drive to reduce industrial accidents pointed to preventive liability as the main weapon of civil law in the fight against the collateral effects of the industrialisation of countries. Provisions on the duty to prevent damage were printed in 'golden letters' but were in reality dead. In practice, liability for compensation for 'industrial damage' was of great importance. All sorts of dangerous *things* inspired the imagination of lawyers, who began to think about shifting the burden of proof from the injured party to the perpetrator of the act. In order to avoid the need for the tortfeasor to prove his innocence, it was decided to abandon fault as the basis of liability and to create the possibility for the tortfeasor to provide positive proof by demonstrating that the damage was caused by force majeure, the fault of the injured party or the fault of third parties. Only in countries such as Poland, where one of the characteristics of force majeure was the externality of the cause, did the scope of liability

[6] See especially Noble (2017), pp. 89–149.

increase to include 'internal' events, i.e. by chance. Criminal law is by its nature repressive towards the offender. In the period of the first industrial revolution, moreover, attention was paid to general prevention (which is essentially criminal prevention) and specific prevention (affecting the perpetrator of a criminal tort). This could be seen especially against the background of the offence of 'bringing about the danger of a catastrophe'. The use of administrative penalties (instead of classical measures of civil law or criminal law) is linked to advances in communications, energy and other branches of the economy. They fulfil either preventive-compensatory functions (typical of civil law) or repressive-preventive functions (typical of criminal law). The advantage of administrative tort liability is the application of the means of implementing administrative liability to collective entities.

3 The Second Scientific and Technological Revolution: Between the Beauty of Provocation and the Beauty of Consumption

As late as the beginning of the twentieth century, Europeans were at the forefront in almost every field: in science, in culture, in the economy, in fashion. With their colonial empires and trading companies, they dominated the entire world. During the period of the 'Eclipse' (between 1914 and 1945), Europe lost its mind. Some European countries were reborn on the ruins of Berlin thanks to US financial aid and the return of Enlightenment ideas from across the Atlantic, enriched with American experience and the latest technology. When the nuclear arms race began in the second half of the last century and the rivalry in the conquest of space became apparent, our world changed beyond recognition. Today, instead of 'beautiful machines', we admire 'magnificent catastrophes'—a symbol of something between the beauty of provocation and the beauty of consumption. They compel us to fight for a clean and healthy environment.

Primum non nocere—this wisdom of life has come to be recognised not only when considering health care, but also in terms of environmental protection. It is expressed among others, the obligation to use *Best Available Technology* (BAT). This legal and moral obligation is an offshoot of the precautionary principle, which has gained citizenship in international, regional and national relations. The implementation of this duty determines whether we can think seriously about our planet. This is required by the 'shared risk' strategy, which forces us to choose between one risk and another and to constantly adapt to new and unpredictable risks. The precautionary principle can be described in the words of Herman from Pushkin's short story *The Queen of Spades*: 'The game occupies me greatly, but I cannot risk what is necessary in the hope of gaining what is superfluous'.

The state of extreme environmental emergency is compounded by the lack of an 'all-powerful sheriff' capable of assessing environmental impacts and controlling the rationality of environmental management. The modern superpowers are unable to play such a role because they have something of a suicidal gene blasting them from within. They are only able to effectively block the resolutions of bodies such as the UN Security Council. The chance of creating an international body with the competence to control risk based on methods such as RCO (*Risk Central Option*) or RCM (*Risk Central Measure*) is slim. Greater hope can be pinned on the development of regional integration of states (including the European Union) in connection with increased protection of public health and the environment. On the other hand, it is difficult to pay much attention to the control carried out by national institutions due to their lack of credibility and their 'game of appearances'.

While liability for 'industrial accidents' shaped its specificity within the bosom of national law, liability for 'magnificent catastrophes' inspired the development of international law. This is reflected not so much in the sphere of general norms and liability for violations of international law (*state responsibility*) and liability for unlawful acts (*state liability*), which are the subject of the work of the International Law Commission and the jurisprudence of international courts[7], but in the sphere of specific norms concerning the obligation to compensate for damage of catastrophic proportions. Liability associated with the conduct of *ultra-hazardous activities* has made its presence felt in the law of the sea, nuclear law[8] and space law as an almost absolute liability. It is characterised by the absence of fault and the limitation of exonerating circumstances to the intentional fault of the injured party and third parties. The scope of this liability has expanded, in particular to include force majeure.

The greatest contribution to the development of standards on liability for violations of international law has been made by the law of the sea. Preventive liability is governed by Article 232 of the 1982 Convention on the Law of the Sea, which obliges States to be responsible for violations of technological and protective standards and rules for controlling their observance by any natural or legal, governmental or non-governmental person conducting activities in the seas and oceans. The principle set out in this 'constitution of the law of the sea' is a model worthy of emulation when working on the responsibility of 'States Parties' in agreements concerning specific bodies of water, including member states of the Helsinki Convention for the Protection of the Marine Environment of the Baltic Sea Area.[9]

---

[7] See Czapliński and Wyrozumska (1999), pp. 431–525.

[8] In my habilitation dissertation *Obligation to Remedy Damage of Catastrophic Proportions* (Brodecki 1978), I presented, among other things, my own draft legislation on liability for nuclear damage, which was accepted by the Polish Parliament when it passed the 'Atomic Law' Act. I have great satisfaction that the Polish legislator was the first in the world to adopt the principle of non-continuation of the statute of limitations for nuclear personal injury, assuming payment from a special compensation fund.

[9] Another appendix to my habilitation thesis included a draft on liability for pollution damage in the Baltic Sea area, the purpose of which was to fulfil the obligation under Article 17 of the Helsinki Convention of 1974. This draft, which I drafted on behalf of the Polish authorities, was not on the agenda of the Helsinki Commission. The parties adopting the new version of the Convention on the

Also, the liability of states for unlawful acts is subject to the law of the sea. Liability for damages is governed by Article 235 of the 1982 Convention of Law of the Sea, which obliges states to compensate for damage to the marine environment and, at the same time, to create a system of indemnification based on compulsory third-party liability insurance and compensation funds.

Thoughts formulated in many of my publications can now be found in Annex VI of the 1991 Protocol on the Protection of the Environment to the Antarctic Treaty, which regulates liability for environmental accidents which have a serious and harmful impact on the Antarctic environment or which threaten to have such an impact imminently.[10] The development of this Protocol has benefited from the debate that has been going on for years under the auspices of the IMO, adapting it to the protection typical of nature reserves.

4 The Third Information Revolution: Beauty on the Web

A new form of object is born, different from the industrial object. It is, in the words of Umberto Eco, 'a fabric invisible to our eye'. The netocratic network creates a holistic system, combining knowledge (knowledge society), dialogue (communication) and reflexivity (social consciousness). The creators of this network try to think, as it were, 'from inside the revolutionary changes' in the market and culture. Sociological 'memes' enrich biological genes, creating new parameters in the 'prespring' of a new technological era. The netocrats include eternalists (philosophers of netocratic society), nexialists (next-generation entrepreneurs) and curators (lobbyists).

The new actors on the world stage convince us that the internet is a haven of freedom. In reality, they are opening up a space ready for everyone to colonise. Information becomes a 'common good',[11] which should be used with extreme moderation. The information infrastructure of the modern state presupposes network security and free access to information. The process of unification of technological

Protection of the Marine Environment of the Baltic Sea Area in 1992 reiterated that the Member States undertake to establish liability rules for pollution damage 'as soon as possible'. One has to be a captive diplomat to repeat this phrase 15 years later.

[10]The text is contained in a work published on the occasion of the 40th anniversary of the establishment of the H. Arctowski Antarctic Station. Ministry of Foreign Affairs, Legal and Treaty Department, *The Antarctic Treaty. A Selection of Documents from the Introduction*, Warsaw, pp. 173–188. I derive my satisfaction from comparing the contents of this Annex with my reflections against the background of the solutions adopted in the CLC/FUND Convention system, which I have commented on, inter alia, in: Llloyd's (*New Definition of Pollution Damage*) and in: Yearbook of Maritime and Commercial Law Quarterly (*Compensation in the Light of the 1984 Protocols to Revise the 1969 CLC and the 1971 Fund Convention*), and in my professorial book *The Modern Law of Transboundary Harm* (Ossolineum, Warsaw 1993).

[11]See, inter alia, Nawrot (2007), pp. 75–88.

and technical issues, i.e. standardisation, plays the most important role in the realisation of these two fundamental goals.[12]

Free culture is based on a balance between anarchy and control. The fight against creators taking and reworking other people's intellectual property and copycats 'chiselling' code and other pirates using other people's ideas in film, music, radio or cable television fascinates copyright warriors. Their lawyers point out that it is difficult to control what is unregulated and to counter the concentration of giants like *Microsoft* in the market. They are in opposition to the *Creative commons* designers who have an interest in the GNU/Linux operating system. The dispute between the defenders of 'sacred property' and the promoters of 'free licences' is still ongoing. And there is no indication that an effective system of international and/or regional control on the web will be established any time soon.

The responsibility for the malfunctioning of the information infrastructure lies specifically with the authorities and services of individual states, which are obliged to interact in the sphere of cybersecurity with private actors and with organisations in international and regional forums.[13] Noting it was determined by the factual connection of this responsibility with the responsibility for the violation of energy security norms in its economic and geostrategic dimension—and consequently—with the responsibility for the violation of environmental security norms, which serves to eliminate or minimise the various threats to human life and health.[14]

5 The Birth of Technological Civilisation: Beautiful Experiments

To observers of the birth of artificial intelligence and 'synergistic reasoning', anything resembling traditional games may seem beautiful. There is a 'neo-Pythagorean' return to the aesthetics of proportion and numbers which is hidden behind. Developments in biotechnology, genetic engineering and 'cyborgisation' are turning robots into new actors in contemporary legal relations. In this metaphysical game, Umberto Eco sees a neo-medieval-style masquerade. Most of the sages warn against being freed from the bonds of Prometheus.

---

[12]The book *Infrastruktura informacyjna nowoczesnego państwa* by (Szafrański and Weydeman 2019, passim) has recently been published. In it, the authors made a general characterisation of the information society, pointed to the legal basis of informatisation processes in Poland and the European Union, and presented the tasks, architecture and resources of this infrastructure.

[13]The concept of cybersecurity does not refer to the posting of prohibited content online (child pornography, hate speech) or legal information but shared without authorisation (infringements of intellectual property rights), as these matters relate solely to the protection of personal rights.

[14]Everything to do with climate change and food security deserves exposure. See, inter alia Adamczak-Retecka and Śniadach (2018), passim.

In the age of artificial intelligence,[15] global security (including ecological security) depends primarily on international cooperation, such as we see on the International Space Station or in projects such as the *Human Genome.*

Project. The sine qua non *for* success on this path is the transformation of the 'international community' (with states as the main actors in the UN) into an 'international community' (a *singleton*, i.e. an order in which there is only one actor at the global level making decisions and wielding decision-making power). Only in this way can the right to secure critical infrastructure be enacted.[16]

The issue of the birth of human-level artificial intelligence (AGI) is of great interest to experts and concern to people. Standard project management techniques are still used when controlling artificial intelligence. On the other hand, we do not know much about the design of robots, as these projects are carried out in secret. Due to the ineffectiveness of the behavioural approach, researchers have to look for new methods of controlling potential with a view to counteracting the explosion of superintelligence and methods of selecting motivation with a view to controlling the consciousness and will of 'thinking and fast learning machines'.

The question of robots' liability for their own acts will be most difficult to resolve without the creation of an artificial intelligence code, as it may not be sufficient to reconstruct *state responsibility* and/or *state liability* and the civil, administrative and criminal liability of individuals to prevent or cause environmental damage. The future Robot Code should define AGI and equip it with a legal personality,[17] and, moreover, create new rules on the preventive liability of AGI for violations of legal norms and the compensatory liability of AGI for damage caused by automated machines,[18] without neglecting the liability of superintelligent robots for international crimes and crimes.[19]

Solving the problem of preventive and indemnity liability will be relatively easy, as environmental insurance can help in this respect: Liability and property insurance (classical civil law instruments) and various types of public funds (classical administrative law instruments),[20] and in the near future, moreover, space insurance.[21]

[15] A number of prominent scholars have written about it, including Bostrom (2016), passim; and Kaku (2018), passim.

[16] See Jaskiewicz-Kamińska (2016), passim.

[17] See, inter alia, Bar (2020), pp. 29–44.

[18] See, inter alia, Wałachowska (n.d.), pp. 57–68.

[19] See, inter alia, Filipkowski (n.d.), pp. 113–128.

[20] Dorota Maśniak writes about this in her excellent monograph Ecological Insurance (Zakamycze 2003), breaking down the barriers to thinking about environmental protection (pp. 15–88), while showing the role of civil liability insurance in environmental protection, i.e. the 'polluter pays' principle (pp. 89–216) and the role of material insurance in environmental protection, i.e. the 'victim pays' principle (pp. 217–264).

[21] The forerunner of 'space insurance' is Katarzyna Malinowska, who, in her habilitation thesis *Space Insurance: International Legal Aspects* (Malinowska 2017), created new contractual templates based on specific contracts concluded by well-known companies such as Lloyd's.

It can be much more complicated to punish robots for crimes (e.g. *self-driving* cars)[22] and even for international crimes (e.g. drone attacks on the enemy without human decision).[23] For we are then dealing with FAULT, constructed on the basis of AWARENESS and WILL. The controversy surrounding the consciousness and will of machines makes it difficult to define the constituent elements of even unintentional and formal crimes committed by robots, as we can only think of such at the current stage of development of artificial intelligence. So only in the future will it be worth thinking about the reaction to robots committing a crime without human involvement, taking into account: moral judgement, penalties and preventive measures.[24] The problem of responsibility for environmental damage caused in outer space will be the most difficult to solve, as outer space is not subject to protection. Today, shooting down one's own satellite in orbit and smashing it to pieces can only entail liability for damage to a foreign space object, not for littering space.[25]

6 Final Conclusions: The Cry of Humanity

After the battle fought at the recent Glasgow climate summit in Poland, we hear the words of the director of the Turów mine who entrusted his workplace to the care of Our Lady of Czestochowa, addressing her with the words of the litany: 'Pray for us'. The question arises as to whether this peculiar relationship between religion and technology still promotes the human and world welfare, or whether it only wants to help man escape from this world? Today, even conservatives are in favour of the *Green Revolution*,[26] confronting ecological problems. This is why people who care about the fate of future generations can hear the cry of the children protesting at the recent climate summit reaching every corner of the world. It can be expressed in the words: 'Saint Socrates and Saint Confucius: pray for everyone'. Their prayer will surely be on the lips of our descendants in the temple on Mars.[27]

---

[22] See Widłak (1978); Zajadło and Zeidler (2021), pp. 159–171.

[23] In 2021 in Libya, a Turkish drone equipped with artificial intelligence attacked enemy troops without a human decision, a UN special report revealed.

[24] Interesting books on the future of criminal law and the philosophy of punishment have been published by K. Mamak. His *Filozofia karania na nowo* (Mamak 2021) is worthy of insightful study.

[25] This is currently the subject of debate in the US in response to Russia shooting down its own satellite and posing a threat to the international space station.

[26] Roger Scruton—a British philosopher, writer and commentator on contemporary events, and at the same time author of the well-known book Green Philosophy—*How to Think Seriously About the Planet* Scruton (2017), passim.

[27] See Brodecki (2021), passim. This booklet is the proverbial 'dot over the i' in my academic work, which I began in earnest with my studies in maritime and space law at University College London under the tutelage of Professor Czeng, and finished with a series of essays under the title 'Sea &

'*Cybersecurity*' and '*Artificial Intelligence Safety Engineering*' are two universal buzzwords reflecting the level of 'safety culture' in the virtual and real worlds. They guide the development of human rights for the benefit of all humanity. The most emphatic expression of 'solidarity rights' today is the aforementioned right to secure critical infrastructure. Its characteristics (networked, long-lived, terrain-intensive), risks (natural and man-made) and effects (natural disasters and technical, social and environmental catastrophes) testify to the existence of an emergency situation. It is referred to as a *major emergency*. Such a situation obliges optimal decision-making in the security management system.

The future of our planet depends primarily on technological and technical security in the IT and AI sectors. Many cyber security experts emphasise the 'incomprehensibility' of the virtual world by those involved in it, citing the slogan '*no security through obscurity*'. In contrast, military and civilian experts in the real world expose any counter-attack from devices over which humans are slowly losing control. This thought is behind the metaphor of '*loose lips sink ships*'. Both attach great importance to prevention.

What seems equally urgent today is the need to create a system of effective international control. For the uncontrolled course of historical change during the greatest transformation of civilisation may intensify the state of chaos and consequently make life on our planet more difficult. Without the creation of a *singleton,* it will not be possible to make a breakthrough in our minds, which—as before the fall of ancient Greece—are dominated by three lines of thought: scepticism, nihilism and hedonism. It will not be possible to break free from these without a new Security Council taking control of the environment within the international community.

The power of the law also depends on the responsibility incumbent on the individual or collective. Already at the end of the twentieth century, cultural theory emerged in sociology and political science, inspiring considerations in the '*Risk and Culture*' strand. It reaches philosophers of law, who expose impartiality and fairness as ideas that provide a balance in the relationship of inter-personal and inter-state responsibility. In environmental protection, preventive liability is leading the way, permeating the international responsibility of states and civil, criminal and administrative, tortfeasors' liability. The low level of legal culture means that it is still not appreciated in the practice of international, regional and national relations. In the real world, what counts above all is compensation liability, the effectiveness of which is ensured by insurance and public compensation funds. They ensure that risks are spread across a wide variety of actors and that the game is played in many arenas.

Space', published, among others, in the series '*Per Mare* ad Astra', published by the Polish Academy of Sciences.

References

Adamczak-Retecka M, Śniadach O (2018) Climate change and food security. The legal aspects with special focus on the European Union. Wydawnictwo University of Gdańsk, Gdańsk

Bar G (2020) Robot personhood, or why we need anthropocentric artificial intelligence. In: Lai L, Świerczyński M (eds) The law of artificial intelligence. C.H. Beck Publishers, Warsaw

Bostrom N (2016) Superintelligence. *Scenarios,* strategies, dangers (original title: superintelligence. Path dangers, strategies), translated by Dorota Konowrocka-Sawa. Helion S.A., Gliwice

Brodecki Z (1978) Obligation to remedy damage of catastrophic proportions. Wydawnictwo University of Gdańsk, Gdańsk

Brodecki Z (2010) Metodologia regulae iuris. In: Komparatystyka kultur prawnych. Wolters Kluwer, Warsaw

Brodecki Z (2021) Temple in the cosmic village, security of future generations in the era of artificial intelligence. EuroPra-law, Warsaw

Czapliński W, Wyrozumska A (1999) *Prawo międzynarodowe publiczne*, Zagadnienia systemowe. C.H.Beck, Warsaw

Filipkowski W (n.d.) Criminal law vis-à-vis artificial intelligence (In:) Law..

Jaskiewicz-Kamińska J (2016) Right to safe critical infrastructure. Europrawo, Warsaw

Jung CG (2017) *Breakthrough of civilisation* (original title: Zivilisation im Übergang), translated by R. Reszke. KR Publishing House, Auckland

Kaku M (2018) The future of humanity. Conquering Mars, interstellar travel, immortality and our destiny beyond earth. (original title: The Future of Humanity. Terraforming Mars, Interstellar Travel, Immortality and our destiny beyond Earth), translated by B. Bieniok and E.L. Łokas. Prószyński i S-ka, Warsaw

Malinowska K (2017) Space insurance: international legal aspects. Wolters Kluwer International B. V, Netherlands

Mamak K (2021) Filozofia karania na nowo. Krakowski Instytut Prawa Karnego, Krakow

Maśniak D (2003) Ecological insurance. Zakamycze, Kraków

Nawrot AM (2007) Knowledge society 9. In: Temple in cyberculture. Technology and law in a knowledge society. University of Gdańsk Publishing House, Gdańsk

Noble DF (2017) *The religion of technology. The divinity of man and the Spirit of invention*, translated by Krzysztof Kornas. Copernicus Center Press, Krakow

Pyć D (2006) Law of sustainable development. Wydawnictwo University of Gdańsk, Gdańsk

Scruton R (2017) Green philosophy: how to think seriously about the planet, translated by J. Grzegorczyk, R. P. Wierzchosławski. ZYSK i S-ka, Poznań

Stelmach J, Brożek B (2004) Legal methods, Krakow

Szafrański B, Weydeman R (2019) Infrastruktura informacyjna nowoczesnego państwa. Military Academy of Technology, Warsaw

Tegmark M (2019) *Life 3.0: being human in the age of artificial intelligence* translated by T. Krzysztoń. Prószyński i S-ka, Warsaw

Wałachowska M (n.d.) Artificial intelligence and the principles of civil liability (in:) Law...

Widłak T (1978) Autonomous road pirate (in:) fascinating paths of the philosophy of law 2, ed. University of Gdańsk, Gdańsk

Zajadło J, Zeidler K (2021) Wolters Kluwer, Warsaw

Part I
Overview of the Environmental Liability and Insurance Regulations

Global Governance of the Environment and Implications for the Insurance Industry

Stephen J. Turner and Claire Bright

Abstract The insurance industry has historically had to respond to risks that corresponded to societal developments, changes in industrial practices and international conflict. Existing challenges for business and industry relating to the risks concerning the environment and society represent a new frontier that requires innovation and strategic assessment.

However, there is another dimension to the challenges faced by the insurance industry which is often overshadowed by the immediate nature of impacts upon the environment and society. This is that global environmental governance itself is changing, as are the responsibilities that businesses have in relation to human rights. The expectations of the international community relating to human rights and the environment, through corporate law, WTO law and international investment law are all changing in ways that will have major implications for the insurance sector.

Therefore, it is arguable that the insurance industry should not only be anticipating physical and commercial risks but engaging more proactively with the processes of change in global governance. The reason for this is due to the pivotal leadership role that the insurance industry can potentially play in the design and development of global governance systems that meet the needs of the international community. This chapter maps out the changes taking place in global governance systems and the important role that the insurance industy can potentially play in those processes.

S. J. Turner (✉)
University of Essex – Essex Law School, Colchester, UK
e-mail: s.j.turner@essex.ac.uk

C. Bright
University of Lisbon, Nova School of Law, Lisbon, Portugal
e-mail: claire.bright@novalaw.unl.pt

K. Malinowska, D. Maśniak (eds.), *Managing Environmental Risks through Insurance*, AIDA Europe Research Series on Insurance Law and Regulation 9,
https://doi.org/10.1007/978-3-031-47602-0_2

1 Introduction

The expectations of the international community are changing in terms of environmental responsibilities and liabilities as the environment itself is changing and in many instances degrading. As a result, environmental governance is evolving at a rapid pace and as part of that, the legal obligations of businesses are undergoing processes of corresponding adaptation and realignment. These developments are inevitably affecting the role of insurance vis-à-vis businesses, individuals and the international community; and this can be forecasted to continue at an increased rate.

The insurance industry has always had challenges in responding to new liabilities whether they be the advent of the motor car,[1] times of war,[2] or modified expectations in terms of professional negligence.[3] Clearly the insurance industry has had to respond to the increased potential of environmental liability faced by business clients resulting from their operations as well as the increased hazards posed to businesses and communities from the changing environment in which they live and work.[4] Extreme weather events including heat waves and flooding create risks for communities and businesses alike.[5] Increasingly there are also specific risks that can arise where parties that have suffered loss as a result of the impacts of climate change seek compensation from those businesses that they see as being responsible. Furthermore, and more broadly businesses need to consider the risks related to the transition to a more environmentally sustainable mode of operation.[6] It is therefore understandable that the insurance industry will need to continue to focus on the different types of environmentally related risks that affect their clients.

Whilst the insurance industry has had the immediate task of responding to these critical challenges, it has to date had less involvement in considering broader global reforms to international economic frameworks that would potentially lead to a revised role for the insurance industry. It can be argued that within an international economy that is putatively in the process of realigning itself towards 'net zero' harm to the environment and 'net zero' greenhouse gas emissions, there is a strong case for the insurance industry to be more integrally involved in the transitions that are taking place within global governance itself.

It is now widely recognised that if major environmental challenges are to be addressed effectively, major actors other than states, whether they be international organisations, businesses and civil society, need to play an integrated part. Indeed, the term 'global environmental governance' has been used in diverse ways,[7] but is often used to refer to governance that includes non-state actors as well as state

[1] Gürses (2020).

[2] Elderton (1938).

[3] Hall (1988), pp. 27–43.

[4] Surminkski (2013), pp. 228–253.

[5] Wouter Botzen (2013).

[6] Alexander (2019).

[7] Speth and Haas (2006) and Kanie et al. (2014).

actors.[8] Within the context of this chapter primary focus is given to the legal aspects of international economic frameworks that play major roles in determining the liabilities of businesses related to the environment and human rights, over and above those that are imposed by states. The reasons for this approach, rather than focussing on multilateral environmental agreements, is due to the fundamental role those international economic frameworks play in determining the commercial business environment that companies operate in, which in turn affects the way that businesses treat externalities.

Certain key international legal and economic frameworks that govern the way that business and industry operate internationally, established after World War II, arguably need to be redesigned or at least realigned, if challenges relating to the environment and human rights are to be successfully addressed. In particular, this chapter considers international trade law, international investment law and the law relating to the responsibilities of corporations. It focusses on these legal regimes as they form crucial pillars of governance that affect business responsibilities relating to the environment and human rights. As a result they inevitably have a direct effect on the insurance services that businesses ultimately require.

This chapter maps out specific aspects of these international legal and economic frameworks, with regard to the potential that they can have to impact the environment and human rights. It specifically includes the issue of human rights alongside the challenges posed by environmental protection, as human rights are so often implicated when the environment becomes degraded.[9] For example, chemicals leaching into a watercourse may create an environmental hazard and a liability but can simultaneously impact upon the rights to life and health of individuals and communities. Similarly, it is now recognised that climate change itself has profound human rights impacts[10] and importantly in 2022, the UN General Assembly recognised through a historic resolution the ‘right to a clean, healthy and sustainable environment’.[11] The linkages between protection of the environment and human rights mean that there is often no clear divide between the two and therefore the responsibilities and liabilities for businesses relating to environmental protection and human rights are in many instances intertwined.[12]

In considering the leadership role that the insurance industry could take in progressive realignments that would transition responsibilities more rapidly towards net zero harm to the environment (including greenhouse gas emissions), this chapter takes into account the shifting expectations of the international community relating to human rights obligations in conjunction with the environment itself. Ultimately, the it indicates the areas where significant adjustments are required.

---

[8]Biermann and Pattberg (2012).

[9]Knox and Pejan (2018).

[10]Turner (2014).

[11]UN GA (2022).

[12]Turner and Bright (2022), pp. 145–165.

In doing so it also highlights the impacts that such realignments could have on insurance regimes and services. Therefore, the analysis of this chapter is to consider those broad issues within the field of global governance to proceed with the argument that the insurance industry as a whole, could or should take a more prominent role in reform processes due to the unique position that it holds as a stakeholder within global environmental governance.

To carry this out, the chapter conducts three stages of analysis, which are as follows. First, it considers the way that the international economic system and the legal landscape it creates for businesses, impacts the environment and human rights. It considers international trade law (WTO law), international investment law, and corporate law and identifies the legal features of those regimes that can be detrimental to the environment and human rights.

The second section considers the way that liabilities for businesses are shifting in relation to the impacts that they can have on the environment and human rights. It draws on the changing culture that has occurred through the human rights and due diligence (HRDD) framework derived from the UN Guiding Principles on Business and Human Rights for the responsibilities of businesses that was subsequently extended to the environment. It indicates a transition of expectation and practice which is underway and uses this to illustrate the potential for further reforms in the coming decades.

The third and final section considers the two aforementioned sections within the context of the ways that the international community could potentially redesign the international economic system in such a way that net zero harm to the environment and the climate could be achieved. In doing this it illustrates the pivotal role that the insurance industry could potentially, and arguably should, play in those reforms. As such it considers a role for the insurance industry that is not only involved in responding to governance changes but playing a more integral part in the design and implementation of those changes.

Overall, this chapter emphasises that all actors whether they be states, businesses, civil society or international organisations have a role in protecting the environment and human rights. It argues that the insurance industry has a much greater role than it has already assumed—and that this represents not only a major challenge but an important responsibility.

2 The International System Under Which Business Operates

This section provides an overview of key aspects of major global international legal and economic frameworks and the responsibilities that they create for corporate actors primarily vis-à-vis protection of the environment but also in relation to human rights too. It does this to demonstrate the ways that they orientate the decision-making of businesses towards commercial maximisation with potential concomitant risks in terms of outcomes for the environment and human rights. It also contextualises these legal and economic frameworks to highlight the changing expectations of the international community relating to them. It is this legal landscape and its relationship with existing business liabilities that paves the way for consideration of the role that the insurance industry can potentially play in the reform of global governance to achieve net zero outcomes for the environment and fully protected human rights.

2.1 The WTO Regime

For decades now concern over the impacts of international trade on the goals of the international community concerning the environment and human rights has led to increased scrutiny of the institutional processes that have been used to achieve trade liberalisation.[13] Where companies engage in international trade whether that be through importation, exportation or both, their businesses are inextricably affected by international trading regimes. Trading regimes inevitably affect the levels of competition that businesses face in the market place and this can have an impact on the extent to which businesses can realistically invest in environmental and human rights related concerns if they are to maintain their positions in markets.

When considering the World Trade Organisation (WTO) it is necessary to primarily consider the General Agreement on Tariffs and Trade.[14] The core obligations of the GATT of 1947 remain fundamental to the way that the WTO creates duties for member states in their trading relationships with each other.[15] It should be noted that those obligations have a strong relationship with regional trade agreements (RTA) and bilateral trade agreements, and these along with international investment law, form what has been described as the 'hard core' of international economic law.[16] In essence, the WTO agreements create a set of principle based legal obligations that member states must observe to be able to access the markets of other member states. The main principles of this system are 'national treatment', 'most-favoured nation status', and the obligation not to impose quantitative restrictions.[17]

Although the WTO has not introduced agreements requiring member states to comply with specific environmental or human rights standards, it has introduced certain agreements that have a relationship with environmental and human rights

[13] Francioni (2001).

[14] General Agreement on Tariffs and Trade 1947.

[15] General Agreement on Tariffs and Trade 1994; Van den Bossche and Prévost (2021).

[16] Van den Bossche and Prévost (2021).

[17] Ibidem.

issues. These include agreements related to technical barriers to trade[18]; food, animal and plant safety[19]; and intellectual property.[20] The traditional argument made by the WTO relating to environmental and human rights issues is that as a regime of trade agreements, it is for other specialist branches of international law to engage with those specific issues and that the WTO does not have the expertise or the remit to do so itself.[21] This may of course appear to be a reasonable argument, but it is also arguable that it reflects a position that only partially acknowledges the power discrepancy between the WTO regime in terms of leverage, when compared to regimes of international environmental and human rights law.[22] For example, the WTO regime includes its binding Dispute Settlement Body (DSB) that has been called upon regularly to make decisions that affect the trading relationships between states, both large and small,[23] but no environmental or human rights regime has that same level of corresponding binding power or authority over member states.

Through the WTO system, a state is able to legally challenge goods being imported into its country on specific grounds. Some of the WTO rules have environmental and human rights implications, and interpretations have been keenly contested.[24] Key to this phenomena have been the issues related to 'process and production methods' (PPMs). In other words, there is a question as to whether a state importing a product can require that it be produced in a manner that meets its own national environmental process and production standards, even if the end product is ultimately no different to those produced domestically. This principle can apply to fishing techniques for example and the extent to which they create bycatch in the process. Traditionally WTO rules have maintained that member states cannot use the PPMs of other countries as a basis upon which to restrict associated imports, but there have been some inroads made in this regard.[25] Nevertheless, the prospect of environmental governance being left to the policies of importing states can be criticised as being an arbitrary and unfair approach that can be partial to economically more powerful states.[26] Some would argue that the WTO itself should be orientated towards the maintenance of internationally agreed standards of environmental and human rights protection as part of an international trading regime.[27]

Whilst it can be understandable from a historical perspective that international trade regimes prioritise access to markets and economic interests above environmental and human rights concerns, the nature of global society in the twenty-first

[18] Agreement on Technical Barriers to Trade 1994.

[19] Agreement on Sanitary and Phytosanitary Measures 1994.

[20] Trade-Related Aspects of Intellectual Property Rights 1994.

[21] Sampson (2005).

[22] Turner (2009).

[23] Herdegen (2016).

[24] Esty (1995).

[25] Turner (2009).

[26] Cooreman (2017).

[27] Esty (2002), pp. 7–22.

century arguably requires a more sophisticated and integrated approach. In part this is because the existing paradigm inevitably places commercial pressure on businesses operating in states that are members of the WTO (currently 164 nations)[28] to compete with each other which can create downward pressure on the maintenance of standards relating to the environment and human rights. Such economic pressure inevitably has an impact on associated outcomes, and affects national law and policymaking accordingly.

For states, there can be legal pressure through the WTO regime related to the environmental or human rights regulations that it introduces. If a member state makes environmental or human rights regulations that could potentially be interpreted as disguised restrictions on international trade, other member states can make legal challenges to the DSB accordingly.[29] Therefore, the WTO regime in providing a rules based system that is in part designed to deter disguised attempts by states to protect their own national markets from imports, and by avoiding engagement in universal standard setting relating to the environment and human rights, inevitably attracts criticism.

The goal of trade liberalisation can be seen as virtuous in the sense that it can liberate 'human beings from governmental constraints on their economic freedom'.[30] However, it has simultaneously been argued that the quest for that economic freedom should not mean the abandonment of 'moral and civil progress of the national and international society'.[31] Therefore, leading authorities have commented that rules to protect the environment and human rights should have kept pace with the rules based system to establish trade liberalisation.[32]

Criticism of this framework and the imbalance of priorities that it represents has not been restricted to academia and civil society. Mainstream international actors have recognised this disparity. For example in 2001, the then Secretary General of the United Nations, Kofi Annan, remarked that the international community

> [c]annot take the onward march of free trade and the rule of law for granted. Instead, we must resolve to underpin the free global market with genuinely global values and secure with effective institutions. We must show the same firm leadership in defence of human rights, labour standards, and the environment as we already do in defence of intellectual property.[33]

It can be argued that if the WTO system should include rules related to intellectual property as it does through the Agreement Trade-Related Aspects of Intellectual Property Rights (TRIPS),[34] it could also adopt standards relating to the environment

---

[28] WTO Membership. Available via https://www.wto.org/english/thewto_e/whatis_e/tif_e/org6_e.htm (Accessed on 19 February 2022).

[29] Herdegen (2016).

[30] Francioni (2001).

[31] Ibidem.

[32] Ruggie (2004), pp. 499–531.

[33] Annan (2001), pp. 19–27.

[34] Trade-Related Aspects of Intellectual Property Rights 1994.

and human rights.[35] Arguments relating to the proper role and function of the WTO have no doubt affected its capacity to develop further. However, whatever role is appropriate for the WTO in terms of environmental governance, it is clear that its agreements form part of a network of rules that influence the way that businesses operate, and this inevitably has an impact on the risks that businesses need to insure. Therefore, potential reform of the obligations that are required of WTO members in relation to the environment and human rights, would inevitably have far-reaching impacts for the insurance industry.

2.2 International Investment Law

Whereas the WTO system was forged from the foundation of the earlier GATT regime with the intention of developing a trade regime that potentially had global applicability, the same type of process has not occurred for international investment law. There is currently no global legal regime for international investment as there is for international trade.[36] Instead there is a plethora of investment treaties (often bilateral in nature) and free trade agreements, which can be referred to as international investment agreements (IIA). Those treaties create rules-based regimes through which investment between host states (those receiving investment) and home states (those states from which investment is sourced whether publicly or privately) is undertaken.[37] The part that these treaties play relating to the responsibilities that businesses have for environmental and human rights issues is significant. This is because they have the potential to affect the degree of regulation and protection that host states require companies to comply with. As with the WTO and RTAs, IIAs are critically important to national economies. Developing countries can be particularly influenced by them as investment is so important to their economies. Prior to the COVID-19 pandemic, levels of foreign direct investment globally were at USD 1.5 trillion in the year of 2019.[38]

IIAs characteristically include two types of rules to maintain regulatory stability. First, rules prohibiting host states from interfering with investments.[39] Such interference can amount to 'expropriation' of an investment. The types of clauses used for this purpose include 'stabilisation clauses' that limit the extent to which changes in regulations by host states can be introduced.[40] This restraint can include regulations relating to the environment and human rights. Second, rules are typically

[35] Turner (2009).

[36] Van Ho (2021), pp. 325–334.

[37] Subedi (2020).

[38] UNCTAD (2021a).

[39] Subedi (2020).

[40] Ibidem.

included which prohibit acts or measures amounting to 'unfair treatment'.[41] The reason why these types of provisions have become particularly controversial is because they are often accompanied by 'choice of law' and dispute settlement clauses which enables investors to take out litigation against host states in tribunals external to a host state, often through the International Centre for the Settlement of Investment Disputes (ICSID) or the United Nations Commission on International Trade Law (UNCITRAL).[42] As a result host states run the risk, if they make changes to their regulatory regimes, of facing highly costly litigation from the companies that have invested in their country.[43]

As such it has been argued that the threat of litigation can act as a disincentive to intervene where human environmental or human rights issues are at stake. Evidence also suggests that the very existence of IIA litigation against states, regardless of the results, leads to a loss of aggregate investment.[44] With regard to human rights, some have argued that IIAs can lead to decisions in arbitral tribunals that are contrary to state obligations vis-à-vis international human rights law[45] and as such are counter to the rule of law.[46] Ultimately IIAs need to achieve a balance between investor risk reduction and the maintenance of the prerogative of host states to regulate in the interests of the public. For this reason, Subedi comments that

> [t]hese challenges can be addressed by fashioning relations between foreign investors and host countries in such a way that foreign investment law is better equipped to balance public and private interests and to pay adequate attention to other competing principles of international law and overall policy objectives of the international community.[47]

It is clear that the existing frameworks for IIAs, when viewed within the context of global environmental governance as a whole, play an important part in the relationship that companies have with the environment and human rights.

At the time of writing there were 2843 Bilateral Investment Treaties (2290 in force) and 420 Treaties with Investment Provisions (324 in force).[48] Different quarters of the international community have sought to develop a global approach to international investment law that would achieve consistency. The OECD has attempted unsuccessfully to negotiate a Multilateral Investment Agreement (MIA)[49] and the WTO has also made efforts within the sphere of international investment which met with resistance.[50] More recently steps have been taken to support

[41] Ibidem.

[42] Cutler (2021), p. 130.

[43] Pelc (2017), pp. 559–583.

[44] Ibidem.

[45] Van Ho (2021), pp. 325–334.

[46] Yilmaz Vastardis (2020), pp. 617–640.

[47] Subedi (2020).

[48] UNCTAD (2021b).

[49] OECD (1998).

[50] Doha WTO Ministerial Declaration (2001), paras 20–22.

developing countries in securing provisions within IIAs that meet the expectations of the UN's Sustainable Development Goals.[51] As the governance framework for international investment comes under closer scrutiny the potential for reform that would have an impact on the insurance industry is significant.

2.3 *Corporate Law*

It can be argued that the influence that international economic law has on the environment and human rights cannot be properly understood without also considering the effect that corporate law has on business decision-making. Corporate law represents an interesting component within the broader international framework of laws that ultimately influence the way that companies strategise and develop business plans. Whilst corporate law itself is not subject to a globally binding international treaty and is generally determined on a state-by-state basis, the nature of corporate law internationally is such that all countries of the world have adopted a formula which is generally ubiquitous and which demonstrates a significant degree of homogeneity. The formula includes certain characteristics that have a profound effect on decision-making relating to the environment and human rights. Those characteristics, if reformed, would inevitably affect business insurance requirements.

There are four specific characteristics of corporate law, that have a major impact upon governance of the environment and human rights; these are separate legal personality, national registration of companies, limited liability and directors' duties. Separate legal personality is fundamental to all companies in whichever jurisdiction they are registered. It is a legal attribute which means that each company is a separate entity in law to all other companies, individuals or organisations, including other companies within a corporate group. Within individual companies, it means that directors and shareholders themselves as individuals are treated as being separate to the companies that they are part of.[52] As such when a company incurs liabilities, the directors and shareholders are shielded from personal liability. The only exceptions to this would be if a shareholder had unlimited liability—which is extremely rare, or if a director or a shareholder had made a personal guarantee relating to any of the company's liabilities, or had committed an offence which led to liability. As the principle of separate legal personality also applies to the different companies within corporate groups,[53] businesses sometimes develop complex corporate structures, involving a number of companies to manage and compartmentalise commercial risks. In terms of the environment and human rights, it can mean that directors, shareholders and even other companies within a corporate group can end up being

[51] UNCTAD (2015).
[52] Roach (2019).
[53] Muchlinski (2021).

legally insulated from specific financial liabilities and this in itself can have the effect of exacerbating risk-taking relating to the environment and human rights.[54]

The second of the associated characteristics of corporate law globally is the fact that there is currently no international system of registration for companies.[55] As a general rule, with some minor exceptions, where a company seeks to operate in a different country to that in which it is domiciled, it will be required to create and register a new company in that jurisdiction, this often means creating a foreign subsidiary.[56] It has been argued that an international system of registration for companies could provide a basis upon which more effective regulation of individual corporations and corporate groups could be effected.[57] An international system of registration for companies could potentially provide the basis upon which compliance with international environmental and human rights standards could be founded. Although within specific sectors compliance and reporting systems have been developed, they are generally non-mandatory, and therefore global governance in this respect can still be regarded as being in its infancy.

The third characteristic that is now integrated throughout corporate law globally is that of 'limited liability'. This legal feature is one of the key reasons for the popularity of the corporate form for business people wherever they are located. It means that shareholders of companies are only liable for the debts of a company up to the amount of money that they have agreed to pay for the purchase of their shares.[58] In some jurisdictions there is the option to register companies that require shareholders to accept 'unlimited liability' but understandably this option is one that is not particularly popular. The advantage of 'limited liability' is that it provides another legal device through which shareholders are insulated from the debts and liabilities of a company. The problem is that in providing this protection, it can result in corporate decision-making that increases risk-taking relating to environmental and human rights, as the shareholders will have limited exposure to those risks in the event that major liabilities arise. It also means that where a company has insufficient funds to cover liabilities relating to the environment or human rights, adequate compensation may not be available where harm or loss is suffered.

The fourth and final characteristic of company law is that all jurisdictions have laws which require the directors of companies to make decisions which benefit the company that they work for.[59] From a commercial perspective these laws are necessary to ensure that the funds that shareholders invest into companies are used for the company's purposes, as the majority of investors seek a return on their investments either through dividends or an increase in share value.[60] Therefore,

[54] Ibidem.

[55] Ibidem.

[56] Backer (2021).

[57] Turner (2014); Turner (2021), pp. 1–31.

[58] Hannigan (2018).

[59] Paolini (2014) and Turner (2014).

[60] Turner (2014).

what are known in some jurisdictions as 'directors' duties' are incorporated into corporate law.[61] These provisions usually create penalties for directors who are in contravention, but serious failures by a director would typically mean that they would lose their job and as such these types of duties are usually self-enforcing.[62]

Directors' duties have been the subject of intense scrutiny for many years and this has resulted in reforms in certain jurisdictions that require directors, or companies themselves, to take the environment and human rights into account in the decisions and strategies that they make. The United Kingdom did so through the Companies Act in 2006,[63] India also in 2013,[64] and more recently France introduced its Loi PACTE[65] which leaves it open for companies to have objectives which do not purely relate to commercial success. Reforms relating to directors' duties and the purpose of companies tie in with the introduction of legal responsibilities to conduct due diligence relating to human rights and the environment; those developments are considered further in section 3 of this chapter. Where changes have been made, there are still questions about their effectiveness and new approaches within the field of corporate responsibility are constantly being considered.[66]

What this means in terms of global governance is that corporate law itself is receiving continued attention as a core component within an international legal framework that has a strong relationship with the environment and human rights. Ultimately associated changes in corporate law can have a major impact upon the liabilities that businesses may have relating to environmental and human rights risks; which necessarily has major implications for the insurance industry.

3 The Changing Face of Responsibility for Businesses

The analysis in section 2 illustrated the way that the legal frameworks of international economic law and corporate law can affect businesses outcomes vis-à-vis human rights and the environment. Attention relating to the impacts that businesses can have on human rights and the environment has gradually changed the expectations of the international community relating to corporate decision-making. Scrutiny at local, national and international levels has therefore led to changing business

---

[61] Andenas and Wooldridge (2009).

[62] Turner (2014).

[63] s. 172 Companies Act (United Kingdom). Available via: https://www.legislation.gov.uk/ukpga/2006/46/contents (accessed on 10.05.2023).

[64] s. 166(2) The Companies Act 2013 (India). Available via https://www.mca.gov.in/Ministry/pdf/CompaniesAct2013.pdf (accessed on 10.05.2023).

[65] PACTE Law, Loi no 2019–486 of 22 May 2019. The Plan d'Action Pour la Croissance et la Transformation des Entreprises (Action Plan for Business Growth and Transformation) Available via: https://www.legifrance.gouv.fr/dossierlegislatif/JORFDOLE000037080861/ (accessed on 10.05.2023).

[66] McCorquodale and Neely (2022).

practices that provide a barometric of the direction of travel which arguably will continue to affect responsibilities for businesses. This section therefore draws on initiatives that have taken place, primarily at the international level, which have gained traction and which provide a prism through which an understanding of what businesses are, who they are responsible to and what their liabilities should be, can be viewed. In doing so it considers a key part of the changing face of responsibilities for businesses and provides a lens through which potential future developments can be understood.

Within this sphere, the United Nations has been particularly active. Whereas the UN has traditionally approached responsibilities for environmental protection through the development of treaty regimes, it has directly addressed businesses in terms of their responsibilities through their impacts upon human rights through alternative methods. As the human rights impacts of businesses are often linked to environmental outcomes, this section examines those developments with a view to understanding their overall impact upon business liability within global governance.

Various approaches to defining business' responsibility in relation to human rights have been followed in the past few decades.[67] In the 1990s, following the scandals around the Southeastern Asian 'sweatshops' supplying international brands such as Nike in the footwear and apparel industry and the resulting protests and boycotts, companies started to respond through the adoption of codes of conduct.

In 1999, the UN Secretary-General Kofi Annan initiated the UN Global Compact[68] at the World Economic Forum in Davos as he invited the business leaders to join the UN's compact of shared values and principles aimed at giving a 'human face to the global market'. The UN Global Compact constituted a new standard for companies to benchmark their conduct against prevailing international law.[69] Indeed, companies wishing to adhere to the initiative are asked to embrace, support and enact, within their sphere of influence, a set of principles in the areas of human rights, labour standards, the environment and anti-corruption. However, the voluntary nature of the UN Global Compact means that it has no effect over the companies who do not wish to participate. In addition, it has been criticised for its lack of teeth, meaning that no real sanction can be imposed on companies who violate the principles that they pledged to respect. Against this backdrop, different strategies were subsequently explored at the UN level.

In 2003, the UN Sub-Commission on the Promotion and Protection of Human Rights presented its *Draft Norms on the Responsibilities of Transnational Corporations and Other Business Enterprises with Regard to Human Rights* (Draft Norms)[70] which constituted a restatement of existing human rights obligations and aimed to extend them to companies as well as states.[71] However, the aspiration to

[67] Bright et al. (2020), pp. 667–697; Bright and Buhmann (2020), pp. 1–18.

[68] United Nations Global Compact (2005).

[69] Ramasastry (2015), pp. 237–259.

[70] United Nations, Commission on Human Rights (26 August 2003).

[71] Ramasastry (2015), pp. 237–259.

impose direct human rights obligations on companies made the Draft Norms very controversial. In 2004, the UN Commission on Human Rights considered them formally but eventually decided not to approve them.

A year later, one of the architects of the Global Compact and Harvard Professor, John Ruggie, was appointed as the Special Representative of the Secretary General on the issue of Human rights and Transnational Corporations and other Business Enterprises with a mandate, among other things, to identify and clarify the standards of corporate responsibility and accountability with regard to human rights. In 2007, he presented the 'Protect, Respect and Remedy Framework' which articulates the differentiated but complementary responsibilities of states and enterprises in preventing, addressing and remedying business-related human rights harms.[72] The Framework is organised around three core principles: (1) the state duty to protect against human rights abuses by third parties, including business enterprises, which derives from the international human rights regime (2) the corporate responsibility to respect human rights which is grounded on social expectations and is part of a company's social licence to operate, and (3) the need for more effective access to remedies, which is a shared responsibility between states and companies.

The Framework was subsequently implemented in the UN Guiding Principles on Business and Human Rights (UNGPs) which were unanimously endorsed by the UN Human Rights Council in 2011 and formed the first authoritative global standards on business and human rights.[73] The approach chosen was one of a soft law instrument which garnered a substantial consensus. The UNGPs have been extremely influential and have paved the way for the legislative developments that are currently taking place. Many of these developments focus on the concept of human rights due diligence which was introduced in the UNGPs and refers to the positive steps that companies need to take, through policies and processes, to identify, prevent, mitigate, and account for the adverse human rights impacts that they may cause or contribute to through their own activities, or that may be linked to their operations, products or services by their business relationships. This has been recognised as a core practice of responsible business conduct and has been incorporated in several other international instruments such as the OECD Guidelines on Multinational Enterprises, revised in 2011 to align with the UNGPs,[74] and the ILO Tripartite Declaration, in its 2017 revision.[75] It has also been extended to other areas than human rights, such as the environment and climate change.

Yet, despite these developments, the implementation of human rights due diligence responsibilities has been very poor in practice for the vast majority of companies. In 2020, the Corporate Human Rights Benchmark assessed the human rights disclosures of 229 global companies across five sectors and revealed that nearly half of the companies assessed (46.2%), failed to score any point on the

[72] United Nations Human Rights Council (2008).

[73] United Nations Human Rights Office of the High Commissioner (OHCHR) (2011).

[74] OECD (2011).

[75] ILO (2017).

human rights due diligence indicators.[76] In Germany, the results of the 2020 monitoring process revealed that only 13–17% of the 455 companies surveyed could show that they adequately met their due diligence obligations as contained in the German National Action Plan for Business and Human Rights.[77] In Portugal, the first National Enquiry on Responsible Business Conduct and Human Rights revealed that less than one in five companies had human rights due diligence processes in place.[78] At the European level, the European Commission Study on Due Diligence Requirements through the Supply Chain surveyed companies across Europe. Just over one-third of business respondents indicated that their companies undertake due diligence which takes into account all human rights and environmental impacts, and amongst those, a large majority specified that their due diligence exercise was limited to first-tier suppliers.[79] The literature has made a connection between the low levels of corporate human rights due diligence practices and the lack of binding legal frameworks at the national or international level.[80] Indeed, the soft law character of the international norms on business and human rights entails that the decision to exercise human rights due diligence remains at the companies' discretion, with no sanction in cases of non-compliance.

In an attempt to address this gap the corporate human rights and environmental due diligence expectations are gradually transforming into a legally binding standard of conduct in an increasing number of jurisdictions where mandatory human rights due diligence legislation is being introduced.[81] For instance, the French Duty of Vigilance law adopted in 2017[82] requires large French companies to establish, effectively implement and disclose a vigilance plan setting out due diligence measures taken in relation to their own activities, the companies under their control, or from the activities of their subcontractors and suppliers with whom they have an established business relationship.[83] In the Netherlands, the Dutch Child Labour Due Diligence Act was adopted in 2019, requiring companies that supply goods or services to Dutch end-users to exercise human rights due diligence in relation to child labour.[84] Recent legislation on mandatory due diligence has also been adopted in Germany and in Norway, and has been put forward in several other jurisdictions.[85] At the EU level, the European Parliament adopted a resolution in March 2021, by a

[76] World Benchmarking Alliance (2020).

[77] German Federal Foreign Office (2020).

[78] Romão et al. (2018).

[79] Smit et al. (2020).

[80] Claire Bright et al. (2020), pp. 667–697.

[81] Macchi and Bright 2020, pp. 218–247.

[82] LOI n 2017–399 du 27 Mars 2017 Relative au Devoir de Vigilance des Sociétés Mères et des Entreprises Donneuses D'ordre (1). Available via: https://www.legifrance.gouv.fr/affichTexte.do?cidTexte=JORFTEXT000034290626&categorieLien=id. Accessed on 10.05.2023.

[83] Savourey and Brabant (2021), pp. 141–152.

[84] Ibidem.

[85] Krajewski et al. (2021), pp. 550–558.

vast majority, with recommendations to the European Commission on corporate due diligence and corporate accountability.[86] The European Commission's Draft Directive on Corporate Sustainability Due Diligence which was introduced in February 2022 is currently being discussed.

In parallel with these legislative developments, the shift towards the increased recognition of legal responsibilities of businesses in relation to human rights and the environment can also be seen in litigation.[87] In particular, cases like the Vedanta case in the UK and the Shell case in the Netherlands have acknowledged that parent companies may, in certain circumstances, owe a duty of care to the workers and local communities affected by the activities of their foreign subsidiaries.[88] In another case against Shell in 2021, the District Court of the Hague found that the parent company had a legal obligation to 'contribute to the prevention of dangerous climate change through the corporate policy it determines for the Shell group' which derives from an 'unwritten standard of care' under Dutch tort law.[89] On that basis, the court ordered the company to reduce its CO_2 emissions by 45% by 2030 relative to 2019 levels. In reaching this decision, the court made an explicit reference to soft law instruments such as the UNGPs and the OECD Guidelines for Multinational Enterprises, thereby highlighting their persuasive authority.[90] More specifically, the court referred to the UNGPs as a 'universally endorsed' and 'authoritative' soft law instrument 'suitable as a guideline in the interpretation of the unwritten standard of care', regardless of whether Shell had committed to them.

The developments in this section are indicative of a response that has occurred through international organisations and national initiatives to the decision-making of companies that to a large extent can be attributed to failure of the legal frameworks of international economic law and corporate law that were described in Sect. 2. Whereas the developments in this section demonstrate the immediate responses of the international community relating to the effects of businesses on human rights and the environment, Sect. 2 addresses some of the seemingly intractable root causes of those issues that are found within systemic frameworks of global governance. Given the expectations of the international community and its priorities these insights can be used to assist in understanding, not only how global environmental governance can be developed to respond effectively but also the role that the insurance industry can play in that process.

---

[86] European Parliament (2021).

[87] Bueno and Bright (2020), pp. 789–818.

[88] Chambers (2021), pp. 519–578.

[89] The Hague District Court (2021).

[90] Bright and Buhmann (2020), pp. 1–18.

4 The Re-design of International Environmental Governance and the Role of the Insurance Industry

When considering global environmental governance and its associated institutions, it is clear that they collectively represent a work in progress. The international community has yet to adopt a system of global governance that adequately protects the environment or human rights in terms of the practices of business and industry. The foregoing commentary indicates that whereas the priorities of past generations may have been well-served through the design of international economic law and corporate law, contemporary priorities relating to the environment and human rights are often not. It has demonstrated that global governance relating to the environment and human rights are integrally linked to the design of international economic law and that of corporate law, to the extent that those legal frameworks include design features which can and often do lead to negative human rights and environmental outcomes. Therefore, there is a very strong case for those frameworks to be redesigned.

A significant degree of sympathy can be afforded to the original designers and architects of corporate law (in the late eighteenth and early nineteenth centuries) and international economic law (at the end of World War II) as they were not to know precisely how globalisation would affect the legal regimes that they were establishing at the time.[91] Nor could they anticipate how those legal regimes could impact, yet to be adopted priorities relating to human rights and the environment. It is clear now that this generation's priorities continue to change; for example the goal of achieving net zero GHG emissions is a relatively recent addition. What these changing priorities arguably elucidate is the need to redesign extant systems of international economic law and corporate law as part of a renewed system of global governance.

As global governance has evolved it has become increasingly clear that the traditional model of state centred international governance that was heavily reliant on international law treaties has been surpassed by the reality of governance involving a range of different actors.[92] Certain scholars such as Koskenniemi have argued that lawyers should be rethinking the activities of expert institutions where power occurs and consider more carefully the way that different regimes, designed to achieve different objectives, intersect with each other.[93] Relevant expertise is found not just within state institutions but within international and private organisations too. These organisations not only represent knowledge bases but they are often key stakeholders in the development of systems of global governance. UN bodies naturally play key roles in global governance, but civil society along with business and industry also will have significant contributions to make. As such when

[91] Turner (2021), pp. 1–31.

[92] Marin and Orsini (2013), pp. 562–589.

[93] Koskenniemi (2011).

consideration is given to the re-design of systems of global governance related to the obligations of business in the sphere of the environment and human rights, it follows that the insurance industry should have an important role to play in specific respects. First, it can be argued that through the knowledge and expertise that it has relating to industrial and environmental risk it can play a significant role. Second, in the understanding that it has in the development of liability regimes and their practical functioning, it can also make a major contribution.

In terms of related research, over a number of years work has been undertaken to systematically analyse global environmental governance with the purpose of redesigning international economic and corporate law frameworks alongside corresponding state law with a view to predisposing business and industry to achieve net zero harm to the environment.[94] This approach is reliant on 'macro-legal analysis' that takes into account the different legal frameworks that exist within international economic law and corporate law, for example, to consider what reforms would be necessary to achieve net zero harm.[95] What is interesting about this approach and the solutions that it provides, is that it argues not only that it is possible to redesign international legal frameworks to achieve net zero harm to the environment, but also that in doing so a key role for the insurance industry would be required if that were to be achieved.

This section summarises two types of reform suggestions that fall within this category. First, where a redesign of international legal and economic frameworks integrates responsibilities for businesses or production processes to result in net zero degradation which would necessitate an insurance safeguard in the event of failure to comply. Second, where international legal and economic frameworks are reformed to incorporate compulsory liability insurance related to the protection of the environment and human rights.

Under the first type of reform, a redesigned legal and economic framework would be predisposed to achieving net zero degradation to the environment and net zero greenhouse gas emissions. The suggested reform would include certain key features that would upgrade existing international legal and economic frameworks.[96] The reform suggestions to achieve this include, the creation of an international registration body for companies, the requirement that all companies achieve net zero degradation of the environment (including greenhouse gas emissions), the associated establishment of an international system of environmental accounting, the establishment of registered suppliers of environmental insurance, and the establishment of registered suppliers of environmental off-sets to enable companies to achieve the net zero requirements.[97] Within this framework corresponding legal obligations would be required through reforms of the WTO, and multilateral development banks. As a result, the insurance industry would provide a crucial service to business, industry

[94]Turner (2017), pp. 237–257.

[95]Turner (2017), pp. 237–257; Turner (2021), pp. 1–31.

[96]Turner (2014).

[97]Ibidem.

and ultimately to the environment to ensure that net zero levels of environmental degradation were achieved.[98]

In the second type of reform framework which would be equally applicable to the protection of human rights as to the protection of the environment, an extended role for compulsory liability insurance (CLI) is envisaged.[99] Under this model, a standard of environmental protection that may be 'net zero' is required of companies along with a concomitant requirement that human rights are 'fully protected'.[100] Whilst it has been recognised that the precise levels of protection that such terms signify would require clarification, the core element of this approach would be to require companies to achieve specific levels of protection of the environment and human rights to protect third party victims and to ensure that the costs of negative impacts would be borne by the companies themselves and not by host governments or the communities affected. CLI has already been implemented effectively in numerous jurisdictions, although it has not been extended so far for the protection of human rights. Whilst it does not represent a magic formula and it requires an effective liability regime to be implemented, it represents an approach that a significant number of governments appear to be willing to adopt.[101] It does have its critics but certainly there is a strong prima facie argument at least, that it could represent a major step forward, especially for individuals, entire communities and regions that suffer environmental degradation and human rights violations without adequate means for redress.[102]

The reform suggestions outlined here have commonalities and overlap in certain ways. However, both implicate the insurance industry as a major player in ensuring that business and industry would achieve net zero harm to the environment and have greater direct responsibility for fully protecting human rights. It is possible of course that a hybrid form of both above-stated models could be envisaged or that a different approach entirely could be adopted. The models act as a basis upon which governance regimes can be reformed and redesigned. However, that reform and design process requires all the relevant stakeholders to be engaged in the consultation processes. The role of the insurance industry, not only as a stakeholder that would be affected but also as a body whose composite expertise would be crucial in the design process is clear. Therefore, engagement of the insurance industry could be said to be a *sine qua non* of effective development and implementation.

---

[98] Ibidem.

[99] Turner and Bright (2022), pp. 145–165.

[100] Ibidem.

[101] Ibidem.

[102] Ibidem.

5 Conclusion

Changes to the environment and the responsibilities that businesses have in relation to the environment have gradually shifted the need for different types of insurance products as a new range of risks have materialised.

What this chapter has demonstrated is that although, as has been recognised, there is an increasing need for environmental insurance within specific sectors, such as those related to climate change,[103] there is a more fundamental change occurring at the global governance level which will have major ramifications for the insurance industry worldwide. This is that existing, international legal and economic frameworks are currently operating in accordance with a post-WWII economic system, which is not responding adequately to the priories of current generations. The international community now expects more from its systems of legal and economic governance and as such there is pressure to change accordingly. These changes have already started to occur and evidence of them has been seen through the developments that have taken place in the expectations of business, as seen in Sect. 3. However, it is clear that the pace of change is currently inadequate if the international community is to be in a position to safeguard people and the planet in the face of growing human rights and environmental challenges.

Therefore, it can be argued that the insurance industry should not merely be anticipating these changes in order to be ready for them from a commercial perspective, but it should be playing a significant and active role in their framing and development. This is because the insurance industry internationally has unique expertise within most business sectors and therefore if there is to be a reframing of business responsibilities through a re-set in the post WWII systems of international economic governance as it relates to human rights and the environment, the insurance industry should play a leading role in that change and in the associated governance redesign that accompanies it.

References

Agreement on Sanitary and Phytosanitary Measures 1994

Agreement on Technical Barriers to Trade 1994

Alexander K (2019) Principles of banking regulation. Cambridge University Press, Cambridge

Andenas M, Wooldridge F (2009) European comparative corporate law. Cambridge University Press, Cambridge

Annan K (2001) Laying the foundations of a fair and fee world trade system. In: Sampson GP (ed) The role of the World Trade Organization in global governance. United Nations University Press, Tokyo, pp 19–27

[103] Wouter Botzen (2013).

Backer LC (2021) The problem of the Enterprise and the Enterprise of law: multinational enterprises as polycentric transnational regulatory space. In: Zumbansen P (ed) The Oxford handbook of transnational law. Oxford University Press, Oxford
Biermann F, Pattberg P (eds) (2012) Global environmental governance reconsidered. MIT Press, Massachusetts
Bright C, Buhmann K (2020) Risk-based due diligence, climate change, human rights and the just transition. Sustainability 13(18):1–18
Bright C, Marx A, Pineau N, Wouters J (2020) Towards a corporate duty of Lead companies to respect human rights in their global value chains? Bus Politics 22(4):667–697
Bueno N, Bright C (2020) Implementing human rights due diligence through corporate civil liability. Int Comp Law Q 69(4):789–818
Chambers R (2021) Parent company direct liability for overseas human rights violations: lessons from the U.K. supreme court. U Pa J Int Law 42:519–578
Claire B, Axel M, Nina P, Jan W, (2020) Towards a corporate duty of Lead companies to respect human rights in their global value chains? Bus Politics 22(4):667–697
Cooreman B (2017) Global environmental protection through trade - a systematic approach to extraterritoriality. Edward Elgar, Cheltenham
Cutler C (2021) Reclaiming sovereignty: resistance to transnational authority and the investor-state regime. In: Zumbansen P (ed) Oxford handbook of transnational law. Oxford University Press, Oxford, p 130
Doha WTO Ministerial Declaration (2001) WT/MIN(01)/DEC/1 (20 Nov. 2001) paras 20–22. Available via: https://docs.wto.org/dol2fe/Pages/FE_Search/FE_S_S009-DP.aspx?language=E&CatalogueIdList=37246&CurrentCatalogueIdIndex=0&FullTextSearch=. Accessed on 10 May 2023
Elderton WP (1938) The impossibility of war risk insurance. Cambridge University Press, Cambridge
Esty D (1995) Greening the GATT – trade, environment and the future. Columbia University Press, New York
Esty D (2002) The World Trade Organisation's legitimacy crisis. World Trade Rev 1(1):7–22
European Parliament (2021) 'European Parliament Resolution with Recommendations to the Commission on Corporate Due Diligence and Corporate Accountability' (2020/2129(INL)), Available via: https://www.europarl.europa.eu/doceo/document/TA-9-2021-0073_EN.html#title2. Accessed on 10 May 2023
Francioni F (2001) Environment, human rights and the limits of free trade. In: Francioni F (ed) Environment, human rights and international trade. Hart Publishing, Oxford
General Agreement on Tariffs and Trade 1947
General Agreement on Tariffs and Trade 1994
German Federal Foreign Office (2020) 'Monitoring the National Action Plan for Business and Human Rights (NAP)', 13 October 2020. Available via: https://www.auswaertiges-amt.de/en/aussenpolitik/themen/aussenwirtschaft/wirtschaft-und-menschenrechte/monitoring-nap/2131054. Accessed on 10 May 2023
Gürses Ö (2020) The law of compulsory motor vehicle insurance. Routledge, Abingdon
Hall KR (1988) Mandatory insurance in Oregon. Competition Law 5(3):27–43
Hannigan B (2018) Company law, 5th edn. Oxford University Press, Oxford
Herdegen M (2016) Principles of international economic law. Oxford University Press, Oxford
ILO (2017) 'Tripartite Declaration of Principles Concerning Multinational Enterprises and Social Policy', Fifth edition, 2017. Available via: https://www.ilo.org/wcmsp5/groups/public/%2D%2D-ed_emp/%2D%2D-emp_ent/%2D%2D-multi/documents/publication/wcms_094386.pdf. Accessed on 10 May 2023
Kanie N, Andresen S, Haas PM (eds) (2014) Improving global environmental governance. Routledge, Abingdon
Knox JH, Pejan R (eds) (2018) The human right to a healthy environment. Cambridge University Press, Cambridge

Koskenniemi M (2011) The politics of international law. Hart, Oxford
Krajewski M, Tonstad K, Wohltmann F (2021) Mandatory human rights due diligence in Germany and Norway: stepping or striding, in the same direction? Bus Hum Rights J 6(3):550–558
LOI n 2017-399 du 27 Mars 2017 Relative au Devoir de Vigilance des Sociétés Mères et des Entreprises Donneuses D'ordre (1). Available via: https://www.legifrance.gouv.fr/affichTexte.do?cidTexte=JORFTEXT000034290626&categorieLien=id. Accessed on 10 May 2023
Macchi C, Bright C (2020) Hardening soft law: the implementation of the UNGPs in domestic legislations. In: Buscemi M, Lazzerini N, Magi L, Russo D (eds) Legal sources in business and human rights - evolving dynamics in international and European law. Brill, Leiden, pp 218–247
Marin JF, Orsini A (2013) Insights from global environmental governance. Int Stud Rev 15:562–589
McCorquodale R, Neely S (2022) Directors duties and human rights impacts: a comparative approach. J Corp L Stud 1-35. https://doi.org/10.1080/14735970.2021.2016147
Muchlinski PT (2021) Multinational enterprises and the law, 3rd edn. Oxford University Press, Oxford
OECD (1998) The MAI Draft Consolidated Text' DAFFE/MAI(98)7/REV1. Available via https://www.oecd.org/daf/mai/pdf/ng/ng987r1e.pdf. Accessed on 10 May 2023
OECD (2011) OECD Guidelines on Multinational Enterprises, 2011 edition. OECD Publishing. Available via: https://www.oecd.org/daf/inv/mne/48004323.pdf. Accessed on 10 May 2023
PACTE Law, Loi no 2019-486 of 22 May 2019. The Plan d'Action Pour la Croissance et la Transformation des Entreprises (Action Plan for Business Growth and Transformation) Available via: https://www.legifrance.gouv.fr/dossierlegislatif/JORFDOLE000037080861/. Accessed on 10 May 2023
Paolini A (ed) (2014) Research handbook on directors' duties. Edward Elgar, Cheltenham
Pelc K (2017) What explains the low success rate of investor-state disputes. International Organisation 71(3):559–583
Ramasastry A (2015) Corporate social responsibility versus business and human rights: bridging the gap between responsibility and accountability. J Human Rts 14:237–259
Roach L (2019) Company Law. Oxford University Press, Oxford
Romão AL, Ferreira AP, Cabrita I, Soarez L, Vaz M (2018) Resultados do I° Inquérito Nacional sobre Conduta Empresarial Responsável e Direitos Humanos. Available via: https://www.dgae.gov.pt/servicos/sustentabilidade-empresarial/responsabilidade-social-das-empresas.aspx. Accessed on 10 May 2023
Ruggie JG (2004) Reconstituting the global public domain—issues, actors, and practices. Eur J Int Relat 10(4):499–531
s. 166(2) The Companies Act 2013 (India). Available via https://www.mca.gov.in/Ministry/pdf/CompaniesAct2013.pdf. Accessed on 10 May 2023
s. 172 Companies Act (United Kingdom). Available via: https://www.legislation.gov.uk/ukpga/2006/46/contents. Accessed on 10 May 2023
Sampson G (2005) The WTO and sustainable development. United Nations University Press, Tokyo
Savourey E, Brabant S (2021) The French law on the duty of vigilance: theoretical and practical challenges since its adoption. Bus Human Rights J 6(1):141–152
Smit L, Bright C, McCorquodale R, Bauer M, Deringer H, Baeza-Breinbauer D, Torres-Cortés F, Alleweldt F, Kara S, Salinier C, Tejero Tobed H (2020) Study on due diligence requirements through the supply chain: Final Report. Study for the European Commission DG Justice and Consumers, 24 February 2020, Available via: https://op.europa.eu/en/publication-detail/-/publication/8ba0a8fd-4c83-11ea-b8b7-01aa75ed71a1/language-en. Accessed on 10 May 2023
Speth JG, Haas PM (2006) Global environmental governance. Pearson/Longman, Delhi
Subedi SP (2020) International investment law—reconciling policy and principle, 4th edn. Hart, Oxford
Surminkski S (2013) The role of risk transfer in encouraging climate investment. In: Dupuy PM, Vinuales JE (eds) Harnessing foreign investment to promote environmental protection in developing countries. Cambridge University Press, Cambridge, pp 228–253

The Hague District Court (26 May 2021) Vereniging Milieudefensie and al. v. Royal Dutch Shell, C/09/571832, Available via: https://uitspraken.rechtspraak.nl/inziendocument?id=ECLI:NL:RBDHA:2021:5339. Accessed on 10 May 2023

Trade-Related Aspects of Intellectual Property Rights 1994

Turner SJ (2009) A substantive environmental right—an examination of the legal obligations of decision-makers towards the environment. Kluwer Law International, Alphen aan den Rijn

Turner SJ (2014) A global environmental right. Earthscan by Routledge, Abingdon

Turner SJ (2017) The use of macro legal analysis in the understanding and development of global environmental governance. Transnational Environ L 6(2):237–257

Turner SJ (2021) Business, human rights and the environment - using macro legal analysis to develop a legal framework that coherently addresses the root causes of corporate human rights violations and environmental degradation. Sustainability 13:12709. https://doi.org/10.3390/su132212709, 1-31

Turner SJ, Bright C (2022) From 'due diligence' to 'adequate redress'. Towards compulsory human rights and environmental Insurance for Companies? Int Community Law Rev 24:145–165

UN GA (2022) 'The Human Right to a Clean, Healthy and Sustainable Environment' UNGA Res. A/76/L.75

UNCTAD (2015) Investment policy framework for sustainable development. Available via https://unctad.org/en/PublicationsLibrary/diaepcb2015d5_en.pdf. Accessed on 10 May 2023

UNCTAD (2021a) World investment report. United Nations Publications, New York

UNCTAD (2021b) Investment Policy Hub. International Investment Agreements Navigator. Available via https://investmentpolicy.unctad.org/international-investment-agreements. Accessed on 10 May 2023

United Nations, Commission on Human Rights (26 August 2003) Sub-Commission on the Promotion and Protection of Human Rights (2003) Norms on the Responsibilities of Transnational Corporations and Other Business Enterprises with Regard to Human Rights. E/CN.4/Sub.2/2013/12/Rev.2 (Draft Norms)

United Nations Global Compact (2005) Available via: https://www.unglobalcompact.org/about/governance. Accessed on 10 May 2023

United Nations Human Rights Council (2008) 'Protect Respect and Remedy: a Framework for Business and Human Rights', Report of the Special Representative of the Secretary-General on the issue of human rights and transnational corporations and other business enterprises, John Ruggie, A/HRC/8/5, 7 April 2008

United Nations Human Rights Office of the High Commissioner (OHCHR) (2011) 'Guiding Principles on Business and Human Rights: Implementing the United Nations "Protect, Respect and Remedy" Framework'. Available via: https://www.ohchr.org/documents/publications/guidingprinciplesbusinesshr_en.pdf. Accessed on 10 May 2023

Van den Bossche P, Prévost D (2021) Essentials of WTO law, 2nd edn. Cambridge University Press, Cambridge

Van Ho T (2021) Obligations of international assistance and cooperation in the context of investment law. In: Gibney M, Erdem Türkelli G, Krajewski M, Vandenhole W (eds) The Routledge handbook on extraterritorial human rights obligations. Routledge, Abingdon, pp 325–334

World Benchmarking Alliance (2020) 'Corporate Human Rights Benchmark - Across sectors: Agricultural products, Apparel, Automotive manufacturing, Extractives & ICT manufacturing, 2020 Key findings'. Available via: https://assets.worldbenchmarkingalliance.org/app/uploads/2020/11/WBA-2020-CHRB-Key-Findings-Report.pdf. Accessed on 10 May 2023

Wouter Botzen WJ (2013) Managing extreme climate change risks through insurance. Cambridge University Press, Cambridge

WTO Membership. Available via https://www.wto.org/english/thewto_e/whatis_e/tif_e/org6_e.htm. Accessed on 10 May 2023

Yilmaz Vastardis A (2020) Investment treaty arbitration as justice bubbles. In: Schultz T, Ortino F (eds) Oxford handbook of international arbitration. Oxford University Press, Oxford, pp 617–640

Environmental Liabilities and Insurance Law in the European Union

Valerie Fogleman

Abstract Each Member State of the European Union (EU) imposes tort liability, including liability from exposure to pollutants and other environmental damage. The liabilities are set out in civil codes, laws of obligations, and similar legislation. Some Member States include liability for pure economic loss as well as bodily injury and property damage. In addition, many Member States impose liability for remediating historic land contamination that continues to pose a risk to human health and the environment.

The predominant environmental permitting legislation in the EU is EU legislation, which is accompanied in most Member States by more extensive national environmental permitting legislation and, in some Member States, environmental liability legislation. Since 2007, EU legislation has imposed liability for preventing and remediating pollution and other environmental damage including damage to natural resources.

Insurance that provides cover for environmental liabilities, including tort claims and costs of remediating environmental damage, differs substantially between Member States. Whereas large and multinational companies tend to have no problem in purchasing environmental insurance policies, the policies are not always available to companies that have sites and/or operations in a single Member State. The policies are widely available to such companies in some Member States but available only to a limited extent or not at all in other Member States. Environmental extensions to general liability policies tend to be widely available in most Member States with the caveat that cover provided by them is limited or severely limited except in Austria and Germany.

A few Member States have imposed mandatory financial security for the prevention and remediation of environmental damage under EU legislation. A much larger number have imposed mandatory financial security on persons that carry out waste

V. Fogleman (✉)
Cardiff University School of Law and Politics, Cardiff, Wales, UK

Stevens & Bolton LLP, Guildford, England, UK
e-mail: foglemanvm@cardiff.ac.uk; valerie.fogleman@stevens-bolton.com

K. Malinowska, D. Maśniak (eds.), *Managing Environmental Risks through Insurance*, AIDA Europe Research Series on Insurance Law and Regulation 9,
https://doi.org/10.1007/978-3-031-47602-0_3

operations or other specified operations. The requirements differ substantially between Member States.

This chapter examines EU and national environmental liabilities, insurance for such liabilities, and mandatory financial security for them.

1 Introduction

This chapter examines European Union (EU) and national law for environmental liabilities and insurance law for such liabilities. The chapter does not attempt to describe national law for each Member State. Instead, it discusses key differences in such laws and provides examples of such laws in individual Member States.

The chapter is structured as follows.

Section 2 examines three types of environmental liabilities: tort law; legislation that imposes liability for remediating historic contamination[1]; and legislation that imposes liability for preventing and remediating current and future pollution and other environmental damage.

Section 3 examines insurance for the environmental liabilities described in Sect. 2. This section describes providers of environmental insurance. It then describes cover for environmental liabilities in general liability and property policies, focusing on environmental extensions that provide cover for some—but not all—liabilities arising from pollution and other environmental damage.

Section 3 continues the examination of insurance for environmental liabilities by discussing environmental insurance policies. These policies specifically provide cover for liabilities that arise from pollution and other types of environmental damage caused by an insured. This section of the chapter begins by discussing the extent of cover provided by such policies, followed by their availability and the demand for them. As discussed, this varies widely depending in large part on the size of businesses that apply for such policies.

Finally, Sect. 4 discusses mandatory financial security requirements for environmental responsibilities and liabilities at an EU and a Member State level. The environmental liabilities discussed include liabilities under the Environmental Liability Directive (ELD)[2] and liabilities for various activities including waste activities.

[1]This chapter uses the words 'contamination' and 'pollution' to refer to damage to land/soil and the word 'pollution' to refer to damage to water and air. The use of the two words is not intended to denote different meanings between them.

[2]Directive 2004/35/EC on environmental liability with regard to the prevention and remedying of environmental damage [2004] OJ L143/56 (consolidated version); https://eur-lex.europa.eu/legal-content/EN/TXT/PDF/?uri=CELEX:02004L0035-20190626&qid=1568193390794&from=EN (accessed on 10.05.2023).

2 Environmental Liabilities

There are three main types of environmental liabilities in Member States in the EU. They are tort law—also called civil liability; liability for remediating historic contamination that continues to pose a risk to human health and the environment; and liability for the prevention, remediation and restoration of current and future pollution and other types of environmental damage.

2.1 Tort Law

Tort law, that is, civil liability for claims for bodily injury, property damage, and economic loss (in some Member States), exists only in Member States' national law. No EU legislation currently imposes liability for such claims although this may change.

In Member States with a civil liability system, tort liabilities are set out in legislation such as Civil Codes, Laws on Obligations and Contracts, Civil Obligations Acts, and Laws of Civil Wrongs. In Member States that have common law (Ireland) or a mixture of civil liability and common law (Cyprus and Malta), the common law imposes liability for torts such as nuisance, negligence and liability for dangerous activities.

2.1.1 Consequential and Pure Economic Loss

As indicated in Sect. 2.1 above, tort law imposes liability for bodily injury and property damage. In addition, civil liability and common law systems tend to impose liability for consequential economic loss (sometimes called relational or indirect economic loss), that is, financial loss that is a direct consequence of bodily injury or property damage. Examples are loss of income suffered by a person whose health is harmed by exposure to pollution resulting in them being unable to work or loss of income suffered by a business due to damage to its property by pollution (such as damage to a fishing boat) on which the business depends for its income.

A limited number of Member States impose liability for pure economic loss, that is, loss in the absence of bodily injury or property damage.

Professors Palmer and Bussani compared pure economic loss claims with consequential economic loss claims as follows:

> [pure economic loss is] loss without antecedent harm to a plaintiff's person or property. Here the word 'pure' plays a central role, for if there is economic loss that is connected to the slightest damage to person or property of the plaintiff (provided that all other conditions of liability are met) then the latter is called consequential economic loss and the whole set of

> damages may be recovered without question. Consequential economic loss (sometimes also termed parasitic loss) is recoverable because it presupposes the existence of physical injuries, whereas pure economic loss strikes the victim's wallet and nothing else.[3]

France is foremost in the EU in recognising pure economic loss claims. Italy, Greece and the Netherlands appear to recognise them, whereas pure economic loss is not recognised in Germany, Portugal or Spain. Some other Member States recognise pure economic loss claims subject to restrictions. For example, Romania recognises claims for pure economic loss in exceptional circumstances. Other Member States impose limitations for them.

Professor Willem van Boom described the reason for limitations on pure economic loss as follows:

> in all European jurisdictions, the concept of causation renders it possible to exclude unwanted floods of claims on the basis of remoteness, unforeseeability, or indirectness of the damage incurred. Whenever a legal system in principle allows claims for pure economic loss, the emphasis is inevitably placed upon causation principles in order to channel claims and to ensure that the right balance between admission and restriction is kept.[4]

2.1.2 Standard of Liability

Civil liability and common law tort systems are based on negligence or fault. In order to bring a claim, the claimant must prove that the act by the defendant that caused harm was carried out negligently or that the defendant was otherwise at fault.

Civil liability and common law tort systems typically also impose strict liability for a narrow category of so-called 'dangerous activities'. Examples in civil liability systems include storing hazardous chemicals or explosives, transporting toxic chemicals, and demolition activities. Other categories of torts subject to strict liability are the custody of dangerous animals that cause damage and, in some Member States, dangerous buildings.

The reasons for the imposition of strict liability for dangerous activities are threefold. First, a person that carries out a dangerous activity benefits—often monetarily—from doing so. Second, the person carrying out the dangerous activity has the power to control risks from it. Third, the person who suffers harm from a dangerous activity has a generally recognised interest in not being harmed by it.

Some Member States have established a middle category between fault-based and strict liability by the creation of a rebuttable presumption. Under this category, the liability system provides for a reversal of the burden of proof for dangerous activities. If the claimant establishes the prerequisites of the tort, the defendant is liable unless it proves that it was not negligent or otherwise at fault.

The imposition of strict liability for harm caused by dangerous activities and other dangerous factors as indicated above is not absolute liability. The same defences that

---

[3] Palmer and Bussani (2007); see also Bussani et al. (2003), p. 113.

[4] van Boom (2004), p. 17.

apply to fault-based liability may also apply to strict liability. Such defences include *force majeure*, the harm having been caused by an action by a third party, and harm that would have occurred despite the tortfeasor exercising care or otherwise taking measures to avoid it.[5]

2.1.3 Scope of Liability

Depending on the Member State, the scope of liability is joint and several or proportionate.

Liability is joint and several when two or more tortfeasors are responsible for a single injury suffered by the claimant. If one or more tortfeasors cannot be located, the remaining tortfeasor(s) are liable for the entire injury.

Liability is proportionate when a tortfeasor is liable only for the proportion of harm caused by it.

2.1.4 Remedies

The typical remedy for a tort is monetary compensation for the harm or loss suffered by the claimant, with the purpose of making the claimant 'whole'. That is, to return the claimant to the state in which the claimant would have been in but for the tort.

Most Member States limit remedies to compensatory damages and/or injunctions to prohibit the defendant continuing to carry out the activities that cause damage or harm.

Provisions for punitive, or exemplary, damages in Member States of the EU are rare.[6]

2.1.5 Limitations Periods

Tort systems typically include limitation periods after which a claim may no longer be brought. The length of such periods varies between Member States and sometimes between torts, depending in large part on individual Member States and the type of claim.

Some Member States have established discovery dates for claims for bodily injury in order to allow claimants to bring actions for harm caused by diseases and other injuries when the disease or injury was not discoverable on the date on which the harm occurred. An example is diseases with long latency periods such as mesothelioma from exposure to asbestos. Under a limitations period with a

---

[5] See Koziol (2012); https://www.jan-sramek-verlag.at/fileadmin/user_upload/Koziol_CompараTortLaw_Eng_0040_2_DRUCK_eBook.pdf (accessed on 10.05.2023).

[6] See Koziol (2008), p. 748.

discovery rule, the accrual period begins on the date that the victim becomes aware—or should become aware—of the harm instead of the date of the injury. Such systems invariably include a long-stop—generally between 12 and 30 years—after which claims may no longer be brought.

2.1.6 Liability Systems Specifically for Environmental Damage

A Member State may also adopt legislation that specifically imposes liability for bodily injury and property damage that arises from environmental damage.

The predominant example is Germany. The German Environmental Liability Act of 10 December 1990 (*Umwelthaftungsgesetz*; UmweltHG) imposes strict liability on the operator of an installation listed in Annex 1 of the Act for death, bodily injury and property damage up to EUR 85,000,000 caused by an environmental impact including damage by substances, vibrations, noise, radiation, gas, vapours and heat.

Annex 1 of the UmweltHG lists 96 types of installations grouped into the following ten categories:

1. mining, energy and heat production;
2. manufacture of products from stone, earth, glass, ceramic, and other construction materials;
3. processing and manufacture of steel, iron, and other metals;
4. manufacture of chemical, pharmaceutical, or petroleum products or their further processing;
5. treatment with organic materials and the manufacture of artificial materials;
6. wood and wood pulp processing;
7. production of food, feed, and agricultural products;
8. waste treatment;
9. storage and disposal of specified materials; and,
10. other facilities, including paint, printing ink, asphalt, etc. production.[7]

The UmweltHG includes a rebuttable presumption according to which an installation is presumed to have caused the damage if, taking into account the facts and circumstances of a case, the installation is likely to have caused it. Likelihood is assessed by considering various factors including: the type of damage; the machines, vehicles, ancillary structures and other facilities that were being used when the damage occurred; the time and place of the damage; operating procedures of the installation; meteorological factors; and the type and concentration of substances that were used and released.

The operator of the installation may rebut the presumption if it shows either that the installation was being operated in accordance with its intended use, specific

[7] See Hoffman (1991), pp. 487, 498 footnote 37.

operating procedures were complied with, and there was no disruption of operations, or that another factor was likely to have caused the damage.[8]

2.2 *Remediation of Historic Contamination*

Liability for the remediation of historic contamination that continues to pose a risk to human health and the environment exists only in the national law of Member States. There is no EU legislation that imposes liability for the remediation of historic contamination. In 2006, the European Commission proposed establishing a Soil Framework Directive that would, among other things, have directed Member States to investigate, assess, and remediate damage to contaminated land in their territories.[9] The Commission withdrew the proposed Directive in 2014[10] following a blocking minority by Austria, France, Germany, the Netherlands and the United Kingdom.[11]

Legislation adopted by Member States focuses on the remediation of contaminated land, with the addition of groundwater and, to a more limited extent, surface water in some Member States (e.g., Belgium, Denmark, Finland, Germany, the Netherlands, Romania, Slovakia).

Member States began introducing such legislation in the early 1980s following the discovery of contaminated sites, especially in Denmark, the Netherlands, and Sweden. In Denmark, a waste dump was discovered that was leaching approximately five tonnes of mercury and other chemicals into the sea at Harboøre Tange.[12] In the Netherlands, hazardous waste was discovered at residential areas in

[8] See Schreier (2020), p. 65, section 3.1; see also Fogleman (2020), section 3.7.2; https://circabc.europa.eu/ui/group/3b48eff1-b955-423f-9086-0d85ad1c5879/library/7d116574-6f1e-47ee-a8d6-b809f1b82b5a?p=1&n=-1&sort=name_ASC (scroll down to 'Study – Financial Security for ELD Liabilities (2020) – reports per Member State') (accessed on 10.05.2023).

[9] Proposal for a Directive of the European Parliament and of the Council establishing a framework for the protection of soil and amending Directive 2004/35/EC (COM(2006) 232 final, 22 September 2006); https://eur-lex.europa.eu/legal-content/EN/TXT/?uri=CELEX:52006PC0232 (accessed on 10.05.2023).

[10] European Commission, Withdrawal of Obsolete Commission Proposals [2014] OJ C153/3; http://eur-lex.europa.eu/legal-content/EN/TXT/PDF/?uri=OJ:C:2014:153:FULL&from=EN (accessed on 10.05.2023).

[11] See Report from the Commission to the European Parliament, the Council, the European Economic and Social Committee and the Committee of the Regions, The implementation of the Soil Thematic Strategy and ongoing activities (COM)2012, 46 final, section 2.4; https://eur-lex.europa.eu/legal-content/EN/TXT/?uri=CELEX:52012DC0046 (accessed on 10.05.2023); see also Heuser (2022), p. 100,053, section 5; https://www.sciencedirect.com/science/article/pii/S266700622200020X (accessed on 10.05.2023).

[12] Church and Nakamura (1994), pp. 41–42; Ministry of the Environment (2003).

Lekkerkerk and Gouderak.[13] In Sweden, a waste dump at Skåne that contained approximately 800 barrels of hazardous waste was discovered.[14]

Nearly all Member States (e.g., Austria, Belgium, Bulgaria, Czechia, Denmark, France, Germany, Italy, Latvia, Lithuania, Luxembourg, Romania, Slovakia, Slovenia, Spain, Sweden) have introduced contaminated land regimes, some of which are highly sophisticated.[15] A notable exception is Ireland due to the Irish Constitution prohibiting the adoption of legislation that imposes retroactive civil liability.[16] The lack of a contaminated land regime does not mean that competent authorities in Ireland do not impose liability on persons that cause land to be contaminated. As in other Member States such as Portugal, competent authorities apply waste management legislation and environmental permitting legislation to require remediation.

Competent authorities in some other Member States (e.g., Austria (federal level), Estonia, Ireland, Latvia, Luxembourg) also apply waste management legislation to remediate contaminated land. Competent authorities in some other Member States that have not adopted a specific regime for remediating contaminated land apply environmental permitting legislation (e.g., Malta).

Some Member States (e.g., Croatia, Czechia, Slovakia) have adopted legislation that imposes liability specifically for the remediation of agricultural land that is contaminated, whilst some other Member States (e.g., Czechia, Estonia, Lithuania) have adopted legislation that imposes liability specifically for the remediation of contaminated forestry land.

A substantial number of Member States that have established liability for remediating contaminated land have also established regimes in which land that is discovered to be contaminated or potentially contaminated by historic pollution is placed on an inventory. In some Member States (e.g., Czechia, Denmark, France, Latvia, Romania, Spain) the inventories are managed at a local or regional level.[17] Screening of sites on the inventories is carried out to assess the degree and nature of

---

[13] See Lewis (1983) http://www.nytimes.com/1983/02/20/weekinreview/following-us-europe-awakens-to-the-dangers-of-toxic-wastes.html (accessed on 10.05.2023); see also Betlem (1995), p. 289, 294.

[14] See Lewis (1983) http://www.nytimes.com/1983/02/20/weekinreview/following-us-europe-awakens-to-the-dangers-of-toxic-wastes.html (accessed on 10.05.2023); Baltic Environment and Energy, Swedish Environmental Policies, History and present regulations (2007), p. 5; see also Fogleman 2015, pp. 42–61.

[15] The following discussion on the contaminated land regimes of Member States is drawn in particular from Fogleman (2021), pp. 100–104; https://ec.europa.eu/environment/legal/liability/pdf/study/FinalReport.PDF (accessed on 10.05.2023) (click on 'Studies' and then 'Study – Facilitating enforcement of the ELD by competent authorities (2021) – Final Report' and 'Studies' and then 'Study – Facilitating enforcement of the ELD by competent authorities (2021) – Member State Report'.

[16] Article 15.5 of the Irish Constitution states, in pertinent part, that Parliament 'shall not declare acts to be infringements of the law which were not so at the date of their commission'. See *Magee v Culligan* [1992] 1 IRLM 223 (per Finlay CJ; provision applies to civil as well as criminal liability).

[17] Pérez and Eugenio (2018), p. 44; https://publications.jrc.ec.europa.eu/repository/handle/JRC107508 (accessed on 10.05.2023).

the contamination or potential contamination in order to determine whether the site should be remediated.

If a site requires remediation and it is not possible to identify a person that is liable for remediating it or a liable person that has the financial ability to do so, the site may be placed—and prioritised—on a list of sites awaiting remedial measures when State funding is available. An example is France, which has an inventory of sites that are potentially or actually contaminated[18] and an inventory that includes details of historic uses of sites that may be contaminated.[19]

Contaminated land regimes in the EU tend to impose primary liability on the person (or persons) that caused the contamination. They also tend to impose secondary liability on current owners and, to a more limited extent occupiers, of contaminated sites that did not cause or permit the contamination (e.g., Austria, Belgium, Bulgaria, Latvia, Spain, Sweden).

Germany is an exception in that it imposes primary liability on the following persons:

- the person that caused the pollution;
- the legal successor of the person that caused the pollution, for example by inheritance or a merger;
- the current owner of the contaminated land;
- the current occupier of the contaminated land; and,
- the former owner of the contaminated land provided that it transferred the land on or after 1 March 1999.

Some Member States (e.g., Austria, Finland, Slovakia, Sweden) have a so-called 'innocent landowner' defence according to which the owner of a contaminated site is not liable if it proves that it did not know and had no reason to know that the site was contaminated when it acquired it.

Some Member States have a more limited innocent landowner defence. For example, in Finland, the owner or occupier of land that was contaminated before the owner or occupier acquired a legal interest in the land is not liable unless the following criteria are met:

- the relevant authority issued, or indicated that it would issue, an order requiring the contaminated land to be remediated before the owner or occupier acquired the land;

[18] Base des sols pollués (BASOL); https://www.data.gouv.fr/en/datasets/base-des-sols-pollues/#description (accessed on 10.05.2023) (in French); see also Darmendrail (2010), p. 277; https://www.researchgate.net/publication/280784366_The_French_approach_to_contaminated_land_management_Legal_framework_and_reclamation_of_former_industrial_sites_in_urban_areas/link/566aa29c08aea0892c4a4ac6/download (accessed on 10.05.2023).

[19] Inventaire des sites pollués (BASIAS); https://www.data.gouv.fr/en/datasets/inventaire-des-sites-pollues/ (in French) (accessed on 10.05.2023).

- the order was not complied with despite the requirement to remediate the contamination having been emphasised and circumstances concerning it having been reported to the police; and either,
- the owner or occupier knew or should have known that an order to investigate or remediate the land had been issued when it acquired the land, or the land was acquired by a person that was or could be required to comply with the order.

In the majority of Member States, liability for the costs of remediating contaminated land is unlimited. In contrast, in some other Member States, such liability is limited. An example of limited liability is Italy, in which a landowner that did not cause its land to be contaminated is secondarily liable. The landowner's liability is limited to the difference between the value of the land when it was contaminated and its value after land has been remediated. A competent authority cannot require the landowner to remediate the land. The authority must carry out the remediation and then claim reimbursement for the cost of doing so from the landowner.

A substantial number of Member States (e.g., Austria, Bulgaria, Estonia, Finland, Italy, Latvia, Romania) have numeric thresholds to indicate when land/soil should be remediated. Some Member States (e.g., Austria, Estonia, Finland, Italy, Slovenia) have more than one threshold depending on the future use of the land, such as residential, industrial and commercial land. Italy has two numeric thresholds: a threshold for concentrated contaminant levels, above which a risk analysis must be carried out; and a risk concentration threshold, above which specified pollutants must be remediated. The assessments apply on a case-by-case basis. Other Member States (e.g., Finland, Hungary, Portugal) have numeric values and a requirement for a risk assessment to be carried out.

Most Member States impose strict liability for remediating contaminated land. A few Member States impose fault-based or strict liability depending on the time at which the land was contaminated. For example, if a site in Finland was contaminated between 1 April 1979 and 31 December 1993 and the person that caused the contamination cannot be found or is not financially viable, the current landowner is required to remediate the land. If, however, no contamination occurred after 1 April 1979, the current landowner is liable regardless of whether it caused the contamination.

The regime in the Netherlands is even more complex. If contamination occurred between 1 January 1975 and 1 January 1987, the current landowner and the person that caused the contamination are liable. If the land was contaminated before 1 January 1975, the current landowner is not liable unless it caused the contamination, was at fault in causing it, and knew or should have known that causing it would result in the State suffering financial harm in the form of the costs of measures to remediate the contamination.

In the Flemish Region of Belgium, three categories of persons are responsible for remediating contaminated land. The operator of a facility or activity for which there is an environmental permit to carry out operations on the land has primary responsibility. If no activities subject to an environmental permit are being carried out, the occupier of the land has secondary responsibility. If there is no occupier or the occupier is exempt from liability, the owner of the land has tertiary responsibility unless the owner can show that another person controls the land. The Flemish system thus differentiates between responsibility and liability for remediating contaminated land/soil. If a person that is responsible for remediating contamination remediates it, that person may claim against the person that is liable for remediating it—assuming of course that the liable person can be found and is financially viable. If the contamination occurred after 29 October 1995, the contamination is 'new contamination' and the operator or occupier is strictly liable. If the contamination occurred before that date, the contamination is 'historic contamination' and detailed rules apply that limit responsibility for the costs of remediating it.

In Hungary, there is a rebuttable presumption that the current landowner is the person that contaminated the land. The landowner may rebut the presumption if it identifies the person that occupied the land and proves beyond a reasonable doubt that the landowner is not liable for contaminating it.

In addition to the above regimes for remediating contaminated land, many contaminated sites are remediated voluntarily during their development under spatial planning and building legislation.

2.3 Remediation of Current and Future Environmental Damage

Liability for the remediation of current and future environmental damage is a mix of EU and non-EU environmental permitting and liability legislation.

2.3.1 Environmental Permitting Legislation

Environmental permitting legislation is the main regulatory legislation for the remediation of land/soil and water pollution and, to a much more limited extent, the remediation of damage to wildlife and ecosystems. There are two types of environmental permitting legislation, EU legislation and national legislation.

The main EU environmental permitting legislation is the Industrial Emissions Directive (IED).[20] Other relevant EU legislation is the Seveso III Directive[21] and the Waste Framework Directive.[22]

2.3.1.1 Industrial Emissions Directive

In 1996, the EU adopted the first Directive on integrated pollution prevention and control.[23] The Directive introduced an EU-wide integrated system of environmental permitting that covered a wide range of installations (and mobile plants) that carried out industrial-related activities.

In 2008, the Directive was codified as the IPPC Directive.[24] The IPPC Directive expanded the permitting system of the 1996 version and increased its scope. The IPPC Directive directed Member States to take necessary measures, among other things, to ensure that 'the operator regularly informs the competent authority of the results of the monitoring of releases and without delay of any incident or accident significantly affecting the environment'.[25] Further, the IPPC Directive directed Member States to:

> take the necessary measures to provide that the competent authorities ensure that installations are operated in such a way that:
>
> (a) the appropriate preventive measures are taken against pollution, in particular through application of the best available techniques; [and]
> (b) no significant pollution is caused.

Conditions in environmental permits issued under the IPPC Directive set out emission limit values (ELVs) for pollutants that are allowed to be discharged or otherwise released from the installation. An ELV is defined as 'the mass, expressed in terms of certain specific parameters, concentration and/or level of an emission,

---

[20] Directive 2010/75/EU on industrial emissions (integrated pollution prevention and control) [2010] OJ L158/25 (consolidated version); https://eur-lex.europa.eu/legal-content/EN/TXT/?uri=CELEX%3A02010L0075-20110106 (accessed on 10.05.2023).

[21] Directive (2012/18/EU) on the control of major-accident hazards involving dangerous substances [2012] OJ L197/1; https://eur-lex.europa.eu/legal-content/EN/TXT/?uri=CELEX:32012L0018 (accessed on 10.05.2023).

[22] Directive 2008/98/EC on waste [2008] OJ L312/3, as amended (consolidated version); https://eur-lex.europa.eu/legal-content/EN/TXT/?uri=CELEX%3A02008L0098-20180705 (accessed on 10.05.2023).

[23] Council Directive 96/61/EC concerning integrated pollution prevention and control [1996] OJ L257/26 (repealed); https://eur-lex.europa.eu/legal-content/EN/TXT/?uri=CELEX%3A31996L0061 (accessed on 10.05.2023).

[24] Directive 2008/1/EC concerning integrated pollution prevention and control [2008] OJ L24/8, art 14(b) (consolidated version) (repealed); https://eur-lex.europa.eu/legal-content/EN/TXT/PDF/?uri=CELEX:32008L0001&from=EN (accessed on 10.05.2023).

[25] Ibid., Article 14(b).

which may not be exceeded during one or more periods of time'.[26] If an operator exceeds an ELV, it may be required to remediate soil and/or groundwater pollution resulting from the emission.

In 2010, the IPPC Directive and six other Directives were recast as the IED. In addition, the IED extended the IPPC Directive to ELVs for further pollutants, extended its application to additional industrial sectors, and strengthened controls on monitoring soil and groundwater and the remediation of pollution.

Approximately 52,000 installations that carry out the following types of industrial activities across the EU are subject to the IED: 'power plants, refineries, waste treatment and incineration, production of metals, cement, glass, chemicals, pulp and paper, food and drink, and the intensive rearing of pigs and poultry'.[27]

An applicant for a permit for an installation subject to the IED must, among other things:

- examine and describe measures to operate the installation so as not to cause any significant pollution, take necessary measures to prevent accidents and to limit their consequences, and avoid the risk of pollution;
- apply best available techniques (BATs);
- prepare, as applicable, a baseline report to assess the state of soil and groundwater pollution by relevant substances when a permit is granted; and,
- prepare a further report when the permit is surrendered and, if significant soil and/or groundwater pollution has occurred, restore the site of the installation to a 'satisfactory state', that is, its state when the permit was granted.

BAT reference documents (BREFs), which have been prepared for many different processes—and are continually being updated—are designed to prevent, reduce and as far as possible eliminate pollution from emissions in order to achieve a high level of protection of the environment.

On 5 April 2022, the European Commission submitted a proposal to revise the IED.[28] The revised IED, when it is adopted, will among other things, strengthen permit controls on emissions of pollutants into the air and waters and extend industrial and agricultural sectors covered by the IED to include the intensive rearing of cattle and mining for specified minerals (but not coal).

---

[26] Ibid., Article 3(5).

[27] See Proposal for a Directive of the European Parliament and the Council amending Directive 2010/75/EU of the European Parliament and of the Council of 24 November 2010 on industrial emissions (integrated pollution prevention and control) and Council Directive 1999/31/EC of 26 April 1999 on the landfill of waste (COM(2022) 156 final, 5 April 2022), explanatory memorandum, section 1; https://eur-lex.europa.eu/legal-content/EN/TXT/?uri=CELEX%3A52022PC0156R%2802%29&qid=1651130627889 (accessed on 10.05.2023).

[28] Ibid.

2.3.1.2 Seveso III Directive

The EU adopted the first Seveso Directive in 1982.[29] In 1996, it adopted the Seveso II Directive[30]; in 2012, it adopted the Seveso III Directive.

The reason for the adoption of the first Seveso Directive was the rupture in 1976 of a reaction vessel containing trichlorophenol at a small chemical facility for pesticides and herbicides in Seveso, Italy. The contents overheated and ruptured the disk of the vessel's safety valve resulting in approximately six metric tonnes of gas containing dioxin, which is highly carcinogenic, to be released into the atmosphere. The gas drifted over Seveso and other nearby small towns, exposing over 37,000 people to high levels of dioxin, resulting in them developing blurred vision, nausea, skin inflammation, and severe chloracne. The release of the gas was not made public for several days, thus causing a delay in evacuating people before they were exposed to the gas. In addition to causing harm to persons exposed to dioxin, children born to women exposed to it were subsequently found more likely to have altered thyroid function than other children. In addition, over 3300 animals were subsequently found dead or slaughtered.

The first Seveso Directive, and the Seveso II Directive, were subsequently amended to take into account, among other things, revisions to EU legislation on the classification of chemicals and public participation.

The Seveso III Directive sets out rules for the prevention of major accidents that involve dangerous substances, and the limitation of their consequences for human health and the environment, with a view to ensuring a high level of protection throughout the EU in a consistent and effective manner.

The Seveso III Directive applies to over 12,000 establishments in the EU at which dangerous substances are stored, mainly petrochemical establishments. The Directive divides the establishments into lower tier and upper tier depending on the amount and type of dangerous substances stored at them. Upper tier establishments are subject to more extensive requirements than lower tier establishments, including requirements:

- to identify and evaluate major hazards, their possible consequences, and prevention and control measures;
- to prepare a safety report to demonstrate that a major accident prevention policy (MAPP) has been prepared and put into effect;
- to submit the safety report to relevant competent authorities;

[29] Council Directive 82/501/EEC on the major-accident hazards of certain industrial activities [1982] OJ L230/1 (repealed); https://eur-lex.europa.eu/legal-content/EN/TXT/?uri=CELEX:31982L0501 (accessed on 10.05.2023).

[30] Council Directive 96/82/EC on the control of major-accident hazardous involving dangerous substances [1996] OJ L10 (consolidated version) (repealed); https://eur-lex.europa.eu/legal-content/EN/TXT/PDF/?uri=CELEX:01996L0082-20120813&from=EN (accessed on 10.05.2023).

- to prepare a safety report that shows the existence of a safety management system (which must include internal and external emergency plans);
- to make all employees aware of the potential for major accidents and be trained to prevent them;
- to test the emergency plan by regular exercises and other appropriate means;
- to review the safety report periodically for effectiveness and suitability;
- to include public participation requirements; and,
- to provide information on safety measures and applicable behaviour to persons that may be affected by a major accident.

Liability is strict and is channelled to the operator. No defences or exclusions apply. The measures and standard of remediation for the prevention and remediation of environmental damage caused by dangerous substances are those that are envisaged to mitigate its medium-term and long-term effects and to prevent any recurrence of such an accident.

The objective of establishing emergency plans for upper tier establishments is to provide 'for the restoration and clean-up of the environment following a major accident'.

The term 'major accident' is defined as:

> an occurrence such as a major emission, fire, or explosion resulting from uncontrolled developments in the course of the operation of any establishment covered by [the Seveso III Directive] and leading to serious danger to human health or the environment, immediate or delayed, inside or outside the establishment, and involving one or more dangerous substances.

Some installations that are subject to the IED are also subject to the Seveso III Directive.

2.3.1.3 Waste Framework Directive

The Waste Framework Directive does not impose liability for preventing or remediating environmental damage. Instead, it established responsibilities which, in some cases, require persons carrying out waste management activities to prevent or remediate damage from waste pollutants.

Article 14(1) of the Waste Framework Directive provides as follows:

> [i]n accordance with the polluter-pays principle, the costs of waste management shall be borne by the original waste producer or by the current or previous waste holders.

Article 3(1) defines the term 'waste' very broadly to mean 'any substance or object which the holder discards or intends or is required to discard'.

Article 3(5) defines a 'waste producer' as:

> anyone whose activities produce waste (original waste producer) or anyone who carries out pre-processing, mixing or other operations resulting in a change in the nature or composition of this waste.

Article 3(6) defines a 'waste holder' as 'the waste producer or the natural or legal person who is in possession of the waste'.

The Waste Framework Directive directs Member States to take necessary measures to ensure that any original waste producer or other waste holder carries out the treatment of waste itself or has such treatment handled by an authorised person. There is no threshold for when a pollutant is waste. In addition, there is no requirement for a substance to cause harm to human health and the environment in order to be waste. Further, the Directive does not contain any defences.

Some Member States implement provisions of the Waste Framework Directive to require original waste producers and waste holders to remediate damage caused by waste and to prevent further damage.

The CJEU has also discussed the close link between responsibility under the Waste Framework Directive and liability for remediating waste pollutants.

The CJEU case of *Van de Walle v Texaco Belgium SA* involved hydrocarbons that had leaked from a tank at a service station in the Brussels-Capital Region. The region discovered water contaminated by hydrocarbons in the cellar of one of its buildings when it was renovating the building. In particular, the region discovered that hydrocarbons were entering the cellar through the wall between the building and the adjoining Texaco service station. Texaco had leased the service station to a manager from 1988 but continued to supply petroleum products as well as controlling bookkeeping and supplies.

In April 1993, Texaco terminated the management contract for the service station. In June 1993, Texaco terminated the lease for it. Texaco denied that it was liable for the contamination but remediated the soil and replaced part of the storage facilities. In May 1994, Texaco ceased carrying out such works. The Brussels-Capital Region, however, considered that further remediation was necessary and paid the costs of the further remedial measures.

The Public Prosecutor brought a prosecution in the Criminal Court of Brussels against Texaco, Mr. Van de Walle, Texaco's managing director, and two other directors, for abandoning waste. The region claimed damages in the criminal proceedings. The court acquitted all the defendants but raised the issue as to whether soil contaminated by an accidental spill of hydrocarbons could be considered to be waste, doubting that this was the case because the soil had not been excavated.

On appeal, the Brussels Court of Appeal stayed the proceedings and requested a preliminary ruling from the European Court of Justice (now the CJEU) as to whether Texaco was a waste producer and/or a waste holder, and whether unexcavated contaminated soil was waste.

The CJEU ruled that the hydrocarbons that had accidentally leaked from the tank were waste, as was the soil polluted by them.[31] The court reasoned that the hydrocarbons could not be separated from the soil until the soil was remediated, and that the fact that the soil had not been excavated was irrelevant. The CJEU ruled

[31] Case C-1/03 *Van de Walle v Texaco Belgium SA* [2004] ECR I-7613, paras 47–50; https://eur-lex.europa.eu/legal-content/EN/TXT/?uri=CELEX%3A62003CJ0001 (accessed on 10.05.2023).

that the manager of the service station was a waste holder. The court commented that Texaco did not possess the hydrocarbons when they had leaked but ruled that Texaco was a waste holder if Texaco had contributed to the poor condition of the tank, had breached contractual provisions between it and the service station manager, or had otherwise contributed to the leakage.[32]

Subsequently, in *Commune de Mesquer v Total France SA*, the CJEU was called on to rule in a further case of whether spilled hydrocarbons were waste.

The case concerned the *Erika,* a small oil tanker, that broke in two in heavy seas on 12 December 1999 approximately 35 nautical miles (approximately 65 km) off the coast of Brittany in France's exclusive economic zone, spiling 19,800 tonnes of heavy fuel oil. The fuel oil was owned by Total France SA which sold the oil to Total International Ltd., which had contracted with ENEL, a large Italian energy company, to transport the oil to Sicily.

The two Total companies eventually paid over EUR 200 million to remediate the waste oil, which had polluted about 400 kilometres of coast, killing over 75,000 birds and other wildlife. The Commune de Mesquer, a municipality whose coast was heavily polluted by the oil, carried out measures to clean up the contamination. The commune subsequently brought an action in the Commercial Court of Saint-Hazaire to claim reimbursement of its costs from the Total companies. The commune's action was unsuccessful as was an appeal to the Court of Appeal of Rennes.

Following a further appeal, the Court of Cassation referred various issues, including whether hydrocarbons that had been accidentally spilled at sea from the wrecked oil tanker and which were then mixed with water and sediment before being washed up on the French coast, were waste.[33]

The CJEU referred to *Van de Walle* and ruled that the hydrocarbons were waste under the Waste Framework Directive. The CJEU also ruled that Total France was a waste holder because it was the possessor and producer of the waste. The court further ruled that Total International could be liable as an original producer or former waste holder if it 'contributed by [its] conduct to the risk that the pollution caused by the shipwreck [would] occur'.[34]

The *Van de Walle* and *Commune de Mesquer* cases raised many issues including whether land in which there was residual contamination must be classified as a landfill and thus require a permit.

In 2008, the EU avoided the issues by including an exception as Article 2(1)(b) in the revised Waste Framework Directive for 'land (in situ) including unexcavated contaminated soil and buildings permanently connected with land'.

---

[32] Ibid., para 60.

[33] Case C-188/07 *Commune de Mesquer v Total France SA* [2008] ECR I-4501, paras 57–59; https://curia.europa.eu/juris/liste.jsf?language=en&num=C-188/07 (accessed on 10.05.2023).

[34] Ibid., para 82.

2.3.1.4 National Environmental Permitting Legislation

Most Member States have extensive environmental permitting legislation, the scope of which includes not only the IED but also the Seveso III Directive as well as facilities not subject to either Directive. Conditions in environmental permits virtually always require the holder of the permit to prevent and remediate pollution to land/soil and water from activities subject to the permit.

If an operator that has a permit under the IED or other environmental permitting legislation breaches a condition of the permit and causes environmental damage, for example, by exceeding an ELV in the permit, there is no need for the damage caused by the discharge to exceed a threshold in order for the operator to be liable. The operator is liable for remediating environmental damage due to having unlawfully discharged the pollutant.

Permits in some Member States such as Finland also require permit holders to remediate damage to biodiversity. For example, Finnish environmental permitting legislation states that if a person breaches a provision of the legislation or regulations pursuant to the primary legislation, the competent authority may, among other things, order them to remediate the damage caused by the breach. Further, an applicant for an environmental permit in Finland must prepare a contingency plan based on a risk assessment in order to prepare for any accidents and to limit their consequences for human health and the environment.

Many Member States have a tiered system of facilities subject to environmental permitting legislation. The systems tend to have two or three tiers. For example, an annex to the applicable Danish legislation lists activities that are subject to the IED, which must therefore have a permit. Another annex lists non-IED activities; these are subject to a simplified notification system based on standard conditions. In Italy, any activity that has an impact on the environment is required to have a permit. In the Netherlands, all facilities, including offices as well as factories, are subject to the environmental permitting system.

Some Member States have a middle tier that requires registration for medium risk activities. Activities in this tier require more than a notification but less than the detailed and lengthy procedures necessary for an environmental permit.

Many Member States include the requirement to prepare an environmental impact permit for proposed projects subject to the Environmental Impact Assessment Directive[35] as part of the permitting process.

There is a trend in Member States towards a single integrated environmental permit for activities subject to the IED, other environmental permitting legislation, spatial planning legislation, and building legislation. An example is the Netherlands, which has a single environmental permit for activities under the IED, approvals for

[35] Directive 2011/92/EU on the assessment of the effects of certain public and private projects on the environment (codified version) [2011] OJ L26 (as amended by Directive 2014/52/EU); https://eur-lex.europa.eu/legal-content/EN/TXT/?uri=CELEX%3A02011L0092-20140515 (accessed on 10.05.2023).

spatial planning, nature conservation permits, construction permits, and logging concessions.

There are still a substantial number of Member States, however, that require separate permits for some of the above activities. For example, there is no single integrated permit for most operations in Austria. Instead, multiple permits may be required under the Industrial Code, Water Management Act, Nature Conservation Act, Forestry Act, and Construction Acts.

Another example of a Member State that requires more than one environmental permit is Italy. Operators subject to the Integrated Pollution Prevention and Control (IPPC/IED) regime must have an integrated IPPC/IED permit. Operators of non-IPPC/IED activities, mostly small and medium sized enterprises, are subject to a separate regime that requires a single environmental authorisation (*L'autorizzazione unica ambientale*).

A hybrid system exists in Ireland, where integrated environmental licences are issued for activities subject to the IED and integrated pollution control legislation, with media-specific licences being issued under other legislation.

Some Member States, including France, also have sophisticated and extensive environmental permitting legislation. The main regime in France is for Installations Classified for the Protection of the Environment (*Installation Classée pour la Protection de l'Environnement*; ICPE). Three main types of facilities are subject to the legislation. Facilities with a high risk of polluting the environment must apply for, and obtain, an authorisation/permit. Facilities with a medium risk of polluting the environment must be registered. Facilities with a low risk of polluting the environment must make a declaration to the relevant competent authority.

In France, the last operator of an ICPE facility is primarily liable for remediating pollution if there is no current operator. If the pollution is caused by non-ICPE activities, the person that caused or contributed to the pollution or person that currently owns or occupies the land (such as a developer) and whose negligence contributed to it are primarily liable. If such persons are not identified, the current owner of the polluted land is liable provided that the current owner was negligent or was otherwise involved with the pollution.

As of the end of 2022, approximately 500,000 facilities were covered by the ICPE regime. They include approximately 15,300 facilities that are registered and approximately 27,900 facilities that have an authorisation. Of the 27,900 facilities that have an authorisation, approximately 6840 are subject to the IED and approximately 1312 are subject to the Seveso III Directive. ICPE also applies to damage to ground and surface water at ICPE facilities.

A separate regime, called Installations, works and activities (*Installations, ouvrages, travaux et aménagements*; IOTA) regulates facilities, buildings, works and developments that affect surface or ground water. There are two classifications for IOTA activities. Facilities that pose a serious risk of damage to water resources or the aquatic environment must have an authorisation. Facilities that do not pose such a risk must make a declaration.

Operators of ICPE and IOTA activities, as well as other specified activities that require an authorisation, have a single integrated permit (*autorisation environnementale*).

In the Netherlands, the requirement under the IED to prepare a baseline environmental survey when an environmental permit is issued and a further environmental survey when operations permanently cease, accompanied by a requirement to remediate the site of the installation to a satisfactory state if necessary applies to all facilities that are subject to national environmental permitting legislation.

2.4 *Environmental Liability Legislation*

Environmental liability legislation is the main liability legislation for the remediation of land/soil and water pollution and damage to biodiversity. There are two levels of environmental liability legislation, EU legislation and national legislation.

2.4.1 Environmental Liability Directive

The main—and only—EU legislation that imposes liability for preventing and remediating environmental damage is the ELD. The ELD does not impose liability for personal/bodily injury, property damage, or economic loss.[36]

The ELD imposes liability on an operator whose 'occupational activity' causes damage to land/soil (land damage), waters under the Water Framework Directive[37] and the Marine Strategy Framework Directive[38] (water damage), and species and natural habitats protected by the Birds Directive[39] and the Habitats Directive[40] (biodiversity damage).

Whilst the term 'occupational activity' does not include activities that are carried out in a 'purely personal or domestic context', the CJEU has held that the term includes all activities that are carried out in an occupational context whether they are

---

[36] Ibid., Article 3(3); ibid., Recital 14.

[37] Directive 2000/60/EC establishing a framework for Community action in the field of water policy [2000] OJ L327/1 (consolidated version); https://eur-lex.europa.eu/legal-content/EN/TXT/?uri=CELEX:02000L0060-20141120 (accessed on 10.05.2023).

[38] Directive 2008/56/EC establishing a framework for community action in the field of marine environmental policy [20008] OJ L164/19 (consolidated version); https://eur-lex.europa.eu/legal-content/EN/TXT/?uri=CELEX%3A02008L0056-20170607 (accessed on 10.05.2023).

[39] Directive 2009/147/EC on the conservation of wild birds [2010] OJ L20/7 (codified version); https://eur-lex.europa.eu/legal-content/EN/TXT/?uri=CELEX:32009L0147 (accessed on 10.05.2023).

[40] Council Directive 92/43/EEC on the conservation of natural habitats and of wild fauna and flora [1992] OJ L206/7 (consolidated version); https://eur-lex.europa.eu/legal-content/EN/TXT/?uri=CELEX:01992L0043-20130701 (accessed on 10.05.2023).

market-related or competitive in nature. The court ruled that such activities included activities that were carried out by a water and soil association.[41]

Damage to land must be remediated if there is a significant risk of an adverse effect on human health.[42] Land damage is not linked to EU legislation. As indicated in Sect. 2.2 above, the European Commission withdrew the proposed a Soil Framework Directive in 2014.

Damage to waters must be remediated if it 'significantly adversely affects . . . the ecological, chemical or quantitative status or the ecological potential', as defined in the Water Framework Directive, of the 'waters concerned', or 'the environmental status' of marine waters as defined in the Marine Strategy Framework Directive.[43]

The ELD is unclear whether an entire water body or only 'waters' must be significantly affected. This is because the definition of water damage refers to waters but the significance criteria refer to classifications of water bodies under the ELD. Some Member States such as Spain require a lowering of the classification of a water body in order for there to be water damage under the ELD.

The European Commission's guidelines on a common understanding of environmental damage, which are based in part on CJEU rulings and which are binding on the Commission (but not other persons), however, state that it is sufficient to affect only part of a water body.[44] Further, the Commission's guidelines state that it is not necessary for an entire water body to be affected; it is sufficient for an activity to affect only part of a water body.[45]

Damage to biodiversity must be remediated if it causes 'significant adverse effects on reaching or maintaining the favourable conservation status of . . . habitats or species [protected by the Birds and Habitats Directives]'.[46] Significance is determined by reference to 'the European territory of the Member States to which the Treaty applies or the territory of a Member State or the natural range of that habitat [or species]'. The ELD is thus unclear whether damage to a species or natural habitat must affect the EU, the territory of a Member State, or the natural range of a habitat or species in order to trigger liability to prevent or remediate the damage. The Commission's guidelines, which as indicated above are based in part on CJEU

[41] Case C-297/19 *Naturschutzbund Deutschland — Landesverband Schleswig-Holstein eV v Kreis Nordfriesland* ECLI:EU:C:2020:533; https://curia.europa.eu/juris/documents.jsf?num=C-297/19 (accessed on 10.05.2023).

[42] ELD Article 2(1)(c).

[43] Ibid., Article 2(1)(b).

[44] Commission Notice, Guidelines providing a common understanding of the term 'environmental damage' as defined in Article 2 of Directive 2004/35/EC of the European Parliament and of the Council on environmental liability with regard to the prevention and remedying of environmental damage 2021/C 118/01 [2021] OJ C118/1, para 151; https://eur-lex.europa.eu/legal-content/EN/TXT/?uri=CELEX%3A52021XC0407%2801%29&qid=1617956961808 (accessed on 10.05.2023).

[45] Ibid., para 151.

[46] ELD Article 2(1)(a).

rulings, state however that it is sufficient for environmental damage to occur only a local level and not at a national or EU level.[47]

Member States may extend the ELD to species and natural habitats that are not listed in the Birds or Habitats Directives but are protected under equivalent national nature conservation legislation.[48] Thirteen Member States have extended liability for preventing and remediating biodiversity damage to nationally or regionally protected sites in some or all of their territory (Austria, Belgium, Cyprus, Czechia, Estonia, Greece, Hungary, Latvia, Lithuania, Poland, Portugal, Spain, Sweden).

The ELD established two liability systems: strict liability and fault-based liability. An operator that carries out activities under 14 pieces of EU legislation listed in Annex III of the ELD is strictly liable for preventing or remediating all three types of damage. An operator that carries out activities that are not listed in Annex III is liable for preventing or remediating biodiversity damage but only if the operator is at fault or negligent.

The ELD includes an option for Member States to apply joint and several or proportionate liability for preventing and remediating environmental damage when multiple operators cause environmental damage.[49] All Member States elected to impose joint and several liability except Denmark, Finland, France, Italy, and Slovakia which impose proportionate liability.

The ELD requires land to be remediated so that it no longer poses a significant adverse effect on human health.[50] In contrast, three types of remediation measures apply to water and biodiversity damage: primary, complementary and compensatory remediation.

Primary remediation consists of measures to remediate waters or biodiversity to their baseline condition, that is, their condition before they were damaged.[51] Complementary remediation consists of measures to provide a similar level of waters or biodiversity and services provided by them if full restoration of the waters or biodiversity is not feasible.[52] Compensatory remediation consists of improvements and other measures to compensate for any interim losses from the damaged waters or biodiversity and services provided by them from the time of the damage to their full restoration.[53]

The requirement to remediate environmental damage does not necessarily mean that a competent authority must require an operator that caused an imminent threat of, or actual, environmental damage to prevent or remediate it before the operator is obliged to do so. The operator's duty to prevent or remediate the damage arises even without the intervention of the authority.

---

[47] Commission Notice, C118/23 – C118/24, para 118.

[48] ELD Article 2(1)(a).

[49] Ibid., Article 9.

[50] Ibid., Annex II, Section 2.

[51] Ibid., Sect. 1(a).

[52] Ibid., Sect. 1(b).

[53] Ibid., Sections 1(c) and (d).

If an operator causes an imminent threat of environmental damage, the operator must carry out necessary preventive measures 'without delay'.[54] If such measures fail to dispel the imminent threat, the operator must notify the competent authority 'as soon as possible'.[55]

If an operator has caused environmental damage, the operator must notify the competent authority 'without delay'[56] and 'immediately' carry out:

> all practicable steps to immediately control, contain, remove or otherwise manage the relevant contaminants and/or any other damage factors in order to limit or to prevent further environmental damage and adverse effects on human health or further impairment of services.[57]

The ELD lists exceptions/exclusions to liability as follows:

- act of armed conflict, hostilities, civil war or insurrection (includes terrorism);
- natural phenomenon of exceptional, inevitable and irresistible character;
- nuclear, marine oil and transportation of dangerous goods conventions;
- diffuse pollution;
- activities the main purpose of which is to serve national defence or international security; and,
- activities the sole purpose of which is to protect from natural disasters.[58]

Mandatory and optional defences also apply. There are two mandatory defences that apply if an operator proves that environmental damage caused by the operator was caused by a third party and occurred despite appropriate safety measures being in place, or the operator proves that the environmental damage resulted from compliance with a compulsory order or instruction from a public authority except one that was consequent on an emission or incident caused by the operator's own activities.[59]

The optional defences, which a Member State may choose to apply are the permit and state-of-the-art defences. The permit defence applies if an operator proves that it was not at fault or negligent and the environmental damage was caused by an emission or event that was expressly authorised by and fully in accordance with the conditions of a permit for activities listed in Annex III of the ELD.[60] The state-of-the-art defence applies if an operator proves that it was not at fault or negligent and the environmental damage was not considered likely to cause environmental damage according to the state of scientific or technical knowledge at the time when the emission was released or the activity occurred.[61]

[54] Ibid., Article 5(1).

[55] Ibid., Article 5(2).

[56] Ibid., Article 6(1).

[57] Ibid., Article 6(1)(a).

[58] Ibid., Article 4; Annexes IV and V.

[59] Ibid., Article 8(3).

[60] Ibid., Article 8(4)(a).

[61] Ibid., Article 8(4)(b).

Sixteen Member States adopted the permit defence (Belgium (regional level), Croatia, Cyprus, Czechia, Denmark, Estonia (except GMOs), Finland (limited), Greece, Italy, Latvia (except GMOs), Lithuania, Malta, Netherlands (limited), Portugal, Slovakia, Spain).

Fourteen Member States adopted the state-of-the-art defence (Belgium (regional level), Croatia, Cyprus, Czechia, Estonia (except GMOs), France, Greece, Italy, Latvia (except GMOs), Malta, Netherlands (limited), Portugal, Slovakia, Spain).

Qualified environmental non-government organisations (NGOs) and members of the public may provide comments/observations to the relevant authority if they consider that environmental damage has occurred.[62] In this respect, the CJEU has ruled that Austrian legislation that precluded the holder of fishing rights in a river downstream of a hydroelectric power plant was unlawful despite the ELD not referring specifically to such a person.[63]

The ELD provides Member States with an option to extend the right to submit comments to an imminent threat of environmental damage.[64] Eleven Member States have not provided the right to NGOs and other qualified persons to submit comments/observations on an imminent threat of environmental damage to the relevant competent authority (Austria, Belgium (Flemish Region and Walloon Region), Bulgaria, Croatia, Cyprus, Finland, Germany, Lithuania, Malta, Slovakia, Slovenia).

If a competent authority denies the request to take action in a purported case of environmental damage—or an imminent threat of such damage, interested person including NGOs may seek a review by an independent court or tribunal of the authority's decision to act or to fail to act.[65]

The ELD does not specify the number of competent authorities that a Member State may direct to implement and enforce the ELD. The number varies greatly between Member States from one competent authority (e.g., Ireland, Malta) to many competent authorities (e.g., Finland, Germany, Spain, Sweden), with the number also depending on the federal structure of some Member States.

The ELD directs Member States to 'encourage the development of financial security instruments and markets' for ELD liabilities[66]; it does not direct them to establish mandatory financial security systems. The potential for mandatory financial security proved to be very controversial, with opposition to it continuing. Czechia, Portugal, Slovakia and Spain have established mandatory financial security systems for ELD liabilities. Ireland has a hybrid system. Italy and Poland have legislative provisions to require such financial security for a limited number of activities. Section 4.2.4 below describes these provisions.

[62] Ibid., Article 12.

[63] Case C-529/15 *Folk v Unabhängiger Verwaltungssenat für die Steiermark* ECLI:EU:C:2017:419; https://curia.europa.eu/juris/liste.jsf?num=C-529/15 (accessed on 10.05.2023).

[64] ELD Article 12.

[65] Ibid., Article 13.

[66] Ibid., Article 14(1).

2.4.2 National Environmental Liability Legislation

As described in Sect. 2.3.1 above, the prevalent legislation that imposes liability for the prevention and remediation of pollution and other environmental damage other than historic pollution is environmental permitting legislation. In some Member States (e.g., Hungary, Italy, Malta, Romania, Slovenia), the same procedures apply to sites contaminated by current and future pollution as well as historic pollution.[67] Other Member States have a separate regime for remediating contaminated land, as described in Sect. 2.2 above.

National environmental liability legislation in a substantial number of Member States includes numerical thresholds for determining when land/soil and water must be remediated. As described in Sect. 2.2 above, the numeric thresholds for land/soil tend to be expressed by concentrations of specified pollutants. In Austria, Bulgaria, Croatia and Portugal, numerical concentrations of pollutants in water quality standards are used to determine whether waters should be remediated.

A major difference between the ELD and national environmental liability legislation is the scope of persons that may be liable for preventing and remediating pollution and other environmental damage caused by them. Whereas the ELD limits the scope to operators, national environmental liability legislation does not have such limitations. That is, any person that causes pollution or environmental damage can be primarily liable under national liability legislation in virtually all Member States.

National liability legislation in some Member States (e.g., Croatia, Estonia, Latvia, Lithuania) requires a person that causes environmental damage to pay compensation to the State if it is not possible to remediate or restore the damage. The legislation sets out the different types of damage to which it applies, including damage to the air, flora and fauna as well as land/soil and waters.

For example, in Latvia, if environmental damage cannot be fully remediated, the person that caused it is required to pay compensation to the State for the necessary costs of restoring environmental values that have been affected or to create equivalent values. Legislation sets out specific monetary rates for environmental damage including damage to water, fauna and flora.

In Lithuania, if damage to land, water, fauna or flora cannot be fully remediated, the person that caused the damage must pay monetary compensation for the damage that cannot be remediated. The amount of compensation is calculated by a specific methodology.

[67] Pérez and Eugenio (2018), p. 18; https://publications.jrc.ec.europa.eu/repository/handle/JRC107508 (accessed on 10.05.2023).

3 Insurance for Environmental Liabilities

The main providers of insurance for environmental liabilities in the EU are commercial insurers.[68] In some Member States (France, Italy, Spain), cover is also provided by re/insurance pools. Also in some Member States, mutuals offer insurance to their members. Further, large companies and groups of companies may establish captives to provide environmental insurance, and other types of insurance.

Insurance for tort environmental liabilities, that is, claims for bodily injury and property damage—and in some Member States pure economic loss—caused by exposure to pollutants may be provided in the body of general liability policies depending on the insurer. Liability for damage to property may also be provided in the body of property damage policies in some Member States, again depending on the insurer. Both types of cover are almost invariably subject to a qualified or absolute pollution exclusion.

General liability and property policies do not provide cover for remediating pollution and preventing further pollution unless cover is provided by an extension. General liability policies in Austria and Germany specifically provide cover for such liabilities.

General liability and property policies across the EU are not standardised with the exception of Austria and Germany, where national insurance associations draft model terms and conditions that their members may decide to use or adapt. As indicated directly above, the model terms and conditions include cover specifically designed for liabilities under the ELD.

Environmental insurance policies in some, but not all, Member States provide much more comprehensive cover by including cover not only for claims for bodily injury and property damage caused by exposure to pollutants but also cover for remediating and preventing further environmental damage. Depending on the insurer, such policies also provide cover for other losses related to pollution as well as other types of environmental damage.

3.1 Providers of Environmental Insurance

Environmental insurance policies and extensions to general liability and property policies are generally provided by commercial insurers. Environmental insurance policies and extensions to general liability policies are also provided in France, Italy and Spain by re/insurance pools. Some very large companies may also establish a

[68] The following discussion on the contaminated land regimes of Member States is drawn in particular from Valerie Fogleman, Improving financial security in the context of the Environmental Liability Directive (ELD); https://circabc.europa.eu/ui/group/3b48eff1-b955-423f-9086-0d85ad1c5879/library/01708073-da51-4db7-8049-6e7141c901f4/details?download=true (scroll down to 'Study – Financial Security for ELD Liabilities (2020) – Final Report') (accessed on 10.05.2023).

captive to provide environmental insurance, either specifically or as part of a combined policy.

3.1.1 Commercial Insurers

A commercial insurer is an insurer that conducts insurance business on a commercial basis. The insurer must be authorised to conduct insurance business by the relevant insurance regulators in the Member State.

Commercial insurers in the Member States of the EU and States in the European Economic Area (EEA) are authorised to carry on insurance business, including offering and placing policies, in all States in the EU and EEA as well as the State in which they are authorised to carry on insurance business. They do this by establishing a branch or agents in the State (called right of establishment) or providing cross-border services across the EEA (freedom of services).

3.1.2 Re/Insurance Pools

Re/insurance pools for environmental liabilities have been established in France, Italy and Spain. All the pools are co-reinsurance consortia, consisting of insurers and reinsurers. Insurers individually underwrite environmental insurance policies—and in some cases environmental extensions to general liability policies—pursuant to terms and conditions established by each pool. Liabilities are then ceded to the respective pool. In addition, each pool provides its members with risk management and claims management support.

Membership of a pool does not mean that an insurer offers policies, or that a reinsurer reinsures them, exclusively through the pool. In addition to membership of the pool, insurers generally underwrite policies, and reinsurers reinsure contracts, outside of it.

The oldest re/insurance pool is Assurpol[69] which was established in France in 1977 as the Groupement d'Intérêt Economique (GIE Garpol), before changing its name to Assurpol in 1989. GIE Garpol was created to provide reinsurance to insurers that provided cover for facilities subject to the ICPE (and subsequently the Seveso Directive (see Sect. 2.3.1.2 above).

The second oldest pool in the EU is Pool Ambiente,[70] which was established in Italy in 1979 as Pool Inquinamento following the 1976 Seveso disaster. In 2019, the pool changed its name to Pool Ambiente. Until 2007, members of the pool provided cover only for civil liabilities from pollution. In 2007, policies issued by the pool included cover for remediating environmental damage.

[69] Assurpol; http://www.assurpol.fr/fr/ (in French) (accessed on 10.05.2023).

[70] Il Pool Ambiente è il Consorzio per l'Assicurazione e la Riassicurazione della Responsabilità per Danni all'Ambiente; https://www.poolambiente.it/ (in Italian) (accessed on 10.05.2023).

The most recent pool is Pool Español de Riesgos Medioambientales,[71] which was established in Spain in 1994. In addition to providing voluntary insurance policies, the pool provides policies specifically designed to provide cover under the system of mandatory financial security for ELD occurrences (see Sect. 2.3.2.1 below).

All the pools offer a range of environmental insurance policies, particularly for small to medium sized enterprises.

3.1.3 Mutuals

A mutual insurance company provides insurance to its members. A primary purpose of a mutual is to share the risk of losses from specified incidents or other occurrences between the members instead of a single member bearing the risk. A mutual may cede risks to a reinsurer or keep the risks within the mutual. The mutual may make an additional call for funding on its members if claims exceed the funding reserve(s) in the mutual. Due to the potential for members of a mutual to be required to pay additional money if a loss occurs, membership is subject to scrutiny and detailed contractual provisions.

Mutual insurance companies tend to be established for specific commercial sectors including the agricultural sector, the shipping sector, public authorities, etc.

For example, Irish Public Bodies (IPB) Insurance was established in 1926 to enable public bodies to become their own insurers. IPB, which is the only indigenous mutual general insurance company that operates in the Irish insurance market, offers an environmental insurance policy that provides cover for ELD and other environmental liabilities, as well as other types of policies.

3.1.4 Captives

Large companies may establish captives to provide insurance as an alternative to purchasing a commercial environmental insurance policy or other types of policies. The sole function of a captive is to insure (or finance risk) for its parent company, other affiliates and sometimes related companies. The captive may, but does not necessarily, purchase reinsurance from commercial reinsurers.

Joint captives may be established to cover risks of more than one company, generally risks for which it is difficult to obtain cover on the commercial insurance market.

Captives tend to be established in jurisdictions that enable favourable tax treatment. Their management may be carried out by specialist teams of brokers.

[71] Qué es el Pool de Riesgos Medioambientales?; https://www.estamos-seguros.es/que-es-el-pool-de-riesgos-medioambientales/ (in Spanish) (accessed on 10.05.2023).

3.2 *Environmental Extensions*

General liability policies provide limited cover for environmental liabilities. Property policies do not tend to provide such cover. This subsection describes cover provided by general liability and property policies to set in context the discussion, which follows, of cover for environmental liabilities provided by extensions to the policies.

3.2.1 General Liability Policies

There are two main types of general liability policies: primary policies and excess policies. If a business wishes to purchase insurance, it will purchase a primary policy. The limit of indemnity in such policies in the EU tends to include costs to defend the insured against third party claims.

If the business wishes to increase the amount of indemnity in the primary policy, it purchases an excess liability policy. As the name implies, excess liability policies provide cover in excess of the limit of indemnity in the primary policy. The policies generally do not provide cover for the costs of defending third party claims.

General liability policies in Member States of the EU have traditionally provided—and continue to provide—cover for third-party claims against an insured for bodily injury and property damage. In addition, general liability policies in Member States that recognise pure economic loss tend to provide cover for third-party claims for pure economic loss.

3.2.1.1 Pollution Exclusions

Virtually all general liability policies offered in Member States of the EU include a pollution exclusion. The exclusions are generally qualified exclusions; they do not bar cover for all harm caused by pollution. Instead, they generally provide cover for sudden and accidental pollution but bar cover for harm caused by gradual pollution.

The exclusions tend to be drafted so that they bar cover for all claims for harm caused by pollution, with a write back of cover (that is, an exception to the exclusion) for harm caused by a pollution incident that occurs on the insured's site and causes off-site bodily injury or property damage during a short period of time.

This does not mean that the policies provide cover for remediating pollution caused by a sudden and accidental incident. As indicated in Sect. 3.2.1 above, cover in virtually all general liability policies except Austria and Germany is limited to third party tort claims.

3.2.1.2 Environmental Extensions

Most of the cover for claims in general insurance policies for remediating pollution and, to a much more limited extent other environmental damage, is provided by environmental extensions. The extensions are offered in the vast majority of Member States.

Except in Austria and Germany (see below), cover provided by the extensions is limited. Cover is generally provided only for remediating offsite soil that is polluted by a sudden and accidental incident on the insured's site. Many do not provide cover for remediating ground, surface or coastal waters.

Some extensions provide cover for a pollution incident only if the insured proves that the incident causing the pollution began and ended within a short, specified period and the insured reports the incident to the insurer within another short, specified period.

Most extensions do not provide cover for environmental damage under the ELD. In particular, they do not tend to provide cover for complementary or compensatory damage under the ELD.

In addition, sub-limits of liability in environmental extensions tend to be very low.

Many, if not most, brokers and operators appear to consider that cover provided by the extensions is much, sometimes very much, more extensive than it actually is.

Cover for ELD and other environmental liabilities is available in Austria pursuant to model terms and conditions of an environmental extension drafted by the Austrian Insurance Association (*Versicherungsverband Österreich*; VVO).

The VVO drafted the extension specifically to provide cover for ELD liabilities, with a sub-limit of liability for compensatory remediation of 50% of the total of primary and complementary remediation.

Although the environmental extension is non-binding, virtually all insurers that offer general liability policies in Austria include the extension, with some insurers adapting the wording of the extension. The vast majority of insureds that purchase general liability policies include it.

The extension does not provide cover for all ELD liabilities. It does not, for example, provide cover for gradual environmental damage, with the caveat that an incident that results in sudden pollution from a gradual process may be considered to be sudden. For example, if corrosion causes a small hole to develop in an oil pipeline, leakage from that hole may be considered to be sudden even if the corrosion that caused the leakage was gradual.

Further, the extension provides cover only if environmental damage is caused by a disruption of, or deviation from, an insured's normal operations. Still further, due to the presence of the extension in a general liability policy, it does not provide cover for remediating environmental damage on the insured's own site.

Cover for ELD and other environmental liabilities is available in Germany pursuant to model terms and conditions for environmental damage (*Umweltschadensversicherung*; USV) drafted by the German Insurance Association (*Gesamtverband der Deutschen Versicherungswirtschaft*; GDV). Although the model terms and conditions are not mandatory, virtually all insurers that offer general liability policies in Germany include them and the vast majority of insureds purchase them or – to a lesser extent—an environmental extension drafted by brokers.

There are two alternatives to the USV:

- General Insurance Conditions for Environmental Damage Basic Insurance (*Allgemeine Versicherungsbedingungen für die Umweltschadens-Basisversicherung*; Basic Cover); and.
- General Insurance Conditions for Environmental Damage (*Allgemeine Versicherungsbedingungen für die Umweltschadensversicherung*) which consists of the baseline wording (*I. USV-Grunddeckung*; Comprehensive Cover), and two optional modules (*II. USV-Zusatzbaustein 1*, and *III. USV-Zusatzbaustein 2*).

The USV are combined with the model terms and conditions for civil law environmental liability (*Umwelthaftpflichtversicherung*; UHV), as standard cover under a separate section in the GDV's non-binding model terms and conditions for public and products liability insurance (*Allgemeine Versicherungsbedingungen für die Betriebs- und Berufshaftpflichtversicherung*; AVB BHV).

The focus of the USV is specifically on pollution liabilities under the ELD, with the exception of the following:

- gradual environmental damage that is not caused by a disruption of the insured's operations;
- environmental damage that exists at a covered site or a divested site before the inception date of the policy;
- the costs of remediating groundwater unless the operator has purchased Comprehensive Cover and the optional module 1 to the Comprehensive Cover;
- preventive measures under the ELD unless the purpose of such measures is to avoid or minimise environmental damage that would otherwise inevitably occur; and,
- environmental damage caused other than by a disruption of the insured's operations.

Due to cover by the USV being provided in a general liability policy, the policy does not provide cover for preventing or remediating pollution or any other environmental damage at an insured's site.

In addition, the USV includes a sub-limit of liability for compensatory remediation under the ELD, with the caveat that individual insurers can adapt the sub-limit.

3.3 Property Policies

Property policies are first party, not third party, policies. They provide cover for losses directly suffered by an insured to property covered by the policy; they do not provide cover for claims by third parties against the insured.

The policies either list risks covered by the policy—such as fire, flood, etc.—or provide cover for all risks with exclusions that bar cover for specified risks.

The policies provide cover for the loss of, or damage to, 'insured property'. The term 'insured property' includes buildings and other structures on the land/site that is insured as well as equipment and/or other types of physical property, depending on the insurer. The policies list property that is within the definition of the term 'insured property'. Land is virtually never within the definition of insured property. Whilst the policies may provide cover for the loss of a tank that is within the definition of insured property and that ruptures, they do not provide cover for remediating land/soil from the ruptured tank.

Property policies typically include a debris removal clause. This is a clause that provides cover for costs incurred by an insured in removing debris following damage caused by a specified risk. Debris removal clauses are limited to the removal of debris from insured property. They do not provide cover for remediating land harmed by the debris.

3.3.1 Pollution Exclusions

Property policies tend to include absolute pollution exclusions. That is, they bar cover for all losses that arise from pollution or other environmental damage. There is no write back of cover for sudden and accidental pollution as there is in many general liability policies.

3.3.2 Environmental Extensions

A few Member States offer environmental extensions to property policies.

For example, insurers based, or with branches, in Finland provide extensions to property policies. The extensions, which provide cover for the costs of remediating and preventing further environmental damage at an insured's own site, tend to be purchased by businesses in order to pay the costs of preventing damage to insured property such as industrial buildings and warehouses.

The extensions are limited in that they provide cover for property damage only from sudden and accidental pollution incidents. In addition to damage to buildings, they typically provide cover for the costs of remediating soil and water provided that the soil or water has been polluted during emergency measures to mitigate damage. They may thus provide enhanced cover for debris removal, that is, removing debris from a fire or other covered risk.

Environmental extensions to property policies are also available in some other Member States (e.g., Belgium, Croatia, Denmark, Estonia, France, Greece) but only to a very limited extent. Cover provided by the extensions is severely limited. They virtually never provide cover for remediating gradual pollution or environmental damage other than pollution. They also do not provide cover for complementary or compensatory remediation under the ELD.

Further, due to cover being provided for first party liabilities for insured property, they do not provide cover for remediating off-site pollution or other environmental damage.

3.4 Environmental Insurance Policies

This section discusses the evolution of the environmental insurance market in the EU, the extent of cover provided by environmental insurance policies, and the availability of, and demand for, such policies.

3.4.1 Evolution of the Environmental Insurance Market

The environmental insurance market in the EU began in the mid to late 1990s when an ever-increasing number of Member States were introducing legislation that imposed liability for remediating contamination. Another major impetus for the growth of the environmental insurance market was the adoption by the EU of the Integrated Pollution Prevention and Control Directive in 1996 and the introduction or extension of national environmental permitting legislation in Member States.

The market grew slowly. Policies that provided cover for remediating and preventing further pollution tended to be available only for large companies and companies that had sites and/or operations in more than one Member State. The underwriting process tended to be especially stringent. Potential insureds were required to provide detailed evidence of environmental management systems at their sites, which were then inspected by underwriters. Cover provided by the policies tended to be restrictive. The majority of policies were offered by affiliates of insurers that offered such policies in the US, where the environmental insurance market was already established.

In 2004, the environmental insurance market in the EU was boosted by enlargement when Czechia, Cyprus, Estonia, Hungary, Latvia, Lithuania, Malta, Poland, Slovakia, and Slovenia joined the EU. Enlargement did not only mean that the EU was much larger than before; it also meant that an additional 10 countries were subject to the IED and other EU environmental legislation and, thus, the potential for liability for preventing and remediating pollution, especially land/soil and water pollution, caused by pollution incidents. In particular, in 2004, the EU's adoption of the ELD provided a major boost to the EU environmental insurance market, resulting in more insurers entering the market.

In 2007, Bulgaria and Romania joined the EU—again adding to the number of Member States subject to EU environmental legislation.

In 2008, adoption of the IPPC Directive to replace the 1996 Directive again widened the scope of businesses subject to environmental permitting. The scope of businesses subject to environmental permitting legislation broadened again in 2010 with adoption of the IED.

In 2013, a study by the Harvard Business School of members of the Federation of European Risk Management (FERMA) stated that, out of the 89 companies and other organisations that had provided comments, 52% stated that they had obtained an insurance policy or other financial security, especially self-insurance, against environmental liabilities as a result of the ELD.[72]

In 2015, Marsh reported that companies that carried out activities listed in Annex III of the ELD had increased their purchase of environmental insurance policies at an annual rate of between 8% and 15% and had increased limits of indemnity by an annual rate of nearly 9%. Marsh also reported, however, that the percentage of companies that carried out non-Annex III activities under the ELD remained the same or had reduced between 2006 and 2014.[73]

In 2016, Marsh noted that the trend of increasing limits of liability in environmental insurance policies had continued, commenting that there had been an average rise in limits of liability for mid-sized companies from an average of EUR 6,900,000 in 2011 to just under EUR 7,900,000 by 2015. The report noted, however, that premiums had tended to decrease rather than increase for multi-year operational risk environmental insurance policies.[74]

Not surprisingly with the increased scope of the IED and national environmental permitting legislation, the number of pollution incidents reported to insurers increased in 2017, with the highest number from the transportation, communications, electricity, gas and sanitary industry sectors, followed by manufacturing, followed by construction especially from waste activities.[75]

The environmental insurance market in the EU has continued to grow, both in the number of insurers that have entered the market, the types of policies issued, its capacity, and the number of policies sold.[76] This trend is almost certain to continue as the scope of businesses subject to environmental liabilities continues to grow. For example, the scope of the IED will increase further when the EU adopts a new version of it, following submission of a proposal to revise it in April 2022.

[72] Harvard Business School (2013). Self-insurance involves a large company setting aside funding for losses in the event of an unanticipated event such as a pollution incident.

[73] See Marsh (2015), pp. 2–3; https://www.marsh.com/content/dam/marsh/Documents/PDF/UK-en/EMEA%20Environmental%20Benchmarking%20Report%202015-11-2015.pdf (accessed on 10.05.2023).

[74] Marsh Environmental Market Update (2016); https://www.marsh.com/content/dam/marsh/Documents/PDF/UK-en/EMEA%20Environmental%20Market%20Update.pdf (accessed on 10.05.2023).

[75] AIG (2018); https://www.aig.co.uk/content/dam/aig/emea/united-kingdom/documents/Insights/eil-claims-2018-uk.pdf (accessed on 10.05.2023).

[76] See Fogleman (2020), pp. 179–183; https://circabc.europa.eu/ui/group/3b48eff1-b955-423f-9086-0d85ad1c5879/library/01708073-da51-4db7-8049-6e7141c901f4/details?download=true (scroll down to 'Study – Financial Security for ELD Liabilities (2020) – Final Report') (accessed on 10.05.2023).

3.4.2 Types of Cover

Environmental insurance policies virtually always provide cover for liabilities imposed by national environmental permitting and liability legislation and the ELD. The reason for this scope is that the ELD imposes liability for environmental damage only if the damage reaches or exceeds specified significance criteria. Businesses would not therefore purchase a policy that did not provide cover for environmental liabilities not covered by the ELD.

Most environmental insurance policies have a menu format in that the policy sets out separate insuring agreements (coverage parts) that an insured may purchase. The insured selects the coverage parts it wishes; there is no requirement to select all of them.

The following describes the main types of environmental insurance policies available to large businesses and, in some cases small and medium sized businesses, with the caveat that their availability depends on individual insurers. In addition, all of them are not available in all Member States, especially for businesses that have operations and/or sites in only a single Member State.

The main types of environmental insurance policies are pollution legal liability (PLL) policies, construction pollution liability (CPL) policies, and environmental consultants' professional services policies.

A PLL policy typically provides cover for some or all of the following risks:

- preventing and remediating pollutants at, on or under the insured's site;
- preventing and remediating pollutants that have emanated from the insured site;
- third-party claims for bodily injury and property damage from exposure to pollutants at or emanating from the insured site;
- third-party diminution of value of property due to pollution incidents at the insured site;
- third-party business interruption losses associated with pollution from the insured site;
- first-party business interruption losses associated with pollution incidents at the insured site;
- remediation of pre-existing contamination at an insured site that was not known to the insured or an environmental manager or director or officer of the company when the policy incepted;
- preventing and remediating environmental damage under the ELD due to environmental damage at or emanating from the insured's site;
- reputational damage suffered by the insured due to a pollution incident at the insured's site;
- transportation of products and waste from the insured's site (but not cover for products liability);
- remediation of waste generated at the insured's site and disposed at an authorised waste disposal site;
- emergency costs; and,
- associated defence costs.

As indicated above and depending on the insurer and the Member State, PLL policies typically provide cover for ELD liabilities. Some policies however limit cover for ELD liabilities to environmental damage caused by pollution; they do not provide cover for ELD liabilities caused by other types of environmental damage. Some also, again depending on the insurer and the Member State, limit cover to losses arising from sudden and accidental pollution incidents. Some policies include claims for bodily injury, property damage and the costs of remediating pollution or other environmental damage at locations where the insured carries out its business operations; others do not do so.

As indicated above, environmental insurance policies tend to have a menu format. A PLL policy that provides cover for the above risks may thus have the following insuring agreements:

- claims for bodily injury and property damage resulting from pollution and other environmental damage in, on, at, under or emanating from the insured's site that result from a pollution incident on the insured's site;
- the costs of remediating and preventing further pollution and other environmental damage in, on, at, under or emanating from the insured's site(s) that arise from a pollution incident on the insured's site;
- the loss of profits caused by the suspension of the insured's operations due to pollution or other environmental damage at the insured's site caused by a pollution incident at the site;
- costs of remediating pollution and other environmental damage in, on, at, under or emanating from the insured's site that arise from pollution or other damage at the insured's site that the insured did not know about, or disclosed to, the insurer when the policy incepted;
- claims for bodily injury and property damage and the costs of remediating pollution or other environmental damage that arise from the transportation of the insured's goods and/or waste;
- costs of advisors and others instructed by the insured to respond to damage to its reputation that arise from a pollution or other environmental damage on the insured's site;
- costs of remediating waste generated by the insured in, on, at, under or emanating from a non-owned disposal site;
- costs incurred by the insured in responding to an emergency; and,
- legal costs to defend a claim for bodily injury and/or property damage, proceedings by an authority to require the insured to remediate or prevent further pollution or environmental damage from an incident at the insured's site.

Various combinations of risks exist. For example, some policies may separate ELD liabilities and non-ELD liabilities into different insuring agreements. Some policies may have separate insuring agreements for emergency costs and/or legal costs; others apply them to all relevant insuring agreements.

Conditions in PLL policies typically require a claim to have been made against the insured during the policy period and notified to the insurer within the policy period. In addition, PLL policies, like other insurance policies set out exclusions (such as capital improvement costs, intentional non-compliance with relevant legislation, and intentional or wilful acts by the insured), claims co-operation clauses, notification clauses, cancellation clauses, etc.

A CPL policy typically provides cover for many of the same liabilities as a PLL policy, with the major difference being that a CPL policy may provide cover not only for the insured's site but also for specified sites at which the insured carries out operations for others.

The policies are generally available to many types of contractors. They may be underwritten for an entire construction project or for periods up to 10 years. They may also include cover not only for ongoing construction projects but also for completed construction projects, in which case they extend the policy period beyond the date of substantial completion of the construction. In such a case, the CPL policy could be written on a losses-occurring basis as well as a claims made and reported basis.

Further, CPL policies may provide cover not only for claims that result from the insured contractor's negligent acts but also from the contractor's errors or omissions such as negligent advice.

Environmental consultants' professional services policies provide cover for claims due to errors or omissions of the insured consultant. They may also be combined with policies that provide cover for claims arising from works carried out by environmental consultants. They may be underwritten for a single project or for a period of up to, say, 3 years depending on the insurer.

3.4.3 Availability and Demand

There is a substantial difference between the availability of environmental insurance policies for businesses with sites and/or operations in a single Member State and those with sites and/or operations in more than one Member State. Environmental insurance policies that provide cover for ELD and other environmental liabilities are widely available from multinational insurers for large businesses that have sites and/or operations in multiple Member States although the policies may be limited in scope.

Much depends on whether reinsurers are willing to offer cover for environmental liabilities in a Member State. Depending on the Member State, reinsurers may exclude cover for environmental liabilities in reinsurance treaties (contracts that provide cover for all risks within a class of business) and offer cover only through facultative contracts (contracts that provide cover for a single risk).

The availability of, and demand for, environmental insurance policies by small to medium sized businesses depends to a large extent on individual Member States.

Environmental insurance policies are widely available for small to medium sized businesses in some Member States (e.g., France, Ireland, Italy, Luxembourg, the Netherlands, Portugal, Slovakia, Spain). Their availability does not necessarily mean that demand for them is good. Whilst demand for them is good in some Member

States (e.g., France, Ireland, Portugal), it is moderate or low in other Member States (e.g., Italy, Luxembourg, the Netherlands, Slovakia, Spain).

Small to medium sized businesses may also purchase environmental insurance policies from co-reinsurance pools in France, Italy and Spain (see Sect. 3.1.2 above).

Environmental insurance policies are also available in Austria and Germany but demand for them is low due to the existence of cover for environmental liabilities in general liability policies.

The availability of environmental insurance policies is heavily influenced by the demand for them. For example, in 2018, one of the largest insurers in Slovenia considered whether to develop an environmental insurance policy in 2018. An assessment carried out by the insurer during 2018 and 2019, however, indicated that demand was low. The insurer therefore decided to postpone its development until demand increased.

Further, the availability and demand for environmental insurance policies is influenced by legislative requirements for mandatory financial security (see Sect. 4 below). For example, legislation in Greece requires a business that manages hazardous waste to have mandatory financial security. Most of the demand for environmental insurance policies in Greece is from businesses that are subject to this requirement. In addition to requiring specified businesses to have insurance—or another type of financial security—introduction of the requirements raises awareness of environmental liabilities.

In some Member States such as Cyprus, environmental insurance policies are only available from a small number of insurers based, or that have branches, in that Member State. The policies tend to be available through 'fronting'. This is a process whereby, for example, a local insurer in Cyprus issues an environmental insurance policy on behalf of another insurer, generally an insurer based in the London environmental insurance market. The local insurer may transfer some, or all, of the risk to the other insurer through a reinsurance agreement and agrees to pay losses covered by the policy and then seek reimbursement through the agreement.

4 Mandatory Financial Security Requirements

There are two main types of environmental financial security requirements: financial security for environmental responsibilities; and financial security for environmental liabilities.

The first type of financial security is for environmental responsibilities such as closing a landfill or restoring land following surface mining. This type of financial security does not tend to be controversial because both the business and the regulatory authority know that such a site must eventually be closed or restored, respectively.

The costs of the closure or restoration can be estimated before the need for them occurs. During operation of the landfill or surface mine (or other type of operations), the business that is operating the site provides information to the regulatory authority on the extent and nature of its operations. The authority and the business then agree on the estimated costs, which may increase or decrease depending on ongoing operations. Instead of requiring the entire amount of estimated costs to be covered at the beginning of operations—before the business has made sufficient profits from which the costs will be paid—the authority may allow the business to accumulate the estimated amount over a specified period of time.

Insurance is generally not a suitable financial security instrument for known environmental responsibilities because insurance provides cover for fortuities not certainties. Applicable financial security instruments therefore tend to be bonds, bank guarantees, trust accounts and other such instruments. As part of the contractual agreement between the business and the authority, insurance may be applied in addition to the above types of financial security in order to cover fortuities such as the time at which a landfill site is closed or a surface mine needs to be restored.

The second type of financial security—for liabilities—is much more controversial because it is for an unknown and unforeseen event such as a pollution incident or other occurrence that may never occur. In this case, it is not possible to estimate the amount of financial security that is required with the accuracy of financial security for environmental responsibilities. The amount of financial security for environmental liabilities may thus be set out in legislation or in the conditions of an environmental permit. The amounts tend to differ depending on the size and nature of the operations carried out by a business, the potential for pollution or other environmental damage in the location of the operation, the existence of an environmental management system, etc. Alternative approaches are to base the amount of financial security on the likely cost of remediating pollution—and sometimes other environmental damage—on an ad hoc basis or on a worst-case basis.

Insurance is a suitable financial security instrument for environmental liabilities and is frequently used to provide evidence of financial security. Insurance policies do not necessarily provide cover only for financial security requirements. The policies are often designed to provide cover for them as part of broader cover for other risks that are not subject to the requirements. In such a case, cover for risks for which financial security is mandated tends to be ring-fenced from risks that are not subject to financial security requirements. For example, an environmental insurance policy may provide cover for remediating pollution from an accident, business interruption due to the accident and related legal expense. In such a case, insurance for remediating pollution could be ring-fenced from insurance for business interruption and related legal costs.

A common feature of financial security requirements is that they tend to be less stringent when the person subject to them is a governmental—rather than a private—person. For example, the requirements may not apply to the operation of activities by the national government, local authorities and other governmental authorities.

4.1 European Union Legislative Requirements

Some EU environmental legislation contains financial security requirements. The Landfill Directive,[77] the Extractive Waste Directive,[78] the Directive on the geological storage of carbon dioxide,[79] the Shipments of Waste Regulation,[80] the Directive on waste electrical and electronic equipment,[81] and the Basic Safety Standards Directive[82] include requirements for financial security. The requirements, however, are all for financial security for environmental responsibilities; they are not financial security requirements for environmental liabilities.

As discussed in Sect. 3 above, insurance is not a suitable instrument for environmental responsibilities with the exception of potential liabilities such as closing a landfill earlier than planned. EU mandatory financial security requirements for environmental responsibilities are thus not a driver for environmental insurance. The above EU requirements are, therefore, not discussed in this chapter except in the context of national legislation that goes beyond the EU law. In some cases, such legislation includes requirements for financial security for environmental responsibilities and environmental liabilities.

4.2 National Legislative Requirements

Some Member States include financial security requirements in their national legislation. The main legislation to include such requirements is national legislation that implements—and goes beyond—EU legislation such as the IED and the Seveso III Directive, as well as waste management legislation.

---

[77] Council Directive 1999/31/EC on the landfill of waste [1999] OJ L182/1; https://eur-lex.europa.eu/legal-content/EN/TXT/?uri=CELEX:31999L0031 (accessed on 10.05.2023).

[78] Directive 2016/21/EC on the management of waste from extractive industries [2016] OJ L102/15; https://eur-lex.europa.eu/legal-content/EN/TXT/?uri=CELEX:02006L0021-20090807 (accessed on 10.05.2023).

[79] Directive (2009/31/EC) on the geological storage of carbon dioxide [2009] OJ L140/114; https://eur-lex.europa.eu/legal-content/EN/TXT/?uri=CELEX%3A32009L0031 (accessed on 10.05.2023).

[80] Regulation (EC) No 1013/2006 on shipments of waste [2006] OJ L190/1 (consolidated version); https://eur-lex.europa.eu/legal-content/EN/TXT/?qid=1454069470717&uri=CELEX:02006R1013-20180101.

[81] Directive 2012/19/EU on waste electrical and electronic equipment [2012] OJ L197/38; https://eur-lex.europa.eu/legal-content/EN/TXT/PDF/?uri=CELEX:32012L0019 (accessed on 10.05.2023).

[82] Directive 2013/59/Euratom laying down basic safety standards for protection against the dangers arising from exposure to ionising radiation [2013] OJ L013/1; https://eur-lex.europa.eu/legal-content/EN/TXT/?uri=CELEX:02013L0059-20140117 (accessed on 10.05.2023).

4.2.1 National Legislation Implementing EU Legislation

Some Member States include financial security requirements for remediating pollution in legislation that implements the IED and/or the Seveso III Directive as well as in permits for IED facilities and/or Seveso III facilities. The requirements thus extend requirements for financial security beyond provisions of the EU legislation.

Eight Member States (Cyprus, Finland (compensation only), France, Ireland, Italy, Malta, Poland (limited), Sweden) have introduced mandatory financial security for integrated pollution prevention and control permits including permits under the IED.

Seven Member States (Finland (compensation only), France, Ireland, Italy, the Netherlands, Slovakia, Sweden) have introduced mandatory financial security for liabilities under the Seveso III Directive. Depending on operations carried out at a facility, both the IED and the Seveso III Directive may apply to it.

Some Member States have a general requirement for financial security under environmental permitting legislation. For example, the Environmental Code in Sweden has a general rule on financial security that applies to all permits, approvals or exemptions pursuant to the Code including the Landfill Directive. The permitting authority may thus make the grant of a permit, approval or exemption subject to the requirement for a financial guarantee.

Ireland has somewhat similar legislation that applies to environmental permits (called licences). There are three types of environmental licences under Irish law: industrial emissions licences for facilities covered by the IED; licences for waste facilities; and Integrated Pollution Control licences for activities that are not covered by the IED. The licences are collectively called Integrated Pollution Control/Industrial Emissions Directive (IPC/IED) licences. Mandatory financial security does not apply to all facilities subject to environmental permitting requirements. Ireland has adopted a risk-based approach that requires financial security only for licensable classes of activities that are considered to be high risk. Conditions in IPC/IED licences require the holder to cover the costs of remediating environmental damage caused by it. More specifically in respect of remedial measures, IPC/IED licences include conditions that require the licensee to have financial security for the costs of remediating and preventing further environmental damage, as well as the costs of closure and aftercare and, depending on the type of licensed facility, restoration of land.

The above measures are listed in the Environmental Liability Risk Assessment (ELRA) for the licensed facility. The measures also include preventive measures to reduce the risk of unexpected incidents that cause environmental damage, with the caveat that whilst these are also included in the conditions of a licence, they are not singly costed for. The scope of financial security requirements for ELRA is similar for all IPC/IED licences. In addition to ELRA, financial security requirements apply to Closure Restoration and Aftercare Management Plan (CRAMP) costs for foreseen events such as closure, restoration and aftercare plans for a licensed facility depending on the facility for which the licence is issued. For example, the conditions of a licence pursuant to the IED require the licensee to ensure that, when the licence is surrendered to the competent authority, the site of the licensed facility is returned to a ‘satisfactory state’, as required by the IED.

4.2.2 Waste Management Legislation

Many Member States have legislation that requires persons that carry out specified activities such as waste management to have financial security to provide a ready source of funds if the activities require pollution or other environmental damage to be remediated.

Eighteen Member States (Belgium (for the remediation of soil pollution), Croatia, Cyprus, Czechia, Denmark (for the remediation of pollution damage from oil tanks), Estonia, Finland (compensation only), France, Germany, Greece, Hungary, Ireland, Italy, Latvia, Lithuania, the Netherlands, Poland, Spain) have introduced mandatory security requirements for activities associated with waste management. The requirements vary from financial security for a variety of waste operations to financial security for the remediation of waste in others, particularly in Belgium and the Netherlands. Some of the requirements apply to civil liabilities arising from waste; others apply to the remediation, removal or other handling of waste.

In some Member States, such as Greece, the financial security requirements apply only to activities concerning hazardous waste. In other Member States, the requirements apply to non-hazardous as well as hazardous waste.

4.2.3 Other Civil and Remediation Liabilities

Financial security requirements are not limited to financial security to pay the costs of remediation measures. Some Member States have introduced mandatory financial security for specified civil liabilities, that is, claims for bodily injury and property damage. They are Austria (gene technology laboratories and other facilities), Croatia (waste management permits including landfill and extractive waste facility permits), Czechia (landfills), Estonia (railways for damage caused by accidental pollution), Finland (scheme requiring companies whose activities involve a significant risk of environmental damage or whose operations generally cause harm to the environment to have financial security for claims for bodily injury, property damage or economic loss when the responsible person cannot be found or is insolvent), Greece (claims for civil liabilities against holders of permits to transport hazardous waste, or to handle, store, dispose of, or recover hazardous waste at operator’s sites), Italy (facilities subject to the Seveso III Directive for insurance for claims for bodily injury and property damage; specified waste operators in the Veneto Region), Lithuania (operators that manage hazardous waste), Poland (operators of storage sites for carbon dioxide), Slovakia (upper tier facilities under the Seveso III Directive), and Spain (hazardous waste treatment sites).

In addition, 22 Member States (Belgium, Croatia, Cyprus, Czechia, Denmark, Estonia, Finland, France, Germany, Greece, Hungary, Ireland, Italy, Latvia, Lithuania, Malta, the Netherlands, Poland, Portugal, Slovakia, Spain, Sweden) have introduced mandatory financial security for remediation liabilities and responsibilities, that is, requirements to remediate environmental damage pursuant to conditions of permits and/or liabilities to remediate environmental damage from potential accidental incidents.[83]

4.2.4 Environmental Liability Directive

As indicated in Sect. 2.3.2.1 above, the ELD encourages but does not direct Member States to adopt mandatory financial security systems for ELD liabilities. Spain, Portugal, Slovakia and Czechia have introduced mandatory financial security systems for them. Ireland has a hybrid system of financial security that includes financial security for ELD liabilities and well as environmental responsibilities. Italy and Poland have adopted a limited number of provisions that requirement such financial security.

4.2.4.1 Spain

Spain was the first Member State to introduce a mandatory financial security system for ELD liabilities. The system was introduced on 23 October 2007 by provisions in the legislation that transposed the ELD into national law. The legislation stated that the system would be introduced by ministerial orders to be approved beginning on 30 April 2010.

Originally, the system was intended to apply to all Annex III operators under the ELD of which there were approximately 300,000. In 2015, the Spanish Government reduced the requirement so that it applies to specified categories of Annex III operators instead of all of them.

Subsequent legislation introduced the mandatory financial security system in phases, with higher risk activities (priority 1) required to have financial security first, followed by medium risk (priority 2), followed by lower risk activities (priority 3).

The first category of operators subject to mandatory financial security was operators of activities subject to the Seveso III Directive and the following activities under the IED: IPPC combustion installations with a total rated thermal input of 50 megawatts or more (IED, Annex I, 1.1); and disposal or recovery, other than

[83] The information concerning the number of Member States as well as the information on mandatory financial security systems for ELD liabilities below is drawn in particular from Fogleman (2020)'; https://circabc.europa.eu/ui/group/3b48eff1-b955-423f-9086-0d85ad1c5879/library/01708073-da51-4db7-8049-6e7141c901f4/details?download=true (scroll down to 'Study – Financial Security for ELD Liabilities (2020) – Final Report') (accessed on 10.05.2023).

landfilling, of hazardous waste with capacity exceeding 10 tonnes per day (IED, Annex I, 5.1), which includes mining waste under the Extractive Waste Directive.

The second category was operators subject to further activities under the IED including oil and gas refineries, facilities to refine petroleum or crude oil, coking plants, facilities for the production of cast iron or raw steel including continuous casting facilities with a capacity of over 2.5 tons per hour, specified chemical facilities, explosive manufacturing facilities, ferrous metal foundries with a production capacity of over 20 tons per day, and landfills for hazardous and non-hazardous waste that receive over 10 tons/day or that have a total capacity of over 25,000 tons.

The third category was the operation of facilities containing extractive/mining waste subject to the Extractive Waste Directive provided the extractive/mining waste was classified as category A (high risk).

The requirement for priority 1 operators to have financial security was effective on 31 October 2018, following by priority two operators on 31 October 2019, followed by priority three operators on 16 October 2021 – except for the intensive rearing of poultry and pigs, mandatory financial security for which was required by 16 October 2022.

The system does not require operators to have financial security for all liabilities under the ELD; financial security is required only for primary—not complementary or compensatory—remediation.

Further, operators of sites at which a verified risk assessment subject to guidelines in UNE Standard 150,008[84] or equivalent rules shows that the cost of primary remediation measures do not exceed EUR 300,000 are not required to have financial security. Nor are operators of sites for which such an assessment shows that the cost of primary remediation measures would be between EUR 300,000 and EUR 2,000,000 provided that the operator has an EU eco-management and audit scheme (EMAS)[85] or an environmental management system certified by the International Organisation for Standardisation (ISO) 14,001 (UNE-EN ISO 14001:1996; ISO 14001) certification.[86] In addition, operators that use specified plant protection products and biocides for agricultural and forestry purposes are not required to have financial security for their operations.

The General Directorate of Environmental Quality and Assessment of the Ministry for the Ecological Transition and the Demographic Challenge (*Ministerio para la Transición Ecológica y el Reto Demográfico*) has developed and published many methodologies, technical instruments, guidance and other documents to assist

[84] See European Standards 150,008:2008, Environmental risk analysis and assessment; https://www.en-standard.eu/une-150008-2008-environmental-risk-analysis-and-assessment/ (accessed on 10.05.2023).

[85] Regulation (EC) No 1221/2009 on the voluntary participation by organisations in a Community eco-management and audit scheme (EMAS) [2009] OJ L342/1 (consolidated version); https://eur-lex.europa.eu/legal-content/EN/TXT/?uri=CELEX%3A02009R1221-20190109 (accessed on 10.05.2023).

[86] An ISO 14001 is an environmental management system certified by the International Organisation for Standardisation (ISO).

operators in carrying out environmental risk analyses, and in determining the amount of financial security.

4.2.4.2 Portugal

There are many differences between the financial security system for ELD liabilities introduced in Spain and the system introduced in Portugal.

In contrast to Spain, Portugal introduced a mandatory financial security system that was effective on the date specified in the legislation that transposed the ELD (1 January 2010) instead of phasing in the requirements.

Also, in contrast to Spain, all Annex III operators under the ELD must have financial security (called financial guarantees). Further, all ELD liabilities (that is, complementary and compensatory remediation as well as preventive measures and primary remediation) are subject to the mandatory financial security system. Still further, there are no exceptions to the Portuguese mandatory financial security system for ELD liabilities and thus no limits in the amount of financial security for operators subject to the exceptions.

In a similar manner to Spain, however, the Portuguese system requires operators subject to mandatory financial security to prepare a risk assessment to determine the amount of financial security that applies to them. Operators may prepare the risk assessment by selecting the detailed methodology prepared by the competent authority, the Portuguese Environment Agency (*Agência Portuguesa do Ambiente*; APA), or they may select another methodology if it is more appropriate to their activities and damage that may be caused to natural resources under the ELD by those activities. The risk assessment may be carried out either by the operator or persons instructed by it.

The amount of financial security for an operator subject to mandatory financial security requirements is based on the estimated costs of measures to prevent or remediate potential environmental damage according to risks from an operator's activities. If the operator carries out measures to reduce the risks and thus minimises them, the amount of required financial security is reduced.

The following financial security instruments and mechanisms are acceptable to the APA:

- insurance policies;
- bank guarantees;
- environmental funds;
- own dedicated funds; and,
- a combination of the above.

All the instruments and/or mechanisms must include provisions to ring-fence liabilities or responsibilities that require mandatory financial security from other liabilities or responsibilities.

Criteria for acceptable insurance policies and details of the other types of financial security instruments and mechanisms are set out on the APA's website.

4.2.4.3 Slovakia

Slovakia introduced a mandatory financial security system for ELD liabilities in its legislation that transposed the ELD into national law. The system became effective on 1 July 2012 to allow time for operators and financial security providers to prepare for its introduction.

Like the system introduced by Portugal, the Slovakian system applies to all operators subject to Annex III of the ELD. Also, like Portugal, all ELD liabilities (that is, complementary and compensatory remediation as well as preventive measures and primary remediation) are subject to the scope of the mandatory financial security system. Further, like Portugal, there are no exceptions to the system.

Similar to the systems in Spain and Portugal, the amount of financial security covered by a financial security instrument or mechanism must correspond to the estimated costs of remedial measures plus the costs of preparing an analysis of the risks and costs of remedying environmental damage that could be caused by the operator's activity.

In order to assist in carrying out a risk assessment of the amount of financial security for environmental damage, the competent authority, the Ministry of Environment (*Ministerstvo životného prostredia*), has published a methodological manual for operators and state administrations. The methodology includes a determination of the amount of financial security and criteria for financial security instruments. A methodological tool, which can be used online as well as offline, is available to calculate the risk. The manual has three annexes that provide examples of an initial environmental risk assessment, selected parts of a detailed environmental risk assessment, and calculations to indicate whether it is necessary to carry out a detailed environmental risk assessment. There is no specified amount or limit of financial security. Instead, the amount depends on the amount calculated in the risk assessment.

Financial security instruments acceptable to the Ministry of Environment are an insurance policy, a bank guarantees, a dedicated account or another appropriate instrument approved by the Ministry.

4.2.4.4 Czechia

Czechia also introduced mandatory financial security for ELD liabilities in the legislation that transposed the ELD into Czech law in 2008. Like Slovakia, the methodology for self-assessment by operators to determine whether they are subject to the mandatory financial security system came into effect on 1 January 2013 in order to allow time to prepare for its introduction.

Unlike Spain, but like Czechia and Portugal, all liabilities under the ELD (complementary and compensatory remediation as well as preventive measures and primary remediation) are subject to the mandatory financial security requirements.

All operators that carry out activities under legislation listed in the equivalent of Annex III of the ELD with specified exceptions must carry out self-assessment for mandatory financial security requirements. Persons subject to the exceptions are specified operators under water law, specifically operators that treat harmful or hazardous substances, or hazardous substances in total quantities below specified limits.

Under the self-assessment system, Annex III operators must carry out a basic risk assessment. If the total amount of 'control points' in the assessment is less than 50, the cost of remediating environmental damage is deemed to be less than CZK 20,000,000 (EUR 819,672). In this case, the operator is not required to prepare a detailed risk assessment.

If the total amount of control points is more than 50, the operator must either submit evidence of financial security to the competent authority or show that it is registered under EMAS or has begun procedures to be registered or shows that it has an ISO 14001 registration or has begun procedures for such registration.

The amount of financial security for ELD liabilities depends on the risk assessment subject to the above amounts. There is no specified amount or limit for financial security.

Acceptable financial security instruments and mechanisms for the mandatory financial security system are a combination of insurance and banking products or a combination of insurance and other products.

4.2.4.5 Ireland

As discussed in Sect. 4.2.1 above, Ireland has a hybrid financial security system for environmental liabilities and environmental responsibilities. Financial security that is required for liabilities in the form of preventing and remediating environmental damage from accidents includes the prevention and remediation of environmental damage under the ELD.

4.2.4.6 Italy

Italy indirectly requires financial security for some ELD liabilities.

The legislation that transposed the ELD states that a person against whom the Ministry of the Environment (*Ministero dell'ambiente*) initiates procedures to reclaim and remediate environmental damage at National Interest Priority Sites (*Siti di interesse nazionale*),[87] or takes related judicial action can propose a settlement that includes an indication of appropriate financial guarantees. It thus appears that there is an intent that the financial guarantee must include the costs of all three

[87] Siti di interesse nazionale are historically contaminated sites subject to State control.

types of remediation measures (primary, complementary and compensatory remediation) under the ELD.

In addition, traders and brokers of waste (that is, persons that do not hold waste themselves) must have financial security for expenses directly or indirectly inherent in or connected with the transportation and disposal of waste, safety measures (including their implementation), remediation, restoration of facilities and contaminated areas. The legislation states that the financial guarantees can be used without prejudice to the overall maximum limit of the guaranteed amount, for the restoration of further damage to the environment pursuant to Part VI of Legislative Decree 152/2006 (*Decreto Legislativo 3 aprile 2006, No 152*), as amended[88] (the legislation that transposed the ELD into Italian law).

4.2.4.7 Poland

Poland has introduced mandatory financial security provisions for ELD liabilities for the following activities: the operation of a landfill, waste collection and waste processing, and specified integrated permits.

In 2012, mandatory financial security for liabilities under the ELD was introduced for operators of landfills. The requirements are in addition to the requirement in the Landfill Directive to have financial security for obligations concerning environmental responsibilities under the permit for the landfill.

In 2018, holders of integrated permits that include authorisation for waste collection and/or waste processing activities were required to have financial security for ELD liabilities.

In 2019, holders of an integrated permit, a permit for gas or dust releases into the ambient air, and/or a permit for generating waste were required to have financial security for ELD liabilities if the relevant competent authority concludes that there is a particularly important social interest related to environmental protection, in particular the risk of substantial deterioration of the state of the environment.

Financial security instruments acceptable for the mandatory financial security requirements for the three above categories of activities are a bank deposit in a dedicated account, a bank guarantee, an insurance guarantee, and an insurance policy.

[88] Decreto legislativo 3 aprile 2006, No 152; https://www.gazzettaufficiale.it/atto/serie_generale/caricaDettaglioAtto/originario?atto.dataPubblicazioneGazzetta=2006-04-14&atto.codiceRedazionale=006G0171 (in Italian). An unofficial version of the Environmental Code is available at https://www.bosettiegatti.eu/info/norme/statali/2006_0152.htm (in Italian) (accessed on 10.05.2023).

References

Cases

Case C-1/03 *Van de Walle v Texaco Belgium SA* [2004] ECR I-7613; https://eur-lex.europa.eu/legal-content/EN/TXT/?uri=CELEX%3A62003CJ0001. Accessed on 10 May 2023
Case C-188/07 *Commune de Mesquer v Total France SA* [2008] ECR I-4501; https://curia.europa.eu/juris/liste.jsf?language=en&num=C-188/07. Accessed on 10 May 2023
Case C-297/19 Naturschutzbund Deutschland — Landesverband Schleswig-Holstein eV v Kreis Nordfriesland ECLI:EU:C:2020:533; https://curia.europa.eu/juris/documents.jsf?num=C-297/19. Accessed on 10 May 2023
Case C-529/15 Folk v Unabhängiger Verwaltungssenat für die Steiermark ECLI:EU:C:2017:419; https://curia.europa.eu/juris/liste.jsf?num=C-529/15. Accessed on 10 May 2023
Magee v Culligan [1992] 1 IRLM 223

Legislation

Commission Notice, Guidelines providing a common understanding of the term 'environmental damage' as defined in Article 2 of Directive 2004/35/EC of the European Parliament and of the Council on environmental liability with regard to the prevention and remedying of environmental damage 2021/C 118/01 [2021] OJ C118/1; https://eur-lex.europa.eu/legal-content/EN/TXT/?uri=CELEX%3A52021XC0407%2801%29&qid=1617956961808
Directive 2008/56/EC establishing a framework for community action in the field of marine environmental policy [20008] OJ L164/19 (consolidated version.); https://eur-lex.europa.eu/legal-content/EN/TXT/?uri=CELEX%3A02008L0056-20170607
Constitution of Ireland; https://www.irishstatutebook.ie/eli/cons/en/html
Council Directive 1999/31/EC on the landfill of waste [1999] OJ L182/1; https://eur-lex.europa.eu/legal-content/EN/TXT/?uri=CELEX:31999L0031
Council Directive 82/501/EEC on the major-accident hazards of certain industrial activities [1982] OJ L230/1 (repealed); https://eur-lex.europa.eu/legal-content/EN/TXT/?uri=CELEX:31982L0501
Council Directive 92/43/EEC on the conservation of natural habitats and of wild fauna and flora [1992] OJ L206/7 (consolidated version); https://eur-lex.europa.eu/legal-content/EN/TXT/?uri=CELEX:01992L0043-20130701
Council Directive 96/61/EC concerning integrated pollution prevention and control [1996] OJ L257/26 (repealed); https://eur-lex.europa.eu/legal-content/EN/TXT/?uri=CELEX%3A31996L0061
Council Directive 96/82/EC on the control of major-accident hazardous involving dangerous substances [1996] OJ L10 (consolidated version) (repealed); https://eur-lex.europa.eu/legal-content/EN/TXT/PDF/?uri=CELEX:01996L0082-20120813&from=EN
Decreto legislativo 3 aprile 2006, No 152; https://www.gazzettaufficiale.it/atto/serie_generale/caricaDettaglioAtto/originario?atto.dataPubblicazioneGazzetta=2006-04-14&atto.codiceRedazionale=006G0171 (in Italian)
Directive (2009/31/EC) on the geological storage of carbon dioxide [2009] OJ L140/114; https://eur-lex.europa.eu/legal-content/EN/TXT/?uri=CELEX%3A32009L0031
Directive (2012/18/EU) on the control of major-accident hazards involving dangerous substances [2012] OJ L197/1; https://eur-lex.europa.eu/legal-content/EN/TXT/?uri=CELEX:32012L0018

Directive 2000/60/EC establishing a framework for Community action in the field of water policy [2000] OJ L327/1 (consolidated version); https://eur-lex.europa.eu/legal-content/EN/TXT/?uri=CELEX:02000L0060-20141120

Directive 2004/35/EC on environmental liability with regard to the prevention and remedying of environmental damage [2004] OJ L143/56 (consolidated version); https://eur-lex.europa.eu/legal-content/EN/TXT/PDF/?uri=CELEX:02004L0035-20190626&qid=1568193390794&from=EN

Directive 2008/1/EC concerning integrated pollution prevention and control [2008] OJ L24/8, art 14(b) (consolidated version) (repealed); https://eur-lex.europa.eu/legal-content/EN/TXT/PDF/?uri=CELEX:32008L0001&from=EN

Directive 2008/98/EC on waste [2008] OJ L312/3, as amended (consolidated version); https://eur-lex.europa.eu/legal-content/EN/TXT/?uri=CELEX%3A02008L0098-20180705Directive 2009/147/EC on the conservation of wild birds [2010] OJ L20/7 (codified version); https://eur-lex.europa.eu/legal-content/EN/TXT/?uri=CELEX:32009L0147

Directive 2010/75/EU on industrial emissions (integrated pollution prevention and control) [2010] OJ L158/25 (consolidated version); https://eur-lex.europa.eu/legal-content/EN/TXT/?uri=CELEX%3A02010L0075-20110106

Directive 2011/92/EU on the assessment of the effects of certain public and private projects on the environment (codified version) [2011] OJ L26 (as amended by Directive 2014/52/EU); https://eur-lex.europa.eu/legal-content/EN/TXT/?uri=CELEX%3A02011L0092-20140515

Directive 2012/19/EU on waste electrical and electronic equipment [2012] OJ L197/38; https://eur-lex.europa.eu/legal-content/EN/TXT/PDF/?uri=CELEX:32012L0019

Directive 2013/59/Euratom laying down basic safety standards for protection against the dangers arising from exposure to ionising radiation [2013] OJ L013/1; https://eur-lex.europa.eu/legal-content/EN/TXT/?uri=CELEX:02013L0059-20140117

Directive 2016/21/EC on the management of waste from extractive industries [2016] OJ L102/15; https://eur-lex.europa.eu/legal-content/EN/TXT/?uri=CELEX:02006L0021-20090807

European Commission, Proposal for a Directive of the European Parliament and of the Council establishing a framework for the protection of soil and amending Directive 2004/35/EC (COM (2006) 232 final, 22 September 2006.); https://eur-lex.europa.eu/legal-content/EN/TXT/?uri=CELEX:52006PC0232

European Commission, Proposal for a Directive of the European Parliament and the Council amending Directive 2010/75/EU of the European Parliament and of the Council of 24 November 2010 on industrial emissions (integrated pollution prevention and control) and Council Directive 1999/31/EC of 26 April 1999 on the landfill of waste (COM(2022) 156 final, 5 April 2022), explanatory memorandum, section 1; https://eur-lex.europa.eu/legal-content/EN/TXT/?uri=CELEX%3A52022PC0156R%2802%29&qid=1651130627889

Regulation (EC) No 1013/2006 on shipments of waste [2006] OJ L190/1 (consolidated version); https://eur-lex.europa.eu/legal-content/EN/TXT/?qid=1454069470717&uri=CELEX:02006R1013-20180101

Regulation (EC) No 1221/2009 on the voluntary participation by organisations in a Community eco-management and audit scheme (EMAS) [2009] OJ L342/1 (consolidated version); https://eur-lex.europa.eu/legal-content/EN/TXT/?uri=CELEX%3A02009R1221-20190109

Other Governmental Documents

Base des sols pollués (BASOL); https://www.data.gouv.fr/en/datasets/base-des-sols-pollues/#description (in French)

Inventaire des sites pollués (BASIAS); https://www.data.gouv.fr/en/datasets/inventaire-des-sites-pollues/ (in French)

Books

van Boom WH (2004) Pure economic loss: a comparative perspective. In: van Boom WH, Koziol H, Witting CA (eds) Pure Economic Loss. Springer, Cham, p 17

Articles

AIG (2018) Burning issues for environmental claims; https://www.aig.co.uk/content/dam/aig/emea/united-kingdom/documents/Insights/eil-claims-2018-uk.pdf. Accessed on 10 May 2023

Assurpol; http://www.assurpol.fr/fr/ (in French). Accessed on 10 May 2023

Betlem G (1995) It's no use crying over spilt chemicals. Maa J Eur Comp Law 2:289

Bussani M, Palmer VV, Parisi F (2003) Liability for pure financial loss in Europe: an economic restatement. Am J Comp Law 51:113

Church TW, Nakamura RT (1994) Beyond superfund: hazardous waste cleanup in Europe and the United States. Georgetown Int Environ Law Rev 7:41–42

Darmendrail D (2010) The French approach to contaminated land management: legal framework and reclamation of former industrial sites in urban areas. J Urban Regeneration Renewal 3:277; https://www.researchgate.net/publication/280784366_The_French_approach_to_contaminated_land_management_Legal_framework_and_reclamation_of_former_industrial_sites_in_urban_areas/link/566aa29c08aea0892c4a4ac6/download. Accessed on 10 May 2023

Fogleman V (2015) 'Landowners' liability for remediating contaminated land in the EU: EU or national law? Part II: national law. Environ Liability 23(2):42–61

Harvard Business School (2013) Environmental Risk Management; A Report by Harvard Business Review Analytical Services

Heuser I (March 2022) Soil governance in current European Union law and in the European green Deal. Soil Secur 6: 100053; https://www.sciencedirect.com/science/article/pii/S266700622200020X

Hoffman WC (1991) Strict pollution liability under Germany's new environmental liability act. Environ Claims J 3:487

Il Pool Ambiente è il Consorzio per l'Assicurazione e la Riassicurazione della Responsabilità per Danni all'Ambiente; https://www.poolambiente.it/ (in Italian)

Koziol H (2008) Punitive damages – a European perspective. Louisiana Law Rev 68:740

Koziol H (2012) *Basic Questions of Tort Law from a Germanic Perspective* 230 (Jan Sramek Verlag); https://www.jan-sramek-verlag.at/fileadmin/user_upload/Koziol_ComparaTortLaw_Eng_0040_2_DRUCK_eBook.pdf. Accessed on 10 May 2023

Lewis P (20 February 1983) 'Following U.S., Europe Awakens to the Dangers of Toxic Wastes' New York Times; http://www.nytimes.com/1983/02/20/weekinreview/following-us-europe-awakens-to-the-dangers-of-toxic-wastes.html. Accessed on 10 May 2023

Marsh (2015) Benchmarking trends: environmental liability directive drives shift in purchasing of environmental impairment liability insurance; https://www.marsh.com/content/dam/marsh/Documents/PDF/UK-en/EMEA%20Environmental%20Benchmarking%20Report%202015-11-2015.pdf. Accessed on 10 May 2023

Marsh Environmental Market Update (September 2016). https://www.marsh.com/content/dam/marsh/Documents/PDF/UK-en/EMEA%20Environmental%20Market%20Update.pdf. Accessed on 10 May 2023

Ministry of the Environment (December 2003) 'Soil contamination: solution to the cheminova toxic waste dump problem' Danish Environment Newsletter No 28

Palmer VV, Bussani M (December 2007) Pure economic loss: the ways to recovery. Netherlands Comp Law Assoc Electronic J Comp Law 11(3): 7

Qué es el Pool de Riesgos Medioambientales?; https://www.estamos-seguros.es/que-es-el-pool-de-riesgos-medioambientales/ (in Spanish). Accessed on 10 May 2023
Schreier V (2020) Pollution insurance – methods, coverage and beneficiaries under German policies; German national report. World congress of the international law association (AIDA) 2018. Zeitschrift für die gesamte Versicherungswissenschaft 1:65

Reports

Baltic Environment and Energy, Swedish Environmental Policies, History and present regulations (Report 3 of the BEE project, 2007)
European Commission, Withdrawal of Obsolete Commission Proposals [2014] OJ C153/3; http://eur-lex.europa.eu/legal-content/EN/TXT/PDF/?uri=OJ:C:2014:153:FULL&from=EN. Accessed on 10 May 2023
European Standards 150008:2008, Environmental risk analysis and assessment; https://www.en-standard.eu/une-150008-2008-environmental-risk-analysis-and-assessment/
Fogleman V (May 2020) Improving financial security in the context of the Environmental Liability Directive (ELD), Member State report for Germany; https://circabc.europa.eu/ui/group/3b48eff1-b955-423f-9086-0d85ad1c5879/library/7d116574-6f1e-47ee-a8d6-b809f1b82b5a?p=1&n=-1&sort=name_ASC. Accessed on 10 May 2023
Fogleman V (31 December 2021) Facilitating Enforcement of the ELD by Competent Authorities' (prepared for European Commission, DG Environment), 100–104; https://ec.europa.eu/environment/legal/liability/pdf/study/FinalReport.PDF. Accessed on 10 May 2023
Pérez AP, Eugenio NR (2018) 'Status of local soil contamination in Europe; Revision of the indicator "Progress in the management contaminated sites in Europe"' (JRC Technical Reports); https://publications.jrc.ec.europa.eu/repository/handle/JRC107508. Accessed on 10 May 2023
Report from the Commission to the European Parliament, the Council, the European Economic and Social Committee and the Committee of the Regions, The implementation of the Soil Thematic Strategy and ongoing activities (COM)2012, 46 final); https://eur-lex.europa.eu/legal-content/EN/TXT/?uri=CELEX:52012DC0046. Accessed on 10 May 2023

Environmental Liabilities and Insurance Law in the United Kingdom

Valerie Fogleman

Abstract Individuals in the United Kingdom (UK) who suffer bodily injury and property damage from exposure to pollutants or other environmental damage have long been able to make claims against persons that caused the damage, with common law torts in England, Wales and Northern Ireland differing from civil law torts in Scotland.

Environmental legislation, especially from the early 1990s, substantially increased the liabilities with the introduction of more extensive environmental permitting and liability legislation. Most environmental legislation in this modern era originated in the European Union (EU). As a result, over 95% of environmental law in the UK is EU law or, as it has been called since the UK left the EU on 31 January 2020, 'retained EU law'.

Since 1998, environmental law in England, Scotland, Wales and Northern Ireland has increasingly diverged in each region as a result of devolution. The environmental is a devolved matter, which means that each government may enact its own environmental legislation. Whereas the extent of the differences was mitigated when the UK was a Member State of the EU, the differences have steadily increased since 31 January 2020.

The increase in environmental liabilities in the modern era of environmental law led insurers in the UK to include a pollution exclusion in public liability policies. At about the same time, some insurers—mostly affiliates of US insurers—began introducing environmental insurance policies for risks across the UK. Insurers subsequently also began offering extensions to public liability policies to provide cover for remediating off-site pollution from sudden and accidental incidents on an insured's site.

This chapter will examine tort and statutory environmental liabilities in the UK and insurance that provides cover for them.

V. Fogleman (✉)
Cardiff University School of Law and Politics, Cardiff, Wales, UK

Stevens & Bolton LLP, Guildford, England, UK
e-mail: foglemanvm@cardiff.ac.uk; valerie.fogleman@stevens-bolton.com

K. Malinowska, D. Maśniak (eds.), *Managing Environmental Risks through Insurance*, AIDA Europe Research Series on Insurance Law and Regulation 9,
https://doi.org/10.1007/978-3-031-47602-0_4

1 Introduction

This chapter examines environmental liabilities and insurance law for such liabilities in the United Kingdom (UK). In doing so, the chapter does not describe all environmental and insurance law in England, Wales, Scotland and Northern Ireland. Instead, it describes common law environmental liabilities in England and Wales and legislative environmental liabilities in England, noting major differences in environmental law in Scotland, Wales and/or Northern Ireland. The chapter then describes insurance law in England and Wales, noting any major differences in insurance law in Scotland and Northern Ireland.

The reason for this focus is due to the complexities of law, especially environmental law, in the UK. These complexities make any attempt to describe all environmental and insurance law in the various jurisdictions of the UK confusing at best.

There are two main types of law in the UK: judge-made law; and legislative (statutory) law. Judge-made law in England, Wales and Northern Ireland is called common law; judge-made law in Scotland is called civil law. Differences in judge-made law in the UK are not limited to differences between common law and civil law; there are also differences between common law between England and Wales (which is the same) and Northern Ireland, where common law is similar to that in England and Wales, but also has differences. The differences in judge-made law exist in both tort law (called delict in Scotland) and contract law.

Traditional judge-made environmental liabilities in the UK are based on tort law. There are thus differences in such environmental liabilities in England and Wales, Scotland, and Northern Ireland.

The construction of insurance policies is based on contract law. There are thus differences in insurance law in England and Wales, Scotland, and Northern Ireland.

The differences in environmental legislation between the different jurisdictions in the UK became more complex as a result of devolution. The environment is a devolved matter. Thus, some environmental legislation may—and does—differ in England and the devolved jurisdictions of Wales, Scotland, and Northern Ireland.

Brexit increased the complexities in environmental legislation between the various jurisdictions in the UK. This is because over 95% of environmental law in the UK is European Union (EU) law. Before Brexit—and despite devolution—each jurisdiction in the UK had roughly the same—or at least similar—environmental law due to the UK being a Member State of the EU. When the UK left the EU, that law became 'retained EU law'. Further complexities have arisen because Northern Ireland is still in the EU single market. Revisions—and suggested revisions—to some environmental legislation in England, Scotland, and Wales since Brexit therefore cannot made in Northern Ireland.

Insurance is not a devolved matter. Whilst judge-made law on the construction of insurance contracts differs between England and Wales, Scotland, and Northern Ireland, legislation on insurance contracts enacted by the UK Parliament is the same for England, Wales, and Scotland, with some small differences in Northern Ireland.

Further, whilst Brexit has had major ramifications for insurance regulatory law and the ability of insurers based in the UK to offer insurance policies throughout the EU by 'passporting', insurance contract law in the UK has not been affected by Brexit with a few notable non-environmental exceptions.[1]

This chapter is structured as follows.

Section 2 examines the common law as it applies to environmental liabilities. This section first discusses the principles of liability followed by a discussion of the main heads of common law tort claims.

Section 3 then describes legislation that imposes environmental liabilities, in particular liability for remediating pollution and other environmental damage. In order to set this discussion in context, Sect. 3 first provides an overview of devolution, followed by the way in which EU legislation was transposed into national law. The section then examines the effect of Brexit on law derived from the EU. This is followed by an overview of the main regimes for preventing and remediating environmental damage.

Section 4 examines the general rules of construction of insurance policies in England and Wales.

Section 5 examines insurance for the environmental liabilities discussed in Sects. 2 and 3. The discussion includes cover for environmental liabilities in general/public liability policies, the withdrawal of such cover and endorsements that write back some of that cover.

Section 6 then examines environmental insurance policies that are designed specifically to provide cover for environmental liabilities. The section includes a discussion of the evolution of the London environmental insurance market and the main types of environmental insurance policies.

Finally, Sect. 7 briefly mentions mandatory financial security requirements for environmental responsibilities and liabilities. It does not, however, discuss these requirements because the main requirements are discussed in the chapter on environmental liabilities and insurance law in the EU due to such requirements in the UK still largely mirroring EU requirements.

[1] One notable exception is insurance for vehicles. In *Vnuk v Zavarovalnica Triglav d.d.*, Case C-162/13 ECLI:EU:C:2014:2146, https://curia.europa.eu/juris/liste.jsf?num=C-162/13, the Court of Justice of the European Union ruled that the Motor Insurance Directive (2009/103/EC) OJ [2009] L263/11; https://eur-lex.europa.eu/legal-content/EN/TXT/?uri=celex%3A32009L0103 (accessed on 10.05.2023) required mandatory motor insurance not only for travel on roads and public places but also in respect of a farm worker who was injured when a reversing tractor with a trailer knocked him off a ladder in a private farmyard. The UK Parliament subsequently removed application of the Directive to vehicles 'other than motor vehicles' that were 'otherwise than on a road or other public place' by the Motor Vehicles (Compulsory Insurance) Act 2022; https://www.legislation.gov.uk/ukpga/2022/25/enacted (accessed on 10.05.2023). The Act applies to England, Wales and Scotland; it does not apply to Northern Ireland.

2 Common Law

There are four main common law actions that are relevant to environmental liabilities. These are nuisance, the rule in *Rylands v Fletcher,* negligence, and trespass, with nuisance being divided into private nuisance, public nuisance, and statutory nuisance.

2.1 Private Nuisance

A private nuisance is an unlawful interference with a person's use or enjoyment of land or some right over or in connection with the land.

Private nuisance is a strict liability tort based on reasonableness between neighbours. In order to be an actionable nuisance, a nuisance must therefore be unreasonable by reference to neighbours. Thus, what may be a nuisance in an affluent area may not be a nuisance in a less affluent area. Whereas a defendant can argue that activities alleged to be a nuisance are part of the character of the locality, this argument is limited in that the activities must not be a nuisance in the first place.[2]

In spite of the locality rule, it is not a defence to state that a claimant came to an existing nuisance. Such an argument is however limited in that if a claimant changes the use of their land by, for example, constructing a building on it, it may be a defence to show that the defendant's pre-existing activity is lawful and was not a nuisance before the change in use of the claimant's land provided that the nuisance is no greater than before the change.[3]

As well as reasonableness between neighbours, there must also be reasonable foreseeability. That is, the claimant must prove, among other things, that the defendant could reasonably have foreseen the harm suffered by the claimant.

In addition to liability for nuisance caused by acts of the defendant, liability also exists for natural nuisances, that is, nuisances caused by the operation of nature, such as a landslip. In such a case, the owner or occupier of the land is subject to a measured duty of care. This means that measures to prevent the escape must be reasonable. For example, a landowner was liable for failing to stop soil and rubble from a large mound on its land falling onto its neighbour's land.[4] A local government that sold land to a developer to build houses and retained land that was higher than the land that was sold, was not liable for failing to construct drainage ditches and a catchpit to stop flooding on the land sold to the developer. Instead, the local

[2] *Coventry v Lawrence* [2014] UKSC 13 [74].

[3] Ibid. [56].

[4] *Leakey v National Trust for Places of Historic Interest or Natural Beauty* [1980] 1 QB 485, 526.

government's measured duty of care was to allow others access to its land and to co-operate with them in their construction of the ditches and catchpit.[5]

It is not a defence to a private nuisance action for a defendant to have an environmental permit for activities carried out on its land. For example, the Court of Appeal rejected an argument by the operator of a landfill that compliance with the permit for the landfill meant that odours from the landfill were not a nuisance to people living near it. The court stated that 'the permit did not, and did not purport to, authorise the emission' of the odours.[6]

Due to private nuisance being a land-based tort, the then House of Lords (now the UK Supreme Court) ruled, in *Hunter v Canary Wharf Ltd*, that a person must have the legal right to exclusive possession of land affected by an alleged nuisance in order to bring a claim. This means that a person that owns or occupies land may bring a claim in private nuisance but not a child or other person who lives with the owner or occupier and who does not have a legal right to the land.[7] The requirement for exclusive possession of land also means that a claim for damages for bodily injury is not available in private nuisance.[8]

A person may be liable for continuing a nuisance as well as creating it. In the landmark case of *Sedleigh-Denfield v O'Callaghan*, the House of Lords held that a person that occupies land and knows, or ought to know, that a nuisance exists, 'continues' the nuisance if the person fails to carry out reasonable measures to end it.[9]

In a much more recent case, the UK Supreme Court held, in 2023, that oil that had washed onshore in Nigeria from an offshore pipeline that leaked for between five and six hours was not a continuing nuisance. The oil had damaged the claimants' fishing, land, mangrove forests, other property and shrines.[10] The judgment and the Court of Appeal's judgment include a detailed review of the law of continuing nuisance.

The foremost remedy for a private nuisance was traditionally an injunction plus damages for past nuisance, with courts being reluctant to award damages for future nuisance. In 2014, however, the UK Supreme Court stated that courts may take the circumstances of the case into account in determining whether to grant an injunction to restrain the defendant from continuing to commit a nuisance or whether to award damages instead. A key factor is the public interest including whether persons other

[5] *Lambert v Barratt Homes Ltd* [2010 EWCA Civ 681 [15]–[19]; see also *House Maker (Padgate) Ltd v Network Rail Infrastructure* [2022] EWHC 1482 (TCC) (rail operator had a measured duty of care to a developer on a site next to a railway station owned and operated by the rail operator to rectify flooding caused to the developer's site by a collapsed drain on the rail operator's land).

[6] *Barr v Biffa Waste Services Ltd* [2012] EWCA Civ 312 [46].

[7] *Hunter v Canary Wharf* [1997] AC 655, 692.

[8] Ibid. [696], [707], [724].

[9] *Sedleigh-Denfield v O'Callaghan* [1940] AC 880, 911–913.

[10] *Jalla v Shell International Trading and Shipping Company* [2023] UKSC 16.

than the claimant would be affected and whether an injunction would result in a loss of jobs.[11]

2.2 Public Nuisance

Public nuisance exists under the law of England and Wales, and Northern Ireland. It does not exist under Scots law.

A public nuisance is an unlawful act or the failure to discharge a legal duty to act when the effect of the act or failure materially affects the reasonable convenience and comfort of a class of people or their health, lives or property. In order to bring a claim, the claimant must have suffered damage over and above damage suffered by the general public.

As with private nuisance, the claimant must prove that the defendant could reasonably foresee the harm suffered by the claimant when the acts that led to the public nuisance occurred.

A public nuisance differs from private nuisance by, among other things, not requiring a claimant to allege that there has been direct interference with enjoyment of their land. Unlike private nuisance, therefore, compensation for public nuisance includes damages for bodily injury. In a ruling on this issue, the Court of Appeal stated that compensatory damages for bodily injuries could be awarded to individuals who claimed that deformities of their arms and hands were caused by their mothers having been exposed during their pregnancies to toxic substances from extensive measures to remediate a seriously contaminated former steelworks site.[12] Lorries that transported toxic materials from the former steelworks had not been covered and had spread some of the materials on roads where their mothers lived. The High Court concluded that the defendant was liable in public nuisance for causing, allowing or permitting dispersal of dangerous contaminants.[13] The court however stated that each claimant must prove that their particular conditions were actually caused by the defendant's actions. The case subsequently settled for an undisclosed amount.

Public nuisance is also a common law crime. Due to the increase in more specific legislative environmental offences since 1990, however, prosecutions have rarely been brought since the early 1990s.

[11] *Coventry v Lawrence* [2014] UKSC 13 [132], [161].

[12] *Corby Group Litigation v Corby Borough Council* [2008] EWCA Civ 463 [29]–[33].

[13] *Corby Group Litigation v Corby Borough Council* [2009] EWHC 1944, [892].

2.3 Rylands v Fletcher

The rule in *Rylands v Fletcher,*[14] which is a subset of nuisance, exists under the law of England and Wales, and Northern Ireland. It does not exist under Scots law.

The rule imposes liability on a person that controls land for the natural consequences of the escape of a substance that the person brought onto, or that accumulated on, the land, provided that the use of the land is 'non-natural'. The rule originated in the 1868 case of *Rylands v Fletcher,* which involved the construction of a reservoir near the claimant's mine. The persons who constructed the reservoir had seen old mine shafts during its construction but had mistakenly concluded that they had been abandoned. The mine shafts were, however, connected to the mine, resulting in water from the reservoir flooding the mine when the reservoir was filled.

As with other actions in nuisance, reasonable foreseeability is a prerequisite to liability under the rule in *Rylands v Fletcher*. In the landmark case of *Cambridge Water Company v Eastern Counties Leather*, the House of Lords ruled that the storage of large quantities of organochlorines, a solvent, in a tannery was 'an almost classic case of non-natural use'.[15] The organochlorines had been spilled by the tannery before 1976 and had then seeped through concrete at the tannery into the ground and had entered the aquifer below the tannery. The organochlorines had then migrated 1.3 miles (just over two kilometres) to a public water abstraction well operated by the Cambridge Water Company. Due to a reduction in the amount of organochlorines allowed by the EU in drinking water,[16] the water company had constructed a new abstraction well to replace the well with the polluted water at a cost of £956,937 (EUR 1,124,622).

The House of Lords discussed the prerequisite for reasonable foreseeability at length, ruling that the tannery was not liable under the rule in *Rylands v Fletcher* because the tannery could not reasonably have foreseen during the pre-1976 operations at the tannery that the organochlorines would cause a nuisance.[17]

Another key factor considered by the court was the potential for the adoption of legislation to impose liability for environmental pollution. Lord Goff, who gave the leading judgment, stated as follows:

> The protection and preservation of the environment is now perceived as being of crucial importance to the future of mankind; and public bodies, both national and international, are taking significant steps towards the establishment of legislation which will promote the protection of the environment, and make the polluter pay for damage to the environment for which he is responsible .... But it does not follow from these developments that a common law principle, such as the rule in Rylands v. Fletcher, should be developed or rendered more strict to provide for liability in respect of such pollution. On the contrary, given that so much

[14] *Rylands v Fletcher* (1868) LR 3 HL 330.

[15] *Cambridge Water Company v Eastern Counties Leather* [1994] 2 AC 264, 309.

[16] The reduction arose from transposition of Council Directive (80/778/EEC) relating to the quality of water intended for human consumption [1980] OJ L229/11; https://eur-lex.europa.eu/legal-content/EN/TXT/?uri=celex%3A31980L0778 (repealed) (accessed on 10.05.2023).

[17] *Cambridge Water Company v Eastern Counties Leather* [1994] 2 AC 264, 306–307.

> well-informed and carefully structured legislation is now being put in place for this purpose, there is less need for the courts to develop a common law principle to achieve the same end, and indeed it may well be undesirable that they should do so.[18]

In a subsequent case, the House of Lords considered whether the rule in *Rylands v Fletcher* should be abrogated. The court considered that the rule had existed for nearly 150 years, whilst acknowledging difficulties with it such as unclear boundaries to it, especially whether the use of land was 'non-natural'. The court concluded that the rule should be kept because the rationale for it was, and remained, valid.[19]

The remedies for an action under the rule in *Rylands v Fletcher* are the same as for nuisance, that is, damages and an injunction to restrain continuance of the activities.

2.4 Negligence

A person that owes another person a legal duty to exercise care is negligent if the person that owes the duty breaches it and the breach causes the other person damage that is a foreseeable consequence of the breach.

A particularly difficult case arises if a claimant develops mesothelioma as a result of the defendant's negligent exposure of the claimant to asbestos. A major reason for this difficulty is the latency period for mesothelioma between the date of the exposure and diagnosis of the disease, which can be up to or even over 40 years. Another major reason is the inability of medical science to prove which asbestos fibre inhaled by the claimant caused the disease. This means that the above test for negligence cannot be applied if more than one person exposed the claimant to asbestos because the claimant will be unable to prove that the defendant breached its duty to the claimant and caused them damage.

In the landmark case of *Fairchild v Glenhaven Funeral Services Ltd*, which involved claims by several former employees against more than one employer each, the House of Lords ruled that a claimant would succeed in a claim against two (or more) defendants if the claimant ('C') proved the following six elements:

- C was employed at different times and for differing periods by employers 'A' and 'B';
- A and B were subject to a duty to take reasonable care or to take all practicable measures to prevent C inhaling asbestos dust because of the known risk that asbestos duty (if inhaled) might cause mesothelioma;
- A and B were in breach of that duty in relation to C during the periods of C's employment by each of them with the result that C inhaled excessive quantities of dust during both periods of employment;
- C is suffering from mesothelioma;

[18] Ibid., 305.

[19] *Transco Plc v Stockport Metropolitan Borough Council* [2003] UKHL 61 [39]–[46], [66].

- any cause of C's mesothelioma other than inhalation of asbestos dust can be effectively discounted; and
- C cannot (because of current limits of science) prove, on a balance of probabilities, that his mesothelioma was the result of his inhaling asbestos dust during his employment by A or B or against both A and B.[20]

The House of Lords subsequently distinguished *Fairchild* in *Barker v Corus (UK) plc,* to rule that an employer that negligently exposes an employee to asbestos resulting in the employee developing mesothelioma is liable to pay compensation proportionate to the risk of exposure to the employee from that employer.[21] In a highly unusual move, the UK Parliament statutorily overrode *Barker* to reinstate joint and several liability as in the *Fairchild* judgment.[22]

As a result of the statutory intervention, the correct test for whether a defendant is liable to a claimant for mesothelioma is whether the defendant materially increased the risk of the claimant contracting the disease, provided that the increase in risk is 'material', that is, not *de minimis*. It is a question for the judge in the facts in a particular case to determine whether the risk is de minimis.[23]

It is important to note that the above test applies only to claims for harm from mesothelioma; it does not apply to any other negligence action including any action in which a claimant develops an asbestos-related disease.

2.5 Trespass

A trespass to land is an unjustifiable direct and immediate interference with the possession of land. It is not necessary to prove that damage has been caused, only that the occupier's right to possession of the land has been infringed. In such a case, however, a court would award only nominal damages.

It is rare for actions in trespass to be brought in environmental cases due to the need for a direct and immediate interference with the possession of land. Most environmental cases do not involve direct and immediate interference but, instead involve indirect interference such as pollution of groundwater by migrating pollutants.

An exception to the general absence of environmental cases in trespass involved an action by a landowner against a company that carried out hydraulic fracturing (fracking). The defendant company had a licence to explore for and exploit petroleum. In carrying out these activities, the company had constructed horizontal wells

---

[20] *Fairchild v Glenhaven Funeral Services Ltd* [2002] UKHL 22 [2].

[21] *Barker v Corus (UK) Plc* [2006] UKHL 20 [113].

[22] Compensation Act 2006, s 3; https://www.legislation.gov.uk/ukpga/2006/29/contents (accessed on 10.05.2023).

[23] *Sienkiewicz (Administratrix of the Estate of Enid Costello Deceased) v Greif (UK) Limited* [2011] UKSC 10 [107]–[112].

at a depth of between 800 and 2900 feet below ground level under the claimant's land. The UK Supreme Court concluded that the defendant's activities were a trespass but awarded only nominal damages because the landowner did not have a licence to drill for petroleum on its land and the UK Parliament had vested interests in petroleum in subsurface land to the Crown.[24]

The UK Parliament subsequently enacted legislation to provide the holder of a permit to exploit petroleum the right to exploit it in 'deep-level land', that is, 'any land at a depth of at least 300 metres below surface level' without permission from the landowner.[25] A main purpose of the legislation was to stop opponents of fracking from buying land through which fracking companies intended constructing horizontal wells as 'ransom land', that is, having the right to bring an action in trespass against them.

2.6 Statutory Nuisance

The Environmental Protection Act 1990 imposes liability for various 'statutory nuisances'.

Section 79(1) of the Act lists the statutory nuisances, which applies in England, Scotland, Wales, and Northern Ireland as follows:

> (a) any premises in such a state as to be prejudicial to health or a nuisance;
> (b) smoke emitted from premises so as to be prejudicial to health or a nuisance;
> (c) fumes or gases emitted from premises so as to be prejudicial to health or a nuisance;
> (d) any dust, steam, smell or other effluvia arising on industrial, trade or business premises and being prejudicial to health or a nuisance;
> (e) any accumulation or deposit which is prejudicial to health or a nuisance;
> (f) any animal kept in such a place or manner as to be prejudicial to health or a nuisance;
> (fa) any insects emanating from relevant industrial, trade or business premises and being prejudicial to health or a nuisance;
> (fb) artificial light emitted from premises so as to be prejudicial to health or a nuisance;
> (g) noise emitted from premises so as to be prejudicial to health or a nuisance;
> (ga) noise that is prejudicial to health or a nuisance and is emitted from or caused by a vehicle, machinery or equipment in a street or in Scotland, road; [and]
> (h) any other matter declared by any enactment to be a statutory nuisance.

The scope of the statutory nuisance regime was restricted when the contaminated land regime (see Sect. 3.4.6 below) came into force. Section 79(1B) of the Environmental Protection Act 1990, as amended by the Environment Act 1995, provides that '[n]o matter shall constitute a statutory nuisance to the extent that it consists of, or is caused by, any land being in a contaminated state'.

Land is defined to be in a 'contaminated state':

---

[24] *Bocardo SA v Star Energy UK Onshore Ltd* [2010] UKSC 35 [90]–[92].

[25] Infrastructure Act 2014, s 32; https://www.legislation.gov.uk/ukpga/2015/7/contents/enacted (accessed on 10.05.2023).

> if, and only if, it is in such a condition, by reason of substances in, on or under the land, that—
>
> (a) harm is being caused or there is a possibility of harm being caused; or
> (b) pollution of controlled waters is being, or is likely to be, caused.

The definitions of 'harm', 'pollution of controlled waters' and 'substance' have the same meanings as Part 2A of the Environmental Protection Act 1990, that is, the contaminated land regime.[26]

The statutory nuisance regime is over 160 years old, having been introduced in the Nuisances Removal Act 1855. The regime then became part of the Public Health Acts until 1990, when it was moved into the Environmental Protection Act 1990.

The statutory nuisance regime is different from common law private and public nuisances in its intent, procedures and remedies.

Local authorities have a duty to inspect their areas from time to time to detect whether any statutory nuisances should be dealt with. They also have a duty to investigate complaints regarding statutory nuisances when it is reasonably practicable for them to do so.[27]

If a local authority determines that a statutory nuisance exists or is likely to occur or recur, the authority contacts the person responsible for the nuisance to request them to abate, prohibit or restrict the nuisance, as applicable. If the person fails to do so, the authority may serve an abatement notice requiring them to abate, prohibit or restrict the nuisance.[28]

The person on whom an abatement notice is served, if they can be located, is 'the person responsible for the nuisance'.[29] If the nuisance has not occurred but is likely to occur, the notice is served on the owner or occupier of the premises at which the statutory nuisance arises.[30]

There is a defence to an abatement notice for statutory nuisances that arise on industrial, trade or business premises, if the person on whom a notice is served shows that they used the 'best practicable means' to prevent or counteract the effect of the nuisance.[31] The term 'practicable' is defined as 'reasonably practicable having regard among other things to local conditions and circumstances, to the current state of technical knowledge and to the financial implications'.[32]

A person on whom an abatement notice is served may appeal it within 21 days of the notice being served on various grounds including that the notice should have

[26]Environmental Protection Act 1990, s 79(1B); https://www.legislation.gov.uk/ukpga/1990/43/contents (accessed on 10.05.2023).

[27]Ibid., s 79(1).

[28]Ibid., s 80(1).

[29]Ibid., s 80(2)(a).

[30]Ibid., s 80(2)(c).

[31]Ibid., s 80(7).

[32]Ibid., s 79(9).

been served on another person, and there was an unreasonably insufficient time to comply with it.[33]

Failure to comply with an abatement notice without a 'reasonable excuse' is a criminal offence, the penalty for which is a fine.[34]

3 Legislation that Imposes Environmental Liabilities

As indicated in Sect. 1 above, the vast majority of environmental legislation in the UK is derived from EU legislation, with differences in some environmental legislation due to devolution. In order to understand environmental liabilities in the UK therefore, the following sections briefly discuss devolution, transposition of EU law into UK law during the time that the UK was a Member State of the EU, and the effect of Brexit. The section then discusses specific legislation that imposes environmental liabilities.

3.1 Devolution

Devolution in the UK began in 1998 with enactment of the Scotland Act 1998,[35] the Government of Wales Act 1998[36] (mostly superseded by the Government of Wales Act 2006),[37] and the Northern Ireland Act 1998.[38] Devolution is not a one-time process; it is ongoing. Subsequent devolution Acts include the Scotland Act 2016[39] and the Wales Act 2017.[40] The scope of devolution is not the same in each devolved region and has not proceeded at the same pace in each one. For example, the UK Parliament devolved more powers to Scotland in 1998 than it devolved to the other regions. Further powers have been devolved to all the regions since 1998 but Wales

[33] Ibid., s 80(3).

[34] Ibid., s 80(4).

[35] Scotland Land 1998; https://www.legislation.gov.uk/ukpga/1998/46/contents (accessed on 10.05.2023).

[36] Government of Wales Act 1998; https://www.legislation.gov.uk/ukpga/1998/38/contents (accessed on 10.05.2023).

[37] Government of Wales Act 2006; https://www.legislation.gov.uk/ukpga/2006/32/contents (accessed on 10.05.2023).

[38] Northern Ireland Act 1998; https://www.legislation.gov.uk/ukpga/1998/47/contents (accessed on 10.05.2023).

[39] Scotland Act 2016; https://www.legislation.gov.uk/ukpga/2016/11/contents/enacted (accessed on 10.05.2023).

[40] Wales Act 2017; https://www.legislation.gov.uk/ukpga/2017/4/contents/enacted/data.htm (accessed on 10.05.2023).

still has fewer devolved powers than Scotland or Northern Ireland; Northern Ireland had fewer devolved powers than Scotland.[41]

Each devolved region has its own legislative and executive branches. Scotland has the Scottish Parliament and the Scottish Government; Wales has the Senedd (Welsh Parliament) and the Welsh Government; Northern Ireland has the Northern Ireland Assembly and the Northern Ireland Executive. Unlike the UK Parliament, which has two Houses—the House of Commons and the House of Lords—the Scottish Parliament, the Senedd and the Northern Ireland Assembly are unicameral; they have only one legislative body.

Devolution is not the same as a federal system. The UK Parliament, which is the legislative body for England, is sovereign. Courts cannot overturn or quash primary legislation enacted by the UK Parliament, although they may overturn secondary legislation. Courts may overturn or quash Scottish, Welsh or Northern Ireland primary or secondary legislation.

The sovereignty of the UK Parliament also means that the UK Parliament may not only legislate on matters that have not been devolved; it may also amend the devolution Acts or enact legislation that overrides them. For example, in a highly controversial move in 2020, the UK Parliament enacted the United Kingdom Internal Market Act.[42] The Act provides that goods produced in or imported into any part of the UK may be freely sold in other parts of the UK. The Act meant for example that Scotland and Wales could not enact legislation that effectively imposed more restrictions on the use of single-use plastics than more limited legislation that had been enacted for England[43] because single-use plastics that were not restricted in England could be freely sold in Scotland and Wales. In order to resolve this particular dilemma, the Welsh Government sought judicial review of the Internal Market Act[44] and the UK Parliament enacted secondary legislation to allow enactment of the Scottish and Welsh legislation.[45]

Five types of matters are involved in devolution. They are:

---

[41] See Wilks (2022); https://www.thenational.wales/news/20088766.explained-devolution-wales-scotland-northern-ireland/ (accessed on 10.05.2023).

[42] United Kingdom Internal Market Act 2020; https://www.legislation.gov.uk/ukpga/2020/27/contents/enacted (accessed on 10.05.2023).

[43] Environmental Protection (Plastic Straws, Cotton Buds and Stirrers) (England) Regulations 2020/971; https://www.legislation.gov.uk/uksi/2020/971/contents/made (accessed on 10.05.2023).

[44] *R (on the application of the Counsel General for Wales) v Secretary of State for Business, Energy and Industrial Strategy* [2021] EWHC 950 (Admin) (denying the application as premature due to the absence of specific legislation), affirmed, *R (on the Application of the Counsel General for Wales) v Secretary of State for Business, Energy and Industrial Strategy* [2022] EWCA Civ 118 (appeal pending).

[45] United Kingdom Internal Market Act 2020 (Exclusions from Market Access Principles: Single-Use Plastics) Regulations 2022/857; https://www.legislation.gov.uk/ukdsi/2022/9780348236101 (accessed on 10.05.2023); see Environmental Protection (Single-use Plastic Products) (Scotland) Regulations 2021/410; https://www.legislation.gov.uk/ssi/2021/410/contents/made The Welsh legislation had not been enacted when this chapter was written (March 2023).

- reserved matters (e.g., trade, energy);
- excepted matters (e.g., defence, international relations);
- devolved matters (e.g., environment, agriculture);
- mixed competency matters (e.g., greenhouse gas emissions trading is energy and environment); and
- silent matters.

Only the UK Parliament can legislate on reserved matters although such matters may be transferred to the devolved governments. Only the UK Parliament can legislate on excepted matters; they may not be devolved. Devolved matters are matters that have been transferred to the devolved governments. Mixed competency matters are, as the name implies, partially devolved and partially reserved. Finally, silent matters are those for which the devolution legislation does not state their status.

3.2 *Transposition of EU Legislation*

The UK joined the EU (then the European Economic Community) on 1 January 1973. When Brexit occurred on 31 December 2020, there was therefore 47 years of EU legislation in the UK including, as indicated in Sect. 1 above, the vast majority of environmental law.

During the time that the UK was a Member State of the EU, as with other Member States, EU Regulations and Decisions entered into force in the precise language of the Regulation or Decision and became directly applicable on the date specified in the Regulation or, if no date was specified, 20 days after their publication in the Official Journal of the EU.

EU Directives were transposed into UK law by Section 2(2) of the European Communities Act 1972.[46] In effect, Section 2(2) provided that Directives could become law in the UK by way of regulations (secondary legislation) provided that the regulations did not go beyond the scope of the Directive that was being transposed.

[46] European Communities Act 1972 (repealed); https://www.legislation.gov.uk/ukpga/1972/68/contents (accessed on 10.05.2023).

3.3 Brexit

The European Communities Act was repealed by Section 1 of the European Union (Withdrawal) Act 2018.[47] Among other things, the 2018 Act created a new category of law called 'retained EU law'.

The following are the three main categories of retained EU law:

- EU-derived law, that is, national law that transposed and implements EU Directives;
- direct EU legislation, that is, EU Regulations and Decisions that were directly applicable in the UK; and
- other 'rights, powers, liabilities, obligations, restrictions, remedies and procedures' that were available in national law through the European Communities Act including rights under EU treaties.

In order to prepare for Brexit after the referendum to leave the EU on 23 June 2016, the UK Government enacted over 600 pieces of secondary legislation that made approximately 80,000 amendments to retained EU law between 2018 and 31 December 2020. The amended legislation came into effect on 31 December 2020. Although most amendments were technical such as removing references to the supervisory powers of the European Commission; other amendments were substantive.

The 2018 Act also retained principles set out in rulings by the Court of Justice of the European Union (CJEU) as well as principles and decisions of UK courts and tribunals that relate to the above three types of retained EU law.

Section 33 of the European Union (Future Relationship) Act 2020[48] provides that, with limited exceptions, relevant national authorities in the UK may amend the law to comply with the Trade and Co-operation Agreement between the UK and the EU.[49] As a result, retained EU law has slowly begun to change.

The UK does not have unlimited power to change retained EU law. The ability to change such law is subject to Article 7.2, the non-regression clause, of the Trade and Co-operation Agreement.

Article 7.2.1 of the Agreement states that the UK and the EU may establish their own policies and priorities for 'environmental levels of protection' (and 'climate level of protection') that each party 'deems appropriate and to adopt or modify its

[47] European Union (Withdrawal) Act 2018; https://www.legislation.gov.uk/ukpga/2018/16/contents/enacted (accessed on 10.05.2023).

[48] European Union (Future Relationship) Act 2020; https://www.legislation.gov.uk/ukpga/2020/29/contents (accessed on 10.05.2023).

[49] Trade and Cooperation Agreement between the European Union and the European Atomic Energy Community, of the one part, and the United Kingdom of Great Britain and Northern Ireland, of the other part; https://assets.publishing.service.gov.uk/government/uploads/system/uploads/attachment_data/file/948119/EU-UK_Trade_and_Cooperation_Agreement_24.12.2020.pdf (accessed on 10.05.2023).

law and policies in a manner consistent with each Party's international commitments'.

Article 7.2.2 provides that:

> A Party shall not weaken or reduce, in a manner affecting trade or investment between the Parties, its environmental levels of protection . . . below the levels that are in place at the end of the transition period [that is, 31 December 2020], including by failing to effectively enforce its environmental law . . . .

Article 7.1.1 defines the term 'environmental levels of protection' as:

> the levels of protection provided overall in a Party's law which have the purpose of protecting the environment, including the prevention of a danger to human life or health from environmental impacts including in each of the following areas:
>
> (a) industrial emissions;
> (b) air emissions and air quality;
> (c) nature and biodiversity conservation;
> (d) waste management;
> (e) the protection and preservation of the aquatic environment;
> (f) the protection and preservation of the marine environment;
> (g) the prevention, reduction and elimination of risks to human health or the environment arising from the production, use, release or disposal of chemical substances; or
> (h) the management of impacts on the environment from agricultural or food production, notably through the use of antibiotics and decontaminants.

As discussed in respect of some of these items in Sect. 3.4 below, legislation imposes liabilities for some of the above categories of 'environmental levels of protection'. The remainder of this section discusses such legislation as well as national non-EU legislation.

3.4 Legislation that Imposes Environmental Liabilities

Businesses and other persons in the UK may be liable for remediating current and future pollution under environmental permitting, water pollution, and waste legislation, and/or legislation that transposed the Environmental Liability Directive (ELD)[50] into national law in the UK. They may also be liable for restoring protected areas under nature conservation legislation.

Businesses and other person may also be liable for remediating past pollution under Part 2A of the Environmental Protection Act 1990 (Part 2A), commonly called the contaminated land regime, and water pollution legislation.

---

[50] Directive 2004/35/CE on environmental liability with regard to the prevention and remedying of environmental damage [2004] OJ L143/56 (consolidated version); https://eur-lex.europa.eu/legal-content/EN/TXT/?uri=CELEX%3A02004L0035-20190626 (accessed on 10.05.2023).

3.4.1 Environmental Permitting Legislation

The Environmental Permitting (England and Wales) Regulations 2016 (2016 Regulations) regulate environmental permitting in England and Wales.[51] Similar legislation exists in Scotland[52] and Northern Ireland.[53]

The 2016 Regulations are the most recent environmental permitting regulations in England and Wales, having superseded environmental permitting regulations issued in 2007 and 2010. The regulations have an integrated approach. The regulations that were issued in 2007 included a single permitting regime for integrated pollution prevention and control that had first been introduced in more limited form in the Environmental Protection Act 1990.

The scope of the regulations was subsequently extended to include waste management, which was previously regulated under separate regulations. The integrated approach has gradually resulted in a broadening of the scope of the regulations to include further activities previously regulated under separate legislation. The 2016 Regulations implement the Industrial Emissions Directive (IED)[54] and the Landfill Directive.[55] In addition, they apply to water discharge consents, groundwater authorisations, radioactive substances permits, mining waste permits, and flood defence consents.

There are two categories of activities/installations under the integrated pollution prevention and control part of the 2016 Regulations; Part A, which is divided into Part A(1) and Part A(2), and Part B. Part A applies to activities and installations that emit more pollutants than Part B activities and installations. Part B installations are regulated only for emissions to air.

The competent authority for Part A permits in England is the Environment Agency (EA); local authorities are the competent authorities for Part B permits. The other competent authorities in the UK are: Natural Resources Wales (NRW) for Part A permits and local authorities for Part B permits in Wales; the Scottish Environment Protection Agency (SEPA) for all permits in Scotland, and the Northern Ireland Environment Agency for Part A permits, with local authorities as the regulators for air pollution in Northern Ireland.

---

[51] Environmental Permitting (England and Wales) Regulations 2016/1154; https://www.legislation.gov.uk/uksi/2016/1154/contents/made (accessed on 10.05.2023).

[52] Environmental Authorisations (Scotland) Regulations 2018/219; https://www.legislation.gov.uk/ssi/2018/219/contents/made.

[53] Pollution Prevention and Control (Industrial Emissions) Regulations (Northern Ireland) 2013/160; https://www.legislation.gov.uk/nisr/2013/160/contents/made (accessed on 10.05.2023).

[54] Directive 2010/75/EU on industrial emissions (integrated pollution prevention and control) [2010] OJ L334/17 (consolidated version); https://eur-lex.europa.eu/legal-content/EN/TXT/?uri=CELEX%3A02010L0075-20110106 (accessed on 10.05.2023).

[55] Council Directive 1999/31/EC on the landfill of waste [1999] OJ L182/1 (consolidated version); https://eur-lex.europa.eu/legal-content/EN/TXT/?uri=CELEX%3A01999L0031-20180704 (accessed on 10.05.2023).

The main regulations that impose liability—in the form of offences—in the 2016 Regulations are Regulations 38 and 12.

Regulation 38(1) of the 2016 Regulations states that:

> It is an offence for a person to—
>
> (a) contravene regulation 12(1), or
> (b) knowingly cause or knowingly permit the contravention of regulation 12(1)(a).

Regulation 12(1) states that:

> A person must not, except under and to the extent authorised by an environmental permit—
>
> (a) operate a regulated facility, or
> (b) cause or knowingly permit a water discharge activity or groundwater activity.

The terms 'water discharge activity' and 'groundwater activity' are defined broadly to include direct and indirect discharges of pollutants into surface and ground waters.

Regulation 38(2) states that 'It is an offence for a person to fail to comply with or to contravene an environmental permit condition'.

All the above offences—like most environmental offences in the UK—are criminal offences. In other words, it is a criminal offence to operate an installation subject to the integrated pollution prevention and control regime without the requisite permit, to cause or knowingly permit such an operation, or to breach conditions of the permit. It is also a criminal offence to cause or knowingly discharge pollutants to surface or groundwater without a permit to do so.

The 2016 Regulations do not directly state that persons subject to them must remediate pollution or other environmental damage caused by them. Instead, conditions in environmental permits typically state that permit holders must not cause pollution. If the holder causes such pollution, it has breached the relevant condition and must remediate the pollution in order to bring itself back into compliance with the permit. As indicated above, it is a criminal offence to breach a condition of a permit. There is thus no significance threshold for remediating such pollution; remediation requirements arise when the relevant permit condition is breached.

Competent authorities have a wide range of powers under the 2016 Regulations and equivalent regulations in Scotland and Northern Ireland. They may issue enforcement, suspension, prohibition and/or revocation notices to holders of permits subject to the regulations. It is a criminal offence to fail to comply with such notices.

The offences described above are important for insurance coverage because there is a close correlation between them and requirements to remediate pollution as described below.

As a general rule, competent authorities do not issue a notice before providing the holder of a permit the opportunity to bring an installation back into compliance with applicable conditions of the permit.

If the competent authority determines that a permit holder has breached one or more conditions of a permit—either during a regular inspection or an inspection in response to a pollution incident—the authority issues a Compliance Assessment

Report (CAR) that details among other things the conditions of the permit that have been breached. The competent authority issues further CARs as the installation brings itself into compliance. If the permit holder does not comply with a notice, the authority may carry out the measures and demand reimbursement of its costs from the holder of the permit.

The permit holder thus knows that if it does not remediate pollution to bring itself back into compliance with its permit, the competent authority may issue a notice to suspend or revoke the permit and may also bring a prosecution against it.

Compliance with the requirements of a CAR does not necessarily mean that the authority will not prosecute the permit holder for breaching the permit or, in a less serious case, issue a warning letter or a caution. Failure to comply with the requirements may however result in the authority seeking greater penalties against the holder or not allowing the holder to enter into an agreement—called an enforcement undertaking—in lieu of a prosecution.

That is, a permit holder that has failed to comply with conditions of the permit by, for example, causing water pollution, may seek to avoid a prosecution by entering into an enforcement undertaking with the authority.[56] In such a case, the person that has breached Regulations 38 and 12 of the 2016 Regulations (or another specified environmental offence under other environmental legislation) offers a package of measures to the authority. Measures include at a minimum remediating the environmental damage and making monetary contributions to environmental charities. They may also include training personnel in pollution prevention, restoring or improving poor quality natural resources, and carrying out civic nature conservation projects.[57] The authority then decides whether to accept the undertaking or to bring a prosecution.

If an offence under the 2016 Regulations is committed by a company with the consent or connivance of a director or officer of the company or a similar person, or if the offence is attributable to such a person's neglect, the director or officer may also be liable for the offence. There is no specific requirement in the 2016 Regulations—or other environmental legislation in the UK—for the director, officer or similar person to remediate the damage. That said, the fact that a person is a director, officer or similar person is not a shield to liability as an individual.

Permits subject to the 2016 Regulations may be transferred in part or in whole subject to notification to the relevant authority or—depending on the type of permit—approval by the authority to ensure that the transferee is a 'fit and proper

[56] Regulatory Enforcement and Sanctions Act 2008, s 50; https://www.legislation.gov.uk/ukpga/2008/13/contents; see, e.g., Environmental Civil Sanctions (England) Order 2010; https://www.legislation.gov.uk/ukdsi/2010/9780111492512/contents; Environment Agency's use of civil sanctions; https://www.gov.uk/government/publications/environment-agencys-use-of-civil-sanctions (accessed on 10.05.2023).

[57] See Environment Agency, Enforcement undertakings accepted by the Environment Agency: 1 January 2022 to 31 May 2022 (updated 22 June 2022); https://www.gov.uk/government/publications/environment-agencys-use-of-civil-sanctions/enforcement-undertakings-accepted-by-the-environment-agency-1-january-2022-to-31-may-2022 (accessed on 10.05.2023).

person' to holder the permit. When a permitted activity ceases definitively, the permit is surrendered to the authority subject to its approval that the surrender meets specified criteria. The requirement under Article 11(h) of the IED to return the site of an installation to a 'satisfactory state' applies only to installations subject to the IED. Additional criteria apply to the surrender of a permit for a landfill.

When the UK left the EU, it was no longer required to follow the best available techniques (BAT) that are required for larger installations subject to the IED. England and the devolved governments are collaborating on developing and setting new BATs, to be called UK BAT Conclusions (BATC). The BATC will be published as statutory instruments and used as the basis for conditions under permits under environmental permitting legislation.[58]

3.4.2 Water Pollution Legislation

As indicated in Sect. 3.4.1 above, the EA and NRW may require the holder of an integrated pollution prevention and control permit to remediate water pollution if the holder has caused the pollution in breach of the relevant condition of its permit.

In addition to such liability for remediating water pollution, the Water Resources Act 1991[59] and Anti-Pollution Works Regulations 1999,[60] which apply in England and Wales, directly impose liability for remediating water pollution on anyone that has caused it. The Act and Regulations may thus be enforced against a person that has caused water pollution and is not required to have an integrated pollution prevention and control permit as well as a person that is required to have the permit but does not have one or a person that has breached the relevant condition of its permit. The same water pollution legislation applies to current and future pollution as well as historic water pollution.

Section 161A(1) of the Water Resources Act authorises the EA and NRW to serve a works notice on a person that has caused any 'poisonous, noxious or polluting matter or any waste matter' to be present in, or to be 'likely to enter, any controlled waters', or has caused 'any controlled waters to be harmed or to be likely to be

[58] See Department for Environment, Food and Rural Affairs, Policy paper: Establishing the Best Available Techniques for the UK (UK BAT) (updated 20 December 2022); www.gov.uk/government/publications/establishing-the-best-available-techniques-for-the-uk-uk-bat/establishing-the-best-available-techniques-for-the-uk-uk-bat (accessed 23 November 2023)

[59] Water Resources Act 1991; https://www.legislation.gov.uk/ukpga/1991/57/contents (accessed on 10.05.2023).

[60] Anti-Pollution Works Regulations 1999/1006; https://www.legislation.gov.uk/uksi/1999/1006/contents/made (accessed on 10.05.2023). The relevant regulations for Northern Ireland and Scotland are the Anti-Pollution Works Regulations (Northern Ireland) 2003/7; https://www.legislation.gov.uk/nisr/2003/7/contents/made (accessed on 10.05.2023); Water Environment (Controlled Activities) (Scotland) Regulations 2011/209; https://www.legislation.gov.uk/ssi/2011/209/contents/made (accessed on 10.05.2023).

harmed'.[61] The term 'controlled waters' is defined to include inland surface waters, groundwater, coastal waters, and territorial waters.[62]

As with notices under the integrated pollution prevention and control regime, the EA and NRW do not automatically serve a works notice against a person that has caused water pollution. Instead, they must reasonably endeavour to consult the person on whom it will be served about the measures specified in it. The Water Resources Act and the Anti-Pollution Works Regulations set out further details concerning works notices including their contents, appeals against them, compensation for the right to enter a third person's land to comply with a notice, hearings on them, and their entry on pollution control registers.

Failure to comply with an anti-pollution works notice is a criminal offence. In addition, if the person on whom the notice is served fails to carry out measures specified in it, the EA or NRW may carry out the measures and bring a cost-recovery action against the person on which the notice was served.

The EA and NRW may also carry out measures to prevent any 'poisonous, noxious or polluting matter or any waste matter' from entering controlled waters when it appears likely that such matter will enter the waters. They are also authorised to investigate and carry out works and operations for the following purposes:

- to remove or dispose of any 'poisonous, noxious or polluting matter or any waste matter [that] is or has been present in, or is likely to enter, any controlled waters';
- to remedy or mitigate any pollution caused by the presence of such matter in the waters; and
- to restore (so far as it is reasonably practicable to do so) the waters, including any flora and fauna dependent on the aquatic environment of the waters, to their state immediately before the matter became present in the waters.[63]

The power of the EA and NRW to carry out the above measures themselves is limited. They may only carry them out if it is necessary to do so 'forthwith' or if they conclude after a reasonable inquiry that there is no person that is responsible for the pollution on whom a works notice may be served.

The EA and NRW may also carry out measures for the above purposes when there is harm to surface or ground water that is not caused by polluting matter. In addition, they may investigate and carry out such measures when it appears to them that there has been, is, or is likely to be, an adverse impact on the condition of any hydromorphological quality element that affects the surface or ground water.[64]

---

[61] Water Resources Act 1991, s 161A(1); https://www.legislation.gov.uk/ukpga/1991/57/contents (accessed on 10.05.2023).

[62] Ibid., s 104.

[63] Ibid., Part VII.

[64] Hydromorphological quality elements are elements that affect the hydrological and geomorphological (water flow, width and depth of the water channel, conditions of riverbeds and banks, etc.) of rivers, lakes and other surface water bodies. They include physical characteristics of water bodies that interact with and affect the biological and chemical quality of water.

If the EA or NRW carry out any of the above works, they are entitled to recover their reasonable costs from the person that caused or knowingly permitted the water pollution or harm.

3.4.3 Waste Removal Notices

The EA and NRW may serve a waste removal notice on the occupier of land on which 'controlled waste' has been unlawfully deposited. The term 'controlled waste' includes virtually any type of waste including municipal, commercial and extractive waste (that is, is waste from mines and quarries).

A waste removal notice requires the occupier to remove the waste and/or to carry out specified measures to eliminate or mitigate its consequences. Failure to comply with a waste removal notice is a criminal offence.

If the person on whom a waste notice is served fails to carry out measures specified in it during the specified time, the authority may carry them out and seek recovery of its costs from the person on whom the notice was served. The occupier may appeal the notice on the following grounds: the occupier did not deposit, knowingly cause or knowingly permit the deposit; or the notice contains a material defect. If there is no occupier of the land on which the waste has been deposited, the EA or NRW cannot find the occupier without incurring unreasonable expense, or if the occupier does not comply with the notice, the EA or NRW, as relevant, may serve a notice on the owner of the site to carry out the measures specified in the notice.[65]

It is a criminal offence to fail to comply with a waste removal notice without a reasonable excuse. If the occupier or owner, as relevant, fails to comply with the notice, the authority may carry out the measures specified in it and recover its reasonable expenses from them.[66]

The EA and NRW may also serve a notice on an occupier to remove waste that was initially lawfully deposited in accordance with a permit or an exemption under

[65] Environmental Protection Act 1990, s 59; https://www.legislation.gov.uk/ukpga/1990/43/contents (accessed on 10.05.2023). There are differing versions of Section 59 for England and Wales (and Scotland). Waste has been unlawfully deposited if the deposit is in breach of Section 33 (1) of the Environmental Protection Act 1990, or regulation 12 of the Environmental Permitting (England and Wales) Regulations 2016/1154; https://www.legislation.gov.uk/uksi/2016/1154/contents/made (accessed on 10.05.2023).

[66] Environmental Protection Act 1990, s 59ZB; https://www.legislation.gov.uk/ukpga/1990/43/contents (accessed on 10.05.2023).

the 2016 Regulations. In addition, if there is a risk of serious pollution to the environment or serious harm to human health from waste at the site, the waste exceeds an exemption, or there is no permit for the site, the EA and NRW may serve a notice that immediately restricts access to the site for up to 72 h to prevent additional waste being brought to it.[67]

In addition, the EA and NRW may apply to a magistrates court for a restriction order for a six-month period, which may be extended.[68] They may also apply to the court for reimbursement of any costs incurred by them in restricting access to the site.[69]

The owner or occupier of the site may appeal a restriction notice on the grounds that they did not keep or dispose of the waste or did not knowingly cause or knowingly permit the waste to be kept or disposed of at the site.[70]

3.4.4 Environmental Liability Directive

The ELD was transposed into law in the UK and is retained EU law. England,[71] Wales,[72] Scotland[73] and Northern Ireland[74] issued separate regulations to transpose and implement the ELD. As with other environmental legislation, different authorities implement the regulations in each region.[75]

The following describes the Environmental Damage (Prevention and Remediation) (England) Regulations 2015 (EDR) in England, noting that the regulations in each region are similar, with the main difference being that liability for damage to species and natural habitats protected by the Birds and Habitats Directives extends to sites of special scientific interest (SSSIs) in England and Wales and areas of special scientific interest (ASSIs)[76] in Northern Ireland, but not to SSSIs in Scotland.

---

[67] Environment Act 1995, s 109A; https://www.legislation.gov.uk/ukpga/1995/25/contents (accessed on 10.05.2023).

[68] Ibid., s 109C-109F.

[69] Ibid., s 109K.

[70] Ibid., s 109L.

[71] Environmental Damage (Prevention and Remediation) (England) Regulations 2015/810; https://www.legislation.gov.uk/uksi/2015/810/regulation/18 (accessed on 10.05.2023).

[72] Environmental Damage (Prevention and Remediation) (Wales) Regulations 2009/995; https://www.legislation.gov.uk/wsi/2009/995/contents (accessed on 10.05.2023).

[73] Environmental Liability (Scotland) Regulations 2009/266; https://www.legislation.gov.uk/ssi/2009/266/contents/made (accessed on 10.05.2023).

[74] Environmental Liability (Prevention and Remediation) Regulations (Northern Ireland) 2009/252; https://www.legislation.gov.uk/nisr/2009/252/contents/made (accessed on 10.05.2023).

[75] The regulations are implemented in England, Scotland, Wales and Northern Ireland, respectively, by the Environment Agency, Natural England, local authorities and the Marine Management Organisation in England; SEPA, NatureScot and Marine Scotland; NRW, local authorities and the Marine Management Organisation; and the Northern Ireland Environment Agency.

[76] ASSIs are the designation for SSSIs in Northern Ireland.

The EDR impose liability on an operator whose activities cause significant damage to land (land damage), waters under the Water Framework Directive[77] and the Marine Strategy Framework Directive[78] (water damage), and species and natural habitats protected by the Birds Directive[79] and the Habitats Directive[80] (biodiversity damage). Following Brexit, sites designated as special protection areas under the Birds Directive and special areas of conservation under the Habitats Directive are called 'national sites' instead of Natura 2000 sites.

Damage to land must be remediated if it causes a significant adverse effect on human health.[81] The scope of liability for land damage is particularly broad. Guidance to the EDR states that it includes respiratory tract effects such as irritation of the nose, throat and respiratory tract, cough, sore throat, and dyspnoea; as well as central nervous system effects including headache, lethargy, drowsiness and decrease in IQ.[82]

Damage to waters must be remediated if it 'significantly adversely affects . . . the ecological, chemical or quantitative status or the ecological potential', as defined in the Water Framework Directive, or 'the environmental status' of marine waters as defined in the Marine Strategy Framework Directive.[83] The EDR track the language of the ELD in this respect.

Damage to biodiversity must be remediated if it causes 'significant adverse effects on reaching or maintaining the favourable conservation status of . . . habitats or species [protected by the Birds and Habitats Directives]'.[84] Again, the EDR track the language of the ELD in this respect.

Damage to SSSIs/ASSIs must be remediated if the damage causes 'an adverse effect on the integrity of the site (that is, the coherence of its ecological structure and

---

[77] Directive 2000/60/EC establishing a framework for Community action in the field of water policy [2000] OJ L327/1 (consolidated version); https://eur-lex.europa.eu/legal-content/EN/TXT/?uri=CELEX:02000L0060-20141120 (accessed on 10.05.2023).

[78] Directive 2008/56/EC establishing a framework for community action in the field of marine environmental policy [20008] OJ L164/19 (consolidated version); https://eur-lex.europa.eu/legal-content/EN/TXT/?uri=CELEX%3A02008L0056-20170607 (accessed on 10.05.2023).

[79] Directive 2009/147/EC on the conservation of wild birds [2010] OJ L20/7 (codified version); https://eur-lex.europa.eu/legal-content/EN/TXT/?uri=CELEX:32009L0147 (accessed on 10.05.2023).

[80] Council Directive 92/43/EEC on the conservation of natural habitats and of wild fauna and flora [1992] OJ L206/7 (consolidated version); https://eur-lex.europa.eu/legal-content/EN/TXT/?uri=CELEX:01992L0043-20130701 (accessed on 10.05.2023).

[81] ELD Art. 2(1)(c).

[82] Department for Environment, Food and Rural Affairs, The Environmental Damage (Prevention and Remediation) Regulations 2009; Guidance for England and Wales (2nd Update, November 2009), 70; https://assets.publishing.service.gov.uk/government/uploads/system/uploads/attachment_data/file/221095/pb13895-indepth-guide-regs09.pdf (accessed on 10.05.2023).

[83] ELD Art. 2(1)(b).

[84] Ibid., Art. 2(1)(a).

function, across its whole area, that enables it to sustain the habitat, complex of habitats or the levels of populations of the species affected)'.[85]

An operator that carries out activities under legislation listed in schedule 2 of the EDR is strictly liable for preventing or remediating all three types of damage. An operator that carries out activities not listed in schedule 2 is liable for preventing or remediating biodiversity damage if the operator is at fault or negligent. The activities in schedule 2 track the language of the ELD.

As in the ELD, the EDR state that land must be remediated so that it no longer poses a significant adverse effect on human health.[86] Also, as in the ELD, three types of remediation measures apply to water and biodiversity damage. Primary remediation consists of measures to remediate waters or biodiversity to their baseline condition, that is, their condition before they were damaged. Complementary remediation consists of measures to provide a similar level of waters or biodiversity and services provided by them if full restoration of the waters or biodiversity is not feasible.[87] Compensatory remediation consists of improvements and other measures to compensate for any interim losses from the damaged waters or biodiversity and services provided by them from the time of the damage to their full restoration.[88]

The requirement to remediate environmental damage does not necessitate the EA or another competent authority to require an operator that caused an imminent threat of, or actual, environmental damage to prevent or remediate it. The operator's requirement to prevent or remediate the damage arises even without the intervention of the authority. If an operator causes an imminent threat of environmental damage, or an imminent threat of damage where there are reasonable grounds to believe that the damage will become environmental damage, the operator must 'immediately . . . take all practicable steps to prevent the damage'.[89] If an operator 'has caused environmental damage, or has caused damage where there are reasonable grounds to believe that the damage is or will become environmental damage', the operator 'must immediately . . . take all practicable steps to prevent further damage'.[90]

Also, as in the ELD, various exclusions to liability apply including diffuse pollution and terrorism.[91] The EDR also state that they do not apply to environmental damage that occurred before 1 March 2009, when they entered into force.[92]

Also, as in the ELD, various defences apply including the permit and state-of-the-art defences, provided the operator was not negligent.[93]

[85] EDR sched 1, para 4.
[86] Ibid., sched 3, para 9.
[87] Ibid., sched 3, para 4.
[88] Ibid., sched 3, para 5.
[89] Ibid., reg 13(1).
[90] Ibid., reg 14(1).
[91] Ibid., reg 8.
[92] Ibid., reg 8(1).
[93] Ibid., reg 19.

Qualified environmental non-government organisations (NGOs) and members of the public may provide comments to the relevant authority if they consider that an imminent threat of, or actual, environmental damage has occurred. They may also seek a review by an independent court or tribunal of the authority's decision to act or to fail to act.[94]

There has only been one litigated case under the ELD in the UK. Fish Legal, a non-profit making organisation, submitted comments to NRW on behalf of an angling society that was one of its members. Fish Legal alleged that the operator of a sewage treatment plant had caused biodiversity and water damage to Llyn Padarn, a lake in a SSSI in Wales.

The High Court concluded that the applicable significance criterion under the ELD was whether there had been damage to the SSSI, as provided by the Welsh Regulations, and not biodiversity or water damage as defined by the ELD. The court concluded that no such damage had occurred.[95] The Court of Appeal upheld the lower court's decision.[96]

3.4.5 Restoring Damage to Nature

Various areas in the UK are protected for their flora, fauna, landscapes or other features. The two types of areas that have the most protection are sites of special scientific interest (SSSIs) (called areas of special scientific interest (ASSIs) in Northern Ireland), and sites that were designated under the Birds Directive[97] and the Habitats Directive[98] when the UK was a Member State of the EU. As indicated in Sect. 3.4.4 above, the latter type of sites, formerly called Natura 2000 or European Sites, are now called national sites. The relevant authorities for both types of sites are Natural England, NRW, NatureScot and/or the Northern Ireland Department of Agriculture, Environment and Rural Affairs in England, Wales, Scotland and Northern Ireland, respectively.

It is a criminal offence for an owner or occupier of land in a SSSI/ASSI to carry out measures that damage the SSSI/ASSI without the consent of the relevant authority, or to fail to comply with a condition in a consent unless they have a reasonable excuse, such as carrying out emergency measures. It is also a criminal

[94] Ibid., reg 29.

[95] *R (on the application of Seiont, Gwyrfai and Llyfni Anglers' Society) v Natural Resources Wales* [2015] EWHC 3578 (Admin).

[96] *R (Seiont, Gwyrfai and Llyfni Anglers' Society) v Natural Resources Wales* [2016] EWCA Civ 797.

[97] Directive 2009/147/EC on the conservation of wild birds [2010] OJ L20/7 (codified version); https://eur-lex.europa.eu/legal-content/EN/TXT/?uri=CELEX:32009L0147 (accessed on 10.05.2023).

[98] Council Directive 92/43/EEC on the conservation of natural habitats and of wild fauna and flora [1992] OJ L206/7; https://eur-lex.europa.eu/legal-content/EN/TXT/?uri=CELEX:01992L0043-20130701 (accessed on 10.05.2023).

offence for any other person intentionally or recklessly to destroy or damage any flora, fauna, or geological or physiographical features of a SSSI/ASSI without a reasonable excuse. In addition to being convicted, the person who causes the damage may be served with an order to restore the damage.

There are two types of restoration notices.

If a person is convicted of destroying or damaging the flora, fauna or geological or physiographical features of an SSSI/ASSI and the person is convicted, the competent authority may make an order to require that person to carry out measures, whether on or outside the boundaries of the SSSI/ASSI to their condition before the damage by the deadline specified in the notice. Failure to comply with a restoration notice without a reasonable excuse is a criminal offence.[99]

If a person is convicted of carrying out measures that, in the opinion of the competent authority are likely to destroy or damage the flora, fauna, or geological or physiographical features by reason of which the site is a SSSI/ASSI, the competent authority may serve a restoration order that requires them to carry out measures to restore the site to its former condition within the deadline specified in the notice. It is a criminal offence to fail to comply with a restoration notice.[100]

If a person is convicted of carrying out measures that appear to the authority to be of a kind that would be likely to destroy or damage protected features of a national site, the authority may serve a nature conservation order that requires that person to restore damaged natural resources. It is a criminal offence to carry out an operation in breach of a nature conservation order without a reasonable excuse.[101] The authority may also serve a stop notice to order the person carrying them out to cease doing so.[102]

3.4.6 Contaminated Land Regime

Part 2A of the Environmental Protection Act 1990 was introduced specifically to require the remediation of land contaminated by historic pollution that continues to pose an unacceptable risk to human health and the environment.[103] The regime applies to England, Scotland and Wales, with some provisions varying depending on

[99] Wildlife and Countryside Act 1981, part II; https://www.legislation.gov.uk/ukpga/1981/69 (accessed on 10.05.2023) (England and Wales); Nature Conservation (Scotland) Act 2004 part 2; https://www.legislation.gov.uk/asp/2004/6/contents (accessed on 10.05.2023); Environment (Northern Ireland) Order 2002/3153, part IV; https://www.legislation.gov.uk/nisi/2002/3153/contents (accessed on 10.05.2023).

[100] Wildlife and Countryside Act 1981, s 31.

[101] Conservation of Habitats and Species Regulations 2017/1012, reg 31; https://www.legislation.gov.uk/uksi/2017/1012/contents/made (accessed on 10.05.2023).

[102] Ibid., reg 28.

[103] Environmental Protection Act 1990, Part IIA Contaminated Land (ss 78A – 78YC); https://www.legislation.gov.uk/ukpga/1990/43/contents (accessed on 10.05.2023).

the different regions. Part 2A does not apply to Northern Ireland, which has not enacted a regime to remediate land that is contaminated by historic pollution.

The primary legislation (Part 2A), which was enacted in 1995, sets out the bare skeleton of the regime. Secondary legislation in the form of regulations for each of England, Scotland and Wales were subsequently introduced to set out procedures and related matters.[104] In 2000, statutory guidance was adopted for each jurisdiction and the regime finally entered into force in all three jurisdictions. The initial statutory guidance for England, which was revised in 2006 and 2012[105] (and guidance for each of Scotland and Wales)[106] sets out the details of the regime.

The main enforcing authorities for Part 2A are local authorities. If a local authority designates a site as 'contaminated land' and the site is determined to be within a category of seriously contaminated sites, called 'special sites', such as serious water pollution or refineries, the EA, NRW or SEPA enforce the regime instead of the local authority.

The respective authority requires persons to remediate contaminated land by serving a remediation notice on them if they do not voluntarily remediate such land.

Local authorities are under a duty to inspect their areas for 'contaminated land', which is defined as:

> any land which appears to the [relevant local authority] to be in such a condition, by reason of substances in, on or under the land, that
>
> (a) significant harm is being caused or there is a significant possibility of such harm being caused; or
> (b) significant pollution of controlled waters is being caused or there is a significant possibility of such pollution being caused.[107]

The term 'harm' is defined as 'harm to the health of living organisms or other interference with the ecological systems of which they form part and, in the case of man, includes harm to his property'.[108] As indicated in Sect. 2 above, the term

---

[104] The regulations for England, Scotland and Wales are the Contaminated Land (England) Regulations 2006/1380; https://www.legislation.gov.uk/uksi/2006/1380/contents/made (accessed on 10.05.2023); Contaminated Land (Scotland) Regulations 2005/658; https://www.legislation.gov.uk/ssi/2005/658/contents/made (accessed on 10.05.2023); Contaminated Land (Wales) Regulations 2001/2197; https://www.legislation.gov.uk/wsi/2001/2197/contents/made (accessed on 10.05.2023).

[105] Department for Environment, Food & Rural Affairs, Environmental Protection Act 1990: Part 2A; Contaminated Land Statutory Guidance (April 2012); https://www.gov.uk/government/publications/contaminated-land-statutory-guidance (accessed on 10.05.2023).

[106] Scottish Government, Environmental Protection Act 1990 – Part IIA Contaminated Land: statutory guidance (7 June 2006); https://www.gov.scot/publications/environmental-protection-act-1990-part-iia-contaminated-land-statutory-guidance/ (accessed on 10.05.2023); Welsh Government Guidance Document; Contaminated Land Statutory Guidance – 2012; https://gov.wales/sites/default/files/publications/2019-08/contaminated-land-statutory-guidance-2012.pdf (accessed on 10.05.2023).

[107] Environmental Protection Act 1990, s 78A(2).

[108] Ibid., s 78A(4).

'controlled waters' includes inland surface waters, groundwater, coastal waters, and territorial waters.[109]

In order for land to be defined as contaminated land, there must be a contaminant linkage—which consists of a contaminant, a pathway, and a receptor. A contaminant is a substance that has the potential to cause, or is causing, significant harm or a significant possibility of significant harm to a receptor, or significant pollution or a significant possibility of pollution of controlled waters.[110] Receptors are human health, ecological systems (including protected areas such as nature reserves), specified types of property (crops, domestically-grown produce, livestock and other owned or domesticated animals), and wild animals subject to shooting and fishing rights. A pathway connects a contaminant with a receptor.

The contaminated land regime is complex. If the enforcing authority determines that there is one or more contaminant linkages at a site, it identifies the legal or natural person(s)—called 'appropriate persons'—that are liable for remediating them. There are two classes of appropriate persons: class A appropriate persons are primarily liable; Class B appropriate persons are secondarily liable.

A Class A appropriate person is the person that 'caused or knowingly permitted' the contaminant(s) to be in, on or under the land. If the enforcing authority cannot find a Class A appropriate person after a 'reasonable inquiry', a Class B appropriate person is liable for remediating the contaminant linkage. A Class B appropriate person is the owner or occupier of the land on which the contaminant linkage is located.[111] If the authority cannot find either a Class A or a Class B appropriate person, the contaminant linkage is an 'orphan linkage' and is remediated at the cost of the relevant enforcing authority.

The statutory guidance includes tests to exclude Class A and B appropriate persons from liability. The tests apply when a freehold interest or a leasehold interest of over 21 years is transferred.

Class A persons are excluded in the order in which they are listed in the exclusion tests. At least one appropriate person must remain in the liability group for a contaminant linkage after the tests have been applied; application of the tests cannot exclude all appropriate persons.

The six exclusion tests for Class A appropriate persons are as follows:

1. excluded activities;
2. payments for remediation;
3. sold with information;
4. changes to substances;
5. escaped substances; and
6. introduction of pathways or receptors.

---

[109] Water Resources Act 1991, s 104.

[110] Environmental Protection Act 1990, s 78A(9).

[111] Ibid., s 78F.

Thus, if application of the fourth test would exclude the only remaining Class A appropriate person, the test is not applied.

As a result of the exclusion tests, it is common practice in commercial transactions involving the transfer of leasehold interests over 21 years and freehold interests in land for parties to the transaction to enter into agreements on liability, as set out in paragraphs 7.29 to 7.30 of the statutory guidance. The two tests most commonly referred to in such agreements are tests two and three.

Test two excludes a person that has made a payment to another person to remediate land provided that the payment is sufficient to cover the costs of remediating it so that it is no longer contaminated land. The test applies if there is a reduction in the sale price of the land as well as a payment for the cost of remediation measures. Language in contracts for the sale or lease of the land typically state that the price has been reduced as well as specifying other criteria to satisfy the test.

Test three excludes a seller that caused or knowingly permitted contamination if the buyer received information before the sale became binding that would reasonably have allowed the buyer to be aware of the presence of contaminants at the site and the broad meaning of that presence. If the buyer is a large commercial organisation or public body and the seller gave the buyer permission to carry out its own investigations of the condition of the land, permission is normally regarded as a sufficient indication that the buyer had information concerning the condition of the land. As with test two, contracts for the sale or lease of land typically include other criteria to indicate that the test is satisfied.

If the buyer under either exclusion test 2 or 3 ceases to exist, liability reverts to the seller.

The exclusion tests for Class B appropriate persons basically exclude the occupier of land (such as a lessee) on which a contaminant linkage exists in lieu of the owner of the land.

In addition to exclusion tests, the statutory guidance includes detailed tests: to apportion liability between persons that remain in a liability group after application of the exclusion tests; to attribute liability between appropriate persons when a measure to remediate contamination involves more than one contaminant linkage; and hardship criteria for an enforcing authority to consider in deciding whether to bear the costs of remediating contaminated land instead of an appropriate person.

Appropriate persons may appeal a remediation notice to the Secretary of State on any ground listed in the contaminated land regulations.[112]

Only four cases have been litigated under Part 2A.

In *Circular Facilities (London) Ltd v Sevenoaks District Council*,[113] the enforcing authority alleged that the developer had knowingly permitted land that it had developed for housing to be contaminated land because the developer knew that contaminants were under the land and remained there after the land had been

[112] Ibid., s 78L.

[113] *Circular Facilities (London) Ltd v Sevenoaks District Council* [2005] EWHC 865 (Admin).

developed. Due to the magistrates court[114] having failed to state in its judgment that the developer had known that such contaminants existed, the High Court ordered a retrial. The case settled before the retrial.

R (on the application of National Grid Gas plc) v Environment Agency[115] involved the remediation of a former gasworks site that had been developed for housing in the 1960s. The EA had remediated the site itself after applying the hardship criteria. The gas company that had owned and operated the site when the contamination occurred no longer existed, having been nationalised—together with other gas companies—by the Gas Act 1948. The gas boards (that had replaced the gas companies) were subsequently privatised by the Gas Act 1986 into a company called National Grid Gas Plc. The House of Lords held that National Grid Gas plc was not liable because statutory language stated that its liabilities included only liabilities that existed before the privatisation in 1986, that is, before Part 2A had existed.

R (on the application of Redland Minerals Ltd) v Secretary of State for Environment, Food and Rural Affairs[116] involved a former chemical works operated by Redland Minerals that had been developed for housing by Crest Nicholson, a property developer. Contaminants were subsequently found in groundwater that had migrated from the site to public drinking water abstraction wells. As a result, the EA served a remediation notice on Redland Minerals and Crest Nicholson. Although Crest Nicholson had not introduced contaminants onto the site, it had demolished buildings and had broken hardstanding on the site, which had allowed rain to cause pre-existing contaminants in the subsurface to seep into groundwater. The Secretary of State determined that Redland Minerals was liable for 85% of the remediation costs and Crest Nicholson was liable for 15%. The High Court subsequently rejected an application by Redland Minerals for judicial review of the Secretary of State's decision.

The fourth and final case, *Powys County Council v Price and Hardwick,*[117] involved a landfill that had been operated by Brecknock Borough Council. In 1996, the council ceased to exist when the Local Government (Wales) Act 1994 and a 1996 Order had transferred its rights and liabilities to the newly created Powys County Council. The Court of Appeal ruled that Powys County Council was not liable under Part 2A for remediating contamination from the former landfill because Part 2A had not come into force until five years after its creation. Thus, Powys County Council had no liabilities that could have been transferred in 1996.

---

[114]The legislation was subsequently revised so that appeals against a remediation notice are to the Secretary of State instead of a magistrates court as indicated above.

[115]*National Grid Gas plc) v Environment Agency* [2007] UKHL 30.

[116]*R (on the application of Redland Minerals Ltd) v Secretary of State for Environment, Food and Rural Affairs* [2010] EWHC 913 (Admin).

[117]*Powys County Council v Price and Hardwick* [2017] EWCA Civ 1133.

4 Rules of Construction of Insurance Policies

Under the law of England and Wales, a court construes an insurance policy like any other contract to give effect to the intention of the parties. The court does this by ascertaining the contextual meaning of the relevant contractual language by referring to the parties' expressed intention.

Words and phrases in a contract/policy are generally given their ordinary or plain meaning. The meaning of words is generally, but not always, their dictionary meaning. There are several exceptions to this general rule. If the prima facie meaning of a word or phrase in the context of the contract is contrary to its commercial purpose when that purpose is ascertained objectively, or if other clauses in a contract indicate that the parties did not intend the word or phrase to have its ordinary or plain meaning, the court may construe the word or phrase to have a different meaning.

If courts have previously ruled on the meaning of a word in an insurance policy, they may presume that the parties intended to use that meaning when the word is used in the same context. There must generally be a line of cases construing the word for this rule to apply. Another exception to the ordinary or plain meaning rule exists if a word or phrase has a meaning that is universally understood by custom and practice in the insurance market.

In determining the meaning of a word or phrase, the UK Supreme Court commented that 'it is necessary to avoid over-concentration on the meaning of single words or phrases viewed in isolation, and to look at the insurance contracts more broadly'.[118] The meaning of a word or phrase 'must [therefore] be set in the landscape of the [policy] as a whole'.[119]

Under the law of England and Wales, courts refer to extrinsic evidence—called the matrix of fact or the factual or contractual matrix. The matrix of fact includes 'absolutely everything which would have affected the way in which the language of the document would have been understood by a reasonable man' except 'the previous negotiations of the parties and their declarations of subjective intent', which 'are admissible only in an action for rectification'.[120]

It is rare for a court that applies the law of England and Wales to determine that a word or phrase is ambiguous.

---

[118] *Employers Liability Policy Trigger Litigation (Durham v BAI)* [2012] UKSC 14 [19].

[119] Ibid. (quoting *Charter Reinsurance Company Ltd. v Fagan* [1997] AC 313, 384 [1996] 2 WLR 726, [1996] 3 All ER 46 (House of Lords)).

[120] *Investors Compensation Scheme v West Bromwich Building Society* [1998] 1 WLR 896, [1998] 1 All ER 98 (House of Lords).

5 Insurance for Environmental Liabilities

General/public liability policies for risks in the UK have traditionally provided—and continued to provide—cover for third-party claims against an insured in nuisance, the rule in *Rylands v Fletcher*, negligence and trespass as well as other specified harms. There is no standard wording for the policies although most policies tend to have similar language. For example, coverage clauses tend to provide cover for 'legal liability' for 'damages' or 'compensation'.

As in the US, public liability policies are occurrence-based. That is, they provide cover for an 'occurrence' (or a similar term such as 'accident') which is defined in relation to the time during which a claimant suffers bodily injury, property damage or another covered harm instead of the time at which a claim is made against the insured. Public liability policies thus have a 'long tail' of liability in that claims may be made against past policies.

Also as in the US, excess general liability policies indemnify insureds for the same types of losses as public liability policies with a key exception being that they generally do not provide cover for defence costs. The public liability policy is the primary policy, providing cover up to a specified limit of liability, with the excess policy (or policies) providing cover above that limit.

Unlike the US, however, public liability policies for risks in the UK rarely—if at all—have a separate duty to defend as well as a duty to indemnify. Public liability policies provide cover for defence costs but the costs are subject to the limit of indemnity. The vast majority of such policies provide the insurer with the right to assume the insured's defence.

5.1 *Pollution Exclusions in Public Liability Policies*

Until 1990, public liability policies did not tend to bar cover for environmental claims. By that time, however, the Association of British Insurers (ABI) had become concerned about the increase in claims concerning harm suffered by exposure to pollutants as well as potential cover for gradual pollution in public liability policies and policies for motor trade premises. The ABI set up a Pollution Working Party, which considered three options:

- totally excluding cover for pollution and establishing a general market pool to provide pollution cover;
- limiting cover to claims arising from sudden, unintended and unexpected pollution incidents; and
- limiting cover to losses arising from sudden, unintended and unexpected pollution incidents and providing an endorsement to write back cover for selected and individually underwritten risks.

In 1991, the Working Party issued its report and concluded that the third option was preferable. The Working Party reasoned among other things that cover for pollution in public liability policies that contained the exclusion would be equivalent to cover offered in other European countries, insurers that had the support of reinsurers could continue to offer cover for losses from gradual pollution on a selective basis, and cover for pollution would be broader than that offered in US general liability policies.

The Working Party's report included a model pollution exclusion that provided as follows:

> This policy excludes all liability in respect of Pollution or Contamination other than caused by a sudden identifiable unintended and unexpected incident which takes place in its entirety at a specific time and place during the Period of Insurance.
>
> All Pollution or Contamination which arises out of one incident shall be deemed to have occurred at the time such incident takes place.

The term Pollution or Contamination was defined as follows:

(i) all Pollution or Contamination of buildings or other structures or of water or land or the atmosphere; and
(ii) all loss or damage or injury directly caused by such Pollution or Contamination.

The ABI exclusion is thus qualified in that it does not bar cover for all claims that arise out of pollution incidents. Instead, it bars cover only for claims that arise out of gradual pollution by including a write-back of cover for incidents that are 'sudden identifiable unintended and unexpected'.

In order to impose an aggregate limit of liability and thus avoid public liability policies being called on to provide cover for harm that continues through several policy periods, the ABI suggested the following language:

> The liability of the Company for all compensation payable in respect of Pollution or Contamination which is deemed to have occurred during the Period of Insurance shall not exceed £... in the aggregate.

The Pollution Working Party emphasised that the pollution exclusion was intended only to be a model due to different terms and conditions in public liability policies and recommended that insurers adopt their own wordings.

In addition to the qualified pollution exclusion, the ABI proposed an endorsement called the Single Event Pollution Trigger Insurance Clause (SEPTIC). The SEPTIC endorsement provides as follows:

> A. All Pollution or Contamination which arises out of one Event shall be deemed to have occurred on the date that the Insured first becomes aware of circumstances which have given or may give rise to such Pollution or Contamination.
> B. The liability of the Company for all compensation payable in respect of all Events which are deemed to have occurred during the Period of Insurance and arising from Pollution or Contamination shall not exceed £... in the aggregate.
>
> If the amount of claim for compensation exceeds the Limit of Indemnity the aggregate shall be reduced in the proportion that the amount which would have been paid by the Company for compensation or pollution or contamination bears to the total

amount which would have been paid by the Company in respect of all compensation had the Limit of Indemnity been unlimited.

C. This Policy/Section shall not apply to any claim arising from Pollution or Contamination if before the current Period of Insurance the Insured had become aware of circumstances which have given or may give rise to such Pollution or Contamination.

D. This Policy/Section shall not apply to Pollution or Contamination which occurred prior to (the Retroactive Date).

For the purpose of this Endorsement the definition of "Pollution or Contamination" shall be deemed to mean:

a. all pollution and contamination of buildings or other structures or of water or land or the atmosphere and
b. all loss or damage or injury directly or indirectly caused by such pollution or contamination.

The Working Party commented that individual insurers may wish to include a sub-clause in the endorsement to refer to their policy's claims notification clause and they may wish to substitute clauses that required notice to be provided 'as soon as possible' to 'immediate notice'.

Few, if any, policies have included the SEPTIC endorsement. Reasons for the absence of such clauses include its potential ambiguity as to whether it writes back cover for pollution and the unwillingness of reinsurers to provide cover for gradual pollution.

Since 1991, however, virtually all public liability policies issued for risks in the UK have included the ABI pollution exclusion, an adaptation of it, or a pollution exclusion issued by the Lloyd's Underwriters Non-Marine Association (NMA) in 1970 (which is also discussed in the chapter on environmental liabilities and insurance law in the US due to being included in some excess policies for US risks).

NMA 1685 provides as follows:

This Insurance does not cover any liability for:

(1) Personal Injury or Bodily Injury or loss of, damage to, or loss of use of property directly or indirectly caused by seepage, pollution or contamination, provided always that this paragraph (1) shall not apply to liability for Personal Injury or Bodily Injury or loss of or physical damage to or destruction of tangible property, or loss of use of such property damaged or destroyed, where such seepage, pollution or contamination is caused by a sudden, unintended and unexpected happening during the period of this Insurance.
(2) The cost of removing, nullifying or cleaning-up seeping, polluting or contaminating substances unless the seepage, pollution or contamination is caused by a sudden, unintended and unexpected happening during the period of this Insurance.
(3) Fines, penalties, punitive or exemplary damages.

This Clause shall not extend this Insurance to cover any liability which would not have been covered under this Insurance had this Clause not been attached.

Neither the ABI qualified pollution exclusion nor NMA 1685 have been interpreted by courts in the UK. Claims that involve interpretation of the exclusions have arisen, but they have been settled out of court.

5.2 *Cover for Costs of Remediation Measures in Public Liability Policies*

A key issue that has been litigated by a court in England is whether a public liability policy provides cover for the costs of remediating pollution. There has only been one reported case on this issue but it has been influential in the development of endorsements, as described below.

The case involved claims arising from a massive fire at a facility that manufactured and packed solvent-based products. As a result of the fire and measures to extinguish it, chemicals in fire-fighting water and foam entered the bed, banks and water in two watercourses. The EA carried out emergency remedial works pursuant to its authority under Section 161 of the Water Resources Act 1991. The works included constructing dams to contain polluted water, pumping the polluted water out, and treating or disposing of it, as well as removing contaminated vegetation on the banks and disposing of it.

The EA subsequently sent two invoices to Bartoline Ltd, the owner and operator of the facility, in the amounts of £608,332.63 and £14,349.15 for reimbursement for the above works.[121] In addition, the EA served an anti-pollution works notice that ordered Bartoline to carry out further remedial works at a cost of £147,988.14 for a total of £770,669.92.[122]

Bartoline made several claims against Royal & Sun Alliance (RSA), which had issued various policies to it including a combined policy that included public liability, employers' liability and property damage. The claims against the public liability section of the policy included the above amount of £770,669.92 for remediating the watercourses. RSA denied the claim.

The public liability section of the RSA policy provided, in pertinent part, that RSA agreed to indemnify Bartoline:

> up to the Limit of Indemnity against legal liability for damages in respect of
>
> A) . . .
> B) accidental loss of or damage to Property
> C) nuisance, trespass to land or trespass to goods or interference with any easement right of air, light, water or way,
>
> . . .
>
> happening during any Period of Insurance in connection with the Business.[123]

Bartoline filed an action against RSA and its brokers, Heath Lambert on the basis that the policy provided cover for the costs of remedial actions. The reported case involves only the claim against RSA and only the public liability section of the combined policy.

[121] *Bartoline Ltd v Royal & Sun Alliance Insurance plc* [2007] All ER (D) 59 (High Court (Mercantile Court)) [6].

[122] Ibid.

[123] Ibid. [13].

Bartoline claimed that its liability to the EA for the emergency works carried out by the EA and/or the costs of complying with the works notice were 'legal liability for damages' within the meaning of the policy. RSA argued that the EA's actions against Bartoline were fundamentally different from the actions of a claimant in a tort cause of action and, thus, were not 'damages'.

HHJ Hegarty QC of the High Court agreed with RSA, concluding that the policy did not provide cover for the costs incurred by Bartoline for remediating the water pollution under the Water Resources Act 1991. The judge rejected Bartoline's argument that he should 'take a wider view of the meaning of the word "damages" ... to give effect to the commercial assumptions underlying the Policy'. He commented that 'I can see no obvious basis for adopting some supposedly "commercial" interpretation of the expression which appears to run counter to established usage'.[124]

Bartoline appealed the High Court's decision to the Court of Appeal but the case settled shortly before the hearing with a confidential settlement.

As stated above, Bartoline has been highly influential in cover the remediation costs under public liability policies. It does not however mean that all public liability policies that include the word 'damages' do not provide cover for the costs of remediating water pollution or other pollution or contamination. Further, the judgment does not mean that policies that include the word 'compensation' do not provide such cover.

For example, the Court of Appeal rejected a narrow 'legalistic' interpretation of the word 'compensation' in a public liability insurance policy. In holding that the word 'compensation' includes exemplary as well as compensatory damages, Simon Brown LJ commented that although:

> the natural and ordinary meaning of "compensation" in the context of a legal liability to pay damages is one which excludes any element of exemplary damages, I cannot accept that this meaning is wholly clear and unambiguous. On the contrary it involves very much a literal, lawyer's understanding of the term and is one which would not command universal acceptance.[125]

As stated in Sect. 4 above, the meaning of the word 'damage' or 'compensation' depends on its meaning in the policy at issue. That said, there are no reported cases in the UK in which either word in a public liability policy has been interpreted to provide cover for remediating pollution or other environmental damage.

---

[124] Ibid. [116].

[125] *Lancashire County Council v Municipal Mutual Insurance Ltd* [1997] QB 897, 904 [1996] 3 WLR 493 (Court of Appeal).

5.3 Environmental Extensions and Endorsements to Public Liability Policies

Following *Bartoline,* some public liability insurers decided to offer endorsements to specified insureds to provide cover for the costs of remediating pollution. The so-called Bartoline endorsements or Bartoline extensions were, however, extremely limited. Some provided cover for remediating pollution only if a claim for property damage or bodily injury had been made against the policy. Most provided cover only for sudden and accidental pollution. Also, because the extensions were to public liability policies, they did not provide cover for remediating pollution that occurred on the insured's property.

5.4 Cover for 'Requests' by a Competent Authority for an Insured to Carry Out Remediation Measures

There is another issue concerning cover for the costs of remediating pollution even if a public liability policy was to be construed to provide cover for such costs. That is, there must be a 'legal liability' on the part of the insured. Under English law, an insured is not legally liable and, thus, not entitled to an indemnity under a public liability policy until its liability has been ascertained and quantified by a judgment, arbitration award or settlement.[126] A 'request' by the EA or another competent authority in the UK to carry out remedial measures does not fall within the first two categories. It also does not fall within the third category unless the claim for which the 'settlement' is reached is covered by the policy.

As described in Sect. 3.4.2 above, the EA and other competent authorities do not automatically serve works notices directly on persons that have polluted water. Instead, the authorities must reasonably endeavour to consult the person on whom it will be served about the measures specified in it. Similarly, the EA and other competent authorities do not serve other notices such as notices under environmental permitting legislation or the contaminated land regime without first consulting the person on whom they would be served about remediating the pollution or contamination and 'requesting' them to remediate it—albeit under threat of potential sanctions. Arguably, 'requests' to carry out remediation measures do not amount to 'legal liability' under a public liability policy.

Further, as described in Sect. 3.4.4, under the EDR, an operator must carry out measures to prevent environmental damage or further environmental damage 'immediately', even before a competent authority begins proceedings against the

[126] *Bradley v Eagle Star Insurance Company Ltd* [1989] 1 AC 957 [1989] 2 WLR 568 (House of Lords); *Post Office v Norwich Union Fire Insurance Society Ltd* [1967] 2 QB 363, [1967] 2 WLR 709 (Court of Appeal); see *Yorkshire Water Services Ltd v Sun Alliance and London Insurance plc (No 1)* [1997] 2 Lloyd's Rep 21 (Court of Appeal).

operator—or is even aware of the imminent threat of, or actual, damage. Thus, even if a Bartoline endorsement had provided cover for remediating environmental damage—which the vast majority did not—it may not have provided the requisite cover.

5.5 Timing of an Occurrence

The issue occasionally arises as to whether an 'occurrence' or an 'event' (both of which words tend to be interpreted synonymously)[127] have taken place during the policy period. There have not been any reported environmental damage cases in the UK in which timing was an issue. The issue has however arisen in third-party claims for harm caused by exposure to asbestos in which the claimant developed mesothelioma (see Sect. 2.4 above).

In *Bolton Metropolitan Borough Council v Commercial Union and Municipal Mutual Insurance*, the Court of Appeal rejected the exposure trigger and adopted the injury-in-fact trigger (see the chapter on environmental liabilities and insurance in the United States) in a case involving a claim against a public liability policy.[128]

The coverage clause of one of the two public liability policies at issue stated that:

> The company agrees to indemnify the insured in respect of all sums which the insured shall become legally liable to pay as compensation arising out of: (a) accidental bodily injury or illness (fatal or otherwise) to any person other than any person employed under a contract of service... with the insured if such injury or illness arises out of and in the course of the employment .... The company will also pay any costs awarded against the insured... In addition the company will pay all costs and expenses incurred with its written consent (a) in defending any claim for compensation...[129]

The other public liability policy at issue in the case contained similar language. The Court of Appeal concluded that no actionable injury existed when the claimant was exposed to asbestos but rather, such an injury occurred either when the malignant tumour was first created or identifiable symptoms first appeared.[130]

In *Durham v BAI (Run Off) Ltd,* the UK Supreme Court unanimously adopted the causation trigger in a claim that tested various phrases in employers' liability policies including 'disease contracted', 'injury sustained', 'bodily injury or disease ... sustained or contracted', and 'sustain any bodily injury or disease'.[131] Lord Mance, who gave the leading judgment, referred to the rules of construction (see

[127] See *American Centennial Insurance Company v Insco Ltd* [1996] Lloyd's Rep LR 407 ('[words] such as "event" and "occurrence" are not easy to define, but ... their meanings are very similar').

[128] *Bolton Metropolitan Borough Council v Commercial Union and Municipal Mutual Insurance* [2006] 1 WLR 1492 (Court of Appeal).

[129] Ibid., 1497.

[130] Ibid., 1502.

[131] *Durham v BAI (Run Off) Ltd* [2012] UKSC 14 [18].

Sect. 4 above) to state that words must be placed in the context of the factual and commercial background of a transaction.[132] He concluded that the causation trigger applied because:

- employment and injury should occur at the same time;
- if an employee was exposed to asbestos but the effects did not manifest themselves until after he was no longer employed, there would be no cover; and
- if the policies were not renewed, cover would no longer exist for historic injuries.[133]

Lord Mance further stated that:

> The natural inference to draw from the references to being engaged in the employer's service and in work forming part of the employer's business process is that it was envisaged that the accident or disease would and should arise out of such service and work, rather than merely occur during it.[134]

In a case involving cover for claims from exposure to asbestos in the reinsurance context, the Court of Appeal was called on to answer the issue of whether an employers' liability insurer that had settled claims without allocating the loss to any particular year of exposure was allowed to present reinsurance claims arising from the claims on a pro rata time-on-the-risk basis.[135]

The court concluded that there was no absolute contractual right to 'spike' claims and that 'spiking' at the reinsurance level was not permissible because reinsurance contracts are justifiably expected to operate to require an insured to allocate its ultimate net loss evenly across the period of exposure.[136] In other words, exceptions for claims for mesothelioma at the insurance level, which exist to ensure that victims are compensated, do not apply at the reinsurance level because the objective of the exceptions has been achieved.

The Court of Appeal granted insurers leave to appeal to the UK Supreme Court, but the case settled shortly before its scheduled hearing.

6 Environmental Insurance Policies

The gap in cover for claims from gradual pollution in public liability policies was one of two major factors that led to the creation of the environmental insurance market in London. The other major factor was enactment of the Environmental Protection Act 1990, which among other things introduced a broader environmental permitting regime than had previously existed.

[132] Ibid. [19].

[133] Ibid. [69]–[75].

[134] Ibid. [27].

[135] *Equitas Insurance Limited v Municipal Mutual Insurance Limited* [2019] EWCA Civ 718 [146].

[136] Ibid. [162].

6.1 Evolution of the London Environmental Insurance Market

The beginnings of the London environmental insurance market occurred in the 1970s with the Clarkson Pool, also called the Environmental Risk Assessment Services pool. After only a few policies were sold however, reinsurers withdrew from it.

In the late 1980s, several chemical companies asked their trade organisation, the Chemical Industries Association (CIA), to assist in obtaining insurance for their environmental liabilities. As a result, the CIA Environmental Impairment Liability Insurance Facility (CEILIF) was launched in December 1989.

The CEILIF policy was a site-specific policy that provided cover up to three years for third-party claims for property damage and bodily injury, legal expenses, remediation costs and 'impairment or diminution of or other interference with any rights or amenity protected by law' that were caused by specified 'environmental impairments' that arose after the policy incepted.

The term 'environmental impairment' was defined as:

> the emission, discharge, release, dispersal, disposal, seepage or escape of solid, liquid, gaseous or thermal contaminants or irritants, including smell, electromagnetic waves, smoke, vapour, soot, fumes, acids, alkalis, chemicals and waste, not or upon the soil, the atmosphere or any watercourse or body of water which changes the natural state or condition of the soil, the atmosphere or any watercourse or body of water and which is related to and is arising out of the Business of the Insured at the locations/sites as shown in the Schedule.

Although the definition of 'environmental impairment' was broad, the policy did not include losses that arose from a 'sudden, unintended and unexpected' environmental impairment or losses that were inevitable or known by the insured before the policy incepted. The exception for sudden, unintended and unexpected environmental impairments could however be removed if an insured wished to have such cover in addition to cover from gradual environmental impairments.

Despite—or because of—its broad cover, the underwriting process was complicated and expensive. In effect, the process sifted out insureds whose activities could cause environmental impairments covered by the policy. In addition, the policy had a short policy period, a high premium, and a low maximum limit of indemnity. Not surprisingly, no CEILIF policies were ever sold. The term 'environmental impairment' however continued to be used in a substantial number of subsequent policies with the result that environmental insurance policies are often still referred to as environmental impairment policies or EIL policies.

After the slow start during the 1970s and 1980s, the London environmental insurance market began to develop in the early 1990s when five insurers entered it.

In January 1991, American International Underwriters (UK) Ltd introduced an environmental insurance policy for site-specific risks, based on policies issued for the US environmental insurance market by its US parent company, American International Group, Inc. In August 1992, the underwriter changed to AIG Europe (UK) Ltd (collectively AIG) when AIG established a dedicated environmental insurance unit in its London offices. In October 1992, AIG introduced an environmental insurance policy specifically for owners and operators of underground storage tanks such as owners and operators of petrol stations. In 1993, AIG expanded its range of environmental insurance policies again by offering a first party policy to property owners and developers for on-site bodily injury, property damage and the cost of remediating accidental pollution on an insured's own site(s).

In Autumn 1991, the Michael Payne syndicate (subsequently R.J. Wallace & Others syndicate) introduced a policy that provided cover for third-party claims for bodily injury, property damage, off-site remediation costs, defence costs, and claims for an 'impairment or diminution of or other interference with any rights or amenity protected by law' caused by an 'environmental impairment' that originated from the insured's premises.

Also in 1991, Swiss Re introduced an EIL policy for general businesses and a policy for newly constructed waste disposal facilities. If an insured that had a waste disposal policy had only a limited number of claims during the operational phase of the facility, Swiss Re would offer the insured the option of refunding a substantial portion of the total premiums or using the accumulated premiums plus interest on them to pay premiums during an extension of the policy for the closure and post-closure phases of the facility.

In mid-1992, the Zurich Insurance Group introduced a site-specific policy as a pilot scheme. The policy provided cover for third-party claims for bodily injury, property damage and remediation costs from gradual pollution that occurred after the policy incepted, and legal expenses. A second layer of the policy was a risk-financing scheme in which the level of premiums and indemnity were influenced by the insured's progress in meeting risk management targets agreed by the insurer and the insured.

In October 1992, ECS Underwriting Ltd, as managing general agent for Reliance National Insurance Company (UK) Ltd, began offering five environmental insurance policies for UK and continental European risks: a site-specific operational risks policy; a first-party policy to property owners and developers; a contractors pollution liability (CPL) policy; a professional liability policy for environmental consultants and environmental laboratories; and a policy that combined the CPL and professional liability policies.

Since the mid-1990s, the London environmental insurance market has substantially expanded, both in the range of policies offered by insurers in the market and the number of insurers that offer policies. In addition, the underwriting process has been greatly relaxed.

Expansion of the market was gradual at first. It was not until the early 2000s that total premiums exceeded £20,000,000, and not until the mid-2000s that they exceeded £50,000,000.

The first major impetus for the growth of the market was enactment of the contaminated land regime in 2000. Enactment of the regime led to the introduction of so-called property transfer policies that provide cover for third-party claims for bodily injury and property damage, remediation of on-site and off-site pollution/contamination, and related legal expenses, provided that the insured was not aware of the contamination when the policy incepted. As the market for these policies matured, insurers began to offer them even if insureds knew that their sites were contaminated. In such a case, insurers may exclude cover for known contaminated areas or known contaminants at an insured site.

A second major impetus for the growth of the market was the EU's adoption of the ELD in 2004. Adoption of the ELD resulted in particular in more insurers entering the market and the development of policies that provide cover for ELD and national environmental liabilities, and the extension of policies that already offered cover for national environmental liabilities to include ELD liabilities.

As the London environmental insurance market developed, major brokers established environmental teams, a development that subsequently resulted in insurers in other parts of the UK offering environmental liability policies, and other brokers providing expertise in placing environmental insurance policies. The growth in the market also resulted in the introduction of specialised teams of environmental loss adjusters.

By 2022, insurers offer the following environmental endorsements to public liability policies, environmental insurance policies, and environmental insurance sections in combined policies.

6.2 Environmental Endorsements and Extensions to Public Liability Policies

As indicated in Sect. 5 above, Bartoline endorsements offered only limited cover. This does not mean that environmental endorsements to public liability policies that are currently offered—which no longer tend to be called Bartoline endorsements—offer only limited cover. It does however mean that they always offer less cover than environmental insurance policies.

There is a large range of environmental endorsements and extensions to public liability policies. They include standardised extensions in the body of public liability policies issued to large businesses as well as optional extensions and endorsements for policies issued to small to medium sized businesses. The number of environmental extensions that are included in public liability policies for large businesses means that there are a larger number of environmental extensions (and endorsements) than there are environmental insurance policies.

Due to environmental endorsements being offered as an addition to public liability policies, they do not provide cover for remediating contamination/pollution on an insured's site; they only provide cover for remediating contamination/pollution that has migrated from such a site. Some endorsements provide cover for third-party claims for bodily injury and property damage as well as the costs of remediating gradual as well as sudden and accidental pollution but most tend not to do so. Some endorsements—referred to as time element endorsements—require the insured to notify the insurer of a pollution incident within a specified time (often hours) after the incident occurs, and for the incident to begin and end within a specified time (usually days) during the policy period. Requirements for pollution incidents to occur and be notified to the insurer within the policy period mean that the policies avoid the long tail of liability of public liability policies.

Some extensions and endorsements provide cover for ELD liabilities as well as liabilities under national law in England, Scotland, Wales and Northern Ireland, but many do not do so. No extensions or endorsements—just as no environmental insurance sections in combined policies and no environmental insurance policies—provide cover only for ELD liabilities. It would not be practical or commercial to do so because, as discussed in Sect. 3.4.4 above, the ELD applies to land, water and/or biodiversity damage only after significance criteria are satisfied; only national liability law applies below this significance threshold. In addition, some extensions and endorsements provide only limited cover for liabilities under national liability legislation whilst some require a claim for bodily injury or property damage to be made in order for the cover under the extension or endorsement to be triggered.

6.3 Environmental Insurance Sections in Combined Policies

Combined policies, which are often designed for specific trades or activities such as agriculture, environmental contractors, etc., tend to provide insurance for a range of risks. Sections in such policies may, depending on the insurer, provide cover for property, public liability, products liability, employers' liability, legal expenses, etc.

Some combined policies for UK risks, especially policies for agriculture and large country estates, may include environmental insurance sections. If they do so, the environmental insurance sections virtually always provide more cover than environmental endorsements but less cover than environmental insurance policies.

When combined policies include a specific section that provides cover for environmental liabilities, cover is underwritten on a claims-made-and-reported basis. That is, a claim against an insured must be made, and reported by the insured to the insurer, during the policy period. There is thus no long-tail of liabilities as in public liability and other policies that are underwritten on an occurrence basis.

6.4 Environmental Insurance Policies

Environmental insurers in the UK offer a wide range of environmental insurance policies, as described below. The vast majority of the policies are underwritten on a claims-made-and-reported basis except for CPL policies which may be underwritten on a claims-made-and-reported basis or an occurrence basis.

Large insurers in the London environmental insurance market offer cover for risks in countries across the world as well as in the UK. For example, they may place policies for environmental risks in a single overseas country as well as policies (insurance programmes) for global businesses to cover their operations in a large number of countries.

Insurers in the London environmental insurance market continue to offer such policies despite Brexit resulting in the loss of passporting rights.[137] In order to do this, many insurers restructured and have affiliated companies in EU Member States as well as the UK that are authorised to carry out insurance business.

The following describes the major environmental insurance policies for UK risks: pollution legal liability (PLL) policies; CPL policies; contractors professional liability policies; environmental consultants' professional services policies; and contaminated land policies. Insurers may also offer other types of policies but they tend to be less common.

For each type of policy, insurers generally have a library of standard endorsements, some with various options within the endorsement. In addition, insurers may draft manuscript endorsements for specific risks.

6.4.1 Pollution Legal Liability Policies

Depending on the insurer, a PLL policy typically provides cover for the following:

- preventing and remediating pollution/contamination at an insured's site from sudden and accidental and/or gradual pollution incidents at the site;
- preventing and remediating pollutants that have migrated from the insured site;
- third-party claims for bodily injury by persons at the insured site;
- third-party claims for bodily injury and property damage from exposure to pollutants originating from the insured site;
- third-party diminution of value of property due to pollution incidents at the insured site;
- third-party business interruption losses associated with pollution from the insured site;
- first-party business interruption losses associated with pollution incidents at the insured site;
- remediation of pre-existing contamination at an insured site that was not known to the insured or a 'responsible person' such as an environmental manager or a director or officer of the company when the policy incepted;
- preventing and remediating environmental damage under the ELD due to environmental damage at or emanating from the insured's site;
- reputational damage suffered by the insured due to a pollution incident at the insured's site;

[137] Member States of the EU and states in the European Economic Area (EEA) are authorised to carry on insurance business, including offering and placing policies, in all Member States as well as the State in which they are authorised to carry on insurance business. They do this by establishing a branch or agents in the State (called right of establishment) or providing cross-border services across the EEA (freedom of services).

- transportation of products and waste from the insured's site (but not cover for products liability);
- remediation of waste generated at the insured's site and disposed at an authorised waste disposal site;
- emergency costs; and
- associated defence costs.

All the above risks are set out as separate coverage parts in a menu format. An insured may therefore, select only the coverage parts that it wishes to purchase. Some policies combine cover for pre-existing contamination and operational risks in a single coverage part; others separate them. In a similar manner, some policies combine cover for preventing and remediating on-site and off-site pollution in a single coverage part; others separate them.

Many, but not all, environmental insurance policies broadly define a 'claim' to include a request by a competent authority to remediate pollution/contamination. A limited number of policies have a restrictive definition.

Typical endorsements for a PLL policy include an endorsement that removes cover for the prevention and remediation of pollution/contamination at an insured site that is to be remediated and developed (offering only off-site cover) until the remediation and development has been carried out. Another typical endorsement allows a large insured automatically to add specified types of sites (such as offices) to a policy during the policy period without the need to notify the insurer of specific details of the sites until a period reporting of them such as every six months. Yet another typical endorsement limits cover for preventing and remediating known pollutants at a site.

If a PLL policy provides cover for operational risks and pre-existing risks, cover for operational risks may be limited, say, to three years, whilst cover for pre-existing contamination may extend to 10 years.

6.4.2 Contractors Pollution Liability Policies

Again, depending on the insurer, a CPL policy typically provides cover for many of the same liabilities as a PLL policy, with the major difference being that a CPL policy may provide cover not only for the insured's site but also for sites at which the insured carries out operations for others.

The policies are generally available to many types of contractors. They may be underwritten for an entire construction project or for periods up to 10 years. They may also include cover not only for ongoing construction projects but also for completed construction projects, in which case they extend the policy period beyond the date of substantial completion of the construction.

Further, CPL policies may provide cover not only for claims that result from the insured contractor's negligent acts but also from the contractor's errors or omissions such as negligent advice.

6.4.3 Environmental Consultants' Professional Services Policies

Environmental consultants' professional services policies provide cover for claims due to errors or omissions of the insured consultant. They may also be combined with policies that provide cover for claims arising from works carried out by environmental consultants.

They may be underwritten for a single project or for a period of up to, say, three years depending on the insurer.

6.4.4 Contaminated Land Policies

A few insurers offer policies that provide cover to businesses for remediating contaminated land at their premises, and sometimes to individuals for remediating contaminated land at their residences. The policies tend to focus on the liabilities arising from the contaminated land regime (see Sect. 3.4.6 above) and tend to be limited in scope.

7 Mandatory Financial Security Requirements

Mandatory financial security requirements for environmental responsibilities exist in the UK under retained EU legislation that implements the Landfill Directive,[138] the Extractive Waste Directive,[139] the Directive on the geological storage of carbon dioxide,[140] the Shipments of Waste Regulation,[141] the Directive on waste electrical and electronic equipment,[142] and the Basic Safety Standards Directive.[143] The mandatory financial security requirements under the above legislation are described

---

[138] Council Directive 1999/31/EC on the landfill of waste [1999] OJ L182/1; https://eur-lex.europa.eu/legal-content/EN/TXT/?uri=CELEX:31999L0031 (accessed on 10.05.2023).

[139] Directive 2016/21/EC on the management of waste from extractive industries [2016] OJ L102/15; https://eur-lex.europa.eu/legal-content/EN/TXT/?uri=CELEX:02006L0021-20090807 (accessed on 10.05.2023).

[140] Directive (2009/31/EC) on the geological storage of carbon dioxide [2009] OJ L140/114; https://eur-lex.europa.eu/legal-content/EN/TXT/?uri=CELEX%3A32009L0031 (accessed on 10.05.2023).

[141] Regulation (EC) No 1013/2006 on shipments of waste [2006] OJ L190/1 (consolidated version); https://eur-lex.europa.eu/legal-content/EN/TXT/?qid=1454069470717&uri=CELEX:02006R1013-20180101 (accessed on 10.05.2023).

[142] Directive 2012/19/EU on waste electrical and electronic equipment [2012] OJ L197/38; https://eur-lex.europa.eu/legal-content/EN/TXT/PDF/?uri=CELEX:32012L0019 (accessed on 10.05.2023).

[143] Directive 2011/65/EU on the restriction of the use of certain hazardous substances in electrical and electronic equipment (recast) [2011] OJ L174/88 (consolidated version); https://eur-lex.europa.eu/legal-content/EN/TXT/?uri=CELEX:02011L0065-20200301 (accessed on 10.05.2023).

in the chapter on environmental liabilities and insurance law in the EU due to the requirements being substantially the same in all Member States.

No jurisdiction in the UK imposes *ex ante* mandatory financial security requirements for ELD liabilities. Regulation 27 of the EDR however authorises a competent authority to serve a notice on a responsible person that owns premises for any costs incurred by the authority in carrying out preventive and remediation measures. The costs and interest accrued on them pursuant to the notice are a statutory charge on the premises and, thus, provide the authority with *ex post* security for the debt. The ELD regulations in Wales and Northern Ireland have identical requirements. There is no equivalent provision in legislation in Scotland.[144]

Cases

American Centennial Insurance Company v Insco Ltd [1996] Lloyd's Rep LR 407
Barker v Corus (UK) Plc [2006] UKHL 20
Barr v Biffa Waste Services Ltd [2012] EWCA Civ 312
Bartoline Ltd v Royal & Sun Alliance Insurance plc [2007] All ER (D) 59 (High Court (Mercantile Court))
Bocardo SA v Star Energy UK Onshore Ltd [2010] UKSC 35
Bolton Metropolitan Borough Council v Commercial Union and Municipal Mutual Insurance [2006] 1 WLR 1492 (Court of Appeal)
Bradley v Eagle Star Insurance Company Ltd [1989] 1 AC 957 [1989] 2 WLR 568 (House of Lords)
Circular Facilities (London) Ltd v Sevenoaks District Council [2005] EWHC 865 (Admin)
Cambridge Water Company v Eastern Counties Leather [1994] 2 AC 264
Charter Reinsurance Company Ltd. v Fagan [1997] AC 313, 384 [1996] 2 WLR 726, [1996] 3 All ER 46 (House of Lords)
Corby Group Litigation v Corby Borough Council [2008] EWCA Civ 463
Corby Group Litigation v Corby Borough Council [2009] EWHC 1944
Coventry v Lawrence [2014] UKSC 13
Durham v BAI (Run Off) Ltd [2012] UKSC 14
Employers Liability Policy Trigger Litigation (Durham v BAI) [2012] UKSC 14
Equitas Insurance Limited v Municipal Mutual Insurance Limited [2019] EWCA Civ 718
Fairchild v Glenhaven Funeral Services Ltd [2002] UKHL 22
Lambert v Barratt Homes Ltd [2010 EWCA Civ 681
Lancashire County Council v Municipal Mutual Insurance Ltd [1997] QB 897 [1996] 3 WLR 493 (Court of Appeal)

[144] See generally Mackie and Combe (2019), p. 83.

Leakey v National Trust for Places of Historic Interest or Natural Beauty [1980] 1 QB 485
House Maker (Padgate) Ltd v Network Rail Infrastructure [2022] EWHC 1482 (TCC)
Hunter v Canary Wharf [1997] AC 655
Investors Compensation Scheme v West Bromwich Building Society [1998] 1 WLR 896, [1998] 1 All ER 98 (House of Lords)
Jalla v Shell International Trading and Shipping Company [2021] EWCA Civ 63
National Grid Gas plc) v Environment Agency [2007] UKHL 30
Post Office v Norwich Union Fire Insurance Society Ltd [1967] 2 QB 363, [1967] 2 WLR 709 (Court of Appeal)
Powys County Council v Price and Hardwick [2017] EWCA Civ 1133
R (on the application of Redland Minerals Ltd) v Secretary of State for Environment, Food and Rural Affairs [2010] EWHC 913 (Admin)
R (on the application of the Counsel General for Wales) v Secretary of State for Business, Energy and Industrial Strategy [2021] EWHC 950 (Admin), *affirmed, R (on the Application of the Counsel General for Wales) v Secretary of State for Business, Energy and Industrial Strategy* [2022] EWCA Civ 118
R (on the application of Seiont, Gwyrfai and Llyfni Anglers' Society) v Natural Resources Wales [2015] EWHC 3578 (Admin)
R (Seiont, Gwyrfai and Llyfni Anglers' Society) v Natural Resources Wales [2016] EWCA Civ 797
Rylands v Fletcher (1868) LR 3 HL 330
Sedleigh-Denfield v O'Callaghan [1940] AC 880
Sienkiewicz (Administratrix of the Estate of Enid Costello Deceased) v Greif (UK) Limited [2011] UKSC 10
Transco Plc v Stockport Metropolitan Borough Council [2003] UKHL 61
Vnuk v Zavarovalnica Triglav d.d., Case C-162/13 ECLI:EU:C:2014:2146, https://curia.europa.eu/juris/liste.jsf?num=C-162/13 (accessed on 10.05.2023)
Yorkshire Water Services Ltd v Sun Alliance and London Insurance plc (No 1) [1997] 2 Lloyd's Rep 21 (Court of Appeal)

Legislation

Anti-Pollution Works Regulations 1999/1006; https://www.legislation.gov.uk/uksi/1999/1006/contents/made (accessed on 10.05.2023)
Anti-Pollution Works Regulations (Northern Ireland) 2003/7; https://www.legislation.gov.uk/nisr/2003/7/contents/made (accessed on 10.05.2023)
Compensation Act 2006; https://www.legislation.gov.uk/ukpga/2006/29/contents (accessed on 10.05.2023)
Contaminated Land (England) Regulations 2006/1380; https://www.legislation.gov.uk/uksi/2006/1380/contents/made (accessed on 10.05.2023)

Contaminated Land (Scotland) Regulations 2005/658; https://www.legislation.gov.uk/ssi/2005/658/contents/made (accessed on 10.05.2023)
Contaminated Land (Wales) Regulations 2001/2197; https://www.legislation.gov.uk/wsi/2001/2197/contents/made (accessed on 10.05.2023)
Council Directive (80/778/EEC) relating to the quality of water intended for human consumption [1980] OJ L229/11 (repealed); https://eur-lex.europa.eu/legal-content/EN/TXT/?uri=celex%3A31980L0778 (accessed on 10.05.2023)
Council Directive 92/43/EEC on the conservation of natural habitats and of wild fauna and flora [1992] OJ L206/7 (consolidated version); https://eur-lex.europa.eu/legal-content/EN/TXT/?uri=CELEX:01992L0043-20130701 (accessed on 10.05.2023)
Council Directive 1999/31/EC on the landfill of waste [1999] OJ L182/1 (consolidated version); https://eur-lex.europa.eu/legal-content/EN/TXT/?uri=CELEX%3A01999L0031-20180704 (accessed on 10.05.2023)
Department for Environment, Food & Rural Affairs, Environmental Protection Act 1990: Part 2A; Contaminated Land Statutory Guidance (April 2012); https://www.gov.uk/government/publications/contaminated-land-statutory-guidance (accessed on 10.05.2023)
Directive 2000/60/EC establishing a framework for Community action in the field of water policy [2000] OJ L327/1 (consolidated version); https://eur-lex.europa.eu/legal-content/EN/TXT/?uri=CELEX:02000L0060-20141120 (accessed on 10.05.2023)
Directive 2004/35/CE on environmental liability with regard to the prevention and remedying of environmental damage [2004] OJ L143/56 (consolidated version); https://eur-lex.europa.eu/legal-content/EN/TXT/?uri=CELEX%3A02004L0035-20190626 (accessed on 10.05.2023)
Directive 2008/56/EC establishing a framework for community action in the field of marine environmental policy [20008] OJ L164/19 (consolidated version); https://eur-lex.europa.eu/legal-content/EN/TXT/?uri=CELEX%3A02008L0056-20170607 (accessed on 10.05.2023)
Directive 2009/147/EC on the conservation of wild birds [2010] OJ L20/7 (codified version); https://eur-lex.europa.eu/legal-content/EN/TXT/?uri=CELEX:32009L0147 (accessed on 10.05.2023)
Directive 2010/75/EU on industrial emissions (integrated pollution prevention and control) [2010] OJ L334/17 (consolidated version); https://eur-lex.europa.eu/legal-content/EN/TXT/?uri=CELEX%3A02010L0075-20110106 (accessed on 10.05.2023)
Environment Act 1995; https://www.legislation.gov.uk/ukpga/1995/25/contents (accessed on 10.05.2023)
Environmental Authorisations (Scotland) Regulations 2018/219; https://www.legislation.gov.uk/ssi/2018/219/contents/made (accessed on 10.05.2023)
Environmental Civil Sanctions (England) Order 2010; https://www.legislation.gov.uk/ukdsi/2010/9780111492512/contents (accessed on 10.05.2023)

Environmental Damage (Prevention and Remediation) (England) Regulations 2015/810; https://www.legislation.gov.uk/uksi/2015/810/regulation/18 (accessed on 10.05.2023)

Environmental Liability (Scotland) Regulations 2009/266; https://www.legislation.gov.uk/ssi/2009/266/contents/made (accessed on 10.05.2023)

Environmental Damage (Prevention and Remediation) (Wales) Regulations 2009/995; https://www.legislation.gov.uk/wsi/2009/995/contents (accessed on 10.05.2023)

Environmental Liability (Prevention and Remediation) Regulations (Northern Ireland) 2009/252; https://www.legislation.gov.uk/nisr/2009/252/contents/made (accessed on 10.05.2023)

Environment (Northern Ireland) Order 2002/3153; https://www.legislation.gov.uk/nisi/2002/3153/contents (accessed on 10.05.2023)

Environmental Permitting (England and Wales) Regulations 2016/1154; https://www.legislation.gov.uk/uksi/2016/1154/contents/made (accessed on 10.05.2023)

Environmental Protection Act 1990; https://www.legislation.gov.uk/ukpga/1990/43/contents (accessed on 10.05.2023)

Environmental Protection (Plastic Straws, Cotton Buds and Stirrers) (England) Regulations 2020/971; https://www.legislation.gov.uk/uksi/2020/971/contents/made (accessed on 10.05.2023)

Environmental Protection (Single-use Plastic Products) (Scotland) Regulations 2021/410; https://www.legislation.gov.uk/ssi/2021/410/contents/made (accessed on 10.05.2023)

European Communities Act 1972 (repealed); https://www.legislation.gov.uk/ukpga/1972/68/contents (accessed on 10.05.2023)

European Union (Future Relationship) Act 2020; https://www.legislation.gov.uk/ukpga/2020/29/contents (accessed on 10.05.2023)

European Union (Withdrawal) Act 2018; https://www.legislation.gov.uk/ukpga/2018/16/contents/enacted (accessed on 10.05.2023)

Government of Wales Act 1998; https://www.legislation.gov.uk/ukpga/1998/38/contents (accessed on 10.05.2023)

Government of Wales Act 2006; https://www.legislation.gov.uk/ukpga/2006/32/contents (accessed on 10.05.2023)

Infrastructure Act 2014; https://www.legislation.gov.uk/ukpga/2015/7/contents/enacted (accessed on 10.05.2023)

Motor Insurance Directive (2009/103/EC) [2009] OJ L263/11; https://eur-lex.europa.eu/legal-content/EN/TXT/?uri=celex%3A32009L0103 (accessed on 10.05.2023)

Motor Vehicles (Compulsory Insurance) Act 2022; https://www.legislation.gov.uk/ukpga/2022/25/enacted (accessed on 10.05.2023)

Nature Conservation (Scotland) Act 2004; https://www.legislation.gov.uk/asp/2004/6/contents (accessed on 10.05.2023)

Northern Ireland Act 1998; https://www.legislation.gov.uk/ukpga/1998/47/contents (accessed on 10.05.2023)

Pollution Prevention and Control (Industrial Emissions) Regulations (Northern Ireland) 2013/160; https://www.legislation.gov.uk/nisr/2013/160/contents/made (accessed on 10.05.2023)

Regulatory Enforcement and Sanctions Act 2008; https://www.legislation.gov.uk/ukpga/2008/13/contents (accessed on 10.05.2023)

Scotland Land 1998; https://www.legislation.gov.uk/ukpga/1998/46/contents (accessed on 10.05.2023)

Scotland Act 2016; https://www.legislation.gov.uk/ukpga/2016/11/contents/enacted (accessed on 10.05.2023)

Scottish Government, Environmental Protection Act 1990 – Part IIA Contaminated Land: statutory guidance (7 June 2006); https://www.gov.scot/publications/environmental-protection-act-1990-part-iia-contaminated-land-statutory-guidance/ (accessed on 10.05.2023)

Trade and Cooperation Agreement between the European Union and the European Atomic Energy Community, of the one part, and the United Kingdom of Great Britain and Northern Ireland, of the other part; https://assets.publishing.service.gov.uk/government/uploads/system/uploads/attachment_data/file/948119/EU-UK_Trade_and_Cooperation_Agreement_24.12.2020.pdf (accessed on 10.05.2023)

United Kingdom Internal Market Act 2020; https://www.legislation.gov.uk/ukpga/2020/27/contents/enacted (accessed on 10.05.2023)

United Kingdom Internal Market Act 2020 (Exclusions from Market Access Principles: Single-Use Plastics) Regulations 2022/857; https://www.legislation.gov.uk/ukdsi/2022/9780348236101 (accessed on 10.05.2023)

Wales Act 2017; https://www.legislation.gov.uk/ukpga/2017/4/contents/enacted/data.htm (accessed on 10.05.2023)

Water Environment (Controlled Activities) (Scotland) Regulations 2011/209; https://www.legislation.gov.uk/ssi/2011/209/contents/made (accessed on 10.05.2023)

Water Resources Act 1991; https://www.legislation.gov.uk/ukpga/1991/57/contents (accessed on 10.05.2023)

Welsh Government Guidance Document; Contaminated Land Statutory Guidance – 2012; https://gov.wales/sites/default/files/publications/2019-08/contaminated-land-statutory-guidance-2012.pdf (accessed on 10.05.2023)

Wildlife and Countryside Act 1981; https://www.legislation.gov.uk/ukpga/1981/69 (accessed on 10.05.2023)

Other Governmental Documents

Aitken, Courtney, Annie Bosse, Sarah McKay and Alasdair Reid, Integrated Pollution Prevention and Control: Developing and Setting of Best Available Techniques (BAT) Framework (Scottish Parliament, 30 June 2022); https://

digitalpublications.parliament.scot/ResearchBriefings/Report/2022/6/30/4ba794cd-bd13-4951-be97-4bbda85ecc2d (accessed on 10.05.2023)
Department for Environment, Food and Rural Affairs, Integrated pollution prevention and control: developing and setting of Best Available Techniques (BAT) provisional common framework (3 February 2022); https://www.gov.uk/government/publications/integrated-pollution-prevention-and-control-developing-and-setting-of-best-available-techniques-bat-provisional-common-framework (accessed on 10.05.2023)
Department for Environment, Food and Rural Affairs, The Environmental Damage (Prevention and Remediation) Regulations 2009; Guidance for England and Wales (2nd Update, November 2009); https://assets.publishing.service.gov.uk/government/uploads/system/uploads/attachment_data/file/221095/pb13895-indepth-guide-regs09.pdf (accessed on 10.05.2023)
Environment Agency, Enforcement undertakings accepted by the Environment Agency: 1 January 2022 to 31 May 2022 (updated 22 June 2022); https://www.gov.uk/government/publications/environment-agencys-use-of-civil-sanctions/enforcement-undertakings-accepted-by-the-environment-agency-1-january-2022-to-31-may-2022 (accessed on 10.05.2023)
Environment Agency's use of civil sanctions; https://www.gov.uk/government/publications/environment-agencys-use-of-civil-sanctions (accessed on 10.05.2023)

References

Article

Mackie C, Combe MM (2019) Charges on land for environmental liabilities: a matter of "priority" for Scotland. J Environ Law 31(1):83
Wilks R (2022) Explained: Devolution in Wales, Scotland and Northern Ireland. The National (23 April 2022). https://www.thenational.wales/news/20088766.explained-devolution-wales-scotland-northern-ireland/. Accessed on 10.05.2023

Managing Environmental Risk Through Insurance: China

Qihao He and Jing Liu

Abstract In the context of China, this chapter explores the role of insurance in compensating for environmental damages and regulating environmental risk. On the one hand, insurance is one of the most promising mechanisms to compensate for damage caused by pollution due to its mechanism to cover environmental pollution accidents. On the other hand, insurance could work as a regulatory tool to mitigate environmental pollution through ex ante governance. However, due to the inherent challenges of environmental risk and China's legal system, insurance faces difficulties in developing environmental insurance products and functioning as theoretically expected. We propose some potential proposals such as mandatory environmental insurance and private-public partnerships which enhance private insurance to address environmental risk.

1 Introduction

Environmental pollution has become one of the most significant issues facing China. With growing economic development, the demand for environmental quality is increasing as well.[1] Environmental tort liability cases are growing rapidly as well.[2] There is increasing discussion on tools to fight against environmental pollution in China.[3] The Chinese leadership also declares to build an "Ecological Civilization" and "to explore a new way of high-quality development oriented by ecological

[1] Guo and Marinova (2011), pp. 1673–1679.

[2] Carpenter-Gold (2015), pp. 241–274.

[3] See, generally, Xue et al. (2007), pp. 669–676; Wu (2020), pp. 63–102; Zhao (2019).

Q. He (✉)
China University of Political Science and Law (CUPL), College of Comparative Law, Beijing, China

J. Liu
Wuhan University, Research Institute of Environmental Law, Wuhan, China
e-mail: jing.liu@whu.edu.cn

K. Malinowska, D. Maśniak (eds.), *Managing Environmental Risks through Insurance*, AIDA Europe Research Series on Insurance Law and Regulation 9,
https://doi.org/10.1007/978-3-031-47602-0_5

priority and green development to ensure harmony between humankind and nature."[4] Traditionally, China has developed two ways to address the issue of environmental pollution and damage compensation. The first one is administrative enforcement of environmental law, and the second one is the immature tool known as public interest litigation.[5]

This chapter is motivated by the application of insurance not only as a financial security tool for environmental damages, but also as a regulatory tool for environmental risk control. As the leading risk management tool, insurance has two functions in managing environmental risks.[6] First, based on the law of large numbers, it could compensate risk-averse environmental individuals exposed to risky activities through risk pooling and risk shifting. Compared to government-provided/subsidized compensation programs, private insurance has been praised due to its lower transaction costs, lower adverse selection, and greater efficiency as a result of competitive markets. Second, when insurers underwrite environmental risk, they have strong incentives to mitigate that risk and any ensuing losses to reduce their payouts.[7] Insurers could control and motivate policyholders' behavior through regulatory techniques to avoid the occurrence of losses and thus contribute to environmental risk reduction.

Currently, environmental insurance products are becoming increasingly available in the Chinese market. Some of these insurance products are strongly promoted and even mandated by the government since the government encourages the use of insurance to manage environmental pollution and the ensuing social disputes. For example, the Regulation on Vessel-Induced Pollution issued in 2009, obliges vessels navigating in the Chinese sea area to buy insurance or seek other financial security coverage.[8] At the local government level, taking Shenzhen city for example, a mandatory environmental pollution insurance system was adopted in the Regulation on Green Finance of Shenzhen Special Economic Zone in 2021, which provided RMB 2.765 billion for the coverage.[9]

However, the environmental insurance market is currently small and not yet that well developed in China.[10] The total premiums of the whole liability insurance market in China are RMB 90.1 billion (7.55% of total non-life premiums) and with low penetration at 0.088% of gross domestic product (GDP) in 2020.[11]

---

[4]Party Documents Research Office of the CPC Central Committee, XI Jingping's Discourse on the Construction Socialism Ecological Civilization (2017). Cited from Wu (2020), pp. 63–102.

[5]Id.

[6]Beck (1992); Baker (2010), pp. 433–447.

[7]Ben-Shahar and Logue (2012), pp. 197–248.

[8]Regulations of the People's Republic of China on the Prevention and Control of Vessel-Induced Marine Environment Pollution (promulgated by the Executive Meeting of the State Council on Sept. 2, 2009, effective Mar. 1, 2010), Art. 53.

[9]Dou (Feb. 24, 2022).

[10]Swiss Re (2019).

[11]Sun (2021), pp. 44, 52–53.

Environmental insurance only stands for a small portion of the liability insurance market (less than 1%), though it would grow significantly over the next few years if the national compulsory environmental liability insurance was implemented successfully.[12]

This chapter explores the role of insurance in compensating for environmental damages and regulating environmental risk. After introducing the theoretical background of insurance and its mechanism to cover environmental pollution accidents, we will discuss the role of insurance as a compensation mechanism for victims of environmental pollution, and the role of insurance as a regulatory tool to mitigate environmental pollution. Finally, this chapter concludes with discussions of the difficulties of environmental insurance in practice, as well as potential proposals such as mandatory environmental insurance and private-public partnerships which enhance private insurance to address environmental risk.

2 Insuring Environmental Risk

Environmental insurance goes by many names in academic research and practice, such as environmental liability insurance, environmental pollution liability insurance, environmental impairment liability insurance, and environmental green insurance. Nevertheless, different names share the same general characteristics, which cover loss or damages caused by unexpected pollution.[13] Before discussing the mechanism of insurance to manage environmental risk, we should pay attention to the insurability of environmental risk since it will affect insurers' willingness to provide coverage.

2.1 *The Insurability of Environmental Risk*

Insurability is a fundamental but flexible concept when insurers consider providing coverage for environmental risks. If risks are uninsurable, insurers would rather not underwrite such policies. However, the boundary of insurability of environmental risk is not fixed. Some risk is insurable at the initial stage, such as asbestos, but then becomes uninsurable due to catastrophic losses beyond the insurer's capability. On the contrary, some risk is uninsurable in the beginning, but then becomes insurable alongside the development of actuarial technology, as a result of which information on the risk is acquired. For example, Oil Pollution Act in the United States established unlimited liability and imposed strict requirements regarding financial security. Many insurers and shipping industries criticized the stringent liability rules

[12] Green Peace (2020); Swiss Re (2019), p. 8.
[13] NAIC (2021).

and predicted that it could result in the withdrawal of many vessels from U.S. trade.[14] The biggest ship insurance provider P&I Clubs refused to act as guarantors under the OPA. Nevertheless, they still provide oil pollution coverage at the price of additional premiums. And gradually, when statistics helped to increase the insurability, many alternatives started to emerge as the guarantors required by law.[15]

The insurance literature often identifies three factors defining insurability: (1) ambiguity of risk, also called uncertainty: the ability to identify and quantify probabilities of predicted losses with sufficient precision; (2) losses and solvency: concern that the most significant possible loss could threaten insurers' solvency; (3) appetite: the desire to underwrite risks at a price policyholder willing to pay.[16] If three factors are all satisfied, a risk is considered to be insurable. This chapter argues that despite some concerns, environmental risks are, in most cases, insurable.

First, chronic environmental risk leads to an increase in the uncertainty associated with the frequency and severity of extreme pollution disasters. When there is "too much" uncertainty, the exposure becomes unmeasurable and unquantifiable, and thus uninsurable. Nonetheless, with the steadily growing body of data on pollution disasters and the development of assessment models which could help estimate potential damages of pollution, environmental risk is evolving away from a highly uncertain line of business.[17]

Second, environmental liability insurance involves concerns and arguments about the potential magnitude of catastrophe losses. In order to address the insolvency concern, outside capital could supplement insurers' capacity. Reinsurance and insurance-linked securitization[18] could provide additional sources to primary insurers. In addition and as a last resort, the government could also contribute to solving this problem.[19]

Third, the asymmetric information problem that affects insurers' underwriting may not be as severe as presumed. The so-called moral hazard might be minimal and even become a moral opportunity due to insurers' governance techniques, as we discussed below.[20] For example, many insurers cooperate with government agencies (e.g., EPA) on auditing and predicting pollution risks and thus have the advantage of the information.

---

[14] Kiern (2011), pp. 1–64.

[15] De La Rue and Anderson (2009), pp. 61–63.

[16] Anderson (1998), pp. 1–23; Kunreuther and Michel-Kerjan (2007), p. 1813.

[17] Swiss Re (2005), p. 14.

[18] Reinsurance can be understood as simply an insurer's insurance. Insurers have protected themselves through private reinsurance contracts whereby portions of their losses from a catastrophic disaster are covered by some type of reinsurance arrangement. Insurance-linked securitization could be regarded as the process of transferring insurance risks from insurers and conveying them to third parties through tradable securities. See Jaffee and Russell (1997), pp. 205–230.

[19] The government has a deep credit capacity due to its ability to raise money through tax or borrow money by issuing debt far more readily than private insurers or reinsurers. See Kaplow (1991), pp. 167–175.

[20] See below Sect. 5. Insurance as Governance for Environmental Risk.

2.2 The Mechanism of Insurance to Cover Environmental Risk

Environmental insurance is an important tool to cover pollution risk due to its expertise in risk management. Its risk management process includes three pillars: risk assessment through underwriting, risk control through service and claim management, and risk finance through pooling.[21] Risk control provides the basis of insurance as governance for environmental damage, while risk finance provides the basis of compensation for environmental damage.

The mechanism of insurance to cover environmental risk could be depicted as follows. Facing the uncertainty of future Environmental pollution disasters, an individual or operator is reasonable to be assumed as risk-averse, "if she considers the utility of a certain prospect of money income to be higher than the expected utility of an uncertain prospect of equal expected monetary value.[22] By covering Environmental pollution, the insurer takes the insured's risk. A risk-averse person would like to transfer risk by paying the premium while insurers are the perfect people to take the transferred risk since the insurers could reduce risk through risk control and risk pooling. Risk pooling is the process of combining a large number of homogeneous exposures into a group, and meanwhile, each individual substitutes the premium (a small fixed cost) into the group for the future uncertain financial loss which is statistically predictable for the group as a whole.[23] Applying the law of large numbers, it enables insurance to play a role in compensating victims if they purchase environmental insurance policies in case of contingency insured against.[24]

Therefore, insurance is often praised as a private market mechanism to cover environmental risks in the law and economic theory.[25] Compared with government-provided compensation programs, insurance has advantages in lowering transaction costs, and is more efficient as a result of completive markets.[26] This mechanism is efficient because it satisfies the "Pareto Efficiency" in which condition no one suffers damage and the individual increases his expected utility through transferring risk.[27]

[21] Thoyts (2010), pp. 286–295.

[22] Cooter and Ulen (2008), p. 50.

[23] Vaughan and Vaughan (2007), pp. 34–44.

[24] The law of large numbers is the basic principle of insurance, which says that for a series of independent and identically distributed random variables, the variance of the average amount of a claim payment decreases as the number of claims increases. See Priest (1996), pp. 219–237.

[25] See Faure and Partain (2019).

[26] Faure and Heine (2011), pp. 117–150.

[27] "Pareto Efficiency," also called "Pareto Optimality," is a state of allocation of resources in which it is impossible to make any one individual better off without making at least one individual worse off, see Seog (2010), pp. 35–39.

2.3 *Insurance (and Potential) Products for Environmental Risks*

Insurance is an attractive mechanism to cover environmental risks in theory. In practice, it is generally held that environmental insurance in China is underdeveloped, due to polluters' low liability risks and non-compulsory insurance options. However, there are still some types of policies provided.

First, the traditional insurance product covering environmental risks is the general liability insurance policy, which was later extended to cover pollution risks. However, pollution is not clearly defined in the policy, and the scope may be limited; there is usually a sub-limit on the coverage for pollution damage, and the general liability insurance only covers accidents, and excludes gradual pollution.[28]

Second, environmental liability insurance ("ELI") is the most important product. Chinese insurers started offering stand-alone ELI after 2007. This type of insurance mainly covers personal injury and property damage caused by pollution, but does not cover specifically pure ecological damage. The cleanup costs—excluding cleanup at polluters' own sites—can be covered either directly under this policy[29] or via an added clause.[30] However, usually, cleanup costs are covered only to the extent that the cleanup may prevent further personal injury or property damage, and the cleanup costs to protect the environment itself are not covered. The restoration costs are usually also excluded.[31]

Third, a still quite rare type is the pollution-site liability insurance policy, which provides coverage for damage to third parties, as well as remediation costs for polluted sites.[32] The risk is covered in the policy provided by Huatai Insurance Company including both new pollution and pre-existing pollution. Moreover, it is defined as a loss that "the insured is legally liable to pay as a result of claims, remediation costs, and associated legal defense expenses" arising out of a "pollution condition on, at, under or migrating from the covered location(s)."[33] Huatai Insurance Company started to provide such a product in 2008. However, three years after beginning to provide this type of insurance, it was reported that the progress was still slow, and the insured were mainly enterprises with foreign-related issues.[34]

---

[28] Faure and Jing (2014), p. 269.

[29] See, for example, China Continent Prop. & Casualty Ins. Co., Environmental Pollution Liability Insurance Terms.

[30] See, for example, China Pacific Property Insurance Co., Ltd., Environmental Liability Insurance, Clean up Costs Clause.

[31] See, for example, China Pacific Property Insurance Co., Ltd., Environmental Liability Insurance, Clean up Costs Clause.

[32] See Horkovich et al. (2013), p. 506.

[33] See Huatai Insurance Company of China (2008), pp. 4–14. More information about Huatai can be found at its website: http://www.ehuatai.com/index.aspx.

[34] See Liu (June 8, 2011).

In addition to pollution-site liability insurance, some other similar products have less extensive coverage. These products cover cleanup costs on polluters' premises as added clauses to environmental liability insurance policies. The added clauses provided by Chang An Insurance Company and Ping An Insurance Company are two examples of environmental third-party liability insurance policies, which use an added clause to provide coverage for cleanup costs on the insured's land.[35]

Finally, pollution risks are covered by general property insurance unless certain damage is explicitly excluded. For example, this could be the case if the property damage to the insured's site is caused by gradual erosion or pollution (i.e., excluding sudden pollution events and pollution events considered unforeseeable by the insurer).

The above insurance (and potential) products for environmental risks show that there are quite a few possibilities to purchase environmental insurance on the market, either explicitly or implicitly, via general—liability or property—insurance policies. However, the number of companies active in the environmental insurance market is limited. For instance, China started experimenting in some local areas to develop the environmental insurance market after 2007. Ten years later, in 2017, it was reported that only 16,000 enterprises bought environmental liability insurance and the revenue from such insurance products accounted for 1% of the total liability insurance revenue.[36] In 2021, one of the experimental areas, Shenzhen started a mandatory environmental pollution insurance program, which provided more substantial incentives for more compensation instruments.

3 Insurance Compensation for Environmental Damage

3.1 Environmental Insurance Market Development: Law and Policy

The literature has primarily argued in favor of the introduction of environmental liability insurance to guarantee both adequate compensations to victims, and avoidance of under-deterrence.[37] When the extent of the damage can exceed the individual wealth of the injurer, an insolvency problem may arise, justifying the introduction of mandatory insurance.[38] General environmental statutes in China, including the revised Environmental Protection Act of 2015 and the new Civil Code of 2021,

[35] See Changan Liability Ins. Corp., Environmental Pollution Liability Insurance Terms for Workplace Cleanup Costs, more information about Chang An please refer to its website https://www.capli.com.cn/; Ping An Pollution Liability Insurance, Cleanup Costs of On-Premises Sites, more information about Ping An please refer to its website http://www.pingan.com/investor/en/index.jsp.

[36] Green Peace (2020).

[37] See Faure and Hartlief (2003), pp. 211–220.

[38] Wagner (2007), p. 110.

are generally silent on compulsory insurance or other financial guarantees; exceptions only exist for marine oil pollution.

Environmental insurance is a new product in China. Only recently have the central and local governments launched pilot programs or regulations for environmental liability insurance. In 2006, the State Council issued the “Several Opinions on the Reform and Development of the Insurance Industry” (Guo Fa [2006] No. 23), proposing to take measures to develop environmental pollution liability insurance. In 2007, the Ministry of Environmental Protection (now the Ministry of Ecology and Environmental Protection,) and the China Insurance Regulatory Commission (now the China Banking and Insurance Regulatory Commission) issued a document requiring local authorities to conduct research and experiments on environmental liability insurance.[39] In 2013, the China Insurance Regulatory Commission and the Ministry of Environmental Protection issued the “Guiding Opinions on Carrying out the Pilot Program of Compulsory Liability Insurance for Environmental Pollution” (Huan Fa [2013] No. 10), proposing to implement a pilot program of compulsory insurance system for enterprises with high environmental risks such as heavy metals. In 2015, the revised Environmental Protection Act stipulated that “the state encourages the purchase of environmental pollution liability insurance” (Article 52). In 2018, the Ministry of Ecology and Environment approved the Draft of Administrative Measures for Compulsory Environmental Pollution Liability Insurance. However, this Draft has still been the draft and has not been implemented till now.[40] Facing intense disputes over the idea of introducing compulsory environmental insurance at the general level, The Ministry of Ecology and Environment has given up the idea to seeking approval of this Draft and tried to limit the mandatory insurance in the field of the treatment of hazardous waste instead.[41]

Local governments also promote a few environmental liability insurance programs. For example, in 2008, the city of Shenyang promulgated the first local regulation, Shenyang Regulation on Preventing Pollution from Dangerous Waste, which is the first local regulation that touched upon environmental liability insurance in China.[42] Under this regulation, insurers are encouraged to establish products to cover environmental liability from dangerous waste. In addition, potential polluters are encouraged to seek such coverage. Since 2013, 21 provinces, including Guangdong, Hubei, Jiangsu, and Guizhou, have successively issued regulations related to environmental liability insurance. Later, Shandong Province and Shenzhen City promulgated local regulations on mandatory environmental liability insurance.

---

[39] See [Guidance on the Development of Environmental Pollution Liability Insurance] (promulgated by the Ministry of Envt’l. Prot. & the China Ins. Reg. Comm’n, Dec. 4, 2007).

[40] The Ministry of Ecology and Environment held a ministerial meeting to review and approve in principle the Administrative Measures for Compulsory Environmental Pollution Liability Insurance (2018) http://www.gov.cn/xinwen/2018-05/08/content_5289087.htm.

[41] See the Draft of Administrative Measures for Environment Pollution Insurance of Hazardous Waste. https://www.mee.gov.cn/xxgk2018/xxgk/xxgk06/202111/t20211119_961008.html.

[42] See [Shenyang Hazardous Waste Pollution Prevention Regulations] (promulgated by the Shenyang City People’s Cong., Oct. 30, 2008, effective Jan. 1, 2009).

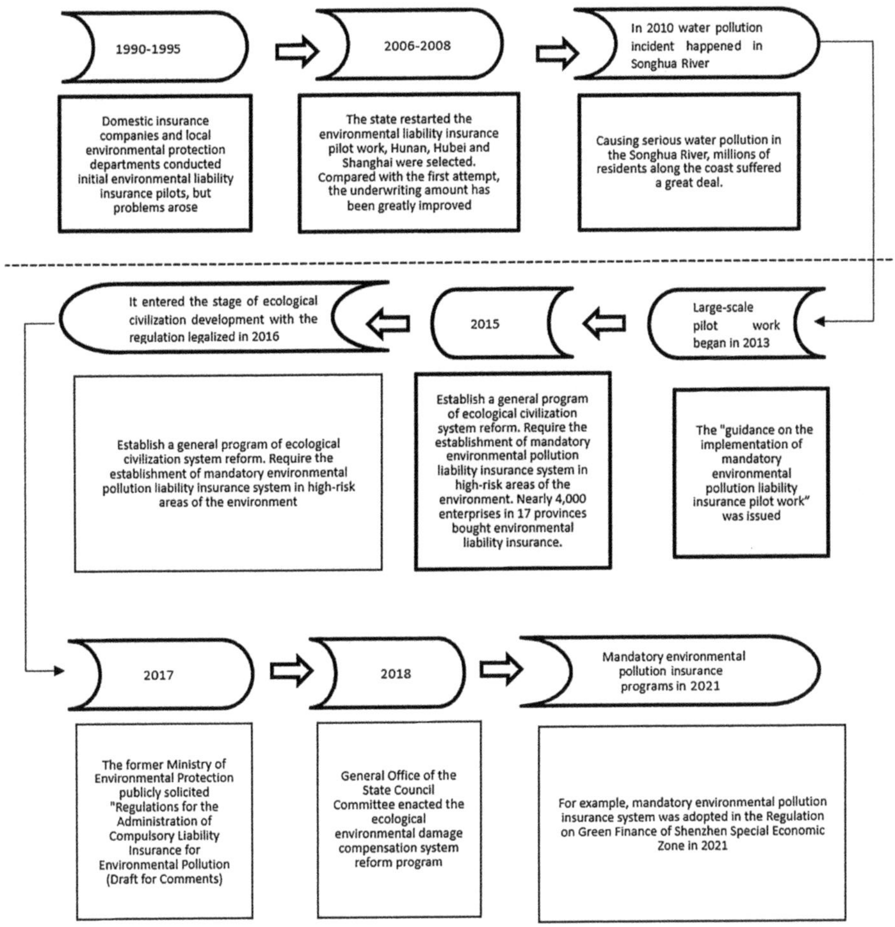

Fig. 1 The legal and practice development of Chinese environmental insurance (Source of Data: Li et al. (2020), pp. 50–55)

Figure 1 depicts the legal development and major practices of environmental insurance in the past decades.

4 Theoretical Analysis of Environmental Insurance Compensation

In this part, we focus on the possibilities for polluters to obtain environmental insurance and thus compensate victims. As a risk management mechanism, insurance offers a unique tool that accords with efficient and fair compensation principles.[43] First, insurance can complement liability rules in compensating and preventing ecological damage. Now insurance possibilities, including general liability insurance policies and specific environmental pollution liability, are widely available. Personal injury and property damage caused by environmental incidents are generally covered. Cleanup costs may also be covered to the extent that they can prevent further personal injury and property damage. Some insurance policies even cover remediation costs on and from the insured sites.[44] Second, in the law and economics literature, private insurance is praised for its lower transaction costs, especially compared to government-provided compensation programs.[45] Insurance compensation system functions well in the competitive market rather than in a bureaucratic government intervention system.

First-party insurance and liability insurance (third-party insurance) are two essential types of insurance. In the first-party insurance system, compensation is awarded directly by the insurer to the victim. It is the victim who buys the insurance. The insurer pays as soon as the damage occurs, making the damage the insured risk.[46] Liability insurance covers the insured's liability for damage caused to other parties, which is defined by the Insurance Law as "the type of insurance of which the insured subject matter is the insured's liability to indemnify a third party according to law."[47] Unlike the first-party insurance funded by victims, in an environmental insurance policy the polluters pay for the premium. Environmental insurance policies focus exclusively on environmental harm, and cover third-party liability for damage from the premises itself, as well as operations with defined extensions; this extends beyond the narrow coverage for industrial accidents under traditional general liability insurance policies.[48]

The environmental insurance policy often uses claims-made clauses for liability coverage. Under a claims-made policy, the claim for damages has to be received by the insured or his insurer within the period of insurance coverage.[49] The policy may also require that the incident leading to the pollution have occurred within a certain retroactive period.[50] Compared to occurrence clauses, it increases the predictability of the insurers. On the other hand, some critics argue that claims-made policies could dilute the deterrent function of liability law.[51] As far as premiums are concerned insurers make a distinction between companies that constitute high environmental risks and companies that do not. The insurer usually appoints an expert for high-risk

[43] Priest (1996), pp. 219–237.
[44] See, for example, Huatai Insurance Company of China (2008), pp. 4–14.
[45] For example, Priest (1996), pp. 219–237.
[46] Faure and Bruggeman (2008), pp. 11–14.
[47] The Insurance Law (2015) Art. 65(4).
[48] Wagner (2009), p. 377.
[49] See Katzman (1988), p. 87 (explaining the claim-made policy).
[50] China Pacific Property Insurance Co., Ltd. [Environmental Liability Insurance], Art. 3.
[51] Abraham (1982), p. 131.

companies to do a risk assessment, with which the to-be-insured company typically cooperates.

5 Insurance as Governance for Environmental Risk

5.1 Regulation by Insurance in Managing Environmental Risk

As a well-known professional risk management mechanism, insurance is regarded as a robust regulatory mechanism in many fields of liability, including automobile accidents, workplace injuries, defamation, corporate and securities liability, medical malpractice, defective products, as well as environmental harms.[52] Environmental insurance does have the potential to regulate insureds' behavior so as to mitigate risks. Scholars of regulation by insurance, also called insurance-as-governance, propose several theoretical explanations for insurance's risk mitigation function.

In theory, insurers have the incentives and the capacity to mitigate risks and the resulting losses. "If an insurer can lower its premiums by lowering its risk of paying claims, it can undercut its competitors by charging lower premiums, thereby attracting more business. Marketplace considerations, rather than altruism, drive insurers to reduce risk."[53] For example, through insurance rate classification, liability insurers can charge experience-rated premiums and thus induce policyholders to "behave more carefully than they would otherwise." In practice, insurance laws' reluctance to prohibit rate classification based on controllable characteristics supports insurers' behavior-control functions.

Regarding capacity, liability insurance can incentivize potential tortfeasors to internalize the costs of the harms they create through its capacity to manage moral hazard and other immoral acts of the insureds.[54] In dealing with environmental risk, insurance is faced with the challenge of moral hazards risk. Due to moral hazard, those who are insured against pollution exercise less care to avoid losses than they would if the damages were not covered by insurers.[55] If moral hazard could not be controlled, liability insurance for polluters, for example, could not compel timely mitigation, but may have socially negative consequences as it could dilute the incentives of the emitters (the potential tortfeasor for environmental disaster victims) to invest in prevention.[56]

---

[52] Baker and Swedloff (2013), pp. 1412–1450.

[53] Cogan Jr. (2016), p. 1522.

[54] Ben-Shahar and Logue (2012), pp. 197–248.

[55] Abraham (2010), p. 7.

[56] Shavell (1982), pp. 120–132; Telesetsky (2010), pp. 691–734.

Besides, insurers have many techniques to reduce risk, and the consensus is that these techniques work reasonably well.[57] Theoretically, risk-based pricing is regarded as the central technique of insurers to risk mitigation. Since the insurance premium is based on the expected overall losses, derived by multiplying loss probability by loss severity, reducing either the probability or the severity of the loss may lower the premium.[58] As long as such reduction cost is lower than the discount of the premium, policyholders would likely undertake mitigation measures to reduce loss probability and/or severity.[59] Besides risk-based pricing, insurers have several other regulatory techniques in underwriting and claim processing. These techniques include, but are not limited to: deductibles, co-payments, contract design, loss prevention services, educational communication with policyholders, claim management, and refusal to underwrite.[60] Through offering effective incentives, applying regulatory techniques, and monitoring policyholders' behavior, insurers have the capacity to remedy the risk of moral hazard, promote policyholders' cost-effective actions, and thus contribute to mitigation.

What has been explained previously about insurance in general also applies to environmental liability insurance. When environmental liability insurance is prevalent and even mandatory, insurance companies could play the role of private regulators, and improves the efficiency of risk mitigation. Empirical examples of insurance minimizing rather than exacerbating moral hazard problems have been found.[61] For example, compared to the government cleanup assurance funds, private insurance induced owners of fuel storage tanks and improved safety by risk-based pricing.[62] It is reported that accidents dropped by more than 20% and saved $ 400 million cleanup-cost in Michigan alone over eight years.[63]

5.2 *Statutory of Rules for Risk Control and Regulatory Techniques of Environmental Insurance*

The above literature has argued mainly to introduce environmental liability insurance as governance to guarantee effective risk mitigation. The Insurance Law of the People's Republic of China, adopted in 1995 and amended or revised in 2002, 2009, 2014, and 2015, has gradually introduced risk control and governance rules.

---

[57] Baker and Siegelman (2013), p. 169.

[58] Molk (2015), pp. 265–277.

[59] Molk (2015), pp. 265–277.

[60] These regulatory tools are widely discussed in a series of articles written by regulation by insurance scholars. For example, Baker and Swedloff (2013), pp. 1416–1423; Ben-Shahar and Logue (2012), pp. 197–248.

[61] See, generally, Freeman and Kunreuther (1997).

[62] Yin et al. (2011), pp. 325–363.

[63] Yin et al. (2011), pp. 325–363.

Article 16 stipulates the insured's duty of disclosure, "[W]here the insurer inquiries about the subject matter insured or about the insured when entering into an insurance contract, the insurance applicant shall tell the truth." Article 21 prescribes the insured's duty to notify after a covered event occurs, "[A]fter knowing the occurrence of an insured incident, the insurance applicant, insured or beneficiary shall notify the insurer in a timely manner." Article 31 requires insurable interest, "[A] insurance applicant shall have an insurable interest. . .. . .[W]here the insurance applicant does not have an insurable interest in the insured when entering into an insurance contract, the contract shall be null and void."

More importantly, Article 51 specifies the insured's duty to protect the subject-matter insured and measures for the insurer's safety inspection and precautions, "[T] he insured shall abide by the state provisions on fire protection, safety, productive operation, labor protection, etc. to maintain the safety of the subject matter insured. The insurer may check the safety status of the subject matter insured according to the contract, and offer written recommendations to the insurance applicant or insured on eliminating unsafe factors or hidden dangers in a timely manner. Where the insurance applicant or insured fails to perform the duty of maintaining the safety of the subject matter insured as agreed upon, the insurer shall have the right to increase the insurance premium or rescind the contract. To maintain the safety of the subject matter insured, the insurer may take safety precautions upon the consent of the insured." Article 52 stipulates the insured's duty to notify of increased risk, "[W]here the degree of peril of the subject matter insured greatly increases during the term of validity of the contract, the insured shall notify the insurer in a timely manner as agreed upon in the contract, and the insurer may increase the insurance premium or rescind the contract as agreed upon in the contract." Article 57 prescribes the insured's obligation to prevent and reduce losses in the event of a covered accident, "When an insured incident occurs, the insured shall endeavor to take necessary measures to prevent or reduce losses."

The Insurance Law provides rules of risk control from a timing framework corresponding to a repetitive circle of risk management as *prevention – response – recovery*: the *ex ante* (before the accident occurs, e.g., Articles 16, 51), *during* (emergency response during a disaster, e.g., Articles 57, 52), and *ex post* (after the disaster, e.g., Article 21).

In practice, as a private regulator, insurance operates stealthily by using technical tools to reduce moral hazards.[64] These technical tools, which almost all insurers use to one degree or another, include risk-based pricing, contract design (e.g., limits, deductibles, copayments, and exclusions), loss prevention, claim management, and refusal to insure. Of course, not all those technical tools will be used by environmental insurers to the same extent in practice.

Risk-based pricing is considered to be the most basic technique for creating incentives to reduce risk.[65] Insurers set premiums to reflect underlying risk levels

---

[64] Heimer (2002), pp. 117–145.

[65] Ben-Shahar and Logue (2012), pp. 197–248.

in order to provide individuals incentives to mitigate losses.[66] Indeed, insurers often adopt feature rating and experience rating in order to signal premium loss prevention. Feature rating means insurers examine the insured's individual risk characteristics and adjust premiums accordingly.[67] For example, as mentioned above, environmental liability policies reward policyholders with premium discounts if they take loss prevention measures, such as replacing fuel tanks constructed with corrosion-prone material; by contrast, the premium will be raised by 10 to 20% due to a prior leak of the fuel tank.[68] Experience rating means insurers gather information about the insured's loss experience during the policy period, and use that information either to make retroactive pricing adjustments or prospective pricing adjustments for future policy periods.[69] Based on the insurer's prediction of the insured's risk preference and behavior performance, the insurer could give the insured a premium discount to the insured or charge a higher premium.[70]

Contract design has also been used to regulate risk both directly and indirectly through deductibles, copayments, coverage amount limits, and exclusions. Deductibles and copayments can mitigate moral hazard directly because they prevent policyholders from shielding themselves entirely from loss.[71] This is one of the tools to control moral hazard: exposing the insured still partially to risk will provide incentives for adequate prevention to the insured. If indeed a portion of the risk remains with the insured, they will exercise greater vigilance.[72] Deductibles are, moreover, a good technique to remedy adverse selection: good risks can signal their lower exposure to risk by choosing a higher deductible. Exclusions can be seen as an indirect way to regulate policyholders, as it excludes certain types of risk or claim from coverage. Intentional pollution, for example, is commonly excluded from environmental liability insurance policies.[73] In addition, environmental claims, too, are often excluded from general liability insurance (CGL) policies, but covered by specialized Environmental Liability Insurance. For example, Environmental Impairment Liability Insurance is typically underwritten and issued on a site-specific basis. However, even for this policy, gradual pollution rather than sudden, abrupt discharges of pollution is generally excluded due to the concerns of moral hazard.[74]

[66] Molk (2015), pp. 265–277.

[67] Ben-Shahar and Logue (2012), pp. 197–248.

[68] Yin et al. (2011), pp. 325–363.

[69] Ben-Shahar and Logue (2012), pp. 197–248.

[70] Ma (2018), pp. 106–125.

[71] "Deductibles require insureds to pay a fixed amount 'out of pocket' to cover insured losses before the insurance coverage kicks in to cover insured losses thereafter. Copayments typically require insureds to bear some fraction of each covered loss claim filed by an insured." See Ben-Shahar and Logue (2012), pp. 197–248.

[72] Baker and Swedloff (2013), pp. 1412–1450.

[73] Ma (2018), pp. 106–125.

[74] Abraham (1988), p. 953.

Environmental insurers are also providing loss prevention services and advising policyholders on how to modify their behavior to mitigate and avoid losses.[75] In other words, loss prevention services serve as ex ante regulation by insurance. Insurers promote loss prevention in a variety of ways, all of which are potentially applicable to environmental insurance.[76] For example, insurers monitor the insureds through loss prevention during the course of the insurance relationship; they conduct research and disseminate new loss-prevention methods; they also cooperate with the state, and promote the legislation of loss prevention laws and regulations; lastly, insurers establish underwriting procedures that make loss prevention activities a precondition to obtaining insurance.[77]

6 Challenges of Environmental Insurance and Potential Proposals

6.1 Difficulties of Environmental Insurance Compensation and Governance

While on the one hand, one may notice theoretical possibilities for environmental insurance coverage, on the other hand, few insurance companies offer environmental insurance. So far environmental insurance has not played a significant role in China.

As far as the ability of environmental insurance to provide adequate compensation for environmental harm in China is concerned, the primary problem is the lack of an adequate institutional and statutory background for creating a market for environmental insurance. Furthermore, given the limited scope of environmental liability, it fails to provide an efficient deterrent effect.[78] If one were to allocate a greater role to liability mechanisms in providing compensation for environmental harm, the question arises as to what extent this liability can actually be covered by insurance. This inquiry is important for victims who may otherwise be confronted with an insolvent defendant. The literature also indicates that insolvency will allow polluters to externalize the harm to society, which can lead to under-deterrence.[79] Low liability deterrence coupled with a lack of a mandatory financial security system leads to a small environmental insurance market in China.

Moreover, serious challenges facing insurers persist as adverse selection exists. Adverse selection is the phenomenon caused by information asymmetry, and means that those with the highest risk are most likely to buy the insurance.[80] Limited

[75] Baker and Swedloff (2013), pp. 1412–1450.

[76] Cohen (1997), pp. 305–352.

[77] Wang (2020), pp. 72–95.

[78] See Faure et al. (2003), pp. 18–50 (discussing the economic analysis of environmental liability).

[79] See, generally, Jost (1996), pp. 259–276.

[80] See Akerlof (1970), pp. 490–491.

information on the side of insurers makes insurance particularly attractive for high-risk companies, which could eventually endanger the insurability of risks.[81] In China, the problem could arise that mainly high-risk companies are interested in purchasing environmental insurance. Given the difficulty of predicting environmental risks, insurers would likely, as the literature predicts, ask for an additional risk premium to cope with their insurer ambiguity.[82] The premium would be around 6% to 8% of the insured amount, compared to on average 0.3% of traditional liability insurance. However, the amount of coverage is relatively low by international standards. It is often only provided for 1 to 2 million RMB from 2015 to 2017.[83]

Third, government involvement makes China's compensation regime a combined civil and administrative system, traditional tort law is insufficient to compensate for environmental damage.[84] Since the government covers most pollution risks due to the concerns of public health and social stability and the probability that polluters will face environmental liability is generally low.[85] This explains low demand for environmental liability insurance, and the penetration rate of liability insurance were only 0.00066% of gross domestic product (GDP) in 2018.[86]

6.2 *Mandatory Environmental Insurance*

There is some debate concerning the introduction of mandatory environmental insurance. At the legislation level, the concern is that lawmakers are attempting to introduce mandatory insurance while simultaneously forcing high-polluting industries to pay environmental protection tax.[87] Some argue that charging a pollution tax from industry, which needs to be paid by permitted installations, and simultaneously requiring the purchase of insurance, makes polluters pay twice. It is suggested that part of the pollution fees paid by industry should be used to purchase environmental liability insurance. Some experts propose to assess environmental risks before the

[81] See, generally, Faure (2007), pp. 83–100.

[82] See, generally, Kunreuther et al. (1993), pp. 71–87.

[83] Green Peace (2020), pp. 9–11.

[84] Faure and Jing (2012), pp. 261–314.

[85] Nagle (2011), pp. 615–620. In addition, historically many enterprises involved in heavy industry were—and to a large extent still are—state-owned enterprises. It leads to an acceptance that the government may be responsible for historic pollution, and therefore, it may be the primary party who should take action to clean up especially historically polluted sites. See Interview with a Representative, Ministry of Environmental Protection (MEP), in Beijing, China (Aug. 23, 2011).

[86] Swiss Re (2019), p. 1.

[87] Previously, the government charged pollution fees according to Regulations on the Administration of Pollution Fees. Later, the pollution fee was replaced by an environmental tax. In 2016, Environmental Protection Tax Act was adopted and came into effect as of Jan. 1, 2018.

operation starts by using an environmental impact assessment, and subsequently requiring the permitting of polluters to include financial guarantees.[88] In practice, some industries with high environmental risks are also required to seek insurance coverage in some local areas.[89] In some local areas where the government has provided subsidies to pay environmental insurance premiums financed from the pollution fee charged from the enterprises.[90] In other areas, the government links environmental insurance with other environmental subsidies and green credit policies.[91]

Meanwhile, low demand arising from an underestimation of, or disregard for, risk can be solved by making insurance mandatory.[92] Mandatory coverage helps to manage adverse selection because it could prevent lower-risk groups from opting out of the pool.[93] Compulsory insurance can help to enhance damage mitigation. Under mandated insurance, industry actors who want to lower their insurance premiums would likely undertake mitigation measures, and thus under the supervision of the profit-motivated insurance industry. It is worth noting, however, that mandatory insurance may cause the subsidy of good risks to bad risks, and lead to less than efficient risk and premium differentiation.[94] Mandatory coverage also have the risks of exaggerating moral hazard and leading to the concentration of insurance market. Therefore, the choice and design of mandatory insurance should be made with caution.

The progressive introduction of a compulsory system can either start from specific geographical areas or certain industries. In some local areas, such as Changsha, the government already requires specific high-risk industries to seek insurance coverage.[95] In certain industries, one of the domains in which insurance compensation and governance seems to work better—not only on paper, but also in practice—is the case involving marine oil pollution. The *Marine Environmental Protection Law* (MEPL) is the primary law in the field of marine environmental

---

[88] Interview with Wang Jin, Professor, Peking University Law School, in Beijing, China (Aug. 24, 2011) (on file with authors).

[89] For example, in Wuxi (a city in Jiangsu Province), some enterprises have been obliged to buy environmental insurance since 2011, depending on their location and type. See Opinions on Implementation of Environmental Liability Insurance in Wuxi (promulgated by the Gov't Office of Wuxi, Feb. 22, 2011).

[90] Wuxi engages in this practice. See Environmental Liability Insurance in Wuxi, Id.

[91] Sichuan is an example. According to a Sichuan Environmental Protection Bureau document, the government, when deciding to offer subsidies on pollution control, should give priority to companies who bought environmental liability insurance. The attendance of environmental liability insurance is also a criterion for examining green credit performance. See [Opinion on the Implementation of the Environmental Pollution Liability Insurance Policy] (promulgated by the Sichuan Envt'l. Prot. Agency, Nov. 30, 2010).

[92] Moss (2004), p. 51.

[93] Kunreuther (1968).

[94] Van Boom (2008), p. 265.

[95] A compulsory system was adopted in Changsha. See Rules on the Management of Environmental Risk Enterprises (promulgated by the Changsha Envt'l. Prot. Agency, Aug. 10, 2009).

protection and pollution prevention.[96] Article 89 of the MEPL stipulates strict liability for marine pollution: "[W]hoever causes pollution damage to the marine environment shall remove the pollution and compensate the losses; in case of pollution damage to the marine environment resulting entirely from the intentional act or fault of a third party, that third [party] shall remove the pollution and be liable for the compensation." In 2009, the *Regulations of the People's Republic of China on the Prevention and Control of Vessel-Induced Marine Environment Pollution* obliged vessels navigating in the Chinese sea area to buy insurance or seek other financial security coverage.[97] Mandatory financial security—like compulsory insurance—for sea-going vessels to cover the risks of marine pollution plays an important role.[98]

7 Public-Private Partnership

While environmental insurance is still new in China, a general compulsory financial security system may not be feasible. Further development of the insurance market can help a progressive introduction of a compulsory system. A public-private partnership, where the government acts as reinsurer of last resort, could help to fill the "capacity gap" of primary insurers and encourage them to underwrite environmental risks. Compared to the private sector, the government has "a deep credit capacity" and can raise money effectively and quickly through tax or issuing debt or government bonds when dealing with catastrophic pollution damages.[99]

Meanwhile, as a reinsurer, the government would not interfere with private insurers' business, including underwriting policies, collecting premiums, and paying claims, thus ensuring that the private insurance market can keep playing a role in environmental risk compensation and governance.

8 Conclusion

This chapter discussed how insurance plays a role in addressing environmental risk. On the one hand, insurance is one of the most promising mechanisms to compensate for damage caused by pollution. On the other hand, through ex ante insurance

---

[96] Marine Environmental Protection Law of the People's Republic of China (promulgated by the Standing Comm. Nat'l People's Cong. on Aug. 23, 1982, revised in 2017).

[97] Regulations of the People's Republic of China on the Prevention and Control of Vessel-Induced Marine Environment Pollution (promulgated by the Executive Meeting of the State Council on Sept. 2, 2009, revised in 2017), Arts. 51, 52.

[98] Faure and Jing (2012), pp. 269–273.

[99] Kaplow (1991), pp. 167–175.

governance, policyholders could take protection and mitigation measures following the incentives offered by risk-based premiums and other regulatory tools. However, due to the inherent challenges of environmental risk and China's legal system, insurance faces difficulties in developing environmental insurance products and functioning as theoretically expected. Mandatory environmental insurance and a public-private partnership, where government intervention contributes to solving both the supply and demand barriers of insurance development, would be potential proposals for consideration.

References

Abraham KS (1982) Cost internalization, insurance, and toxic tort compensation funds. Va J Nat Resour Law 2:123–148

Abraham KS (1988) Environmental liability and the limits of insurance. Columbia Law Rev 88: 942–988

Abraham KS (2010) Insurance law and regulation, 5th edn. Foundation Press

Akerlof G (1970) The market for "lemons": quality, uncertainty and the market mechanism. Q J Econ 84:488–500

Anderson D (1998) Development of environmental liability risk management and insurance in the United States: lessons and opportunities. Risks Manag Insur Rev 2:1–23

Baker T (2010) Insurance in sociolegal research. Annu Rev Law Soc Sci 6:433–447

Baker T, Siegelman P (2013) The law and economics of liability insurance: a theoretical and empirical review. In: Arlen J (ed) Research handbook in the economics of tort. Edward Elgar Publishing, pp 169–196

Baker T, Swedloff R (2013) Regulation by liability insurance: from auto to lawyers professional liability. UCLA Law Rev 60:1412–1450

Beck U (1992) Risk society: towards a new modernity. Sage Publications

Ben-Shahar O, Logue KD (2012) Outsourcing regulation how insurance reduces moral hazard. Mich Law Rev 111:197–248

Carpenter-Gold D (2015) Note, castles made of sand: public-interest litigation and China's new environmental protection law. Harv Environ Law Rev 39:241–274

Cogan JA Jr (2016) The uneasy case for food safety liability insurance. Brooklyn Law Rev 81(4): 1495–1553

Cohen GM (1997) Legal malpractice insurance and loss prevention: a comparative analysis of economic institutions. Conn Insur Law J 4:305–352

Cooter R, Ulen T (2008) Law & economics. Pearson

De La Rue C, Anderson CB (2009) Shipping and the environment: law and practice. Informa, London

Dou Y (Feb. 24, 2022) Shenzhen mandatory environmental pollution liability insurance achieves full coverage of environmentally high risk enterprises. Shenzhen Special Zone Daily. Available at https://baijiahao.baidu.com/s?id=1725633424073523735&wfr=spider&for=pc

Faure M (2007) Is risk differentiation on European insurance markets in danger? Maastricht J Eur Comp Law 14:83–100

Faure M, Bruggeman V (2008) Catastrophic risks and first-party insurance. Conn Insur Law J 15:1–52

Faure M, Hartlief T (2003) Insurance and expanding systemic risks. OECD

Faure M, Heine K (2011) Insurance against financial crises? N Y Univ J Law Bus 8:117–150

Faure MG, Jing L (2012) New models for the compensation of natural resources damage. Ky J Equine Agric Nat Resour Law 4:261–314

Faure M, Jing L (2014) Compensation for environmental damage in China: theory and practice. Pace Environ Law Rev 31:226–309
Faure M, Partain R (2019) Environmental law and economics: theory and practice. Cambridge University Press
Faure M et al (eds) (2003) Deterrence, insurability, and compensation in environmental liability. Springer
Freeman PK, Kunreuther H (1997) Managing environmental risk through insurance. Springer, Dordrecht
Green Peace (2020) Problems and analysis of environmental pollution liability insurance in China. Available at https://www.greenpeace.org.cn/eli-report-20201207/
Guo X, Marinova D (2011) Environmental awareness in China: facilitating the greening of the economy. In: Chan F, Marinova D, Anderssen RS (eds) MODSIM2011: 19th international congress on modelling and simulation, pp 1673–1679. https://mssanz.org.au/modsim2011/D12/guo.pdf
Heimer C (2002) Insuring more, ensuring less: the costs and benefits of private regulation through insurance. In: Baker T, Simon J (eds) Embracing risk: the changing culture of insurance and responsibility. University of Chicago Press, pp 117–145
Horkovich RM et al (2013) Site pollution liability insurance. In: Environmental liability and insurance recovery. American Bar Association
Huatai Insurance Company of China (2008) Limited Premises Pollution Liability Insurance
Jaffee D, Russell T (1997) Catastrophe insurance, capital markets, and uninsurable risks. J Risk Insur 64:205–230
Jost P (1996) Limited liability and the requirement to purchase insurance. Int Rev Law Econ 16(2): 259–276
Kaplow L (1991) Incentives and government relief for risk. J Risk Uncertain 4:167–175
Katzman M (1988) Pollution liability insurance and catastrophic environmental risk. J Risk Insur 55:75–100
Kiern L (2011) Liability, compensation, and financial responsibility under the Oil Pollution Act of 1990: a review of the first decade. Tulane Marit Law J 36:1–64
Kunreuther H (1968) The case for comprehensive disaster insurance. J Law Econ 11(1):133–163
Kunreuther HC, Michel-Kerjan EO (2007) Climate change, insurability of large-scale disasters, and the emerging liability challenge. Univ Pa Law Rev 155:1795–1842
Kunreuther H et al (1993) Insurer ambiguity and market failure. J Risk Uncertain 7:71–87
Li W et al (2020) Environmental pollution liability insurance: American experiences and Chinese practices. Chin J Environ Manag 2:50–55
Liu X (June 8, 2011) How to promote environmental liability insurance? China Insurance News Network. Available at http://www.sinoins.com/101288/101475/59505.html(China)
Ma N (2018) Construction of the legal system of environmental liability insurance and environmental risk control. Chin J Law 1:106–125
Molk P (2015) Private versus public insurance for natural hazards: individual behavior's role. In: Gardoni P et al (eds) Risk analysis of natural hazards. Springer, pp 265–277
Moss D (2004) When all else fails: government as the ultimate risk manager. Harvard University Press
Nagle JC (2011) How much should China pollute? Vermont J Environ Law 12:591–632
NAIC, Environmental Insurance (last updated 7/9/2021). Available at https://content.naic.org/cipr-topics/environmental-insurance#:~:text=Issue%3A%20Environmental%20insurance%20(also%20known,liability%20and%20property%20insurance%20policies
Priest GL (1996) The government, the market, and the problem of catastrophe loss. J Risk Uncertain 12:219–237
Seog SH (2010) The economics of risk and insurance. Wiley
Shavell S (1982) On liability and insurance. Bell J Econ 13:120–132
Sun Q (2021) China Insurance Market Report 2021. Economic Science Press
Swiss Re (2005) Innovating to Insure the Uninsurable

Swiss Re (2019) China Liability Insurance Market Trend Report
Telesetsky A (2010) Insurance as a mitigation mechanism. Pace Environ Law Rev 27:691–734
Thoyts R (2010) Insurance theory and practice. Routledge
Van Boom WH (2008) Insurance law and economics: an empirical perspective. In: Faure M, Stephen F (eds) Essays in the law and economics of regulation - in honour of Anthony Ogus. Intersentia, Antwerp/Oxford/Portland, pp 253–276
Vaughan EJ, Vaughan TM (2007) Fundamentals of risk and insurance. Wiley
Wagner G (2007) (Un)insurability and the choice between market insurance and public compensation systems. In: van Boom WH, Faure M (eds) Shifts in compensation between private and public systems. Springer Vienna, pp 87–112
Wagner G (2009) Tort law and liability insurance. In: Faure M (ed) Tort law and economics. Edward Elgar Publishing, pp 377–405
Wang W (2020) Research on environmental liability insurance system. JiLin University Press
Wu W (2020) The reform of the compensation system for ecological and environmental damage in China: natural resources, environmental enforcement, and legislation. Nat Resour J 60:63–102
Xue L et al (2007) Environmental governance for China: major recommendations of a task force. Environ Polit 16(4):669–676
Yin H, Kunreuther H, White MW (2011) Risk-based pricing and risk-reducing effort: does the private insurance market reduce environmental accidents? J Law Econ 54(2):325–363
Zhao X (2019) Developing an appropriate contaminated land regime in China: lessons learned from the US and UK, 2nd edn. Springer

Environmental Liabilities and Insurance Law in the United States

Valerie Fogleman

Abstract State common law in the United States (US) has long imposed liability for bodily injury and property damage caused by persons that expose individuals to pollutants as well as causing other harm to them. In the 1970s, the scope of liability for environmental damage was substantially increased when the US Congress enacted extensive permitting legislation for waste, water and air pollution. Among other things, the legislation required permit holders to clean up environmental damage caused by their operations. In 1980, the scope of environmental liabilities was increased again when Congress introduced a programme, called the Superfund programme, and liability for cleaning up historic land contamination that continued to pose a serious risk to human health and the environment. The legislation also introduced liability for restoring damage to natural resources.

Enforcement of the Superfund programme resulted in insureds being liable for many millions of dollars of costs for cleaning up the contamination. In turn, insureds claimed against their commercial general liability policies, resulting in massive litigation. Another result of the increased environmental legislation was the introduction of pollution exclusions in primary and excess general liability policies. In turn, various insurers developed environmental insurance policies that specifically provide cover for the liabilities as well as policies that provide evidence of mandatory financial security for specified environmental liabilities.

This chapter examines environmental liabilities in the US, insurance for them, and mandatory requirements for insurance policies and other financial security instruments and mechanisms.

V. Fogleman (✉)
Cardiff University School of Law and Politics, Cardiff, UK

Stevens & Bolton LLP, Guildford, England, UK
e-mail: foglemanvm@cardiff.ac.uk; valerie.fogleman@stevens-bolton.com

K. Malinowska, D. Maśniak (eds.), *Managing Environmental Risks through Insurance*, AIDA Europe Research Series on Insurance Law and Regulation 9,
https://doi.org/10.1007/978-3-031-47602-0_6

1 Introduction

This chapter examines environmental liabilities and insurance law in the United States of America (US). In keeping with other chapters on environmental liabilities in European Union (EU) and non-EU countries, the chapter focuses on environmental liabilities in the inland US rather than from offshore oil and gas operations or shipping.

Section 2 of the chapter provides an overview of environmental liability law in the US. First, Sect. 2 examines the common law torts of nuisance, the rule in *Rylands v Fletcher* and/or liability for an abnormally dangerous activity, negligence, and trespass. The second part of Sect. 2 provides an overview of legislative requirements for the remediation of pollution/contamination. Liabilities for remediating current and future pollution tend to arise from environmental permitting legislation. Most liabilities for remediating past pollution that continues to pose a risk to human health and the environment arise from the federal Comprehensive Environmental Response, Compensation, and Liability Act (CERCLA or Superfund) and state mini-CERCLA legislation that is based on—but is not necessarily the same as—CERCLA.

Section 3 examines insurance for the environmental liabilities described in Sect. 2. This section discusses cover for environmental liabilities in general liability insurance policies, in particular the comprehensive general liability policy (now called the commercial general liability policy; collectively CGL policy) and, to a lesser extent in excess general liability policies. The section discusses, among other things, the history of cover for remediating pollution in these policies including pollution exclusions, claims against the policies for remediating pollution, and the withdrawal of cover for pollution-related claims. This history has had a massive influence on cover that is now available in the US for environmental liabilities in general liability policies.

Section 4 then examines environmental insurance policies that were designed specifically to provide cover for environmental liabilities. The section includes a discussion of the evolution of the environmental insurance market in the US including its growth, demise and subsequent re-growth, and the various types of environmental insurance policies.

Finally, Sect. 5 examines the main types of mandatory financial security requirements for environmental responsibilities and liabilities in the US. Financial security requirements for environmental responsibilities are not a driver for environmental insurance because the requirements are for eventualities that will necessarily occur. In contrast, financial security requirements for environmental liabilities are a driver for environmental insurance because insurance covers fortuities, that is, events that may—or may not—occur.

2 Environmental Liabilities

There are three main types of environmental liabilities in the US that pose risks for operators and owners and occupiers of land: (1) third party claims for bodily injury and property damage under state common law; (2) proceedings for the remediation of contaminated land and polluted water and the removal of waste under federal and state legislation; and (3) proceedings for the assessment and restoration of natural resource damage under federal and state legislation.

2.1 Common Law

As a general rule, claims for bodily injury and property damage are brought under the common law of the relevant state, with a limited number being brought under state statutory tort law. Louisiana is an exception due to the application of civil—not common—law.

Tort law is state law. The prerequisites for each tort thus differ between individual states. This chapter therefore focuses on the general principles of common law torts that are set out and summarised in the American Law Institute's highly influential Restatements of the Law of Torts. There are three editions of Restatements of the Law of Torts: the Restatement of Torts (published in 1939); the Restatement (Second) of Torts (published in 1976); and the Restatement (Third) of Torts, which is superseding the Restatement (Second) of Torts.[1]

The Restatements of the Law of Torts cover a wide range of areas of common law. They are not primary legislation and do not state the law of individual states. Instead, they 'restate' common law rules as a series of principles. The highest civil courts and legislatures in some states have adopted—and in some cases modified—specific principles so that they have become law in that state.

There are four main types of common law torts: public and private nuisance; the rule in *Rylands v Fletcher* and/or liability for an abnormally dangerous activity; negligence; and trespass. Depending on the state, other categories of torts include negligent and intentional infliction of emotional distress, fear of cancer or another disease, and medical monitoring.

Exposure to, and other effects of, a wide range of pollutants can cause bodily injury, property damage and related economic loss. Sources of pollutants include hydrocarbons and other pollutants in surface and ground water; pollutants, including waste, on and in land; lead and other pollutants in ambient and indoor air; and asbestos, mould and lead paint in structures.

The US and state constitutions entitle a claimant in a common law tort action to demand a jury to decide the facts of an action. Virtually all actions for common law

[1] Superseded areas of tort law are Liability for Physical and Emotional Harm (2010/2012), Apportionment of Liability (2000), Products Liability (1998), and Liability for Economic Harm (2020).

torts are thus heard by juries, which make factual findings based on the evidence presented to them. Judges make conclusions of law.

In addition to compensatory damages, the law of most, but not all, states authorise punitive damages. In order to be entitled to punitive damages, a plaintiff must – depending on the state – prove that the defendant acted recklessly, unlawfully, fraudulently, or with a conscious or wanton disregard for the known rights or safety of the plaintiff. Also, again depending on the state, the amount of punitive damages that are recoverable may be capped.

As well as bringing an individual action or an action with other claimants, a person that suffers harm may bring a class action, subject to applicable rules of civil procedure.

2.1.1 Nuisance

There are two types of common-law nuisance: private nuisance; and public nuisance.

Private nuisance is a substantial and unreasonable interference with another person's interest in the use and enjoyment of land, or a non-trespassory and unreasonable invasion of another person's interest in land.

Nuisance is based on reasonableness between neighbours, that is, balancing the rights of neighbouring owners and occupiers of land to the reasonable use and enjoyment of their land. The Restatement of Torts states that the standard of liability for nuisance can be intentional, negligence, or strict liability. Depending on the state, this situation has remained since the first Restatement was published.[2] Damages for bodily injury and property damage are available, again with specifics depending on the state in which an action is brought or the applicable state law. An example of a private nuisance action involving environmental liabilities is a claim for property damage caused by the migration of pollutants in groundwater from the defendant's site that results in the poisoning and deaths of livestock on an adjoining farm.

Public nuisance is an unreasonable, unwarranted, or unlawful interference with a right that is common to the general public. In contrast to a private nuisance, public nuisance must affect more than one person—sometimes an entire community or neighbourhood depending on the state. A person who makes a claim for public nuisance must suffer damage that is different from the damage suffered by the general public. An example of a public nuisance action is a claim for bodily injury caused by the pollution of a public water supply system by the defendant. Another example is the use of a site for the disposal of toxic waste. In one case, people living near a clearing in a wood that was used by the defendants to store and dispose of over 100 deteriorating drums of liquid hazardous waste succeeded in a nuisance action.

[2]See Dillard and Brogdon (presentation, May 2017), p. 10 (citing Restatement (First) of Torts s 822 (1930)); https://www.nortonrosefulbright.com/-/media/files/nrf/nrfweb/imported/20161031%2D%2Dnuisance-cases-against-energy-companies-in-texas-pennsylvania-and-other-areas-with-signifi.pdf (accessed on 10.05.2023).

Explosions at the site had resulted in a massive fire. The court had no difficulty in concluding that the defendants had caused a private and public nuisance and issued an injunction to prevent them accepting further waste and to clean up the existing contamination.[3] The site eventually became a Superfund site (see Sect. 2.2.2).

A nuisance may be permanent or continuing. Depending on the state, the differentiating factor may be whether the nuisance is capable of being discontinued or abated as well as, or instead of, the time period during which it takes place. For example, the Maine Supreme Judicial Court decided that there was a factual issue as to whether a permanent or continuing nuisance existed in a case in which the plaintiff had acquired land that was contaminated by waste that had been deposited before 1978. The court stated that there was an issue of fact as to whether the contamination could be cleaned up and, thus, abated. Under Maine law, a continuing nuisance exists if the nuisance is capable of being abated. If the nuisance could be abated, the plaintiff's cause of action would not be barred because a continuing nuisance results in a new cause of action for each day during which the nuisance continues. If the nuisance could not be abated, the plaintiff's cause of action would be barred by the 6-year limitation period under Maine law for a nuisance.[4]

Public nuisance may be an offence as well as a civil action. The introduction of specific offences in statutory law in many states has however abrogated the tort of nuisance as a criminal offence.

The remedies for nuisance are compensatory damages for past (and in some cases future) harm and/or an injunction to prohibit the continuance of the nuisance.

2.1.2 Rule in *Rylands v Fletcher* and Liability for an Abnormally Dangerous Activity

The rule in *Rylands v Fletcher* imposes strict liability on a person that controls land for the natural consequences of the escape of a substance that the person brought onto or that accumulated on the land provided that the use of the land is 'non-natural', that is, not of common usage.[5]

The principle of liability in *Rylands v Fletcher* is the origin of the 'abnormally dangerous activities' test of strict liability in section 20 of the Restatement (Third) of Torts (formerly in Sections 519 and 520 in the Restatement (Second) of Torts).[6]

Section 20 provides that a person that carries out an abnormally dangerous activity (that is, an activity that is not of common usage and that creates a foreseeable

---

[3] *O'Neil v Picillo*, 682 F. Supp. 706 (D. R.I. 1988), *affirmed*, 883 F.2d 176 (first Circuit 1989), *certiorari denied*, 493 U.S. 1071 (1990).

[4] *Jacques v Pioneer Plastics, Inc.*, 676 A.2d 504 (Me 1996).

[5] See Cornell Law School, Legal Information Institute, 'Abnormally Dangerous Activity'; https://www.law.cornell.edu/wex/abnormally_dangerous_activity#:~:text=DEFINITION,is%20exercised%20by%20all%20actors (accessed on 10.05.2023).

[6] Sections 519 and 520 of the Restatement of Torts refer to an 'ultrahazardous' activity.

and highly significant risk of bodily injury or property damage) is strictly liable for the injury or damage that results from the activity. It is not necessary for the defendant to know that its activity was abnormally dangerous; it is sufficient that the defendant should have known or had reason to know that it was abnormally dangerous. It is also not a defence for the defendant to have exercised reasonable care in carrying out the activity.[7]

An example of an abnormally dangerous activity is the storage of hazardous chemicals near residences but not necessarily if the surrounding area is not sensitive. An oil company's disposal of wastewater from its oil production activities was determined to be an abnormally dangerous activity under Utah law because the disposal site was next to a residence that used well water for household purposes.[8] In another case, the Maryland Court of Appeals, that state's highest court, explained that if petroleum had leaked from an underground storage tank into an aquifer that was used for drinking water, the leak 'might' be abnormally dangerous but not if it occurred on a commercial site that was not surrounded by residences.[9]

In some states, the plaintiff is required to prove that the storage is abnormally dangerous in the specific case at issue. As indicated in the above examples, states that have adopted the abnormally dangerous activity test tend to construe the test narrowly.

The remedies for actions brought under the rule in *Rylands v Fletcher* and/or liability for an abnormally dangerous activity are damages and/or an injunction to prohibit the continuance of the activity.

2.1.3 Negligence

A person may bring an action in negligence against a person that breached the legal duty of care owed to the person bringing the action if the breach caused that person damage that is a foreseeable consequence of the breach. The plaintiff must show that the defendant's activities were the actual and proximate cause of the harm suffered by the plaintiff.

The defendant's breach of duty must be shown to have occurred when the harm was caused. In an action for property damage caused by pollutants that seep into groundwater from a pit on the defendant's land and migrate to the plaintiff's land, it may thus be difficult to prove that the person that disposed of the pollutants many years ago was negligent when the prevailing best practice at the time was such disposal.

An example of an unsuccessful action in negligence arose from claims that companies that had sold batteries to a battery recycling facility in Alabama owed a duty of care to residents of the surrounding area. The residents claimed that lead had

---

[7] Ibid.

[8] *Branch v Western Petroleum, Inc.*, 657 P.2d 267 (Utah 1982).

[9] *Rosenblatt v Exxon Company*, 335 Md. 58, 642 A.2d 180 (1994).

leaked from the batteries and had caused bodily injury and property damage to them. The court concluded that the sellers could not have foreseen that the recycling facility would misuse the batteries.[10]

Some states recognise an action in negligence per se. Section 14 of the Restatement (Third) of Torts sets out the prerequisites of such an action as follows. The plaintiff must show that the defendant breached a statute or regulation without an excuse for doing so and the breach caused the plaintiff damage that is a consequence of the breach. Section 15 sets out exceptions including the legislation not being clear and the defendant having exercised due care to attempt to comply with the legislation.[11]

Depending on the state, the breach of legislation may create a presumption of negligence. The harm caused to the plaintiff must be of the same type that the legislation is designed to prevent and the plaintiff was the type of person that the law was designed to protect.

The remedy for an action in negligence and negligence per se is damages.

2.1.4 Trespass

Trespass is an intentional act that results in a direct physical entry or invasion of another person's exclusive possessory interest in land without that person's permission. Depending on the state, the intentional act that results in the entry or invasion may be indirect as well as direct. For example, under Alabama law, a plaintiff may show that an invasion of their land affected an interest in their exclusive possession of that land, the invasion was intentional, the harm was reasonably foreseeable, and the invasion caused substantial actual damage.[12]

There is no need for the trespass to have caused harm to the plaintiff although in such a case, damages are likely to be nominal.

Similarly to nuisance, a trespass may be permanent or continuing. Also, similarly to nuisance, states differ as to whether the trespass ceases when the defendant's wrongful act ceases or whether it continues throughout the time that the harm from the wrongful act could reasonably be abated.

The remedies for trespass are damages for the trespass and, in some states, an injunction to remove the trespass.[13]

---

[10] *Thompson v Mindis Metals, Inc.*, 692 So. 2d 805 (Ala. 1997).

[11] See Cornell Law School, Legal Information Institute, 'negligence per se'; https://www.law.cornell.edu/wex/negligence_per_se#:~:text=According%20to%20Restatement%20(Third)%20of,statute%20is%20designed%20to%20protect (accessed on 10.05.2023).

[12] *Borland v Sanders Lead Company*, 369 So. 2d 523 (Ala. 1979).

[13] See Roisman and Wolff (2010), pp. 159–60.

2.2 *Remediation of Pollution*

Requirements to remediate pollution differ depending on whether the pollution occurs currently or in the future or whether the land or water was polluted in the past. The main legislation that sets out requirements for remediating current and future pollution is environmental permitting legislation. The main legislation that sets out requirements for remediating past pollution is CERCLA.

2.2.1 Environmental Permitting

Federal and state authorities may require persons that deposited waste or that caused water to be polluted without, or in breach of the conditions of, a permit to remove the waste and to remediate the pollution.

The main federal environmental permitting statutes relevant to a discussion of environmental insurance are the Clean Water Act (CWA)[14] which regulates discharges of pollutants into waters of the US, and the Resource Conservation and Recovery Act (RCRA)[15] which regulates the handling, treatment, storage, disposal and transportation of non-hazardous and hazardous waste.

Other major federal environmental permitting statutes include the Clean Air Act (CAA)[16] which regulates air quality and air pollution from stationary and mobile sources, and the Safe Drinking Water Act (SDWA)[17] which regulates public drinking water supply and systems and the quality of drinking water from surface and ground water. This chapter does not discuss the CAA or the SDWA except to note that federal environmental statutes do not establish causes of action for cleaning up air pollution or providing compensation for harm caused by it. Actions for such clean-up costs and compensation have been rejected by most courts that have heard them.[18]

The CWA, RCRA (and the CAA and SDWA) are implemented by the federal government and the states pursuant to co-operative federalism. Under this system, the US Environmental Protection Agency (EPA) has regulatory, oversight and enforcement duties. The EPA promulgates regulations to implement and enforce the statutes under delegated powers from the US Congress, including the establishment of national standards and the review of state standards. Individual states submit plans to the EPA detailing how they will implement and enforce the federal legislation in their state. The plans include state equivalents of the federal statutes

[14] 33 United States Code ss 1251 et seq.

[15] 42 United States Code ss 6901 et seq.

[16] Ibid., ss 7401 et seq.

[17] Ibid., ss 300f et seq.

[18] See Tanaka et al. (2021) sect. 7; https://uk.practicallaw.thomsonreuters.com/0-503-4622?transitionType=Default&contextData=(sc.Default)&firstPage=true (accessed on 10.05.2023).

and regulations. The state statutes and regulations must be at least as stringent as the federal statute and regulations.

Individual states submit their plans to the EPA. If the EPA approves the plan, the state requests the EPA to delegate authority to it to implement and enforce its plan in lieu of the EPA implementing and enforcing the federal legislation in that state. The EPA retains the right to oversee implementation of the state legislation as well as independent enforcement authority.

When the federal statute and/or the EPA's regulations are amended, the state must update its plan to include the amendments and seek approval of the updated plan from the EPA in order to implement and enforce them.

Environmental permits in the US are not integrated. Instead, separate permits are required for activities under the CWA and RCRA (and other statutes).

Discharges of effluent from point sources (that is, discernible, confined and discrete conveyances including outfalls, etc.) into waters of the US require a National Pollutant Discharge Elimination System (NPDES) permit. In states in which the requisite plan under the CWA has been approved by the EPA, the relevant state authority is the regulatory authority for administering the permit. Also under the CWA, the US Army Corps of Engineers or authorised state authorities issue so-called Sect. 404 permits that authorise discharges of dredged or fill material into waters of the US. The term 'waters of the United States' is controversial because it defines the CWA's scope of jurisdiction. The term, which has been subject to rulings by the US Supreme Court as well as several rulemakings by the EPA and the US Army Corps of Engineers, includes waters that are not navigable in the traditional sense.[19]

If the holder of an NPDES permit breaches its conditions, the regulatory authority may order it to cease further discharges, remediate pollutants (including pollutants in sediments) in surface water from discharges that breached the permit's conditions. A person that unlawfully discharges dredged or fill material into waters of the US may also be required to remove the unlawfully discharged material and remediate affected wetlands and waters. If the liable person does not carry out the above remediation, the regulatory authority may carry it out and seek reimbursement of its costs in doing so from the liable person.

A person that discharges effluents from a point source or discharges dredged or fill material into waters of the US without or in breach of the terms and conditions of a permit is subject to civil and criminal sanctions. The penalties are substantial, with

[19] See, e.g., *Rapanos v United States*, 547 U.S. 715 (2006); see also US Environmental Protection Agency and US Army Corps of Engineers, Department of Defense, The Navigable Waters Protection Rule: Definition of 'Waters of the United States', 85 Federal Register 22,250 (21 April 2020), *vacated and remanded by Pascua Yaqui Tribe v US Environmental Protection Agency*, No. CV-20-00266-TUC-RM (D. Ariz. Aug. 30, 2021). The EPA and the US Army Corps of Engineers issued a new final rule with a revised broader definition of 'waters of the United States' on 8 September 2023. US Environmental Protection Agency and US Army Corps of Engineers, Department of Defense, Revised Definition of 'Waters of the United States', 8 Federal Register 61,964 (2023).

daily fines subject to periodic rises for inflation, as well as imprisonment. In addition to actions by the EPA and/or US Army Corps of Engineers, state authorities may bring additional actions under analogous state legislation.

RCRA established a framework for the management of hazardous and non-hazardous waste. Among other things, RCRA requires a company or other person that generates hazardous waste above a specified threshold, or that transports hazardous waste, to obtain a generator identification number (RCRA Site ID) from the EPA. RCRA also requires owners and operators of treatment, storage and disposal facilities (TSDFs) for hazardous waste to obtain a RCRA Site ID and to have a permit to operate the facility. Further, RCRA established controls on the ownership and operation of underground storage tanks that store petroleum or hazardous substances. Section 5 below describes mandatory financial security requirements for TSDFs and underground storage tanks.

As indicated above, the programme for hazardous waste is operated pursuant to co-operative federalism. States have the lead role in regulating underground storage tanks under RCRA under this system. States also have the lead role in implementing the programmes for non-hazardous waste including disposal facilities.

2.2.2 Comprehensive Environmental Response, Compensation, and Liability Act

In the late 1970s, the US Congress recognised that the broad range of major environmental legislation introduced by it during the 'Environmental Decade' of the 1970s did not include legislation that was specifically designed to require the clean up of sites that were contaminated by historic pollution. The absence of specific legislation was particularly acute due to the discovery of severely contaminated sites, in particular Love Canal in New York State at which a school had been constructed over a pit that contained approximately 25,000 tons of chemical waste. In response, the US Congress enacted CERCLA on 11 December 1980. Subsequently, states enacted their own mini-CERCLA legislation.

2.2.2.1 Clean-up Costs

CERCLA established a national programme called the Superfund programme to clean up contaminated land. When the EPA discovers or is notified that a contaminated site may pose a serious threat to human health or the environment, contamination at the site is investigated and assessed to determine whether it needs to be remediated. Part of this process includes—for more seriously contaminated sites—application of a screening process called the hazard ranking system. Sites that receive a specified high score under this system, may be entered onto the National Priorities List (NPL), the list of the most seriously contaminated sites in the US.

The NPL, which is implemented and enforced by the EPA as part of the Superfund programme, includes federal and non-federal facilities.[20] Federal facilities are sites that are owned and/or operated by a department, agency or other body of the US, in particular the Departments of Defense, Energy and the Interior. A non-federal facility is any site other than a federal facility. The EPA implements the NPL for non-federal facilities. The relevant federal governmental body has a major role in implementing the NPL together with the EPA for facilities owned and operated by it. Either the EPA, states, or both implement and enforce requirements for the remediation of sites that are not seriously contaminated enough to be listed in the NPL. There are two types of clean-up measures (called 'response actions'); remedial actions (generally long-term measures) and removal actions (shorter-term measures).

The number of historically contaminated sites proved to be much larger than Congress had anticipated when, as part of CERCLA, it established the Hazardous Substance Response Trust Fund, generally known as Superfund, as a revolving fund to provide funding for implementation and enforcement of the Superfund programme. The trust fund was initially established at US$1.6 billion (EUR 1,596,168,000) for 5 years in 1980.[21] In 1986 after recognising the large scale of the programme, Congress re-authorised the trust fund at $8.5 billion (EUR 8,480,025,000) for 5 years as part of the broad revision of CERCLA by the Superfund Amendments and Reauthorization Act (SARA). In 1986, the US Congress discontinued the trust fund and various dedicated taxes that had been established to fund it. Since that time, Congress has funded the Superfund programme by annual appropriations to the EPA.

Discontinuation of the trust fund does not mean, however, that contaminated sites, including sites on the NPL, have all been cleaned up and that further seriously contaminated sites have not been discovered. As of 23 February 2023, there were 1335 sites listed on the NPL, of which 1177 were non-federal and 158 were federal. A total of 453 sites had been deleted from the NPL, of which 436 were non-federal and 17 were federal. Perhaps most surprisingly—over 40 years after the NPL was established—a further 37 sites were proposed for listing on it, of which 35 were non-federal and two were federal.[22]

Liability under CERCLA is strict, mitigated joint and several, and retroactive. There are no monetary limits to liability for clean-up costs.

Each of the following elements must be shown for there to be liability for clean-up costs:

---

[20] Federal sites are sites that are owned or operated by a department, agency or other body of the US including the Departments of Defense, Energy and the Interior. These bodies have a substantial role in cleaning up their facilities.

[21] 42 United States Code s 9631(a) (repealed).

[22] US Environmental Protection Agency, Superfund: National Priorities List (NPL); https://www.epa.gov/superfund/superfund-national-priorities-list-npl (accessed on 10.05.2023).

- the site is a 'facility'[23] or 'vessel',[24]
- from which there has occurred a 'release'[25] or a threatened release,
- of a 'hazardous substance',[26]
- into the 'environment,' and,
- the person is a 'potentially responsible party' (PRP).

The term 'facility' is broadly defined to include any area in which a hazardous substance is located including roadsides, pipes and stables as well as buildings and hazardous waste landfills. The term 'vessel' is also broadly defined as 'every description of watercraft or other artificial contrivance used, or capable of being used, as a means of transportation on water'.

The term 'release' is also broadly defined, subject to various exclusions, as:

> any spilling, leaking, pumping, pouring, emitting, emptying, discharging, injecting, escaping, leaching, dumping, or disposing into the environment (including the abandonment or discarding of barrels, containers, and other closed receptacles containing any hazardous substance or pollutant or contaminant)....

A release occurs if any quantity of a hazardous substance, however minimal, enters the 'environment'. A 'threatened release' is necessarily much broader.

The term 'environment' is also broadly defined to include navigable waters, coastal waters and 'any other surface water, ground water, drinking water supply, land surface or subsurface strata, or ambient air within the United States or under the jurisdiction of the United States'.

Over 700 substances are defined as 'hazardous substances' by reference to RCRA, the CWA and the CAA. Notably, petroleum in its unused and unadulterated form is excluded from the definition of a 'hazardous substance' under CERCLA. Instead, liability for remediating unused and unadulterated oil is imposed by the Oil Pollution Act.[27]

Four categories of 'persons' may be PRPs:

- owners or operators of a facility;
- owners and operators of a facility at the time of a 'disposal' of a hazardous substance;
- persons that arranged to dispose of or treat a hazardous substance at a facility; and,
- persons that transported a hazardous substance to a facility selected by them.

The term 'person' is broadly defined as:

---

[23] 42 United States Code s 9601(9). The vast majority of proceedings under CERCLA involve facilities.

[24] Ibid., s 9601(28).

[25] Ibid., s 9601(22).

[26] Ibid., s 9601(14).

[27] 33 United States Code ss 2701 et seq.

> an individual, firm, corporation, association, partnership, consortium, joint venture, commercial entity, United States Government, State, municipality, commission, political subdivision of a State, or any interstate body.[28]

The term 'disposal' is defined by reference to RCRA as:

> the discharge, deposit, injection, dumping, spilling, leaking, or placing of any solid waste or hazardous waste into or on any land or water so that such solid waste or hazardous waste or any constituent thereof may enter the environment or be emitted into the air or discharged into any waters, including ground waters.[29]

The 'disposal' of a hazardous substance includes even a minor disturbance of it and has been interpreted by some courts to include passive migration.[30]

The third category, persons that 'arranged to' dispose of or treat[31] a hazardous substance, is the largest category of PRPs especially because it is not required that such a PRP knew or knows the location at which its hazardous substance is disposed. Such PRPs have thus included persons whose used oil was collected and transported to an oil recycling facility and persons that disposed of lead acid batteries or transformers containing polychlorinated biphenyls (PCBs) at a scrap yard in addition to persons that arranged to dispose of hazardous substances at landfills.

The final category of transporters is also broad and includes a person that moved contaminated soil during the grading of a site that was being developed.[32]

CERCLA does not impose secondary liability. The application of company law, however, means that many persons may be secondarily liable including parent companies, shareholders, directors and officers, lenders, successor companies, and trustees and receivers if they otherwise meet the criteria to be PRPs. Protections were added in amendments to CERCLA and subsequent regulations under it for some secondarily liable persons such as lenders.[33]

CERCLA includes a limited number of defences—albeit narrow defences. A PRP has a defence to liability under CERCLA if it proves by a preponderance of the evidence (51% or more) that the release or threatened release of a hazardous substance was caused solely by an act of God, an act of war, the act of a unrelated third party, or a combination of them.[34] In an additional defence to liability under CERCLA introduced by SARA colloquially called the 'innocent purchaser' defence, a PRP has a defence if it carried out 'all appropriate enquiries' into the previous ownership and uses of a facility in accordance with specified 'generally accepted good commercial and customary standards and practices' on or before the date that it

[28] 42 United States Code s 9601(21).

[29] Ibid., s 9601(29); see, ibid., s 6903(3).

[30] See, e.g., *United States v CDMG Realty Company*, 96 F.3d 706 (3d Circuit 1996) (hazardous substances at a closed landfill dispersed by drilling operations may be a disposal).

[31] The term 'treatment' is defined by reference to its (very broad) meaning in RCRA. 42 United States Code s 9601(29) referring to ibid. s 6903(34).

[32] *Tanglewood East Homeowners v Charles-Thomas, Inc.*, 840 F.2d 1568 (fifth Circuit 1988).

[33] 42 United States Code s 9601(20)(A).

[34] Ibid., s 9607(b).

acquired the facility and took 'reasonable steps' to stop any continuing release, prevent any threatened future release, and to 'prevent or limit any human, environmental, or natural resource exposure to any previously released hazardous substance'.[35]

In order not to deter the redevelopment of 'brownfield' sites, CERCLA was again amended in 2002 to provide a defence to a bona fide prospective purchaser subject to specified conditions.[36] Also in 2002, CERCLA was amended to exempt a contiguous property owner from liability from migrating polluted groundwater.[37]

In enacting CERCLA, the US Congress was aware that it was imposing liability on PRPs to clean up contamination when most PRPs had not breached any laws in causing the contamination and, in some cases, had complied with best practices when they disposed of hazardous substances. CERCLA, as amended by SARA, thus includes onerous provisions to ensure that the EPA can successfully bring administrative proceedings against PRPs without delay to a clean-up taking place.

The EPA has the following three options in enforcing CERCLA.

First, the EPA may issue a notice letter that 'requests' one or more PRPs to clean up a contaminated site. If the EPA has determined that 'there may be an imminent and substantial endangerment to the public health or welfare or the environment because of an actual or threatened release of a hazardous substance from a facility' and the PRPs do not clean up the site, the EPA issues a unilateral administrative order—called a section 106 order—to require them to clean it up.[38] If a PRP does not comply with the order, the EPA may ask the US Department of Justice (DOJ) to request a court to enforce the order and/or to seek civil monetary penalties during the period in which the PRP did not comply with it.[39] The penalties have steadily risen to reflect inflation. As of 6 January 2023, the penalties were up to $67,544 per day for breaches of Sect. 106 orders issued after 2 November 2015 for penalties issues on or after 6 January 2023.[40]

Second, the EPA may ask the DOJ to request a court to order PRPs to clean up the site.[41] As above, the DOJ may seek penalties for the period during which a PRP failed to comply with the order.

Third, the EPA may clean up the site and then seek to recover its costs by notifying the PRPs of their potential liability, sending a notice letter to request

[35] Ibid., s 9601(35)(A).

[36] Ibid., s 9601(40).

[37] Ibid., s 9607(q)(1).

[38] Ibid., s 9606(a).

[39] The EPA and other federal administrative authorities and departments do not bring judicial actions themselves. Instead, the DOJ brings judicial actions on their behalf.

[40] US Environmental Protection Agency, Civil Monetary Penalty Inflation Adjustment, 88 Federal Register 988 (6 January 2023).

[41] 42 United States Code s 9606(a).

reimbursement or, if the EPA does not receive reimbursement, requesting the DOJ to bring a judicial cost-recovery action.[42] If the EPA has cleaned up the site itself, the DOJ may seek recovery on behalf of the EPA of the EPA's clean-up costs and punitive damages of up to three times the amount incurred by the EPA in cleaning up the site.[43]

A PRP cannot judicially review the EPA's actions until a site has been cleaned up, the DOJ, on behalf of the EPA, seeks to enforce a unilateral administrative order, or the DOJ brings a judicial action to recover costs incurred by the EPA in cleaning up the site.[44] CERCLA, as amended by SARA, prohibits a court from having jurisdiction to consider such an action. As a result of the prohibition of judicial review of the EPA's actions until the above have occurred, most clean ups under CERCLA are carried out pursuant to settlements.

If the EPA enters into a settlement with a PRP, the settlement is documented by an administrative order on consent or a consent decree (which must first be lodged with a court). Both include a period for public consultation before they are considered and, if agreed by the EPA or the relevant court following the public consultation period, issued. In addition, both must be in the public interest and must expedite the clean-up.[45] Further, a consent decree must include specified conditions including an agreement that the PRP will pay stipulated penalties if it breaches the decree.[46]

Also, both contain a covenant by which the EPA agrees not to pursue the settling PRP for future liability under CERCLA based on the hazardous substance that has been remediated in compliance with the order or decree. The covenant not to sue is generally subject to a 'reopener' which reserves the EPA's right to require the settling party to carry out further clean-up actions for unknown conditions, facts that were not known to the EPA at the time of the settlement (such as the PRP having disposed of a larger quantity of hazardous substances at the site), and failure of the clean-up actions. Thus, even if a PRP settles with the EPA, there is no guarantee that further actions will not follow.

The EPA has several settlement policies to encourage settlements with PRPs. For example, CERCLA authorises the EPA to settle with *de minimis* PRPs, that is, PRPs that made a negligible contribution of hazardous substances to a Superfund site.[47] In order to be entitled to a *de minimis* settlement, the settlement must involve a minor proportion of the clean-up costs at a site, the EPA must determine that the settlement is practicable, and the EPA must also determine that the settlement is in the public interest.

---

[42] Ibid., ss 9604(a), 9607.

[43] Ibid., s 9607(c)(3).

[44] Ibid., s 9613(h).

[45] Ibid., s 9622(f)(1).

[46] Ibid., s 9621(e)(2).

[47] Ibid., s 9622(g).

Another settlement policy authorised by CERCLA is for *de micromis* PRPs, that is, PRPs that have contributed an even smaller proportion of hazardous substances to a contaminated site than *de minimis* PRPs.

As a general rule, it is very beneficial for a PRP that falls into the above categories to settle with the EPA. This is because CERCLA, as amended by SARA, authorises contribution actions by PRPs against other PRPs.[48] A PRP that enters into a settlement with the EPA (or state authority if it is the 'lead agency' at a Superfund site), however, is automatically protected from such contribution actions.[49]

2.2.2.2 Natural Resource Damage

In addition to imposing liability for cleaning up contaminated sites, CERCLA imposes liability for damage to 'natural resources', known as natural resource damage. Proceedings for natural resource damage differ markedly from proceedings brought by the EPA for cleaning up contamination.

CERCLA defines 'natural resources' as:

> land, fish, wildlife, biota, air, water, ground water, drinking water supplies, and other such resources belonging to, managed by, held in trust by, appertaining to, or otherwise controlled by the United States . . . any State or local government, any foreign government, any Indian tribe, or, if such resources are subject to a trust restriction on alienation, any member of an Indian tribe.[50]

Only 'natural resource trustees', that is trustees of federal, state, Indian and foreign natural resources may bring proceedings for natural resource damage. The trustees are generally the heads of governmental agencies for natural resources such as the US Secretaries of the Interior and Commerce and state equivalents. Persons that are liable for natural resource damage are the same PRPs that are liable for cleaning up contamination.

In order to establish liability for natural resource damage, a natural resource trustee must prove that there was a 'release' or threatened release of a 'hazardous substance' from a 'facility' into the 'environment' and that the injury to, destruction of, or loss of the natural resource was caused by the release.[51] This liability is more stringent that liability for cleaning up contamination because the trustee must prove that there was an actual injury to a natural resource and that the injury was the result of the release of a hazardous substance. That is, the trustee must prove that there is a causal link between the release of the hazardous substance and the injury to the natural resource. In comparison, the EPA need prove only that an actual or threatened release of a hazardous substance led to the incurrence of clean-up costs whether or not such costs resulted from the PRP's action or omissions.

---

[48] Ibid., s 9613(f)(1).

[49] Ibid., s 9613(f)(2).

[50] Ibid., s 9601(16).

[51] Ibid., s 9607(a)(4).

Further, unlike liability for clean-up costs, liability for natural resource damage is limited to $50 million (EUR 49,761,250) for one release or any one incident involving a release.[52] Still further, unlike the imposition of retroactive liability under CERCLA for clean-up costs, liability for natural resource damage applies only if the damage to a natural resource and the release of a hazardous substance occurred after 11 December 1980, the date on which CERCLA was enacted.[53]

In addition to liability for restoring natural resources, PRPs are liable for the costs of assessing the damage. Thus, PRPs are liable for the following in respect of natural resource damage:

- costs of restoring a damaged natural resource to its baseline condition or its replacement by the acquisition of an equivalent natural resource;
- costs of any emergency restoration measures;
- lost use of the natural resource from the time it was damaged until it is fully restored or replaced;
- reasonable and necessary costs of assessing the above damage including administrative costs and expenses; and,
- interest on amounts that are recoverable.[54]

A claim for the lost use of a natural resource takes the form of compensation for losses that arise from the use or non-use of the resource from the time that it was damaged until it is restored. Use values include consumptive uses such a fishing, hunting, drinking groundwater as well as non-consumptive (passive) uses such as photographing a natural resource, swimming, hiking and camping.

The costs of cleaning up a Superfund site and paying for damage to natural resources can be huge. The large size of sites that are listed on the NPL—and the costs of remediating them—is illustrated by the Bunker Hill Superfund site, albeit one of the largest Superfund sites. Mining for lead, zinc and silver has been carried out in the area since 1883, resulting in soil, groundwater and surface water contamination as well as historic emissions from lead smelters. The site covers an area of 1500 square miles (3885km^2) including 166 miles (267 km) of rivers and a 21 square mile (54 km^2) core area called the 'box'.

The EPA listed the site on the NPL in 1983 since which time the EPA, state authorities, Indian tribes and PRPs have been involved in its remediation and restoration. Clean-up actions include remediating approximately 7000 residential gardens, commercial properties and parks and other public areas, and the restoration of mining and milling sites, railways, recreation areas and drinking water.[55] The total

[52] Ibid., s 9607(c)(1)(D).

[53] Ibid., s 9607(f)(1).

[54] 43 Code of Federal Regulations s 11.15.

[55] Idaho Department of Environmental Quality, Bunker Hill Superfund Site; https://www.deq.idaho.gov/waste-management-and-remediation/mining-in-idaho/bunker-hill-superfund-site/ (accessed on 10.05.2023).

costs of cleaning up the site and restoring natural resources at it has been estimated at $2 billion (EUR 1,986,550,000).[56]

Not surprisingly given the huge costs involved, there has been litigation concerning liability for cleaning up the site and the scope and nature of the clean up and natural resource damage. Costs arising from the litigation include $180 million (EUR 179,079,300) from a settlement between the Hecla Mining Company and the EPA, money from litigation involving other mining companies, and $435 million (EUR 432,774,975) from the bankruptcy of the American Smelting and Refining Company, Inc. (ASARCO).[57] In addition, a settlement for natural resource damage in the Coeur d'Alene Basin at the Superfund site between the US and the Coeur d'Alene Tribe and seven mining companies was for $59,625 (EUR 59,306) plus a specified amount of future proceeds from future ore smelting activities.[58]

3 General Liability Policies

The Superfund programme and state mini-Superfund programmes have had a massive effect on the insurance industry not only in the US but also Europe. The main types of re/insurance policies that have been affected are general/public liability policies, excess policies, and reinsurance treaties for both types of policies.

[56] See Malinowski (2010); https://www.law360.com/articles/196191/epa-hacks-away-at-2b-idaho-superfund-case (accessed on 10.05.2023).

[57] US Environmental Protection Agency, Superfund Site: Bunker Hill Mining & Metallurgical Complex, Smelterville, Idaho, Cleanup Activities; https://cumulis.epa.gov/supercpad/SiteProfiles/index.cfm?fuseaction=second.cleanup&id=1000195#content (accessed on 10.05.2023). See, e.g., *United States v Asarco, Inc.*, 214 F.3d 1104 (ninth Circuit 2000); *United States v Asarco, Inc.*, 430 F.3d 972 (ninth Circuit 2005); US Department of Justice, Hecla Mining Company to Pay £263 Million in Settlement to Resolve Idaho Superfund Site Litigation and Foster Cooperation (13 June 2011); https://www.justice.gov/opa/pr/hecla-mining-company-pay-263-million-settlement-resolve-idaho-superfund-site-litigation-and; (accessed on 10.05.2023) US Department of Justice, Department Of Justice, EPA Reach Agreement with Two Idaho Mining Companies to Secure Wastewater Treatment and Remove a Barrier to New Mining Operations (12 March 2018); https://www.justice.gov/opa/pr/department-justice-epa-reach-agreement-two-idaho-mining-companies-secure-wastewater-treatment (accessed on 10.05.2023)The total amount for clean up and restoration from the ASARCO bankruptcy was $1.79 billion (EUR 1,784,531,550). See US Environmental Protection Agency, Case Summary: ASARCO 2009 Bankruptcy Settlement; https://www.epa.gov/enforcement/case-summary-asarco-2009-bankruptcy-settlement (accessed on 10.05.2023).

[58] US Department of the Interior, Trustees Settle Natural Resource Damage Claims at Bunker Hill Superfund Site in Idaho (19 January 2012); https://www.doi.gov/restoration/news/Coeur-dAlene-CD-entered#:~:text=The%20settling%20companies%20will%20pay,the%20Coeur%20d'Alene%20Basin (accessed on 10.05.2023).

3.1 *Types of General Liability Policies*

The most common general liability policy in the US that was affected by CERCLA and mini-CERCLAs was the CGL policy, which was designed by the Insurance Services Office (ISO), was standardised in the 1940s and has been amended many times since then.

CGL policies—like other general liability policies—indemnify the insured for legal liabilities incurred by the insured for third-party claims for bodily injury and property damage and other harms such as personal and advertising injury caused by acts or omissions of the insured. In addition to the duty to indemnify in such policies, there is an additional duty to defend the insured against third-party claims. Whereas cover for indemnified costs is subject to a limit of liability, cover for defence costs is unlimited.

As a general rule, CGL and other general liability policies are occurrence-based. That is, the policies provide cover for an 'occurrence' (or a similar term such as 'accident') which is defined in relation to the time during which a claimant suffers bodily injury, property damage or another covered harm instead of the time at which a claim is made against the insured. General liability policies thus have a 'long tail' of liability in that claims may be made against past policies.

Excess policies indemnify insureds for the same types of losses as general liability policies. as their name implies, they are excess to primary policies. That is, the general liability policy, as the primary policy, provides cover up to a specified limit of liability. An excess policy provides cover above that limit. There may be many layers of excess policies especially for large insureds with operations in many states and other jurisdictions. For example, an insured may have a primary general liability policy with a limit of liability of $5 million (EUR 4,973,675), an excess liability policy with a limit of liability of $5 million excess the limit of the primary policy, and another excess liability policy with a limit of liability of £10 million (EUR 9,947,350) excess the limit of the first excess policy. In this simplified example, there are three layers of cover: $5 million by the primary policy; $5 million excess $5 million by the first excess liability policy; and $10 million excess $10 million by the second excess liability policy for a total of $20,000,000 (EUR 19,894,700). If the excess policy is underwritten by London market insurers, especially insurers at Lloyd's, they are typically subscription policies. That is, they are underwritten by more than one—sometimes many—insurers. In a subscription policy, each insurer specifies its limit of liability.

Unlike general liability policies, excess policies typically do not provide cover for defence costs. As a general rule, the insurer in an excess general liability policy has a right to participate in the defence of the insured but not a duty to do so. If cover is provided for defence costs, it tends to be subject to the limit of liability for indemnified costs.

3.2 State Regulation of Insurance

Insurance law in the US is state law.[59] This means among other things that each state has its own statutes, regulations and policies that govern the regulation of insurance and insurers that carry out business in that state. State insurance regulatory bodies must approve versions of the CGL and other general liability policies (as well as other types of insurance policies) before they may be offered for sale in that state. Insurers that offer such policies must also be authorised by the state regulatory bodies. This means that although the wording of the CGL policy is standardised—albeit subject to amendments by individual insurers—the standardised wording must be authorised by each state before it is offered for sale and the insurer that offers it for sale must be authorised to carry out insurance business in each state in which it is sold.

In contrast, excess and other surplus line policies are subject to less regulation. A surplus lines policy provides cover for risks that are not covered by state-approved policies offered for sale by insurers that are admitted to carry out business in a state. There is no need for the wording of such policies to be approved by each state or for an insurer that offers such policies to be admitted to carry out business in the state, although the sale of such policies is subject to eligibility requirements by individual states.

Surplus lines policies must, however, be offered for sale through a surplus lines broker licensed by the state insurance regulatory authority to place (sell) non-approved policies from non-admitted insurers in a state. The non-admitted insurer must also be listed by the state insurance regulatory authority as an authorised non-admitted insurer and must file its policy forms and rates with the state authority. In contrast to approved wordings offered for sale by admitted insurers, the regulation of surplus lines policies is focused on individual sales of such policies, that is, the surplus line transaction rather than the policy.[60]

3.3 State Insurance Law

As indicated above, insurance law in the US is state law. In addition to each state governing the business of insurance in that state, the judiciary in each state has its own rules for the interpretation—called rules of construction—for insurance policies. The rules are based on rules of construction in contract law with some

[59] The McCarran-Ferguson Act, codified at 15 United States Code ss 1011–1015, provides that the 'business of insurance ... shall be subject to the laws of the several states which relate to the regulation or taxation of such business').

[60] See generally National Association of Insurance Commissioners, Surplus Lines (last updated 11 May 2022); https://content.naic.org/cipr-topics/surplus-lines (accessed on 10.05.2023).

significant differences due to the contract being interpreted being an insurance policy.

A basic rule—with the proviso that the rules differ between individual states—is that a court will construe an insurance policy in order to determine the mutual consent of the parties when they entered into it. Words and terms in the policy are interpreted in the context of the policy as a whole. If a court determines that a word or term is ambiguous, that is, susceptible to more than one reasonable meaning, it may examine extrinsic evidence to determine its meaning. Courts in some states examine extrinsic evidence in order to determine whether a word or term is ambiguous.

An insured has the burden of proving that an insurance policy provides cover for a claimed loss. If the insured does so—and the insurer disputes coverage—the insurer has the burden of providing that an exclusion or another provision of the policy applies to deny cover.

Some courts have adopted the 'reasonable expectations doctrine'. According to this doctrine, a court does not rely solely on the terms and conditions of the policy but may consider whether extrinsic evidence shown by the insured leads to a conclusion that the insured's reasonable expectations concerning the scope of cover provided by the policy were not met even though the terms and conditions of the policy bar cover.

The application of state courts' rules of construction means, for example, that the highest court in one state may interpret words in the CGL policy—and other standardised policies—differently than the highest court in another state. As discussed below, this has had major implications for the interpretation of the CGL policy and issues related to cover for environmental liabilities.

3.4 Pollution Exclusions

The CGL policy and most primary and excess general liability policies did not—and do not—provide cover for liabilities to remediate contamination/pollution or to restore natural resources that have arisen from the wide range of federal and state environmental legislation that has been enacted since the 1970s.

Before 1969, such policies did not have exclusions to bar claims from such liabilities. There was no need to do so because most federal and state legislation enacted before the 1970s did not impose the onerous environmental liabilities introduced in legislation since 1970. In addition, claims under common law torts for bodily injury and property damage caused by exposure to contamination or pollution were relatively infrequent.

3.4.1 Commercial General Liability Policies

In 1969, following the oil spill from offshore drilling near Santa Barbara, California, and the increased exposure to insurers for claims from gradual pollution incidents, the Insurance Rating Board (IRB), a predecessor of the ISO, drafted an optional endorsement to the CGL policy that barred cover for bodily injury or property damage caused by an occurrence other than a 'sudden and accidental' occurrence. The exclusion, called a qualified pollution exclusion because of the write back of cover for sudden and accidental occurrences, bars cover for:

> bodily injury or property damage arising out of the discharge, dispersal, release or escape of smoke, vapors, soot, fumes, acids, alkalis, toxic chemicals, liquids or gases, waste materials or other irritants, contaminants or pollutants into or upon land, the atmosphere or any water course or body of water; but this exclusion does not apply if such discharge, dispersal, release or escape is sudden and accidental.

In 1971, when the US Congress had begun introducing major environmental statutes, the IRB included the qualified pollution exclusion in the body of the proposed revision of the CGL policy. In 1973, the revised CGL policy was issued with the exclusion in it.

In 1983, in *Jackson Township Municipal Utilities Authority v Hartford Accident & Indemnity Company*,[61] the New Jersey Court of Appeals interpreted the term 'sudden and accidental' in the qualified pollution exclusion to mean 'unexpected and unintended'. The court held that the insurer had a duty to defend a municipal utility company that was claimed to have negligently polluted groundwater from a landfill resulting in bodily injury and property damage.

The effect of the case on the provision of cover for environmental liabilities was almost instantaneous. By 1984, most reinsurance treaties no longer provided cover for environmental liabilities for risks in the US. Also in 1984, states began approving the use of an endorsement that barred all cover for pollution from the CGL policy.

In 1986, the ISO incorporated an absolute pollution exclusion into the body of the standard CGL policy that was similar to the 1984 endorsement. The exclusion not only barred cover for bodily injury and property damage from 'the actual, alleged or threatened discharge, dispersal, release or escape of pollutants', it also barred cover for '[a]ny loss, cost, or expense arising out of any governmental direction or request that you test for, monitor, clean up, remove, contain, treat, detoxify or neutralize pollutants'.

The term 'pollutants' was defined as:

> any solid, liquid gaseous or thermal irritant or contaminant, including smoke, vapor, soot, fumes, acids, alkalis, chemicals and waste. Waste includes materials to be recycled, reconditioned or reclaimed'.

---

[61] *Jackson Township Municipal Utilities Authority v Hartford Accident & Indemnity Company*, 186 N.J. Super. 156, 451 A.2d 990 (1982).

The ISO subsequently issued various amendments to the absolute pollution exclusion for the CGL policy including application of the exclusion to the personal injury coverage clause.

In 1988, the ISO issued a 'total pollution exclusion' as an optional endorsement to replace the absolute pollution exclusion in the body of the CGL policy. The total pollution exclusion was broader than the absolute pollution exclusion in that it also barred cover for claims that arise from products liability, completed operations and specified off-site operations carried out by an insured. The exclusion also made the causal link between the damage and harm suffered by a claimant less stringent, thus making it easier for an insurer to prove the exclusion.

By the mid-1990s, some insurers began to offer endorsements that provided limited cover for pollution incidents on a time element or claims-made basis. That is, the endorsement provides cover for bodily injury or property damage caused by an incident that begins and ends and is reported to insurers within specified times during the policy period. For example, a time element endorsement may provide cover for bodily injury and property damage that arises from the discharge, dispersal, release or escape of pollutants provided that the discharge, dispersal, release or escape begins and ends within 72 h during the policy period and is reported to insurers within 14 days after it begins. The time element clause endorsements may be used to limit or replace the absolute pollution exclusion in the body of a standard CGL or other general liability policy.

3.4.2 Excess General Liability Policies

The Lloyd's Underwriters Non-Marine Association (NMA) first drafted a qualified pollution exclusion for general liability policies in 1959. The exclusion which was directed mainly at pollution risks from subsurface oil and gas was rarely used however.

In 1970, the NMA published a broader qualified pollution exclusion called NMA 1685. NMA 1685 bars cover for:

1. Personal Injury or Bodily Injury or loss of, or damage to, or loss of use of property directly or indirectly caused by seepage, pollution or contamination, provided always that this paragraph (1) shall not apply to liability for Personal Injury or Bodily Injury or loss of or physical damage to or destruction of tangible property, or loss of use of such property damaged or destroyed, where such seepage, pollution or contamination is caused by a sudden, unintended and unexpected happening during the period of this Insurance.
2. The cost of removing, nullifying or cleaning up seeping, polluting or contaminating substances unless the seepage, pollution or contamination is caused by a sudden, unintended and unexpected happening during the period of this Insurance.
3. Fines, penalties, punitive or exemplary damages.

This Clause shall not extend this Insurance to cover any liability which would not have been covered under this Insurance had this Clause not been attached.

Also in 1970, the NMA published an absolute pollution exclusion called NMA 1686. NMA 1686 bars cover for:

1. Personal Injury or Bodily Injury or loss of, damage to or loss of use of property directly or indirectly caused by seepage, pollution or contamination.
2. The cost of removing, nullifying or cleaning-up seeping, polluting or contaminating substances.
3. Fines, penalties, punitive or exemplary damages.

NMA 1685 and NMA 1686 have tended to be used in excess general liability policies underwritten by the London market for US risks.

3.5 Claims for Past Pollution

As indicated in Sect. 3.4 above, cover for claims for bodily injury and property damage from environmental liabilities in general liability policies for risks in the US is severely limited; cover for clean-up costs is barred subject to being covered by optional endorsements. The main reason for the lack of broader cover is the interpretation by a substantial number of courts of provisions in the CGL and other general liability policies to provide cover for claims for historic pollution incidents under CERCLA.

This section briefly discusses judicial rulings on the following key issues concerning whether the CGL and other general liability policies provide cover for claims arising from CERCLA and state mini-CERCLAs:

- duty to defend administrative proceedings;
- duty to indemnify and a legal obligation to indemnify;
- clean-up costs as 'damages';
- timing of an 'occurrence';
- ISO qualified pollution exclusion;
- NMA 1685; and.
- absolute and total pollution exclusions.

The section focuses on the 1973 standard version of the CGL policy because insurance coverage claims against the CGL policy were predominantly brought against this version of the policy.[62] The section also focuses on claims under CERCLA whilst recognising that provisions of state mini-CERCLAs may differ from CERCLA.

[62]The discussion in the following section is drawn from Aylward (2018); https://www.morrisonmahoney.com/resource/673-50-state-environmental-coverage-case-law-survey-2018 (accessed on 10.05.2023) and Fogleman (2005); chap. 12.

3.5.1 Duty to Defend Administrative Proceedings

The duty to defend in the 1973 standard CGL policy obliged the insurer 'to defend any *suit* against the insured seeking damages' (emphasis added).[63] There has been a split in courts that have been called on to rule on this issue.

As discussed in Sect. 2.2.2 above, the EPA implements and enforces the Superfund programme and state environmental authorities implement and enforce mini-CERCLAs. Both the EPA and state authorities do this by sending notice letters to PRPs and issuing a unilateral administrative order if a PRP does not respond positively to a notice letter.

Some courts have held that the word 'suit' includes administrative procedures in actions brought under CERCLA. The reasoning behind this conclusion is that notice letters and unilateral administrative orders are the functional equivalents of a lawsuit because of their coercive and adversarial nature. The counter argument is that the word 'suit' means a civil action that begins when a claim is filed in a court, unambiguously means a lawsuit, and that the EPA has discretion to choose whether to issue administrative proceedings or to request the DOJ to file a lawsuit on its behalf. Some courts have reached a hybrid conclusion depending on the language in a notice letter or order.

3.5.2 Duty to Indemnify and a Legal Obligation to Indemnify

The 1973 standard CGL policy obliged an insurer to 'pay on behalf of the insured all sums which the insured shall become legally obligated to pay as damages because of ... bodily injury or ... property damage'.

As discussed in Sect. 2.2.2 above, CERCLA and mini-CERCLA's have usually been enforced by administrative—rather than judicial—proceedings with the exception, in some cases, of consent orders filed with a court after a settlement was reached between the EPA (or state authority) and a PRP. As with the issue of whether the 1973 CGL policy required an insurer to defend an insured in the absence of a suit, the issue also arose whether an insured was 'legally obligated' to pay clean-up costs when there were no judicial proceedings requiring the insured to do so. That is, if an insured negotiates and enters into an administrative consent order with the EPA or a state authority in the absence of judicial proceedings against the insured or the insured enters into a judicial consent order in the absence of other judicial proceedings, is the insured 'legally obligated' to pay clean-up costs?

As with the issue concerning the duty to defend a suit in the absence of judicial proceedings, there has been a split between courts on this issue.

Some courts have held that the insurer had a duty to indemnify the insured because the nature of the obligation to clean up a contaminated site is the same regardless of whether judicial proceedings have been filed. Some courts also

[63] The word 'suit' was subsequently defined in the 1986 version of the CGL policy.

reasoned that it was sufficient for a statute—such as CERCLA—to impose strict liability for cleaning up a site. Other courts have held that there must be judicial proceedings that require an insured to clean up a contaminated site and that an insured is not 'legally obligated' to do so in the absence of such proceedings.

3.5.3 Clean-up Costs As Damages

The 1973 standard version of the CGL policy provided that the insurer:

> will pay on behalf of the insured all sums which the insured shall become legally obligated to pay *as damages* because of . . . bodily injury or . . . property damage (emphasis added).

The policy further provided that the insurer was obligated to 'defend any suit against the insured seeking *damages* on account of such bodily injury or property damage' (emphasis added).

The policy did not define the word 'damages'.

This issue was particularly crucial because a ruling that clean-up costs are not 'damages' means that the costs are not covered by the CGL standard policy. As described in Sect. 3.1 above, CGL and other general liability policies indemnify the insured for legal liabilities incurred by the insured for third-party claims for bodily injury and property damage and other specified harms. The 1973 version of the standard CGL policy—and virtually all excess general liability policies underwritten when the 1973 version was used—did not include clean-up costs as a specified harm.

During the 1980s, courts that ruled on the issue tended to conclude that clean-up costs were not within the meaning of the term 'damages'. This trend changed in 1990, however, when the highest courts of California, Massachusetts, Minnesota, North Carolina and Washington concluded that clean-up costs were within the term 'damages'.[64] The trend then became virtually irreversible in favour of insureds.

The reasoning by courts that concluded that clean-up cost were 'damages' included the word 'damages' being considered to be ambiguous, thus construing the ambiguity against insurers. Some courts applied the rules of construction to conclude that the ordinary and non-technical meaning of the word 'damages' includes clean-up costs and that such costs are the functional equivalent of compensation for property damage. Some other courts applied public policy arguments to conclude that it would be unfair for liability for the costs of cleaning up contamination to depend on the manner in which the claim was brought and that insureds should be encouraged to clean up contamination rather than subsequently receiving a

[64] See *AIU Insurance Company v Superior Court,* 51 Cal. 3d 807, 274 Cal. Rptr. 820, 799 P.2d 1253 (1990); *Hazen Paper Company v United States Fidelity & Guaranty Company,* 407 Mass. 689, 555 N.E.2d 576 (1990); *Minnesota Mining & Manufacturing Company v Travelers Indemnity Company,* 457 N.W.2d 175 (Minn. 1990); *C.D. Spangler Construction Company v Industrial Crankshaft & Engineering Company*, 326 N.C. 133, 388 S.E.2d 557 (1990); *Boeing Company v Aetna Casualty & Surety Company*, 113 Wash. 2d 869, 784 P.2d 507 (1990).

demand from the EPA and other authorities to reimburse them for costs incurred in cleaning up contamination.

The minority of courts that held that clean-up costs were not 'damages' reasoned that CERCLA distinguishes between clean-up costs and natural resource damage, and that clean-up costs are injunctive or restitutionary relief and not monetary compensatory.

3.5.4 Timing of an Occurrence

The 1973 standard CGL policy provided that:

> The company will pay on behalf of the insured all sums which the insured shall become legally obligated to pay as damages because of
>
> A. bodily injury or,
> B. property damage.

to which this insurance applies, caused by an occurrence.

The word 'occurrence' was defined as:

> an accident, including continuous or repeated exposure to conditions, which results in bodily injury or property damage neither expected nor intended from the standpoint of the insured.

The term 'property damage' was defined as:

1. physical injury to or destruction of tangible property which occurs during the policy period, including the loss of use thereof at any time resulting therefrom, or,
2. loss of use of tangible property which has not been physically injured or destroyed provided such loss of use is caused by an occurrence during the policy period.

The term 'bodily injury' was defined as:

> bodily injury, sickness or disease sustained by any person which occurs during the policy period, including death at any time resulting therefrom.

The insured bears the burden of proving that an 'occurrence' happened during the policy period.

By the time that the number of insurance coverage cases involving environmental liabilities had become substantial, courts had already been called on to determine the timing of an 'occurrence' in asbestos-related claims. The CGL standard policy clauses set out above are not precise with regard to the timing of bodily injury suffered by an insured in such claims, especially claims for bodily injury from mesothelioma. This is because mesothelioma has a long latency period so that there is a time lag of up to or over 40 years between the time that an individual is exposed to asbestos and the time at which mesothelioma is manifested or diagnosed.

In ruling on asbestos-related claims, courts developed four theories to determine the time at which 'bodily injury' occurred: the exposure theory; the manifestation theory; the injury-in-fact or actual injury theory; and the continuous or multiple trigger theory. When insurance coverage cases under CERCLA and state mini-CERCLAs arose, the highest courts of a substantial number of states had already adopted trigger theories that they then applied to the environmental cases.

Application of the exposure trigger to claims for clean-up costs requires insurers that underwrote policies that were in force when land or water was exposed to pollutants to respond to a claim for property damage. Adoption of this trigger means that insurers that underwrote CGL and other general liability policies many years before the EPA or state authority brought a claim for clean-up costs were determined to provide cover for the damage subject to other terms and conditions of the policy.

Application of the manifestation trigger to such claims requires insurers that underwrote general liability policies when the property damage manifested itself—or was discovered—to respond to the claims, again subject to other terms and conditions of the policy.

Application of the injury-in-fact trigger means that any general liability policy that was on the risk on the date(s) when actual damage occurred must respond.

Finally, the continuous trigger combines the exposure, injury-in-fact and manifestation triggers.

Application of the triggers can have a significant effect on the extent of cover provided by the CGL and excess general liability policies. If a court applies the exposure trigger, claims are concentrated on older policies that may not include pollution exclusions. Conversely, application of the manifestation trigger concentrates claims on newer policies that are more likely to have pollution exclusions. If, for example, the contamination was discovered after 1986, the absolute or total pollution exclusions would apply. Application of the continuous trigger—and less so the injury-in-fact trigger—results in claims being spread over many years.

Further, if an insured has primary and excess general liability policies, application of the manifestation trigger concentrates claims into a single policy year, with application of the exposure trigger concentrating claims into more, but still a limited number of, policies. Application of the continuous trigger meanwhile spreads claims across a longer time period.

In addition, application of the manifestation trigger means that excess policies are more likely to be triggered versus application of the continuous trigger, which means that claims tend to be concentrated on primary policies. That is, application of the manifestation trigger concentrates claims in a single year that is more likely to reach the limit at which the excess general liability policies apply. Application of the continuous trigger spreads the claims across multiple primary general liability policies so that the claims are much less likely to reach that limit.

3.5.5 ISO Qualified Pollution Exclusion

As discussed in Sect. 3.4.1 above, the 1973 CGL standard policy bars cover for bodily injury or property damage unless the 'discharge, dispersal, release or escape [of pollutants] is sudden and accidental'. Whilst the insurer has the burden of proving that an exclusion applies, the courts are split on whether the insurer—or the insured—has the burden of proving that an exception to an exclusion applies.

More crucially, the courts are split on the meaning of the term 'sudden and accidental'. This matters because the contamination at most sites that have been cleaned up under CERCLA and state mini-CERCLAs is gradual contamination that sometimes occurred over many years.

Some courts have concluded that the term 'sudden and accidental' is unambiguous and has only a temporal meaning. Many reasons have been given for this conclusion including the following:

- the plain and ordinary meaning of the word 'sudden' has a temporal element;
- the word 'sudden' does not add anything to the term 'sudden and accidental' unless it has a temporal element;
- the word 'sudden' means abrupt when it is read in the context of the entire policy; and,
- the word 'accident' is generally understood to mean 'unexpected and unintended', therefore the word 'sudden' would be redundant unless it had a temporal meaning.

Reasons for the conclusion that the word 'sudden' is ambiguous and not intended to be limited to a temporal meaning include the following:

- the word 'accident' in the definition of an 'occurrence' does not have a temporal meaning, therefore, the word 'accidental' in the pollution exclusion does not have a solely temporal meaning;
- if insurers intended the word 'sudden' to have only a temporal meaning, they would have defined the term to include such a meaning;
- the drafting history of the qualified pollution exclusion by the ISO indicates that the term 'sudden' was not intended to have only a temporal meaning; and,
- the split between the courts on the meaning of the word 'sudden' suggests that the word can reasonably be read to have more than one meaning.

3.5.6 NMA 1685

As indicated in Sect. 3.4.2 above, excess general liability policies for US risks at the time when the 1973 version of the standard CGL policy was in force tended to include NMA 1685.

In contrast to the large number of cases that have ruled on the meaning of the ISO qualified exclusion, only a few courts have construed the meaning of NMA 1685. Some of these courts have ruled that the word 'sudden' in the term 'sudden, unintended and unexpected' in the exception to the exclusion is ambiguous and can have a meaning that is not temporal as well as a temporal meaning. For example, the Colorado Supreme Court concluded that a reasonable reading of the term 'sudden, unintended and unexpected' is 'unprepared for, unintended and unexpected.[65]

Other courts have ruled that the word 'sudden' is unambiguous and has only a temporal meaning. For example, the Delaware Supreme Court ruled that the word 'sudden' in the term 'sudden, unintended and unexpected' 'clearly and unambiguously includes a temporal element synonymous with abrupt'.[66]

3.5.7 Absolute and Total Pollution Exclusions

There are far fewer insurance coverage cases concerning absolute and total pollution exclusions in post-1986 CGL and excess general liability policies than coverage cases concerning the qualified pollution exclusion.

Many of the cases that concern these exclusions focus on the meaning of the word 'pollutants'. For example, the Georgia Supreme Court ruled, in a case concerning a claim for carbon monoxide poisoning, that carbon monoxide was within the definition of a 'pollutant' in the absolute pollution exclusion.[67] The Missouri Supreme Court ruled that the absolute pollution exclusion is unambiguous and that toxic emissions from lead smelting were 'unequivocally a pollutant under the plain meaning of the term'.[68]

Some courts have ruled that the exclusions are limited to 'environmental pollution'. For example, the Wyoming Supreme Court ruled that the total pollution exclusion did not bar cover for a claim concerning hydrogen sulphide gas that poisoned and killed a worker in an oil field. The court discussed the history of the exclusion and its purpose in barring cover for clean-up costs under federal and state legislation. The court stated that '[w]e cannot believe that any person in the position of the insured would understand the word "pollution" in this exclusion to mean anything other than environmental pollution'.[69]

It is not possible to reconcile rulings on the absolute and total pollution exclusions. For example, the Alabama Supreme Court stated that:

> Our review and analysis of the entire body of existing precedent reveals that there exists not just a split of authority, but an absolute fragmentation of authority. Cases may be found for and against every issue any litigant has ever raised, and often the cases reaching the same conclusion as to a particular issue do so on the basis of differing, and sometimes inconsistent, rationales.[70]

---

[65] *Public Service Company of Colorado v Wallis & Companies,* 986 P.2d 814 (Colo. 1999).

[66] *E.I. du Pont de Nemours & Company v Allstate Insurance Company,* 693 A.2d 1059 (Del. 1997).

[67] *Reed v Auto-Owners Insurance Company*, 667 S.E.2d 90 (Ga. 2008).

[68] *Doe Run Resources Corporation v American Guarantee & Liability Insurance Company,* 531 S.W.3d 508 (Mo. 2017).

[69] *Gainsco Insurance Company v Amaco Production Company,* 53 P.3d 1051 (Wyo. 2002).

[70] *Porterfield v Audubon Indemnity Company,* 956 So. 2d 789 (Ala. 2002).

4 Environmental Insurance Policies

The introduction of environmental liabilities in federal and state legislation and the limitation and then exclusion of cover for environmental liabilities in the CGL and other general liability policies led some insurers to develop environmental liability policies that specifically provide cover for such liabilities. A further reason was requirements for mandatory financial security for environmental liabilities, as examined in Sect. 5 below.

4.1 Evolution of the Environmental Insurance Market

The environmental insurance market in the US began, albeit slowly, in the late 1970s. The first policies to be introduced during this era were for losses arising from sudden and accidental pollution consisting of claims for bodily injury and property damage, clean-up costs for pollutants that had migrated or were likely to migrate from an insured's site, and the costs of cleaning up hazardous substances that had been disposed off-site. Despite less than five insurers issuing environmental insurance policies at that time, the market grew rapidly due to the demand for them.

In addition to the increase in legislation that imposed liability for environmental risks, another driver for the demand was the introduction of mandatory financial security for environmental liabilities during the operational phase of TSDFs (see Sect. 2.2.1 above and Sect. 5 below).

By 1986, however, the environmental insurance market collapsed, leaving only one insurer that offered broad environmental insurance policies and a few insurers that offered restrictive cover with low policy limits and high deductibles. Three reinsurers remained in the market but they all offered cover for environmental liabilities only on a facultative basis rather than by treaty.

The main reason for the collapse in the environmental insurance market was a change in the EPA's policy for implementing the Superfund programme. Before 1986, the EPA had tended to use money from the Superfund to clean up sites and then seek reimbursement of its costs from PRPs, with the result that it recovered only a small percentage of the costs. Under the new policy of 'enforcement first', the EPA actively pursued PRPs to clean up contaminated sites at their cost.

In the second half of the 1980s, the environmental insurance market began to grow again. Most of the growth however resulted from an increase in the number of lines of coverage rather than an increase in capacity. By the late 1980s, environmental insurance policies had been introduced for operational risks from sites other than TSDFs. As discussed in Sect. 2.2.1 above, legislation that required such sites to have environmental permits, and the number of sites subject to such requirements, increased throughout the 1970s and 1980s.

A further driver for environmental insurance was the increase in the number of environmental consultants and contractors. The increase was due to the remediation of sites under the Superfund and state mini-Superfund programmes and, especially, the risk of liability under CERCLA and mini-CERCLAs. A particular driver for policies for environmental consultants was the substantial revision of CERCLA by SARA in 1986, to include, among other things, the 'innocent purchaser' defence (see Sect. 2.2.2.1 above). In order to fall within the defence, it was necessary for purchasers of land to instruct environmental consultants to carry out 'all appropriate enquiries' into the previous ownership and uses of the land that was being purchased. Existence of the defence meant that environmental consultants began to be instructed in the vast majority of commercial transactions.

Another major driver for the growth in the number of environmental insurance policies was increased awareness of liabilities under CERCLA that arose after the EPA cleaned up contamination at a farm and then began proceedings to recover its costs against the bank that had foreclosed on the farm and continued to own it for four and a half years. In 1986 in a judgment that was widely publicised in the lending community, a court in Maryland concluded that the bank was a PRP.[71]

A further driver was the introduction of programmes by states to facilitate the redevelopment of 'brownfield' sites, that is, 'abandoned, idled or under-used industrial and commercial facilities where expansion or redevelopment is complicated by real or perceived environmental contamination'.[72] Many states introduced these programmes in the 1980s and 1990s to provide incentives, such as grants and favourable tax treatment, to remediate these sites.

Yet another driver was the Base Realignment and Closure Act (BRAC) and other programmes by the US Department of Defense and the US Department of Energy to sell military bases to the private sector. Insurers designed environmental insurance policies specifically to cover risks involving in buying and redeveloping the sites.

A further driver was the continued introduction of mandatory financial security requirements for environmental liabilities, as discussed in Sect. 5 below.

By 2000, four insurers, with a total of approximately $1.2 billion (EUR 1.151 billion) in annual premiums led the US environmental insurance market.[73]

Despite this growth, there remains room for substantial further growth due largely to the lack of understanding about environmental insurance policies and restricted cover for environmental liabilities in general liability (and property) policies.

In 2019, the National Association of Insurance Commissions (NAIC) stated as follows:

> a great number of insureds are often mistakenly under the impression they are covered for pollution releases under their general liability and property policies. However, these policies either restrict or completely exclude such coverage leaving their policyholders exposed to potentially very costly risks.
>
> ...

---

[71] *United States v Maryland Bank & Trust,* 632 F. Supp. 573 (D. Md. 1986).

[72] US Environmental Protection Agency, Handbook of Tools for Managing Federal Superfund Liability Risks at Brownfields and Other Sites (EPA 330-B-98-001, November 1998).

[73] Hannah (2000), pp. 4–5; https://www.irmi.com/articles/expert-commentary/the-us-environmental-liability-insurance-market (accessed on 10.05.2023).

> Given that many . . . brokers also do not fully understand pollution exclusions in general liability policies, the principal constraint in the market for environmental insurance seems to be the product distribution channel. For a long time [brokers] have been instructed with technically inaccurate information regarding pollution exclusions. Thus, if [brokers] do not understand how policy exclusions work, they cannot inform and educate their clients about the need to buy environmental insurance.[74]

The NAIC subsequently repeated its concerns in 2022 as follows:

> A major concern in the market is a great number of insureds mistakenly believe they are covered for pollution releases under their general liability and property policies. However, these policies either restrict or exclude such coverage, leaving their policyholders exposed to potentially costly risks.
>
> Litigation regarding coverage of environmental risks is often the result of misinterpretation of policies whose language about pollution points more to exclusion than coverage. Specialists argue that if there is not an explicit insuring agreement for losses caused by pollutants, the coverage is not true environmental insurance. Often, policyholders were not aware of their environmental loss exposures nor were they informed about environmental insurance coverage options.
>
> Given that many agents and brokers also do not fully understand pollution exclusions in general liability policies, the principal constraint in the market for environmental insurance seems to be the product distribution channel. Agents have long been instructed with technically inaccurate information regarding pollution exclusions. Thus, if agents do not understand how policy exclusions work, they cannot inform and educate their clients about the need to buy environmental insurance.[75]

In 2022, the NAIC reported that the environmental insurance industry was entering a 'transformative' era, with the market becoming mature. The NAIC stated that the market was estimated to be approximately $2 billion (EUR 1,986,550,000) in annual premiums, with its growth outpacing that of the general property and casualty market.[76]

---

[74] National Association of Insurance Commissioners (2019); https://cc.bingj.com/cache.aspx?q=National+Association+of+Insurance+Commissioners%2c+%e2%80%98Environmental+Insurance%e2%80%99&d=4600524307961009&mkt=en-GB&setlang=en-GB&w=ktOsQSHMhz8sE6Kj6bSi2vwecR_FxzDY (accessed on 10.05.2023).

[75] National Association of Insurance Commissioners, 'Environmental insurance' (last updated 23 June 2022); https://content.naic.org/cipr-topics/environmental-insurance (accessed on 10.05.2023).

[76] Ibid; see also Aon, Environmental Market Status Q1 2021; https://www.aon.com/getmedia/9337eb54-3e93-4098-8b4b-8e3bbf412368/Environmental-Market-Status-Q1-2021_Final.aspx; Watson (2019); https://www.wtwco.com/en-US/Insights/2019/11/insurance-marketplace-realities-2019-fall-update-environmental (accessed on 10.05.2023).

4.2 *Types of Environmental Insurance Policies*

There are many types of environmental insurance policies for US risks. This section describes the following main types of environmental insurance policies offered by insurers for such risks:

- Pollution legal liability (PLL) policies;
- Contractors pollution liability and professional liability policies;
- Environmental consultants professional service policies;
- Cost cap policies;
- Lender liability policies;
- Owner/contractor controlled environmental insurance programmes; and.
- Finite risk policies.[77]

Other types of environmental insurance policies include asbestos and lead abatement policies for businesses carrying out such operations; products pollution liability policies for risks from products such as remediation equipment; and policies for claims concerning pollution control equipment and tanks.

4.2.1 Pollution Legal Liability Policies

A PLL policy provides cover, depending on the insurer, for a wide range of liabilities arising from contamination including the following:

- remediation of contamination at and migrating from the insured's site from gradual as well as sudden and accidental pollution;
- third-party claims for bodily injury and property damage from pollutants at or migrating from the insured's site;
- natural resource damage claims for such damage at the insured's site or emanating from it;
- remediation of pollution from waste from an insured's site following its disposal at an authorised waste disposal site;
- business interruption at the insured's site from pollution incidents that occur at the site;
- remediation of pre-existing contamination at the insured's site provided that the insured did not cause it and was not aware of the contamination when it acquired the site;
- costs of emergency measures to remediate contamination or pollution; and,
- associated legal expenses.

Cover for the remediation of pre-existing contamination is sometimes covered by separate policies called property transfer policies.

---

[77] Much of this section on the types of environmental insurance policies is drawn from Fogleman (2020); https://ec.europa.eu/environment/legal/liability/studies.htm (accessed on 10.05.2023).

4.2.2 Contractors' Pollution Liability and Professional Liability Policies

Contractors' pollution liability and professional liability policies provide cover for many different types of contractors. The contractors' pollution liability part of the policy provides cover for contractors that own and occupy a job site for the same type of liabilities as a PLL policy. Policies for this part tend to be offered on a blanket basis for an entire construction project or for periods of up to 10 years.

The contractors' professional liability part of the policy provides cover for negligent acts, and errors and omissions. Cover is provided to many types of contractors. The policy also provides cover for claims for bodily injury and property damage, remediation measures and related legal expenses as a result of pollution conditions caused by contracting and completed operations carried out by or on behalf of a contractor. Contracting operations are operational risks during construction. Completed operations are operations carried out by a contractor after the date of substantial completion of the construction, thus extending the policy period beyond this date.

In addition to being offered as a combined policy, the two coverage parts may be offered as separate policies.

Although, depending on state law, it may not be mandatory for contractors to have such policies, clients often decline to instruct contractors that do not have it.

4.2.3 Environmental Consultants Professional Service Policies

Environmental consultants professional service policies, which are sometimes called errors and omissions policies, provide cover for advice provided by environmental consultants as well as activities carried out by them. As with contractors although, depending on state law, it may not be mandatory for environmental consultants to have such policies, clients often decline to instruct consultants that do not have it.

4.2.4 Cost Cap Policies

A cost cap policy, sometimes called a remediation stop loss policy, provides cover for unanticipated cost overruns in the remediation of a contaminated site. These policies usually require detailed negotiations between the insurer and the insured because they are based on the estimated remediation costs—which must be understood by the insurer as well as the insured and its broker.

The policies tend to have an excess of a buffer of between 5 and 10% of the cost of the project above the estimated costs of carrying out the remediation.

4.2.5 Lender Liability Policies

A lender liability policy provides cover for the outstanding balance of a loan if land that is collateral for the loan becomes contaminated or, unknown to the insured, is already contaminated. The policies provide protection to the lender by avoiding the lender having to foreclose on the property and potentially becoming liable for its remediation.

4.2.6 Owner/Contractor Controlled Environmental Insurance Programmes

An owner controlled environmental insurance programme provides wrap around cover for bodily injury and property damage and the costs of remediating contamination to the owner or developer of a site that is being developed or redeveloped for third-party claims. In addition to providing cover for the owner during the construction phase of the project, they also provide cover for sub-contractors as additional insureds.

A contractor controlled environmental insurance programme is similar to an owner controlled environmental insurance programme except that it focuses on environmental liabilities due to the contractor not owning the land that is being developed. The policy combines PLL and contractors' professional liability policies. As with contractors' pollution liability policies, the policy may be extended to provide cover for completed operations as well as contracting operations.

Both types of policies may bar cover for specified sub-contractors such as those that carry out high risk works such as demolition or are below a specified size.

4.2.7 Finite Risk Policies

A finite risk policy provides cover for businesses that know they must remediate contamination at a site but do not know the time at which they must do so. The policy consists of a specified amount and an insurance policy. The insured pays the specified amount and a premium to the insurer for a specified amount of time (the policy period).

If the insured is required to remediate the contamination during the policy period, the specified amount plus the policy are used to pay the costs up to the limit of indemnity in the policy. If the insured is not required to remediate the contamination during the policy period, the insurer returns the specified amount plus a percentage of interest earned on that amount during the policy period to the insured.

Some finite risk policies also provide cover for third-party claims for bodily injury and property damage during the policy period.

5 Mandatory Financial Security Requirements

Mandatory financial security for environmental responsibilities and liabilities has existed for over 40 years in the US, with the requirements steadily increasing from the 1980s to have become a trend that shows no signs of abating.[78]

In order to impose mandatory financial security, a competent authority must be able to identify the person who is required to provide evidence of it. The typical means of doing this is to impose financial security requirements as a condition of an environmental permit. Financial security that is required for remediating contamination meanwhile, arises because the person that must provide evidence of it has already been identified.

This section describes the difference between mandatory financial security for environmental responsibilities and mandatory financial security for environmental liabilities. The section then describes the different types of mandatory financial security instruments and mechanisms. Finally, the main categories of financial security requirements for environmental responsibilities and liabilities are discussed.

5.1 Mandatory Financial Security for Environmental Responsibilities and Liabilities

There is a crucial difference between mandatory financial security requirements for environmental responsibilities and such requirements for environmental liabilities. Financial security for environmental responsibilities tends to be non-controversial because the event that triggers the requirement for financial security, such as the closure of a facility, inevitably arises. Financial security for environmental liabilities, however, is controversial. This is because such requirements oblige an owner or operator of a facility or other structure to provide evidence of its ability to remediate pollution or meet third-party claims for bodily injury or property damage from pollution only if there is an accidental release of pollutants from the facility or structure—an event that may never arise.

Whereas it is possible to estimate the costs of environmental responsibilities by reference to, say, the amount of waste at a landfill, it is more difficult to estimate the cost of environmental liabilities. Requirements for financial security for environmental liabilities in the US therefore tend to be based on minimum levels for various categories of operators. As discussed in Sect. 5.3.1 below, the levels tend not to change after they have been established by legislation.

[78]Much of this section on mandatory financial security requirements is drawn from Fogleman (2020); https://ec.europa.eu/environment/legal/liability/index.htm (accessed on 10.05.2023).

5.2 Types of Mandatory Financial Security Instruments and Mechanisms

As discussed below, there are many types of financial security instruments and mechanisms.

The main financial security instruments for environmental liabilities in addition to insurance are trust funds, bonds, and letters of credit. The main financial security mechanisms are self insurance, and corporate guarantees.

Another term for self-insurance is financial test. The mechanism is based on the operator providing evidence that it is above a certain size (as determined by its net working capital or net worth) and that it would have sufficient money to pay a claim without obtaining financial security in advance from a third party. A corporate guarantee is based on the parent or other affiliate of the operator providing evidence that it is above a specified size (as again determined by its net working capital or net worth) and could therefore pay a claim without the operator obtaining financial security in advance from a third party. Both are obviously only as good as the continued financial viability of the operator or affiliated company.

Insurance is not typically used as evidence of financial security for environmental responsibilities because it provides cover for fortuities and not certainties. Insurance may however be a component of evidence of financial security together with a dedicated source of funding to provide cover for the risk of the costs of, say, closing a landfill exceeding the estimated costs or closure of the landfill occurring before sufficient funds have been accumulated in the dedicated funding instrument. Insurance may also be a component of a financial security requirement that combines evidence of environmental liabilities and environmental responsibilities.

When insurance is an acceptable type of financial security, it is subject to specified details that may include the following. If a term in the policy is inconsistent with the certificate or endorsement that must be provided as evidence of financial security, the policy is statutorily amended to be consistent with the certificate or endorsement. Insurers may be required to certify that the wording of the policy is identical to the certificate or endorsement.

The insurance policy must generally be assignable to a successor owner or operator of the facility to which the policy applies. If the purpose of the policy is to provide a minimum level of financial security for a potential environmental liability, the indemnity limit of the policy must equal or exceed that level. The minimum level of the policy must generally exclude legal and similar fees and expenses. That is, any additional cover provided by the policy must be over and above cover provided for the subject matter of the financial security requirement.

In addition, exclusions in a policy that provides financial security for cleaning up contamination are generally limited to bodily injury and property damage from a pollutant, natural resource damage and civil and criminal penalties. The above restrictions mean that an insured may satisfy financial security requirements by an insurance policy that provides cover for environmental liabilities that are not subject to the financial security requirements as well as environmental liabilities that are subject to the requirements. In such a case, cover for the financial security requirements is ring-fenced from other cover provided by the policy.

Further, the insurer and the insured may only cancel a policy after providing a specified time period of notice to the regulatory authority. This requirement provides the regulator with time to continue the policy if it wishes.

Reasons for the cancellation may be limited to non-payment of premiums. In this respect, an insured and insurer may be required to provide proof of payment of the premium before the regulatory authority agrees that it has received adequate evidence of financial security.

5.3 *Main Financial Security Requirements*

A wide range of federal and state environmental legislation includes financial security requirements for environmental responsibilities and liabilities. This section discusses the following main types of such requirements: transportation of hazardous substances and materials; TSDFs, non-hazardous waste facilities; underground storage tanks; and the remediation of contamination.

5.3.1 Transportation of Hazardous Materials

The Motor Carrier Act 1980[79] was introduced as part of the federal government's deregulation of the interstate trucking industry. Among other things, the Act requires commercial businesses that transport 'oil', 'hazardous materials', 'hazardous substances' and 'hazardous waste' to have evidence of financial security.[80] The above terms are defined by reference to whether they are 'capable of posing an unreasonable risk to health, safety and property when transported in commerce' and whether they have been designated as 'hazardous'.[81] The harm covered by the financial security are 'public liability, property damage, and environmental restoration'.[82]

Regulations under the Act define the term 'environmental restoration' as:

> restitution for the loss, damage, or destruction of natural resources arising out of the accidental discharge, dispersal, release or escape into or upon the land, atmosphere, watercourse, or body of water of any commodity transported by a motor carrier. This shall include the cost of removal and the cost of necessary measure taken to minimize or mitigate damage to human health, the natural environment, fish, shellfish, and wildlife.[83]

---

[79] 49 United States Code ss 31131 et seq.

[80] Ibid., s 31139(d).

[81] 49 Code of Federal Regulations s 171.8.

[82] 49 United States Code s 31139(d).

[83] 49 Code of Federal Regulations s 387.5.

The amount of financial security that is required depends on the type of carriage, including the weight of the vehicle and the commodity (hazardous materials, hazardous substances, etc.) that is transported. Most hazardous substances transported in bulk in a vehicle with a weight rating of 10,001 or more pounds (4536 kg) require financial security in a minimum of $5,000,000 (EUR 4,908,750).

A carrier may provide evidence of financial security by insurance, a guarantee, a surety bond issued by a bonding company authorised to do business in the US, or qualification as a self-insurer.[84]

5.3.2 Hazardous Waste Treatment, Storage and Disposal Facilities

Owners and operators of TSDFs and hazardous waste management units (HWMUs; such as containers, tanks, containment buildings, waste piles and surface impoundments) are subject to both environmental responsibility and environmental liability requirements.[85]

The requirements are based on the phase of the TSDF or HWMU, that is, the operational phase during which hazardous waste is treated, stored or disposed; the closure phase; or the post-closure (aftercare) phase.

5.3.2.1 Environmental Responsibility Requirements

Environmental responsibility requirements are based on ensuring that the owner or operator of a TSDF or HWMU has sufficient financial means for the closure and post-closure phases. Activities that must be carried out during the closure phase include closing the TSDF or HWMU, removing all the waste from it, decontaminating or removing equipment, and cleaning up surrounding soil. Activities that must be carried out during the post-closure phase include monitoring, record-keeping and other long-term maintenance for at least 30 years after closure.[86]

If the owner or operator of a HWMU closes the unit pursuant to 'clean closure' requirements including closing tanks, surface impoundments and removing waste piles, it is not required to have evidence of financial security for post-closure activities. There is no need for such financial security because, as indicated above, all waste and contamination would have been removed from the unit and surrounding soil.

---

[84] 49 United States Code s 31139(f)(1).

[85] See generally US Environmental Protection Agency, Financial Assurance Requirements for Hazardous Waste Treatment, Storage and Disposal Facilities; https://www.epa.gov/hwpermitting/financial-assurance-requirements-hazardous-waste-treatment-storage-and-disposal (accessed on 10.05.2023).

[86] 40 Code of Federal Regulations s 264.117(a)(1).

The amount of financial security that is required is based on the estimated amount of money that would be paid to a third party to carry out measures specified in the permit for the TSDF or HWMU. The estimated amounts are adjusted annually during the operational phase of the TSDF or HWMU.

The owner or operator of a TSDF or HWMU that is not owned by the federal or a state government may provide evidence of financial security by the following instruments:

- a trust fund[87];
- a surety payment bond or performance bond together with a standby trust fund[88];
- an irrevocable letter of credit together with a standby trust fund[89]; and,
- an insurance policy.[90]

In addition, evidence of financial security may be provided by the following mechanisms:

- self insurance or financial test according to net working capital criteria or tangible net worth criteria[91]; and,
- a corporate guarantee from a direct corporate parent company, a corporate grandparent, a sibling corporation or a company that has a 'substantial business relationship' with the owner or operation of the facility or unit.[92]

A company has a 'substantial business relationship' with another company if there is a pattern of recent or ongoing business transactions that satisfies the administrator of the relevant regional office of the EPA.[93]

It is not necessary fully to fund a trust fund or a standby trust fund. Instead, the funds may generally be accumulated over a specified period of time.

The requirements for financial security are set out in detailed regulations that include templates for each type of instrument and mechanism. The template for an insurance policy is a certificate of insurance/endorsement.

5.3.2.2 Environmental Liability Requirements

Financial security requirements apply to TSDFs during its operational phase. During this phase, the owner or operator must have financial security for 'bodily injury and

[87] Ibid., s 264.143(a) or s 265.143(a).

[88] Ibid., ss 264.143(b), (c) or s 265.143(b).

[89] Ibid., s 264.143(d) or s 265.143(c).

[90] Ibid., s 264.143(e) or s 265.143(d).

[91] Ibid., s 264.143(f) or s 265.143(e).

[92] Ibid., s 264.143(f) or s 265.143(e).

[93] See 'RCRA Subtitle C Financial Assurance: Instrument Review', ASTSWMO Training Conference, Oklahoma City, OK, 15 August 2017; http://astswmo.org/files/Meetings/2017/HWMM_Workshop/Presentations/Pease.pdf (accessed on 10.05.2023).

property damage to third parties caused by sudden accidental occurrences' that arise from operations at the facility or a group of facilities.[94] Examples of sudden accidental occurrences include releases of hazardous waste caused by a fire or explosion, that is abrupt releases rather than continuous or repeated releases.

Land-based TSDFs must also have financial security for third-party bodily injury and property damage caused by a facility's or group of facilities' 'nonsudden accidental occurrence'. Examples of nonsudden accidental occurrences include a leak of liquid waste from a landfill or a surface impoundment that pollutes groundwater.

The minimum levels of financial security have not been revised since they were phased in between 1983 and 1985. They are as follows.

The minimum level of financial security required for third-party bodily injury and property damage from a sudden and accidental occurrence is $1000,000 (EUR 992,335) for each occurrence, with an aggregate annual limit of $2,000,000 (EUR 1,984,670). The minimum level of financial security required for third-party bodily injury and property damage from a nonsudden and accidental occurrence is $3,000,000 (EUR 2,977,005), with an aggregate annual limit of $6,000,000 (EUR 5,953,500). The requirements for sudden and nonsudden and accidental occurrences may be combined with a minimum level of $4,000,000 (EUR 3,969,000) for each occurrence with an aggregate annual limit of $8,000,000 (EUR 7,938,000).

Claims may be made directly against insurers and other providers of financial security if the insured is in bankruptcy proceedings or if a claim that arises from activities that are subject to mandatory financial security cannot be made against the insured because a court cannot obtain jurisdiction over the insured despite acting with reasonable due diligence.[95]

The following are acceptable financial security instruments:

- a financial test or self-insurance;
- a financial guarantee;
- an irrevocable letter of credit;
- an insurance policy;
- a surety bond;
- a trust fund; and,
- a combination of the above.[96]

Trust funds and standby trust funds must be fully funded. Unlike trust funds and standby trust funds for environmental responsibility requirements, funds for them may not be gradually accumulated.

[94] 40 Code of Federal Regulations s 264.147(a).

[95] 42 United States Code s 6924(t)(2).

[96] 40 Code of Federal Regulations s 264.147.

5.3.2.3 Non-hazardous Waste Facilities

States set financial security environmental responsibility and environmental liability requirements for solid waste treatment, transfer and disposal facilities including landfills.

The types of instruments and mechanisms tend to be the same as those for TSDFs.

5.3.2.4 Underground Storage Tanks

Financial security requirements for owners and operators of underground storage tanks that contain 'regulated substances' were introduced by RCRA in 1988 together with technical requirements for such tanks. A 'regulated substance' is defined as petroleum and 'any hazardous substance' under CERCLA except hazardous waste.[97]

The owner or operator of an underground storage tank is liable for third-party claims for property damage and bodily injury caused by a sudden or nonsudden and accidental release of a regulated substance from the tank, and the cost of corrective actions to remediate contamination from the release of the contents of the tank.[98]

The term 'bodily injury' is defined according to applicable state law with the proviso that it does 'not include those liabilities which, consistent with standard insurance industry practices, are excluded from coverage in liability insurance policies for bodily injury'.[99]

In a similar manner, the term 'property damage' is defined according to applicable state law with the proviso that it does 'not include those liabilities which, consistent with standard insurance industry practices, are excluded from coverage in liability insurance policies for property damage'. The definition further states as follows: 'However, such exclusions for property damage shall not include corrective action associated with releases from tanks which are covered by the policy'.[100]

As with the minimum levels of financial security for TSDFs, the minimum levels of financial security for underground storage tanks have not changed since they were introduced in 1988.

The minimum levels for financial security for underground storage tanks that contain petroleum are based on a per occurrence level as follows:

- $1000,000 (EUR 992,335) for petroleum marketers or tanks that handle an average of over 10,000 gallons (37,854 litres) of petroleum each month based on an annual throughput for the previous calendar year; and

---

[97] 42 United States Code s 6991(7); see, ibid., s 9601(14).

[98] Ibid., s 6991b(d).

[99] 40 Code of Federal Regulations s 280.92.

[100] Ibid.

- $500,000 (EUR 496,182.50) for all other owners or operators of underground storage tanks.[101]

The minimum levels for financial security for underground storage tanks that contain petroleum are based on an aggregate basis are as follows:

- $1000,000 for owners and operators of 1 to 1000 underground storage tanks; and
- $2,000,000 (EUR 1,986,550,000) for owners or operators of 101 or more underground storage tanks.[102]

Acceptable financial security instruments are as follows:

- a financial test or self insurance;
- a corporate guarantee;
- a letter of credit;
- a surety bond;
- a trust fund;
- membership in a risk retention group; and,
- a combination of the above.[103]

As with other financial security requirements issued by the EPA, the regulations set out detailed requirements including a pro forma for each type of financial security instrument.[104] The pro forma for insurance is a certificate of insurance or an endorsement from a qualified insurer or a risk retention group.[105]

5.3.2.5 Remediation of Contamination

As described in Sect. 2.2.2.1 above, the US EPA enters into unilateral administrative orders and consent decrees with PRPs that set out the terms and conditions under which the PRPs agree to remediate sites in the Superfund programme. Both the orders and decrees include financial security requirements to ensure that the PRP will have sufficient funding to carry out the remediation or if not, the EPA can use the money set aside by the financial security requirements to remediate the site itself.

According to the guidance issued by the EPA to its regional offices, acceptable instruments include insurance policies as well as trust funds, financial test, financial guarantees, payment or performance bonds and letters of credit.

The guidance states that an insurance policy must be between the PRP and an authorised insurer. The policy must also provide that the insurer agrees to pay claims

[101] Ibid., s 280.93(a).

[102] Ibid., s 280.93(b).

[103] Ibid., ss 280.95 to 280.03; see, ibid., s 280.94.

[104] Ibid., s 280.97.

[105] Ibid.

by the EPA against the PRP or the policy in connection with issues related to the site that is being cleaned up.[106]

References

Cases

AIU Insurance Company v Superior Court, 51 Cal. 3d 807, 274 Cal. Rptr. 820, 799 P.2d 1253 (1990)
Boeing Company v Aetna Casualty & Surety Company, 113 Wash. 2d 869, 784 P.2d 507 (1990)
Borland v Sanders Lead Company, 369 So. 2d 523 (Ala. 1979)
Branch v Western Petroleum, Inc., 657 P.2d 267 (Utah 1982)
C.D. Spangler Construction Company v Industrial Crankshaft & Engineering Company, 326 N.C. 133, 388 S.E.2d 557 (1990)
Doe Run Resources Corporation v American Guarantee & Liability Insurance Company, 531 S. W.3d 508 (Mo. 2017)
E.I. du Pont de Nemours & Company v Allstate Insurance Company, 693 A.2d 1059 (Del. 1997)
Gainsco Insurance Company v Amaco Production Company, 53 P.3d 1051 (Wyo. 2002)
Hazen Paper Company v United States Fidelity & Guaranty Company, 407 Mass. 689, 555 N.E.2d 576 (1990)
Jackson Township Municipal Utilities Authority v Hartford Accident & Indemnity Company, 186 N.J. Super. 156, 451 A.2d 990 (1982)
Jacques v Pioneer Plastics, Inc., 676 A.2d 504 (Me 1996)
Minnesota Mining & Manufacturing Company v Travelers Indemnity Company, 457 N.W.2d 175 (Minn. 1990)
O'Neil v Picillo, 682 F. Supp. 706 (D. R.I. 1988), *affirmed,* 883 F.2d 176 (1st Circuit 1989), *certiorari denied,* 493 U.S. 1071 (1990)
Porterfield v Audubon Indemnity Company, 956 So. 2d 789 (Ala. 2002)
Public Service Company of Colorado v Wallis & Companies, 986 P.2d 814 (Colo. 1999)
Rapanos v United States, 547 U.S. 715 (2006)
Reed v Auto-Owners Insurance Company, 667 S.E.2d 90 (Ga. 2008)
Rosenblatt v Exxon Company, 335 Md. 58, 642 A.2d 180 (1994)
Tanglewood East Homeowners v Charles-Thomas, Inc., 840 F.2d 1568 (5th Circuit 1988)
Thompson v Mindis Metals, Inc., 692 So. 2d 805 (Ala. 1997)
United States v Asarco, Inc., 214 F.3d 1104 (9th Circuit 2000)
United States v Asarco, Inc., 430 F.3d 972 (9th Circuit 2005)
United States v CDMG Realty Company, 96 F.3d 706 (3d Circuit 1996)
United States v Maryland Bank & Trust, 632 F. Supp. 573 (D. Md. 1986)

Legislation

33 United States Code

[106] Office of Site Remediation Enforcement (2015), pp. 6–7; https://www.epa.gov/sites/production/files/2015-04/documents/fa-guide-2015.pdf (accessed on 10.05.2023).

40 Code of Federal Regulations
42 United States Code
43 Code of Federal Regulations
49 Code of Federal Regulations
49 United States Code
McCarran-Ferguson Act, codified at 15 United States Code, Sections 1011-1015
US Environmental Protection Agency, Civil Monetary Penalty Inflation Adjustment, 87 Federal Register 1676 (12 January 2022)
US Environmental Protection Agency and US Army Corps of Engineers, Department of Defense, The Navigable Waters Protection Rule: Definition of 'Waters of the United States', 85 Federal Register 22,250 (21 April 2020), *vacated and remanded by Pascua Yaqui Tribe v US Environmental Protection Agency*, No. CV-20-00266-TUC-RM (D. Ariz. Aug. 30, 2021)
US Environmental Protection Agency and US Army Corps of Engineers, Department of Defense, Revised Definition of 'Waters of the United States', 86 Federal Register 69,372 (2021)

Other Governmental Documentation

'RCRA Subtitle C Financial Assurance: Instrument Review' (15 August 2017) ASTSWMO Training Conference, Oklahoma City, OK; http://astswmo.org/files/Meetings/2017/HWMM_Workshop/Presentations/Pease.pdf. Accessed on 10 May 2023
Idaho Department of Environmental Quality, Bunker Hill Superfund Site; https://www.deq.idaho.gov/waste-management-and-remediation/mining-in-idaho/bunker-hill-superfund-site/. Accessed on 10 May 2023
Memorandum from Kenneth Patterson (21 January 2022) Director, Regional Support Division, Office of Site Remediation Enforcement, US Environmental Protection Agency to Regional Superfund Legal Branch Chiefs, Regions 1–10; https://www.epa.gov/system/files/documents/2022-01/106b-penalty-matrix-mem-2022.pdf. Accessed on 10 May 2023
Office of Site Remediation Enforcement (6 April 2015) Office of Enforcement and Compliance Assurance (OECA), U.S. Environmental Protection Agency, 'Guidance on Financial Assurance in Superfund Settlement Agreements and Unilateral Administrative Orders', 6–7; https://www.epa.gov/sites/production/files/2015-04/documents/fa-guide-2015.pdf. Accessed on 10 May 2023
US Department of Justice (13 June 2011) Hecla Mining Company to Pay £263 Million in Settlement to Resolve Idaho Superfund Site Litigation and Foster Cooperation; https://www.justice.gov/opa/pr/hecla-mining-company-pay-263-million-settlement-resolve-idaho-superfund-site-litigation-and. Accessed on 10 May 2023
US Department of Justice (12 March 2018) Department Of Justice, EPA Reach Agreement with Two Idaho Mining Companies to Secure Wastewater Treatment and Remove a Barrier to New Mining Operations; https://www.justice.gov/opa/pr/department-justice-epa-reach-agreement-two-idaho-mining-companies-secure-wastewater-treatment. Accessed on 10 May 2023
US Department of the Interior (19 January 2012) Trustees Settle Natural Resource Damage Claims at Bunker Hill Superfund Site in Idaho; https://www.doi.gov/restoration/news/Coeur-dAlene-CD-entered#:~:text=The%20settling%20companies%20will%20pay,the%20Coeur%20d'Alene%20Basin. Accessed on 10 May 2023
US Environmental Protection Agency, Case Summary: ASARCO 2009 Bankruptcy Settlement; https://www.epa.gov/enforcement/case-summary-asarco-2009-bankruptcy-settlement. Accessed on 10 May 2023
US Environmental Protection Agency, Financial Assurance Requirements for Hazardous Waste Treatment, Storage and Disposal Facilities; https://www.epa.gov/hwpermitting/

financial-assurance-requirements-hazardous-waste-treatment-storage-and-disposal. Accessed on 10 May 2023
US Environmental Protection Agency, Superfund Site: Bunker Hill Mining & Metallurgical Complex, Smelterville, Idaho, Cleanup Activities; https://cumulis.epa.gov/supercpad/SiteProfiles/index.cfm?fuseaction=second.cleanup&id=1000195#content. Accessed on 10 May 2023
US Environmental Protection Agency, superfund: National Priorities List (NPL); https://www.epa.gov/superfund/superfund-national-priorities-list-npl. Accessed on 10 May 2023

Report

Fogleman V (May 2020) Improving Financial Security in the context of the Environmental Liability Directive (prepared for the European Commission, DG Environment, Contract No 07.0203/2018/789239/SER/ENV.E.4); https://ec.europa.eu/environment/legal/liability/studies.htm. Accessed on 10 May 2023

Books

American Law Institute (1930) Restatement (first) of torts. American Law Institute, Philadelphia
American Law Institute (1965) Restatement (second) of torts. American Law Institute, Philadelphia
Aylward MF, *Environmental Insurance Litigation: A State By State Case Law Survey* (Morrison Mahoney, Summer 2018 edition); https://www.morrisonmahoney.com/resource/673-50-state-environmental-coverage-case-law-survey-2018. Accessed on 10 May 2023
Cornell Law School, Legal Information Institute, 'Abnormally Dangerous Activity'; https://www.law.cornell.edu/wex/abnormally_dangerous_activity#:~:text=DEFINITION,is%20exercised%20by%20all%20actors. Accessed on 10 May 2023
Cornell Law School, Legal Information Institute, 'negligence per se'; https://www.law.cornell.edu/wex/negligence_per_se#:~:text=According%20to%20Restatement%20(Third)%20of,statute%20is%20designed%20to%20protect. Accessed on 10 May 2023
Fogleman V (2005) Environmental liabilities and Insurance in England and the United States. Witherby & Co Ltd, Livingston
US Environmental Protection Agency (November 1998) Handbook of Tools for Managing Federal Superfund Liability Risks at Brownfields and Other Sites (EPA 330-B-98-001)

Articles

Aon, Environmental Market Status Q1 2021; https://www.aon.com/getmedia/9337eb54-3e93-4098-8b4b-8e3bbf412368/Environmental-Market-Status-Q1-2021_Final.aspx. Accessed on 10 May 2023
Dillard SC, Brogdon LH (May 2017) 'Nuisance cases against energy companies in Texas, Pennsylvania, and other areas with significant or developing oil and gas exploration' (presentation); https://www.nortonrosefulbright.com/-/media/files/nrf/nrfweb/imported/20161031%2D%2Dnuisance-cases-against-energy-companies-in-texas-pennsylvania-and-other-areas-with-signifi.pdf. Accessed on 10 May 2023

Hannah J (May 2000) 'The U.S. Environmental Liability Insurance Market – Reaching New Frontiers' (International Risk Management Institute); https://www.irmi.com/articles/expert-commentary/the-us-environmental-liability-insurance-market. Accessed on 10 May 2023

Malinowski N (24 September 2010) 'EPA Hacks Away At £2B Idaho Superfund Case'; https://www.law360.com/articles/196191/epa-hacks-away-at-2b-idaho-superfund-case. Accessed on 10 May 2023

National Association of Insurance Commissioners (7 January 2019) Environmental Insurance; https://cc.bingj.com/cache.aspx?q=National+Association+of+Insurance+Commissioners%2c+%e2%80%98Environmental+Insurance%e2%80%99&d=4600524307961009&mkt=en-GB&setlang=en-GB&w=ktOsQSHMhz8sE6Kj6bSi2vwecR_FxzDY. Accessed on 10 May 2023

National Association of Insurance Commissioners, Surplus Lines (last updated 11 May 2022); https://content.naic.org/cipr-topics/surplus-lines. Accessed on 10 May 2023

National Association of Insurance Commissioners, 'Environmental insurance' (last updated 23 June 2022); https://content.naic.org/cipr-topics/environmental-insurance. Accessed on 10 May 2023

Roisman AZ, Wolff A (2010) Trespass by pollution: remedy by mandatory injunction. Fordham Environmental Law Review 21(1):157

Tanaka P, Saretsky M, Ni D, Foote M, Swanson M (1 May 2021), 'Environmental law and practice in the United States: overview' (Thomson Reuters Practical Law); https://uk.practicallaw.thomsonreuters.com/0-503-4622?transitionType=Default&contextData=(sc.Default)&firstPage=true. Accessed on 10 May 2023

Watson WT (13 November 2019) 'Insurance Marketplace Realities 2020 – Environmental; https://www.wtwco.com/en-US/Insights/2019/11/insurance-marketplace-realities-2019-fall-update-environmental. Accessed on 10 May 2023

Environmental Civil Liability in the Mercosur Region South America

Maria Kavanagh, Ricardo Peralta Larrain, and Roxana Corbrán

Abstract In this chapter, from a theoretical approach, we deal in this first section with environmental responsibility, environmental damage in the Argentine Republic, civil liability derived from ecological damage, the causality assumption, the role of the judge in the environmental process, and the sanctions to environmental damage. Under the subheading Environmental Protection, we develop the precautionary principle as an instrument of environmental policy and management, the Role of the Judge in environmental protection and its powers to issue precautionary measures, and the Responsibility of the State and its obligation to take appropriate measures for environmental protection. On the other hand, we analyze under this same title the prevention and cessation of the damage, and the preventive claim of the damage with the cardinal rule of the principle of prevention. With a comprehensive vision, we raise the issue of environmental insurance, we analyze from the empirical point of view, the three regulations that give rise to it, and we mention in the jurisprudence of three leading cases. Finally, we conclude with environmental damage and insurance activity, with reference to Joint Resolution 2/2019 of the National Insurance Superintendence that expresses the basic guidelines for the contractual conditions of insurance policies.

In the second section of chap. 6, from a theoretical approach, we analyze the Environmental Constitutional Guardianship as protection of the environment; the Environmental Impact Assessment Law that provides for the protection of the environment, the prevention of environmental impact, and the recomposition of the damaged environment. On the other hand, under subheading Environmental Damage, we interpret Article 3 of Law No. 17,283 followed by the statement of

---

M. Kavanagh (✉)
UMSA University of the Argentine Social Museum, Buenos Aires, Argentina

R. P. Larrain
Universidad Católica de los Andes & Universidad Alberto Hurtado & Escuela de Seguros de Chile, Santiago, Chile
e-mail: rperalta@vyaa.cl

R. Corbrán
UDELAR, Montevideo, Uruguay

K. Malinowska, D. Maśniak (eds.), *Managing Environmental Risks through Insurance*, AIDA Europe Research Series on Insurance Law and Regulation 9,
https://doi.org/10.1007/978-3-031-47602-0_7

objective/subjective responsibility. Under the subheading Procedural Legal System, we analyze the particularities of the system. Regarding Urgent Consideration Law No. 19,889 and the environment, it is worth mentioning that the rule gives rise to the creation of the Ministry of the Environment. To conclude, in relation to the project of the Norm on Environmental Responsibility being studied in the Parliament, the future regulation of said provision will determine the terms, limits, and conditions of environmental insurance.

In the third section of chap. 6, we discuss the topics related to environmental responsibility in Chilean legislation. Under the subheading Concepts, we develop the precepts of Law No. 19,300 on General Bases of the Environment and the general regulations on civil liability derived from environmental damage. On the other hand, we analyze the role of the state represented by the government entities responsible for authorizing and supervising activities that produce environmental impacts or contamination and the procedural legal system in case of environmental infractions. Finally, and applying a global approach to what is discussed in this section, we consider it relevant to mention the environmental liability policy marketed by the Chubb de Chile insurer.

1 Argentinian Republic: Environmental Civil Liability

Maria Kavanagh

1.1 *Introduction*

The life of man unfolds around certain physical circumstances that surround him, with which he is linked and takes advantage of to satisfy his needs. This environment is what we call environment. In other words, the environment is a system made up of natural and artificial elements that are interrelated and that are modified by human action.

Not any environment is appropriate for human life, we speak of an environment in "acceptable living conditions" which means not only favorable situations for the preservation of physical and mental health but also a healthy environment as established in Article 41 of the National Constitution, and also for the maintenance of "emotional and aesthetic qualities of the environment that surrounds man." "A clean, pure environment, without pollution or contamination is appropriate for a healthy life."[1]

[1] Mosset Iturraspe et al. (2011), p. 39.

In the Argentine Republic, the legally protected asset of environmental law has two areas: the natural sphere, which includes the layer of soil, water, and air that surrounds the planet, and a cultural area that includes the historical, urban heritage, and the social environment of the Man.

In our country, environmental protection acquired constitutional rank with the reform of the Constitution of 1994, consecrating in its Article 41 the preservation of the environment.[2] "All inhabitants enjoy the right to a healthy, balanced environment, suitable for development human and so that productive activities satisfy present needs without compromising those of future generations; and they have a duty to preserve it." Environmental damage will generate, as a priority, the obligation to recompose, as established by law.

The authorities will provide for the protection of this right, for the rational use of natural resources, for the preservation of the natural and cultural patrimony and of biological diversity, and for environmental information and education. It corresponds to the Nation to dictate the norms that contain the minimum protection budgets, and to the provinces, those necessary to complement them, without those altering the local jurisdictions. The entry into the national territory of currently or potentially dangerous waste, and radioactive waste is prohibited.

The right to a healthy environment: implies that the health of human beings is not damaged, impeded, or put at risk or danger, the term "healthy" refers to the one that facilitates the installation of people in an environment favorable to their well-being. It must allow the life of the beings that naturally compose it and never prevent it. Apt for human development goes without saying that it refers to the integral development of the human being, implies equity and well-being for all men.

1.2 Environmental Damage

The General Environmental Law, in its Article 27, classifies as environmental damage of collective incidence any relevant alteration that negatively modifies the environment, its resources, the balance of ecosystems or collective goods or values. When addressing the issue of environmental damage, we warn that has a linear relationship with sustainable development, it goes without saying that Article 41 of the Magna Carta speaks of the "right to a healthy, balanced environment, suitable for human development and for productive activities to satisfy present needs without compromising those of future generations". It is not a common damage, it must play a double structure: the preventive and the repairing.

The assumption of causality, between the fact of the natural or legal person, asset or liability by action or omission and the environmental damage, must mediate an "adequate causal relationship" in our legal system, if the adequate causality is reached after a practical investigation of the judge, avoiding arbitrariness in judging

[2] Constitución de la Nación Argentina 1996 6° edición Editorial Astrea.

the relationship of the facts. In comparative law, the German Unwelthg Law generally provides for a presumption of responsibility for a series of cases, improving the position of the victim, and facilitating the proof of the budget. On the other hand, and briefly, when the damage can be described as "collective" or plural in terms of the agents that originate it, a group of polluters, companies, or entities that contribute to its cause or aggravation, the theories of an anonymous author, member of a perfectly identified group, in the case that the authors are not anonymous but known, but that they discuss the proportion in which each one contributes to the contamination, for such questions the denominated ones are applicable: the theory of alternative causality, qualified by a sector "Dutch theory" (alternative causaliteit), the theory of market participation (industry-wide or enterprise theory of liability), and the theory of proportionality.

Civil liability derived from ecological damages was interpreted as objective, suggesting that along with the objective attribution of responsibility, compulsory insurance for activities with a high accident rate should be implemented, articulated with guarantee funds and prompt payment mechanisms. It is worth mentioning Solidarity 3 expressed in the General Environmental Law No. 25,675. In its Article 31, the norm establishes that "if in the commission of collective environmental damage..." Commission by action or omission. Collective damage not because of the plurality of its perpetrators but because it "affects the community," the citizenry, the people in general ("... two or more people have participated"—plural authors, natural or legal persons), regardless of the degree of participation or intervention; "... or it is not possible to accurately determine the extent of the damage caused by each person responsible..." Legitimate multiple or plural liabilities. With a real collaboration but of debatable amount and seriousness, in this case it is precisely what happened in the *Riachuelo* case.[3]

1.2.1 The Role of the Judge in the Environmental Process

The General Law of the Environment No. 25,675, in its Article 32, says "The environmental judicial jurisdiction will be the one that corresponds to the ordinary rules of competition..." The intervening judge may order all the necessary measures to order, conduct or prove the harmful acts in the process, in order to effectively protect the general interest.[4]

[3]"Mendoza, Beatriz S. and others against the National State and others on damages derived from the environmental contamination of the Matanza Riachuelo River."

[4]Mosset Iturraspe et al. (2011), p. 150.
http//www.argentina.gob.ar <ley-25675-79980>textoTitulo Daño Ambiental artículo 31.

1.2.2 Sanctions for Environmental Damage

The sentence to recompose the environment is the most chosen sanction, since it returns things to the previous state, because the damage disappears. It is the maximum of commutative justice: it erases injustice. The sentence to compensate personal damages; material or patrimonial damages and non-pecuniary damages in this case, parallel to the pure ecological damage suffered by the community, an individual may suffer individual moral damage or the destruction of the landscape.

The Judiciary must be the promoter of the protection of good environmental management, recognizing, in compensation claims, the principle in dubio pro environment.

1.2.3 Condemnation Against Collective Damage

The expression "collective damage" has a double meaning: damage caused by multiple agents or damage suffered by a plurality of people, multiple victims.

Article 30 of the General Environmental Law, "Produced collective environmental damage. . ." Produced as a synonym for "caused" or "cause." The norm regulates the effects of the already existing damage and not the mere danger or the eventuality of its occurrence. It alludes to the civil route, without dealing with the criminal and administrative ones. For these reasons, it is necessary to determine the legitimized assets, holders of shares. ". . . they will have legitimacy to obtain the recomposition of the damaged environment. . ." The text starts with two details: (a) it refers only to the collective environmental damage, leaving aside the individual or personal damage that agrees action for the victim, and (b) mentions the basic or preferred sanction, the recomposition of the environment and leaves aside the compensation.

". . . the Ombudsman and non-governmental associations for environmental defense, as provided for in article 43 of the National Constitution. . ." collective interests are protected in the strict sense. ". . . and the national, provincial or municipal State. . ." The role of the public administration, in the defense, management, and study of environmental impact, particularly in the face of collective damage, is of the highest hierarchy.

1.3 Environmental Protection[5]

Environmental protection is a constitutional process based on Articles 41 and 43 of the National Constitution, which include the conceptions and visions that inform the protection of natural resources, the ecosystem, water and ecological reserves, in short, the environment, considered as a transcendent good of collective belonging of the community and humanity. What typifies the environmental protection action is to seek the recomposition, the cessation and reparation for acts harmful to the environment. Hence, it is a collective process whose focus and configuration elements of the specific judicial case lie in the possible existence of environmental damage.

A particular kind of protection that will respond to the express guidelines of Article 30 of Law No. 25,675 of National Environmental Policy provides that "Once the collective environmental damage has been produced, they will have legitimacy to obtain the recomposition of the damaged environment, the affected, the Ombudsman and the non-governmental associations for environmental defense, as provided for in article 43 of the National Constitution, and the national, provincial or municipal State, likewise, will be entitled to the pertinent recomposition or compensation action, the person directly affected by the harmful event that occurred in their jurisdiction." After deducting the claim for collective environmental damage by any of the indicated holders, the rest may not file it, which does not impede their right to intervene as third parties. Without prejudice to what is indicated above, any person may request, through an amparo action, the cessation of activities that generate collective environmental damage.

The norm thus specifically receives environmental protection, as a useful way to provide environmental law with the effectiveness and executive action that its legal protection requires. As such, it must be an expeditious and fast way in order to guarantee the effective defense of a right of a collective nature of the importance of the environment.

The summary and collective are merged into a single procedural scenario against the impetus of the objective, constituting the matrices to which its director (judge) must respond.

1.3.1 The Preeminence of the Precautionary Principle

The precautionary principle is part of the instruments of environmental policy and management, which are located in the ex ante or pre-damage stage and leads to the need to adopt effective measures based on costs to prevent environmental degradation. Any action that is part of a process of this nature must be under the guidance of the precautionary principle, as it constitutes one of the fundamental legal guidelines

[5]Revista de Derecho ambiental-Doctrina, Jurisprudencia, Legislación y Práctica 2014 N° 40 Oct/Dec Director Cafferata, N. Pág. 236/255 Editorial Abeledo Perrot Argentina.

to resolve conflicts that arise when an injury to the environment is invoked, which supports the protection of anticipation.

1.3.2 The Role of the Judge in Environmental Protection

The various requirements and aspects of environmental matters raise the role of the judge in the direction, conduct and participation in the process exceeding the classic procedural powers, elaboration of creative sentences and activists with erga omnes effect, destined to make effective the constitutional mandates, ensuring values, behavior, and attitudes that contribute to the environmental education of the community.

From the environmental paradigms, the judge assumes an active and leading role in order to achieve compliance and observance of the minimum environmental budgets.

The first tool that the judge has in these processes is the ex officio impulse, due to the singularity of a process where social projection rights are at stake, which reveals the inconvenience of depositing the disposition of the procedure in the heads of the parties. and with it, the arbitrator of the procedural times.

Within this framework, the judge has broad powers to order the precautionary measures that he deems necessary to prevent the damage from worsening or to prevent its production. He becomes admissible all those actions suitable to achieve adequate and effective guardianship of him, whether they take the form of precautionary measures or channel a true early guardianship. In this context, the court has the duty to notify the parties of the existence of a collective process, as well as of the different instances through which it is going through in order to properly safeguard the right to defense.

In the same sense, all the notification, participation and publicity requirements of a conflict of this magnitude find protection in a tool coined by constitutional law: public hearings. Within the framework of orality that public hearings provide, the judge is faced with the certain possibility that enables him to know the different plots of an environmental conflict, through the participation of all interested parties.

In relation to the subject, another tool of inestimable value in processes of these characteristics is the participation of the so-called amicus curiae, their intervention in matters of collective importance represents an important contribution for the court since it allows the intervention of people not only interested in the problem but also, because they are people with knowledge in the matter, they can provide a better perspective to the judge.

Regarding the principle of elasticity or flexibility, this alludes to the fact that the court must adapt the requirement of the formalities provided for in the rules of procedure to the achievement of the purposes of constitutional processes. In this regard, the International Court of Human Rights has said that the process is a means to achieve justice and that justice cannot be sacrificed for the sake of mere formalities.

In terms of legitimation, environmental protection as a collective process requires affectation with this scope, in this sense it is worth mentioning that environmental damage constitutes a two-faced phenomenon since, as indicated by doctrine and jurisprudence, it houses environmental damage. collective and individual, hence the jurisdictional activity must be projected in both directions—the collective and the individual—in order to achieve a comprehensive solution to the environmental case raised.

On the other hand, the intervention of the Public Prosecutor's Office arises from the normative correlation between Articles 41 and 43 of the National Constitution and Articles 27 and 30 of the General Environmental Law, it has been estimated that the Public Prosecutor's Ministry is part of and must be given intervention in this class of processes.

At the level of evidence, in the dispositive system, the judge reconstructs the truth but on the basis of what has been provided by the parties, because of which it may happen that the reconstruction shows a truth different from the historical one, essentially formal.

The informal and the preventive are combined to prevail in the matter of proof both in relation to the probative initiative, as in the processing and even with respect to its value implications in order to achieve a conviction regarding the environmental situation in question.

Within the evidentiary measures referring to damage to the environment, the judge can and should resort to the environmental impact study (EIA), whose usefulness is aimed at identifying, preventing and interpreting the environmental impacts of certain acts, actions or authorizations in the environment in which they occur.

This study, which requires the activity of specialized technical agencies, the assistance of entities interested in environmental issues, and the public participation of the citizenry, makes it possible to prepare an opinion or declaration regarding environmental impact.

Regarding the sentence, in principle the judge must respect the constitutional limits of the division of functions and cannot advance beyond seeking the defense of rights through mandates in pursuit of a result. Sometimes it becomes imperative to resort to the help of other disciplines or specialized agencies in the matter in order to equip themselves with the necessary elements to form the jurisdictional conviction.

For its part, the execution of sentences tending to environmental recomposition is a complex process and requires monitoring by the courts within the framework of the officiousness and prevention that flows throughout the previous process, in order to ensure fidelity and compliance with what is ordered.

1.4 State Responsibility for Damage to the Environment

The state has the obligation to take the appropriate measures for environmental protection, to protect men, animals, and plants from any type of environmental alteration. These objectives oblige the state towards the citizens, since it must protect them against any injury that through these elements (climate, humidity, water, environmental purity) they may suffer, but also protect the owners of natural resources.

The protection of the environment has as its immediate goal not only the care of nature itself, but the care of man and his quality of life, through the satisfaction of his vital needs.

1.4.1 Environmental Prevention

The principle of prevention appears regulated in Article 41 of the National Constitution and in international instruments of supra legal rank Article 75 para 22 first paragraph. Since the reform of the National Constitution in 1994, with the incorporation of Article 41, the subjective right of the inhabitants to live in a healthy and balanced environment has been regulated.

Regarding the first paragraph, when analyzing Article 41, Dr. Daniel Alberto Sabsay maintains that said provision qualifies the environment as "healthy, balanced..." and it must be emphasized that in this system it could only be achieved that. It possesses these qualities when the activities to be carried out allow it to meet the objective in time to satisfy the needs of present generations without depriving future generations of them. In this way, the notion of sustainable or sustainable development is incorporated into our constitutional text, which today places the environmental variable as necessary in making any decision that makes the development of an organized community.[6]

Consequently, it must be understood—with respect to Article 41—that it follows that the protection must be preventive. Then individuals and groups must be guaranteed to intervene against an eventual threat that looms against the preservation of the environment.

On the other hand, Law No. 25,675 has adopted a definition of the principle of prevention restricted to certain aspects. Article 4 says: "Principle of prevention: The causes and sources of environmental problems will be addressed in a priority and integrated manner, trying to prevent the negative effects that may occur on the environment."

---

[6] Sabsay, D.A.; "*El Desarrollo Sustentable en un Fallo de la Justicia Federal*"; Publicado en: El Derecho. Diario de Jurisprudencia y Doctrina. AñoXXXV/N°9355 (10/10/97), Buenos Aires, p. 1.

1.4.2 Prevention and Cessation of Damage[7]

The unified digest speaks of three civil liability functions: one reparatory—the traditional one—and two new ones: preventive and punitive. Traditionally, the compensable damage was only the one that had already occurred. The real one. Existing. Accomplished. When speaking of future damage, reference was made to a detriment that was necessarily going to take place, the germ of it already existing.

According to this position, legal action could not be taken, in the face of a simple threat of damage, there was no right to prevent damage, nor therefore, a claim directed towards that objective. In the unification of the Civil and Commercial Code, mechanisms are established to put into practice this preventive function of damage. Article 1710 expresses the duty to prevent damage. Every person has the duty, insofar as it depends on them, to: (a) avoid causing unjustified damage; (b) adopt, in good faith and in accordance with the circumstances, reasonable measures to prevent damage from occurring, or reduce its magnitude; if such measures avoid or reduce the magnitude of a damage for which a third party would be responsible, he has the right to be reimbursed by the third party for the value of the expenses in which it occurred, in accordance with the rules of enrichment without cause; (c) not aggravate the damage, if it has already occurred. To which is added, in terms that we understand predominantly procedural the following:

Article 1711: Preventive Action. Preventive action proceeds when an unlawful action or omission makes the production of damage, its continuation or aggravation foreseeable. The concurrence of any attribution factor is not required.

Article 1712: Legitimation. Those who demonstrate a reasonable interest in preventing the damage are entitled to claim.

Article 1713: Judgment. The sentence that admits the preventive action must provide, at the request of a party or ex officio, definitively or provisionally, obligations to give, do, or not do, as appropriate; it must weigh the criteria of the least possible restriction and the most suitable means to ensure the effectiveness in obtaining the purpose.

1.4.3 Preventive Claim of Environmental Damage Itself

If the damage to the environment did not occur and there are indications that it may occur, the preventive claim will only have the purpose of preventing the risk of damage from passing to the phase of concrete damage. This mandate to avoid harm has a special dimension when it comes to the environment. It is worth remembering the presence and validity of the principle of prevention, the cardinal rule in this specific area contemplated in Article 4 of the General Environmental Law. Here the pertinent measures, to give, to do or not to do, make up a sentence of conviction,

[7]Revista de Derecho ambiental-Doctrina, Jurisprudencia, Legislación y Práctica 2016 N° 45 Enero/Marzo Director Cafferata, N. Pág. 96/105 Editorial Abeledo Perrot Argentina.

with a final nature, necessarily dictated at the request of a party and prior bilateralization. The judgment in this process of autonomous knowledge may not be issued ex officio by the judge, and considering that the issuance of the ruling was made prior to bilateralization, in no case may it be provisional.

On the other hand, within the framework of this damage prevention process, understood as a trial of knowledge, there may be a need to adopt urgent measures. This is so, since otherwise the protective possibility of the institute could be frustrated. In this autonomous trial, provisional—precautionary—measures may be issued to ensure the effectiveness of the process.

In summary with the environmental preventive claim, it seeks to avoid or minimize damage to the environment. Cautiously, the same objective can be achieved immediately and provisionally. With the compensation claim, patrimonial reparation is generally sought. As a precaution, an attempt must be made to preserve the solvency of the debtor.

1.5 Environmental Liability Insurance[8]

The issue of environmental insurance in Argentina arises from three laws: National Law No. 25,612 on the Comprehensive Management of Industrial Waste and Service Activities, Law No. 25,670 on Minimum Budgets for the Management and Elimination of PCBs, and Law No. 25,675 General Law of the Environment. These three laws require companies to have environmental insurance, which causes a problem, all polluting companies or companies that generate risky environmental situations have to anticipate the damage they may cause to the environment.

The logic of these regulations is that if society benefits by consuming a product that damages or puts the environment at risk, the employer must calculate and incorporate that risk into the price of the product. At the same time, information is provided to the market about the true value of the product that is consumed and the consumer can decide if the product is "worth what it costs." In this way, environmental insurance and the laws that require it in our country generate a framework of rules that provide more information to the markets and freedom to consumers and users.

The concept of insurance is closely linked to the concept of damage. Environmental insurance can be defined as that intended to cover the expenses caused by environmental damage. Environmental damage is a modern concept, while the right to the environment was incorporated by the National Constitution in 1994 in Article 41 and later by jurisprudence. According to the constitutional framework, Dr. Bidart Campos states that "there is a subjective right of human beings to a dignified and healthy environment, which can be classified within the attributes of personality and more specifically in the right of man to the safety of his body and to their physical

[8]Paz et al. (2006), p. 2.

and mental health that connects with their own right to life, which is the first of all." In summary, damage to the environment is that damage to the environment that endangers the survival of man on earth.

Environmental damage can be classified into: (1) Personal, patrimonial, and economic in which there is damage to the environment, but there are individuals affected individually, it is the classic mechanism of civil liability, for these civil liability insurances are applied and governed by the classic mechanisms of civil law. In this case, minimizing risk is essential, since as the risky or harmful action is reduced, there will be a direct decrease in the premium for risk reduction. (2) Pure ecological damage, which is the environmental damage suffered by the elements of nature without falling on people or things legally protected, indirectly affecting the quality of life of the various living beings of the planet, for these there are variables that make their operation difficult, these difficulties range from legitimacy to demanding the repair of the damage and on the other hand the big problem is the valuation of the damage. In most environmental issues the damage is not repairable, despite this impossibility until today the only possible answer is with money.

1.5.1 Characteristics of Environmental Damage

(1) Regarding the number of victims, it is generally extensive: a large number of victims (a neighborhood, a region).
(2) In many cases, the authors cannot be determined (numerous industries or companies that discharge into the same watercourse).
(3) They are related to specialized activities or specific techniques, unknown to the victims.
(4) In general, it is serious damage to the environment, although for people it is not relevant at first.

1.5.2 Types of Insurance

By virtue of the types of damages and the risk of their occurrence, it is generally possible to speak of two large types of risks.

Ad. 1) Environmental risk due to an emergency or an accidental situation, an example of this type of risk is a truck that transports a dangerous substance and suffers an accident spilling the substance.

Environmental insurance against this type of risk already works correctly in developed countries and in ours there are several companies that have taken out policies abroad. These insurances require plans and continuity of control by the insurance company. They require constant monitoring systems and mechanisms in order to avoid or at least minimize the possibility of changes occurring.

Ad. 2) The other risk that it is not yet known how to insure is the risk for what a product may cause in the future or for the hidden damage that a company has generated up to the present. A paradigmatic case of the damage that a product can cause in the future is that of asbestos. In the 70s they were a great discovery, they were widely used in construction for their great insulating property, today we know that asbestos is highly polluting and there is a large number of lawsuits for the effect on the health of the population caused by exposure to asbestos.

In summary, we can say that in the most advanced countries, environmental insurance that provides for damage to the environment caused by accidental situations is working correctly, while those that try to insure the possible future effects of a substance are still under discussion.

In reality, with these damages there is nothing to insure since the harmful event has already occurred, so the only thing left would be to repair the damage. There are several insurance companies that are offering environmental insurance, the premiums are very expensive, since there are no statistical data on the possibility of accidents occurring. Most of the insured companies are those that have ISO 14000 because it is believed that by having a good environmental management system, accident risks are minimized, thus they have affordable premiums.

Not knowing the risk cannot be insured, most companies are beginning to register and quantify their accidents at this time due to the requirements of the Occupational Health and Safety Law, until now there are few that have statistics on the issue. One way that companies can obtain an affordable premium for environmental insurance is to minimize risks, through documents and business action plans that demonstrate the minimization of risks of accidents, spills, etc. Insurers hire external companies to audit companies that want to insure themselves environmentally, auditors are expensive and their work is charged to the company to be insured.

1.5.3 Law No. 25,670: Minimum Budgets for the Management and Elimination of PCBs

Article 9 of the PCBs Law requires that every natural or legal person must ensure the recovery of possible environmental damage and cover the risks to the health of the population that their activity could cause. This is something extremely difficult to ascertain, as for example there is still disagreement about the health risks caused by PCBs.

Article 15 requires that before 2005 all holders of PCBs must submit to the enforcement authority a program for the elimination or decontamination of devices that contain them, with the objective that by 2010 there will be no equipment with PCBs installed in the country.

In 2005, by Resolution 313/2005, the Ministry of Health and Environment enabled the Integrated National Registry of PCB Holders, which will work within the scope of the National Directorate of Environmental Management.

In 2006, by Resolution 56/2006, the Nation's Ombudsman made a recommendation to the Executive Power for the immediate Regulation of the Law of Minimum Budgets for Environmental Protection called PCB's Management and Elimination Law No. 25,670 which has public order characteristics, since the term to comply with the constitutional obligation of regulation will expire in 2003.

The Executive Branch by Regulatory Decree No. 853/2007 regulated Law No. 25670, establishing the Ministry of Environment and Sustainable Development of the Cabinet of Ministers as the enforcement authority.

In 2010, the Matanza Riachuelo Basin Authority by Resolution 34/2010 establishes: That, accordingly, Resolution No. 158/08 of the Federal Environmental Council (COFEMA) states that it is the Superintendence of Insurance of the Nation, which must inform about the offer of insurance policies for environmental damage of collective incidence. That there are policies on the market that conform to the aforementioned objective of environmental protection.

The National Insurance Superintendency, on August 26, 2008, approved the Surety Insurance Plan for environmental damage of collective incidence, presented by an insurance company and in turn, the Ministry of Environment and Sustainable Development, within the framework of the powers provided for in Article 3 of the aforementioned Joint Resolution, issued the prior environmental approval.

Subsequently, the same Superintendence of Insurance of the Nation, through provisions, expanded the list of entities authorized to operate surety insurance for environmental damage of collective incidence, which gives a growing market.

The regulatory background indicates that, in the Province of Buenos Aires, the Provincial Directorate for Sustainable Development of the Provincial Organization for Sustainable Development, through Provision No. 4059, established as an environmental policy measure, to require natural or legal persons whose activities are achieved by Joint Resolution No. 98/07 and No. 1973/07 of the Ministry of Finance and the Ministry of Environment and Sustainable Development of the Nation, included in an Annex, which prove compliance with the provisions of Article 22 of the Law No. 25,675 for the purpose of obtaining permits, authorizations and/or renewals with based on Law No. 11,459 and its Regulatory Decree No. 1741/96 and on Law No. 5965 and its Regulatory Decree No. 3395/96. All this, without prejudice to the intervention that corresponds to the Provincial Waste Department in the cases of presentation of annual sworn declarations, according to Law No. 11,720 and complementary legislation and Decree No. 23/07.

The Matanza Riachuelo Basin Authority, by virtue of Law No. 26,168, is responsible for the control and prevention of pollution of industrial origin, the execution of the Comprehensive Environmental Sanitation Plan, and in summary, it could be affirmed, tend to the development of all regarding the tasks of recomposition of the collective environmental damage, of the Matanza Riachuelo Basin.

The Court of the 1st Federal Instance of Quilmes, in execution of the sentence issued by the Supreme Court of Justice of the Nation, of 07/08/08, in re "Mendoza, Silvia B. and others c/ National State and others s/ damages derived from environmental contamination," by resolution of 06/12/09, urged the Matanza Riachuelo Basin Authority to urgently regulate the requirement established in Article 22 of General Environmental Law No. 25,675, to be demanded in the area of your competence.

The Board of Directors of the Matanza Riachuelo Basin Authority, approved a Registration Plan for all industrial and service establishments in the Basin, which includes in the sworn statement that integrates it, an item related to the status of insurance for damages environmental.

The Resolution of the Matanza Riachuelo Basin Authority No. 01/08, defines who are polluting agents. Therefore, any industrial or service establishment, located in the Matanza Riachuelo Basin, declared a polluting agent, carries out a concrete or potentially risky activity for the environment, for which reason it is consequently affected by the legal obligation to have one of the insurance instruments provided for in Law No. 25,675, Article 22 and concordant.

That it is necessary to adequately promote, the implementation by the industries located in the Matanza Riachuelo Basin, of some of the forms of insurance provided for in the General Environmental Law No. 25,675, and concordant regulations, to guarantee the necessary funds and the consequent obligation of recomposition of the same, of base in addition, Constitutional.

The Ministry of Environment and Sustainable Development by Resolution 840/2015 creates the Integral PCB Management Program. The functions of the Program will be:

Develop actions regarding the integral management of PCBs, in order to comply with the international commitments assumed through Law No. 26,011, regarding the elimination of PCBs. Organize and manage the Integrated National Registry of PCB Holders, created by Article 7 of Law No. 25,670.

On the other hand, both the Directorate of Hazardous Waste and the Transboundary Movements Unit, both of the National Directorate of Environmental Control of the Undersecretariat for Environmental Control and Enforcement and Pollution Prevention of this Secretariat participate in the integral management of PCBs elimination, through the application of the Law on Hazardous Waste No. 24,051 and the Law approving the Basel Convention on the Control of Transboundary Movements of Hazardous Waste and its Elimination No. 23,922, respectively, noting the need to concentrate the relevant information in order to identify problems, needs and develop strategies for the environmentally sound management of PCBs.

Law No. 25,612: Comprehensive Management of Industrial Waste Law No. 25,612 on the Comprehensive Management of Industrial Waste and Service Activities states that all transporters must ensure the recovery of possible environmental damage that their activity may cause.

The same regulations state that the natural and legal persons responsible or owners of waste storage, treatment and final disposal plants must ensure the recovery of possible environmental damage that their activity could cause. Among the objectives of the law that are listed in its Article 4, is to minimize the potential "risks" of waste at all stages of comprehensive management and to promote the cessation of discharges that are hazardous to the environment, In addition to reducing the amount of waste that is generated and, of the generic ones, guaranteeing environmental preservation, the protection of natural resources, the quality of life of the population, the conservation of biodiversity, and the balance of ecosystems; as well as promoting the use and transfer of clean and appropriate technologies for environmental preservation and sustainable development.

In its Article 6, it contains the absolute prohibition on the import, introduction and transport of all types of waste, coming from other countries to the national territory, and its air and maritime spaces, except for the transit of waste provided for in international agreements and that is of residues that are included by regulation and that the interested parties demonstrate, in a reliable manner, that they will be used as inputs for industrial processes.

The National Gas Regulatory Entity by Resolution 3587/2006 resolved: Approve the Minimum Argentine Standards for Environmental Protection in the Transportation and Distribution of Natural Gas and Other Gases through Pipes (NAG 153). Repeal Resolution No. 186/95.

Article 4 stipulates that companies that carry out works and services for the subjects mentioned in Article 3 must apply and adopt the regulations provided for in these regulations, as well as the manuals, plans and studies approved by the regulated subject that hires them.

Article 6 establishes: For the construction of new gas pipelines, branches, networks, and their complementary facilities, the provincial or municipal regulations that establish procedures for consultations or public hearings must be complied with prior to carrying out the projects. The subjects mentioned in Article 3 must submit to the regulatory authority, the information detailed below: copy of the minutes or certifications of proof of the acts of consultation or public hearing held; copy of the definitive project of the enterprise; Protocols of the Preliminary Environmental Study, the Environmental Impact Study and the specific Environmental Protection Plan for the scheduled work.

The Secretary for Environmental Control and Monitoring and the National Agri-Food Health and Quality Service by Resolution 1/2019 establishes in its Article 1: Approval of the Regulatory Framework for the Production, Registration and Application of Compost, in accordance with the prescriptions provided for in this resolution.

In its Article 2, the purpose of this standard is to define the possible applications and establish the necessary requirements that the compost made from organic waste separated at source and collected in a differentiated manner must meet, for the purposes of its registration, ensuring sustainable management and promoting its production, use and application in the different provincial jurisdictions.

The Government Secretariat for the Environment and Sustainable Development by Resolution 19/2019 approves: The technical standard for the Agricultural application of Digestate from anaerobic digestion plants.

1.5.4 Law No. 25,675: General Environmental Law

Article 4 of the General Environmental Law establishes the Principle of Responsibility which says: "the generator of degrading effects on the environment, current or future, is responsible for the costs of preventive or corrective restoration actions, without prejudice to the validity of the corresponding environmental responsibility systems." This means that any person who causes damage to the environment, must repair it.

This norm, sanctioned in the year 2002, incorporates in the positive legal system of the country in its Article 22 the obligation to take out insurance so that any natural or legal person, public or private, who carries out activities that are risky for the environment will have the obligation to take out insurance. coverage insurance with sufficient entity to guarantee the financing of the recomposition of the damage that in its type could produce. In Article 28, the regulations establish that "Whoever causes damage to the environment is responsible for its restoration to the previous state of its production, in the event that it is not technically feasible, the substitute compensation determined by the intervening ordinary justice must be deposited in the Fund of Environmental Compensation that is created hereby, which will be administered by the enforcement authority, without prejudice to other legal actions..."

Decree 1638/2012 establishes in its Article 1, in order to comply with the provisions of Article 22 of the General Environmental Law No. 25,675, two types of insurance may be contracted: (a) Surety insurance for environmental damage of collective incidence (b) Collective Incident Environmental Damage Liability Insurance.

There is a scheme that requires that everything be returned to the state prior to the damage and in the event that this cannot be done, money is deposited in the Environmental Compensation Fund, which will be dedicated to repairing different environmental damages.

Other types of damage such as health, property and moral/psychic damage will commonly derive from environmental damage, but even when such derivatives exist and are proven, residual environmental damage will remain due to deterioration or impairment of the environment, not only natural but social in the terms of Article 41 of the National Constitution.

1.5.5 Leading Cases

We analyze the jurisprudence of three leading cases:

(I) In a decision by the Chamber of Chamber H in a lawsuit by Subterráneos de Buenos Aires del Estado against the owners of a Shell service station, in the sentence obliges to remove all the soil contaminated by the spilled hydrocarbons, decontaminate that land and return it to its place of origin or bring uncontaminated soil, all of this under Avenida 9 de Julio in the City of Buenos Aires.

(II) The second case occurred in a lawsuit in the town of Magdalena in the Province of Buenos Aires, against Shell-Capsa for the oil spill that the oil tanker Estrella Pampeana caused on the coast of said town and whose ruling requires that the correctly the waste caused by the spill and recompose the ecosystems of the locality. The traditional insurer is excluded from the sentence, so Shell will have to bear the costs of rebuilding the ecosystem on its own. The insurer will not take responsibility because surely the policy that she had signed with Shell did not include environmental aspects.

Twenty-three years after the oil spill in front of the city of Magdalena, the only one in Argentina and the largest in freshwater in world history, the economic reparation agreed between the Executive of that Buenos Aires district and the Shell company has not yet materialized. owner of the oil tanker that collided with another ship carrying containers in the Río de la Plata.

Ten years after that environmental disaster, in March 2009, an Agreement for USD 9.5 million was signed to put an end to the municipality's claim. The text included a clause that said it did not imply "acknowledgment of any responsibility" on the part of the defendants, Shell and the company responsible for the other ship that was involved in the crash. The Agreement was submitted that same year to a popular plebiscite that obtained 77% support, and was later approved by the local Deliberative Council unanimously by all forces. At present, there is no longer any environmental damage from the spill of the 5 million liters of oil that affected the fauna, flora, water, commercial exploitations and the inhabitants of the area at the time, basically due to the time elapsed. The Justice has not yet approved the homologation of that Agreement, a necessary requirement for the municipality to finally collect financial compensation from Shell.

(III) Mendoza cause. The cause began in July 2004, when a group of residents, led by Beatriz Silvia Mendoza and 16 other people, filed a lawsuit demanding the recomposition of the environment and the creation of a fund to finance the sanitation of the basin, holding the following actors responsible for damages: • The National State, the Province of Buenos Aires and the Autonomous City of Buenos Aires. • Forty-four neighboring companies to overturn hazardous waste directly into the river, for not building treatment plants, for not adopting new technologies and for not minimizing the risks of their productive activity. The National State was sued when the denounced situation occurred on a navigable and interjurisdictional waterway, with respect to which it has regulatory and control powers, under the terms of Art. 75, incs. 10 and 13 of the National Constitution. The Province of Buenos Aires is sued for having the original domain over the existing natural resources in its territory, in accordance with Arts. 121 and 124 of the National Constitution. And the Autonomous City of Buenos Aires is sued in its capacity as corribereña del Riachuelo, which constitutes, in the area of its jurisdiction, a property of its public domain.

The object of the claim is compensation for damages suffered as a consequence of the contamination of the Matanza Riachuelo Basin (in order to repair the supervening disability, expenses for medical treatment, expenses for new filing, moral damage, psychological damage suffered by mothers, fathers and their children, the comprehensive future damage of the expenses that will have to be made to free the children from the contamination they carry in their organism, and the loss of rental value of the properties they inhabit); and the cessation of pollution and recomposition of collective environmental damage (Art. 41 of the National Constitution and

Art. 30 of Law No. 25,675—General Law of the Environment). The Matanza-Riachuelo Basin covers an area of more than 2200 km^2 in which some 5 million inhabitants live and constitutes a region with multiple pollution problems. Less than 4 km from Plaza de Mayo, is the neighborhood known as Villa Inflamable. It is located in the vicinity of the Petrochemical Pole, historically polluting, and partially located on land resulting from the filling of a swamp area (contaminated). The *Mendoza* case originated in that neighborhood—in which the Supreme Court of Justice ordered the sanitation of the stream—and is designated by the Matanza Riachuelo Basin Authority as one of the most critical territories. For all these reasons, Villa Inflamable is included in the first phase of the Relocation process that must be carried out to protect the rights of the affected residents. Ms. Beatriz Mendoza worked professionally at the San Martín de Porres Sanitary Unit, located within the Dock Sud Petrochemical Pole, where studies were carried out that demonstrated the contamination of the inhabitants with lead, benzene and toluene, among other chemical agents. used in petrochemical operations in the area.

On June 20, 2006, the Supreme Court of Justice of the Nation ordered the defendants to present a plan to clean up the basin, and the companies to report on the measures taken to stop and reverse the contamination of the basin. zone. The Court divided the claim of the neighbors into several files, one of them was compensation for the individual damages suffered by each one, to repair the expenses for medical treatment, moral and psychological damage and the new establishment of the families. The Court declared itself competent to study the collective damage, that is, the part of the claim that requests that the environment be recomposed and that sanitation works be carried out. "The prevention of future damage has an absolute priority, since these are acts that will continue to produce contamination. Secondly, the recomposition of environmental pollution must be pursued and, finally, in the event of irreversible damage, compensation," says the court. In September 2006, the first public hearing was held before the Court, in which the National Government and the governments of the Province of Buenos Aires and the Autonomous City of Buenos Aires presented a Plan for the Sanitation of the Riachuelo and the creation of a Committee of Interjurisdictional Basin. It contemplates the relocation of the population of Villa Inflamable, which was identified as one of the neighborhoods in the most critical situation. In February 2007, the second public hearing was held, in which the progress made since the presentation of the Sanitation Plan. On July 8, 2008, the Supreme Court of Justice issued a historic ruling in the case "Mendoza Beatriz Silvia and Others v. National State and Others S/Damages and Damages (Damages derived from the environmental contamination of the Matanza-Riachuelo River)" where it was determined who is responsible for carrying out the actions and sanitation works, the term in which they must be executed, leaving open the possibility of imposing fines in the case of non-compliance. On the other hand, the Highest Court entrusted the Nation's Ombudsman and the NGOs with the formation of a Collegiate Body for the control of the Sanitation Plan.

In the month of February 2023, within the framework of the judicial sentence Mendoza Beatriz v. the National State issued by the Supreme Court of Justice of the

Nation, whose execution is processed before Federal Court No. 2 of Morón, the Municipality of Esteban Echeverría carries out the relocation of the families that live on the banks of the Arroyo Ortega, in the neighborhoods of La Morita and San Ignacio de El Jagüel. Said sentence provides for the provision of a healthy, balanced and suitable environment for human development to the neighbors who are within the towpath of lagoons and streams or areas highly floodplains of the Matanza Riachuelo Basin. The families are relocated to the new housing complex in the Montecarlo neighborhood of Monte Grande Sur are part of the people registered between 2011 and 2016 in the sector determined by the court. On the other hand, there are various regulations that modify the General Environmental Law, we have taken those corresponding to the month of January 2023.

The National Executive Branch by Decree 2/2023 Igneous Emergency: the growing number of sources of forest, rural, grassland and interface fires in our country constitutes a worrisome multi-causal phenomenon that demands the adoption of immediate measures, through maximum coordination and cooperation between the organizations to which this issue is transversal.

During the year 2022 these massive and repeated fires in different critical areas of the country continued to acquire an alarming dimension and represent a serious threat both to the environment and its ecosystems and to the heritage, health and lives of people. The situation, caused by mainly anthropic activities whose consequences are aggravated by climate change, continues to harm different ecoregions of the country and generate harmful consequences on native and implanted forests, natural protected areas, agricultural areas, prairies, pastures, scrublands and wetlands.

The Ministry of Environment and Sustainable Development by Resolution 27/2023 Creates the National Organic Valorization Program, the general objectives establish:

Formulate national organic reduction and recovery goals in pursuit of resource optimization, carbon footprint reduction, promotion of the circular economy and compliance with sustainable development goals.

Provide technical and regulatory advice to national, provincial and municipal public institutions and civil organizations in relation to modalities, scales, requirements, methodologies for the recovery of organic waste, and the materials derived from it.

Promote the creation of a Federal Network for the Valuation of Organics with the participation of the various actors involved in the matter.[9]

1.5.6 Insurance Features

It is worth mentioning before introducing ourselves to the subject, that from the moment there is damage it is necessary that there is someone who must pay for it, it

[9]El DiarioSur Esteban Echeverría. Año XVI N° 687 2023-2-26 Pág. 22. Buenos Aires -Argentina.

may be that the victim himself takes charge, that the state takes charge, the one that generated the damage or the one who benefited from that damage. It is the political power that is in charge of determining who will be responsible for the environmental damage that is generated; the way in which the costs of recovering the damage caused must be distributed must be determined by the legislative and executive powers.

The judge, unlike the other powers, has the obligation to rule. In other words, it must provide a solution to the conflict that is presented to it, given the lack of laws or regulations applicable to a case, it does not exempt itself from failing and to do so it must refer, based on its knowledge and understanding, to constitutional and/or jurisprudential texts. used to solve similar cases.

The environmental reality is very different from all aspects of traditional justice, in many cases it is the judges who must make decisions since the elected powers do not provide fair and applicable legal solutions. There are laws that are a framework for dealing with issues such as a comprehensive system of guarantees or environmental insurance, both are instruments proposed and required by law. To this is added the option of a Restoration Fund and a Compensation Fund. The purpose of the law is the prevention and reduction of environmental risk, as well as the assurance of guarantees so that companies can repair the damage without disappearing.

In the case of insurers, the main drawback is the lack of definition and measurement of risk, since there are neither reliable statistics nor a clear regulatory framework to determine when damage is generated. On the other hand, the lack of clarity is added to determine the number of insured, since it is difficult to determine who the law includes when it refers to those who carry out "an activity that is risky for the environment."

To define risk, it must be taken into account that it is uncertain, future and beyond the control of the insured. Therefore, the fraud is eliminated. Risk is the possibility of an event occurring and for this it would be necessary to establish certain coverage limitations. It is not clear in the law what type of insurance is required of the company. There are several possibilities: Damage Policy that can be in two forms: (1) Civil Liability Policy, in this case it is Civil Liability, in this case, a limit should be placed on the policy, that is, determine how much the policy covers; (2) Claim made on the basis of claims, the insurer covers the claim during the term of the policy, even if the damage was caused before contracting the policy (retroactivity). In the event that the insured announces, within the policy coverage period, that an event has occurred that may generate damage and future claims, the insurer should be liable for this event, even if the claim occurs after the policy expires. Some claim made policies cover up to two years after the end of the policy term.

What is the degree of recomposition? Article 28 of the General Environmental Law says "return to the original state," this implies unlimited liability. How is the damage caused? Unexpectedly or gradually, and sometimes there is no cause of the damage. In this case, joint and several liability is sought.

As far as risks are concerned, if the risks are not well defined it is impossible to take out insurance. Another issue is that of recomposition. It is not possible to return everything to the previous state. Even if in some cases it is technically possible to do so, the cost can be enormous. What must be recomposed is the condition, not the state, that is, for example, a soil continues to have the parameters of a soil suitable for agriculture or industry, even if it is not the same as in its original state. When companies carry out activities, it is perfectly possible to define risks, including gradual ones. Insurance is undoubtedly necessary, as is a fund for what insurance cannot cover. You must work on the risks, in order to minimize them and obtain a safer habitat.

1.5.7 Environmental Damage and Insurance Activity

From the reform of the National Constitution in 1994, the new Article 41 is incorporated, which introduces among its precepts the figures of both damage and environmental recomposition, establishing the general principle that whoever causes damage to the environment must restore the affected resource to its previous state, or alternatively and in cases where it is impossible, compensate by substitute means those who are harmed by ecological or environmental damage.

The novel institution of environmental damage, accompanied by other instruments such as environmental insurance and repair and remediation funds, will provide the state and the regulated community itself with the necessary tools for the evaluation of environmental risks. These tools will also allow a remediation efficient and effective management of environmental liabilities, with quantifiable costs and regulatory parameters established on an objective basis.

The industrialization of Latin America and Argentina was accompanied by a significant migration from the rural peripheries to the cities and large metropolitan regions. This scheme of urbanization with industrialization was, however, a spontaneous product of events and almost never was prosecuted through adequate planning or regulation that would mitigate its effects on the environment and the natural resources directly affected.

As a consequence of this spontaneous growth, the locations of polluting activities and their actions and impact on the environment of polluting activities and their actions and impact on the environment of the main cities of Argentina have been accompanied by a proliferation of high-risk environmental liabilities. for the environment, affecting in some cases private properties and in others public property when not directly the health of the community.

In this context, by joint Resolution 2/2019[10] the National Insurance Superintendence (SSN) and the Government Secretariat for the Environment and Sustainable Development (SGAYDS) approved the Basic Guidelines for the Contractual Conditions of Damage Insurance Policies Environmental Collective Advocacy.

[10]htpps:// www.revistaestretegas.com.ar/contenidos/5219 Publicado 2019-11-27.

The standard contains an Annex that details issues such as Subjects of the Contract, Application Authority, Purpose and Scope of Coverage and other basic Guidelines for all the coverage of the Collective Incident Environmental Insurance.

In this sense, it is important to remember that by Decree 447/2019, the Executive Branch expanded the range of coverage, allowing the contracting of policies with "Risk Transfer or other financial instruments or insurance plans" that are approved by both the SSN and by SGAYDS.

Both this norm and the current resolution are based on the inter-ministerial table formed by the SSN, the SGAYDS, the Ministry of Production and the Chief of Staff, in October 2018, precisely with the objective of implementing actions, generating new environmental management tools and establish a commitment to sustainable development.

Article 2 of the new resolution provides that prior to the approval of the collective incidence environmental damage insurance plans, on the one hand the SSN will review the current technical-contractual elements and the SGAYDS will verify compliance with current environmental requirements.

Insurers that already have insurance plans for environmental damage previously, will have to send to the SSN, within 30 days of publishing the new resolution, an affidavit signed by the president of the entity and a report from an independent lawyer of the company, realizing that they conform to the new guidelines. Among the foundations of the norm, it refers to Article 22 of the General Environmental Law (Law No. 26,675) and confirms that it is a type of coverage where the protected legal right is the collective environment and whose owner is the community. In this sense, it has the purpose of providing operation to the instrument of the collective ODS, with the purpose of providing predictability and operability to the regulatory system of the Mandatory Environmental Insurance instrument.

Likewise, it considers the inclusion of a franchise appropriate, since it constitutes an effective instrument for the prevention of accidents by the policy holder and/or insured.

In the Annex, it refers to those insurances with risk transfer. These coverages may establish franchises that may not exceed 5% of the Minimum Insurable Amount of Sufficient Entity that will be established by the Government Secretariat for Environment and Sustainable Development. Finally, it explains that based on the accumulated experience, it is appropriate to establish a minimum period of validity of the coverage of one year.

2 The Republic of Chile: Brief Review on Some Topics Related to Environmental Responsibility in Chilean Legislation

Ricardo Peralta Larrain

2.1 Concepts

Law No. 19,300 of the year 1994 defines necessary words in this matter, namely:

Environment: The global system made up of natural and artificial elements of a physical, chemical or biological, socio-cultural nature and their interactions, in permanent modification by human or natural action and which governs and conditions the existence and development of life in its multiple manifestations.

Environmental Damage: Any significant loss, decrease, detriment or impairment inflicted on the environment or one or more of its components;

Pollution: The presence in the environment of substances, elements, energy or a combination of them, in concentrations or concentrations and permanence higher or lower, as appropriate, than those established in current legislation.

Consequently, our legislation establishes that pollution is a kind of environmental damage, not a synonym. This allows us to conclude that there are many ways to cause damage to the environment, other than pollution itself, such as climate change or the irrational use of natural resources, among others.

2.2 General Rules on Civil Liability Derived from Environmental Damage

There are mainly three rules that regulate the bases of this type of liability, without prejudice to a number of specific rules for some particular risks, such as transportation, mining, construction, etc. Such basic norms are those contained in the Political Constitution of the State of 1980, the aforementioned Law No. 19,300 and residually, the ubiquitous Civil Code 1857, which regulate as follows:

Political constitution; Article 19 No. 8 that guarantees: The right to live in a pollution-free environment. It is the duty of the State to ensure that this right is not affected and to protect the preservation of nature. The law may establish specific restrictions on the exercise of certain rights or freedoms to protect the environment, Law No. 19,300 of the year 1994 Title III Article 51 provides: Anyone who negligently or maliciously causes environmental damage will be liable for it in accordance with this law. However, the rules on liability for damage to the environment contained in special laws shall prevail over those of this law.

The Civil Code regulates what is not provided for in other laws in accordance with the general rules of civil liability.

2.2.1 The Victim

We must clarify that the victim, who suffers the damage, can be anyone, there is no legal limitation on that, but on who can exercise certain actions:

The actor is distinguished according to the type of action in question, which can be of two kinds:

i. *Indemnity*: Anyone who has suffered the damage or loss.
ii. *Reparation*: Municipalities, for the events that occurred in their respective communes and the State of Chile.

Deducted claim for any of the above, may not file the others, which is a common restriction in these matters in comparative law. Such restriction is limited to the active subjects of the action, but it does not make both actions incompatible as Article 53 of Law No. 19,300 states when it says:

> Once environmental damage has occurred, action is granted to obtain reparation for the damaged environment, which does not preclude the exercise of ordinary compensation action by the directly affected party.

The action to obtain the repair of the damaged environment will not proceed when the person who committed the damage satisfactorily executed a repair plan approved by the Superintendence of the Environment.

2.2.2 Responsibility of a Subjective Nature

European systems in general have opted for the "polluting, paying" principle of an objective nature or without fault, however the Chilean legislator opted for the subjective route, without doubts or interpretations when saying:

> Anyone who negligently or maliciously causes environmental damage will be liable for it in accordance with this law.

Notwithstanding this subjectivity, the law also establishes a presumption of responsibility "if there is a violation of environmental quality standards, emissions standards, prevention or decontamination plans, special regulations for cases of environmental emergencies or the rules on environmental protection, preservation or conservation, established in this law or in other legal or regulatory provisions."[11] Law No. 19,300, on Bases of the Environment, and its corresponding regulations on the Environmental Impact Assessment System have not established the obligation of companies to take out insurance for environmental damage as a general rule, since for certain dangerous activities such as, for example, the maritime transport of hydrocarbons and other dangerous substances, based on a strict liability regime, insurance is mandatory.

This, because in cases of strict or strict liability, it was a necessary system that would give victims the certainty that compensation for pollution damage.

[11] http//www.Derechoymedioambiente.uc.cl 2.2 Historia de la Ley Pag. 6; accessed on 14.06.2023.

2.2.3 The Causal Relationship in Environmental Damage

We know that subjective responsibility is the one that requires the fault of the agent of the damage, this does not mean that it does not require cause and in this regard our specific law does not establish its own form, consequently the Civil Code governs, however in those cases in which the responsibility it is presumed, there will only be room for compensation, if a cause-to-effect relationship between the infringement and the damage produced is proven.

In simple terms, to have access to compensation, the causal relationship between the fault and the damage claimed by the victim must be proven, who bears the burden of proof.

2.2.4 Prescriptio No Faction: Exception to the General Rule

The general rule provided by the 1857 codifier states that the actions prescribe in five years from the "perpetration of the act" that gives rise to the damage. Article 63 of Law No. 19,300 makes an exception to this norm because although they establish the same term of five years, its computation is different and something totally alien to our history, novel if you want to our civil legislation, but not to the norms that govern the matter in other countries, as the aforementioned article provides that "Environmental action and civil actions arising from environmental damage will prescribe within a period of five years, counted from the evident manifestation of the damage." This way of setting the beginning of the prescription period is what gave rise to the "claims made" policy system in the Anglo-Saxon insurance trade, always adverse to what is colloquially called the "long tail" prescription that defies the certainty that the statistics required in insurance matters, on which various authors have dealt in the last 30 years.

Government entities responsible for authorizing and supervising activities that produce environmental impacts or contamination. There is a set of entities in our legal system whose function is the aforementioned, such as the Ministry of the Environment, on which the supervisory body depends, which is the Superintendence of the Environment, as well as an Environmental Impact Assessment System.

The law also created an Environmental Protection Fund, which is the administrator of the money allocated judicially to repair the environment.

The superintendence's function is to "execute, organize and coordinate the monitoring and control of the Environmental Qualification Resolutions, the measures of the Prevention or Environmental Decontamination Plans, the content of the Environmental Quality Standards and Emission Standards, and the Management Plans, when appropriate."[12]

[12] https://vlx.cl>vid>servicio-superintendencia-ambiente, accessed on 14.06.2023.

2.3 *Procedural Legal System in Case of Environmental Offenses*

This system works in Chile at two levels: The administrative one that depends on the Executive Power and the Judiciary:

i. *Administrative*:

   The municipalities will receive complaints made by citizens for non-compliance with environmental regulations and will notify them to the Superintendency of the Environment so that it can process them.

   Single window system.

ii. *Judicial*

   There are Environmental Courts, specialized in this matter, which are part of the Judiciary and are incorporated into its organic structure. Such courts have the particularity of being made up not only of lawyers, but there are also judges who must hold the professional title of engineer.

Chilean companies concerned about the environment are becoming more numerous, in this context the insurance industry, adding to this trend, offers special products to encourage business interest. The Chubb de Chile insurer sells a policy contract with the following characteristics in the insurance market.

The traditional Civil Liability contract protects against a one shot environmental accident, that is, the consequences of it up to 72 h after the incident, but what happens if the accident has consequences beyond this period of time?

The environmental responsibility policy covers one shot contamination but also gradual contamination, that is, everything that may occur after 72 h of the contingency. We exemplify with a hypothetical case: a truck that transports chemical compounds, and after an accident on public roads, spills its load. Cleaning is done, but part of this residue reaches a water spring, and this water is consumed by a person. This particular contingency is not included in the contamination coverage of a traditional civil liability policy.

The environmental responsibility policy covers this and other associated variables, such as environmental contamination of properties—of the insured himself and of third parties, including cases where a contractor is the cause of the incident -, damage to natural resources, transportation, decrease in the patrimonial value of the goods that belong to third parties, business interruption of the insured himself and even crisis management.

Most companies, whatever the nature of the operation, are exposed to situations of this type. Another example that we take is a company that renews computer equipment and discards it without an adequate process, contaminating a mixed area with chemical products, affecting third parties. Any productive activity where organic components are handled, such as fruit packing, or a vineyard, are also subject to environmental risks that may have consequences beyond the 72-h contingency.

Another relevant aspect to consider is the seismic condition of Chile, which increases the probabilities of this type of contingency. Our country's protocol for handling chemical waste is very strict for this reason. Environmental regulations have become more complex both in Chile and in the world, along with the increase in operations that involve risks in this area. This type of insurance converses with the regulatory development that Chile has undergone in recent years and that we believe will become a plus for any venture that seeks to establish a green, sustainable and environment-conscious operation.

3 Environmental Civil Liability in the Eastern Republic of Uruguay

Roxana Corbrán

3.1 Environmental Constitutional Protection

The protection of the environment in Uruguay has constitutional recognition since the reform of the Constitution promulgated in 1997. Article 47 para 1 of the Constitution of the Republic establishes that the protection of the environment is of general interest and that people must refrain from any act that causes serious depredation, destruction or contamination of the environment. Said article was regulated through Law No. 17,283 of November 28, 2000 called the General Law for Environmental Protection, which establishes the fundamental rights and duties as well as interpreting the constitutional text.

3.2 Environmental Impact Assessment Law

Law No. 16,466 on environmental impact assessment, declared of general and national interest, provides for the protection of the environment against any type of depredation, destruction or contamination, as well as the prevention of negative environmental impact or harmful and, where appropriate, the recomposition of the environment damaged by human activities.

This regulation considers the negative or harmful environmental impact to be any alteration of the physical, chemical or biological properties of the environment caused by any form of matter or energy resulting from human activities that directly or indirectly harm or damage: I. Health, safety or quality of life of the population,

II. The aesthetic, cultural or sanitary conditions of the environment, and III. The configuration, quality and diversity of natural resources.

It establishes as a fundamental duty of every person, physical or legal, to refrain from any act that causes an environmental impact that translates into depredation, destruction or serious contamination of the environment.

The law provides for administrative and criminal sanctions, whoever causes depredation, destruction, or contamination of the environment in violation of the provisions of the law will be civilly responsible for all the damages caused, and must also take charge, if materially possible, of the actions leading to its recomposition. When the damages caused by said violation are irreversible, the person responsible for them must take charge of all the measures tending to their maximum reduction or mitigation, without prejudice to the administrative, civil or criminal responsibilities that may correspond.

3.3 Environmental Damage

The definition of environmental damage arises from Article 3 of Law No. 17,283 as any significant loss, decrease or detriment that is inflicted on the environment. However, the obligation to restore the environment is provided for in Article 4 of Law No. 16,466, promulgated on January 19, 1994.

The environmental damage itself is that which affects the environment, although it is not possible to identify a particular injured party or interested party, but rather corresponds to an indeterminate group of people. The doctrine thus distinguishes environmental damage itself, insofar as it harms the environment itself, from damage due to environmental causes, which directly affects people or their property. Environmental damage, both in our legal system and in comparative law, presents its own characteristics. One of them is related to representation to promote the relevant process. Article 42 of the General Process Code (approved by Law No. 15,982 of October 18, 1988) establishes the rules of representation in the case of the so-called diffuse interests; providing that, in case of issues related to the defense of the environment, as in other issues that belong to an indeterminate group of people, the Public Ministry, the current Ministry of the Environment, the institutions or associations will be indistinctly entitled to promote the relevant process of social interest that according to the law or in the opinion of the court guarantee an adequate defense of the committed interest, as well as any interested party without any other requirement. However, even with specific provisions regarding environmental damage and diffuse interests, there are few provisions on relevant issues for the effectiveness of legal actions aimed at rebuilding the damaged environment. In a process of several decades, the environment in our country has clearly deteriorated, which, however, has not been accompanied by an increase in legal proceedings that have as their object the recomposition of environmental damage. A possible explanation for the low number of cases on this subject, may be the difficulty that exists to achieve a sentence that accepts a claim that has as its object the recomposition of the damaged environment.

3.4 Objective-Subjective Liability

In our law, the doctrinal discussion has been raised about the type of liability that applies to this kind of damage, insofar as it can be understood as subjective or objective. It has been pointed out that the rule in our law is subjective responsibility (Article 1319 of the Civil Code), which also applies to judicial processes with claims tending to restore the damaged environment. Therefore, in principle, the culpable behavior must be proven (subjective responsibility), in addition to requiring proof of the causal link between the illegal act and the damage caused, which in itself is enormously difficult from a practical point of view. Liability for environmental damage appears to be incipiently regulated by Article 4 of Law No. 16,466, although it does not expressly clarify the type of liability that should be applied with respect to such damage, when it has been understood that strict liability must be consecrated to an express text. That article establishes that, without prejudice to the administrative and criminal sanctions indicated by law, whoever causes depredation, destruction or contamination of the environment in violation of the provisions of the articles of said law, will be civilly responsible for all damages caused, and must take charge, in addition, if materially it were possible, of the actions leading to its recomposition. Therefore, to date there has not been expressly legislated in our legal system on the liability regime for environmental damage, and there is only one express reference to strict liability in any case of environmental damage. Article 10 of Law No. 16,688 of December 22, 1994 establishes an objective and joint liability, with respect to the owners or operators of ships, aircraft operators, naval artifacts, facilities established on land or underwater platforms. that have caused contamination, the payment of expenses for cleaning the water, compensation for damages or for any other service that, as a consequence of the fact, the General Command of the Navy, any other intervening body or company designated by the shipowner, should have carried out. owner of the ship or naval artifact. All this may imply greater difficulty and lack of legal certainty when determining responsibility for environmental damage.

3.5 Procedural Legal System

Since environmental damage is collective damage, we must point out the particularities that refer to the legitimacy provided by Article 42 of the General Process Code (CGP), which provides that in matters related to the environment: it will be legitimized indistinctly to promote the pertinent process, the Public Ministry, any interested party and the institutions or associations of social interest that, according to the law or in the opinion of the Court, guarantee an adequate defense of the committed interest. On the other hand, Article 220 of the CGP establishes that:

> The sentence handed down in processes promoted in defense of diffuse interests (article 42) will have general effectiveness, unless it is acquittal due to lack of evidence, in which case, another legitimized party may raise the issue again in another process. Another important norm to highlight and of vital importance is Law 17220 that prohibits the introduction in any form of all types of hazardous waste in the areas of national jurisdiction of the hazardous waste or residues referred to in article 3 of the law that establishes that hazardous waste or waste shall mean all those substances or objects, whatever their origin, that are thus categorized by the regulations, taking into account those physical, chemical, biological or radioactive characteristics that constitute a risk to the environment, including human, animal or plant health.

Notwithstanding other categories that may be provided for in national legislation and as long as they are not expressly defined by the regulations, radioactive wastes and those considered as such according to subparagraph a) of paragraph 1 are included among the hazardous wastes covered by this law. Article 1 and Annexes 1 and 111 of the Basel Convention on the Control of Transboundary Movements of Hazardous Waste and its Elimination, approved in Basel (Switzerland), on March 22, 1989, and its amendments.

Article 6 establishes: When there are reasons to presume that through a means of transport it is intended to illegally introduce hazardous waste, the competent authorities will order the appropriate preventive measures.

3.6 Urgent Consideration Law No. 19,889 and the Environment

On July 9, 2020, Law No. 19,889, the Urgent Consideration Law, was promulgated, in Section V Efficiency of the State, in Chapter I Article 291, provides for the Creation of the Ministry of the Environment, which will have jurisdiction on the matters indicated in this law. Article 292. (Conduction of the sectoral policy) - The Executive Branch will establish the national environmental policy, environmental management and sustainable development and conservation and use of natural resources, which it will execute through the ministry that is hereby created. Law in the matter of its competence.

The non-governmental organization (NGO) Ecologistas Unidos de Uruguay, in the hearing with the Study Commission of the Urgent Law Project for consideration by the Senate, proposed various points to be discussed, among others environmental education, an issue that was added to the text of the regulations in question.

3.7 Standard on Environmental Responsibility

The environmental responsibility standard is under treatment in the Parliament of Uruguay. The purpose of the regulation is to regulate the liability action in the case of environmental damage, promoted by a legitimized party representing diffuse interests. Establishes strict liability for both individuals and legal entities (extending liability to the acting authorities and professionals) obliged to rebuild and reestablish the situation prior to the occurrence of the damage in accordance with Article 4 of Law No. 16,466. Precautionary measures are planned, liability solidarity, compulsory insurance and the statute of limitations is 30 years from the time the environmental damage was committed, from its termination if it was continued, or from the time the environmental damage could be detected if its effects were not manifestly perceptible.

This bill expressly establishes strict liability for environmental damage related to diffuse interests, whose purpose is the recomposition of the environment. This follows the trend of comparative law (in countries such as Germany, Argentina, Spain, Ecuador, the United States of America, and Great Britain), and the suggestion by the doctrine of environmental law, both national and foreign. The legal system does not establish substitute compensation for cases in which the recomposition of the environment is not materially or technically feasible, as it exists in other legislations (such as in Argentina, by virtue of the General Environmental Law, Law No. 25,675). Therefore, the bill provides for substitute compensation, which must be determined by the intervening court, and deposited in the National Environmental Fund (FONAMA), created by Article 454 of Law No. 16,170 of January 10, 1991. These funds could be used for the purposes of the State carrying out ex officio recovery and recomposition plans (literal H of Article 7 of Law No. 17,283), and improve environmental conditions in our country.

On the other hand, this bill establishes solidarity with regard to those responsible for environmental damage (Article 4), clarifying that if two or more people participated in the commission of that damage, they will all be jointly and severally responsible for the recomposition of environmental damage, without prejudice to the right of repetition between them, in a solution that also appears in comparative law. The same article proposes that any person who uses subcontractors, intermediaries or labor suppliers will be jointly and severally liable for the environmental damage caused by them. All this in order to avoid hiring certain figures that could be used to avoid liability for environmental damage, as has been warned and resolved in Labor Law, for example through Law No. 18,099 of 24 January 2007, and Law No. 18,251 of January 6, 2008. Article 5 of the bill provides for the regime applicable to other obligated subjects, providing that in the event that the damage is caused by legal persons, they will also be their authorities and professionals responsible, if there has been fraud or negligence, and to the extent of their participation. Other of the particularities of environmental law is reflected in the causal relationship. The diffuse nature of this type of damage offers a series of difficulties in identifying the causal link. That is why the doctrine understands that in environmental law, the interested party should not demonstrate this causal relationship with scientific accuracy, but a probability close to certainty or a high probability could suffice. In this sense, the bill proposes in its Article 7 that in procedures whose objective is the recomposition of the environment, the causal relationship will be understood to have been verified when there is a high probability that a certain natural or legal person has caused the damage, and that Such subjects will have the burden of proving that they have not been responsible for the environmental damage whose recomposition or repair is pursued. All this in order to settle the evidentiary difficulty that exists in this type of responsibility, and that can also explain the lack of environmental trials in our law. The jurisprudence of our country tends—increasingly—to impose the burden of proof on those who are in the best condition to provide the evidence, and taking into account the particularities of the parties. The bill also establishes a more flexible regime in figures proper to Procedural Law, such as precautionary measures. In comparative law, it has been noted that in this type of process it may not be possible or convenient to set a counter-injunction, due to the particularity of environmental issues, the nature of the protected assets, as well as the general incidence of their affectations. Article 7 establishes that in cases in which the precautionary measure is aimed at protecting the environment and the petitioner has justified the danger of environmental damage, the court will consider this case as an exceptional case for the purpose of exempting from the counter-injunction provision. in accordance with the provisions of numeral 5) of Article 313 of the General Process Code.

On the other hand, Article 8 of the bill establishes the obligation to contract an ***Environmental Insurance***, for certain activities, constructions or works from which risks to the environment may arise. The future regulation of said provision will determine the terms, limits and conditions of the environmental insurance. The obligation to take out insurance of this nature does not entail a comprehensive solution to environmental damage, but it operates as a complementary measure, since certain preventive measures are required (essential function of the regulations related to environmental law and foreseen as a principle of environmental policy in the literal B of Article 6 of Law No. 17,283), for the granting of coverage, will result in a reduction in risk, tending to protect the environment.

Finally, an issue that is also complex to determine with the current legal regime, is the existing limitation period for actions aimed at rebuilding the damaged environment. In comparative law, the statute of limitations generally exceeds 20 years, although countries such as Spain have established a term of 30 years. Regarding the computation of said period, the solution already provided for the prescription of administrative offenses committed against the rules of environmental protection was adopted, in the manner provided in Article 169 of Law No. 19,535 of September 25, 2017. We understand that prevention is the most important thing, but reality leads us to forms of reparation or restitution when unwanted damage has occurred, so it is to be expected that a liability regime that tries to avoid the damage to nature and therefore human life, animal, plant, and environment.

References

Código Civil 2023 Equipo Editorial Thomson Reuters Chile
Código Civil de la República Oriental del Uruguay. Comentado, anotado y concordado
Código Civil y Comercial de la Nación Ley 26.994 Di Lalla Ediciones 2014
Código General del Proceso 2016 Gómes Santoro, F. Editorial La Ley de Uruguay
Constitución de la Nación Argentina 1996 6° edición Editorial Astrea
Constitución de la República Oriental del Uruguay de 1.967. 5ª Edición 2017 Fundación de Cultura Universitaria
Constitución Política de Chile. Edición Oficial 25ª Edición 2022 Editorial Jurídica de Chile
El DiarioSur Esteban Echeverría. Año XVI N° 687 2-26-2023 Pág. 22. Buenos Aires –Argentina
htpps:// htpps:// www.saij.gob.ar/corte-suprema-justicia-nacion-Municipalidad de Magdalena c/ Shell CAPSA y otros. Sentencia 3 de Mayo de 2007
htpps:// servicios.infoleg.gob.ar Ley 25.612 Gestión Integral de Residuos Industriales
htpps:// servicios.infoleg.gob.ar Ley 25.670 Presupuestos Mínimos para la Gestión y Eliminación de los PCB's
htpps:// servicios.infoleg.gob.ar Ley 25.675 Ley General del Ambiente
htpps:// www.revistaestretegas.com.ar/contenidos/5219 Publicado 2019-11-27
htpps:// www.saij.gob.ar/corte-suprema-justicia-nacion- Mendoza Beatriz Silvia y ots. c/ Estado Nacional y ots. 2006/2008
htpps:// www.scba.gob.ar Subterráneos de Buenos Aires Sociedad del Estado c/propietario estación de servicio Shell CNCIV Sala H 01/10/1999
https://www.impo.com.uy> bases>leyes > 16170
https://www.impo.com.uy> bases>leyes > 16466
https://www.impo.com.uy> bases>leyes > 16688
https://www.impo.com.uy> bases>leyes > 17220
https://www.impo.com.uy> bases>leyes > 19889
Ley N° 19300 Sobre bases generales del medio ambiente. Biblioteca del Congreso Nacional de Chile/BCN. Ministerio Secretaría General de la Presidencia. Promulgación 03-01-1994
Marino López A. 5ª Edición. 2021
Mosset Iturraspe J, Hutchinson T, Donna EA (2011) *Daño Ambiental* Tomo I 2ª.ed. Cap. I Pag. 39 Editorial Rubinzal Culzoni Editores Santa Fe
Ossandón Rosales J (2022) Daño Ambiental y significancia 1ra edición Rubicon Editores https://www.chubb.com/cl-es
Paz A et al El Seguro Ambiental (2006) LexisNexis Argentina Pág 2/17
Revista de Derecho ambiental-Doctrina, Jurisprudencia, Legislación y Práctica 2014 N° 40 Oct/Dec Director Cafferata, N. *El amparo ambiental. Proceso en defensa delambiente* Palacio de Caerio, S,; Junyent de Dutari, P. Pág. 236/255 Editorial Abeledo Perrot Argentina
Revista de Derecho ambiental-Doctrina, Jurisprudencia, Legislación y Práctica 2016 N° 45 Enero/ Marzo Director Cafferata, N.*Novedades protectorias del ambiente en elCódigo Civil y Comercial Unificado* Pág. 96/105 Camps, C. Editorial Abeledo Perrot Argentina
Sabsay D. "*El Desarrollo Sustentable en un Fallo de la Justicia Federal*"; Publicado en: El Derecho. Diario de Jurisprudencia y Doctrina. AñoXXXV/N°9355 (10/10/97), Buenos Aires, p 1

Part II
The Practice of Insurance Coverage of the Environmental Risks

Environmental Insurance Product

Malwina Lemkowska

Abstract The unclear meaning of the terms "environment" and "risk" and, as a result, the ambiguous concept of "environmental risk" makes one look for protection from this risk in many insurance products. However, not all of them bear the attributes of an environmental insurance product. This chapter proposes a definition of an environmental insurance product, with environmental underwriting as its main determinant. The basic classification of environmental insurance was indicated, and—from a historical perspective—the process of its evolution was presented.

1 Environmental Risk: Notion

The concept of risk has troubled humanity for ages. Over the years, however, various categories of risk have been treated with varying importance. Environmental risk, as it is understood today, had not received proper attention until the twentieth century.

It is extremely difficult to determine the scope of the term environmental risk. The problem lies mainly in the ambiguity of the two components of this notion: namely, the definitions of environment and risk. What also seems to be raising substantial doubts is the description of sources of perils, leading to the materialisation of risk. Indicating the subject of risk, which can be identified as individual or collective (social), is essential as well. Additionally, various fields of science and diverse areas of socio-economic activities call for separate scopes of the aforementioned terms. Therefore, it is absolutely essential to formulate them more accurately in order to fulfil the aim of the present compilation.

Subject literature and documents referring to environmental issues provide a wide array of definitions for "**environment**", beginning from the most general (e.g. "the

M. Lemkowska (✉)
Poznań University of Economics and Business, Poznań, Poland
e-mail: malwina.lemkowska@ue.poznan.pl

K. Malinowska, D. Maśniak (eds.), *Managing Environmental Risks through Insurance*, AIDA Europe Research Series on Insurance Law and Regulation 9,
https://doi.org/10.1007/978-3-031-47602-0_8

surrounding in which the organisation operates”[1] or “the place where we all live”)[2] to the detailed ones (e.g. “physical and biological surrounding of man, whether this environment is ‘natural’ or it is affected by man’s actions”[3] or “the surrounding which offers man physical sustenance and affords him the opportunity for intellectual, moral, social and spiritual growth, where both aspects of man’s environment, the natural and the man-made, are essential to his well-being and to the enjoyment of basic human rights”[4]). Next to the functional approach to the environment, the definitions that identify particular elements of the environment become particularly relevant for insurance.[5] Among the latter ones, the legal definitions are primarily valid. They operationalise the objective scope of the legal protection of the environment. Hence, e.g., the English Environmental Protection Act[6] defines “environment” as consisting of all, or any, of the following media: air, water and land, and the medium of air includes the air within buildings and the air within other natural or man-made structures above or below ground. Abundant US legislation assumes various definitions of the environment, depending on the regulatory purpose; e.g., the National Environmental Policy Act[7] points to environmental classes, including, but not limited to, the air; the aquatic ecosystem, including marine, estuarine and freshwater; and the terrestrial environment, including, but not limited to, the forest, dryland, wetland, range, urban, suburban and rural environment. The Comprehensive Environmental Response, Compensation, and Liability Act (CERCLA)[8] defines “environment” as “(A) the navigable waters, the waters of the contiguous zone, and the ocean waters of which the natural resources are under the exclusive management authority of the United States under the Fishery Conservation and Management Act of 1976, and (B) any other surface water, groundwater, drinking water supply, land surface or subsurface strata, or ambient air within the United States or under the jurisdiction of the United States”. Also, the suspended draft of the German environmental law[9] proposed a uniform definition of the environment, which enumerated its elements, such as animals, plants, biological diversity, soil, water, air, climate and

[1] Point 3.2.1 of the standard. ISO (2015) Environmental management systems – Requirements with guidance for use. ISO 14001:2015, Geneva.

[2] WCED World Commission on Environment and Development (1987) Our Common Future (Brundtland Report). http://www.un-documents.net/our-common-future.pdf. (access 10.05.2023).

[3] United Nations Economic and Social Council (1969) Problems of the Human Environment. Report of the Secretary-General (U’Thant’s Report). https://digitallibrary.un.org/record/729455 (access 10.05.2023).

[4] United Nations Conference on the Human Environment (1972) Report: Stockholm Declaration, A/Conf 48/14/rev.1. http://www.un-documents.net/aconf48-14r1.pdf. (access 10.05.2023).

[5] Larsson (2009), 156 and next; Duikers and Bischofs (2019), 11–13.

[6] Environmental Protection Act of 1990 (c. 43).

[7] The National Environmental Policy Act of 1969 (42 U.S.C. § 4321 et seq.).

[8] Comprehensive Environmental Response, Compensation and Liability Act (CERCLA) of 1980, (42 U.S.C. § 9601 et seq.).

[9] Umweltgesetzbuch (UGB) Entwurf (2008). https://www.umweltbundesamt.de/sites/default/files/medien/1/dokumente/ugb1_allgem_vorschriften.pdf. (access 10.05.2023).

landscape, as well as cultural and other material assets (environmental assets). The project's failure contributed to various, often incoherent, definitions in German law.[10] The definition of the environment as a list of its distinguishable elements is rather commonplace in many other state regulations,[11] as well as international ones, like the Lugano Convention[12] or the Draft Principles of the International Law Commission (ILC) on the allocation of loss in the case of transboundary harm arising from hazardous activities.[13] It has to be said here that the collection of elements that constitute the environment is not uniform among various legal acts, such as in the case of the two latter documents; the difference lies in "cultural heritage", which is excluded from the definition of the environment in the Draft Principles of ILC.

Defining the environment as an enumeration of its components is primarily useful in regulations that refer to the liability for environmental damage. In legal systems, a violation of an element of the environment or the relations between the elements as well as the damage done to its or their functionalities are eligible bases for victims' claims or the remedial duties of the authors of the damage. Component-based definitions of the environment are therefore crucial to the construction of most products of environmental insurance.

The ambiguity of the notion of environment is accompanied by a lack of a uniform **concept of risk** in research processes. Over centuries, the concept of risk has been defined numerous times in legal regulations, standards and guidelines. Similarly, the scientific approach to risk has continuously evolved over time; as a result, present-day scholars tend to use multiple definitions of risk, which are frequently incompatible or incoherent.[14] In the past, there were numerous, albeit fruitless, attempts to curb this vagueness. Not one of the proposed definitions was accepted by all researchers or practitioners within various fields of social activity. Nevertheless, one common element among the various definitions is that they all refer to categories that materialise in the future and values that defining subjects

---

[10] E.g. Bundes-Immissionsschutzgesetz in der Fassung der Bekanntmachung vom 17. Mai 2013 (BGBl. I S. 1274; 2021 I S. 123), das zuletzt durch Artikel 1 des Gesetzes vom 18. August 2021 (BGBl. I S. 3901) geändert worden ist; Gesetz über die Umweltverträglichkeitsprüfung in der Fassung der Bekanntmachung vom 18. März 2021 (BGBl. I S. 540), das durch Artikel 14 des Gesetzes vom 10. September 2021 (BGBl. I S. 4147) geändert worden ist.

[11] The Polish Act of 27th April 2001 The Law on Environmental Protection (unified text Dz.U. 2020 item 1219); The Environment (Protection) Act of India, act no. 29 of 1986.

[12] Convention on civil liability for damage resulting from activities dangerous to the environment (Lugano, 1993). https://www.ecolex.org/details/treaty/convention-on-civil-liability-for-damage-resulting-from-activities-dangerous-to-the-environment-tre-001166/?q=Convention+on+civil+liability+for+damage+resulting+from+activities+dangerous+to+the+environment%2C+. (access 10.05.2023).

[13] International Law Commission (ILC) (2006) Draft principles on the allocation of loss in the case of transboundary harm arising out of hazardous activities. https://legal.un.org/ilc/texts/instruments/english/commentaries/9_10_2006.pdf. (access 10.05.2023).

[14] Aven (2010), pp. 623–631; Rejda and McNamara (2017), p. 20; Renn (1998), pp. 49–71; Vaughan and Vaughan (2008), pp. 1–11.

subscribe to. This is reflected in the construction of particular definitions that are emotionally charged (e.g. peril, loss, damage, failure) and contain reference to goals and expectations.

In the course of risk studies, two essential trends were established. The first one (more prevalent) approaches risk as the derivative of the attributes of its objective sources. In line with this trend, risk is objective and independent of an individual person's beliefs; it is assessed in accordance with expertise (with the use of such measurements as the probability of the realisation of an occurrence or the probable scope of damage), and the attitudes of individuals to an objectively existing risk are determined by their perception of this risk. The other trend treats risk as a subject-centred, individual, subjective phenomenon. It does not enable the risk to be identified by external entities because it is determined by a host of endogenous conditions referring to the subject of risk. Hence, the attributes of risk are always different, depending on the subject to which the risk refers. Such an approach makes it possible, when analysing risk, to use measurements of damage materialisation probability or the potential scope of this damage. It does not, at the same time, eliminate the possibility of using probabilistic methods of risk assessment. The values of these measures, however, will remain varied, depending on the subject of risk to which they refer.

The analysis of the subjective factor in risk studies makes the pragmatic conclusions of both trends converge with each other. In the trend that treats risk as subject centred, the subjective factor determines the risk itself. Its biased assessment, in turn, is a permanent/constant, albeit presented in a multifaceted way, element that unites scientific concepts in studies based on the objective approach to risk.[15] The subjective factor predominantly affects the wide spectrum of research problems.

The first group of research problems stems from the question of why people perceive risk in different ways.[16] Numerous concepts of risk perception determinants have been studied for many years. They comprise such approaches as the techno-scientific approach, the comprehensive personality model, the psychometric model, and the value-belief-norm theory.[17] The essential factor that differs from the above concepts is the significance attributed to particular determinants of the risk perception process.[18] Janmaimool and Watanabe[19] suggest classifying the scientifically elaborated risk perception concepts into one of the following four groups. The first—the group of cultural concepts—attributes crucial relevance to social factors affecting the determination of risk. The paradigm of axiomatic measurement (group 2) prioritises the individual dimension of risk perception determination. In the psychometric paradigm (group 3), risk perception is derived from both physical attributes of

[15] Aven and Renn (2010), p. 10; Anantho (2008), p. 3; Sandman (2012), pp. 6–12; Altonoğlu et al. (2017), p. 436.

[16] Chauvin et al. (2007), p. 171.

[17] Altonoğlu et al. (2017), p. 437.

[18] Kaczała (2017), p. 282.

[19] Janmaimool and Watanabe (2014), p. 6294.

a risk (i.e. voluntariness, knowledge of risk, or its potentially catastrophic impact) and psychological as well as cognitive factors. The fourth group is the most interdisciplinary in its character. Risk perception is developed in two stages within this approach. First, it is determined by external factors (i.e. the manner in which information about risk is communicated). Next, the image of the risk is interpreted individually or collectively, which, in turn, is a process moulded by internal factors.

Empirical studies have identified numerous factors (both intrinsic and extrinsic) that determine perceptions of environmental risk. The system of risk perception has turned out to be exceptionally elaborate and diverse. Perception-moulding factors differ depending on a person's residence, exposure to exogenous risk,[20] race and ethnic group, educational background, level of income, political views,[21] and spatial and time distance.[22] Research findings have not always been consistent. Alhakami and Slovic,[23] for instance, demonstrated that the higher the benefits that were equated with risk-generating activities, the lower values were allocated to risk perception. Gregory and Mendelsohn,[24] on the other hand, noticed that individual risk assessment is embedded in perceiving the benefits of engagement in a given activity (through a decrease in these benefits). Quite conversely, the studies by Janmaimool and Watanabe[25] showed that the higher the assessment of the benefits of an activity was, the higher was the perception of the risk referring to it.

The recognition of the factors determining risk perceptions caused researchers to develop recommendations with reference to the process of risk communication.[26] A suitable adaptation of the method of communication to the profile of risk and the factors determining its perception by a particular entity (groups of entities) results in its effectiveness.[27] Communication principles must therefore change dynamically, along with the evolution of the surroundings of the subject of risk.[28]

Another group of research problems was connected with the assessment of the impact of risk perception on attitudes to risk. In the 1980s, it was demonstrated that risk perception determines the importance ascribed to the means of control of that risk.[29] Risk perception, next to such factors as individual or collective awareness of problems (e.g. environmental ones), access to information, experiences and administrative tools like sanctions or subsidies, is a determinant of the decision-making process of the subject of risk. In the past, the impact of perceptions on the type of

---

[20] Janmaimool and Watanabe (2014), p. 6307.

[21] Macias (2016), pp. 124–126.

[22] Shengxiang et al. (2012), p. 224. The effects of risk materialisation which were distant in terms of time and space were assessed as lower than the current and proximate ones.

[23] Alhakami and Slovic (1994), pp. 1085–1096.

[24] Gregory and Mendelsohn (1993), pp. 259–264.

[25] Janmaimool and Watanabe (2014), p. 6307.

[26] Seeger (2006), pp. 232–244; Allen et al. (2017), pp. 422–440.

[27] Janmaimool and Watanabe (2014), p. 6308.

[28] Kasperson (2014), pp. 1233–1239; Renn (2014), pp. 1277–1281.

[29] Slovic et al. (1980), p. 202.

action taken was studied with reference to various risk categories (e.g. natural disaster risk,[30] health risk[31] and various types of social activities, e.g. nature-related risk in farming[32]).

Hence, the subjective factor is of crucial significance to the range of actions taken in order to control risk (especially including the development of the insurance market), regardless of whether it determines the risk itself or merely its perception. This is because the demand for insurance either is derived from the identification of a particular individual risk category by the potential insured individual (subjective approach to risk) or results from a definite perception of an objectively existing risk (objective approach to risk). In both of these cases, increasing the demand for insurance requires a suitable level of awareness concerning the area that the risk refers to.

Within the lengthy and abundant history of risk studies, it was only in the mid-twentieth century, which is rather late, that **environmental risk** became a subject of research interest. The social need for environmental protection has however been identified for many centuries. The environmental risk that it referred to assumed a different dimension in each historical period. Its perception resulted from a disparate bundle of values followed in the past (e.g. the value of natural resources used to facilitate the military) and a variety of social causes (such as the protection of towns against epidemics). In the twentieth century, environmental risk started to be linked to technological development.[33] At first, the prevalent view was the one concerning the control of technology which would enable efficient risk prevention (a so-called deterministic approach). Soon, however, it became evident that this particular risk required much more attentive research, so first attempts at risk assessment using probabilistic methods were made. Despite this, until the mid-twentieth century, the benefits resulting from the exploration of technology were believed to outbalance the costs represented by the materialisation of environmental risk. It was only in the 1960s that environmental issues were recognised as socially relevant. The statement by United Nations Secretary General U'Thant at the 23rd session of the UN Assembly in 1968, followed a year later by the publication of a document called "Problems of the Human Environment", marked the symbolic beginning of a contemporary approach by the international community to the issue of environmental risk. From that moment onwards, a range of documents have been compiled at the international level (i.a. the level of United Nations, Organisation for Economic Cooperation and Development, the European Union, the African Union, and the Association of South-East Asian Nations or the Program for Supporting the Environment of the South-Pacific Region), as well as at the local level (ecological policies of the different countries in the world), aimed at establishing the framework for the activities of the community with a view to environmental risk. In the wake of

[30] Kaczała (2019), pp. 113–120.

[31] Brewer et al. (2007), pp. 136–145.

[32] Toma and Mathijs (2007), pp. 145–157.

[33] Stankiewicz (2008), p. 32.

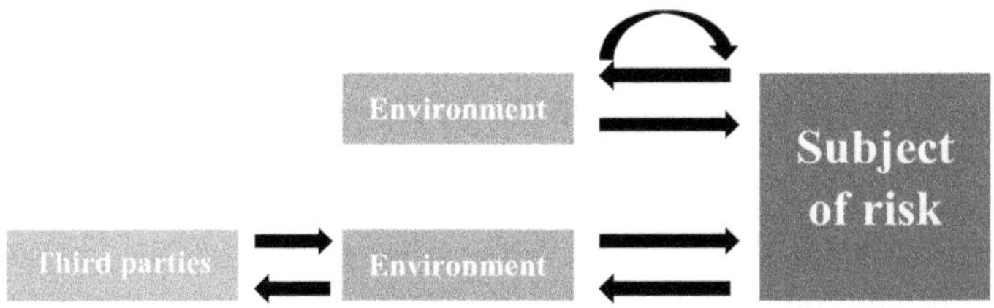

Fig. 1 Relation Between the Subject of Risk and the Environment. Source: By author

this creative activity in the area of environmental protection, intensified regulatory steps were taken.

It was only as a result of the aforementioned activities that the identification of the environment (its elements and their functions) as a value (direct or indirect) led to a broader scientific exploration of the subject of environmental risk. The studies of this subject were, however, evidently intensified only at the start of the new millennium[34] and clearly stemmed from the increasingly common, on a global scale, restrictive regulations that establish the principles of environmental damage liability.

In the past 50 years, the scientific approach to environmental risk (just as to risk in general) has evolved significantly. The evolution referred to how entities were granted entitlements to define the values that are violated by the materialisation of environmental risk. At first, only experts (engineers for the most part) were given the right to establish the values and estimate risk attributes. Such a perspective indeed narrowed the array of values considered that would be violated by the materialisation of environmental risk. Nevertheless, with time, social science scholars have built an ample and versatile catalogue of values connected with the environment, which were identified by subjects of risk at various levels of economic system organisation (micro-micro, micro, meso, macro and global). On the grounds of social sciences, environmental risk was not approached as an ontological being. Conversely, within the epistemological approach, individual factors were studied (such as individuals' psychological traits), as well as cultural patterns that determine the identification or perception of risk.[35]

It is therefore not surprising that in the course of the aforementioned evolution of the various approaches to environmental risk, it was recognised that its sources may be derived from a host of environmental problems, beginning with a lawn fouled with animal faeces to climate change caused by the emissions of greenhouse gases.[36] Risk originates from all types of relations of the subject of risk with the environment. The subject of environmental risk can be a natural person, a legal entity or an organisation without legal status, as well as a social group whose property or

[34] Bamberg and Möser (2007), pp. 14–25; Xu et al. (2017), pp. 35–50; Janmaimool and Watanabe (2014), pp. 6292–6293; Altonoğlu et al. (2017), p. 437; Rowe and Frewer (2004), p. 513.

[35] Douglas and Wildavsky (1982), p. 20.

[36] Dryzek (2005), p. 25.

personal interests may be infringed as a result of the relations they have with the environment (Fig. 1).

Environmental risk is not the only category generated by relations between the subject of risk and the environment presented in the diagram above as it only results from the accidental impact on environmental elements. It must be emphasised here that the term "accidental" should not relate to the event itself that infringes on the elements of the environment; it denotes the impact on the environment the scope of which is inadvertent and socially unacceptable.

The impact on the environment frequently results from commonly accepted consequences of human activity. The long-term character of this impact and the accumulation of its consequences lead one to identify yet another risk category, i.e. climate risk. Climate risk is a hybrid of nature-related risk (where the sources of peril are the forces of nature, such as hurricanes, rainfalls, air temperature etc.) and social risk (when the source of peril is human activity). Climate risk and other types of nature-related risk should definitely be distinguished as separate from the category of environmental risk.

Essentially, it is possible to distinguish three groups of **subjects of environmental risk**. Firstly, environmental risk subjects are the potential or actual operators who have caused environmental damage. Because a significant amount of such damage occurs due to pollution (i.e. emissions of substances or energy that may have a harmful effect on human health or on the condition of the environment, may inflict damage onto material goods, may deteriorate the aesthetic qualities of the environment or may interfere with other justified ways of using the environment), the damage-causing operator is the polluter at the same time. The consequences of the materialisation of environmental risk may be twofold for the operator who is at fault. First, it may lead to his financial liability (civil, administrative) for the consequences of the damage done. Second, own emissions may result in the infringement of property or personal interests of the polluter. The scope of the liability of the operator at fault is derived from the legal system within which they operate. There is no uniform legal framework that would mark, in an international sense, the range of the preventive and remedial duties of the potential or actual polluter. Also, there is no universal, globally applicable legal **definition of environmental damage**, while particular legal acts narrow the notion down to suit the purpose of the given regulation. International legal acts (conventions) treat environmental issues in a "spotlight" manner.[37] Environmental damage refers therein to a particular type of activity (e.g. under the Convention on liability and compensation for damage in

[37] One of the few exceptions to such "spotlight" regulations is the 1993 Lugano Convention (Convention on civil liability for damage resulting from activities dangerous to the environment (Lugano, 1993). https://www.ecolex.org/details/treaty/convention-on-civil-liability-for-damage-resulting-from-activities-dangerous-to-the-environment-tre-001166/?q=Convention+on+civil+liability+for+damage+resulting+from+activities+dangerous+to+the+environment%2C+. (access 10.05.2023)). The document regulated the liability for the broadly meant environmental damage without limitations regarding the type of activity, emissions or elements of the environment. The convention, however, never came into force.

connection with the carriage of hazardous and noxious substances by sea[38]), the type of emissions (as contained in the Convention on civil liability for oil pollution damage[39] or the Protocol to amend the international Convention on civil liability for oil pollution damage[40]) or a precisely defined element of the environment (e.g. the seas) (Convention on the Law of the Sea[41]). International regulations serve the purpose of solving the problem of cross-border environmental damage[42]. They establish the rules for remedying the damage, which are in force only when the affected area spreads over the territories of several different countries. At the same time, they leave it at the discretion of the particular state legislators to pass the liability regulations concerning pollution confined to the area of a particular country. Such a design of a legal system does not make it possible to use a single binding definition of environmental damage. The analysis of environmental risk and environmental insurance as a broad approach that reaches beyond either the framework of a particular legislation, a single type of emission or an element of the environment justifies reference to non-legal scholarly works. In accordance with the broadest, non-legal terminology, environmental damage encompasses both primary damage (done to the elements of the environment) and secondary damage (done to a person or property or the financial losses of indirectly affected parties).[43]

J.S. Dryzek[44] points out that there are two dimensions of environmental problems: one regarding ecosystems and one concerning social systems (decision-making systems—be they individual or collective decisions) which determine the scope of the impact of environmental damage on the operator who causes it. Dryzek qualifies both systems as extremely complex. When it comes to ecosystems, he emphasises the limitations in the area of knowledge about nature, both on an individual level and in scientific (social) terms. The lack of awareness of the details concerning relations that occur in ecosystems leads to the omission of certain present-day activities from the catalogue of the ones that are hazardous to the environment, while some changes in the environment are either entirely unrecognised or considered to be harmless. It is difficult to explicitly categorise

[38] Convention on liability and compensation for damage in connection with the carriage of hazardous and noxious substances by sea (London, 1996). https://www.ecolex.org/details/treaty/international-convention-on-liability-and-compensation-for-damage-in-connection-with-the-carriage-of-hazardous-and-noxious-substances-by-sea-1996-tre-001245/. (access 10.05.2023).

[39] Convention on civil liability for oil pollution damage (Brussels 1969). https://www.ecolex.org/details/treaty/international-convention-on-civil-liability-for-oil-pollution-damage-tre-000120/. (access 10.05.2023).

[40] Protocol to amend the international Convention on civil liability for oil pollution damage (London 1984). https://www.ecolex.org/details/treaty/protocol-to-amend-the-international-convention-on-civil-liability-for-oil-pollution-damage-tre-000839/. (access 10.05.2023).

[41] Convention on the Law of the Sea (Montego Bay 1982). https://www.un.org/depts/los/convention_agreements/convention_overview_convention.htm. (access 10.05.2023).

[42] Khalatbari and Poorhashemi (2019), pp. 21–28.

[43] Swiss Re (2007) Insuring environmental damage in the European Union, 9.

[44] Dryzek (2005), pp. 8–9.

particular actions as definitely favourable to the environment or as ones acting against it.[45] Consequently, it is not an easy task to describe the scope of environmental damage. There have been instances of remedial actions taken that—against all expectations—aggravated the damage that had been done to the environment.[46] At the social system level, it is the liability regulations, their evolution and interpretation as well as the victims' level of legal and environmental awareness that determine the scope of the impact of environmental risk materialisation for the damage-causing entity. In the past, remedial duties were imposed via regulations on operators with regard to secondary environmental damage. Liability for primary damage has been an aftermath of the later legal acts, e.g. the United States's Resource Conservation and Recovery Act[47] or the Comprehensive Environmental Response, Compensation, and Liability Act[48] and Great Britain's Environmental Protection Act.[49] Along with a powerful promotion of pro-environmental social attitudes at the global or macro levels of economic systems, as well as expanding the activities of public and non-governmental organisations or think-tanks, the victims' legal and environmental awareness is increasing as well. Therefore, polluters may expect a systematic growth in the scope of the consequences of environmental risk materialisation. Another interesting issue—still lacking an unambiguous interpretation—is the scope of liability for damage occurring due to the regular (not accidental) activities of entities.[50]

Another group of subjects of environmental risk is the victims of emissions generated by a third party. The victims may be individuals (natural persons, legal entities, or other organisations whose property or personal interests have been infringed due to changes in the elements of the environment), or they may constitute a group that collectively uses particular elements of the environment. Such a group may have a local (e.g. local community), countrywide and also global character. The particular elements of the environment can also be private property (land) or can constitute the common good (air), which determines the type of risk assigned to

---

[45] Fisher et al. (2013), pp. 22–23.

[46] E.g., installation of taller chimneys that carried pollution emissions high enough into the atmosphere so as not to infringe the property interests of particular third parties in an identifiable way. They did, however, in the long term, cause depletion of the ozone layer (Fisher et al. (2013), p. 618), cleansing the Alaskan coast beaches following the Exxon Valdez tanker oil spill by means of hot water under pressure, which turned out to be deadly for many marine fauna species which had survived the oil spill itself (Exxon Valdez Oil Spill Trustee Council (1999) Exxon Valdez Oil Spill Restoration Plan, Update on Injured Resources and Services. https://www.arlis.org/docs/vol1/41089450.pdf. (access 10.05.2023)).

[47] The Resource Conservation and Recovery Act (RCRA) of 1976 (42 U.S.C. § 6901 et seq.)

[48] Comprehensive Environmental Response, Compensation and Liability Act (CERCLA) of 1980, (42 U.S.C. § 9601 et seq.).

[49] Environmental Protection Act of 1990 (c. 43).

[50] Cf. the case of Native Village Kivalina v. ExxonMobil Corp. (Johnson (2013), 557–563) or the case of Peruvian farmer, Saul Luciano Lliuya v. RWE AG (Peruvian farmer sues German Energy giant for contributing to climate change (2017). In: The Guardian. www.theguardian.com. (access 10.05.2023)).

particular victims. The consequences of risk realisation with reference to the group of entities mentioned above may be manifold. For instance, they may amount to diminishing the value of fixed property, the infringement of personal interests such as health in particular as well as limitations on opportunities to benefit from the environment (e.g. a beach closed due to contamination) or a reduction in biodiversity as an element of natural heritage.

Finally, the last group of subjects of risk includes the state. On the one hand, the state should be understood as a social organisation that encompasses (in the context of the presently researched subject matter) a group of victims affected by a violation of the environment as their common good. On the other hand, though, the public authority, which is a defining element of the state within its three-pronged concept,[51] has its unique interest (different from the interest of the victims) in maintaining the adequate condition of the environment. The interest of thus the broadly understood state exceeds the limits of property interest according to civil law regulations, and it may take on two forms. Firstly, the constellation of the elements of the environment determines the supply of natural resources and the natural properties of the country, which, in turn, affects its attractiveness for tourism as well as the development of some sectors of the economy and—indirectly—state budget revenues. Secondly, each state functions within a particular system of values. Regardless of such a system being (or not) embedded in formal regulations, its protection seems indispensable from the point of view of the state. In the era of sustainable development paradigm, i.e. recognising the impact of natural heritage protection on economic growth and the need to remedy each environmental damage leaving aside the activities of the operator who caused it, it is the state alone, more often than not, that is ultimately burdened with the costs of remedial actions. This duty can be perceived either in terms of a constitutional obligation of the public authority[52] or as a task that is directly derived from the signed international agreements (such as the Protocol Concerning Cooperation in Combating Pollution of the Mediterranean Sea by Oil and Other Harmful Substances in Cases of Emergency[53]), which do not necessarily constitute laws. Both types of obligations emphasise the individual interest (separate from the victims' interest) of the state within its authority.

The wide array of categories of the subjects of environmental risk makes the risk materialisation consequences discernible at every level of economic systems, from micro-micro to micro-, meso-, macro- or the global level. Each level has at its disposal a different collection of means to control risk. Proactive behaviour is particularly welcome and encouraged (as opposed to reactive behaviour, the

[51] Seidler et al. (1993), p. 33.

[52] Rakoczy (2008), p. 14.

[53] Protocol Concerning Cooperation In Combating Pollution Of The Mediterranean Sea By Oil And Other Harmful Substances In Cases Of Emergency, (Barcelona, 1976). https://www.ecolex.org/details/treaty/protocol-concerning-co-operation-in-combating-pollution-of-the-mediterranean-sea-by-oil-and-other-harmful-substances-in-cases-of-emergency-tre-000541/?q=Protocol+Concerning+Cooperation+In+Combating+Pollution+Of+The+Mediterranean+Sea+By+Oil+And+Other+Harmful+Substances+In+Cases+Of+Emergency. (access 10.05.2023).

so-called "end-of-pipe" activities), i.e. the behaviour that is aimed at stifling the pollution "at source" and removing the causes and consequences thereof as close to its place of origin as possible. The statements above emphasise the importance of actions undertaken by polluters themselves, be they potential or actual ones. They also indicate the relevance of environmental insurance, which makes it possible to take timely action "at source".

2 Environmental Insurance Product: Structure

The comprehensive approach—presented above—to the interaction between the environment and the subject of risk leads to broadening the notion of environmental insurance. Protection against environmental risk can be found indeed within many products of property insurance and individual insurance. Aside from specialist environmental insurance, one can enumerate here civil liability insurance, fixed property insurance, automobile or financial insurance and, finally, health or life insurance. Hence, environmental hallmarks can be found both in products that do not exclude environmental perils from the catalogue of causes of risk materialisation but at the same time do not include these perils into a designated risk category (e.g. sickness insurance, where the insurer does not identify the causes of the illness) and in those that, by naming the risk or including a distinctive clause, enable the insurance to cover environmental risks.

Therefore, considering the legal and doctrinal definitions of insurance, one can assume that **environmental insurance** is an economic instrument wherein the insurer undertakes to pay a defined benefit should one or more of the following occurrences take place:

(1) Liability (civil or administrative) arises due to adverse impacts on the environment (**environmental liability insurance**).
(2) Damage to the insured's property interest other than that connected to giving rise to liability caused by pollution or another type of violation of the elements of the environment.
(3) Infringement of the insured's personal interests caused by pollution or another type of violation of environmental elements.

The most important part of the thus understood environmental insurance refers to the insurance mentioned in point 1 above. Should it become commonplace as proposed, the relevance of insurance types mentioned in the two further points would be marginalised. However, the importance of these two points remains valid when the insured individuals themselves are the subjects exerting adverse impacts on the environment. Also, this is the case when the rule of law does not include the damage-causing operator or any other party's liability for environmental damage.[54] In most of the remaining cases, the insurer is entitled to the right of recourse against the polluter.

According to the presented approach, natural disaster insurance does not belong in the category of environmental insurance, which results from the above description of the scope of the environmental risk concept.

Despite the frequently unquestionable cover for the impact of environmental damage (e.g. in life insurance, death caused by an industrial breakdown and the resulting pollution can also be treated as an insurance accident), environmental risk is only analysed at the underwriting stage for a limited range of products. The fact that the insurer identifies an environmental peril in the course of product development determines the validity of this peril's symptoms when providing insurance cover, especially the *underwriting* process.[55] Hence, the criterion of the *underwriting* scope should be decisive by assigning the product to the environmental insurance category. Considering this approach, it is difficult to predict the future scope of this category. At present, the dominant type of the thus understood environmental insurance is the specialised (environmental) legal liability insurance products as well as other liability products that involve protection initiated on the basis of appropriate clauses. In the course of market development, products such as *business interruption* insurance, personal insurance as well as other financial insurance (connected with, e.g., the issue of securities linked to the materialisation of environmental risk) should be expected within the broadened environmental insurance product range and not only in the leading insurance markets.

3 The Origins of Environmental Insurance: Historical Approach

The USA is the cradle of the thus regarded environmental insurance.[56] Its dynamic, uneven development in this country, marked with manifold doubts and issues, reflects the multitude of aspects within products, the level of their complexity and the unpredictability of the results. Until the early 1970s, the cover of property and personal loss due to changes in the environment was available without major limitations; it rarely involved meeting the aforementioned defining criterion of underwriting. American insurers, however, began to experience the growing costs resulting from environmental damage, which ultimately led to the introduction of the clause into general liability insurance, which excluded the insurers' liability for pollution which was intentional and expected by the insureds connected with their

[54] It refers, among other things, to the pure economic loss.

[55] Broadly understood as the process of assessment, selection and classification of risk.

[56] Pollock (2012), p. 199 and next.

operations (e.g. regular chimney emissions into the air).[57] The clause seemed to emphasise the insurers' readiness only for covering the financial impact of sudden and accidental occurrences, i.e. those that constitute the basis for the materialisation of environmental risk, as presented in this compilation. With the passing of time, however, as a response to numerous catastrophes generating environmental damage, such as Love Canal, which led to the involvement of the state and federal authorities, the insureds began to make increasing numbers of claims to insurance companies under general liability contracts concerning the costs they had incurred as a result of environmental disasters. Negotiations between the insurers and the policyholders or the insureds focussed on the interpretation of the terms "sudden and accidental" in the context of the pollution incidents and the reply to the question of whether the liability insurers had intended to cover the environmental damage and what kind of damage would be actually covered.

The insureds emphasised that the 1973 exclusion clause was in fact a form of confirmation of the classical definition of an insurance accident and that its purpose was to exclude the expected and intentional damage connected with the violation of the natural environment from the insurers' liability. On the other hand, the insurers went beyond the interpretation of a random occurrence and asserted that they had intended to eliminate all liability for damages caused by the violation of the environment, except for the damage that was sudden and accidental according to the time criterion, e.g. a sudden catastrophic fuel leakage (explosion, crack etc.).

Interpretational inconsistencies between the parties to the insurance contract were often settled in court, which, in turn barely developed uniform and clear jurisprudence. Interpreting the exclusion clause to the insurers' detriment led to holding them accountable for the need to remedy the damage that they had never intended to cover and had not considered in the process of premium calculation. Consequently, insurance contract terms and conditions were becoming more and more restrictive. The turmoil that ensued from the interpretation of the clauses, however, became a challenge that other insurers took. They saw the opportunity in the niche that was created due to the introduction of the exclusion clause. As a result of the above, the first products of environmental impairment liability insurance[58] came into life. Until 1980, in the USA, only two insurers offered autonomous environmental insurance products; in 1983, this number grew to 40 insurers.[59] Insurance companies—while assessing environmental risk as relatively high—often chose to establish subsidiaries, i.e. new, separate units dedicated only to the environmental type of business. In this way, they tried to protect the remaining part of their insurance-related activity from the costly environmental damage. Soon it turned out that the initial

[57] Insurance Information Institute. Environmental liability insurance. The role of private insurance in industrial accidents. https://www.iii.org/article/environmental-liability-insurance. (access 10.05.2023).

[58] According to sources, the first autonomous environmental insurance in the USA was offered in 1977 Dybdahl (2017), p. 3.

[59] Hester and Harrison (2001), p. 146.

apprehension concerning the high loss burden was well justified and the insurers had not in fact been prudent enough. As many of them had neglected the sufficient process of environmental risk assessment, they faced compensation payments, which literally crushed their operations.[60] Consequently, following a brief debut in the early 1980s, the market stalled, and at the end of 1984, there was just one insurer remaining that offered autonomous environmental insurance products on the American market.[61]

From that moment onwards, the American environmental insurance market cautiously embarked on a development path that was long and initially fraught with obstacles. In 1986, the exclusion clause was introduced into the standard specimen forms of liability insurance contracts, which practically eliminated all the liability of insurers for the impact of pollution from classical liability insurance. Once more, this move provided the insurance sector with a motivation to develop autonomous environmental insurance products. Initially, insurers offered very modest cover for environmental risk, which was accompanied by high premiums and restrictive underwriting practices. Such an attitude resulted from the reinsurance market's cautious approach to covering this kind of risk, which was justified by prior experiences as well as the dynamic changes taking place in the area of regulations concerning the pollution of the environment. In response to excessively high insurance premiums, many companies undertook to self-insure their exposure to risk. The situation altered slightly when insurers began to experience positive technical results in the area of environmental activities. Since the claims filed under environmental insurance contracts are usually of a catastrophic dimension, while their frequency is limited, it was possible in the long term for insurers to accumulate reserves that were adequate to the scope of risk they covered. Moreover, the long-term perspective contributed to the great strides made with regard to data collection on environmental risk, which enabled the insurers and reinsurers alike to comprehend its specific character.[62]

Given all of the above, it was only in the late 1990s that the market for environmental insurance began to develop dynamically. It seems that the willingness of companies and federal and state offices to retrieve the usefulness of formerly contaminated property provided encouragement for the introduction of new environmental insurance products.[63] Initially, the most powerful players in the environmental insurance market in the USA were AIG, Reliance National Insurance Company, Zurich Insurance Company and Kemper Environment. In 2013, more

[60] Cf., i.a., the case of North River Insurance Company, which insured the partnership RSR Corporation against environmental risks in 1981. Soon after the insurance contracts were signed, the insurer faced massive claims against RSR filed by private individuals (infringement of property and personal interests) as well as by government agencies (Wagner 2013).

[61] Hester and Harrison (2001), p. 146.

[62] Hannah (2000).

[63] Wagner (2013), p. 2.

than 35 insurers offered various types of environmental risk cover.[64] However, the peak insurance capacity of the market with regard to environmental risk was seen between the years 1998 and 2005.[65] Parallel to that, between 1998 and 2007, the offered scope of insurance is believed to have been the widest and at most affordable prices. In the following years, the experiences of increased claims as well as the impact of the financial crisis on the balance sheets became the main determinants of the product range offered by insurers.

The US environmental insurance market is a very dynamic and changeable one. It is possible to notice two processes occurring parallel to each other. Firstly, insurers continuously verify their willingness to insure certain types of environmental risks that are covered by the products already existing on the market. The remarkable fact is that the more experienced insurers are typically far more conservative in their approach to underwriting than the remaining companies. The history of the environmental insurance market also involves the resignation of a long-term specialist from providing cover for certain types of risk. For instance, AIG went out of the market for insurance products such as secured creditor policies offered to financial institutions on the ground of the unacceptable scale of claims based on such policies.[66]

The incremental value of the benefits paid out by insurers also resulted in—albeit temporarily—the disappearance of a product line. The group of products affected by this phenomenon was the so-called Cleanup Cost Cap. This kind of insurance constituted a definite minority within the market. Unlike the majority of other products, they did not refer to liability for adverse effects on the environment exerted in the future or past events of unknown occurrence or consequences; they dealt with the already identified contamination for which the necessity to conduct remedial action had been approved. The cover addressed the potential increase in the cost of the remedial process, which was hard to predict for the subject of risk.[67]

The disappearance of certain types of insurance products has been accompanied by the continuous introduction of new ones. This is the insurance sector's response to the market demand, moulded by the growing awareness of the detrimental impact that the changing environment has on individuals, business entities or whole communities. Natural sciences point to an ever-greater network of interdependencies between various types of emissions or other forms of impact on the environment and human life, health and social activity. The notion of pollution continues to evolve due to the expanding collection of harmful substances and types of energy that may be emitted into the air, water, soil or earth, and this does not only apply to activities traditionally considered as creating the risk of damage occurrence in the environment. Environmental risk can be identified by an ever broader array of organisations; hence, the products offered by insurers are not only focussed on high-carbon

[64] Wagner (2013), p. 2.

[65] Dybdahl (2016).

[66] Wagner (2013), p. 3.

[67] Wagner (2013), p. 10.

industrial activity, but they are also directed at schools, hospitals and other low-carbon entities. The scope of the cover can reach well beyond the effects of traditional pollution or contact with such harmful substances as asbestos; it can also encompass, e.g., the impact of mildew or some types of bacteria (such as legionella) inside water installations on the health and life of water users.[68]

The American environmental insurance market has been the indisputable forerunner when it comes to offering cover for environmental risk. It is assumed that autonomous environmental insurance in Europe is approx. 15 years younger than the American products.[69] One of the first European countries that entered the fast development track in the area of environmental risk insurance is Great Britain. Its particular market development stages were almost identical to those in the USA. Until the 1990s, it was difficult to identify environmental insurance products on the British market according to the hereby presented definition. Environmental risk was covered by the standard insurance protection of civil liability insurance without an individual evaluation distinguished within the insurance premium. The milestone event in the development of the British market took place in the early 1990s. Namely, in April 1991, the Association of British Insurers (ABI) recommended a standard clause to be included in the terms and conditions of civil liability insurance that limited the insurance cover to sudden, identifiable, unintended and unexpected events that materialise fully within a particular time and place as well as during the insurance period.[70] The clause excluded the cover for areas that were particularly relevant to high-risk sectors. Therefore, organisations that were especially vulnerable to environmental risk materialisation were unable to find cover for both gradual and sudden polluting accidents. The clauses excluding insurers' liability for environmental damage resulted from new regulations passed in 1990 that remarkably tightened the polluters' obligations and burdened them with significant costs. Such market conditions, i.e. involving tough legal requirements and additionally supplemented with the non-existent or limited cover for environmental risk in civil liability insurance – just like in the USA – sparked the creation of specialised environmental insurance products called Environmental Impairment Liability (EIL). The market was filled by several specialised insurers as well as numerous

---

[68] Arthur J. Gallagher & Co (2017) Environmental Risk and Insurance Discussion for Schools, School District and School Pools, 4. https://financedocbox.com/Insurance/75776704-Gallagher-environmental-practice-environmental-risk-and-insurance-discussion-for-schools-school-districts-and-school-pools.html. (access 10.05.2023).

[69] Aon (2011) Commercial Risk Europe Technical Briefing: Insuring pollution and environmental damage, 7. http://www.aon.com/risk-services/environmental-articles/article_cre-env-ins-briefing.jsp. Accessed 6 Sept 2019. Some of the sources report that the first specialised environmental insurance was offered by Lloyd's of London in 1979 (UNEP Finance Initiatives (2003) Risk, The Environment and The Role of The Insurance Industry, 16. https://www.unepfi.org/fileadmin/documents/risk_environment_insurance_epavic_2003.pdf. (access 10.05.2023).

[70] Sanders et al. (1993), p. 585.

Lloyd's syndicates. From the outset, the British product range was strongly supported by the heavily experienced American market.[71]

The USA and Great Britain have indeed created a huge platform of experience in the area of environmental risk cover, which is transferred efficiently into many other states. The pace of development of other markets, however, depended on many local particularisms, and within the conditions of an open economy and the free transfer of insurance technology, it was rarely the lack of insurers available that determined the level of the market maturity. For instance, the environmental insurance market in Ireland grew at a much slower pace than that in the United States and Great Britain, although many British underwriters have also been operating on the Irish market in the field of environmental risk for many years. The reason for this situation was the highly restrictive law that was implemented in the American and British systems under a much more severe regime than in Ireland. This means that the barriers to development must be sought on the demand side of the market, not on the supply one.[72]

The evolution of environmental insurance, which had taken so many years, finally led to generating an ample product range. Over time, the essential insurance offered within the markets of the Anglo-Saxon culture was environmental liability insurance, i.e. Pollution Legal Liability (PLL) or Environmental Impairment Liability (EIL), and contractors' environmental liability insurance, i.e. Contractors Pollution Liability (CPL). Both product types mostly cover the financial impact of pollution, such as compensations and benefits paid out to third parties, the costs of remedying the violated elements of the environment or legal costs. In the case of the first product type (PLL, EIL), the cover is provided only for pollution the source (or several sources) of which can be precisely located according to the contract terms. Contrary to the above, contractors' insurance (CPL) allows for the potential materialisation of the polluting event in the area that belongs to a third party, where the contract is being executed. Insurance products also take into account the peculiarities of project implementation and multi-layered execution. As a result, the market also offered customised products to chief contractors in the event of the subcontractors being insured insufficiently (General Contractors Pollution Liability).

Except for the products above, environmental risk cover was offered within more comprehensive products, which, next to the consequences of polluting accidents, also covered other aspects of the insured's operations. One may give several examples: Environmental and General Liability Exposures, Contractor Operations and Professional Services as well as Errors and Omissions (E&O), which guarantee the cover to damage resulting from mistakes committed by professionals in the course of providing their services, including engineering and environmental consulting services. The insurance market has also developed products that are complementary to the popular liability insurance, which is a hybrid of *first-party*

---

[71] Sanders et al. (1993), p. 587.

[72] Fanagan et al. (2012/2013).

and *third-party* products[73] (e.g. Owner's Protective Professional and Environmental Liability), which cover the damage whose costs exceed the limits of a typical contractor liability policy.[74]

Still another type of environmental insurance product was intended for very narrow categories of business activities or operations connected with a specific substance harmful to the environment, i.e. asbestos or lead. This group includes insurance for above-ground and underground tanks against the pollution caused by the release of their contents. In this group of products, one should also mention insurance—offered on the American market—for owners of property where asbestos content may be suddenly released, causing damage to person or property. Another example is liability insurance against damage to person or property arising due to professional entities' operations aimed at the removal of asbestos or lead. The scope of cover in the above products, additionally expanded to cover the adverse effects of all other projects aimed at environment remediation, could also be included in the master policy.

Specialist environmental insurance products have also been created for the transportation sector. These were either products complementary to standard automobile insurance, which excluded liability for damage done to property or person and environment remediation costs caused by pollution, or products intended for cargo owners, covering the owner's liability for damage done to persons or property and the cost of environment remediation caused by a pollutant release from the cargo.

The insurance sector also offered specific cover in connection with the operations of waste management companies, where the process of closing down requires preparation and following a closure schedule. The closure process is expected to lead to a safe, stable, self-balancing condition of the reclaimed environment, which should also be sustained after the closure procedures, when the post-closure action is still taken (monitoring, maintenance). Insurance cover makes it possible to bear the costs of both the closure procedures and actions in accordance with plans after the company is closed down.

The catalogue of insurance cover for environmental risk in the history of the environmental insurance market closes with the offer for financial institutions. Insurance products guaranteed cover for banks offering loans secured by property against pollution claims that could arise on that property. The insurer's liability was limited to the value of the borrower's debt towards the bank.

Most environmental liability insurance products were based on claims-made triggers. This means that an insurance accident the occurrence of which determines

[73] Insurance covering different sorts of construction projects constituted a very wide product range offered by insurance companies. The main factor that differentiated the products was the insurance beneficiary – be it project teams, engineers, contractors or possibly the project owners themselves. Various forms of insurance cover for this kind of activity frequently included the cover for environmental risk (Polini 2008).

[74] The necessity to conclude a contractor's liability insurance contract with a specified minimum guaranteed amount was indicated as a condition for the insurance cover.

the payment of the insurance benefit is actually the submission of a claim to the insurer for environmental damage. The moment of the occurrence of the damage itself, its disclosure or an event that caused its occurrence only matters to the extent to which the retrospective date has been set in the policy. Act committed was a trigger primarily in products related to the release of asbestos, or damage resulting from the implementation of activities connected with asbestos or lead reduction. The act committed trigger was also used in products that go beyond protection only in terms of environmental risk, including, in particular, insurance for the activities of professional service contractors.[75]

Discussion of the product-rich market development within the Anglo-Saxon culture does not exhaust the issue of the evolution of the global market for environmental insurance. To make it complete, at least one example from the continental system needs to be presented. In Germany, the concept of covering selected environmental damage in a systematic and separate manner appeared as early as 1965. It was the outcome of the Water Act, the so-called Wasserhaushaltsgesetz (WHG), passed in 1957. The insurance sector required 8 years to respond to regulatory issues with an insurance proposal. What was prepared—complementary to the basic offer—was the insurance terms aimed at the cover of liability for damage in waters (WHG—Zusatzbedingungen), which were widely used both among enterprises and private individuals—fixed property owners. This type of insurance evolved, to the benefit of both policyholders and insurers, until the 1980s. Initially, the costs related to the resulting losses turned out to be lower than expected, which made it possible to increase the sums insured without changing the amount of the insurance premium. The success of the product was due to, i.a., a favourable regulatory environment that promoted the obligation of policyholders to apply preventive and repressive measures aimed at minimising moral hazards. In 1979, the insurance cover was extended to two other parts: cover of damage related to the insured's own property and bearing the preventive costs incurred due to the direct threat of damage. The above was a systemic innovation in the context of the scope of insurance products previously offered on the German market and at the same time was an early harbinger of changes in the area of environmental liability brought about by the regulations of the European Union after more than 20 years.[76]

The year 1983 brought uncertainty onto the environmental insurance market in Germany when the regulator focussed on historical pollutants, through the analysis of which significant progress was made in the technical and systemic tools for measuring them. Consequently, public administrations revised the limit values for previously known polluting substances and introduced limits for new types of pollutants. Research on historical pollution has also led to a clear distinction between pollution that is generated at a specific point in time and the one that has an impact over a long period. This resulted in growing concerns about the scope of insurance cover and increased activity in the process of creating legal regulations. The

[75] Hannah (2000).

[76] Wiedenlübbert (2001), pp. 153–154.

Environmental Liability Act adopted in 1990[77] and the Environmental Damage Act developed in 2007[78] determined the offer of environmental insurance products[79] in the following years. It was assessed as complicated, difficult to comprehend and different from international standards.[80] The extensive and non-transparent product range in Germany was largely derived from the nature of legal regulations. Environmental law has not been codified in one place there, and regulations relating to environmental damage issues can be found in acts within various areas of law (civil, administrative, public and criminal).[81] As a result, elements of cover for environmental risk could be seen in the products of business liability insurance (Betriebshaftpflichtversicherung), product liability (Produkthaftpflichtversicherung), environmental liability insurance (Umwelthaftpflichtversicherung) and environmental damage insurance (Umweltschadensversicherung).[82] For example, damage caused by a defective product, which consists in disturbing the population of a protected animal species, was covered by environmental damage insurance (Umweltschadenversicherung). The same product, through its impact on the environment, could also cause personal injury. The insurance cover was provided for this damage within product liability insurance (Produkthaftpflichtversicherung). However, if the need for product liability rested with the manufacturer of environmental protection devices and their components, the environmental liability product (Umwelthaftpflichtversicherung)[83] was more appropriate. The scope of cover for all the above-mentioned insurance products was described in Germany in the model of the general terms and conditions of insurance drawn up by the Association of German Insurers (Gesamtverbandes der Deutschen Versicherungswirtschaft (GDV)). Theoretically, since the establishment of the European Community Single Insurance Market in 1994, the German insurance market has enjoyed full formal freedom in shaping the general terms and conditions of insurance. During the first decade, however, it was not practically used.[84] To this day, the patterns developed by GDV determine the insurance market very strongly, but the presence of international insurers more and more often allows for the

[77] Umwelthaftungsgesetz vom 10. Dezember 1990 (BGBl. I S. 2634), das zuletzt durch Artikel 6 des Gesetzes vom 17. Juli 2017 (BGBl. I S. 2421) geändert worden ist.

[78] Umweltschadensgesetz (2007) in der Fassung der Bekanntmachung vom 5. März 2021 (BGBl. I S. 346).

[79] Der Schutz der Umwelt und die betriebliche Haftpflicht, Schwerpunkt: Industrie- und Gewerbeversicherung (2011). Versicherungswirtchaft 17, 1212.

[80] Der Schutz der Umwelt und die betriebliche Haftpflicht, Schwerpunkt: Industrie- und Gewerbeversicherung (2011). Versicherungswirtchaft 17, 1212.

[81] Deutsche Rück (2018) Einführung in die Umweltversicherung, 2. https://www.deutscherueck.de/fileadmin/Downloads/Umweltversicherung_Deutsche_Rueck_2018.pdf. Accessed 21 Sept 2021.

[82] Der Schutz der Umwelt und die betriebliche Haftpflicht, Schwerpunkt: Industrie- und Gewerbeversicherung (2011). Versicherungswirtchaft 17, 1214.

[83] Der Schutz der Umwelt und die betriebliche Haftpflicht, Schwerpunkt: Industrie- und Gewerbeversicherung (2011). Versicherungswirtchaft 17, 1212, 1214.

[84] Maśniak (2003), p. 146.

cross-border transfer of insurance technology and experience, thanks to which new products are created bottom-up (out of the initiative of individual insurers), often more transparent than GDV models.

Apart from economically highly developed countries, such as the USA, the European Union countries or Australia, signs of activity in the field of building protection against environmental risk were also identified in other parts of the world (e.g. Asian and Latin American markets). Despite the fact that the insurance sector often declared the lowest possible premiums for environmental risk cover,[85] the barrier to the development of these markets still could often be put down to the purchasing power of the demand side. It is because one should not accept the assumption that insurance premiums declared as low meant a reasonable price from the point of view of a potential insurance buyer. In many developing countries, insurance cover remained beyond the financial capacity of entities that could potentially cause environmental damage. The low level of premiums was assessed from the point of view of the loss ratio in the insurance sector. In this sense, low premiums mean a minimum level sufficient to cover all environmental losses. In the past, the high loss ratio of environmental insurance and the need for significant additional risk charges (due to the difficulty in assessing exposure to risk and its volatility) often meant that the price offered by insurers remained unacceptable for many potential insurance buyers.

In developed markets, in turn, apart from the purchasing power of the demand side, the complexity of the offer also turned out to be a barrier to market development. The lack of product standardisation generated problems on the part of the client (who was unable to evaluate the offer), the broker (comparing two environmental insurance products took the broker several hours to analyse) and the insurers (who faced the problem of developing individual protection conditions, which was burdened with high risk).[86]

In view of the saturation of the supply side, a proposal was put forward to focus on the insurance awareness of potential buyers,[87] i.e. building up their damage and protection experience with reference to environmental risk. The above task can be performed by the insurance sector itself: insurance companies and insurance

---

[85] Dybdahl (2016).

[86] Dybdahl (2016).

[87] Dybdahl (2016).

brokers,[88] as well as the regulator (the state, through various administrative units, in various forms of public activity[89]).

Legal Documents

Bundes-Immissionsschutzgesetz in der Fassung der Bekanntmachung vom 17. Mai 2013 (BGBl. I S. 1274; 2021 I S. 123), das zuletzt durch Artikel 1 des Gesetzes vom 18. August 2021 (BGBl. I S. 3901) geändert worden ist

Comprehensive Environmental Response, Compensation and Liability Act (CERCLA) of 1980, (42 U.S.C. § 9601 et seq.)

Convention on civil liability for damage resulting from activities dangerous to the environment (Lugano, 1993). https://www.ecolex.org/details/treaty/convention-on-civil-liability-for-damage-resulting-from-activities-dangerous-to-the-environment-tre-001166/?q=Convention+on+civil+liability+for+damage+resulting+from+activities+dangerous+to+the+environment%2C+. (access 10.05.2023)

Convention on civil liability for oil pollution damage (Brussels 1969). https://www.ecolex.org/details/treaty/international-convention-on-civil-liability-for-oil-pollution-damage-tre-000120/. (access 10.05.2023)

Convention on liability and compensation for damage in connection with the carriage of hazardous and noxious substances by sea (London, 1996). https://www.ecolex.org/details/treaty/international-convention-on-liability-and-compensation-for-damage-in-connection-with-the-carriage-of-hazardous-and-noxious-substances-by-sea-1996-tre-001245/. (access 10.05.2023)

Convention on the Law of the Sea (Montego Bay 1982). https://www.un.org/depts/los/convention_agreements/convention_overview_convention.htm. (access 10.05.2023)

Environmental Protection Act of 1990 (c. 43)

Gesetz über die Umweltverträglichkeitsprüfung in der Fassung der Bekanntmachung vom 18. März 2021 (BGBl. I S. 540), das durch Artikel 14 des Gesetzes vom 10. September 2021 (BGBl. I S. 4147) geändert worden ist

[88] The interest of insurance brokers in the area of environmental insurance was often limited. The low demand for environmental risk protection did not encourage brokers to develop their competencies in the field of environmental insurance. A certain kind of motivation for them could be to highlight the responsibility of independent brokers for not taking into account environmental insurance products in the developed risk management systems and the resulting insurance programmes. The exposure of insurance brokers to this type of liability risk, albeit high, has not yet found expression in the claims of victims even on the American market. Therefore, it is difficult to expect its significance in the much less developed environmental insurance markets in the near future (Dybdahl 2016).

[89] Including increased enforcement activity of legal acts, i.e. execution of environmental liability to the full extent specified in legal regulations.

Protocol Concerning Cooperation In Combating Pollution Of The Mediterranean Sea By Oil And Other Harmful Substances In Cases Of Emergency, (Barcelona, 1976). https://www.ecolex.org/details/treaty/protocol-concerning-co-operation-in-combating-pollution-of-the-mediterranean-sea-by-oil-and-other-harmful-substances-in-cases-of-emergency-tre-000541/?q=Protocol+Concerning+Cooperation+In+Combating+Pollution+Of+The+Mediterranean+Sea+By+Oil+And+Other+Harmful+Substances+In+Cases+Of+Emergency. Accessed 21 Sept 2021 (access 10.05.2023)

Protocol to amend the international Convention on civil liability for oil pollution damage. (London 1984). https://www.ecolex.org/details/treaty/protocol-to-amend-the-international-convention-on-civil-liability-for-oil-pollution-damage-tre-000839/.(access 10.05.2023)

The Environment (Protection) Act of India, act no. 29 of 1986

The National Environmental Policy Act of 1969 (42 U.S.C. § 4321 et seq.)

The Resource Conservation and Recovery Act (RCRA) of 1976 (42 U.S.C. § 6901 et seq.)

Umweltgesetzbuch (UGB) Entwurf (2008). https://www.umweltbundesamt.de/sites/default/files/medien/1/dokumente/ugb1_allgem_vorschriften.pdf. (access 10.05.2023)

Umwelthaftungsgesetz vom 10. Dezember 1990 (BGBl. I S. 2634), das zuletzt durch Artikel 6 des Gesetzes vom 17. Juli 2017 (BGBl. I S. 2421) geändert worden ist

Umweltschadensgesetz (2007) in der Fassung der Bekanntmachung vom 5. März 2021 (BGBl. I S. 346)

Ustawa z dnia 27 kwietnia 2001 r. Prawo ochrony środowiska (unified text Dz.U. 2020 item 1219)

References

Alhakami AS, Slovic PA (1994) Psychological study of the inverse relationship between perceived risk and perceived benefit. Risk Anal 14:1085–1096. https://doi.org/10.1111/j.1539-6924.1994.tb00080.x

Allen D, Coles E, Kankaanranta T, Mcmullan C, Mobach D, Norman A, Perko T, Pylvas K, Wijngaards N (2017) Good practices and innovation in risk communication. In: Poljansek K (ed) Science for Disaster Risk Management 2017: knowing better and loosing less, Brussels, pp 422–440

Altonoğlu BD, Atav E, Sönmez S (2017) The investigation of environmental risk perception and attitudes towards the environment in secondary school students. The Turkish Online Journal of Educational Technology December: 436–444

Anantho S (2008) Risk Perception and Sustainable Development in Thailand. https://www.academia.edu/7423455/Risk_Perception_and_Sustainable_Development_in_Thailand. Accessed 10 May 2023

Aon (2011) Commercial Risk Europe Technical Briefing: Insuring pollution and environmental damage. http://www.aon.com/risk-services/environmental-articles/article_cre-env-ins-briefing.jsp. Accessed 10 May 2023

Arthur J. Gallagher & Co (2017) Environmental Risk and Insurance Discussion for Schools, School District and School Pools. https://financedocbox.com/Insurance/75776704-Gallagher-environmental-practice-environmental-risk-and-insurance-discussion-for-schools-school-districts-and-school-pools.html. Accessed 10 May 2023

Aven T (2010) On how to define, understand and describe risk. Reliab Eng Syst Saf 95(6):623–631. https://doi.org/10.1016/j.ress.2010.01.011

Aven T, Renn O (2010) Risk management and governance. Springer, New York

Bamberg S, Möser G (2007) Twenty years after Hines, Hungerford, and Tomera: a new meta-analysis of psycho-social determinants of pro-environmental behavior. J Environ Psychol 27: 14–25. https://doi.org/10.1016/j.jenvp.2006.12.002

Brewer NT, Chapman GB, Gerrard M, Gibbons FX, McCaul KD (2007) Meta-analysis of the relationship between risk perception and health behaviour: the example of vaccination. Health Psychol 26(2):136–145. https://doi.org/10.1037/0278-6133.26.2.136

Chauvin B, Hermand D, Mullet E (2007) Risk perception and personality facets. Risk Anal 27(1): 171–185. https://doi.org/10.1111/j.1539-6924.2006.00867.x

Der Schutz der Umwelt und die betriebliche Haftpflicht, Schwerpunkt: Industrie- und Gewerbeversicherung (2011). Versicherungswirtchaft 17

Deutsche Rück (2018) Einführung in die Umweltversicherung. https://www.deutscherueck.de/fileadmin/Downloads/Umweltversicherung_Deutsche_Rueck_2018.pdf. Accessed 10 May 2023

Douglas M, Wildavsky A (1982) Risk and culture. An essay on the selection of technological and environmental danger. University of California Press, Berkeley, as cited in Mesjasz C (2018) Podejście konstruktywistyczne w zarządzaniu ryzykiem. Studia Ekonomiczne Zeszyty Naukowe 359:18–36

Dryzek JS (2005) The politics of the earth, environmental discourses, 2nd edn. Oxford University Press, Oxford

Duikers J, Bischofs V (2019) Grundlagen des Umweltrechts. Zentrum für Fernstudien und Universitäre Weiterbildung, Koblenz-Landau

Dybdahl DJ (2016) A Big Picture on Environmental Insurance. https://www.irmi.com/articles/expert-commentary/environmental-insurance-overview. Accessed 10 May 2023

Dybdahl DJ (2017) Users Guide to Environmental Insurance. American Risk Management Resources Network

Exxon Valdez Oil Spill Trustee Council (1999) Exxon Valdez Oil Spill Restoration Plan, Update on Injured Resources and Services. https://www.arlis.org/docs/vol1/41089450.pdf. Accessed 10 May 2023

Fanagan A, Roberts A, Mc Henry N, Milne J (2012/2013) Practical Law, Multi-Jurisdictional Guide 2012/2013. Environment. Ireland. www.practicallaw.com/environment-mjg. Accessed 10 May 2023

Fisher E, Lange B, Scotford E (2013) Environmental law, text, cases, and materials. Oxford University Press, Oxford

Gregory R, Mendelsohn R (1993) Perceived risk, dread, and benefits. Risk Anal 13:259–264. https://doi.org/10.1111/j.1539-6924.1993.tb01077.x

Hannah J (2000) The U.S. Environmental liability insurance market-reaching new frontiers. www.irmi.com. Accessed 21 Sept 2021

Hester RE, Harrison RM (eds) (2001) Assessment and reclamation of contaminated land. Issues in environmental science and technology. The Royal Society of Chemistry

Insurance Information Institute. Environmental liability insurance. The role of private insurance in industrial accidents. https://www.iii.org/article/environmental-liability-insurance. Accessed 21 Sept 2021

International Law Commission (ILC) (2006) Draft principles on the allocation of loss in the case of transboundary harm arising out of hazardous activities. https://legal.un.org/ilc/texts/instruments/english/commentaries/9_10_2006.pdf. Accessed 21 Sept 2021

ISO (2015) Environmental management systems – Requirements with guidance for use. ISO 14001: 2015, Geneva

Janmaimool P, Watanabe T (2014) Evaluating determinants of environmental risk perception for risk management in contaminated sites. Int J Environ Res Public Health 11(6):6291–6313. https://doi.org/10.3390/ijerph110606291

Johnson N (2013) Native Village of Kivalina v. ExxonMobil Corp: Say Goodbye to Federal Public Nuisance Claims for Greenhouse Gas Emissions. Ecol Law Q 40(2):557–563

Kaczała M (2017) Empirical Analysis of Farmers' Winterkill Risk Perception. In: Nešleha J, Plíhal T, Urbanovský K (ed) European Financial Systems 2017. Proceedings of the 14th International Scientific Conference. Masaryk University, Brno

Kaczała M (2019) Systemowe ryzyko suszy rolniczej a ubezpieczenia. Wydawnictwo UEP, Poznań

Kasperson R (2014) Four questions for risk communication. J Risk Res 17(10):1233–1239. https://doi.org/10.1080/13669877.2014.900207

Khalatbari Y, Poorhashemi A (2019) "Environmental Damage": Challenges and opportunities in International Environmental Law. CIFILE J Int Law 1(1):21–28. https://doi.org/10.30489/cifj.2019.93906

Larsson ML (2009) Legal definition of the Environment and Environmental Damage. Stockholm Institute Law. www.scandinavianlaw.se/pd/38-7.pdf. Accessed 21 Sept 2021

Macias T (2016) Environmental risk perception among race and ethnic groups in the United States. Ethnicities 16(1):111–129. https://doi.org/10.1177/1468796815575382

Maśniak D (2003) Ubezpieczenia ekologiczne. Zakamycze, Kraków

Peruvian farmer sues German Energy giant for contributing to climate change (2017). In: The Guardian. www.theguardian.com. Accessed 21 Sept 2021

Polini T (2008) Owners Protective Professional Indemnity Insurance. https://www.irmi.com. Accessed 21 Sept 2021

Pollock JM (2012) The general liability policy. In: Guevera DL, Deveau FJ (eds) . Environmental liability and insurance recovery, ABA Publishing, pp 199–246

Rakoczy B (2008) Komentarz do ustawy o zapobieganiu szkodom w środowisku i ich naprawie. LexisNexis, Warszawa

Rejda GE, McNamara MJ (2017) Principles of risk management and insurance, 13th edn. Pearson

Renn O (1998) Three decades of risk research: accomplishments and new challenges. J Risk Res 1(1):49–71. https://doi.org/10.1080/136698798377321

Renn O (2014) Four questions for risk communication: a response to Roger Kasperson. J Risk Res 17(10):1277–1281. https://doi.org/10.1080/13669877.2014.940601

Rowe GR, Frewer LJ (2004) Evaluating public participation exercises: a research Agenda. Sci Technol Human Values October:512–556. https://doi.org/10.1177/0162243903259197

Sanders D E A, Boulton R J, Jones S M, Shepley S M (1993) UK Environmental Pollution. General Insurance Convention. GISG Working Party

Sandman PM (2012) Responding to Community Outrage: Strategies for Effective Risk Communication. Falls Church.

Seeger MW (2006) Best practices in crisis communication: an expert panel process. J Appl Commun Res 34(3):232–244. https://doi.org/10.1080/00909880600769944

Seidler G, Groszyk H, Malarczyk J, Pieniążek A (1993) Wstęp do nauki o państwie i prawie. Wydawnictwo UMCS, Lublin

Shengxiang S, Qiang L, Chaoqun M (2012) A probability-time & space trade-off model in environmental risk perception. J Risk Res 15(2):223–234. https://doi.org/10.1080/13669877.2011.634515

Slovic P, Fischhoff B, Lichtenstein S (1980) Facts and fears: understanding perceived risk. In: Schwing RC, Albers WA (eds) Societal risk assessment: how safe is safe enough? Plenum Press, New York. https://doi.org/10.1007/978-1-4899-0445-4_9

Stankiewicz P (2008) Ryzyko i konflikt. Strategie zarządzania konfliktami technologicznymi w Polsce. Dissertation, Uniwersytet Mikołaja Kopernika

Swiss Re (2007) Insuring environmental damage in the European Union. www.swissre.com. Accessed 10 May 2023

Toma L, Mathijs E (2007) Environmental risk perception, environmental concern and propensity to participate in organic farming programmes. J Environ Manage 83:145–157. https://doi.org/10.1016/j.jenvman.2006.02.004. Accessed 10 May 2023

UNEP Finance Initiatives (2003) Risk, The Environment and The Role of The Insurance Industry. https://www.unepfi.org/fileadmin/documents/risk_environment_insurance_epavic_2003.pdf. Accessed 10 May 2023

United Nations Conference on the Human Environment (1972) Report: Stockholm Declaration, A/Conf 48/14/rev.1. http://www.un-documents.net/aconf48-14r1.pdf. Accessed 10 May 2023

Vaughan EJ, Vaughan T (2008) Fundamentals of risk and insurance, 10th edn. John Wiley & Son

Wagner AM (2013) Current insurance policies for insuring against environmental risks. Greenbaum Rowe Smith & Davis LLP. www.greenbaumlaw.com. Accessed 10 May 2023

WCED World Commission on Environment and Development (1987) Our Common Future (Brundtland Report). http://www.un-documents.net/our-common-future.pdf. Accessed 10 May 2023

Wiedenlübbert R (2001) Assekuranz, Ökologie und Risiko: Versicherungen als Mitgestalter des ökologischen Generationenvertrages. Deutscher Universitäts-Verlag GmbH, Wiesbaden

Xu G, Feng X, Li Y, Chen X, Jia J (2017) Environmental risk perception and its influence on well-being. Chinese Manage Stud 11(1):35–50. https://doi.org/10.1108/cms-12-2016-0261

Websites

https://tsibinc.com/insurance-services/owners-protective-professional-indemnity. Accessed 10 May 2023

Prevention in Environmental Insurance

Katarzyna Malinowska

Abstract The goal of the chapter is to analyse the preventive aspect of insurance covering environmental risks. This seems important for a few reasons. Firstly, the general goal of environmental liability insurance is to follow the liability legal regime, which has started including prevention as an inherent part of the environmental liability regime. Secondly, it coincides with the visibly changing paradigm of the role of insurance, i.e., from risk transfer to risk prevention, which can be observed in many new innovative insurance products, which are slowly infiltrating the general function of insurance. Environmental risks seem to be a very relevant field for enhancing new forms of insurance prevention, in both the macro- and micro-scales. What is more, it is interesting to consider prevention as a field for cooperation between the insurance industry and governments (for example in the form of prevention funds). Thus, a thesis can be made about the synergistic effect of environmental liability legislation and the preventive function performed by insurance. Also, another issue appears, i.e. whether prevention as an express part of the insurance contract needs to be regulated in private law as an emanation of the principle of good faith or the principle of indemnity or could eventually be taken into account as part of insurance market regulation as a reflection of sustainable development. Thus, it will be discussed the issue of whether prevention can be directly linked to sustainable development on both the level of the insured organisations (or individuals) and the level of societies.

K. Malinowska (✉)
College of Law, Kozminski University, Warsaw, Poland
e-mail: katarzynamalinowska@kozminski.edu.pl

K. Malinowska, D. Maśniak (eds.), *Managing Environmental Risks through Insurance*, AIDA Europe Research Series on Insurance Law and Regulation 9,
https://doi.org/10.1007/978-3-031-47602-0_9

1 Introduction: Prevention in the Regime of Liability for Environmental Damages

As was stated in a recent report of the United Nations, "One of the most fundamental actions that the insurance industry can take to advance environmental risk management is the continued investment in and support for environmental risk assessments, risk surveys and risk reduction strategies (. . .). This approach leads to the alignment of interests and a strong commitment from both the insured and insurer to prevent a dangerous and potentially lethal [risks]. By aligning environmental risk assessments in a similar way, there is an opportunity for insurers and insureds to reduce environmental risks." [1]

The above quote may be taken as a motto of this chapter as its goal is to analyse the preventive aspect of insurance covering environmental risks. The method used in this chapter is twofold. The problems will be analysed, firstly, from the point of view of the general preventive function of insurance, including environmental pollution insurance (macro approach) and, secondly, based on the way environmental insurance contracts work, especially through the precautionary obligations of the insured and cooperation between the insured and insurer (micro approach). Such aspects affecting insurance as new technologies will also be taken into account. This forms part of the problem of the changing paradigm of the nature of insurance from "just" risk transfer to risk prevention.

The preventive function in environmental insurance coverage is not only due to insurance legislation or practice. It is indeed strictly related, influenced by and reinforced by current environmental legislation adopted worldwide, as has been analysed in Part I. To cite a few instances enacted in response to widely recognized environmental disasters, consider the reforms initiated following the Deepwater Horizon explosion and subsequent oil spill in the Gulf of Mexico. These reforms represent the most assertive and comprehensive changes to offshore oil and gas regulation and oversight in U.S. history were launched.[2] As many analyses show, the most recent disasters, such as the abovementioned Deepwater Horizon explosion, could have been fully avoided should adequate preventive measures be applied. What was missing was "a culture of tighter safety and more experienced regulators might have prevented the BP Deepwater Horizon leak".[3]

[1] *One example from the property insurance market is the boiler inspection process that exists in many jurisdictions where the boiler insurer is required to undertake the inspections.* UN Report, June 2022.

[2] https://www.boem.gov/about-boem/regulations-guidance/regulatory-reforms. The other environmental laws to be mentioned include: *Examples of legal frameworks for environmental liability are the Comprehensive Environmental Response, Compensation, and Liability Act (CERCLA) in the US, the Environmental Liability Directive in the EU, the Prevention and Integral Management of Wastes in Mexico, the Act on Liability for Environmental Damage and Relief Thereof in the Republic of Korea, and the Environmental Protection Law in China.*

[3] https://www.technologyreview.com/2010/06/10/26736/how-to-prevent-deepwater-spills/; also see the opinion that: "The sad fact is that this was an entirely preventable disaster".

Having the above in mind, it seems possible to discuss the role of environmental pollution insurance with respect to its impact on the prevention of pollution risks or the mitigation of the related damages. It comes from the historical evolution of liability insurance in general. As has been stressed, liability insurance policy terms and insurance markets have emerged in response to specific policy and regulatory requirements and various types of insurance are designed to meet regulatory requirements. This concerns the most popular—motor third-party liability insurance as well as workers' compensation.[4] Thus, the first natural incentive for the preventive function of environmental pollution insurance is to look for relevant provisions in environmental legislation.

The legislation in force for several years now places prevention among the three basic functions of environmental law, alongside preservation and restoration. While the first one consists of taking measures to preserve the existing state of natural elements, the restorative aspect consists of leading the environment to the desired state. Preventive measures, on the other hand, aim to avoid the materialisation of the damageable event. This function is currently regarded as one of the most important roles of the environmental law regime. It is directly reflected in the provisions of the law around the world (such as the EU regime included in the Environmental Liability Directive), which imposes an obligation on entities undertaking activities that may have a negative impact on the environment to prevent such an impact and on entities undertaking activities whose negative impact on the environment is not yet fully recognised to take all possible preventive measures in a precautionary manner. Moreover, those likely to cause environmental pollution are obliged to bear the costs of preventing such pollution.

The prevention principle supported by the concept of the precautionary approach, as one of the most prominent developments in modern international environmental law, has been included in many international instruments. Despite no uniform understanding of its meaning, the principle included in the 1992 Rio Declaration[5] is widely recognised by states and provides practical guidance on the development and application of international law. Its principle 15 proclaims: "in order to protect the environment, the precautionary approach shall be widely applied by States according to their capabilities".[6] In European Acquis Communautaire, the principle of prevention may be found already in the Maastricht Treaty, where it was stated that "the Community policy on the environment (. . .) shall be based on the precautionary principle and on the principles that preventative action should be taken, that environmental damage should as a priority be rectified at source and that the polluter should pay. Environmental protection requirements must be integrated into the

[4]UN Report June 2022.

[5]Rio Declaration On Environment And Development Included In The Report Of The United Nations Conference On Environment And Development* (Rio De Janeiro, 3-14 June 1992).

[6]IISD 2020 International Institute for Sustainable Development, The precautionary principle, October 2020.

definition and implementation of other Community policies." [7] Mainly, the European Union, in its legislative efforts, adopts the international regime implemented independently by its member states. It was visible in particular in maritime law. Finally, international standards have been also implemented in EU legislation (see Part I). Directive 2004/35/EC established, inter alia, a common framework for liability, with a view to preventing and remedying damage to animals, plants, natural habitats and water resources as well as damage affecting the land. However, the preventive measures, as per the Directive's regime, not only include private entities' liabilities but are also addressed to public authorities as the ones in charge of ensuring that responsible operators take or finance the necessary preventive or remedial measures themselves.[8]

With the above in mind, the possibility of environmental damage insurance fulfilling its preventive role should be analysed. This is intriguing not only in the context of the overarching objective of environmental liability insurance to align with the legal liability regime but also considering the evolving paradigm of the insurance role. This shift, observed in numerous innovative insurance products, is gradually transitioning from mere risk transfer to a more proactive stance in risk prevention, influencing the broader function of insurance. Environmental risks seem to be a very relevant field for enhancing new forms of insurance prevention, in both the macro- and micro-scales. What is more, it is interesting to consider prevention as a field for cooperation between the insurance industry and governments (for example in the form of prevention funds). Thus, a thesis can be made about the synergistic effect of environmental liability legislation and the preventive function performed by insurance.

2 Insurance as a Prevention Tool

Insurance is traditionally a form of risk management, and its function has always gone beyond purely compensatory aspects. An auxiliary but important function of insurance is undoubtedly risk prevention as it is considered to be the most rational method of loss control. Insurance methodology even points out two basic but equal functions of insurance—compensation and prevention.[9] It is also argued that conducting an insurance business without prevention would be unprofitable. Through prevention, an insurer's claims process can become more sustainable and sometimes also become a factor for competitive struggle in the insurance market.[10] However, the importance of the preventive function not only is due to the above

[7] Maastricht Treaty, 1992, Article 130r.

[8] Noussia (2022). ISSN: 0966-1646.

[9] T. Sangowski, Ubezpieczenia Gospodarcze, pp. 102–103.

[10] Ibidem, pp. 100–101.

competitive, market-based factors but also comes from the social role played by insurance.[11] In this context, it can complement the social and organisational role played by states, especially in the area of catastrophes and climate change. And while insurance prevention has potentially obvious benefits for the insured themselves, the insurance being in place potentially affects a moral hazard. The insurer's prevention activities are supposed to eliminate or reduce hazards. Thus, though the doctrine and even sometimes legislation entrust insurers with a preventive function, the legal regulations in that respect do not go much further than the general function (such as financing road safety campaigns or funding fire extinguishers, etc.) and provide only a general regulation on the level of individual insurance relations.

The issue of insurance prevention can be analysed in at least two ways: as a moral and business model and as a statutory duty. The first one can have its roots in the historical aspect of insurance prevention. The issue requires the social, legal and technical insurance contexts to be considered simultaneously.[12] What was the traditional dogma of insurance nowadays seems to be shown as a new type of business model of insurers. We can find this in such statements as that by Andrea Keller, *Head Automotive & Mobility Solutions, Swiss Re*, who says that "technological possibilities are there, but not used beneficially for preventing risks.[13] The insurers stress that their role in risk prevention consists of supporting risk mitigation by their policyholders via improvements in the effectiveness of communications tools, combined with increased access to broadband Internet connections and smartphones. Emerging technologies and innovation in connected devices have the potential to enhance the contribution of insurance to risk reduction. A number of insurers have begun to encourage the use of connected devices, such as water leak detectors and smart smoke detectors, among their policyholders, which is done by offering discounts on premiums for policyholders willing to install these devices and share the generated data with insurers. An increasing number of insurance companies are offering their policyholders connected device packages as a risk mitigation service.[14] The second perception needs the legal analysis of the legal, statutory and contractual duties of the parties to the insurance contract, which shall be presented in Sect. 4 below.

Examining insurance through the lens of legal policy and general insurance principles, it is apparent that its role goes beyond merely transferring risk from the insured to the insurer. It also encompasses covering preventive actions related to the insured risk.[15] Risk prevention in insurance has been recently promoted in relation to some risks and some products that can make direct use of new technologies, such as

[11] The fire insurance that emerged just after the great fire in London in 1666 was strictly related to the activity of fire brigades aiming at limiting the risk of fire. https://www.london-fire.gov.uk/museum/history-and-stories/early-insurance-brigades-brigades/.

[12] T. Sangowski, Ubezpieczenia Gospodarcze, pp. 102–103.

[13] The Geneva Association (2021).

[14] Adb And Oecd (2020); (Meagher 2019); Schlesinger and Venezian (1986), pp. 227–38.

[15] Such as good faith, indemnity, reasonable expectations.

the Internet of Things, and similar tools. This, however, seems to be limited to a kind of business model. The question worth investigating is whether insurance may go beyond the concept of a business model and whether it can become an inherent part of underwriting and distribution activities in insurance. If so, the next question emerges—whether prevention as an express part of the insurance contract needs to be regulated under private law as an emanation of the principle of good faith or the principle of indemnity or could eventually be taken into account as part of insurance market regulation as a reflection of sustainable development.

The other approach should also be taken into account. Seminal theoretical papers highlight that insurance and risk-reducing protective measures are substitutes.[16] According to the theory, insurance would discourage individuals from investing in loss reduction measures unless they are rewarded with a reduction in their premiums. This behaviour may lead to moral hazards when individuals take fewer risk-reducing measures after purchasing insurance and to adverse selection when they are mainly individuals with a high risk who demand insurance. And it is still difficult for the insurer to distinguish between high- and low-risk individuals. These two problems arise from information asymmetries in the sense that the higher risk-taking by the insured is not observed by the insurer and, therefore, not reflected in a higher-risk-based premium.[17] Recent works over the past decade reveal other patterns, however, according to which some insured individuals may view additional measures to limit risk ex ante as complements to insurance and thus implement more of these measures than the uninsured do, for example, because they are (highly) risk averse. Such behaviour can lead to both taking insurance and engaging in risk prevention measures.[18] Other empirical research has in turn shown that some individuals who engage in moral hazard have a higher demand for insurance coverage, except for highly risk-averse individuals with a high-perceived risk who do not engage in moral hazard and are willing to pay for insurance coverage.[19] The above heterogeneity in the relation between insurance coverage and risk reduction shows that additional factors enhancing risk prevention need to be chased.

One important issue related to enhancing the preventive function of insurance is the impact of new technologies. As technology changes, risks also change in terms of type, level and geographies.[20] Among the factors publicly discussed are finer risk segmentation and pricing, lower operating expenses, automated interactions with clients as well as broader and more varied sources of funding for insurance companies. Though this is all undoubtedly crucial for grasping new opportunities, it is

---

[16] Ehrlich and Becker (1972), pp. 623–648, Available at SSRN: https://ssrn.com/abstract=961496; Arnott and Stiglitz (1988), pp. 383–413.

[17] Botzen et al. (2019), .pp. 167–188; Akerlof (1970), pp. 488–500; Rothschild and Stiglitz (1976), pp. 629–649 The MIT Press Stable URL: http://www.jstor.org/stable/1885326.

[18] This has been termed advantageous selection Meza and Webb (2001), pp. 249–262; Cohen and Siegelman (2010); Einav et al. (2013), pp. 178–219.

[19] Op. cit.

[20] Schwedel et al. (2021).

claimed that going beyond risk transfer towards risk mitigation and prevention will be a critical factor for insurers and customers in the riskier world. In environmental risks, technology will undoubtedly soon be playing a more and more important role, such as risk monitoring systems with sensors that can detect pollution and improve remote and continuous soil, air and groundwater monitoring.[21] Insurers have a great role to play in terms of not only compensating but also participating in the prevention of the damageable event or the mitigation of its impact. The same may be said about reinsurers, which act indirectly but efficiently, especially in emerging economies, in such a way as to bring the best practices and expertise as well as through the aggregation of data. All this altogether has an impact on policymakers in determining if relevant legislative actions have the desired effect. It contributes to the cultivation of a "prevention culture".

As has been stressed in the UN Report, "It is crucial that all parties create a culture of prevention and a vibrant and supportive insurance ecosystem that can enable environmental pollution liability insurance to grow and support businesses in their endeavours while better understanding, preventing and reducing pollution risks and other environmentally-damaging events".[22]

3 Environmental Insurance Prevention and New Technologies

Loss prevention is an area where new technologies can play a significant and relatively uncontroversial role. This includes not only the identification of factors that increase the risk of damageable events but also the ability to react quickly when there is a chance that their impact will be reduced. In this regard, the Internet of Things (IoT) may be mentioned, as well as advanced image analysis tools, such as satellites.[23] At the stage of underwriting, the potential of new technologies is to identify risky behaviours in insureds, but at the post-contracting stage, the role of the insurer may consist of stimulating the insureds' behaviour by encouraging or imposing good practices on insureds to mitigate loss events. Finally, the possibility of predicting the outcome of the insureds' behaviours, or even of tracking the behaviour of the insureds by relying on connected devices, may be mentioned. The monitoring of the driving style of telematics devices, for example, not only serves to assess risk but also has a significant and ad hoc influence on the behavioural

[21] United Nations, Report on 'Managing environmental, social and governance risks in life &health insurance business' June 2022, https://www.unepfi.org/wordpress/wp-content/uploads/2022/06/PSI-Life-Health-ESG-Guide.pdf.

[22] Ibidem.

[23] Insurance Institute Of Canada (2021). Ai And Big Data. Implications For The Insurance Industry In Canada.

pattern of a driver aware of the presence of such a device.[24] This trend has started to be common in various types of insurance and is claimed to be a new business model in insurance, one based on new types of risk assessment and behaviour-based pricing.[25]

The same, if not greater emphasis, can be placed on environmental insurance, wherein access to data, along with new sources and methods of analysis, serves as crucial tools for identifying and assessing risks. In particular, the new technology can play an important role in such areas as detecting pollution and improving remote and continuous soil, air and groundwater monitoring. It seems quite obvious that insurers may and should play an active role in the development of these systems.[26] Data from new sources, better processed and in increased amounts, have the potential to facilitate the implementation of advanced risk management and early warning systems. These, in turn, enable timely interventions, not only to reduce the frequency of the events insured but also to reduce the severity of damage when risks materialise. The significance of the data for risk prevention purposes is confirmed by the research presented in the UN Report. The survey presented indicates that insurers lack crucial data preventing them from maximizing the potential of environmental insurance. Specifically, the missing information pertains to the preventative measures taken by policyholders to mitigate pollution.[27]

The use of new technologies can therefore help expand the application of environmental insurance and can aid in strengthening its function (or even transforming it), from "merely" protecting against the consequences of an event insured to predicting and preventing risk materialisation.[28] Such an expectation has been confirmed in the survey made by the earlier mentioned researchers of the UN Report. The question about the positive outcome of environmental insurance brought an answer showing that better risk management and hazard reduction are some of the key benefits of environmental pollution liability insurance, together with better risk identification and greater risk awareness. This may correspond with the possibilities given by the new technologies with respect to creating models to predict the frequency and severity of damageable events.[29] Thus, it seems that risk prevention can be recognised as part of an environmental insurance arrangement, not only as an additional or enhanced insurance service but also as its inherent ingredient.[30]

---

[24] Swedloff (2020).

[25] (L).

[26] United Nations. New risks, new opportunities: Harnessing environmental pollution liability insurance for a sustainable economy A global study by UN Environment Programme's Principles for Sustainable Insurance Initiative. June 2022.

[27] United Nations, Report on 'Managing environmental, social and governance risks in life &health insurance business' June 2022, https://www.unepfi.org/wordpress/wp-content/uploads/2022/06/PSI-Life-Health-ESG-Guide.pdf.

[28] Keller (2020).

[29] Insurance Institute Of Canada (2021). Ai And Big Data. Implications For The Insurance Industry In Canada.

[30] *Ibidem.*

Environmental insurance not only fulfils a systemic role in protecting individuals (both physical persons and corporations) but also plays a vital role in protecting the *res communae*—environment. The widespread exploitation of the environment on a global scale highlights that the fundamental approach to effectively managing risks is through prevention. The role of insurers cannot be different, and the awareness thereof is gaining more and more acceptance from all stakeholders. Risk prevention becomes the natural ingredient of insurance coverage. As a result, insurers are beginning to demand risk monitoring systems from policyholders, offering incentives in the form of premium reductions or good coverage terms for policyholders who effectively monitor pollution risks. Such methods should, however, not appear as merely business models by innovative insurers but be systemically introduced to the legal systems of environmental and insurance laws. Legal solutions should be supported by investment in prevention system technologies by insurers and governments (alongside policyholders). A strong approach to loss prevention is a must not only in the future but also at present.[31] Moreover, the expanded capabilities in insurance prevention may transform numerous uninsurable risks into insurable ones. This has obvious implications for the principle of inclusiveness, which must become more than a theoretical idea. An equally important trend is preventing risk as part of a holistic risk valuation approach by insurers.[32] This holistic approach, known as the "risk prevention framework", gives the potential to change risk management processes within both insurance organisations and the insureds' organisations.

Prevention is directly linked to sustainable development both on the level of insured organisations (or individuals) and on the level of societies. This emerging approach shows increasing results in preventing avoidable economic losses and reducing risk exposure, which brings benefits to all stakeholders—insurers, policyholders and society (including state expenses for medical care, social security, catastrophic funds payments, etc.). In fact, a better understanding of a policyholder's risk exposure can help all the parties involved. Insurers make data-informed decisions and define more adequate terms of coverage and in this way are able to limit their risk exposure and offer more competitive products. The insureds in turn are incentivised to improve internal risk management, which results in reflecting improvements and good practices in insurance premiums. As a result, society and stakeholders as a whole may become less exposed to risks. Over time, not only insurers but all sectors may become more economically, socially and environmentally sustainable.[33]

Digital technologies that give rise to ever-increasing amounts of data and ever-more-penetrating insights might make for more accurate pricing and reduce

---

[31] United Nations, Report on 'Managing environmental, social and governance risks in life &health insurance business' June 2022, https://www.unepfi.org/wordpress/wp-content/uploads/2022/06/PSI-Life-Health-ESG-Guide.pdf.

[32] Arthur D. Little 2018, Loss Prevention Framework For Insurance Companies. An Innovative Approach To Measuring And Controlling Risk. Https://Www.Adlittle.Com/Sites/Default/Files/Viewpoints/Adl_Loss_Prevention_Framework_For_Insurance_Companies.Pdf.

[33] Ibidem.

maintenance and downtime. This logically leads to a model whereby policyholders pay premiums not just in order to be compensated for damages they might incur but also for services that predict and help prevent that risk materialising. As has been stressed by the McKinsey report, "insurers of the future will pay more of a risk avoidance role and less of a risk mitigation one".[34]

The issue of a paradigm shift in the purpose of insurance services and their added value seems to be a necessary development trend. This is pointed out not only by insurers themselves, who see it as a new business model, but also by insurance researchers, economic trendsetting organisations and think tanks, such as the Geneva Association, etc. The question that needs to be answered is whether the law, especially insurance law, supports adequately this trend.

4 Risk Prevention in Insurance Law

Analysing the issue of prevention in insurance law, we have to abandon the general perspective and enter the land of precise notions that define insurance activity, insurance services as well as the duties of the parties to the insurance contract. In order to identify the legal tools related to risk prevention and mitigation in insurance, the notion of risk should also be pre-defined. Of the many different definitions, it seems reasonable to choose those in ISO 3100 seems reasonable. This recognises risk as a combination of the probability of a hazardous event and its consequences on the organisation. Risk prevention is directly related to the predictability of the risk. A useful definition, therefore, is one that encompasses measures and actions taken in advance in order to prevent new risks or hinder their development and strengthening. Thus, by prevention, one should understand both the measures aimed at avoiding the materialisation of the risk, i.e. the event insured—known also as "precautionary measures"—and those aimed at preventing [avoiding or diminishing] the consequences of an accident that actually happened, which can also be called the "mitigation of loss". If we look at the goal of preventative actions, which is the ultimate reduction of costs, as well as the unavoidable nature of natural hazards such as earthquakes, volcanos and hurricanes, it seems obvious that from an economical and axiological point of view, all the above actions should be acknowledged as risk prevention. It is claimed that risk prevention aims to systematically reduce the likelihood of a risk occurring,[35] though given the definition of risk, prevention may act on both the elements, i.e. the likelihood of the event happening, and its impact. Risk prevention methods include all techniques and management practices that help prevent unnecessary or foreseeable risks.[36]

---

[34] Mckinsey (2017).

[35] Https://Www.Lawinsider.Com/Dictionary/Risk-Prevention.

[36] Https://Managementmania.Com/En/Risk-Prevention-Methods.

4.1 Insurance Solvency Regulations

The exploration of the role of law in relation to the preventive capabilities of insurers primarily revolves around examining regulations governing insurance activities. Some analysis has been done on the basis of solvency rules, specifically taking the Solvency II Directive [37] as an example. As Solvency II states, "In order to promote good risk management and align regulatory capital requirements with industry practices, the Solvency Capital Requirement should be determined as the economic capital to be held by insurance and reinsurance undertakings (. . .). That economic capital should be calculated on the basis of the true risk profile of those undertakings, taking account of the impact of possible risk-mitigation techniques, as well as diversification effects. In addition, 'risk-mitigation techniques' have been defined and mean, "all techniques which enable insurance and reinsurance undertakings to transfer part or all of their risks to another party."

Risk mitigation techniques form a part of the risk management system in insurance companies.[38] This, however, seems to be applied at the general level of managing the insurer and does not refer to actions at the level of individual insurance contracts. It is regulated therefore solely in the context of solvency requirements (see Articles 100 and 108 of the Solvency II Directive).[39] Only a few examples of insurance laws in Europe proclaim expressly the preventive role of insurance services. These include Polish and Hungarian laws. It has been stated in the recitals to the Hungarian insurance law: "In the interest of protecting the interests of policyholders, promoting self-support, enhancing confidence in insurance and insurance companies, strengthening the role of the insurance industry in general and of the insurance companies in the nation's economy, enhancing the feasibility and reliability of the insurance industry, as well as the guarantees for insurance services, (. . .) promoting the role of insurance companies in preventing damage; furthermore, taking into account the requirement of compliance with the legislation of the European Union and that insurance industry is to achieve a level in terms of governing principles, quality and security it provides to market players (. . .), Parliament has adopted the following act" (Hungarian Law on Insurance Business; Act LXXXVIII of 2014). An additional illustration is found in Polish insurance law, which outlines activities directly associated with the reinsurance business. This list

[37] Directive 2009/138/EC of the European Parliament and of the Council of 25 November 2009 on the taking-up and pursuit of the business of Insurance and Reinsurance (Solvency II) (recast) (Text with EEA relevance), *OJ L 335, 17.12.2009.*

[38] Insurance And Reinsurance Undertakings Must Have In Place An Effective Risk-Management System Comprising Strategies, Processes And Reporting Procedures Necessary To Identify, Measure, Monitor, Manage And Report, On A Continuous Basis The Risks, At An Individual And At An Aggregated Level, To Which They Are Or Could Be Exposed, And Their Interdependencies.

[39] When Calculating The Solvency Capital Requirement, Insurance And Reinsurance Undertakings Must Take Account Of The Effect Of Risk-Mitigation Techniques, Provided That Credit Risk And Other Risks Arising From The Use Of Such Techniques Are Properly Reflected In The Solvency Capital Requirement.

encompasses endeavors in statistics, actuarial science, risk analysis, investments, and activities aimed at preventing or alleviating the impact of an insured event, with financing sourced from the prevention fund. It also includes actions that prevent or mitigate the effects of random events, with corresponding financing from the prevention fund, as stipulated in the Insurance and Reinsurance Law.[40] In view of technological, economic and social changes, this status of insurance law regulating insurance activity and services sounds unsatisfactory and seems to not only limit the justified interests of the insureds but also act to the detriment of the insurers. The hope for change comes from the new ESG legislation.

4.2 *Environmental Sustainability Governance and Insurance Prevention*

The above short analysis of the solvency rules shows that the preventive function of insurance has not yet been explored sufficiently on the level of regulatory measures. Although the enhancing role of insurance in risk prevention is the task of insurers, it seems that a regulatory response is yet to come. The signs of the changing paradigm are visible in the ESG regulations and the way they are interpreted.

The UN Report on "Managing Environmental, Social and Governance Risks in Life & Health Insurance Business" indicates many examples where ESG risks may be mitigated by insurers' good practices in sharing knowledge. First, it is worth noting that on 1 August 2022, ESG rules have been introduced into the solvency and insurance distribution regimes. They affect the internal system of risk management and governance of the insurers and also have an impact on product oversight and governance in such a way that environmental sustainability factors need to be taken into account in the course of product design, testing and distribution.[41] Though at first sight there is no link between these factors and insurance prevention, experts tend to interpret the whole ESG regime in such a way that it should enhance cooperation between the insurer and the policyholder so as to share information on risks with the aim of reducing exposure. Also, the UN Report identified the major tasks of insurers, which encompass the promotion of "good risk management practices to prevent and reduce various forms of pollution (...) through capacity building programmes and events to better educate clients, regulators and

[40] Art. 278. 1. An Insurance And Reinsurance Undertaking May Establish A Prevention Fund Of An Amount Not Exceeding 1% Of The Premium Written At Equity In The Last Financial Year.

[41] Commission Delegated Regulation (EU) 2021/1256 of 21 April 2021 amending Delegated Regulation (EU) 2015/35 as regards the integration of sustainability risks in the governance of insurance and reinsurance undertakings; Commission Delegated Regulation (EU) 2021/1257 of 21 April 2021 amending Delegated Regulations (EU) 2017/2358 (EU) 2017/2359 as regards the integration of sustainability factors, risks and preferences into the product oversight and governance requirements and for insurance undertakings and insurance distributors and into the rules on the conduct of business and investment advice for insurance-based investment products.

policymakers on the required capabilities to manage environmental risks and help make insurance solutions affordable, accessible and sustainable". Strictly related to that is the potential of cooperating with "environmental regulators and policymakers on the development of the necessary legal and regulatory frameworks to manage environmental pollution risks, and to ensure enforcement of environmental protection laws and regulations".[42]

4.3 *Communication Between the Parties and Transparency as a Prevention Tool*

Another angle for examining the issue of prevention in insurance involves considering the fundamental principles that have evolved over centuries within the insurance practice. Thus, indemnity and good faith might be taken into account as a starting point for considering the parties' obligations in that respect. The established rule is that both parties are obliged to maintain a high level of transparency with respect to the risk being subject to insurance coverage. This might gain a new perspective when related to the new technologies (as mentioned in Sect. 3 above) being a powerful tool for gathering and analysing risk data. It may be of importance, especially where new technologies give a high level of risk prediction in real time. Such an approach suggests that the preventive potential of insurance is expressed not only in technical actions but also in the form of communication between the parties, with the objective of risk prevention. This form of cooperation should be ensured by the legal system regulating insurance, in particular the provisions regulating insurance contracts. It is interesting to investigate whether this obligation lies only on the side of the insured or whether also the insurers should *be obliged to communicate information on the risk, with the potential to prevent the event insured or* to mitigate its consequences. At the current state of laws (at least in Europe), insurers are not obliged to share information on risk, even when it might be crucial for the purpose of mitigating or preventing a potential event. The only document (being unfortunately still merely a soft law recommendation) that refers to information on the performance of insurance contracts is PEICL,[43] where the insurer should, at the demand of the policyholder, report all matters relevant to the performance of the contract. Having this in mind, it seems that even if no explicit information duties are imposed on the insurers, we can place these duties within one of the established insurance contract principles, such as reasonable expectations or good faith.

[42] United Nations, Report on 'Managing environmental, social and governance risks in life &health insurance business' June 2022, https://www.unepfi.org/wordpress/wp-content/uploads/2022/06/PSI-Life-Health-ESG-Guide.pdf.

[43] Principles of European Insurance Contract Law.

Reports in the business press show that new technologies and data capabilities have the potential to reduce claims payouts, but there, the doctrine is nearly silent about the legal consequences of the above for the nature of insurance as a method of risk management.[44] This reality has not been so far described in the context of insurance contract principles, and that subject has been analysed mostly in terms of a new business model that is applied by insurers only when it may bring more profits. The legal questions are still waiting for answers. The regulatory solution may come not from insurance contract law but from the abovementioned ESG standards. In that particular field, researchers are beginning to recognize the potential of sharing insurers' knowledge on risk and highlighting it as a tool for mitigating risks.[45]

So far, it seems that the technology has been applied by insurers mainly for the purpose of checking up on policyholders' intentions and proper behaviour rather than for preventing the event insured. The insurers cannot, however, still just play the role of an indifferent observer even when they are technically capable of interfering or improving the chances of preventing the event insured. The technology raises questions about the role of the insurer in the insurance contract or—even more broadly—about the role of insurance in the risk management process. These questions are also about compliance with using new technologies in line with the established principles of insurance contracts, such as good faith, reasonable expectations and indemnity. They also concern issues about whether new tools and technical possibilities can naturally create new obligations for insurers that would satisfy the abovementioned principles of insurance contracts.

4.4 *Precautionary Duties of the Parties in Insurance Contract*

The meaning of prevention, precaution or mitigation looks clear when we discuss the general function of insurance, but it becomes more problematic when it comes to the obligations of the parties to the insurance contract. The conventional meaning of prevention concerns the obligation of the insured to prevent the polluting event or to mitigate its consequences. As has been, however, stressed by experts, the term "mitigation" is also used when the policyholder is obliged to take action to prevent the event that has not happened.[46] Thus, it is practical to assess what the statutory duties of the parties to the insurance contract are that may help enforce the prevention role of insurance.

[44] Schwedel et al. (2021).

[45] United Nations, Report on 'Managing environmental, social and governance risks in life &health insurance business' June 2022, https://www.unepfi.org/wordpress/wp-content/uploads/2022/06/PSI-Life-Health-ESG-Guide.pdf.

[46] The many meanings of environmental mitigation coverage (16.02.2016), https://chivaroli.com/meanings-environmental-mitigation-coverage/ accessed on 30 November 2022.

Historically, the prevention of the event insured from happening and the mitigation of the loss were totally in the hands of policyholders. They were reflected in the legal provisions regulating the insurance contract, which in various legal cultures established similar sets of duties evolving in the most prominent insurance principles. These are mentioned in the previous section: the principle of good faith, related to risk declaration, as well as the obligation to behave as a "prudent uninsured", expressed in the obligation to prevent the event and mitigate the loss.

The legal provisions and the structure of insurance contracts have been developed in most of the EU Member States in the nineteenth and twentieth centuries. They reflected the state of the art of technology at the time, including ways to obtain risk data. The manner of collecting information and the number of data available to insurers, as well as the manner and time of processing data, were in a completely different place than today. This applies not only to the availability of data, the type of data, the formats in which the data were collected and the possibilities and speed of processing but also to the range of data available, not only because it was not available but also because it was not foreseeable or it was hoped that this type of data would be widely available. At the time the insurance contract legislation was drafted, it was not possible to predict how quickly such data would be processed, what the cross-referencing and merging of data might be or what the sources of the data might be.

Additionally, at the time when the insurance contract regulations were created, certain risks not only seemed unimaginable, but they actually did not exist in people's minds. For the same reason, they were not anticipated by insurers. There is no doubt that they followed economic and business trends; progressive development and potential and developmental risks were inherently of interest to them in terms of the insurance products they could offer. The last 20 to 30 years have, however, seen a dramatic change in the format, purpose and formula of insurance, both non-life and life. Dynamically, developing science and technology allows data of a completely different type, with a wider range, to be captured, and allows it to be processed in an uncharacteristically fast and accurate way. This puts insurers in a decidedly privileged position. The insurer has not only the data it can ask for from the client but also the data it can obtain from many different sources, not involving or even without the knowledge of the potential insured. The amount of this data can be unimaginable and obtainable immediately. This new reality has been noticed by regulators and has been addressed in the regulation concerning the use of artificial intelligence [47] and proposing the concept of open insurance.[48]

At the present state of insurance contract laws, prevention, in the form of "precautionary actions", was imposed solely on the policyholder. Despite some differences, the nature of these obligations is consistent across jurisdictions. A

[47] Proposal For A Regulation Of The European Parliament And Of The Council Laying Down Harmonised Rules On Artificial Intelligence (Artificial Intelligence Act) And Amending Certain Union Legislative Acts, Com/2021/206 Final

[48] Eiopa 2021, Open Insurance: Accessing And Sharing Insurance-Related Data. Discussion Paper.

common trend in this regard can be seen in the PEICL regulations. Article 4:101 of PEICL says: "A precautionary measure means a clause in the insurance contract, whether or not described as a condition precedent to the liability of the insurer, requiring the policyholder or the insured, before the insured event occurs, to perform or not to perform certain acts. A 'precautionary measures' clause that allows an insurer to refuse to pay all or some of a claim for non-compliance with it, is only effective to the extent the loss was caused by the policyholder or the insured." The above concept of precautionary measures taken before the materialisation of the risk has been regulated only in a few countries. It is so in Finland and Sweden, where certain obligations were introduced by law. In accordance with Article 31 of the Finnish Law on Insurance Contracts, the terms of an insurance contract may include provisions on devices, apparatuses, procedures or other arrangements introduced with the aim of preventing or restricting the occurrence of bodily injury, property damage or loss or on guidelines to the effect that the person using or managing the property insured must have certain skills (precautionary guidelines). The insured must comply with the precautionary guidelines. Comparably, the German and Swiss laws focus on certain actions to be taken by the insured before the event insured occurs, but only if they were provided for in the contract.[49] According to the VVG (2008) §28 ("Non-observance of an incidental obligation"): (1) In the event of the non-observance of an incidental obligation which the policyholder must fulfil towards the insurer prior to the occurrence of an insured event, the insurer may terminate the contract.

Many more insurance laws provide for the statutory obligations of *sauvetage* in case the risk materialises. In accordance with Swiss law, *Lors du sinistre, l'ayant droit est obligé de faire tout ce qui est possible pour limiter le dommage. S'il n'y a pas péril en la demeure, il doit requérir les instructions de l'entreprise d'assurance sur les mesures à prendre et s'y conformer.* [2] *Si l'ayant droit contrevient à cette obligation d'une manière inexcusable, l'entreprise d'assurance peut réduire l'indemnité au montant auquel elle serait ramenée si l'obligation avait été remplie.* The same rule has been provided for under Spanish,[50] Polish, Belgian and Dutch laws.[51] According to the position of the French doctrine, an insurer can draft a "precautionary measures" clause so that it delimits cover by defining the risk, by excluding cover or by forfeiting cover if the insured does not comply with the clause (*déchéance*). It is not clear, however, whether a causal link between non-compliance and loss is a relevant consideration. In addition, the insurer can stipulate that cover will only commence if the policyholder implements certain "preventive measures". The insured bears the onus of proving compliance with the "preventive measures". The insurer can also provide for a reduction of cover to the extent that the insured's non-compliance with a "preventive measure" is causally linked to the loss. The

[49] Basedow et al, Principles Of Insurance Contract Law, 2016 Otto Schmidt, p. 188

[50] In Spain, The Insured Or The Policyholder Must Use The Means At Their Disposal To Mitigate The Consequences Of The Event Insured.

[51] Basedow et al, Principles Of Insurance Contract Law, 2016 Otto Schmidt, p. 189

insured's due diligence, negligence or intent is irrelevant, though it cannot unilaterally terminate a contract for non-compliance with the above obligations.[52] More complicated regulations are present in English law. The concept of precautionary measures is represented by a concept of promissory warranty that "is a common law notion and is very similar to a 'precautionary measures' clause. It is a promise or representation by an insured to an insurer about future conduct, or that a state of affairs will continue after the contract is made. It is a condition precedent to liability and must be literally, strictly and exactly complied with."[53]

Summing up, according to insurance contract laws, most precautionary measures encumber the policyholder, which should behave as a "prudent uninsured"; take reasonable precautions, considering all reasonable steps to safeguard the object of insurance; and aim at minimising the loss by acting to reduce the financial implications of a loss. On the other hand, despite the insurer enjoying much better access to information on the risk being imminent, it is obliged to "just" reimburse the costs of mitigating the loss (after the event insured took place). With this in mind, it is worth considering whether the structure of the insurance contract, its relevant regulations as well as the legal provisions regarding the distribution of insurance products and the conduct of insurance activity can be interpreted in a way that takes into account the current technological reality and the possibilities of the insurers – the insurers are obliged to actively participate in risk prevention and to a certain extent, especially if their current technological capabilities may go well beyond the tools and data available to most of the insureds.

The literal analysis of the laws binding across Europe does not bring a satisfactory result as regards balancing the rights and duties of the parties, though both aim at the best management of the risk, and one of them (insurer) is not even compelled to warn the insured of any impending and threatening insurance accidents that the insured could have prevented had they obtained the relevant knowledge available to the insurer or, at the very least, had a better chance of mitigating the damages of the accident.[54]

5 Prevention and Mitigation Clauses in Environmental Insurance Contracts

Risks covered by environmental liability insurance manifest themselves either as sudden events or gradual events that can take many years to be identified. It is important to note that coverage is typically only provided for accidental pollution events and is not designed to cover systemic pollution. Although there are

[52] The French Position: Professor Anne Pélissier, Montpellier I University, Montpellier, France, Aida 2012, Precautionary Measures, P. 15.

[53] The English Position: John Habergham, Myton Law Ltd, Lawyers, Hull, England, Aida 2012, Precautionary Measures, P. 11

[54] Basedow et al., Principles Of Insurance Contract Law, 2016 Otto Schmidt, p. 261.

differences across jurisdictions, environmental liability insurance typically covers losses involving pollution or other contaminants that result in bodily injury, property damage, clean-up costs or business interruption. In some jurisdictions, insurance covers the costs of mitigation and emergency response, public relations and crisis containment expenses or costs.[55]

In the absence of regulatory solutions that deal satisfactorily with insurance prevention, it is necessary to turn to insurance practice to discern how insurance prevention works in environmental insurance. Addressing insurance prevention in environmental insurance terms can be considered a market standard. Insurance terms and conditions strictly distinguish between risk prevention and "emergency" situations when an insurance accident has already occurred and the only thing left to do is to limit the consequences of its damage.

At the pre-risk stage, the insured is usually required to take measures to mitigate or counteract the risk, which are often called "special risks" in the terms and conditions of insurance. Thus, one can encounter clauses according to which *the Policyholder shall be obliged to remove special risks which, according to the circumstances, the Insurer may have demanded and has demanded in letters to the Policyholder. The special risks shall be deemed to include in particular an increase in the probability of an accident occurring.* This clause gets full meaning when interpreted in view of the consequences of failure to implement preventive actions. In case of a failure to comply with the duties, the insurer may be relieved *of any liability for losses occurring after the time limit indicated by the Insurer as a result of failure to remove the risk indicated, insofar as such failure has influenced the occurrence or extent of the loss.* Though the clause seems to concern the prevention of risks, in fact, it concerns more the identification of the risks insured and the level of insurability. The insurer is decided to cover certain types of risks and is not going to cover the risks increased or other "special risks" identified and included in the letter to the insured (as above). In consequence, the obligation in the above clause does not concern the duty to prevent the risks covered effectively by insurance but focuses on the risks that are not to be covered. The actions of the policyholder with respect to the removal of the "special risks" seem to have the character of a guarantee that the special risks will be removed by the insured.

Actual preventive duties are imposed on the insured in other clauses. The standard wording of insurance terms requires the insured to "act with due diligence in performing all acts designed to avoid or limit the extent of loss covered under the insurance". These clauses concern acts of due diligence by the insured, which may be taken on various stages of risk entanglement. Such actions by the policyholder are aimed at avoiding the loss, as well as limiting its extent. This means that they can and should be taken both before an insured event occurs and after it occurs, before its full damaging consequences develop.

In this aspect, the environmental insurance regulation affects the wording of environmental policies and their prevention clauses. Due to the liability elements

[55] Ibid.

resulting from the environmental legislation, most environmental insurance contracts also include coverage for "emergency response" activities. In the majority of the terms, there are clauses requiring the policyholder to notify the insurer and obtain approval for any emergency response activities before those response activities are taken. Usually, also the time frames for notification are set (such as 48 or 72 hours). In some insurance contracts, the insurer's approval is required only when engaging outside experts, which the internal costs of the policyholder are covered automatically. There are also clauses that prohibit the insured from incurring any remediation costs without the written consent of the insurer, except in the event of imminent or serious danger to human health or the environment.

Naturally, in the face of a rapidly evolving damage situation, it is often difficult to delineate precisely when there is still a phase of the prevention of a damageable event and when the damage mitigation phase starts. For this reason, contract clauses adopt a kind of fiction, providing that the *cover for insured costs of preventive action is limited to the costs of action taken within 72 hours following the first indication of the occurrence of an imminent threat of environmental damage.* [56] This is undoubtedly important in the face of some insurance legislation providing for a statutory obligation to reimburse preventive costs incurred only after the occurrence of an event insured (for example Polish law). In such a situation, the insurer, unless it has undertaken to bear the prevention costs of an event insured, will not be obliged to reimburse them at all. For this reason, it is worth paying attention to the time frames included in contract clauses as regards the reimbursement of prevention costs.[57] In this respect, it is worth noting also that through third-party liability insurance and first-party insurance, which partly complement each other and partly overlap, loss prevention and loss mitigation measures are financed prior to or in the initial stages of a liability loss.[58] An illustrative instance of the exact distinction between mitigation and prevention costs can be found in the Chubb insurance terms. According to these terms "the costs of Remedial Action will mean not only direct Remedial Action Costs, supplementary Remedial Action Costs, compensatory Remediation Costs but also preventive Action Costs. These mean The costs associated with the necessary measures that would have to be taken to prevent imminent environmental pollution."[59]

Having in mind the modest regulation of the insurer's obligations with respect to the prevention and mitigation of loss in contemporary insurance contract laws, still the situation of the insured results mostly from the policy wordings, which is complicated by the fact that there are various approaches represented by different jurisdictions. The statutes provide for the insurers' obligations only in a narrow scope, limiting these usually to the cost coverage of the mitigation actions taken after

[56] *ERGO Hestia Terms of insurance.*

[57] Kellner et al. (2010).

[58] Chapter XII Financial Assurance Issues: Germany, Austria, Italy and Spain, p. 319.

[59] https://www.chubb.com/content/dam/chubb-sites/chubb-com/pl-pl/products/environmental-liability/documents/pdf/owu-ppl-chubb-v-2017.pdf (Access 10.05.2023).

the risk materialises. *The coverage offered usually refers to "mitigation expense"(e.-g. if the subcontractor's insurance coverage is exhausted and the insured is responsible for payment of a claim, mitigation expense may pay for loss in excess of the subcontracted professional or contractor).*[60] Such an approach is far inadequate to the real possibilities that the insurers these days have in their hands, which could actually contribute to the prevention of losses.

6 Conclusions

Insurance is built on the foundation of trust between the insurers and the customers. This fundamental promise of protection and reliability cannot be compromised. The worldwide insurance protection gap, which has been noticed in recent years, is a good place to start strengthening that trust. Based on this premise, it may be claimed that the obligation on insurers to be actively involved in preventive (or so-called mitigation measures) results from the above grounds.

Based on the above analysis, it becomes clear that the modern premise of insurance, and in fact of an insurance contract, should not only be to provide compensation in the event insured but also to support the insured with regard to the range of risks covered before they materialise. In fact, the inclusivity approach with respect to risk prevention should be applied as an inherent element of insurance coverage. Thus, the most important challenge for the insurers can be to shift from a product-centric to a customer-centric approach, as well as to shift from offering not just insurance products but also services of prevention and mitigation actions as part of their promise. This is possible especially given that insurers have expertise that no one else has, making them valuable partners in the ecosystems that are evolving to offer customers both risk prevention and risk mitigation services. The lack of express regulatory duties in that respect should not stop us from applying the well-established principles of utmost good faith and reasonable expectations, which should serve the changing technological landscape.

What is, however, missing in this regulatory picture is the possible new potential that may be played by insurance as a result of the technological revolution. A new paradigm seems to emerge in the face of changing risks and the use of new technologies and data processing. New technological possibilities available to insurers, for example the risk analysis model, concern both new sources of data and new methods of processing them, and the effect of this technological change is the increasing predictive and protective potential of the insurance coverage and, thus, increasing its preventive function. The preventive potential of insurance contracts may help develop the sustainable model of insurance as a risk management tool at the level of social policy. The first symptoms of the changing paradigm of

[60] https://chivaroli.com/meanings-environmental-mitigation-coverage/; accessed on 30 November 2022.

insurance may be seen in such emerging or increasing risks as cyber or environmental risks.

References

Adb and Oecd (2020) Leveraging technology and innovation for disaster risk management and financing. Manila/Paris

Akerlof GA (1970) The market for "Lemons": quality uncertainty and the market mechanism. Q J Econ 84(3):488–500. https://doi.org/10.2307/1879431

Arnott RJ, Stiglitz JE (1988) The basic analytics of Moral Hazard. Scand J Econ 90(3), Information and Incentives. Vol. 1: Organizations and Markets, pp 383–413

Botzen W, Deschenes O, Sanders M (2019) The economic impacts of natural disasters: a review of models and empirical studies. Rev Environ Econ Policy. 13:167–188. https://doi.org/10.1093/reep/rez004

Cohen A, Siegelman P (2010) Testing for Adverse Selection in Insurance Markets, https://doi.org/10.1111/j.1539-6975.2009.01337.x

Ehrlich I, Becker GS (1972) Market insurance, self-insurance, and self-protection. J Polit Econ 80(4):623–648, Available at SSRN: https://ssrn.com/abstract=961496

Einav L, Finkelstein A, Ryan SP, Schrimpf P, Cullen MR (2013) Selection on Moral Hazard in health insurance. Am Econ Rev 103(1):178–219

Keller B (2020) Promoting responsible artificial intelligence in insurance. The Geneva Association—International Association for the Study Of Insurance Economics, Zurich

Kellner L et al (2010) Insurance coverage issues for third-party businesses and municipalities with losses due to the oil rig explosion in the Gulf of Mexico, Insurance Coverage Alert, Dickstein Shapiro LLP

McKinsey (2017) Digital disruption in insurance: cutting through the noise

Meza D, Webb D (2001) Advantage selection in insurance market. RAND J Econ 32:249–262. https://doi.org/10.2307/2696408

Noussia K (2022) Global offshore energy installations: implications for environmental pollution liability insurance in relation to major oil spill incidents. Eur Energy Environ Law Rev 32(2). ISSN: 0966-1646

Rothschild M, Stiglitz J (1976) Equilibrium in competitive insurance markets: an essay on the economics of imperfect information. Q J Econ 90(4):629–649. The MIT Press Stable, http://www.jstor.org/stable/1885326

Schlesinger H, Venezian E (1986) Insurance markets with loss-prevention activity: profits, market structure, and consumer welfare. Rand J Econ 17(2) [Rand Corporation, Wiley], pp 227–238, https://doi.org/10.2307/2555386

Schwedel A, Judah M, Goosens G (2021) The future of insurance: as risks mount, insurers aim to augment protection with prevention. Bain & Company Inc

Swedloff R (2020) The new regulatory imperative for insurance. Boston College Law Review

The Geneva Association (May 2021). From Risk Transfer To Risk Prevention – How The Internet Of Things Is Reshaping Business Models In Insurance. Authors: Isabelle Flückiger And Matteo Carbone

Loss Adjustment in the Environmental Insurance and the Role of the Loss Adjuster

Mark Vos

Abstract The chapter focuses on the loss adjustment service under an Environmental Impairment Liability cover. Within the loss adjustment aspects, the chapter will encompass the actions to be taken, starting from notifying the authorities, developing and implementing the remediation plan, and maintaining geotechnical, hydrological, or baseline and biotope investigations. Finally, the remediation operation is the last part of the loss adjustment process.

Considering the above complexity of the environmental damages, the role of the loss adjuster seems invaluable.

1 Introduction

What is loss adjustment in the first place?

The word explains itself, that service is about the adjustment of a loss, but we need to specify the meaning of the loss and the meaning of the adjustment. In the British insurance market, loss adjustment is the service to define a covered loss falling within the description, meaning, and intent of the policy wording taken out to cover a specific risk.

The major role in the loss adjustment process is played by the loss adjuster. However, a Chartered Loss Adjuster is a degree granted after having passed a range of certificates and exams on insurance law, and professional exams of cases at the Chartered Institute of Loss Adjusters in the United Kingdom.[1] The Chartered loss adjuster, as the professional is judging over cover under the policy and therefore provisionally recommending insurers in the interpretation of the claim and calculated loss. The United Kingdom is, however, a very specific jurisdiction in that

[1]Membership organisation for claims professionals associating over 4500 members, see more: https://www.cila.co.uk/. Access 23 March 2023.

M. Vos (✉)
Global P&C Loss Adjusting and Consulting, The Hague, The Netherlands
e-mail: Markvos@globalpandc.com

K. Malinowska, D. Maśniak (eds.), *Managing Environmental Risks through Insurance*, AIDA Europe Research Series on Insurance Law and Regulation 9,
https://doi.org/10.1007/978-3-031-47602-0_10

respect. Outside the United Kingdom, this profession is provided with specialists having a bachelor's or master's degree and having obtained local insurance law. In comparison to the Chartered Loss Adjuster, the loss adjuster is generally a specialist reviewing the insured interest and intended cover of the policy but leaves the final conclusion of the policy liability to insurers and pending markets inclusive consulting the Insurance Brokers, who had placed the risk in the market.

The European Federation of the Profession of Loss Adjusting Experts Associations (www.FUEDI.eu),[2] representing the associations of the national profession in a number of countries in Europe, rather describes the profession Loss Adjusting Experts encompassing the profession of loss adjusters as well as Experts in the field of insurance claims.

The professional loss adjusting expert is assigned to investigate cause and extent and support the claim services of a notified claim under an insurance policy.

As this chapter is focussing on environmental-related claims, the services are already narrowed down to claims in the environmental context, but the legal angle of the approach is defined by the insurance policy. This means that the approach can be based on:

- Environmental Impairment Liability insurance, the so-called EIL covers
- General Liability inclusive accidental environmental incidents
- Cargo Liability of trucked/shipped cargo
- Maritime-insurance-related environmental incidents with barges, boats, and ships, inclusive of onshore and offshore installation

The main difference between the covers is that perils resulting in losses should be related to incidents or gradual contaminations. Moreover, there are covers specifically only covering liability to third parties, but other policies also include own property.

The intention of this chapter is to raise a selection of aspects, which are part of the loss adjustment and which form part of the focus to be applied by the loss adjusting expert and his science experts to manage an environmental incident under an insurance contract. Having in mind the above, this chapter focuses on the loss adjustment service under an Environmental Impairment Liability cover. The loss adjusting expert may bring a professional proactive approach in case the exposed liability is insured and may take a less proactive involvement when the policy on behalf of which he is assigned is not meant to cover the relevant risk and therefore the loss.

[2] European Federation of Loss Adjusting Experts, an organisation comprising fifteen national loss adjusting associations, each representing loss adjusting experts in their own countries. These loss adjusting experts who are qualified in their own country are recognised as FUEDI-ELAE or FUEDI-NLAE depending on their level of qualification. FUEDI is recognised by the European Commission as the representative body for all professional loss adjusters in Europe. See more on www.fuedi.eu; access on 23 March 2023.

2 Loss Adjustment Process

2.1 The First Response

The sequence of actions in relation to the loss adjustment process includes the first response, investigating the cause, notifying the authorities, as well as developing and implementing the remediation plan and maintaining geotechnical and hydrological or baseline and biotope investigations. Finally, the remediation operation is the last part of the loss adjustment process.

The first response after a notified incident is often defining a successful further evolvement of the incident and associated insurance file consisting of the insurance policy and related documentation collected from both parties to insurance. Pending the nature of the incident a difference may exist, when an environmental incident is discovered by general soil, groundwater, and/or surface water investigations, or when a pipeline ruptures or a shore tank starts to leak suddenly. In the latter case, one needs to nominate an imminent response team to coordinate the first emergency measures, like the closing of the ruptured area, the closing of valves and the sealing of the pipeline section, the placing of oil booms in waterways etc., whilst in the other case, the incident may have occurred in the past or is still occurring without a clear root cause.

On the basis of the governance and responsibility principles like ESG, the management of every insured is required to act promptly. It is therefore of eminent importance that every insured has a Business Response Plan and an Emergency Response Plan in case of an incident, and in this case for an environmental first response. Within the management, officers should be assigned to lead the response and make funds available. Additionally, they need to nominate operational management, and pre-agreed contractors should be called upon to provide their emergency services. Further, a production officer should consider the impact on production and sales, and the marketing officer should consider the response to the market in the field of sustainability of supplies to vendors and Press Releases to clients and News Papers. The finance officer has to release funds to allow budget committees or other financial procedures to operate without any major hindrance. And last but not least, the officer involved in having contact with the insurance market should contact its insurance broker and or its insurer to notify the incident.

The notification of the incident to the insurer is of major importance, as it is the access to the emergency and loss adjusting services agreed with, provided, or supported by insurers. The insurers' first reaction is to nominate a loss adjuster specialising in the field of environmental impairment liability claims. The appointed adjuster may start to act as a kind of incident manager if an environmental incident of some calibre does have a major impact on the organisation. As example of situations like that can be given pipelines. They may be taken out of service, areas may be fenced off for investigations and containment of the contaminating chemical compounds etc. should be taken into account All these emergency measures directly impact the normal operations and logistics of a company.

In addition to the incident management role of the loss adjusting expert, such a professional can discuss and release adequate support to assist the insured to prevent the imminent spread of the loss as much as possible. Further, the services under the policy may extend to the involvement of environmental specialists to investigate the options to contain and remediate the evolving loss. The loss adjusting expert and/or the insurance company can see to it that these services are made available within the time frame set.

2.2 The Cause and Authorities

Parallel to the emergency response, a team is assigned to analyse the incident and to notify the authorities, which may fence off the area and may want to lead the investigations into the root cause.

Nevertheless, the difference in the circumstances surrounding the loss and the proximate cause of the loss should be stressed. It means that in a short time after the incident, it will become evident, whether the discovery is related to an incident of the day of discovery or that it must have been related to something in the past but still unknown. To provide a simple example a pipeline fracture overground is detected earlier than a pipeline fracture underground, which may have grown over the days, weeks, months, or years. This means that the exposed contaminated area may differ substantially.

Without any doubt, historical reports should be reviewed, permits, previous water and soil sampling analysed, and procedures should be scrutinised. All of the above should be effected to learn from the past and to support analysis into the root cause, which will ultimately result in amending operational procedures or changes in the design of process systems. It is also likely that material defects are found during that stage of the operation, which fuels a new set of measures to drive a refurbishment of the plant.

2.3 Nature and Extent of Damage

Still, the question remains, what constitutes damage? Part of the aspects discussed above related to the cost for emergency response, marketing response to the client base, support to the authorities, and involvement of its own senior technical staff in a root cause analysis and further technical consequences resulting from the incident and the findings. This array of cost headings needs to be considered and isolated for further review in line with the policy coverage by the loss adjusting expert.

The situation needs to be analysed on environmental damage to the First Party, i.e., insured land/plant site, and Third Party Property of neighbouring property. The neighbouring property may be public property like roads, railway tracks, and waterways and also private and or business property. In addition to the above, the sewage, stormwater drainage, and waterways may have become the conduit to spread the chemical contaminant to adjoining areas. Pending on the professional Emergency Response Plan, the spread may be broad and reach for example Natura 2000 areas. Therefore, the loss adjusting expert will need to communicate with all these parties. It will now become more evident that the loss adjusting expert is more of an incident manager in the context of environmental impairment policy.[3]

2.4 Remediation Plan

Whatever area is contaminated, the insured is obliged to develop and execute a remediation plan in order to remediate the contaminant. The development of the remediation plan is not always simple. For example, an overground pipeline fracture generally results in a prompt response ensuing in containing the area for remediation, whilst an underground pipeline fracture, of which the leakage was discovered by accident, will have contaminated a wider area. The same applies to pollutants leaving the chimney stack having contaminated a wide area around the site or regular accidental threshold incidents in the process wastewater systems or presently evolving new regulations in combination with highly sensitive laboratory analysers allowing to bring contaminant thresholds from ppm (parts per million) to ppb (parts per billion) or even ppt (parts per trillion). All these incidents require remediation, the cost of which needs to be presented to the loss adjusting expert managing the loss adjustment of the policy in question.

A remediation plan can only be drafted when the area that needs to be remediated is known, as well as what contaminant needs to be remediated and to what level. In these situations, it is not unusual to find historic site contaminations or even contributing contamination from neighbouring companies/sites. It is clear that adequate chemical analysis is to be made to define the appropriate measures, but also to involve neighbouring parties in further developments of the file. The remediation measures are dependent on the concentrations, and the nature of the contaminant, like a vaporising organic chemical compound, tends to disperse in the soil downwards but releases evaporating gases upwards, whilst a leakage of sticky oil may ensue in very local contamination.

[3] The division of the 'first party' and 'third party' risks is well known to the insurance market. First-party, which refers to losses directly borne by the policyholder (or insured) firm, and Third-party, which refers to damages alleged by clients or other third parties for which the policyholder firm may be liable. See for example: Environmental Insurance and Risk Management Tools Glossary of Terms; https://www.epa.gov/sites/default/files/2015-09/documents/ei_glossary_06.pdf; access 23 March 2023.

It now already shows that the word incident manager for the loss adjustment process demonstrates a wider role instead of approving costs on behalf of insurers.

2.5 Geotechnical and Hydrological Investigations

The concentrations mentioned above are dependent on the volume of leakage, the time that elapsed before the discovery, and the nature of the soil. The geological and geotechnical conditions are contributing to the spread as the chemical compounds are using preferential pathways to benefit from the lack of resistance. Simply said clay layers are more resistant to allowing spread than sand layers or even pebble zones along a waterway.

It means that a widespread network of monitoring wells is to be drilled to analyse the various concentrations and preferential spread direction. However, the spread direction may be influenced by the nature of the geotechnical conditions, but also from the hydrological conditions. Therefore, in addition to the geological and geotechnical soil conditions, an investigation needs to be set up for the hydrological patterns and flow directions.

These flow directions are important as they tend to fuel the spread of chemical compounds at the groundwater level or aquifer layer. When the flow direction proves to be dominant the seasonal effects of rains season will need to be considered as well, as the impact of low river water levels resulting in a 'pull' function of groundwater to the river versus a 'push' function with high river water levels or even floods may have a contributing impact.

From a geological perspective, there is not necessarily one groundwater level i.e., aquifer as low permeable horizontal layers can have historically been deposited to build more than one aquifer, as a result of which the remediation needs to be carried out at different depth levels. In addition to the groundwater/aquifers and or river flow, the migration of the chemical compounds can cross state or national borders, for which different governmental bodies may get involved. The investigations into the geological and geotechnical aspect of permeability and the presence and contribution of aquifers and dominant hydrological patterns result in an investigation with a range of technical parameters.

2.6 Baseline and Biotope Investigations

The technical investigation may suffice when the remediation is to be carried out in an industrial area, but when the contaminant has spread or is still spreading to a flora and fauna region or even to a Natura 2000 area, i.e. an EU-registered designated protection zone, the remediation needs to extend to a recovery of the damage to 'nature'. Damage to nature needs to be defined on the basis of a baseline investigation, which will report on the specific species of interest. The species of interest will have been registered under the Natura 2000 regulation, but when such Natura 2000 area is not existing the sensitive species need to be defined, and the biological impact on these species need to be monitored.

Under the transposed EU Environmental Liability Directive,[4] guidelines and regulations will have been drawn up in the EU Member States to adhere to. As per national legislation, these guidelines and regulations must be considered and met. In this place, it should be noted that (as the EU Commission's report stated) 'several Member States failed to comply with the deadline for transposing the ELD and that only by mid-2010 had it been transposed by all 27 Member States. Also, it has been noted that due to the discretionary powers awarded in the ELD and to the significant lack of clarity and uniform application of key concepts as well as to underdeveloped capacities and expertise, the transposition of the ELD into national liability systems has not resulted in a level playing field. For a long time after the implementation deadline, it has been totally disparate in both legal and practical terms, with great variability in the number of cases between Member States; is therefore of the opinion that additional efforts are required to enable regulatory standardisation to take place across the EU.'[5]

It may therefore occur that the remediation plan needs to encompass the damage to nature and the remediation thereof—remediating the biological impact to enable, say fish to return and exist again in the impacted area—or to compensate the damage to nature by providing additional species of the same nature at other locations. It may also be that the entire impact on the habitat is considered by for example monitoring snails. The principle applied is based on the assumption that when the snails have returned to their original concentration at their normal habitat, then the biological impact to the habitat must have been remediated.

3 Primarily, Complementary and Compensatory Remediation

During the discussion of the various steps, the remediation can actually be divided into different stages as illustrated in Fig. 1.

In the sketch above, one can notice the baseline being the normal habitat conditions. At the moment of the incident, the condition of the habitat reduces its conditions and may recovery as a 'Normal Recovery Path' over the years. But by spending extra work to reduce the exposure or remove the contaminant the recovery

[4]Directive 2004/35/CE of the European Parliament and of the Council of 21 April 2004 on environmental liability with regard to the prevention and remedying of environmental damage; OJ L 143 30.4.2004, p. 56.

[5]See more: https://www.europarl.europa.eu/doceo/document/TA-8-2017-0414_EN.html; access on 23 March 2023. As well as European Environmental Bureau, Position paper on the Environmental Liability Directive, June 2023. https://eeb.org/wp-content/uploads/2022/09/ELD-Position-Paper-FINAL.pdf.

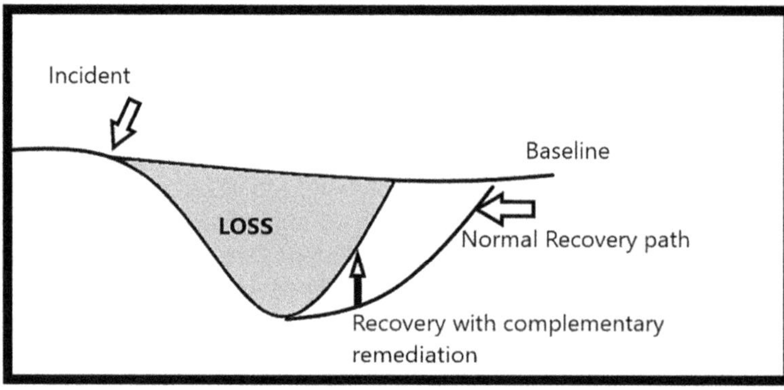

Fig. 1 Stages of remediation etc. Source: By author

period is reduced indicate by 'Recovery with complementary remediation'. Nevertheless, the habitat conditions were affected, and species of a kind were permanently lost. Such loss of habitat and species needs to be reinstated and or compensated when such replacement is not possible.

The remediation plan, therefore, needs to address the above aspects of the different stages under review.

3.1 The Remediation Operation

As described above the emergency measures and the remediation plan needs to address the nature and extent of the chemical compounds, the spread by the geological, geotechnical, and hydrological conditions, as well as its impact on the habitat and the prevailing regulations on maximum allowable thresholds in ppb or ppt.[6]

When the aquifer is situated close to the surface, excavation of the seat of the incidents may be a very effective option. It will become already more complex, when excavation is not possible, allowed, or not feasible, when the aquifer is at considerable dept. In those cases extraction techniques are available to extract the concentrated chemical compound mass at dedicated pumping wells, drilled at the various location to enable extraction by pumping or other. When the chemical contaminant is a Volatile Organic Compound, the physical state will not only be fluid but also gaseous resulting in the need to extract the vapours by means of a dedicated vacuum extraction network to remove the gaseous state of the chemical compound. This process is known as soil vapour extraction. It is without saying that a mass balance is

[6]Parts per billion (ppb) and parts per trillion (ppt) are the most commonly used terms to describe very small amounts or trace levels of contaminants in our drinking water. https://www.secnav.navy.mil/eie/Pages/DrinkingWaterConcentrations.aspx.

to be drawn up covering the anticipated volume of the spill and the total collected recovery.

Ultimately the remediation plan and selected remediation techniques need to be presented to the authorities to receive a permit for action. The plan will include removal, filtering, and neutralising techniques (please see the figure below) to prevent further spread after the recovery of the contaminant. It is without saying that a full plan and a permit may consume a lot of time, which can be considered a waste of time when prompt action is required. For this reason, open and pro-active dialogue with the authorities, the assigned experts, and the insurers, as well as the loss adjusting expert will allow prompt emergency measures and a continued activities leading to a full remediation plan, whilst no time is lost during the need to take measures to control the spread of the spill.

Controlling the spill may require installing a hydrological barrier model to isolate the plume from the non-contaminated area around the seat of the incident (see Fig. 2).

The objective of the remediation plan is to remediate the spill in total or to such an extent that the authorities accept the existing concentration level to remain behind and leave it to natural attenuation viz bacterial activity to break down the remnants. The proof of such natural degradation will be a part of this strategy. It is without saying that in the overall mass balance the contribution of natural attenuation can be included as of the day of the incident. Pending the nature and extent of the chemicals, the remediation may take a few months, a few years to many years, when the widely applied forever chemicals like PFAS nowadays have to be considered.

3.2 The Compensatory Remediation

Ultimately, the purpose of remediation is to bring the habitat back to its baseline conditions. It is evident that from the day of notification, information and evidence need to be registered to define the 'Baseline' condition.

In that respect, it is worth noting that Ecological consultants can contribute to the registration of such conditions of habitat and species, flora and fauna, or even underground biotopes with worms, etc. representing fertile soil. Where breeding locations are destroyed, major investments may need to be undertaken to bring the breeding activity back; otherwise, the lost breeding colony may never come back and may have selected other areas, which may need additional cultivation. Such additional cultivation of the breeding area is then considered compensatory remediation. The same applies to the deepening of riverbeds or creeks and improving embankments to facilitate better restoration of fish life. In one case, port authorities requested grass plants at the bottom of the port to support the faster recovery of snails and worm species in the sediments after an incident with a ruptured shore tank containing acids.

The major question is, however, what should be compensated?

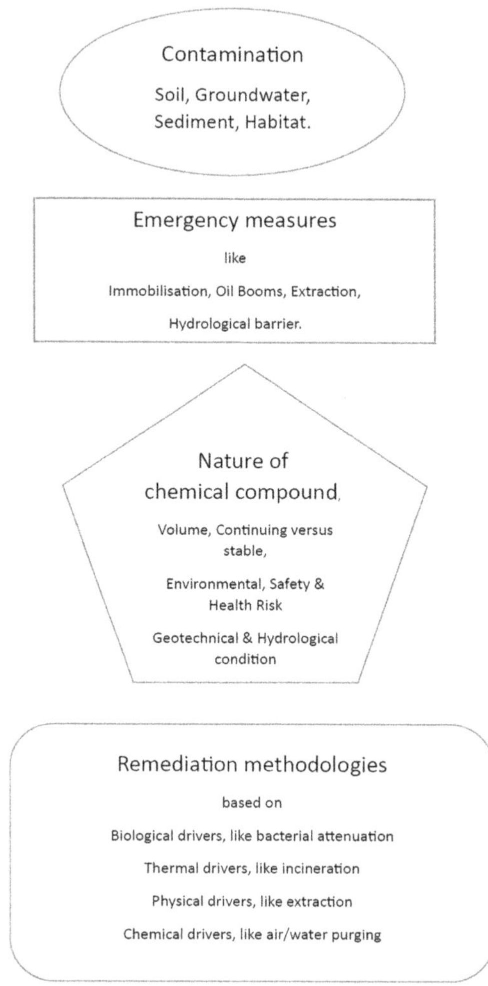

Fig. 2 Incident response and remediation methodologies Source : by author

For this answer, a compensation model has developed viz. the formula of the Habitat Equivalency Analysis (HEA),[7] which calculates the service at a pre-loss condition against the post-loss condition, where recovery periods are required. In addition to the HEA also financial loss and economic loss of the region may need to be included like pollutions resulting from the Deep-Water Horizon incident in the Gulf of Mexico, as a simple example.[8]

[7]For further reference please see Joshua Lipton, Ece Özdemiroglu, David Chapman, and Jennifer Peers; Equivalency Methods for Environmental Liability, published by Springer under ISBN 978-90-481-9811-5.

[8]Kyriaki Noussia (2012).

3.3 *Recovery of Insured and Uninsured Cost*

It is understood that in the wide array of activities after a spill, from remediation to operational conditions, the cost will be added up at the financial department. The loss adjustment by the loss adjusting expert depends very much on the nature of the peril being covered or not, and the extent of coverage, and the nature of the exclusion of the insurance policy taken out.

Ultimately not only the applicable deductible but also loss of sales market over a shorter or longer period can be translated into a capital loss. It is without saying that such capital loss can be broken down in multiple aspects of the business to consider, but may include press releases to balance the loss of image, and marketing efforts to recover a commercial status. For this reason, both the operation and the insurers, who have indemnified the insured loss, have an interest in whether the root cause can be attributed to and recovered from a liable party.

The root cause analysis together with the review of a potential breach of contracts or regulations by contractors or the insured will need to show the direction to a recovery potential of the capital loss sustained by the insured and the insurer viz, its subrogation rights after a legitimate payment under the policy. Proper evidencing of the facts and statements made in the early days of the discovery of the incident and securing the recovery rights under the different laws and regulations need to ensure a potential successful recovery.

4 Conclusions

The loss adjustment is the ultimate result of the professional approach and commitment of the loss adjusting expert and its support by expert specialists, as well as the professional competencies of the insured.

The loss adjusting expert is therefore more the incident manager to initiate and enact action when a vacuum in management of the incident is becoming evident, whilst the Insured is focussing on maintaining its business after the first weeks of attention to the incident.

On the other side, the loss adjusting expert is a respected professional assigned by the insurer to assist the insured and the insurer to respond to the policy taken out of its risks.

References

European Environmental Bureau, Position paper on the Environmental Liability Directive, June 2023. https://eeb.org/wp-content/uploads/2022/09/ELD-Position-Paper-FINAL.pdf

Joshua Lipton, Ece Özdemiroglu, David Chapman, and Jennifer Peers; Equivalency Methods for Environmental Liability, published by Springer under ISBN 978-90-481-9811-5

Kyriaki Noussia K (2012) Environmental pollution liability and insurance law ramifications in light of the deepwater horizon oil spill. In: Basedow J, Magnus U, Wolfrum R (eds) The Hamburg Lectures on Maritime Affairs 2009 & 2010. Hamburg Studies on Maritime Affairs, vol 23. Springer, Berlin, Heidelberg. https://doi.org/10.1007/978-3-642-27419-0_7

Part III
Specific Issues

Liability for Wastes and Its Insurance

Dorota Maśniak

Abstract The study is the result of an analysis of EU legal conditions supporting rational ecological waste management. The starting point for a deeper analysis was the creation of a conceptual apparatus related to the definition of insurance waste risk. The use of insurance as financial security for claims related to waste management is influenced by the principles of EU law: the polluter pays principle or the extended producer responsibility principle. American jurisprudence was also analyzed in order to find an answer to the question of to what extent the American insurance market is prepared to cover this type of risk. The American insurance market can be considered mature, also in the field of waste insurance, as indicated by the analysis of selected judgments.

1 Introduction

During the COVID-19 pandemic, due to lockdowns, waste production decreased in commercial and industrial sectors as factories and offices were completely or partially shut down. However, the amount of urban waste from residential areas has increased. The reopening of production facilities at the beginning of 2021 and the rising vaccination rates have led to an increase in waste generation.

The global waste management market size was valued at USD 1,293.70 billion in 2022 and is expected to grow at a compound annual growth rate (CAGR) of 5.4% from 2023 to 2030. [1] The market is expected to be driven by stringent government regulations. Waste law has become one of the most extensive and complex segments of environmental law in international law, regional law such as EU law, and the

[1] Waste Management Market Size, Share & Trends Analysis Report By Service Type (Collection, Transportation, Disposal), By Waste Type, By Region, And Segment Forecasts, 2023–2030 https://www.grandviewresearch.com/industry-analysis/global-waste-management-market/toc.

D. Maśniak (✉)
University of Gdansk, Gdańsk, Poland
e-mail: dorota.masniak@prawo.ug.edu.pl

K. Malinowska, D. Maśniak (eds.), *Managing Environmental Risks through Insurance*, AIDA Europe Research Series on Insurance Law and Regulation 9,
https://doi.org/10.1007/978-3-031-47602-0_11

domestic law of many countries around the world. As far as international law is concerned, the greatest importance should be attributed to two conventions: the Convention on the Prevention of Marine Pollution by Dumping of Wastes and Other Matters[2] and the International Convention on the Control of Transboundary Movements of Hazardous Wastes and Their Disposal.[3] At EU level, we are currently dealing with the third Waste Directive.[4] EU legislation on waste management is very extensive. Therefore, the further part of the study focuses primarily on regulations linking the issues of waste management with the financial market through the requirement of financial security.

The aim of this study is to analyze the EU legal conditions supporting rational ecological waste management. In order to achieve this objective, it proved necessary to establish a conceptual apparatus related to the definition of insurance waste risk. US case law has also been analyzed in order to find an answer to the question of how well the insurance market is prepared to cover this type of risk. The US insurance market can be considered mature, also in the field of environmental insurance, hence the selection of rulings issued in the United States. The issues, being the subject of court disputes, can be useful information for shaping legal norms and insurance conditions.

2 Waste Risks

2.1 Wastes and By-Products

Webster's Third New International Dictionary defines "wastes" as "damaged, defective or superfluous material produced during or left over from a manufacturing process or industrial operation; material not usable for the ordinary or main purpose of manufacture." As an example of such "waste," the dictionary mentions "material rejected during a textile manufacturing process and either recovered for reworking (as yarn) or used usually for wiping dirt and oil from hands and machinery."

EU law adopts a very general definition linking waste to the holder's decision to discard it. According to the definition adopted in the Waste Directive and used in the entire EU waste management legislation, "waste" means any substance or object that the holder discards or intends or is required to discard. The legislator resigned from providing a catalog of waste (Article 3 (1) of the Directive), leaving such a catalog for a separate category of "hazardous waste" (Article 3 (2) of the Directive). A

---

[2]Convention on the Prevention of Marine Pollution by Dumping of Wastes and Other Matters, written in London, Moscow, Washington, and Mexico City on 29.12.1972, called the London Convention.

[3]Basel Convention on the Control of Transboundary Movements of Hazardous Wastes and their Disposal written in Basilea on 22.03.1989, called the Basil Convention.

[4]Directive 2008/98/EC of the European Parliament and of the Council of 19 November 2008 on waste and repealing certain Directives, *OJ L 312, 22.11.2008, p. 3–30 called Waste Directive.*

definition of waste based on the act of discarding and not on the value of the material could be problematic. Unfortunately, it is not clear what is meant by discarding. This definition corresponds to a moving reality, where waste streams become more and more problematic due to the variety and complexity of all the new products available on the market, especially in the electric and electronic field. The case law of the Court of Justice, which has opted to emphasize the environmental protection aspects of the Waste Directive, is of fundamental importance for the comprehension of the notion of waste. The Court has adopted a case-by-case approach, considering all the factual circumstances involved. In general, the Court has opted to emphasize the environmental protection aspects of the Directive, as a result of which it has applied the definition of waste and considered any attempt to interpret this definition restrictively to be incompatible with the Directive.

There is a significant problem in the product-waste relationship. It is also visible in the difficulties in distinguishing waste from by-products that are not treated as waste under EU waste law. A production residue ("a substance or object, resulting from a production process, the primary aim of which is not the production of that item") that fulfills the conditions of Article 5 (1) Waste Directive is a by-product: "1. it may be considered not to be waste as referred to in Article 3 (1), but as to be a by-product only if the following conditions are met: (a) further use of the substance or object is certain; (b) the substance or object can be used directly without any further processing other than normal industrial practice; (c) the substance or object is produced as an integral part of a production process; and (d) further use is lawful. It has to be decided on a case-by-case basis".

The waste hierarchy set out in Article 4 of the Waste Directive indicates the preferred waste treatment options because they deliver the best environmental outcome. The priority order is as follows: prevention, preparing for reuse, recycling, other recovery (e.g., energy recovery) and disposal in landfills. It closes the loop between product and waste by introducing the principle of life-cycle thinking.

A necessary element for waste to achieve the "end-of-waste" status is for the waste to serve a useful purpose, substituting other materials. It is the essence of a recovery operation. The Court of Justice of the EU has given guidance in a number of rulings as to when a material can be regarded as something that an enterprise wishes to use rather than a substance or object that is discarded.[5] According to Article 6 of the Waste Directive, waste can achieve, after undergoing a recovery operation, a nonwaste status. The criteria must meet the following cumulative conditions: (1) the substance or object is commonly used for specific purposes, (2) there is a market or existing demand for such a substance or object, (3) the substance or object fulfills the technical requirements for the specific purpose and meets the existing legislation and standards applicable to products, and (4) the use of

[5] See, for instance, the judgments: Palin Granit (case C-9/00), Saetti (case C-235/02), Euro Tombesi (joined cases C-304/94, C-330/94, C-342/94 and C-224/95), and Inter-Environmental (case C-129/96).

the substance or object will not lead to overall adverse environmental or human health impacts.[6]

Due to their environmental impact, special subgroups of waste are hazardous waste (distinguished by particularly negative impact). The EU legislator defines them through their hazardous properties, listed in Annex III to the Waste Directive. A waste is considered hazardous if it has one or more hazardous properties (more on this subject below). The second group of waste distinguished in the Waste Directive is biowaste, defined as "biodegradable garden and park waste, food and kitchen waste from households, restaurants, caterers and retail premises, and comparable waste from food processing plants." The selective collateral of biowaste makes the composting and digestion of biowaste environmentally safe.

2.2 *Hazardous Waste*

There is a strict specification in EU law "in order to prevent or limit, as far as possible, the potential negative effects on the environment and on human health due to inappropriate management" (recital 14 of the Preamble to the Waste Directive). In order to encourage a harmonized classification of waste and ensure a harmonized determination of hazardous waste, waste and hazardous waste have been classified in the Community according to the list of waste types as recently established by Commission Decision 2000/532/EU.[7] Member States should encourage the separation of hazardous compounds from waste streams where it is necessary to achieve environmentally sound management (recital 28 of the Preamble to the Waste Directive). According to Article 7.1 of the Waste Directive, "the inclusion of a substance or object in the list shall not imply that it is waste in all circumstances." The EU legislator emphasized that hazardous waste is a subgroup of waste; that is, qualifying it as waste requires meeting the characteristics referred to in Article 3.1. A Member State may consider waste as hazardous waste if, even though it does not appear as such on the list of waste, it displays one or more of the properties listed in Annex III to the Waste Directive. The list shall take the origin and composition of the waste into account and, if necessary, the concentration limits. On the other hand, "where a Member State has evidence to show that a specific waste that appears on the

[6]There is an important link between the end-of-waste criteria and Regulation (EC) No 1907/2006, i.e. the EU regulation on chemical substances. As emphasized by the Waste Directive guidelines, issued by the Commission in 2012 (https://ec.europa.eu/environment/waste/framework/pdf/guidance_doc.pdf), whoever places the material on the market for the first time after it has achieved the "end-of-waste" status must ensure that the material meets the relevant requirements under the applicable products regulation.

[7]Decision 2000/532/EC of 3 May 2000 replacing Decision 94/3/EC establishing a list of wastes pursuant to Article 1(a) of Council Directive 75/442/EEC on waste and Council Decision 94/904/EC establishing a list of hazardous waste pursuant to Article 1(4) of Council Directive 91/689/EEC on hazardous waste (OJ L 226, 6.9.2000, p. 3).

list as hazardous waste does not display any of the properties listed in Annex III, it may consider that waste as non-hazardous waste" (Article 7 of the Waste Directive).

The control of hazardous waste management is achieved through the prohibition on mixing hazardous waste. According to this principle, "hazardous waste shall not be mixed, either with other categories of hazardous waste or with other wastes, substances or materials. Mixing shall include the dilution of hazardous substances" (Article 18 of the Waste Directive). This prohibition is also the basis of the waste disposal legislation. According to the provisions of the Landfill Directive, hazardous waste should be disposed of in separate landfills (Article 4 of the Landfill Directive). This solution affects the risk assessment of hazardous waste storage. On the one hand, it facilitates such an assessment by specifying the waste, but on the other hand, it constitutes a risk that is difficult to accept for the insurer due to the high probability of environmental damages caused by hazardous waste management.

2.3 *Waste Management*

As early as 1997, the Council of the European Union in its resolution[8] confirmed "that waste prevention should be first priority of waste management, and that re-use and material recycling should be preferred over energy recovery from waste" (recital 7 of the Waste Directive). Recognizing a very broad understanding of the concept of waste management and linking it with the abovementioned (after Article 4 of the Waste Directive) waste hierarchy, focusing on the environmental impacts of waste generation and management throughout the life cycle of resources, is part of the environmental protection objectives set out in Article 191 of the Treaty on the Functioning of the European Union, which include "reasonable and rational use of natural resources."

Figure 1 (below) is an illustration of the types of operations covered by the concept of Waste Management under EU waste law.

The EU legislator defines collection as "gathering of waste, including the preliminary sorting and preliminary storage of waste for the purpose of transport to a waste treatment facility" (Article 3 (10) of the Waste Directive), and recovery "means any operation the principal result of which is waste serving a useful purpose by replacing other materials which would otherwise have been used to fulfill a particular function, or waste being prepared to fulfill that function, in the plant or in the wider economy"(Article 3 (15) of the Waste Directive). Recycling was distinguished as a special type of recovery "by which waste materials are reprocessed into products, materials or substances whether for the original or other purposes. It includes the reprocessing of organic material but does not include energy recovery and the reprocessing into materials that are to be used as fuels or

[8]Resolution of 24 February 1997 on a Community strategy for waste management OJ C 76, 11.3.1997, p. 1.

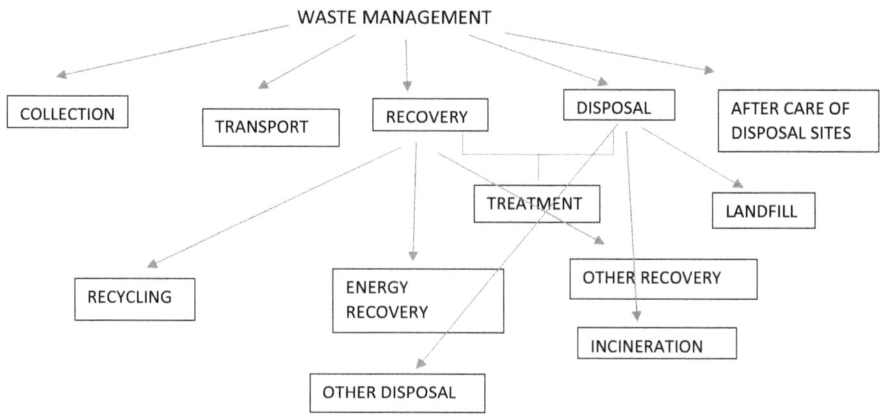

Fig. 1 Waste management – types. Source: own study

for backfilling operations" (Article 3 (17) of the Waste Directive), whereas disposal "means any operation which is not recovery even where the secondary consequence of the operation is a reclamation of substances or energy" (Article 3 (19) of the Waste Directive).

Such a broad approach to the concept of waste management, related to the waste hierarchy, results in a different degree of environmental impact of different types of operations. Some of them (such as landfills or incineration) are recognized as significant threats to humans and the environment and others (such as recycling) as forms of waste management preferred from the point of view of environmental protection. This means that the risks associated with each type of waste management will generate various insurance needs.

Ranked as the lowest in the waste hierarchy, landfill (as a type of disposal) generates such environmental risks as methane emissions from biodegradable waste contributing to global warming and local hazards such as the risk of fires and explosions, risks of water pollution from leachate (liquor) from waste decomposition, nonsustainable use of resources by land use, noise and odor harmful to human and animals life. Some carbon compounds may be retained in the landfill for long periods (sequestered) and so are not returned to the atmosphere as CO2. Incineration (as another type of disposal) generates risks: emissions of harmful air pollutants such as NOx, SO2, HCl, fine particulates and dioxin, emissions of carbon dioxide from fossil-derived waste (e.g. plastics) and N2O contributing to global warming, fly ash and residues from air pollution control systems require stabilization and disposal as hazardous waste.

At the same time, however, incineration is associated with more preferred forms of waste management, which puts this operation above landfills in the waste hierarchy. The energy recovered from incineration can replace fossil fuels, thus avoiding carbon dioxide emissions. The bottom ash can be reused as secondary aggregate, and metals can be recovered from the bottom ash for recycling.

In comparison to the disposal methods mentioned above, recycling is characterized by its positive impact on the environment. It saves energy as generally less energy is required to manufacture products from recycled feedstocks and hence emissions of pollutants. The recycling process prolongs the supply of finite resources (e.g., metal ores) – contributes to the sustainable resource use. Equally important is that it avoids impacts associated with the extraction of virgin material (e.g., the mining of ores and sand, the cutting down of old growth forest to produce wood for paper).[9] The so-called recycling insurance, which takes into account the specificities of such activities, can be an answer to such activities.

3 Principles Supporting the Development of Waste Insurance

3.1 The Holder-Pays Principle as a Modification of the Polluter-Pays Principle

The "polluter-pays" principle is a guiding principle at the European and international levels.[10] "The waste producer and the waste holder should manage the waste in a way that guarantees a high level of protection of the environment and human health" (recital No. 26 of the Waste Directive). According to this principle, waste disposal costs should be borne by the waste holder or by the previous holders or producers of the products (Article 14 of the Waste Directive). The importance of this principle is also indicated by the EU legislator in the Landfill Directive in the context of waste landfilling, who deems it necessary to "take into account any damage to the environment caused by a landfill" (recital No. 5).

Under EU law, the term "waste holder" includes the scope of the waste producer. In accordance with Article 3 (6), "waste holder" means the waste producer or the natural or legal person that is in possession of the waste. However, "waste producer" means "anyone whose activities generate waste (original waste producer) or anyone who carries out pre-processing, mixing or other operations resulting in a change in the nature or composition of this waste"" (Article 3 (5) of the Waste Directive). The status of a waste producer is therefore a factual state and results from the conducted activity or the fact that the waste was generated. The status of a waste producer can also be obtained as a result of the provision of the service of demolition, the renovation of facilities, the cleaning of tanks or devices, as well as cleaning, maintenance, and repair.[11]

The "holder of waste" is therefore a broader concept than the generator and involves both the generation of waste and the fact of possession. The use of the

---

[9] Smith et al. (2001), p. 19 https://ec.europa.eu/environment/pdf/waste/studies/climate_change.pdf.

[10] Bugge (2009), pp. 411–428, also Maśniak (2021), p. 95.

[11] Dmowska (2019), p. 135.

term "holder," rather than "owner," indicates the intention of the EU legislator to broadly define the personal scope of application of the "polluter pays" principle; the reference is to the holder of waste. A holder is a person who is in possession of waste as an owner, as well as a person who actually is in possession of waste as a user, pledgee, lessee, or tenant or having any other right that entails specific authority over the waste owned by another person. Possession is thus a form of ownership determined by the factual element in the form of the holder's relationship to the waste – regardless of the legal basis for that possession. The holder's relationship to the waste must be actual; i.e., it provides the holder with the ability to affect the waste. The Polish doctrine emphasizes that the holder cannot be required to maintain physical contact with the object at all times; it is sufficient that they have such a possibility.[12] The possibility of recognizing a certain factual authority as possession does not depend on the holder's direct control over the object. In light of this reasoning (common in the civil legislation of many Member States), the holder of waste does not lose its status as holder (self-ownership) if the waste is put to use by means of a lease or rental. In addition to actual authority (*corpus*), possession has a second element, i.e. its exercise by a specific entity in its own interest (*animus rem sibi habendi*). [13]

The holder takes control of the waste as soon as it is actually acquired, and if they act in their own interest, they do not lose this possession by giving the waste to another entity for transportation. That is, at this point, they assume responsibility for waste management and bearing the costs of waste disposal and other costs of repairing the environmental damage caused by the waste. The permanence of the authority over waste in the self-interest of those deciding to acquire a waste holder status is evidenced by an administrative decision. Due to the far-reaching licensing of waste management, the role of the administrative authority affects the inherently civil law relationship of possession. It is also important from an insurance point of view since the requirement for financial security (more about it below) often arises already at this stage. However, one must agree with the view that under EU waste law, a holder is also understood as an illegal holder who does not have the permit in the form of an administrative-legal decision for waste management and is not exempt from the obligation to apply for such a permit.[14] Excluding such a holder from the "polluter pays" principle would contradict the objectives of the rule.

A waste transporter is also a waste holder, especially when the transport of waste is carried out without the required documents, which indicate the waste holder transferring the waste and the waste holder to whom the waste is to be delivered.[15] The recognition of the transporter as the holder raises doubts due to the difficulty of

[12] Gniewek and Machnikowski (2017), Kunicki (1966).

[13] Cf. Skowrońska-Bocian and Warciński (2020).

[14] See. Górski (2005), p. 46.

[15] Expressed in Ustawa z 20.07.2018 o zmianie ustawy o Inspekcji Ochrony Środowiska oraz niektórych innych ustaw (Dz.U. poz. 1479) – art. 24 ust 4 a.

proving the permanence of the authority in the transport.[16] The waste holder is also the owner of the surface land with regard to the waste on the property.

3.2 Extended Waste Producer Responsibility Principle in EU Law

The principle introduced by the Waste Directive refers to a producer of a product, by which the EU legislator means "any natural or legal person who professionally develops, manufactures, processes, treats, sells or imports products" (Article 8 (1) of the Waste Directive). It follows from the definition that the German importer of Chinese products will also be understood as a producer of a product; i.e., it is an entity that places a product on the EU market. According to this model, the producer is liable during the entire life cycle of the product, including the phase in which it has become waste. EPR (extended producer responsibility) ensures that the producers are financially and/or organizationally responsible for waste management, from designing and manufacturing, in a way that minimizes resource consumption, to recycling and the disposal of a product that is easy to dismantle (recital no. 27 of the Waste Directive). Then waste is not an unwanted burden but a profitable resource. Producers invent and produce sustainable products (which have lower environmental impacts and are easily recyclable).

Thinking of a product in terms of waste, the management of which is a phase in the entire life cycle of the product, is a great and costly challenge for a manufacturer. Hence, there is the obligation for Member States to create incentives "to encourage the design of products in order to reduce their environmental impacts and the generation of waste in the course of the production and subsequent use of products, and in order to ensure that the recovery and disposal of products that have become waste take place" (Article 8 (2) of the Waste Directive) without endangering human health or harming the environment. The EU legislator indicates the criteria to be followed by the Member States in the implementation of legislative or nonlegislative measures to ensure that any producer of the product has extended producer responsibility. They include 1) technical feasibility; 2) economic viability; 3) overall environmental, human health, and social impacts; and 4) the proper functioning of the internal market (Article 8 (3) of the Waste Directive). According to Article 8 (1) of the Waste Directive, "such measures may include the acceptance of returned products and of the waste that remains after those products have been used, as well as the subsequent management of the waste and financial responsibility for such activities." In addition, EPR shifts the responsibility for waste management upstream to the producer and away from municipalities. [17]

[16]Widely. J. Dmowska, Obowiązki wytwórcy . . .,p. 137.

[17]Thieffry (2022).

The implementation of the EPR is indeed organized at various degrees by specific directives: Directive on batteries and accumulator,[18] Directive on packaging and packaging waste,[19] Directive on end-of-life vehicles,[20] and Directive on waste electrical and electronic equipment (WEEE),[21] generally focused on recovery and recycling targets laid down by legislation and constituting its ultimate goal. To the extent regulated by the abovementioned directives, the principle of extended producer liability should be considered mandatory. Due to the minimal nature of harmonization, states may extend the application of this principle to other activities as well (e.g., in France).

From the point of view of the topic of this paper, the example of producers of electrical and electronic equipment is relevant. Under the ERP, the producer is obliged to guarantee and finance the free collection of waste equipment. Small equipment (such as a hairdryer) should be collected by shops selling the producer's products. The producer is obliged to recycle waste equipment at a certain percentage, which increases in accordance with EU standards. An additional financial instrument supporting the producer's financial responsibility is the product fee, which is an alternative to meeting the standards for recycling used equipment. A producer that fails to meet the applicable standards is obliged to pay a product fee. Because of the risk of the producer's insolvency, the EU legislator imposes an obligation to provide financial security in the case of failure to pay the product fee (more on this below).

4 Waste Insurance as Mandatory EU Financial Security

4.1 EU Mandatory Financial Security Requirements

The main EU legislation that includes mandatory financial security provisions for environmental responsibilities for waste are the Landfill Directive,[22] the Extractive Waste Directive,[23] the Shipments of Waste Regulation, and the Directive on waste electrical and electronic equipment. Eighteen Member States (Belgium, Croatia, Cyprus, the Czech Republic, Denmark, Estonia, France, Germany, Greece,

[18] Directive 2006/66/EC of the European Parliament and of the Council of 6 September 2006 on batteries and accumulators and waste batteries and accumulators and repealing Directive 91/157/EEC) OJ L 266, 26.9.2006, p. 1.

[19] European Parliament and Council Directive 94/62/EC of 20 December 1994 on packaging and packaging waste (OJ L 365, 31.12.1994, p. 10).

[20] Directive 2000/53/Ec of the European Parliament and of the Council of 18 September 2000 on end-of-life vehicles (OJ L 269, 21.10.2000, p. 34).

[21] Directive 2012/19/EU of the European Parliament and of the Council on waste electrical and electronic equipment [2012] OJ L197/38.

[22] Council Directive 1999/31/EC on the landfill of waste [1999] OJ L182/1.

[23] Council Directive 2016/21/EC on the management of waste from extractive industries [2016] OJ L102/15.

Hungary, Ireland, Italy, Latvia, Lithuania, the Netherlands, Poland, Croatia, and Spain) have introduced mandatory financial security that goes beyond EU legislation requirements for activities associated with waste.

The Landfill Directive was adopted to prevent or mitigate the negative effects on the environment from landfilling waste as much as possible. The Directive does this, among other measures, by (1) requiring the disposal of hazardous waste, nonhazardous waste, and inert waste in separate landfills; (2) specifying types of waste that cannot be disposed of in landfills; (3) banning landfilling waste that does not meet specified waste acceptance criteria; and (4) requiring landfills to satisfy technical and financial security requirements.

The Landfill Directive requires the operator to have financial security to meet the closure and postclosure obligations under its permit. Article 8 (a) (iv) of the Landfill Directive directs the Member States to take measures to ensure that competent authorities do not issue a landfill permit unless they are satisfied, among other things, that "adequate provisions, by way of a financial security or any other equivalent, on the basis of modalities to be decided by Member States, has been or will be made by the applicant prior to the commencement of disposal operations to ensure that the obligations (including after-care provisions) arising under the permit ... are discharged and that the closure procedures required by [the Landfill Directive] are followed. This security or its equivalent shall be kept as long as required by maintenance and after-care operation of the site in accordance with [the Landfill Directive]."

The purpose of the Extractive Waste Directive (also called the Mining Waste Directive) is, as stated by Article 1 of the Directive, to provide for "measures, procedures and guidance to prevent or reduce as far as possible any adverse effects on the environment, in particular water, air, soil, fauna and flora and landscape, and any resultant risks to human health, brought about as a result of the management of waste from the extractive industries." Recital 25 states, among other stipulations, that operators of extractive waste facilities must "lodge a financial guarantee or equivalent in accordance with procedures to be decided by the Member States ensuring that all the obligations flowing from the permit will be fulfilled, including those relating to the closure and after-closure of the waste facility. The financial guarantee should be sufficient to cover the cost of rehabilitation of the land affected by the waste facility, which includes the waste facility itself, as described in the waste management plan prepared ... and required by the ... permit, by a suitably qualified and independent third party." The Directive requires the operator to have financial security for obligations under its permit, including postclosure measures and the rehabilitation of land affected by the waste facility.

The Commission has issued technical guidelines on financial security pursuant to the Extractive Waste Directive.[24] The guidelines state that the Member States shall base the calculation of the financial guarantee for a waste facility on the following:

[24]Commission Decision of 20 April 2009 on technical guidelines for the establishment of the financial guarantee in accordance with Directive 2006/21/EC of the European Parliament and of the

(1) its likely impact on human health and the environment; (2) the definition of rehabilitation, including its after use; (3) applicable environmental standards and objectives, including the physical stability of the waste facility, minimum quality standards for soil and water resources, and the maximum release rates of contaminants; (4) technical measures required to achieve environmental objectives, especially measures aimed at ensuring the stability of the facility and limiting environmental damage; (5) measures required to achieve objectives during and post closure, including land rehabilitation, postclosure treatment, and monitoring if required, and, if relevant, measures to restore biodiversity; (6) the estimated time scale of impacts and required mitigation measures; and (7) an assessment of the costs necessary to ensure land rehabilitation, closure, and postclosure, including the possible monitoring or treatment of contaminants.

The Waste Shipment Regulation[25] implements the Basel Convention and the OECD Decision on the control of transboundary movements of waste[26] in the EU. The Regulation lays down the procedures for transboundary shipments of waste within the EU and between the Member States and third countries, including a ban on the export of waste for disposal. Article 4 (5) of the Regulation states, among other stipulations, that a financial guarantee or equivalent insurance must be established and declared in the notification for the shipment of waste. Article 4 (5) further provides that the financial guarantee or equivalent insurance shall be submitted as part of the notification document before the start of the shipment. Article 6 sets out the requirements for a financial guarantee or equivalent insurance. It must cover (1) transport costs; (2) recovery or disposal, including any necessary interim operations; and (3) the storage of waste for 90 days. Article 6 (2) states that the purpose of financial security is to provide for the shipment or recovery of waste when it cannot be carried out as intended or the shipment, recovery, or disposal is illegal. According to Article 6 (5), the financial guarantee or equivalent insurance shall be valid for and cover the notified shipment and completion of the recovery or disposal of the notified waste. In 2010, the Commission carried out a study to analyze the practices in the Member States with regard to financial guarantee or equivalent insurance, as set out in Article 6 of the Shipments of the Waste Regulation. The correspondents, pursuant to Article 54 of Regulation (EC) No 1013/2006 on shipments of waste (WSR), agreed that there is no need to develop a common European method for calculating the financial guarantee or equivalent insurance.[27]

Council concerning the management of waste from extractive industries (notified under document number C(2009) 2798) *OJ L 101, 21.4.2009, p. 25–25.*

[25] Regulation (EC) No 1013/2006 on shipments of waste [2006] OJ L190/1 (consolidated version).

[26] OECD, Decision of the Council C(2001)107/Final concerning the control of transboundary movements of wastes destined for recovery operations as amended by C(2004)20; Decision of the Council C(2001)107/Final concerning the control of transboundary movements of wastes destined for recovery operations as amended by.

[27] Method of Calculation of the Financial Guarantee and Equivalent Insurance pursuant to Art. 6 of Regulation (EC) No 1013/2006 on shipments of waste in the Member States - A Compilation Document.

In the draft of the new Shipments of Waste Regulation 2021,[28] the provisions on financial security have not changed.

The EU adopted the first Waste Electrical and Electronic Equipment Directive in 2002 to improve the collection, treatment, and recycling of waste electrical and electronic equipment (WEEE). Article 8 (3) of the WEEE Directive requires the Member States to ensure that the producers or third parties acting on their behalf establish systems to provide for the recovery of WEEE using the best available techniques. The systems may be established individually or collectively by producers. Article 12 (3) states that the guarantee may be in "the form of participation by the producer in appropriate schemes for the financing of the management of WEEE, a recycling insurance or a blocked bank account." Recital 23 states that the purpose of the requirement is "to prevent costs for the management of WEEE from orphan products from falling on society or the remaining producers." Most Member States have established compliance schemes to satisfy the requirement for a financial guarantee. The compliance schemes also enable producers to meet other requirements of the WEEE Directive. As a result, most WEEE producers have not taken out bank guarantees or purchased insurance.[29]

4.2 *Insurance Contract vs. Other Types of Financial Security*

The interference of the EU legislature in insurance instruments in waste management is characterized by a kind of liberality allowing the choice of collateral—either by the entity applying for a permit for a specific waste management activity or by the administrative body. The directives cited above are not uniform in these issues. However, it can be assumed that the administrative body issuing the permit has the final say on the issue of financial security. It should be taken into account that in all cases, financial security is a requirement for the activity of the entity concerned: landfill manager, mining plant, or electronic equipment producer.

What we are dealing with is financial security of a compulsory nature for a specific entrepreneur, which, however, cannot be treated as compulsory (or even mandatory) insurance. There is a kind of competition between different financial instruments as instruments for securing claims of public entities. The EU legislator limits itself to imposing "financial security or any other equivalent" (Landfill Directive), a "financial guarantee or equivalent" (Extractive Waste Directive), a "financial guarantee or equivalent insurance" (Shipments of Waste Regulation), and, most specifically, "the form of producer's participation in appropriate WEEE management financing schemes, a recycling insurance or a blocked bank account"

---

[28] Proposal for a Regulation of the European Parliament and of the Council on shipments of waste and amending Regulations (EU) No 1257/2013 and (EU) No 2020/1056, Brussels, 17.11.2021 COM(2021) 709 final 2021/0367 (COD).

[29] Fogleman (2020), p. 117.

(WEEE Directive). As can be seen, there is a lack of uniformity in the formulation of the safeguards imposed by the EU legislator. Such a general wording is in the spirit of harmonization and allows the Member State to adapt the requirement to the level of national financial market development. National legislation, therefore, usually indicates a specific financial security from which the security is chosen in a particular case.

For example, in Poland, in accordance with the provisions of the Waste Act,[30] which is an expression of the implementation of the Landfill Directive, the waste management entity, in order to undertake and carry out its activities, is obliged to present financial security in the form of (1) a bank deposit, (2) a bank guarantee, (3) an insurance guarantee, or (4) an insurance policy. The security in the form of a bank guarantee, an insurance guarantee, or an insurance policy shall be submitted to the authority approving the landfill operation manual. The purpose of such action is to secure the claims of the administrative authority (Marshal of the voivodship or director of the regional environmental protection authority) for the occurrence of negative effects on the environment and environmental damage in connection with the operation of the landfill (damage to protected species, protected habitats, waters, land surface). In accordance with the wording of Article 125 of the Waste Act, the bank guarantee, insurance guarantee, or insurance policy should state that, in the event of the occurrence of negative effects on the environment or environmental damage, the bank or insurer will cover the liabilities in the event that the competent authority (Marshal of the voivodship) decides to use the funds from the security of claims for the remedy of these effects unless these actions have not been performed by the landfill manager at his own expense (similarly, Article 48a (17) of the Waste Act). The requirement of such a declaration, as well as its content, may constitute a significant factor hindering the use of insurance as the required contract security. One has to agree with the view that limiting the obligation to activate security to situations where the landfill manager has failed to remedy adverse environmental effects or environmental damage at its own expense is hardly acceptable under insurance law, but it also raises broader doubts. The purpose of the security is to satisfy claims against the security holder, i.e. to discharge the obligation of personal performance. This is the intention behind the conclusion of an insurance contract, including environmental insurance. The policyholder acquires insurance protection in return for a relatively low premium in relation to the costs they would have to bear if the covered event occurred. In this way, the policyholder protects their property interests by transferring a part of their financial responsibility to another entity—the insurer.[31] This immanent feature of insurance can be a barrier in choosing this form of security.

Difficulties in the use of insurance are indicated by the specific case of Zakład Utylizacji Odpadów Sp z o.o. (Waste Treatment Plant), which applied for an

---

[30] Ustawa z dnia 14 grudnia 2012 r. o odpadach Dz. U. 2013 poz. 21 (Waste Management Act of 14 December 2012).

[31] Orzechowska (2021a), p. 51.

integrated permit to operate a thermal waste conversion facility issued by the Marshall of the Wielkopolskie Voivodship as a competent authority in this matter. In accordance with Article 48a (1) to (4) of the Waste Act, it was obliged to obtain a permit for waste processing as a waste holder that is not the operator of a landfill to which the abovementioned Article 125 of the Waste Act applies. Obtaining of the permit requires the establishment of a security for claims in the amount to cover the costs of substitute performance of: (a) a decision ordering the removal of waste from a place not intended for its landfill or storage, (b) the removal of waste or the negative effects or damage to the environment caused in the event of withdrawal of the permit, or (c) the removal of waste or residues after a firefighting action or the removal of the negative effects or damage to the environment. The operator of the installation—Zakład Utylizacji Odpadów Sp z o.o.—declared the form and amount of claims security in the form of an insurance policy for the insured amount of PLN 1,500,000 (in words: one million five hundred thousand zlotys). In accordance with Article 48a (7) of the Waste Act, the Marshal of the Wielkopolskie Voivodship specified the abovementioned form and amount of the claims security in their decision. According to Article 48a (10) of the Waste Act, Zakład Utylizacji Odpadów presented the original insurance policy to the authority. The authority stated that the submitted policy did not meet the requirements set out in the provisions of the Waste Act, in particular with regard to the insurer's statement concerning the payment of obligations to the competent enforcement authority, and obliged the operator to resubmit a document confirming the establishment of security of claims meeting the condition referred to in Article 48a (5) of the Waste Act.[32] In response to the above, Zakład Utylizacji Odpadów changed the form of the claimed security—from an insurance policy to a bank guarantee. The Marshal of the Wielkopolskie voivodship, by way of a decision, redefined the abovementioned form (bank guarantee) and the amount of the claimed security (amount: PLN 1,500,000).[33]

Failure to include a statutory statement in the insurance policy may result from at least two reasons: (1) incorrect understanding of the insurance policy as a legal transaction and (2) the essence of the insurer's benefit which amounts to insurance protection in relation to the assumed risk of an uncertain event.[34] The first reason is

[32]The wording of paragraph 5 of Article 48 a reads: '5. The bank guarantee, insurance guarantee or insurance policy shall state that at any time, until a final decision on the return of the bank guarantee, insurance guarantee or insurance policy referred to in paragraph 18 is issued, in the event of adverse effects on the environment or environmental damage within the meaning of the Act of 13 April 2007 on prevention of damage to the environment and its remediation, arising as a result of the entity's failure to comply with the obligations set out in this Act, including the obligations arising from its waste collection permit or waste processing permit, or the need to remove waste from a place not intended for its storage or landfill, the bank or insurance company shall pay the obligations to the authority enforcing these obligations.

[33]Decision of the Marshal of the Wielkopolskie voivodship of 30.11.2020, DSR-II-2.7222.34.2019 https://bip.umww.pl/artykuly/2826939/pliki/20210316115713_7222.34.pdf.

[34]Instead of many Maśniak (2022), p. 1225.

characteristic of continental law, where the insurance policy is only a document confirming the conclusion of an insurance contract.[35] It does not constitute a source of obligation, and the statements contained therein only confirm the content of the contract concluded by implication. Unfortunately, the provision of the Polish Waste Act explicitly refers to the insurance policy as financial security that loses its nature. This results in the administrative body focusing on the content of the policy. The second reason seems to be of key importance in examining the adequacy of the insurance contract as a financial security for claims of administrative authorities to cover the costs of substitute performance of activities related to the removal of negative changes in the environment—resulting from an administrative decision issued on the basis of specific provisions concerning a particular waste management entity (landfill operator, waste holder, producer of waste shipped abroad). The purpose of the security is to secure the payment of obligations to the enforcement authority of the waste manager. Such assurance requires a specific definition of the concept of an insured accident—a concept that is crucial to the formation of the insurance relationship. According to the established insurance doctrine, an insurance accident means the materialization of an insurance risk that is an event independent of the will of the policyholder (insured) and is characterized by uncertainty.[36] The solution may be an appropriate definition of an insurance accident by the insurer in the insurance conditions. This is possible in property insurance other than liability insurance—which depends on the liability of the insured due to its accessory nature. The Polish Civil Code stipulates that in liability insurance, "the insurer undertakes to pay compensation, specified in the contract, for damage caused to third parties against whom the insurer or the insured is liable" (Article 822 of the Polish Civil Code). Assuming that an insurance accident will be the issuance of a final decision of the competent enforcement authority on the allocation of funds from the claims security, established to cover the costs of substitute performance during the insurance period, does not negate the attribute of uncertainty—immanent to an insurance accident?[37] Such a definition solves the problem raised in the doctrine of adjusting the scope of insurance protection of the security to the extent expected by the legislator, requiring the release of funds regardless of whether there is a direct risk of damage to the environment.[38]

The specificity of the financial security established to "ensure that all obligations arising from the permit have been fulfilled" (recital 28 of the Preamble to the Landfill

[35] Fuchs (2009), pp. 19–26.

[36] The definition of a fortuitous event adopted in the Polish Insurance and Reinsurance Act of 11 September 2015, OJ 2015 No 1844 (Article 3(1)(57)) reads "a fortuitous event - a future and uncertain event, independent of the will of the policyholder or the insured, the occurrence of which causes damage to personal property or property, or an increase in property needs on the part of the policyholder or another person covered by the insurance protection".

[37] Such a solution is already used in the insurance market, but it is unfortunately a rarity – Environmental Protect General Terms and Conditions of Indemnity Insurance for Environmental Damages - the General Terms and Conditions, of Colonnade Insurance S.A.

[38] Orzechowska (2021b), pp. 79–82.

Directive) also affects the temporal scope of protection. It is in the interest of the environmental authority, and arguably in the context of the Directive, to assume that the security covers all obligations owed to the waste manager, regardless of when they arise. Such a solution is not acceptable to insurers. Hence, the prerequisites used on the insurance market stipulating that the insurance protection covers accidents resulting from negligence committed by the insured person up to 3 years preceding the beginning of the insurance period should be indicated in the insurance contract.[39]

Such insurance, properly "tailored" to the needs imposed by EU law, can hardly be considered third-party insurance. As insurance of preventive and remedial costs related to waste management, it should be classified under insurance group 16 (insurance of various financial risks). This classification is all the more justified when we bear in mind that they represent an alternative to insurance guarantees—an insurance activity whose object is financial risk.

A comparison of national solutions that reflect the implementation of EU financial security rules shows the absence of environmental insurance as the sole means of financial security for measures such as the closure or aftercare of a landfill or other waste facility. Insurance may be used to provide cover for the risk of taking measures, say, to close a landfill or waste facility exceeding the estimated costs of closure, when the operator is being required to close the landfill or waste facility before the planned date, or in the event of environmental damage arising from incidents during closure or aftercare. Other financial security instruments, such as bank guarantees, deposits, or bonds, however, are required to cover the estimated costs of closure and aftercare. This is because the insurance covers fortuities but not certainties. However, the statement that "insurance may be part of the financial security for responsibilities only to the extent that liabilities may arise from them" does not see the opportunity offered by financial risk insurance and focuses on third-party insurance (liability insurance).[40]

5 Waste Risks as Insurance Risk in the USA: Ambiguous Wording

5.1 Waste Risk as Content of Pollution Exclusion in Insurance Conditions: In the Light of Case Law

Thinking about the insurance of environmental risks in the context of liability insurance is also characteristic of the US. Most CGL (Commercial General Liability) insurance policies available in the US insurance market adopt a pollution exclusion policy language that is similar to the language used in the standard Insurance Services Office form, as evidenced by definitions adopted by insurers involved in

[39] Environmental Protection - the General Terms and Conditions, of Colonnade Insurance S.A.

[40] Fogleman (2020), p. 48.

litigation.[41] "Pollutants" are defined in the policy as "any solid, liquid, gaseous or thermal irritant or contaminant, including smoke, vapor, soot, fumes, acids, alkalis, chemicals, and waste."[42] "Pollutants means any solid, liquid, gaseous, or thermal irritant or contaminant, including smoke, vapor, soot, fumes, acid, alkalis, chemicals, and waste. Waste includes material to be recycled, reconditioned or reclaimed."[43] The policy defined pollutants as "any solid, liquid, gaseous, or thermal irritant or contaminant, including smoke, vapor, soot, fumes, acids, alkalis, chemicals, and waste."[44] As can be seen, in all conditions. "waste" is treated as a "pollutant" excluded from the scope of protection.

The supreme courts in California, Illinois, and Louisiana all determined that the pollution exclusion was ambiguous. These courts developed three separate interpretations of pollution under the absolute pollution exclusion. Although the California Supreme Court attempted to provide a uniform interpretation of the absolute pollution exclusion, lower courts in California have not always utilized this interpretation. One lower California court circumvented the Supreme Court's interpretation by finding the pollution exclusion clause unambiguous, which required a very different analysis from that used by the Supreme Court.[45]

The importance of the identified problem is highlighted by the analysis of the Ortega Rock Quarry v. Golden Eagle Insurance Corp. case, where the California Courts of Appeal interpreted the absolute pollution exclusion clause. Ortega Rock Quarry claimed damages from its insurance provider for claims arising out of the Environmental Protection Agency's (EPA's) order and lawsuit that resulted from the placement of fill dirt and rocks in the quarry along the access road. Ortega Rock Quarry claimed damages that arose from the quarry placing the fill dirt and rocks, along the access road, that later flowed into the stream.

The insurance company refused to cover the action under the absolute pollution exclusion because it argued that the dirt and rocks were pollutants. The court determined that the pollution exclusion was not ambiguous and refused to cover the claim. In reaching this conclusion, however, the court never explicitly explained why dirt and rocks could be commonly regarded as pollution. The lower court's decision in the Ortega Rock Quarry case also reveals the problem that can arise when lower courts do not apply the interpretation suggested by the state supreme court. When lower courts fail to apply the supreme court's interpretation of pollution, the expectation gap increases because both insureds and insurance providers become uncertain about whether the supreme court's test would be used by lower courts in the future. After determining that the pollution exclusion is ambiguous, courts should apply a three-factor analysis to determine whether an alleged pollutant is,

---

[41] Meeks (2009), p. 828.

[42] See: Bituminous Cas. Corp. v. Sand Livestock Sys., Inc., 728 N.W.2d 216 219 (Iowa 2007).

[43] Clendenin Bros., 889 A.2d at 390.

[44] Nav-Its, Inc. v. Selective Ins. Co., 869 A.2d 929, 932 (N.J. 2005).

[45] See Ortega Rock Quarry v. Golden Eagle Ins. Corp., 46 Cal. Rptr. 3d 517, 527-32 (Cal. Ct. App. 2006). But see Garamendi v. Golden Eagle Ins. Co., 25 Cal. Rptr. 3d 642, 646 (Cal. Ct. App. 2005).

in fact, pollution, which would then trigger the application of the CGL's pollution exclusion. These three factors are (1) whether the alleged pollutant is mainly of natural or chemical origin, (2) whether the alleged pollutant is typically hazardous by the way it caused the harm, and (3) whether the insured is typically a polluter.

In the Ortega Rock Quarry case, the alleged pollution was created when a rock quarry released rocks and dirt into a creek to maintain the access road that was washed away when the creek flooded. As a preliminary matter, the court first found that the pollution exclusion was ambiguous, so it applied the proposed three-factor analysis of pollution. First, the court would consider the composition of the alleged pollution to determine whether it was of natural or chemical origin. In this case, the first factor is easily determined because rocks and dirt are natural materials. In fact, this is an abnormally clear case because the rocks and dirt in question did not contain any potential chemical material. Since the alleged pollutant consists of natural materials, this factor suggests that the alleged pollutant does not fall within the definition of pollution in the pollution exclusion. Next, the court would apply the second test factor: whether the alleged pollutant is typically hazardous because of the way it caused the damage. In this case, the rocks and dirt were hazardous because of the way they caused the damage. Here, the fact that the rocks filled the stream is the damage, and this is the exact damage that the insureds and insurance providers would have considered when deciding whether rocks could be hazardous pollution. This is therefore different from a case where a toxic chemical was hazardous because of the damage it could cause if ingested but instead caused the damage because it was wet and someone slipped on it. In this case, the parties likely understood that the reason that rocks could pollute is because the rocks could interfere with a waterway, and thus the rocks were actually hazardous in this case for that reason—because they filled the stream. This factor, therefore, would suggest a finding of pollution under the pollution exclusion.

Finally, in the Ortega Rock Quarry case, the court would apply the third factor: whether the insured was a polluter. In this case, the insured operated a rock quarry. A rock quarry is a type of business that risks polluting through the use of chemicals in typical mining operations or inadequately disposing of waste material, which could include excess rocks and dirt. Typically, one would expect that a rock quarry can pollute by releasing various chemicals used in the mining process and not by releasing rocks and dirt that were used to build up a washed-out road. Therefore, since a rock quarry does not typically pollute by repairing an access road with rocks and fill, in this case, the quarry would not be considered a polluter with respect to this specific pollution. Although this factor would support defining various chemical discharges from the quarry as pollutants, it does not similarly suggest this conclusion if the pollutants were rocks and dirt used to reinforce a road. In the facts presented before the court, this factor counts against applying the pollution exclusion. In this case, considering the expectations of the parties, two factors suggest that the rocks and dirt were not pollutants, and one factor weighs in favor of the rocks being pollutants. Specifically, the first factor strongly weighs against the finding of pollution because the rocks and dirt did not contain any potential chemical material. The third factor also weighs against the finding of pollution but is less conclusive because a rock quarry may be commonly thought of as a polluter in numerous other circumstances. In contrast, the second factor strongly suggests that there was pollution because the rocks and dirt caused the damage because of the way that they were hazardous. Since two factors weigh in favor of finding the alleged pollutant to not be pollution, it would be presumed that the rocks and dirt in this case were not pollutants covered by the pollution exclusion. Considering the expectations of the insured and insurance provider supports this presumption and suggests that the court should find that the rocks and dirt were not pollution under the exclusion. In this case, both parties would probably not expect that the exclusion applies to something that was completely natural, even though the damage caused was typical. Because of this analysis, the court would find that the rocks and dirt were not pollution as defined by the pollution exclusion.[46]

In the Ross Dev. Corp. v. Fireman's Fund Ins. Co. case,[47] the US District Court for the District of South Carolina, Charleston Division, ruled that both qualified and absolute pollution exclusions preclude coverage for elevated levels of metals and acidic pH conditions in the soil, groundwater, and sediment at the policyholder's former property located in Charleston, South Carolina. The US Court of Appeals for the Fourth Circuit affirmed such a conclusion.[48] The incident occurred on the Ashley River in Charleston, where the Planters site was producing phosphate fertilizers. The US Environmental Protection Agency (USEPA) subsequently discovered environmental impacts associated with the manufacturing operations at the site, including elevated levels of metals, particularly lead and arsenic in soil, groundwater, and sediment, as well as acidic pH conditions. In 2005, the property's then owner claimed for the reimbursement of remedial action incurred in accordance with regulations of the Comprehensive Environmental Response, Compensation, and Liability Act (CERCLA).[49] In the course of the court proceedings, it was established that pyrite was burned on the land owned by Planters and pyrite slag was produced, which was a by-product of Planters' production activities. Pyrite slag is the source of the vast majority of arsenic and much of the lead contaminating the site. Planters disposed of hazardous waste at the site by dumping the pyrite slag and cleaning the chambers that were used to produce sulfuric acid. Due to the arsenic contamination, there was a need to carry out remediation activities at the site. In the situation where the joint and several liability of the successive owners of the site was acknowledged, the question arose as to the insurer's liability under the insurance contract covering environmental property damage to the site. Due to the specific nature of the damage, i.e., long-term soil contamination, the insurance terms of several years (1972–1990) were taken into account.

46 See: Ortega Rock Quarry v. Golden Eagle Ins. Corp., 46 Cal. Rptr. 3d 517, 519-20 (Cal. Ct. App. 2006);. as cited in: Meeks (2009), p. 849.

47 Ross Dev. Corp. v. Fireman's Fund Ins. Co., 910 F.Supp.2d 828 (DSC 2012).

48 Ross Dev. Corp. et. al. v. PCS Nitrogen Inc., Case No. 12-2059 (4th Cir. 2013) (unpublished).

49 Comprehensive Environmental Response, Compensation, and Liability Act (CERCLA) (42 USC 9601-9675).

The landowner had both a contractual liability insurance agreement as an owner and lesser and a general liability insurance (CGL) agreement. The insurance terms and conditions under which the contract was concluded included standard qualified pollution exclusions. "This insurance does not apply: (f) to bodily injury or property damage arising out of the discharge, dispersal, release or escape of smoke, vapors, soot, fumes, acids, alkalis, toxic chemicals, liquids or gases, waste materials or other irritants, contaminants or pollutants into or upon land, the atmosphere or any water course or body of water; but this exclusion does not apply if such discharge, dispersal, release or escape is sudden and accidental."

An absolute exemption was included in the conditions subsequently in force (1987–1990), which read: "This insurance does not apply to: f. (1) 'Bodily injury' or 'property damage' arising out of the actual, alleged or threatened discharge, dispersal, release or escape of pollutants:

(a) At or from premises you own, rent or occupy; (b) At or from any site or location used by or for you or others for the handling, storage, disposal, processing or treatment of waste; (c) which are at any time transported, handled, stored, treated, disposed of, or processed as waste by or for you or any person or organization for whom you may be legally responsible; or (d) At or from any site or location on which you or any contractors or subcontractors working directly or indirectly on your behalf are performing operations: (i) if the pollutants are brought on or to the site or location in connection with such operations; or (ii) if the operations are to test for, monitor, clean up, remove, contain, treat, detoxify or neutralize the pollutants. (2) Any loss, cost, or expense arising out of any governmental direction or request that you test for, monitor, clean up, remove, contain, treat, detoxify or neutralize pollutants. Pollutants means any solid, liquid, gaseous or thermal irritant or contaminant, including smoke, vapor, soot, fumes, acids, alkalis, chemicals and waste. Waste includes materials to be recycled, reconditioned or reclaimed."[50]

The insured questioned the validity of the application of the insurer's exclusion of liability under the terms of insurance. It took the view that pyrite slag, a by-product of Planters' historic production operations at the site, was not considered waste because it had value as a material for use in road construction and stabilization. The court did not accept the arguments of the insured-polluting plaintiff. It took the view that the polluter's interpretation of the term "waste" was too restrictive, focusing on whether the slag had a utility purpose not directly related to the insured's production activities. In the court's view, many by-products can be reused or recycled, giving them a certain value—in a context other than their original use. This does not mean that a by-product is not "waste" in relation to the production process in which it arose. Referring to waste as a by-product of the manufacturing process in the Ross case, the court stated that "the term *waste material* unambiguously includes pyrite slag, a byproduct of Ross's fertilizer production suitable only for low-value uses such as filling in low-lying land and road beds." Referring to the insured's argument that the absolute pollution exclusion did not apply because there

[50] La Porta (2014), pp. 350–351.

was no evidence that the pyrite slag was "handled, stored, disposed of, processed, or treated as waste," the district court found that the pyrite slag produced by Planter's production activities clearly fell within the definition of waste (Id., 835). The district court noted that the insurer's exclusion of liability specifies that waste "includes materials to be recycled, reclaimed or reconditioned," which is contrary to the position that a by-product of production must be completely useless or worthless to be qualified as waste. In the court's view, the use of pyrite slag in a way that provided some benefit did not mean that there was no utilization. The court claimed that the insured placing pyrite slag in the soil at the site constituted a "disposal" of "waste." Accordingly, any financing of "property damage" resulting from the "actual, alleged or threatened discharge, dispersal, release or escape of pollutants" on the site is excluded from the insurer's liability under the so-called absolute exclusion provided for in the conditions of insurance (CGL).[51]

The insured also argued that pyrite slag was not a pollutant per se. They argued that only the components of pyrite slag that were released as a result of certain environmental processes were pollutants. The insured further argued that pyrite slag, when placed on the ground surface as a fill material or a road base, did not constitute a pollutant because the arsenic and lead components contained in the slag had not been released. According to the insured, "it is only when those compounds are separated from the pyrite slag that any pollutants are, in fact, discharged into the environment." The court rejected the insured's arguments, taking the opinion that the compounds contained in the pyrite slag would have entered the soil and water sources in the "normal and natural course of events without any further human action." The court also referred to the method of release, claiming that "the fact that these pollutants may have escaped from their container slowly rather than immediately has no bearing on whether Ross discharged pollutants into the environment." In the court's view, there is no doubt that arsenic and lead do not lose their pollutant status because they are not released immediately upon discharge into the environment.

According to the insured, even relying on the definition used by the court, pyrite slag does not constitute "waste material" subject to exclusion from insurance protection. Pyrite slag was not a "damaged, defective or superfluous material" or a material rejected from the production process and "reclaimed" for other purposes. For the fertilizer industry, pyrite slag was a commodity for immediate use in many processes, including soil stabilization and road construction. Their value was so high that suppliers of pyrite often retained ownership of the slag. From the producer's point of view, the slag was used for its "usual and main purpose," had a significant value, and was not waste. The insured's arguments aimed to prove that pyrite slag did not fall within the definition of waste covered by the so-called absolute exclusion because it was not "materials to be recycled, reconditioned or reclaimed." It argued

[51] Ross Dev. Corp. v. Fireman's Fund Ins. Co., 910 F.Supp.2d 828 (DSC 2012) as cited in: La Porta (2014).

that the slag was usable in its original state and did not need to be adapted, made ready, returned to a prior condition, restored, rescued, made available, or obtained.

The county court did not formulate a clear rule that the production of by-products constitutes waste within the meaning of the absolute pollution exclusion in terms of the insurance in all circumstances. The court suggested that the answer depends to some extent on whether the by-product has a limited value or utility, as well as whether it is a commercially valuable product. However, it emphasized that a by-product does not cease being waste simply because it has some value or utility. Referring to the contamination provided for in the terms and conditions of the insurance to include "material to be recycled, reconditioned or reclaimed," the county court emphasized that waste may have some value that does not preclude it from qualifying as waste (for the purposes of the exclusion). Logically, the fact that the insured's production waste pollutes the environment once it enters the environment should not depend on its degree of utility. The insured's production waste is still waste for pollution exclusion purposes, even if it has some use.[52]

US case law on this issue, however sparse, seems to be internally consistent. The Grain Dealers Mut. Ins. Co. v. Farmers Alliance Mut. Ins. Co. case[53] concerned fly ash that had been buried on the property by the insured. The court stated that the ash constituted waste as a by-product despite the argument that it had a generally recognized productive use. Thus, the court upheld the exclusion of the insurer's liability on the basis of the absolute exclusion of pollution from insurance protection.

In the Pipefitters Welfare Educational Fund v. Westchester Fire Ins. Co. case,[54] the extent of the absolute exclusion of contamination was examined in relation to scrap metal. The court took the view that waste that is "marketable" and "useful" is still waste and rejected the insured's argument stating that scrap metal was not waste because it was a "marketable and useful product," finding that scrap fell within the definition of waste, which included "material to be recycled, reconditioned or reclaimed."

In the Independent Petrochemical Corp. v. Aetna Cas. And Sur Co. case,[55] the entrepreneur mixed the insured's dioxin waste with oils and sprayed the mixture on unpaved roads and horse paddocks to suppress dust. The court rejected the insured's position that the spraying of the mixture did not constitute pollution within the meaning of exclusion in the insurance terms and conditions because the mixture was used for beneficial purposes, arguing that the waste in question was a by-product and that the alleged damage resulted from its improper disposal.

[52] La Porta (2014), p. 356.

[53] Grain Dealers Mut. Ins. Co. v. Farmers Alliance Mut. Ins. Co., 2001 US Dist. LEXIS 24299, *23 (W.D. Okla 2001).

[54] Pipefitters Welfare Educational Fund v. Westchester Fire Ins. Co., 976 F.2d 1037 (7th Cir. 1992).

[55] Independent Petrochemical Corp. v. Aetna Cas. And Sur Co., 1988 U.S. Dist. LEXIS 15839 (DDC 1988).

5.2 Waste Risk in Environmental Insurance

Ambiguous clauses in the insurance terms and conditions are a barrier to the development of environmental insurance and effective coverage of waste risks.[56] The customer may experience negative consequences due to defects and ambiguity in the insurance terms and conditions. This is illustrated by a case involving a dispute between the insured and the insurer over the availability of funding for the costs of removing construction and demolition debris that was improperly buried on the insured's property by a contractor commissioned by the insured for the demolition of the building, site clearance, and site grading services.

In Picerne, the insured entered into an environmental liability insurance contract with AISLIC for their property in Fort Bragg, North Carolina. Picerne was commissioned by PBG of North Carolina, Inc. (PBG), for demolition, site cleaning, and leveling services. The contractor was obliged to dispose of waste related to the performed works. The waste in question consisted of "concrete, broken wood, painted wood, rebar, metal piping, white goods and vegetation (including tree trunks, tree limbs, tree stumps and mulch created from chipped trees." To achieve this goal, by breaking the law, PBG dug large pits on the insured's property, threw waste into them, and covered them with soil. Picerne argued that all this took place without their knowledge or consent.

Sometime later, the relevant environmental authority accused Picerne of violating environmental legislation and creating a "non-conforming solid waste disposal site/ open dump." The insured was obliged to stop depositing and move all waste from this property to an appropriate disposal facility within 30 days. Costs incurred amounted to \$250,000. The insurer refused to cover the costs, arguing that the waste in question did not constitute pollution within the meaning of the insurance conditions. Pollution condition is specifically defined in the policy as "the discharge, dispersal, release or escape of any solid, liquid, gaseous or thermal irritant or contaminant, including, but not limited to, smoke, vapors, soot, fumes, acids, alkalis, toxic chemicals, medical waste and waste materials into or upon land, or any structure on land, the atmosphere or any watercourse or body of water, including groundwater, provided such conditions are not naturally present in the environment in the amounts or concentrations discovered." The court argued that recognizing the materials as waste does not in itself authorize it to be considered contamination within the meaning of the insurance terms and rejected the insured's arguments, who referred to the common understanding of an "irritant or contaminant" related to an open list of examples that could qualify as condition pollution. The interpretation of this concept was crucial in the case. The AISLIC insurer replied that there was extensive case law that defined pollution as "covering hazards traditionally considered harmful to society or the environment," and in this case, the waste in question was not "hazardous and did not pose a significant risk to human health, the soil or the

[56]Picerne-Military Housing, LLC v. American Intern. Specialty Lines Ins. Co., 650 F.Supp.2d 135 (D.R.I.09).

surrounding environment." The case was pending before the courts for 4 years and did not end with a settlement favorable to the insured.[57]

The doctrine emphasizes that a broader definition of pollution in insurance terms and conditions would be a solution to this problem. In addition, if the policyholder has been adequately informed of the risks of the demolition project that caused the damage, the policyholder may have taken appropriate steps to ensure that the contractor properly disposed of all waste material resulting from the project.[58]

References

Bugge C (2009) The polluter pays principle: dilemmas of justice in national and international contexts. In: Ebbesson J, Okowa P (eds) Environmental law and justice in context. Cambridge University Press

Dmowska J (2019) Obowiązki wytwórcy i posiadacza odpadów. In: Prawo o odpadach. Wybrane problemy, red. B. Rakoczy, Warsaw

Fogleman V (2020) Improving financial security in the context of the Environmental Liability Directive

Fuchs D (2009) Charakter prawny polisy ubezpieczeniowej w prawie polskim a przedmiotowy zakres zastosowania Konwencji Wiedeńskiej o umowach międzynarodowej sprzedaży towarów z 1980 r. Przyczynek do wykładni norm międzynarodowego prawa handlowego, Rozprawy Ubezpieczeniowe I nor 1(6)I

Gniewek E, Machnikowski P (2017) Kodeks cywilny. Komentarz, Wroclaw

Górski M (2005) Gospodarowanie odpadami w świetle prawa wspólnotowego i polskiego prawa wewnętrznego. Poznań

Huenke AD (2013) Environmental insurance policies are negotiated contracts and not commodities. Environ Claims J 25(3)

Kunicki A (1966), Critical gloss on the judgment SN z 3.06.1966 r. , II CR 412/68, OSPIKA 1967/ 10, no. 234

La Porta AJ (2014) A waste is a waste: if it polluted it should be excluded. Environ Claims J 26(4): 348–356

Maśniak D (2021) Wykorzystanie ubezpieczeń do naprawy szkód w środowisku o rozmiarach katastrofalnych, Prawo Morskie tom XL, Gdańsk

Maśniak D (2022) Umowa ubezpieczenia. In: Kodeks cywilny. Komentarz, ed. Małgorzata Balwicka-Szczyrba, A. Sylwestrzak, Warsaw

Meeks C (2009) The pollution delusion: a proposal for a uniform interpretation of pollution in general liability absolute pollution exclusions. Geo Wash Law Rev 77

Orzechowska R (2021a) Environmental liability of the operator – financial tools to mitigate the consequences of environmental liability with insurance. In: Malinowska K, Maśniak D, Tarasiuk A (eds) Environmental risk and insurance

Orzechowska R (2021b) Odpowiedzialność podmiotu korzystającego ze środowiska – narzędzia mitygacji finansowych konsekwencji odpowiedzialności za szkodę w środowisku za pomocą ubezpieczeń, Prawo Asekuracyjne Nr 1/2021

Skowrońska-Bocian E, Warciński M (2020). In: Pietrzykowski K (ed) Kodeks cywilny Tom I. Komentarz do Art. 1–449. Warsaw, Art. 336

---

[57] Picerne-Military Housing, LLC v. American Intern. Specialty Lines Ins. Co., 650 F.Supp.2d 135 (D.R.I.09).

[58] Huenke (2013), pp. 229–232.

Smith A, Keith B, Steve O, Kathryn R, Judith B (2001) Waste Management Options and Climate Change. Final report to the European Commission, DG Environment, July 2001, https://ec.europa.eu/environment/pdf/waste/studies/climate_change.pdf
Thieffry P (2022) Extended Producer Responsibility. https://www.era-comm.eu/EU_waste_law/stand_alone/part_3/index.html

Underwriting Environmental Risks for Carbon Capture Usage and Storage (CCUS) Coverage: Challenges and Best Practices Forward

Kyriaki Noussia

Abstract The Paris Agreement on climate change is calling for mitigating techniques, such as carbon capture, use, and storage (CCUS) to reduce carbon emissions. Insurance can help carbon (CO2) mitigation and promote the tackling of the pace of acceleration of climate change. This chapter proposes to examine the international environmental law regime and the contribution of CO2 capture to the resolution of the climate change problem and to evaluate the role of insurance for CCUS technology and consider parameters of insurance coverage in terms of CCUS, as such coverage. The provision of adequate insurance cover will allow a real expansion in the deployment of the CCUS technology at a large scale. It will assess new solutions in insurance products for CCS coverage to offer guidance to the insurance market on how to obtain better coverage and to provide insurers with a window of opportunity to grow their product base and encourage lobbying efforts for legislation favorable to the insurance industry. Such enactment of specific further statutory regulations will offer great benefits to the insurance market and potential policyholders as it will provide benefits such as the lowering of the price of CCS liability insurance.

1 Introduction

The Paris Agreement on climate change is calling for mitigating techniques, such as carbon capture, use, and storage (CCUS), to reduce carbon emissions. Because CCUS technology offers CO2 mitigation options without cobenefits, there has been no big expansion in it so far, but the solution for this could be a robust regulatory and legal regime that will enhance the use of CCUS as a gatekeeper for environmental protection and ultimately for the mitigation of the pace of occurrence of climate change. CCUS technologies can help meet the COP15 and thereafter climate change targets. To do that, special environmental climate change and other

K. Noussia (✉)
University of Reading, School of Law, Reading, UK
e-mail: k.p.noussia@reading.ac.uk

K. Malinowska, D. Maśniak (eds.), *Managing Environmental Risks through Insurance*, AIDA Europe Research Series on Insurance Law and Regulation 9,
https://doi.org/10.1007/978-3-031-47602-0_12

risks will need to be identified to be covered by adequate insurance. This chapter discusses the international environmental law regime and the contribution of CO2 capture to the resolution of the climate change problem, and it also examines the role of insurance as a crucial mitigating mechanism in minimizing the negative outcomes that may arise out of potential damage caused in the operation and transportation of CO2 via the use of CCUS technology, and in doing so, it considers parameters of insurance coverage in terms of CCUS and what insurance should be underwritten to provide cover throughout the operation of CCUS. It discusses the way such insurance risks should be identified and worded, the potential deductibles and exclusions, and the need for special insurance cover for environmental pollution and other environmental risks, as well as cyber risks.

2 Climate Change and International Legal Regulatory Instruments: Brief Overview and Correlation with CCUS

The United Nations Framework Convention on Climate Change (UNFCC), which entered into force in 1994,[1] was the first international treaty agreed to contribute to the tackling of international climate change. The main deficit of the UNFCC was that it did not impose any strict requirements for signatories but simply highlighted the need for further scientific work into climate change and solutions. In 1997, the Kyoto Protocol constituted the first legal instrument to impose international targets on developed countries, requiring them to reduce their emissions for compliance with targets allocated via a "top-down" approach;[2] however, it did not have the support of a good number of signatories; hence, a new approach to international climate law was needed.[3] This was achieved and depicted in the Paris Agreement, which was created with an overall aim of keeping global temperature rise this century to well below 2 degree Celsius above preindustrial levels and also with the further vision to limit this even further to 1.5 degrees Celsius[4]—and to do so, parties were required to set their own "nationally determined contributions" (NDCs), and in addition, the Paris Agreement also contains provisions relating to the conservation and enhancement of sinks and reservoirs of greenhouse gas emissions (Article 5),[5] inter alia.

[1] United Nations Framework Convention on Climate Change, 9 May 1992, (1992) U.N.T.S. 1771, 31(4) I.L.M. 849, entered into force 21 Mar. 1994.

[2] Green et al. (2014), p. 1064.

[3] The Guardian (2011), Canada pulls out of Kyoto Protocol https://www.theguardian.com/environment/2011/dec/13/canada-pulls-out-kyoto-protocol, 2011 (access 10.05.2023).

[4] Paris Agreement, 12 Dec. 2015, (2015), 55(4) I.L.M. 740 (2016), entered into force 4 Nov. 2016, https://unfccc.int/files/meetings/paris_nov_2015/application/pdf/paris_agreement_english_.pdf, art 2. (access 10.05.2023).

[5] Paris Agreement, 12 Dec. 2015, (2015), 55(4) I.L.M. 740 (2016), entered into force 4 Nov. 2016, https://unfccc.int/files/meetings/paris_nov_2015/application/pdf/paris_agreement_english_.pdf, art 5. (access 10.05.2023).

Such carbon sinks and reservoirs are systems (often natural) that absorb carbon dioxide from the atmosphere, e.g., plants, forests, soil, the ocean, as well as man-made equivalents, i.e., carbon capture, use and storage (CCUS). CCUS adheres to a larger process of capturing CO2, transporting it with the usage of either a pipeline or a ship, using it, and then storing it.[6] The Intergovernmental Panel on Climate Change (IPCC) has divided the CCUS operation and procedure into three phases, i.e., firstly the phase of separation of CO2, then its transport to storage and its use, and, finally, its long-term isolation from the atmosphere.[7]

Because it is impossible to fully prevent the emission of carbon into the atmosphere, a mechanism is needed to help absorb some of this carbon and mitigate against the harm it can cause, hence the emergence of CCUS as a mitigating method to prevent the accelerated pace of climate change occurrence. Critics of CCUS state that prevention is better than mitigation as a strategy and policy mechanism and that CO2 is not extinguished via the use of CCUS; however, CCUS can prevent further global warming and help reverse climate change effects.[8] Therefore, this chapter will discuss the international legal and insurance challenges surrounding CCUS perceived as a mitigation tool for tackling climate change.

In international conventions and laws, CCUS has neither been expressly prohibited nor authorized, and in many cases, the international legal instruments needed amendments, which were not easy to accomplish in a short time. Some of the challenges encountered in the regulation of CCUS have been addressed via international legal instruments such as the Basel Convention, the United Nations Convention on the Law of the Sea (UNCLOS), and the London Convention. In the Basel Convention, a substance is categorized as "hazardous waste," and under the Convention, parties are bound by a number of general obligations relating to the manner in which they handle the waste. In it, the provisions under Article 4(2) on measures to reduce hazardous wastes and other wastes to a minimum, on the availability of adequate disposal facilities, and on the safeguarding of acts of pollution prevention from those involved in the management of hazardous wastes and the minimum transboundary movement of hazardous wastes and the ban of their export to developing countries, or countries that have forbidden its import, relate to CCUS.[9] However, as CO2 is not listed in any of these annexes, it is argued that its transportation is not restricted by the Basel Convention;[10] nonetheless, the fact that CO2 bears some hazardous characteristics of Annex III of the Convention in

[6]Tucker (2018), p. 31.

[7]Metz et al. (2005).

[8]United Nations (1987), Report of the World Commission on Environment and Development: Our Common Future.https://sustainabledevelopment.un.org/content/documents/5987our-common-future.pdf (access 10.05.2023).

[9]Basel Convention on the Control of Transboundary Movements of Hazardous Wastes and their Disposal, 22 March 1989, (1989), 1673 U.N.T.S. 126), article 4(2).

[10]Raine (2008), p. 353.

certain circumstances[11] has meant that perhaps it falls within the remit of the scope and application to it of the Basel Convention if mixed with other hazardous substances;[12] however, no consensus as to this interpretation has been reached. UNCLOS[13] in Article 192 contains a general obligation on states to "protect and preserve the marine environment,"[14] and Article 195 states that "in taking measures to prevent, reduce and control pollution of the marine environment, States shall act so as not to transfer, directly or indirectly, damage or hazards from one area to another or transform one type of pollution into another."[15] It is not clear as to whether CO2 constitutes a hazardous substance or pollutant, but UNCLOS has certain restrictions for the transportation of CO2 by ship or pipeline concerning the exact ocean area of CO2 transportation. Regarding the use of pipelines in territorial seas, all states involved where the pipelines will cross need consent to this operation, and it is also possible that states can object to the use of pipelines in their exclusive economic zone and continental shelf. Regarding the transportation of CO2 by ship, this is permitted, and overall, UNCLOS does not prohibit CCUS operations so long as they do not contravene its provisions. The London Convention[16] and the 1996 London Protocol,[17] in force as of 2006, do not allow the dumping of various substances listed in Annex I and presuppose a state permit for substances in Annex II, and again, CO2 is not listed as an Annex I or II substance; hence, it is not prohibited. The 2007 proposal to amend Annex I of the London Protocol to include CCS in the permitted activities sets out in which cases CO2 can be dumped.[18] It is argued by the 2008 Legal and Technical Working Group on Transboundary CO2 Sequestration Issues that Article 6 prohibited the export of CO2 from one contracting party to other countries.[19] This was rectified via the 2009 Resolution LP.3 (4) by means of an amended text for Article 6, stating that although the export of wastes or other matter to other countries for dumping or incineration at

---

[11] Basel Convention on the Control of Transboundary Movements of Hazardous Wastes and their Disposal, 22 March 1989, (1989), (1673 U.N.T.S. 126), annex IV.

[12] Romeiro and Parente (2012); United Nations, (2012), Transboundary carbon capture and storage project activities: Technical Paper. https://unfccc.int/resource/docs/2012/tp/09.pdf (access 10.05.2023).

[13] United Nations Convention on the Law of the Sea 1982, (1982), 1833 UNTS 3.

[14] United Nations Convention on the Law of the Sea 1982, (1982), 1833 UNTS 3, art 192.

[15] United Nations Convention on the Law of the Sea 1982, (1982), 1833 UNTS 3, art 195.

[16] Convention on the prevention of marine pollution by dumping of wastes and other matter 1972, (1972), (London) 26 UST 2403, TIAS 8165; UKTS 43 (1976) Cmnd. 6486, 11 ILM (1972) 1294. In force 30 August 1975. Replaced by the 1996 Protocol. 1046 UNTS 120.

[17] Protocol to the Convention on the prevention of marine pollution by dumping of wastes and other matter, (1997), 36 ILM (1997) 7. In force March 2006. Amended in 2006.

[18] UCL Carbon Capture Legal Programme (2007), CO2 transport for storage: Regulatory regimes – Convention on the Control of Transboundary Movements of Hazardous Wastes and their Disposal, 1989 (Basel Convention) https://www.ucl.ac.uk/cclp/ccstransport-int-waste-basel.php (access 10.05.2023).

[19] Report of the 1st Working Group of the Legal and Technical Working Group on Transboundary CO2 Sequestration (25 - 27 February 2008), (2008), [IMO Document LP/CO21/8].

sea is forbidden, the export of carbon dioxide streams for disposal in accordance with Annex 1 may occur upon states' agreement. This amendment is in force as of 2019 via the enactment of Resolution LP.5(14),[20] which finally overcomes the prohibitions for CCUS, previously encountered via the London Protocol.

3 Assessment of Underwriting Coverage for CCUS Operations: The Risks Involved and the Coverage to Be Obtained

Existing insurance coverage for physical damage and liability exposures is not adequate to cover all risks involved. Ordinary liability policies are not suitable for environmental cover as there is no coverage for precaution costs, and pollution is not a sudden but a gradual event, needing special liability wording. Risks include construction, physical damage, wreck removal expenses, pollution, casualty, and property damage coverage for covering cleanup and third-party liability. Liability might be agreed to be capped, but this hinders the allocation of pragmatic sums to be indemnified and to reflect the damage in the case of an incident from CCUS. However, caps in liability sums allow the noncollapse of the market as the private insurance market cannot holistically respond to major incidents.[21] The challenges imposed by the use of the CCUS technology and the magnitude and volume of the pollution risks it bears urge for the establishment and agreement of new liability caps in relation to the future availability and provision of environmental pollution liability insurance,[22] including coverage for liability during postclosure care and long-term stewardship of CCUS operations.[23] For CCUS operations, insurance coverage is sparsely underwritten for risks and coverage for general liability, property damage (first party), business interruption, physical damage; however, the development and progress of the CCUS technology will result in such coverage being broadly offered.[24] Given the anticipated wide use of the CCUS technology in stopping the accelerated pace of the occurrence of climate change, the need for bespoke insurance products for environmental harm from CCUS, including cyber coverage, will emerge. Such insurance products will need to pertain to offer coverage for a longer period given the gradual character of the occurrence of environmental harm.[25]

[20] Resolution LP.5(14) on the Provisional Application of the 2009 Amendment to Article 6 of the London Protocol (adopted 11 October 2019).

[21] Faure and Wang (2017), p. 236.

[22] Ibid.

[23] Wilson et al. (2009), pp. 4575–4582.

[24] Marsh, UK Cyber Security (2015), The Role of Insurance in Managing and Mitigating the Risk: Technical Report, UK HM Government, 2015. https://www.marsh.com/uk/insights/research/uk-cyber-security-role-of-insurance-in-managing-mitigating-risk.html (access 10.05.2023).

[25] Lebsworth (2017) (access 10.05.2023).

4 Assessment of CCUS as a Solution to Mitigate Climate Change

To limit global warming to the levels anticipated by the 2015 Paris Agreement, the overall net emissions of greenhouse gases need to be zero by 2050, and beyond that, net-negative emissions will need to be sustained. However, the goal of zero emissions is not easy to achieve and, to some extent, seems unrealistic if no additional helping measures are employed, as even within the current move to a low-carbon economy, global emissions are still rising, and some sectors will need a long period to fully decarbonize some sectors; hence to balance, reverse, and draw to the negative, the emission level will require billions of tons of negative emissions up to and after 2050.[26] Hence, scaling the deployment of carbon removal technologies and activities will be central to keeping global warming in the long term, and it follows that insurance and reinsurance can help toward the achievement of the above set goals in that they assist in the scaling up of the carbon removal industry; i.e., they can assist into improving the bankability of carbon removal projects by providing compensation for losses in the case of adverse events via the provision of contractor-all-risk policies for all construction- and infrastructure-related risks and losses and via standard property insurance for technology infrastructure or those resulting from natural disasters and also through the provision of environmental pollution liability insurance to cover risks and losses related to long-term liability exposures, such as in the case of carbon storage reversal. Another contribution of the insurance and reinsurance sector is via the provision of financing for removal projects and infrastructure via a net-zero emission asset portfolio strategy so as to achieve also the balance of long-term liabilities.[27]

5 Solutions for Broader Insurance Coverage for CCUS

Solutions pertaining to broader, more effective insurance coverage include the state liability of the host state for the storage of CO2 or third-party liability insurance to provide financial security affordable premiums and realistic insurance deductibles to avoid the formation of a "hard" insurance market due to high premiums or extended deductibles. The market needs to develop to include a widespread provision of CCS-related risks and CCS risks in transportation and embrace the insurability of the risk and not just reject it due to the severity of the risk in the fear of an environmental accident.[28] Overall, the insurance sector is uniquely positioned to offer support via risk management knowledge and transfer solutions and insurance

[26] Repmann et al. (2021) (access 10.05.2023).

[27] Ibid.

[28] HWLebsworth, Insurance issues for CCS, H W Lebsworth, (2017) Insurance issues for CCS, https://hwlebsworth.com.au/insurance-issues-for-carbon-capture-and-storage/ (access 10.05.2023).

for emerging new risks via long-term investment to help finance measures to mitigate the effects of climate warming.[29] Traditionally, the insurance market has been underwriting CO2-related risks through property and casualty insurance, such as traditional property insurance for property value risks and business interruption, as well as via general third-party and product liability and/or employer's liability or motor, professional liability or environmental liability risks or via specialty lines (marine, agricultural, engineering, cyber, credit and surety, etc.). The challenges posed pertain to the structuring and pricing of insurance offerings as CCUS processes are still in the early stages of development, and not much loss data are available historically to help quantify and monetize the risk exposure and needs. To the lack of loss history challenge, one can add as another challenge to insurability the complexity and interdependency of the value chains involved, especially for hybrid and technological solutions. In addition, for the case of storage reversal, contingency plans and financial securities need to exist, and insurance can be one mode for achieving such financial security. The main challenge for the insurance industry has always been the case of insuring for CO2- and CCUS-related tail risks, hence leading to the uninsurability of some liabilities for CCUS, and hence, this has not allowed the vast deployment of the CCUS technology. However, and notwithstanding the lack of historical data for losses and the lack of known risk management processes available to operators, the insurance industry has identified four challenging risk exposures, i.e., CO2 leakage risk, decommissioning cost risk, premature determination and possession risk, and value-chain integration risk. Also, given that many existing operational CCUS risks can be handled via existing risk mitigation and risk transfer options, the following policy types can help offer the insurance of CCUS. In effect, construction-all-risk insurance can cover risks for physical damage to construction works, damage to existing property, and third-party liability from construction works; property damage and business interruption insurance can provide cover to have all assets reinstated or replaced in the event of damage or destruction; general third-party liability insurance can provide cover against the loss of, or damage to, third-party property and personal injury, death, or disease to persons, including environmental liability; control of well insurance can provide cover for the injection wells related to CO2 injection; and directors and officers (D&O) liability insurance can provide cover to project partner's directors and offices for private liability.[30]

Zurich offers a CCS policy covering the below: bodily injury, property damage, cleanup costs, or natural resource damages resulting from a pollution event that happens as a direct result of carbon injection and storage operations and is within, at, under, or migrating from the storage location; the loss of business income and reasonable and necessary expenses to the extent resulting from either a pollution event or a geo-mechanical event, including induced seismicity within, at, under, or migrating from the storage location; reasonable and necessary costs, charges, and

[29] Repmann et al. (2021) (access 10.05.2023).

[30] Liang and Voysey (2012) (access 10.05.2023).

expenses incurred by the insured to bring an "out of control" well "under control"; loss as a result of a claim for bodily injury, property damage, natural resource damages, or cleanup costs sustained by a third party resulting from a pollution event that happens during transportation of the gas stream; and losses that the insured has to pay as a result of bodily injury, property damage, cleanup costs, or natural resource damages resulting from a geo-mechanical event, including induced seismicity. [31]

With regards to CO2 leakage, a "carbon allowance reimbursement insurance" type of policy could be introduced as an "all risks" insurance for the injection phase providing cover for all leakage from damage to wells. In addition, other environmental insurance policies could be modified to provide coverage for gradual seepage through faults and fractures. A policy as such would exclude defects in the design, plan, specification, materials, or workmanship; normal wear and tear; gradual deterioration or normal corrosion; and earthquake—however, if included, it would result in the aggregation of risks given the geographic focus of this market, normal settling, or shrinking or expansion in land. For the limitation of liability, this would be determined by the declaration of the volume of stored CO2 to be insured up front, and the insurer and insured would need to agree on the emission allowance price for leakage based either on a minimum and maximum cap figure or on a moving average based on the previous few years' price. A deductible would also be expected as there would be an expectation that the insured would retain a primary portion of the risk. Challenges in such a type of insurance would be the annual renewal, which allows the premium to reflect the gradual nature of risk exposure in the injection phase, but from a CCS operator investment point of view, it would entail cost uncertainty, and such a challenge could be handled by introducing a multiyear policy, e.g., a 3-year policy, renewable on a rolling annual basis.[32] In addition, the limited insurance market capacity will also limit the indemnity available and make insurance a noncomprehensive solution. There is also discussion on whether the trigger in terms of such a policy should be the proximate cause itself or the regulatory decision on the quantum of loss. The inevitable time gap between the two elements of the proximate cause and of the regulatory decision on the quantum of loss will result in that the time needed will exceed the duration of the usual 12 month duration of policies. This is something for tghe parties to consider as this will also denote if the policy is on a "claimsoccurrence" basis (with the proximate cause being the relevant trigger) or on a "claims-made" basis (with the regulatory decision being the relevant trigger). The latter method entails the risk of delaying insurance coverage renewal until a regulatory decision is reached.[33] Regarding decommissioning, operators need provide financial security to get a permit. Again, theuncertainty involved in the time needed for the decommissioning phase makes its insurability difficult, hence alternative arrangements other than insursnce coverage would need to be arranged to help

[31] Ibid, p. 25.

[32] Ibid, p. 35.

[33] Ibid, p. 37.

manage this risk.[34] For premature determination and possession risk insurance coverage whereby the operator faces incurring financial liabilities if its storage license is temporarily or permanently withdrawn due to incompetence or insolvency, the problem is that these circumstances are hard to classify as accidental or fortuitous, and such risk cannot easily be insurable as it would also mean that there is a moral hazard element entailed if an operator could transfer the risk of their own incompetence or insolvency to an insurer. Finally, the risk of value-chain integration denotes the risk faced by all parties of the loss of revenue because of failure on the part of the CCS value chain. As most unexpected interruptions to a CCS value chain have a fortuitous element, business interruption is a reasonable cover for such risk for assureds that have suffered a reduction in revenue due to operations interrupted by an insured peril, and as a result, pre-loss operations are no longer possible to be maintained.[35] The amount able to be claimed corresponds to the amount of consequential loss resulting from the interruption of business upon damage to property, the calculation being based on a gross profit basis or on the gross profit ratio multiplied by the turnover, the limitation of liability being usually a cap of a certain percentage of revenue and also a combined deductible with property damage insurance being able to be agreed.[36] In addition, credit insurance coverage can be used for mitigating credit risk within the CCS value chain, while commercial property damage cover could be extended to cover the accidental event leading to a loss of another party, and machinery insurance is to be added to business interruption cover for failures in CCS operation. In the case of a serious interruption event, if the original pipeline becomes a stranded asset, the coverage for the building of a new pipeline and storage means that unknown future CO2 prices or the uncertain cost and future value of pipeline infrastructure can limit the insurers' capacity to provide coverage.[37]

6 Conclusions

The goal of reducing our greenhouse gas emissions gives us an opportunity to search for and develop solutions: solutions to addressing our current emissions as well as solutions that create new approaches for our economy to produce less or even no CO2. A robust liability framework for CO2 capture, use, and storage undoubtedly represents a positive first step toward addressing a difficult regulatory issue. Ensuring the environmentally safe deployment of CCUS through the minimization of leakage must remain a priority so as to fully profit from the deployment of this technology and also supplement climate change mitigation efforts. While efforts

[34] Ibid, p. 50.

[35] Ibid, pp. 53–55.

[36] Ibid, p. 55.

[37] Ibid, pp. 53, 55, 57.

have been made in international environmental law to confirm that the capture, transportation, and storage of CO2 legally fits within the London Protocol, the Basel Convention remains an area that has not been clearly clarified. Hence, future amendments to international environmental law legalizing CCUS are due in order to ensure that this method can effectively be used, and liability will need to be capped so as to further allow insurability to operate. Also, insurers and assureds need to bear in mind that environmental pollution is usually gradually occurring; hence, due to the "sudden" and "unexpected" loss of coverage in property casualty policies, such cover is not appropriate for environmental pollution incidents, and regulatory and insurance industry action is needed to help maintain a "soft" insurance market and hence allow the wide deployment of CCUS.

Our discussion has also shown that proposed insurance coverages entail challenges. As discussed above for CO2 leakage, a carbon allowance reimbursement insurance type of policy would face challenges, such as the fact that alternative risk transfer mechanisms might allow the transfer of losses beyond the capacity of traditional insurance, but there are significant technical and commercial barriers to be addressed before such an option is commercialized and widely used, and for the present, it is challenging to say the least to transfer such risk in its entirety using insurance because the need for insurance policies to indemnify against a defined risk exposure means that as liability is regulated at present, there will be residual risk for operators.[38] For decommissioning insurance, the uncertainty of defining the time for the decommissioning phase poses barriers and insurance to be employed herewith as an effective risk transfer.[39] Regarding the type of insurance namely premature determination and possession risk insurance, the two main proximate causes of operator incompetence or insolvency act as barriers to insurability due to the moral hazard on the side of the assured, and this has to be clustered as an uninsurable risk.[40] For value-chain integration, risk coverage is available as most unexpected interruptions to a CCS value chain classify as fortuitous, sudden, and accidental and can be covered by business interruption insurance when the effect is temporary interruption; however, the difficulty lies in defining a quantum of loss for events related to permanent interruption whereby traditional insurance policy models are not easy to be applied.[41]

Operators need to be aware that bespoke insurance coverage will be needed; however, to a large extent, the involved risks are covered by existing risk transfer options. In terms of insurance options, the traditional coverage options apart, existing insurance products could be modified to transfer CO2 leakage risk, and to reach a status of soft market largely insuring CCUS, we need to maintain an increased demand from the industry and broad market participation. Regulators need to be aware that because insurance can only be provided for defined liability,

---

[38] Liang and Voysey (2012), pp. 44–45.

[39] Ibid, at 52.

[40] Ibid at 55.

[41] Ibid at 56.

in the case of CCUS, this is not always a holistic solution as uncapped liability will remain uninsured and hinder investments and CCUS deployment. Operators will still face residual, uncapped liability, which is considered a roadblock for investors. Governments need to consider putting a cap on CO2 leakage risk availability and introduce measures to avoid moral hazard, as well as an insurance risk transfer solution so as to reduce uncertainty for the CCUS industry and augment insurability options, hence allowing CCUS to be vastly and widely deployed for the sake of social and environmental benefits.[42]

References

Faure M, Wang H (2017) The use of financial market instruments to cover liability following a major offshore accident. In: Faure M (ed) Civil liability and financial security for offshore oil and gas activities. CUP, p 236

Green J, Sterner T, Wagner G (2014) A balance of bottom-up and top-down in linking climate policies. Nat Clim Change 4(12):1064

Lebsworth HW (2017) Insurance issues for CCS. https://hwlebsworth.com.au/insurance-issues-for-carbon-capture-and-storage/

Liang X, Voysey A (2012). Managing liabilities of European Carbon capture and storage: a climatewise Report on developing commercially viable insurance solutions. ClimateWise, CUP, pp 22–23. http://www.climatewise.org.uk/storage/_website-2012/collaborations/ccs/ClimateWise%20CCS%20Report%20Nov%202012%20-%20Full%20Report.pdf

Marsh (2015) UK Cyber Security: The Role of Insurance in Managing and Mitigating the Risk: Technical Report, UK HM Government. https://www.marsh.com/uk/insights/research/uk-cyber-security-role-of-insurance-in-managing-mitigating-risk.html

Metz B, Davidson O, de Conick H, Loos M, Meyer L (2005) Carbon dioxide capture and storage. CUP

Raine A (2008) Transboundary transportation of CO2 associated with carbon capture and storage projects: an analysis of issues under international law. Carbon Climate Law Rev 4:353

Repmann M, Schelke O, Collin D, Prasad S (2021) The insurance rationale for carbon removal solutions. Swiss Re, p 1 https://www.swissre.com/dam/jcr:31e39033-0ca6-418e-a540-d61b8e7d7b31/swiss-re-institute-expertise-publication-insurance-%20rationale-for-carbon-removal-solutions.pdf

Report of the 1st Working Group of the Legal and Technical Working Group on Transboundary CO2 Sequestration (25–27 February 2008) [IMO Document LP/CO21/8]

Romeiro V, Parente V (2012) Carbon capture and storage and the UNFCCC: Recommendations to address trans-boundary issues. Low Carbon Econ 3:130; United Nations. Transboundary carbon capture and storage project activities: Technical Paper. https://unfccc.int/resource/docs/2012/tp/09.pdf

The Guardian (2011) Canada pulls out of Kyoto Protocol https://www.theguardian.com/environment/2011/dec/13/canada-pulls-out-kyoto-protocol

Tucker T (2018) Carbon capture and storage. IOP Publishing Ltd, p 31

UCL Carbon Capture Legal Programme. CO2 transport for storage: Regulatory regimes – Convention on the Control of Transboundary Movements of Hazardous Wastes and their Disposal, 1989 (Basel Convention) https://www.ucl.ac.uk/cclp/ccstransport-int-waste-basel.php

[42] Ibid, at 57.

United Nations (1987) Report of the World Commission on Environment and Development: Our Common Future. https://sustainabledevelopment.un.org/content/documents/5987our-common-future.pdf
Wilson E, Klass A, Bergan S (2009) Assessing a Liability Regime for CCS. https://doi.org/10.1016/j.egypro.2009.02.277

Liability for Environmental Damages in Aviation

Małgorzata Polkowska

Abstract This chapter is a basic introduction to international liability for environmental damages in aviation. It defines environmental law in the context of aviation. This discipline is quite new and important. It concerns private international aviation law. It is worth mentioning that this discipline is not based on only one international act or convention, but it consists of different regulations: on the global and regional scales. Environmental damages (aircraft emissions or aircraft noise) are connected to the liability of different entities, such as airlines, airport operators, or others, so is necessary to know the rules in case to eliminate risks connected to civil aviation. All aviation actors should be involved in creating international standards and regulations in environment liability.

1 Introduction

Environmental law in aviation concerns airlines, airports and air navigation services. This means that this discipline is broad and complex and still needs to be clarified for the sake of safe operations. Aviation lawyers and insurers are also involved in it to eliminate risks in civil aviation.

With the continuing economic advances and progress in science and technology in the aviation industry, environmental awareness has become a worldwide consensus. Reducing emissions and aircraft noise, discussing alternative fuels and combating environmental protection are the global goals.[1]

[1] Abeyratne (2012), p. 74.

M. Polkowska (✉)
Law and Administration Faculty, War Studies University, Warsaw, Poland

War Studies University, International and UE Departament, Poland, Warsaw, Polska
e-mail: m.polkowska@ron.mil.pl

K. Malinowska, D. Maśniak (eds.), *Managing Environmental Risks through Insurance*, AIDA Europe Research Series on Insurance Law and Regulation 9,
https://doi.org/10.1007/978-3-031-47602-0_13

Environmental issues related to aviation are directly related to global climate change. This topic is very important and is described by various experts around the world. It refers to aircraft noise around airports and has a significant impact on water or air quality. Therefore, business aviation must follow international environmental standards in this regard.

2 International Regulations

More than 10 years ago, environmental challenges became one of the emerging aviation issues. Member States (103) of the International Civil Aviation Organization (ICAO) gave a strong mandate and a roadmap for the Organization to act on climate change. ICAO is very active in the environmental protection area and cooperated closely during the summit of the United Nations Climate Change (UNCC) in Paris (in December 2015). Although the United Nations Framework Convention on Climate Change (UNFCCC) does not specifically refer to emissions from aviation, its coverage includes emissions from all sources.

One of the commitments of the Convention is that the parties to the Convention compile national inventories of their emission source. The goal of the so-called Paris Agreement is to limit global warming to well below 2, preferably to 1.5 degrees Celsius, compared to preindustrial levels. To achieve this long-term temperature goal, countries aim to reach a global peaking of greenhouse gas emissions as soon as possible to achieve a climate-neutral world by mid-century. The Paris Agreement is a binding agreement, which brings all nations into a common cause to undertake ambitious efforts to combat climate change and adapt to its effects. The Kyoto Protocol from 1997[2] followed, in pursuit of the UNFCCC objectives. According to Article 2(2) of the Protocol provides, the parties shall pursue limitation or reduction of emissions of certain greenhouse gases from aviation and marine bunker fuels, working through the International Civil Aviation Organization[3].

It should be mentioned here also that in light of the obligations under the above international regulations, the European Commission proposed a scheme for greenhouse gas emission allowance trading. The first of such a scheme was established in 2003.[4]

[2]https://unfccc.int/kyoto_protocol (accessed 27-12-2021). Kyoto Protocol entered into force on 16 February 2005. Currently, there are 192 Parties to the Kyoto Protocol. The Kyoto Protocol operationalizes the United Nations Framework Convention on Climate Change by committing industrialized countries and economies in transition to limit and reduce greenhouse gas (GHG) emissions in accordance with agreed individual targets. In Doha, Qatar, on 8 December 2012, the Doha Amendment to the Kyoto Protocol was adopted for a second commitment period, starting in 2013 and lasting until 2020. The amendment entered into force on 31 December 2020.

[3]https://unfccc.int/sites/default/files/resource/docs/cop3/l07a01.pdf (accessed 27-04-2023).

[4]Bakker (2015), pp. 3–13.

International aviation became the first global sector to adopt global aspirational goals for carbon dioxide (CO2) emissions—2 percent fuel efficiency improvement per year and carbon neutral growth from 2020—and a "basket of measures" to progress toward these goals.

In 2013, during the following session of the ICAO Assembly, commitment toward this climate change strategy was reaffirmed and enabled ICAO to take the necessary actions to realize the set ambition by incentivizing innovative aircraft technologies, implementing more efficient operations, facilitating the use of sustainable alternative fuels and creating a global market-based measure, the Carbon Offsetting and Reduction Scheme for International Aviation (CORSIA).

These achievements have required the increased involvement of ICAO's traditional partners and cooperation with new governmental and non-governmental organizations, industry bodies and research institutes.[5]

According to the Annual Report by ICAO Council 2019,[6] about 80 States, representing more than 70% of those engaged in international aviation activity, announced their intention to voluntarily participate in CORSIA in 2021. It was the reason for updating the existing ICAO standards and Guidance material on noise, local air quality and climate change.[7]

In 2018, the first edition of Annex 16—Environmental Protection, Volume IV – Carbon Offsetting and Reduction Scheme for International Aviation (CORSIA), was approved.[8] The main objective of the mechanism is to maintain a zero increase in CO2 emissions in civil international aviation from 2021 in relation to emissions from 2019 to 2020. Obligations to compensate and reduce CO2 emissions will come into force in 2021, but the first obligations on the part of air carriers and countries will take place already in 2019 and will concern, inter alia, monitoring of emissions. The participants of the mechanism will be air operators carrying out international transport with aircraft with MTOW> 5700 kg, emitting more than 10,000 tons of CO2 per year, excluding humanitarian, medical and firefighting flights.

Currently, work is underway in the Group of Experts on Climate Change under the Directorate for Climate Action within the structures of the European Commission (EC) on the implementation of the provisions of this Annex to the law of the European Union. The Commission plans to implement the provisions by amending the Directive on the EU Emissions Trading System (EU ETS), along with delegated acts. The aim of the work is to integrate the CORSIA mechanism with the EU ETS as much as possible, which is to avoid the duplication of obligations arising from these systems.

[5]ICAO Environmental Report -Aviation and Environment; Destination green - The next chapter, 2019, p. 4.

[6]ICAO Annual Report of the Council 2019, https://www.icao.int/annual-report-2019/Pages/progress-on-icaos-strategic-objectives-environmental-protection-corsia.aspx (access 26-04-2023).

[7]Revenue tonne kilometres (RTK). The revenue load in tonnes multiplied by the distance flown.

[8]https://www.icao.int/environmental-protection/CORSIA/Pages/SARPs-Annex-16-Volume-IV.aspx (access 20-04-2023).

The development of the CORSIA Central Registry (CCR) was initiated by a selected supplier. The ICAO Council also approved the 2019 version of the ICAO CO2 Estimation and Reporting Tool (CERT) to help with the monitoring and reporting of international aviation CO2 emissions by aeroplane operators under CORSIA. Meanwhile, the organization set up several regional workshops and webinars on CORSIA to assist states in the monitoring, reporting and verification of CO2 emissions.

Under the ICAO umbrella, a few bodies were established. One of them is TAB (Technical Advisory Body), which has the objective of making recommendations to the Council regarding eligible emission units for use under CORSIA. The Council agreed on a list of 19 TAB members and approved the Terms of Reference (TOR) for TAB. The Council also approved the Emission Unit Criteria (EUC) to be used by TAB in undertaking its task to assess emission unit programmes against the EUC.

The Committee on Aviation Environmental Protection (CAEP) are held regularly to discuss technical recommendations to address aircraft noise, as well as emissions affecting local air quality and global climate[9].

These recommendations included proposals for amendments to Annex 16 – Environmental Protection, Volume I – Aircraft Noise,[10] Volume II – Aircraft Engine Emissions[11] and Volume III — Aeroplane CO2 Emissions,[12] including the recommendation on a new standard for non-volatile particulate matter (nvPM) mass and number engine emissions, to be incorporated into Annex 16, Volume II. In addition, CAEP agreed to recommend amendments to all four volumes of the Environmental Technical Manual (Doc 9501)[13] to facilitate the implementation of the Standards and Recommended Practices (SARPs) contained in Annex 16.

The CAEP made a number of recommendations associated with airports and operations, such as an Eco-Airport Toolkit e-collection, the first global horizontal flight efficiency (HFE) analysis, reports on the state of aircraft end-of-life and recycling; and on performance-based navigation and community engagement. One recommendation was about to use the results of the combined Aviation System Block Upgrade (ASBU)[14] B0/B1 environmental analysis to facilitate decision-

[9]https://www.icao.int/environmental-protection/pages/caep.aspx (access 23-08-2021).

[10]https://www.ulc.gov.pl/_download/ltt/certyfikacja_organizacji/Za%C5%82%C4%85cznik_16_tom_I.pdf (access 23-04-2023).

[11]https://www.ulc.gov.pl/_download/ltt/certyfikacja_organizacji/Za%C5%82%C4%85cznik_16_tom_II.pdf (access 23-04-2023).

[12]https://www.ulc.gov.pl/_download/prawo/prawo_miedzynarodowe/konwencje/Za%C5%82%C4%85cznik_16_tom_III.pdf (access 23-04-2023).

[13]https://www.icao.int/environmentalprotection/Documents/Doc_9501_ETM_Vol_III_SGAR%202017.pdf (access 20-04-2023).

[14]ASBU methodology is a programmatic and flexible global approach that allows all Member States to advance their Air Navigation capacities based on their specific operational requirements. The Block Upgrades aim to enable aviation to realize the global harmonization, increased capacity, and improved environmental efficiency that modern air traffic growth now demands in every region around the world.

making on the implementation of ASBU Block 0 and Block 1. CAEP also recommended the first integrated independent expert technology goals assessment, including new aircraft noise, nitrogen oxides (NOx) emissions and fuel efficiency technology goals for the aviation sector. Some expertise referring to supersonic transport and engine technology (SST) in case to better understand of airport noise impact were also recommended.[15]

Another important element of ICAO's basket of measures to mitigate climate change is sustainable aviation fuels (SAF). They play an important role in reducing CO2 emissions from aviation. Three problem representations were identified in ICAO's alternative jet fuel strategy: the increasing contribution of international aviation to climate change, the technological limitations to constraint and reduce the necessary carbon emissions, and the uncertainty around future jet fuel prices and availability.[16] Although ICAO presumes that time will be needed to deploy such fuels at scale, it is encouraging that the technologies for SAF production already exist today: the challenge is to accelerate SAF deployment, reduce its cost, and ensure the environmental integrity of SAF production. The ICAO Assembly requested States to recognize existing approaches to assess the sustainability of alternative fuels that should contribute to local social and economic development while avoiding competition with food and water. In that regard, work is ongoing to expand these sustainability criteria, which will be subject to the ICAO Council's approval upon the completion of the CORSIA Pilot Phase (end of 2023).[17]

ICAO's alternative jet fuel strategy supports and promotes the development and consolidation of supply chains of alternative fuels for international aviation through its Member States. It was originally developed within ICAO's Program of Action on International Aviation and Climate Change, and it encompasses a broad range of activities, including research and development (R&D), certification, financial assistance, monitoring, verification and evaluation (MRV), technology transfer, capacity building, etc.[18]

ICAO's Global Framework for Aviation Alternative Fuels (GFAAF) created in 2009 is a platform for sharing examples of policy implementation, results and lessons learned. The main target is to help the Member States accelerate the development and adoption of alternative jet fuels.[19]

---

[15] ICAO Annual Report of the Council 2019, https://www.icao.int/annual-report-2019/Pages/progress-on-icaos-strategic-objectives-environmental-protection-corsia.aspx (access 26-04-2023).

[16] M. S. Baledón, N. Kosoy "Problematizing" carbon emissions from international aviation and the role of alternative jet fuels in meeting ICAO's mid-century aspirational goals, Elsevier, https://www.ncbi.nlm.nih.gov/pmc/articles/PMC7148887/#__ffn_sectitle.

[17] ICAO Environmental Report Aviation and Environment; Destination green - The next chapter, 2019, p. 114.

[18] M. S. Baledón, N. Kosoy "Problematizing" carbon emissions from international aviation and the role of alternative jet fuels in meeting ICAO's mid-century aspirational goals, Elsevier, https://www.ncbi.nlm.nih.gov/pmc/articles/PMC7148887/#__ffn_sectitle.

[19] ICAO Journal, Green Airports, vol. 73 no. 1, p. 29 https://www.icao.int/publications/journalsreports/2018/7301_en.pdf (access 20-04-2023).

The international community cooperates with ICAO on the subject of climate change and its impact on aviation. Such organizations as the International Air Transport Association (IATA), Airports Council International (ACI), Civil Air Navigation Services Organisation (CANSO), International Coordinating Council for Aerospace Industries Associations (ICCAIA), International Coalition for Sustainable Aviation (ICSA) and many others are combating climate change, which remains a top priority. They have committed to cut CO2 emissions in half by 2050 with innovative technologies, sustainable aviation fuel and improved operations and infrastructure. They offer different programmes to help the industry (airlines, airports or air service providers) improve its sustainability, as well as share best practices on environmental protection (reducing noise and managing waste responsibly).

3 National Responsibilities

According to Article 31 of the Chicago Convention 1944[20] (Certificates of Airworthiness), every aircraft engaged in international navigation shall be provided with a certificate of airworthiness issued or rendered valid by the State in which it is registered. Those certificates are issued by the national civil aviation authorities. They are responsible for fulfilling all requirements and standards: international (International Civil Aviation Organization (ICAO), Annex 16, standards and procedures[21]) or regional (European Union regulations, such as parliament directives or Council regulations[22]).

Civil aviation authorities are responsible for implementing international and regional laws internally and, based on them, for issuing certificates for aircraft noise and emissions. For example, the noise certificate states that the aircraft should comply with the relevant requirements of Volume I of Annex 16 to the Convention on International Civil Aviation. This is one of the conditions necessary to be allowed to use it. In EU states, European aviation law applies. In Article 9.2 (Chapter II section I) of the mentioned EU Regulation 2018/1139 (Airworthiness and

[20] Convention on International Civil Aviation - Doc 7300 https://www.icao.int/publications/Documents/7300_cons.pdf.

[21] Annex 16 ICAO Environmental Protection.

[22] Regulation (EU) 2018/1139 of the European Parliament and of the Council of 4 July 2018 on common rules in the field of civil aviation and establishing a European Union Aviation Safety Agency, and amending Regulations (EC) No 2111/2005, (EC) No 1008/2008, (EU) No 996/2010, (EU) No 376/2014 and Directives 2014/30/EU and 2014/53/EU of the European Parliament and of the Council, and repealing Regulations (EC) No 552/2004 and (EC) No 216/2008 of the European Parliament and of the Council and Council Regulation (EEC) No 3922/91 (Text with EEA relevance.)

environmental protection), it is provided, inter alia, that "…as regards noise and emissions, those aircraft and their engines, propellers, parts and non-installed equipment shall comply with the environmental protection requirements contained in Amendment 12 of Volume I, in Amendment 9 of Volume II, and in the initial issue of Volume III, all as applicable on 1 January 2018, of Annex 16 to the Chicago Convention".

The essential requirements for compliance with environmental protection requirements set out in Annex III to Regulation 2018/1139 apply to products, parts and non-installed equipment to the extent that the provisions of the Chicago Convention referred to above do not contain environmental protection requirements.

The most important supervising body for aviation in Europe is the European Union Aviation Safety Agency (EASA). This Agency's mission is to provide safe air travel for EU citizens in Europe and worldwide, and the vision is to provide even safer and greener civil aviation. EASA has published a noise database, and EU countries are required to issue such certificates strictly according to the data provided there. EASA respects not only the noise measurement procedures and permissible levels given in volume I of Annex 16 ICAO but also the limitation on the application of the requirements to older aircraft despite the fact that such types and models appear in its database. Chapter 6 of Annex 16 ICAO exempts the following aeroplanes with a maximum certified take-off mass of up to 8618 kg from the obligation to conduct noise certification and, thus, to have a noise certificate: aeroplanes designed as agricultural or firefighting and aerobatic aeroplanes and aeroplanes for which the application for a type certificate was submitted before 1 January 1975 or the certificate of airworthiness for a particular aeroplane was first issued before 1 January 1980. EU States strictly follow those rules, and all operators should remember that when flying to countries where airport noise is charged, such as Germany, a much higher fee is charged for landing without a noise certificate.

Some Civil Aviation Authorities and regional organizations established its own policies and guidelines on environment, such as Federal Aviation Administration in the US,[23] or strategies (the EU Aviation Strategy[24]) and reports (European Aviation Environmental Report)[25] focusing on progress of aviation sector, technology and design of aviation industry (including noise level aspects), efficiency of Air Traffic Management and Operations (saving emissions aspects), airports (the means of verifying aircraft noise, the Airport Carbon Accreditation programme), Market-Based Measures (to address the climate impact of aviation, CORSIA, air quality, etc.).

[23] https://www.faa.gov/regulations_policies/policy_guidance/envir_policy/ (access 30-04-2023).

[24] https://ec.europa.eu/transport/modes/air/environment_en (access 30-04-2023).

[25] https://ec.europa.eu/transport/sites/default/files/2019-aviation-environmental-report.pdf (access 30-04-2023).

4 Environmental Liability: Case Studies

Noise issue is a big problem in society. People who live close to airports suffer from the noise of ascending and descending aircraft. Aircraft noise may significantly impact the mental and physical health of people who live below the flight paths of commercial and private aeroplanes. Since the 1970s, numerous studies have found aircraft noise linked to stress, hypertension, sleep disturbances, work-related performance, and learning and academic performance. Annex 16, Volume I, addresses aircraft noise.

In 2001, the ICAO General Assembly adopted a balanced approach to environmental harm. Under this approach, noise problems are to be addressed in two stages (first, a longer-term comprehensive assessment is made of all sources of noise, and second, four measures are to be implemented: quieter aircraft, land-use planning and management, noise abatement operational procedures and operating restrictions). Each airport identifies a noise problem based on objective data, considers all available alternatives for addressing the noise issue and selects the most cost-effective approach. There are many cases that address the issue of aircraft noise at night. In one of them, the Belgian regional environmental authority imposed financial penalties on an air transport company for the infringement of the national legislation on noise abatement in the urban environment due to night-time aircraft noise.[26]

There are two types of mechanisms for reducing aircraft noise: curfews that prohibit take-offs or landings during certain prescribed periods, typically at night, and slots. Those rules must be followed by airport authorities. There are some lawsuits, such as in the United Kingdom[27] which upheld an environmental review of expansion of London's Stansted Airport from a single runway that concluded, inter alia, additional air noise. In one of the cases of the US Supreme Court, it was held that in light of the comprehensive nature of the federal regulation of aircraft noise, the Federal Aviation Administration and the Environmental Protection Agency had plenary jurisdiction over airport noise, pre-empting local municipal or state control.[28] In another case,[29] the Court recognized that Congress had placed in the public domain, as a public highway, the navigable airspace above the minimum safe altitude of flight – at that time 500 feet by day and 1000 feet by night for air carriers. However, the Court recognized that if a property owner is to have full

[26] European Air Transport SA v Collège d'environnement de la Région de Bruxelles-Capitale and another, (Case C-120/10) Before the Court of Justice (First Chamber) 8 September 2011 [2012] 1 C.M.L.R. 19.

[27] Carol Barbone, Brian Ross (on behalf of Stop Stansted Expansion) v The Secretary of State for Transport, The Secretary of State for Communities and Local Government, Case No: CO/10952/2008 High Court of Justice Queen's Bench Division Administrative Court 13 March 2009 [2009] EWHC 463 (Admin) 2009 WL 635004.

[28] City of Burbank v. Lockheed Air Terminal, 411 U.S. 624 (1973).

[29] United States v. Causby, 328 U.S. 256, 259, 66 S.Ct. 1062, 90 L.Ed. 1206.

enjoyment of his land, he must have exclusive control of the immediate reach of the enveloping atmosphere, the super adjacent airspace below the altitude that Congress appropriately determines to be a public highway.

Thus, the Court determined that flights over private land are not a taking unless they are so low and so frequent as to be a direct and immediate interference with the enjoyment and use of the land. In the case of Phillips v. Montgomery County, a nuisance-type taking occurred when a governmental entity with eminent domain power interfered with a landowner's beneficial use and enjoyment of the property.[30]

A similar case happened in Canada. The trial judge found a new airport runway at the Vancouver International Airport that caused noise nuisance to the plaintiffs substantially enhanced the utility of an airport that was "of immense utility to the public at large". He nevertheless concluded that the burden imposed on the plaintiffs, who were nearby property owners, exceeded what was reasonable and therefore created a nuisance.[31]

In one of the EU cases,[32] the court stated that an environmental impact assessment that has not been carried out does not, in principle, by itself, according to EU law and without prejudice to the rules of national law, which are less restrictive as regards State liability, confer on an individual the right to compensation for purely pecuniary damage caused by a decrease in the value of his property as a result of the environmental effects of a project. However, it is for the national court to determine whether the requirements of EU law applicable to the right to compensation, including the existence of a direct causal link between the breach alleged and the damage sustained, have been satisfied.[33]

5 Concluding Remarks

Environmental law in aviation is a set of many regulations at the international, regional and national levels. All aviation partners are engaged in this process of combating climate change. Because the subject is so crucial, there are also legal cases that show that the balance between society and business needs was always a challenge worldwide. Aviation is an important contributor to the global economy, satisfying society's mobility needs. Green technology (including alternative fuels) is costly, so UN international bodies battle to compromise it. Environmental regulations and the engagements of ICAO Member States make climate change in aviation

[30] Phillips v. Montgomery County, 2013 WL 3378952, Tenn.Ct.App., 2013.

[31] Susan Heyes Inc. v. Vancouver (City), 2011 CarswellBC 269, British Columbia Court of Appeal, 2011.

[32] Leth v Republik Österreich and another, (Case C-420/11) Before the Court of Justice (Fourth Chamber) [2013] 3 C.M.L.R. 2.

[33] Dempsey (2013). https://www.mcgill.ca/iasl/files/iasl/aspl_633-2015-dempsey-environmental_law.pdf (access 13-07-2021).

a priority. The pending question is whether there is a possibility to meet all aspirational goals in the aviation environment in the post-COVID-19 era.

Websites

https://unfccc.int/kyoto_protocol (accessed 23-04-2023)

https://unfccc.int/sites/default/files/resource/docs/cop3/l07a01.pdf (accessed 23-04-2023)

https://www.icao.int/environmental-protection/CORSIA/Pages/SARPs-Annex-16-Volume-IV.aspx (access 20-08-2021)

https://www.icao.int/environmental-protection/pages/caep.aspx (access 23-04-2023)

https://www.ulc.gov.pl/_download/ltt/certyfikacja_organizacji/Za%C5%82%C4%85cznik_16_tom_I.pdf (access 23-04-2023)

https://www.ulc.gov.pl/_download/ltt/certyfikacja_organizacji/Za%C5%82%C4%85cznik_16_tom_II.pdf (access 23-04-2023)

https://www.ulc.gov.pl/_download/prawo/prawo_miedzynarodowe/konwencje/Za%C5%82%C4%85cznik_16_tom_III.pdf (access 23-04-2023)

https://www.icao.int/environmentalprotection/Documents/Doc_9501_ETM_Vol_III_SGAR%202017.pdf (access 20-04-2023)

https://www.faa.gov/regulations_policies/policy_guidance/envir_policy/ (access 30-08-2021)

https://ec.europa.eu/transport/modes/air/environment_en (access 30-04-2023)

https://ec.europa.eu/transport/sites/default/files/2019-aviation-environmental-report.pdf (access 30-04-2023)

References

Abeyratne R (2012) Aeronomics and law. Fixing anomalies. Springer, p 74

Bakker M (2015) Including aviation in the European Union scheme for emission allowance trading: stimulating global market-based measures. J Air Law Commer Winter 80(1):3–13

Baledón MS, Kosoy N. "Problematizing" carbon emissions from international aviation and the role of alternative jet fuels in meeting ICAO's mid-century aspirational goals. Elsevier, https://www.ncbi.nlm.nih.gov/pmc/articles/PMC7148887/#__ffn_sectitle

Carol Barbone, Brian Ross (on behalf of Stop Stansted Expansion) v The Secretary of State for Transport, The Secretary of State for Communities and Local Government, Case No: CO/10952/2008 High Court of Justice Queen's Bench Division Administrative Court 13 March 2009 [2009] EWHC 463 (Admin) 2009 WL 635004

City of Burbank v. Lockheed Air Terminal, 411 U.S. 624 (1973)

Convention on International Civil Aviation - Doc 7300. https://www.icao.int/publications/Documents/7300_cons.pdf

Dempsey PS (2013) Environmental Law and Sustainability in International Aviation. https://www.mcgill.ca/iasl/files/iasl/aspl_633-2015-dempsey-environmental_law.pdf (access 13-04-2023)

European Air Transport SA v Collège d'environnement de la Région de Bruxelles-Capitale and another, (Case C-120/10) Before the Court of Justice (First Chamber) 8 September 2011 [2012] 1 C.M.L.R. 19

ICAO Annual Report of the Council (2019). https://www.icao.int/annual-report-2019/Pages/progress-on-icaos-strategic-objectives-environmental-protection-corsia.aspx. Accessed 23-04-2023

ICAO Annual Report of the Council 2019., https://www.icao.int/annual-report-2019/Pages/progress-on-icaos-strategic-objectives-environmental-protection-corsia.aspx (access 26-04-2023)

ICAO Environmental Report Aviation and Environment; Destination green - The next chapter, 2019, p. 114

ICAO Environmental Report -Aviation and Environment (2019) Destination green - The next chapter, p 4

ICAO Journal, Green Airports, vol. 73 no. 1, p. 29 https://www.icao.int/publications/journalsreports/2018/7301_en.pdf (access 20-08-2021)

Leth v Republik Österreich and another, (Case C-420/11) Before the Court of Justice (Fourth Chamber) [2013] 3 C.M.L.R. 2

Phillips v. Montgomery County, 2013 WL 3378952, Tenn.Ct.App., 2013

Regulation (EU) 2018/1139 of the European Parliament and of the Council of 4 July 2018 on common rules in the field of civil aviation and establishing a European Union Aviation Safety Agency, and amending Regulations (EC) No 2111/2005, (EC) No 1008/2008, (EU) No 996/2010, (EU) No 376/2014 and Directives 2014/30/EU and 2014/53/EU of the European Parliament and of the Council, and repealing Regulations (EC) No 552/2004 and (EC) No 216/2008 of the European Parliament and of the Council and Council Regulation (EEC) No 3922/91 (Text with EEA relevance.)

Susan Heyes Inc. v. Vancouver (City), 2011 CarswellBC 269, British Columbia Court of Appeal, 2011

United States v. Causby, 328 U.S. 256, 259, 66 S.Ct. 1062, 90 L.Ed. 1206

Liability for Environmental Damage in Outer Space and Its Insurance

Katarzyna Malinowska and Kaja Hopej

Abstract In the ongoing discussion on space sustainability, an important aspect concerns the regime of liability for damages caused to the space environment. Apart from the general regulations that can be found in the canon of international space law, specific provisions for environmental protection are scarce. Despite many efforts, it has not yet been possible to create international regulations of a universal and binding nature that would adequately protect the outer space environment. The process of creating such regulations also seems to be ineffective due to the dynamic development of the commercial space sector and, consequently, the growing amount of space debris, which poses a real threat not only in space but also on Earth. In response to this challenge, many countries are referring environmental issues to the national liability regime related to indigenous space activities. Internationally recognized guidelines and standards that minimize the risk of damage are helpful in this regard, but their application may be questionable due to their heterogeneous nature. This implies considerable legal uncertainty, not only for the interests of the state but especially for private entities that have to meet the relevant requirements. The aim of the authors is to indicate the existing liability regime for environmental damage in space based on both international law and national space legislation. Environmental law has received particular attention in this analysis. Furthermore, the authors present legislative gaps that need to be filled in order to meet current challenges regarding sustainable space development. In addition to indicating the elements of the space environment, the authors seek to identify the spatial aspect of outer space. Finally, the authors propose space insurance as an incentive tool for protecting the space environment.

K. Malinowska (✉)
College of Law, Kozminski University, Warszawa, Poland
e-mail: katarzynamalinowska@kozminski.edu.pl

K. Hopej
Central European Academy, Budapest, Hungary

K. Malinowska, D. Maśniak (eds.), *Managing Environmental Risks through Insurance*, AIDA Europe Research Series on Insurance Law and Regulation 9,
https://doi.org/10.1007/978-3-031-47602-0_14

1 Introduction

The phenomenon of the current NewSpace era is the fact that outer space has become a territory where the direction of action is increasingly beginning to be set by private entities. The aforementioned segment highlights the trend toward the most modern and advanced technology, which creates the right environment for the development of competition among private entities. Consequently, the virtually unlimited exploration and use of space is associated with the occurrence of increasing damage and pollution to the space environment. A wide variety of space debris, i.e. old satellites, nonfunctioning satellites, jettisoned spent rocket stages, and other space objects, accumulate a huge stock of debris in outer space.[1] As of today, the number of debris tracked by the Space Surveillance Network and stored in their catalogs is about 32,300. However, the estimated number of explosions, collisions, and breakups resulting in fragmentation is approximately 640. The total mass of all space objects (including satellites) in orbit of the Earth is over 10,700 tones. [2]

Observation of the recent circumstances in space has prompted the international community to engage in extensive discussions regarding space activities in the context of environmental issues. They become even more urgent in view of the recent ASAT tests (direct-ascent anti-satellite (DA-ASAT) test) performed by some of the countries. An example of it can be the Russian ASAT test, in order to destroy a defunct Soviet satellite—Cosmos 1408.[3] As a consequence, thousands of new debris appeared in outer space, which threatened the astronauts on the International Space Station (ISS), forcing them to undertake evacuation measures. The destruction of one 10-tonne satellite can generate, according to the Union of Concerned Scientists,[4] 5000 to 15,000 debris pieces greater than 10 cm; 8 to 14 million debris pieces between 1 mm and 1 cm; and 250,000 to 750,000 debris pieces between 1 cm and

[1]Hutagalung et al. (2020), p. 1.

[2]*Space debris by the numbers* https://www.esa.int/Safety_Security/Space_Debris/Space_debris_by_the_numbers, Information last updated on 22 December 2022 (access: 16.04.2023).

[3]When destructive ASAT weapons collide with satellites, they can create thousands to millions of pieces of debris that can orbit the Earth for decades at extremely high speeds. According to the Union of Concerned Scientists, the destruction of a single 10-ton satellite can generate: (1) **8 to 14 million** debris pieces between 1 mm and 1 cm in size (2) **250,000 to 750,000** debris pieces between 1 cm and 10 cm (3) **5000 to 15,000** debris pieces greater than 10 cm. The debris from destructive ASAT testing adds to the **8800 metric tons** of space debris that is already floating around in space. Since space debris can travel at speeds up to **29,000 km/h** (roughly 8 km/s), even millimetre-sized fragments are massive threats to other objects in orbit. In fact, the International Space Station (ISS) has conducted **29** debris avoidance manoeuvres since 1999, which involve rerouting to avoid potential collisions with debris pieces. https://www.visualcapitalist.com/sp/anti-satellite-weapons/?fbclid=IwAR3F0tmIu1bw3QAMxUnRUJQBq_CW1AESinAvg8gqZEeITAj1rG0WhZ0Bi3s. (access: 16.04.2023).

[4]https://www.ucsusa.org/sites/default/files/2019-09/debris-in-brief-factsheet.pdf.

10 cm.[5] Another case that highlighted the problem involved a Note Verbale addressed to the Secretary General of the United Nations under Article V of the Outer Space Treaty (OST)[6] reporting two close encounters between the China Space Station and Starlink satellites launched by the commercial Space Exploration Technologies Corporation (SpaceX) of the United States of America. As a consequence of these events, for safety reasons, the China Space Station implemented preventive collision avoidance control.[7] Apart from the property damage that may be caused by the above, the debris floating in the orbit endangers more and more the future safe use and exploration of the outer space.

The existing liability regime included in the space treaties[8] and other instruments of international law does not fulfill its function when it comes to bearing responsibility for environmental damage caused in outer space. It is crucial to note that attempts to regulate the environmental aspects of outer space exploration and in particular the issue of space debris have not brought until today any substantial effects. No binding regulations in this area have been successfully adopted in spite of the efforts of the COPUOUS.[9] The need to create a coherent global approach for the protection of the space environment is still pending.[10] However, as the issue of

---

[5] *Anti-Satellite Weapons: Threatening the Future of Space Activities* https://www.visualcapitalist.com/sp/anti-satellite-weapons/?fbclid=IwAR3F0tmIu1bw3QAMxUnRUJQBq_CW1AESinAvg8gqZEeITAj1rG0WhZ0Bi3s (access: 15.04.2023).

[6] According to the Art. V of the OST, '[. . .] States Parties to the Treaty shall immediately inform the other States Parties to the Treaty or the Secretary-General of the United Nations of any phenomena they discover in outer space, including the moon and other celestial bodies, which could constitute a danger to the life or health of astronauts.'

[7] Note verbale dated 3 December 2021 from the Permanent Mission of China to the United Nations (Vienna) addressed to the Secretary-General.

[8] Treaty on Principles Governing the Activities of States in the Exploration and Use of Outer Space, including the Moon and Other Celestial Bodies, adopted by the General Assembly in its resolution 2222 (XXI), opened for signature on 27 January 1967, entered into force on 10 October 1967 (The 'Outer Space Treaty'); Convention on International Liability for Damage Caused by Space Objects, adopted by the General Assembly in its resolution 2777 (XXVI), opened for signature on 29 March 1972, entered into force on 1 September 1972 (The 'Liability Convention'); Convention on Registration of Objects Launched into Outer Space, adopted by the General Assembly in its resolution 3235 (XXIX), opened for signature on 14 January 1975, entered into force on 15 September 1976 (The 'Registration Convention'); Agreement on the Rescue of Astronauts, the Return of Astronauts and the Return of Objects Launched into Outer Space, adopted by the General Assembly in its resolution 2345 (XXII), opened for signature on 22 April 1968, entered into force on 3 December 1968 (The 'Rescue Agreement'); Agreement Governing the Activities of States on the Moon and Other Celestial Bodies, adopted by the General Assembly in its resolution 34/68, opened for signature on 18 December 1979, entered into force on 11 July 1984 (The 'Moon Agreement').

[9] The United Nations Committee on the Peaceful Uses of Outer Space. https://www.unoosa.org/oosa/en/ourwork/copuos/index.html.

[10] K. Malinowska, M. Szwajewski *Licensing Small Satellites In Modern World. Is 'Flag Of Convenience' Only A Legal Issue? Engineering and project management approach to the licensing requirements. Comparative Study.*

environmental risk is a legitimate concern, a growing number of states started recognizing it by referring to environmental damage in their space laws.

Apart from the basic space law instruments enacted separately by the states, there are several other standardization activities that, although staying beyond the strictly regulatory aspect, contribute to the gradual uniformity process of space activities, at least on a technical level. Examples of this include the initiative to set standards for all European Space Activities (ECSS), as well as the endeavors in the area of mitigating space debris, which on the global level took the form of the Space Debris Mitigation Guidelines, as well as the European Code of Conduct and even ISO standards for space.[11]

The authors' aim within this study is to present the current status of the legal framework on international space law in the context of the environment as well as on the level of EU regulations and national legislation. The increasing availability of commercial spaceflight has led to situations that require clear and consistent regulations. Therefore, special attention has been given to *de lege ferenda* postulates as the conclusions reached in this chapter can be used to formulate regulation proposals concerning liability for damage caused in the outer space environment. The other goal is to consider the insurability of environmental damage through compulsory insurance, which is an instrument of risk management adopted in the majority of those countries that enacted the national space laws.

2 Basic Notions and Concepts

2.1 Outer Space Environment

Hundreds of billions of galaxies are located in the outer space environment studied so far, consisting of tens or even hundreds of billions of stars. Some of them, perhaps most, are equipped with their own planetary systems. The best-studied and most familiar elements of space are the so-called near-Earth objects (NEOs). This term describes any comet, asteroid, or meteorite as a macro object that has the potential to collide with or fly past the Earth. These objects include those with a diameter of a few centimeters that burn high in the Earth's atmosphere and also those capable of causing huge explosions by penetrating deep into the Earth's atmosphere. The source of these types of objects may be those that arose from comets. However, they can come as a result of the collision fragmentation and the evolution of orbits of larger asteroid bodies located in the region of the solar system, in the main asteroid belt between Jupiter and Mars.[12] In accordance with the calculations of NASA JPL

[11] Malinowska (2017), p. 63.

[12] *'At this low end of the NEO size distribution the objects are thought mainly to arise as a result of **collisional fragmentation and orbital evolution of larger asteroidal bodies** in the main asteroid belt, a region of the Solar System lying between Mars and Jupiter approximately 2.1–3.3 times the*

CNEOS, the number of objects close to Earth in 2018 reached the number 17,459.[13,14] There are also astronomical sources outside the solar system that can significantly affect the entire outer space ecosystem. They are of particular importance in the context of cosmic explosions causing, among other things, cosmic rays, high-energy electromagnetic radiation, or radioactive nuclei.[15] The above shows the complexity of the outer space environment. However, for the purposes of this study, the authors focus on natural physical objects or those resulting from human activity.

A legal definition of the space environment does not exist in any international regulations. In addition, only a few countries included a mere reference to outer space itself in their national space laws. This implies that, from a legal point of view, various components of the outer space environment can be taken into account with reference to the activities undertaken by humans within the outer space exploration.[16] We can also try to apply by analogy the definitions of the environment worked out by the general environmental law, dealing with "terrestrial" environment. It can prove to be useful in the context of further analysis of the liability for damage caused in the outer space environment. As an example, the EU Environmental Liability Directive does not define "environment," but instead includes a definition of natural resources ("natural resources" means protected species and natural habitats, water and land). The definition of "environment" may be taken from some national jurisdictions (for example, in Polish law on environmental protection), where "environment" has been defined as a set of natural elements, including those transformed by man. In particular (i.e., this is an exemplary catalog—the most important ones), these are inland waters, air, land surface, minerals, plant and animal world, as well as both natural and human-transformed landscape and climate and other elements of biodiversity, including their interactions. Though this definition does not expressly include outer space, it could be taken as an analogy.

Nevertheless, before recognizing the elements of the space environment, it is worth identifying the spatial aspect of outer space. In this context, again it must be stressed that no international definition has been adopted, and what is more, lots of controversies appear in the doctrine. As a consequence of the many discussions at the forum of the United Nations, two main theories have appeared: "functionalists" and "spacialists." Functionalists (Stephan Meyer and N.M. Matte, among others) oppose the geographical division of space and believe that the basis for the division should be created by international aviation law based only on the range of aircraft. Spacialists, on the other hand, consider it necessary to make such a division since the

distance (1 astronomical unit, AU) of the Earth from the Sun. Some, however, come from comets, and the examples of Chelyabinsk and Tunguska illustrate both sources.'; see also Wilman and Newman (2018), pp. 17–19.

[13] https://cneos.jpl.nasa.gov/ca/ (access: 16.04.2023).

[14] Wilman and Newman (2018), p. 22.

[15] Wilman and Newman (2018), p. 82.

[16] Philip de Man (2016), p. 207.

problems affecting each of them are quite different and should be covered by separate legal regimes. The determination of the space boundary has remained an unresolved problem since the beginning of the so-called Space Age. It is not stipulated by the Outer Space Treaty. International organizations and UNCOPUOS have repeatedly put the topic on the agenda of their meetings but without results. States have not shown enough political will to finally regulate the issue in international law. As a result, only some of them have dared to adopt national regulations on the space frontier by law. As a result of the increased activity of states in space and the advent of the so-called new era in space—characterized by a growing number of small users among those gaining access to it—discussions on the space frontier are gaining importance. Also, in a survey addressed to entrepreneurs and professionals operating in the Polish space sector in 2021, there was no shortage of questions about the legitimacy of establishing a space boundary in law. One of the questions was as follows: Should a future Polish law on space activities set a so-called lower space limit, among other things, to ensure legal certainty? If so, at what height should it run?

The norms of the international agreements that make up the canon of international space law do not specify at what height above the Earth's surface (above sea level) space begins (the so-called lower limit of space). It is also difficult to decode any customary norm of international law (international custom) of a universal nature in this regard. "Only" conventionally it is assumed that the lower limit of space runs at an altitude of 100 km above the surface of the Earth, counting from sea level. Such a value is taken into account, among others (for its purposes), by the International Aeronautical Federation (Fédération Aéronautique Internationale (FAI)). According to the glossary of terms in the general section of the MFL Sporting Code (FAI), "space" should be understood as the space 100 km above the Earth's surface.[17]

In response to those disputes and mostly for practical reasons of licensing space activities, some of the countries have introduced the definition of outer space itself into their national space laws. Three of them, namely, Australia, Denmark, and Kazakhstan, took a spatial approach, referring to the distance of 100 km from the Earth as the criterion of applying space law. The South African law also defines "outer space," but in a functional way as it means the space above the surface of the Earth from a height at which it is, in practice, possible to operate an object in orbit around the Earth. The Belgian law, though it does not define outer space, in its definition of a space object and its definition of flight and guidance, refers to launching it on an orbital trajectory around the Earth or to a destination beyond the Earth's orbit.[18]

Apart from the definition of the outer space environment, the regulatory gaps on all levels (international as well as national) exist also within the elements that may form the outer space environment. In particular, the question arises whether it

[17] Kłoda et al. (2022).

[18] Malinowska (2017), p. 76.

consists of only the natural elements or also those that arose as a result of human activity in outer space.

New types of human activities in outer space, such as in-orbit servicing[19] or space mining, bring questions about the natural resources of celestial bodies being the component of the outer space environment. In that respect, we can also observe a lack of a commonly accepted definition in general international law. The legal concept of defining celestial bodies was proposed in 1966 as part of the work of IISL Working Group III and was as follows: "celestial bodies, in the sense of the Treaty, are all natural objects in outer space and within the solar system, the natural utilization of which by a State or group of states should not modify their natural orbits nor consume them."[20] Reference to this type of resource is made in the Moon Treaty;[21] Article 11 of this Treaty declares that the Moon and its natural resources are "the common heritage of mankind," which, however, does not result in providing an explicit definition thereof. A further reference to binding international law is found in Article 44 section 2 of the Constitution and the Convention of the International Telecommunication Union (ITU), which requires Member States to bear in mind that "radio frequencies and any associated orbits, including the geostationary satellite orbit, are limited natural resources." The United Nations Committee on the Peaceful Uses of Outer Space (UNCOPUOS) Subcommittee follows this type of language in recent reports.[22] However, this type of attempted wording is not specified and may raise many questions of interpretation.

Apart from the above natural elements, we have to mention the man-made objects introduced into outer space. In this sense, special attention should be paid to the increasing amount of space objects, which are no longer active ones and quite often out of control. The definition of debris has been first proposed in the Inter-Agency Space Debris Coordination Committee (IADC) Technical Report of 1999[23] and still seems to fit the goal. It was repeated in the UN Guidelines.[24] According to the Report, "space debris are all man-made objects, including their fragments and parts, whether their owners can be identified or not, in Earth orbit or re-entering the dense layers of the atmosphere that are non-functional with no reasonable expectation of their being able to assume or resume their intended functions or any other functions for which they are or can be authorized." In practice, space debris usually consists of parts of satellites or launch vehicles, including spent rocket stages, defunct satellites, collision fragments, lens caps, and even an astronaut's tool bag. Further debris is

[19] See more in Malinowska (2020).

[20] de Man (2016), p. 138.

[21] Agreement Governing the Activities of States on the Moon and Other Celestial Bodies of 18 December 1979.

[22] de Man (2016), p. 139, 141.

[23] Technical Report on Space Debris, Text of the Report adopted by the Scientific and Technical Subcommittee of the United Nations Committee on the Peaceful uses of Outer Space, United Nations, New York 1999 (A/AC.105/720) p. 2.

[24] United Nations Office For Outer Space Affairs, Space Debris Mitigation Guidelines of the Committee on the Peaceful Uses of Outer Space, Vienna 2010.

created by fragments from in-orbit breakups and degradation. The nonfunctioning feature distinguishes space debris from operational satellites and natural meteoroids that pass through Earth's orbit. The categories of debris include (1) mission-related objects (parts released during the mission operation); (2) fragments, including intentional destructions, accidental breakups during operation, breakups after mission termination, as well as in-orbit collisions; and, lastly, (3) mission-terminated spacecraft and rocket bodies.[25] The notion of space debris has also been stated in EU Regulation 2021/696, where space debris has been defined as any space object, including spacecraft or fragments and elements thereof in Earth's orbit or reentering Earth's atmosphere, that is nonfunctional or no longer serves any specific purpose, including parts of rockets or artificial satellites or inactive artificial satellites.[26] In addition, some of the countries attempt to define space debris in their internal space laws. This has been undertaken by, among others, the UK[27] and the UAE.[28] These definitions in general mirror or are similar to the concept included in the IADC,[29] United Nations Office for Outer Space Affairs (UNOSA),[30] European Space Agency (ESA),[31] or National Aeronautics and Space Administration (NASA)[32] guidelines.

To summarize the considerations in this section, it should be pointed out that there is no definition of the space environment in regulations at any legislative level. Nevertheless, for the research purpose of this chapter, the space environment should include both natural elements and space objects, including space debris. In addition, an important element of the considerations defining the space environment is the delineation of its spatial boundaries, a problem that generally does not exist on the grounds of terrestrial environmental regulation. The suggested concept of the space

[25] Malinowska (2017), p. 202.

[26] Article 2(4) Regulation (EU) 2021/696 of the European Parliament and of the Council of 28 April 2021 establishing the Union Space Programme and the European Union Agency for the Space Programme and repealing Regulations (EU) No 912/2010, (EU) No 1285/2013 and (EU) No 377/2014 and Decision No 541/2014/EU.

[27] 'Fragmentation debris' means debris that is emitted as a result of an explosion or deflagration; Implementing Act: *The Space Industry Regulations 2021.*

[28] 'Space Debris: A Space Object that has no role or purpose, or the remains thereof, and the materials, waste, or fragments resulting therefrom, whether in Outer Space, including the Earth's orbit or inside the Earth's atmosphere. Federal Law No. (12) of 2019 Issued on 19/12/2019 Corresponding to 22 Rabi' Al-Akhar 1441H. On the regulation of the space sector'.

[29] 'Space debris are all man made objects including fragments and elements thereof, in Earth orbit or re-entering the atmosphere, that are non functional'.

[30] 'Space debris is defined as all man-made objects, including fragments and elements thereof, in Earth orbit or re-entering the atmosphere, that are non-functional'.

[31] 'Space debris is defined as all non-functional, artificial objects, including fragments and elements thereof, in Earth orbit around the Earth or re-entering into Earth's atmosphere. Human-made space debris dominates the natural meteoroid environment, except around millimetre sizes.'

[32] 'Orbital debris is any human-made object in orbit about the Earth that no longer serves a useful function. Such debris includes nonfunctional spacecraft, abandoned launch vehicle stages, mission-related debris, and fragmentation debris.'

environment is pertinent for subsequent discussions on potential harm to this environment and the establishment of regulations governing liability for such harm.

2.2 *Damage to the Environment of Outer Space*

In the context of liability for damage to the space environment, the authors decided to characterize it, taking as criteria the sources and consequences of such damage. A wide range of national legislation refers to the concept of "damage," the comparative analysis of which also falls within the scope of this chapter.

Since, as previously noted, defining the space environment from a legal perspective is very difficult, it is useful, in the authors' view, to focus on the causes giving rise to such damage in order to examine liability. The sources of damage to the space environment include, among others, explosions, collisions, or aerodynamic breakups. These causes may occur in the course of launch operations, during satellite operations, and during prelaunch preparations. Due to the subject matter of this chapter, the authors focus on the consequences that may occur in the space environment.

There is a variety of threats to the space environment. They include explosions, breakups, or collisions of space objects. Explosions do not happen always during the launch, but they also occur after the separation from the launch vehicle, during the operation phase, or during the manned flight (e.g., Apollo 13 mission) or reentry (Columbia shuttle). Similar to the launch phase, when a satellite explodes in orbit, it typically leads to both complete loss of the satellite and serves as a significant contributor to space debris, potentially triggering subsequent collisions. Apart from the explosions, the breakup of the space objects in outer space causes further debris. The meaning of breakup is quite broad as it is usually explained as any event generating fragments, and from this point of view, it also includes explosions caused by chemical or thermal energy from propellants, pyrotechnics, etc. However, it is not necessarily related to an explosion and may occur without it, as an independent occurrence, for example, as a rupture caused by an increase in internal pressure, as well as a breakup caused by energy from collision with another object.

The risk of collision between two satellites or between a satellite and debris, though it is still perceived as low,[33] cannot be excluded and is recognized by experts as a growing hazard (especially if attention is paid to the context of the aforementioned Note Verbale addressed to the Secretary General of the United Nations). This is mostly due to the increasing amount of space debris, only a small part of which is trackable objects. The risk of collision is usually assessed by the launching states at

[33] The level of the risk of space debris can be a bit misleading. It is still calculated as low when the probability factor is taken into account on an equal basis with the severity of consequences. Such an approach needs to be changed, as a part of the changing perception of the black swan risks. As recent history shows, the black swan events may affect whole civilization and they should not be ignored only due to the not so high probability.

every phase of the mission. As analyses show, there are several collision alerts yearly, meaning that at least a conjunction between satellites is threatening. However, it should be noted that collision avoidance measures are mainly taken for satellites placed in the LEO,[34] as well as for the International Space Station. The analyses show that the threat of collision can be increasing, along with the growth of a space object operating in orbit in spite of the improving precision in maneuvering. Collisions may be followed by the explosion or breakup (or both) of the satellite (s) involved. So far, the most famous collision occurred in 2009, when the inactive Russian satellite Cosmos collided with an Iridium 33 communication satellite, the effect of which was breakup and a debris cloud.[35]

Attempting to analyze the liability for damage in the outer space environment, firstly, it should be noted that the space treaties, including the Liability Convention, do not define environmental damage and, what is more, do not include the liability regime for environmental damage. The space treaties that would be the most relevant for analyzing the liability for damage are the Outer Space Treaty of 1967 and the Liability Convention of 1972. The reasons why they do not define damage to the space environment nor do they deal with liability for this specific type of damage are due to the time when the space treaties were negotiated and adopted. At that time, the problem of pollution of the space environment did not exist at all due to the initial stage of human space exploration. Therefore, the treaties' definition of damage is very general and means loss of life, personal injury or other impairment of health; or loss of or damage to property of States or of persons, natural or juridical, or property of international intergovernmental organizations.

Thus, for a general understanding of environmental damage, it seems appropriate to refer to the definition contained in the Regulation of the European Parliament and of the Council of 11 July 2007 (Rome II). Recital 24 of the Rome II Preamble provides a definition of environmental damage, which *should be understood as meaning adverse change in a natural resource, such as water, land or air, impairment of a function performed by that resource for the benefit of another natural resource or the public, or impairment of the variability among living organisms.*

Defining the concept of damage in space-law-related legislation has been undertaken, among others, by Australia, Belgium, and Indonesia. In the context of the first two countries, damage is defined with reference to the Liability Convention (as mentioned above). In the case of Australia, some dualism has been introduced; i.e., damage in relation to a space object has the same meaning as in the Liability Convention, while in relation to a high-powered rocket, it "means loss of life, personal injury or other impairment of health or loss of or damage to property of persons."[36] Belgium, on the other hand, in addition to defining damage in the manner laid down in Article 1 LC, introduces, by law, the liability of the Belgian state, which, for such damage, extends to Belgian citizens, whether they are natural

---

[34] *Low Earth Orbit.*

[35] Malinowska (2017), pp. 216–219.

[36] Space (Launches and Returns) Act 2018.

or legal persons (with the exception of persons participating in the activities in question).[37] Indonesia defines damage as "any condition that results in loss of life, bodily injury or other damage to health, as well as loss of or damage to state property or to natural and legal persons and the property of international intergovernmental organizations."[38] The country that refers to environmental damage is France, which includes in its definition damage to, inter alia, the environment.[39]

3 Liability for Damages in the Outer Space Environment: International Framework

The most important treaties related to aspects of the space environment that the authors believe should be highlighted are the Outer Space Treaty (OST), the Liability Convention (LC), and the Convention on Registration of Objects Launched into Outer Space (RC).

3.1 Outer Space Treaty (OST)

The initial regulations of the OST Treaty provide for general principles regarding the freedom of exploring outer space for the benefit and interests of all countries. However, this freedom is subject to certain limitations.[40] The first sentence of Article IX states that "In the exploration and use of outer space, including the Moon and other celestial bodies, States Parties to the Treaty shall be guided by the principle of co-operation and mutual assistance and shall conduct all their activities in outer space, including the Moon and other celestial bodies, with due regard to the corresponding interests of all other States Parties to the Treaty." One of such constraints is the issue of environmental protection, where States Parties to the Treaty are obliged to conduct space research and the exploration of celestial bodies in such a way as to avoid their harmful contamination and adverse changes in the Earth's natural environment (as a result of the introduction of extraterrestrial matter), taking appropriate measures, if necessary. In addition, where there are reasonable grounds to conclude that an activity may cause "potentially harmful interference with activities of other States Parties," it is possible to request a consultation regarding such activity. OST refers to the issue of liability in Article VII, which provides for general international liability for the damage caused by a space object,

[37] Loi du 17 septembre 2005 relative aux activités de lancement, d'opération de vol ou de guidage d'objets spatiaux.

[38] Undang-undang tentang keantariksaan. [Law No. 21 of 2013 on Space Activities].

[39] Loi relative aux operations spatiales.

[40] Hutagalung et al. (2020), p. 4.

as does Article VI, which stipulates that "States Parties to the Treaty shall bear international responsibility for national activities in outer space."

The approach taken by the Outer Space Treaty causes the imposition of all international obligations on States Parties in order to ensure that private entities act in accordance with the OST.[41] The Treaty "provides for comprehensive international liability for damage caused by a space object, but is the framework convention."[42] The fundamental principles of the OST were expanded in the Liability Convention, according to which the signatory states are responsible for all acts and omissions of all their natural or juridical persons and of their government agencies.[43]

3.2 *Liability Convention (LC)*

The legal regime providing compensation for damage caused by space objects has been established in the Liability Convention (LC). The LC in Article 2 imposes absolute liability on the launching state "to pay compensation for damage caused by its space object on the surface of the earth or to aircraft in flight." Liability for causing damage to the space environment, despite the broad list of situations envisaged in Article 1 ("loss of life, personal injury or other impairment of health; or loss of or damage to property of States or of persons, natural or juridical, or property of international intergovernmental organizations"), is very difficult to establish. What can be easily seen is that the enumeration of potential harm refers not to the space environment itself but to physical damage to property and persons.[44]

The core subject of the LC is liability for damage caused by space objects at any stage of space operations, which also includes launch operations, as long as it involves a space object being capable of inflicting damage on third parties. The broad scope of the LC sets out the liability for damage caused at any time in the space object's life, regardless of whether the space object is operated and under the control of its owner or whether such control is lost for whatever reason. However, it does differentiate the principles of liability depending on where the damageable effects occur. Thus, if damage takes place on the surface of the Earth or to an aircraft in flight, the liability is absolute, and "in the event of damage being caused elsewhere than on the surface of the earth to a space object, of one launching state or to persons or property on board such a space object by a space object of another launching state," the liability is based on fault. The universal value of the LC and its victim-oriented approach should be appreciated despite the fact that it has been applied only once since its adoption.[45] This is probably caused, among other

[41] K. Nakamura, *Space Debris and Liability Schemes under International Law,* p. 4.

[42] Dennerley (2018), p. 282.

[43] Manikowski (2006), p. 6.

[44] Pietkiewicz (2019), p. 219.

[45] This situation concerned the Canadian's claim against the Soviet Union for compensation for damages caused by the re-entry and crash in 1978 of Cosmos 954, the Soviet satellite. It was based primarily on the 1972 Liability Convention.

things, by the fact, that, at the international level, the liability for damage is attributed exclusively to the state fulfilling the prerequisites of being the launching state, regardless of whether the damage was caused by the state or by nationals remaining under its jurisdiction and cannot be enforced by private space entities.[46]

It should be emphasized that the Convention provides for liability for damage caused by space objects, and launching states cannot be held liable for the mere presence of orbital debris in space if no harm to third parties is caused. Consequently, it seems that there are no sufficient legal incentives to prevent this type of pollution, specifically by the production of orbital debris (i.e., debris or micro debris particles).[47]

3.3 Registration Convention (RC)

The subject matter of the Registration Convention relates strictly to the scope of application of the OST and LC. Its purpose is to ensure the legal effect of their provisions in terms of the safety of outer space exploration and enforcing the liability and responsibility regime. Thus, it does not enlarge or clarify the scope of application but refers to the above treaties. The importance of the RC for the practical aspects of space activity is introducing certain rules concerning the control, jurisdiction, and related registration requirements to be implemented by the launching states in their domestic laws.[48]

In the context of this Convention, it is important to emphasize the necessity of identifying a space object in order to assign liability for space damage. The issue of the space debris problem in relation to RC is explained by Howard Baker: "The extent to which provisions are made in space law for the identification of space refuse is determined by the extent to which identification of space objects is provided for under the Registration Convention."[49]

It happens that countries that have their objects in space are not listed in the relevant registers in this respect (due to a lack of appropriate regulation at the national level), which poses problems in identifying the "producers" of the space debris. In the absence of such identification, the Liability Convention is practically inapplicable.[50]

---

[46]Malinowska (2017), p. 22.

[47]U.S. Congress, Office of Technology Assessment, Orbiting Debris: A Space Environmental Problem-Background Paper, OTA-BP-ISC-72 (Washington, DC: U.S. Government Printing Office, September 1990). p. 31.

[48]Malinowska (2017), p. 23.

[49]Baker (1989), p. 55, 64.

[50]U.S. Congress, Office of Technology Assessment, Orbiting Debris: A Space Environmental Problem-Background Paper, OTA-BP-ISC-72,Washington, DC: U.S. Government Printing Office, September 1990, page 31.

3.4 UN Resolutions

Already in its 2000 Resolution (symbol: A/RES/55/122), the General Assembly recommended that more attention should be paid to all matters relating to the protection and the preservation of the space environment, especially those that could potentially affect the Earth's environment.[51] Furthermore, the resolution calls for continued research in the collision aspect of space objects, the development of improved technology for monitoring space debris, and the collection and dissemination of space debris data. Developing appropriate and affordable strategies to minimize the impact of space debris on future space missions has become an important goal.

The above assumptions were confirmed in the next resolution from 2013 (symbol: A/RES/ 68/74), which once again noted "the need to maintain the sustainable use of outer space, with particular emphasis on reducing the amount of space debris and ensuring the safety of operations in space and minimize the potential harm to the environment." In its most recent resolution adopted in 2017, the General Assembly recognized that space science applications and technologies that enable a better understanding of the universe and Earth and contribute to advances in environmental monitoring, among other things, have grown significantly in space-faring countries.

The resolutions of the UN are, however, not internationally binding instruments. They constitute only recommendations to the Member States but nevertheless have moral significance in terms of public opinion. According to the authors, the threat to the space environment, as well as liability for causing damage in the space environment, is not sufficiently addressed in the five United Nations space treaties. Over the past years, a number of guidelines and standards have been developed at the international level, specifically to reduce space debris. However, these are nonbinding in nature. In addition, many countries have adopted appropriate regulations and related procedures in their national regulations, so to some extent, an attempt has been made to apply international disaster consequence regulations to national space operations.[52]

---

[51] Resolution adopted by the General Assembly [on the report of the Special Political and Decolonization Committee (Fourth Committee) (A/55/569)].

[52] Steinkogler (2016), p. 212.

4 European Union and European Space Agency Tools for Protecting the Outer Space Environment

4.1 *Code of Conduct*

Environmental instruments have been developed in the European Code of Conduct for Space Activities initiated by the European Union.[53] The elements in the Code are consistent but provide more detail and justification relative to the Inter-Agency *Space* Debris Coordination Committee (IADC) guidelines. The Code applies to projects carried out by the European Space Agency as well as to entities in Europe and European entities carrying out their activities outside Europe. The voluntary implementation of the Code of Conduct should be applied also by national space agencies as well as their contractors. The Code also relates to all space systems and launch vehicles orbiting or intended to orbit the Earth.[54] "The aims of the measures and recommendations presented in the Code of Conduct are to preserve the outer space from the uncontrolled growth of space debris in the future, and to protect space systems from the hazard due to existing debris generated by past space activities."[55] This document provides numerous guidelines for management measures, design measures, and operational measures.

4.2 *EU Space Programme*

The new European Union Space Programme was adopted in April 2021 by the European Commission. The implementation of such a document was prompted by the need to increase the competitiveness and innovation potential of space industries within the EU by supporting scientific and technological progress. Special attention has been given to small and medium-sized enterprises (SMEs), innovative enterprises, and start-ups.[56]

Article 4, paragraph 1, subparagraph e, establishes as the objective of the program to "enhance the safety, security and sustainability of all outer space activities pertaining to space objects and debris proliferation, as well as space environment, by implementing appropriate measures, including development and deployment of technologies for spacecraft disposal at the end of operational lifetime and for space debris disposal." Special importance was also given to already existing programs, for

---

[53] https://www.unoosa.org/documents/pdf/spacelaw/sd/2004-B5-10.pdf access 23 March 2023.

[54] Popova and Schaus (2018), p. 11.

[55] European Code of Conduct for Space Debris Mitigation p. 2.

[56] REGULATION (EU) 2021/696 OF THE EUROPEAN PARLIAMENT AND OF THE COUNCIL of 28 April 2021 establishing the Union Space Programme and the European Union Agency for the Space Programme and repealing Regulations (EU) No 912/2010, (EU) No 1285/2013 and (EU) No 377/2014 and Decision No 541/2014/EU.

example, COPERNICUS, which aims to provide autonomous access to knowledge by supporting the Union in taking independent decisions and actions in the field of, inter alia, the environment. The program implements space activities in Earth observation, satellite navigation, space research, innovation, and connectivity as well as establishes the European Union Agency for the Space Programme (EUSPA).

5 National Space Laws

5.1 Bottom-Up Universalism on the Level of Principles?

As the issue of environmental risk is a legitimate concern, a growing number of states refer to environmental damage in their space laws. Examples of this can be found in France, Kazakhstan, Belgium, and the Netherlands. In the absence of strict legal measures that enforce financial accountability for environmental harm, the technical regulations governing space operations permits are intricately tied to environmental considerations, though their efficacy is uncertain. The launching states started to address the environmental issues at least with respect to debris mitigation, managed at the stage of the authorization process. Such management regulations at various regulatory levels exist in Austria, Belgium, France, Hong Kong, Argentina, etc.[57]

The provision of Article 10 of the Dutch Rules Concerning Space Activities can be taken as an example. It states that "if an incident occurs or has occurred that may jeopardize the safety of persons and goods, environmental protection in outer space, the maintenance of public order or national security, or otherwise cause damage, the license-holder shall take the steps to limit or mitigate the damage to the extent possible." However, it is not clear, in the context of incurring liability for environmental damage, whether there is an obligation to compensate for such damage, in particular because the duty to compensate arising from a recourse claim by the state responsible under international law does not extend to environmental damage. [58]

Closely related to environmental aspects are the technical rules concerning authorization for space operations. The criteria for licensing space operations and the associated environmental prerequisites are grounded in regulations such as those in Belgium. These regulations outline the conditions for obtaining a license for space missions, emphasizing the operator's responsibility to implement fundamental environmental precautions. In Belgian law, prior to the issuance of a permit, appropriate examinations are carried out by one or more experts. Such preliminary examination is carried out to assess the potential environmental impacts in space or on Earth. The Hong Kong regulation[59] is of a similar shape; the obtained license may in particular

[57] Malinowska (2017), p. 228.

[58] Carpanelli and Cohen (2013), http://www.iislweb.org/docs/Diederiks2013.pdf.

[59] Cap. 523 Outer Space Ordinance.

contain conditions obliging the licensee to conduct its activities in such a way as to prevent the contamination of outer space or unfavorable changes in the Earth's environment. In Austrian law,[60] a permit is issued if "the space activity does not cause harmful contamination of outer space or celestial bodies or adverse changes in the environment." In Kazakhstan's Law on Space Activities,[61] environmental regulations are much more extensive. Compensation for environmental damages resulting from space activities, according to Kazakh law, is provided on a voluntary basis or on the basis of a court decision in accordance with the laws of the Republic of Kazakhstan.[62] Regulations of the Law on Space Activities refer to the environmental legislation of the Republic of Kazakhstan imposing on participants of space activities the obligation to conduct production environmental control.[63] One novelty among national space regulations deserves attention, namely, the ban on the use of space hardware and (or) stellar bodies for negative impacts on the environment.[64]

This type of regulation is also contained in Indonesian Law Number 21/ 2013 on Space Activities. Article 8(e) states that "Space Activities are prohibited to: [...] conduct activities that may cause contamination and/or damages to the Earth and Space environment as well as harmful to the Space Activities including the destruction of Space Objects." Nevertheless, Indonesian law lacks the practical conditions necessary to prevent such pollution because space regulations do not incorporate policies to prevent the harmful potentials of, among others, space debris.[65]

A visible problem that arises is the lack of binding regulations at the national level or a clear implementation of the already existing guides issued by international initiatives[66] on how to prevent pollution of the space environment and what detailed steps to take when such pollution occurs. Countries are trying to meet this challenge by introducing technical procedures in their implementing legislation.

5.2 *Technical Requirements and Guidelines*

The consequence of the current status of international law is that there are no coherent technical patterns of sufficient granularity that would incentivize the protection of the outer space environment. This causes the launching states to adopt various (or no) definitions of the spacecraft, notion of space debris and decide on adoption of the prevention and mitigation measures on the national level. No

[60] Bundesgesetz über die Genehmigung von Weltraumaktivitäten und die Einrichtung eines Weltraumregisters (Weltraumgesetz).

[61] Law of the Republic of Kazakhstan on Space Activities (No.528-IV of 6 January 2012).

[62] Ibidem.

[63] Ibidem. Art. 28.

[64] Ibidem. Art. 30.

[65] Hutagalung et al. (2020), p. 5.

[66] Initiatives such as IADC, ISO.

coherence on including small satellites in the regime is observed. Though all space-faring states should be interested in adopting similar measures and tools, enabling the avoidance of liability based on fault (if the damage is caused in outer space—according to the LC), it is an insufficient argument, and the practice shows that no international coherence in this respect leads rather to the diversification of the requirements and flags of convenience (India case).[67] This in turn proves to be counter-effective on a global scale.

On the international level, we have to base solely on nonbinding instruments, such as rules adopted by the IADC or the 2007 UNCOPUOS Space Debris Mitigation Guidelines. Looking at the scope of application of the guidelines, first, the scope of application should be distinguished. "The IADC Space Debris Mitigation Guidelines are applicable to mission planning and the design and operation of spacecraft and orbital stages that will be injected into Earth orbit. Organisations are encouraged to use these Guidelines in identifying the standards that they will apply when establishing the mission requirements for planned spacecraft and orbital stages. Operators of existing spacecraft and orbital stages are encouraged to apply these guidelines to the greatest extent possible."

Such nonbinding instruments at the international level are the COPUOS—Space Debris Mitigation Guidelines[68] and the IADC Guidelines. However, the lack of homogenous technical patterns causes decisions to adopt mitigation and preventive measures, which must be taken at the national level. The lack of a solution to the problem at the international level results, however, in a lack of consistency between countries in terms of technical criteria for avoiding and mitigating risks from space debris, among other things. An example of a solution to this issue would be missions launched by NASA and ESA as these entities adopted clear criteria to that effect.[69] The guidelines also provide general guidance for action to be taken by satellite operators in order to implement the goal of preventing and minimizing debris. Emphasis has been placed on the need for organizations, in the planning and operation of spacecraft and orbital stages, to systematically incorporate measures for mitigating space debris throughout the life cycle of the spacecraft or orbital stage. This includes integrating such mitigation measures from the initial mission requirement analysis and definition phases. In order to manage the implementation of space debris mitigation measures, it is recommended that a feasible Space Debris Mitigation Plan be established and documented for each program and project. The Mitigation Plan should include the following items: (1) a management plan addressing space debris mitigation activities, and (2) a plan for the assessment and mitigation of risks related to space debris, including applicable standards. No further criteria for

[67] https://spacelaws.com/articles/space-licensing-in-india/. (access 16.04.2023).

[68] Space Debris Mitigation Guidelines of the Committee on the Peaceful Uses of Outer Space, endorsed by the Committee on the Peaceful Uses of Outer Space at its fiftieth session and contained in A/62/20 Minutes.

[69] K. Malinowska, M. Szwajewski, *Licensing Small Satellites In Modern World. Is 'Flag Of Convenience' Only A Legal Issue? Engineering and project management approach to the licensing requirements. Comparative Study.*

assessment were proposed. Having this in mind, the guidelines, although useful as a first step, cannot be regarded as a sufficient tool. Their general nature can only indicate the path to be followed by much more specific technical tools.

If we, however, look at the technical regulations on a global level, we can easily notice that apart from some attempts to regulate the issue of space debris, there is a general lack of any rules in this respect. Even the soft model of ADR (active debris removal) guidelines is too general to ensure a coherent global approach to ADR. Therefore, there is a need to investigate not only statutory laws but also licensing requirements on the technical level.

6 Space Insurance as a Tool for Incentivizing the Protection of the Outer Space Environment

Insurance has always been one of the most important methods of risk management. This has also been the case in the space sector. As the list of national space legislation grows longer, so does the demand for liability insurance for damages caused by space objects, including space debris resulting from space exploration. Indeed, liability insurance is becoming, in the vast majority of these legislation pieces, one of the basic conditions for obtaining a license for space activities. Thus, as a condition for carrying out space activities, it is usually a requirement for the operator to take out liability insurance and maintain coverage throughout the period of carrying out licensed activities. The insurance is intended to protect the interests of the state, in particular, against incurring the high costs of improper space activities of private entities. In view of such a specifically defined purpose of space object liability insurance, its scope will generally coincide with the content of the operator's, and usually the state's, obligation under the provisions of the Liability Convention. And with a broad approach to the definition of damage and increasing attention to space pollution, insurers will soon face the dilemma of covering damage resulting from the dramatically increasing number of space debris in orbit. This, in turn, may give rise to more vigorous efforts to not only prevent the creation of new space junk but also to remove existing ones.

Already, initiatives in this regard (in-orbit servicing leading to bringing space junk to earth and repairing active satellites) are supported by insurers.[70] Still, however, space debris as a source of space environmental damage is a silent risk due to the deficiencies of the environmental liability regime in the space sector. Recent works on sustainability in outer space exploration will hopefully bring an expected change, and space insurers will also have a chance of contributing to reversing the trend. This can be achieved in a way that is not even tied to specific regulations (except for the imposition of insurance), but through bottom-up action by insurers. These actions can consist of assessing risks based on technological

[70] See more Malinowska (2020).

standards aimed at avoiding the generation of space junk, and as a result, insurers propose insurance terms, including premiums, appropriate to the amount of risk. In extreme cases, insurers, deeming the risk of generating space junk too high, may deny coverage. Insurers thus have a chance to play an important role as market regulators.

7 Conclusions

Within the *Corpus Iuris Spatialis*, regulations regarding the space environment, especially in the context of liability for damages caused therein, are negligible and very general. Efforts at the United Nations, European, and national levels are progressing towards safeguarding the outer space environment. This is in response to the significant accumulation of space debris in Earth's orbit, coupled with an evolving commitment to sustainable development. An important aspect coming to the fore is not only the question of liability but also the definition of what the space environment is and for which specific actions liability should be borne. The delimitation of space and the analogy with environmental law may be helpful, but the space sector, which is a very specific and challenging area from various perspectives, requires an interdisciplinary approach and an appropriate interpretation of the definition of damage to the space environment. Finally, insurance as an important risk management instrument has become common in most of those countries that have enacted national space laws. Współpraca

References

Baker HA (1989) Space debris: law and policy in the United States. Univ Colo Law Rev 60:55, 64

Carpanelli E, Cohen B (2013) Interpreting 'Damage Caused by Space Objects' under the 1972 Liability Convention. Proceedings of International Institute of Space Law, Eleven International Publishing, Beijing, China, 2013., http://www.iislweb.org/docs/Diederiks2013.pdf

de Man P (2016) Exclusive use in an inclusive environment the meaning of the non-appropriation principle for space resource exploitation. Springer, Leuven, p 207

Dennerley JA (2018) State liability for space object collisions: the proper interpretation of 'fault' for the purposes of international space law. Eur J Int Law 29(1):282

Hutagalung JM, Tobing CI, Debastria J, Amanda RT (2020) Space debris as environmental threat and the requirement of Indonesia's prevention regulation. IOP Publishing

Kłoda MT, Malinowska K, Malinowski B, Polkowska M (2022) Polskie prawo kosmiczne – wyzwania i kompromisy [Polish space law – challenges and trade-offs]. Przegląd Sejmowy 3/2022

Malinowska K (2017) Space insurance. International legal aspects. Wolters Kluwer, The Netherlands

Malinowska K (2020) Risk management and insurance of on-orbit servicing. In: Frollich A (ed) On-orbit servicing: next generation of space activities. Studies in space policy, vol 26. Springer, Cham. https://doi.org/10.1007/978-3-030-51559-1_2

Malinowska K, Szwajewski M. Licensing Small Satellites In Modern World. Is 'Flag Of Convenience' Only A Legal Issue? Engineering and project management approach to the licensing requirements. Comparative Study
Manikowski P (2006) Examples of space damages in the light of international space law. Poznań University of Economics, p 6
Pietkiewicz M (2019) Protection of the space environment against space debris pollution. Uniwersytet Warmińsko-Mazurski w Olsztynie, p 219
Popova R, Schaus V (2018) The legal framework for space debris remediation as a tool for sustainability in outer space
Steinkogler C (2016) Small satellites and space debris mitigation. In: Marboe I (ed) Small satellites: regulatory challenge and chances. Brill Nijhoff, Leiden
U.S. Congress, Office of Technology Assessment, Orbiting Debris: A Space Environmental Problem-Background Paper, OTA-BP-ISC-72,Washington, DC: U.S. Government Printing Office, September 1990
Wilman RJ, Newman CJ (2018) Frontiers of space risk, natural cosmic hazards & societal challenges. Taylor & Francis Group, United States

Liability for Pollution Damage to the Marine Environment

Dorota Pyć

> If anyone intentionally spoils the water of another . . . let him not only pay damages, but purify the stream or cistern which contains the water—*Plato.*

Abstract This chapter discusses some aspects of liability for pollution damage caused to the marine environment, focusing on the general obligations developed mainly under the law of the sea, which requires States to take measures to prevent, reduce, and control the pollution of the marine environment. The United Nations Convention on the Law of the Sea (UNCLOS) reaffirms the principle of civil liability of natural and legal persons for marine pollution, but it is the responsibility of States to ensure that claims are pursued in accordance with their legal systems in order to obtain prompt and adequate compensation or to otherwise provide indemnity for the damage caused. Despite nearly three decades from the entry into force of UNCLOS, the obligation of States to further develop international law not only concerning international responsibility but also civil liability is still extremely valid.

D. Pyć (✉)
University of Gdańsk, Faculty of Law and Administration, Maritime Law Department, Gdańsk, Poland
e-mail: dorota.pyc@prawo.ug.edu.pl

K. Malinowska, D. Maśniak (eds.), *Managing Environmental Risks through Insurance*, AIDA Europe Research Series on Insurance Law and Regulation 9,
https://doi.org/10.1007/978-3-031-47602-0_15

1 Introduction

Marine pollution[1] causing damage to the marine environment is a global issue.[2] The introduction of pollutants into the seas and oceans as a side effect of human activities on land, at sea, and in the air negatively affects the health and biodiversity of the marine environment. Undoubtedly, awareness of the complexity of pollution damage impacts the ecosystem of the World Ocean contributes to the development of methods of managing marine pollution risks through prevention, control, and responsibility. For many decades, special legislative attention has been focused on improving the legal instruments for the effective management of pollution from ships.[3] Oil pollution from ships is a particular threat to the marine environment.[4]

The widely perceived principle of preventing marine pollution is included in legal standards, mainly in international conventions.[5] However, it does not ensure the full and effective protection of the environment. Therefore, methods are used to introduce marine pollution management measures aimed at the ecological balance of the marine environment.[6] Moreover, the prevention of pollution causing irreversible changes in the marine environment is supported by the introduction of stringent standards in European Union law.[7] This chapter discusses some aspects concerning the importance of liability for pollution damage to the marine environment, focusing

[1] Definition of marine pollution for the purpose of the IOC Working Group is: "introduction by man of substances into the marine environment resulting in such deleterious effects as harm to living resources, hazards to human health, hindrance to maritime activities including fishing, and reduction of amenities," Report of SCOR/ACMMR Working Group 22 on Marine Pollution, p. 25, https://scor-int.org/Publications/WG22-1967.pdf; see also: Environmental Capacity. An Approach to Marine Pollution Prevention; GESAMP (IMO/FAO/UNESCO/WMO/WHO/IAEA/UN/UNEP), Joint Group of Experts on the Scientific Aspects of Marine Pollution, Rep. Stud. GESAMP, nr 30, Rome 1986, www.gesamp.org/site/assets/files/1207/environmental-capacity-an-approach-to-marine-pollution-prevention-en.pdf.

[2] Harrison (2017); Argüello (2020), pp. 101–118; Braverman (2023).

[3] The Annexes to the MARPOL Convention on the Prevention of Pollution from Ships divide pollution into six categories: oils; noxious liquid substances in bulk; harmful substances carried by sea in packaged form, sewage from ships, garbage from ships and air pollution from ships; https://www.imo.org/en/About/Conventions/Pages/International-Convention-for-the-Prevention-of-Pollution-from-Ships-(MARPOL).aspx.

[4] Faule and Hui (2003), pp. 242–253.

[5] Dow (1999), pp. 414–424; Attard (2016) *passim*.

[6] Laine et al. (2021), p. 112724.

[7] Case C-308/06: Judgment of the Court (Grand Chamber) of 3 June 2008 (reference for a preliminary ruling from the High Court of Justice of England and Wales, Queen's Bench Division (Administrative Court)) — The Queen on the application of International Association of Independent Tanker Owners (Intertanko), International Association of Dry Cargo Shipowners (Intercargo), Greek Shipping Co-operation Committee, Lloyd's Register, International Salvage Union v Secretary of State for Transport (Maritime transport — Ship-source pollution — Directive 2005/35/EC — Validity — United Nations Convention on the Law of the Sea — Marpol 73/78 Convention — Legal effects of the Conventions — Ability to rely on them — Serious negligence — Principle of legal certainty), OJ C 183, 19.7.2008, p. 2–3.

on general obligations developed in the law of the sea, which required States to take measures to prevent, reduce, and control the pollution of the marine environment and to specify the legal bases and premises for liability, as well as the methods of repairing the damage and compensation.[8]

2 Marine Environment

In a normative sense, the marine environment has not been universally defined to use this term in a unified meaning in international conventions. However, it is well recognized in the literature that the marine environment is the space of saltwater and the airspace above it, the seabed and ocean floor, and the subsoil thereof, which are inhabited by various species of fauna and flora, as well as other components, both natural and anthropogenic.[9] The marine environment includes the seawater (water column), the waters connected to the sea, the airspace above the sea, and the areas classified as sea basins, as well as the coastal belt. The marine environment is an area of economic activity (e.g., shipping, fishing and aquaculture, seabed mining, off-shore energy) and is regulated by international agreements that introduce norms, standards, and recommended practices of a preventive nature, aimed at reducing, preventing, and controlling the pollution of the marine environment.

3 Pollution of the Marine Environment

Historically, most marine pollution cases have involved ship-source spills of oil. An effective prevention of marine pollution is the implementation of preventive measures against shipping practices. The vast majority of these measures have their source in international conventions,[10] which require States Parties to implement legal instruments and enforce an efficient mechanism for monitoring compliance, as well as define legal sanctions when a violation of the law has occurred. Violation aimed at preventing marine pollution results in legal responsibility and liability. Standards specifying the obligation to prevent damage to the marine environment (e.g. as a result of pollution or marine pollution), i.e., preventive measures

[8] Liability and Compensation for Ship-Source Oil Pollution: An Overview of the International Legal Framework for Oil Pollution Damage from Tankers, UNCTAD 2012, https://unctad.org/system/files/official-document/dtltlb20114_en.pdf.

[9] Charney (1994), p. 883.

[10] E.g.: International Convention for the Prevention of Pollution from Ships – MARPOL; Convention on the Prevention of the Marine Pollution by Dumping of Wastes and Other Matter – LC; International Convention on the Control of Harmful Anti-fouling Systems on Ships – AFS; International Convention for the Control and Management of Ships' Ballast Water and Sediments – BWM; Convention on the Protection of the Marine Environment of the Baltic Sea Area.

(e.g. technical, protective, operational) and standards constituting the basis for inspection (by competent inspection authorities—flag state inspection, port state inspection), are the core of the legal structure in regard to the widely understood prevention of marine pollution. The obligation to prevent marine pollution is a minimum requirement of many multilateral international agreements. According to the law of the sea, States are required to take measures to prevent, reduce, and control the pollution of the marine environment from any source. According to the United Nations Convention on the Law of the Sea (UNCLOS),[11] these are those measures that are necessary to ensure that activities under States' jurisdiction and control are not causing damage through pollution (Article 194 UNCLOS).

The United Nations Convention on the Law of the Sea defines pollution of the marine environment as the introduction by man, directly or indirectly, of substances or energy into the marine environment, including estuaries, which results or is likely to result in such deleterious effects as harm to living resources and marine life, hazards to human health, hindrance to marine activities, including fishing and other legitimate uses of the sea, impairment of quality for use of sea water and reduction of amenities (Article 1(4) UNCLOS), and also contains some general obligations, *inter alia*, to: protection and preservation of the marine environment (Article 192), cooperation of States Parties to protect and preserve the marine environment (Article 197), provision of technical assistance to developing countries (Article 202), monitoring of threats (Article 204) and assessment of the potential consequences of activities in the marine environment (Article 206), the adoption of legislation by States Parties to reduce, prevent and control pollution of the marine environment from various sources (Article 207), ensure the implementation of regulations (Article 213) and the responsibility of States for failure to comply with international obligations regarding the protection and conservation of the marine environment (Article 235). UNCLOS contains provisions on the prevention, control, and reduction of the pollution of the marine environment from different sources and also for the mitigation of pollution damage.[12]

UNCLOS introduced the principle of responsibility of States for the fulfillment of their international obligations in terms of the protection and preservation of the marine environment.[13] It concerns the liability of States for damages caused by marine pollution, as well as the liability of States for damages resulting from the violation of the obligation to prevent marine pollution, including the obligation to adapt domestic law and standards to the norms of international law. States are responsible under international law. Preventive responsibility is related to the obligation to prevent damage, which also includes nonaccidental pollution (in some cases difficult to identify). UNCLOS reaffirms the principle of civil liability of natural and legal persons for marine pollution, but it is the responsibility of States

[11] United Nations Convention on the Law of the Sea, https://www.un.org/depts/los/convention_agreements/texts/unclos/unclos_e.pdf.

[12] Roland Holst (2022), pp. 250–252.

[13] Article 192 UNCLOS.

to ensure pursuing claims in accordance with their legal systems in order to obtain prompt and adequate compensation or to otherwise satisfy the damage suffered.[14]

UNCLOS refers to liability for pollution damages. According to its provisions, States are fully responsible for the fulfillment of their international obligations regarding the protection and preservation of the marine environment (Article 235-(1) UNCLOS). This requires ensuring the legal compliance of domestic law with international law (*inter alia*, with conventional legal norms), above all by indicating the entity obliged to repair the damage, specifying the legal bases and premises for liability, as well as the method of repairing the damage and the amount of compensation. States shall ensure that recourse is available in accordance with their legal systems for prompt and adequate compensation or other relief in respect of damage caused by pollution of the marine environment by natural or juridical persons under their jurisdiction. In order to provide prompt and adequate compensation in respect of all damages caused by the pollution of the marine environment, States are obliged to cooperate in the implementation of existing international law and the further development of international law relating to responsibility and liability for the assessment of and compensation for damages and the settlement of related disputes, as well as, where appropriate, the development of criteria and procedures for the payment of adequate compensation, such as compulsory insurance or compensation funds (Article 235(3) UNCLOS).

Preventive liability is a form of administrative (or administrative and criminal) liability. Administrative liability in environmental protection law is a legally regulated possibility of launching legal measures against a specific entity due to its activity that violates the state of the environment, implemented in forms and procedures specific to the administration. Moreover, administrative liability can be characterized as follows: (1) administrative and legal liability covers only those consequences of activities violating the state of the environment, which are formulated in norms; (2) liability is always subject to a specific entity; (3) liability can be tied and activated only due to the activity of a specific entity that violates the state of the environment; (4) activity violating the state of the environment should be understood as any harmful activity, even if it is legally permitted by the standards of acceptable pollution and/or an administrative decision; (5) the distinction of administrative responsibility is made according to the method of its investigation, and not according to the content.

The implementation of administrative responsibility is aimed at eliminating or limiting environmental pollution (marine, inland water). When determining the cause of this liability, the occurrence of natural damage to the marine environment is, in this sense, objective. Moreover, it is crucial to determine the state of the environment, including the extent of exceedances of permissible pollution levels specified by law and/or administrative decisions (impact on the occurrence of damage).

[14] Jackson (2005), pp. 74–95.

Table 1 The main international and EU legal instruments

	Marine pollution substances or activities	Legal instruments
1.	Persistent oil carried by a tanker that causes, or threatens to cause, pollution damage	1992 Civil Liability Convention as amended 1992 Fund Convention 2003 Supplementary Fund Protocol
2.	Bunker oil carried by any other type of ship that causes, or threatens to cause, pollution damage	2001 Bunker Oil Convention
3.	Hazardous and/or noxious substances other than persistent oil or bunker oil carried by a ship that causes, or threatens to cause, pollution damage	1996 HNS Convention and its Protocol (not yet in force)
4.	Activities of an operator causing environmental damage (or the risk thereof) within some specific zones not being covered by CLC and FUND	Domestic legislation transposing Directive 2004/35/EC (Environmental Liability)

Created by author

4 Damage to the Marine Environment (Environmental Damage)

The process of developing the concept of environmental damage and marine pollution damage itself began in the 1980s.[15] Their structural elements are characteristic of all the damages caused to the natural environment. The damage caused to the marine environment consists primarily of damage to fauna and flora (including the impairment of marine environment).[16] In this context, damage as well as pollution damage have been defined in several conventions; for example damage means any impact on the living or nonliving components of that environment or those ecosystems, including harm to atmospheric, marine or terrestrial life beyond that which is negligible or which has been assessed and judged to be acceptable pursuant to the Convention on the Regulation of Antarctic Mineral Resource Activities (CRAMRA, Article 1(15)).[17] Pollution damage means loss or damage caused outside the ship by contamination resulting from the escape or discharge of oil from the ship, wherever such escape or discharge may occur, provided that compensation for impairment of the environment other than loss of profit from such impairment shall be limited to costs of reasonable measures of reinstatement actually taken or to be undertaken (Civil Liability Convention (CLC), Article 1 (6)) (see Table 1). Ship-source oil pollution may arise as a result of major accidents, such as collisions as well as groundings, and also in the course of ordinary cargo operations, such as loading and unloading or bunkering activities at terminals.

Pollution damage means loss or damage outside the installation caused by contamination resulting from the escape or discharge of oil from the installation

[15] Brodecki (1983) *passim*.

[16] Birnie (1993), pp. 1–22.

[17] https://documents.ats.aq/recatt/att311_e.pdf.

and includes the costs of preventive measures and further loss or damage outside the installation caused by preventive measures (Convention on civil liability for oil pollution damage resulting from exploration for and exploitation of seabed mineral resources, Article 1 (6)).[18]

5 Liability for Damage to the Marine Environment

Liability for damage is understood as an obligation for the responsible entity to bear the costs of restoring the marine environment. Under the strict liability regime, this obligation does not require proof of negligence or regulatory noncompliance. Remediation is usually conducted by the entity responsible for the pollution damage to the marine environment based on an administrative or court order in accordance with a specific cleanup project. In a public health or environmental emergency, public authorities can directly proceed with remediation and then recover the remediation costs from the liable entities.[19]

In order to prevent environmental degradation and the loss of biodiversity in the European Union, as well as to regulate the issue of liability for damages, legal norms were adopted in 2004 to increase the level of environmental protection in EU Member States. Directive 2004/35/EC of the European Parliament and of the Council of 21 April 2004 on environmental liability with regard to the prevention and remedying of environmental damage[20] introduced the concept of environmental damage into EU law.[21] Directive 2004/35/EC is also applicable at sea. Environmental damage, as defined by the Directive, comprises damage to protected species and habitats (based on the Habitats and Birds Directives[22]), water damage (based on the EU Water Framework Directive[23]), and land damage. The Directive defines preventive and remedial measures. “Preventive measures” means any measures taken in response to an event, act, or omission that have created an imminent threat of environmental damage, with a view to preventing or minimizing that damage.

[18] https://www.iflos.org/wp-content/uploads/Convention-on-Civil-Liability-for-Oil-Pollution-Damage-Resulting-from-Exploration-for-and-Exploitation-of-Seabed-Mineral-Resources.pdf.

[19] EU States Claims Management Guidelines. Claims arising due to maritime pollution incidents, EMSA 2012, updated 2020, https://www.emsa.europa.eu/publications/inventories/item/720-eu-states-claims-management-guidelines-claims-arising-due-to-maritime-pollution-incidents.html.

[20] OJ L 143, 30.4.2004.

[21] Schütte (2019), pp. 459–460.

[22] Directive 2000/60/EC of the European Parliament and of the Council of 23 October 2000 establishing a framework for Community action in the field of water policy, OJ L 327, 22.12.2000, p. 1–73.

[23] Council Directive 92/43/EEC of 21 May 1992 on the conservation of natural habitats and of wild fauna and flora OJ L 206, 22.7.1992, p. 7–50; Directive 2009/147/EC of the European Parliament and of the Council of 30 November 2009 on the conservation of wild birds (Codified version), OJ L 20, 26.1.2010, pp. 7–25.

"Remedial measures" means any action, or a combination of actions, including mitigating or interim measures, to restore, rehabilitate, or replace damaged natural resources and/or impaired services or to provide an equivalent alternative to those resources or services.

The remedying of environmental damage, in relation to water or protected species or natural habitats, is achieved through the restoration of the environment to its baseline condition by way of primary, complementary, and compensatory remediation. Primary remediation is any remedial measure that returns the damaged natural resources and/or impaired services to, or toward, their baseline condition; complementary remediation is any remedial measure taken in relation to natural resources and/or services to compensate for the fact that primary remediation does not result in fully restoring the damaged natural resources and/or services; and compensatory remediesis any action taken to compensate for interim losses of natural resources and/or services that occur from the date of damage occurring until primary remediation has achieved its full effect.

"Interim losses" means losses that result from the fact that damaged natural resources and/or services are not able to perform their ecological functions or to provide services to other natural resources or to the public until primary or complementary measures have taken effect. It does not consist of financial compensation to members of the public. This Directive is not applicable to incidents falling within the scope of international compensation regimes.

6 Liability and Compensation for Ship-Source Pollution

6.1 International Liability and Compensation Regime

In 1967, the Torrey Canyon[24] oil tanker disaster caused a "culture shock." No one could believe that liability for damage caused by the oil pollution of the sea was dependent on the fault of the shipmaster (while liability for other accidents was usually based on the principle of risk) and that the amount of compensation was limited to amounts close to the value of the ship (which was with traditional principles of maritime law). Significant lack of public acceptance contributed to the abandonment of blame as the basis for the shipowner's civil liability for maritime accidents and the increase of compensation limits for victims of pollution. The new liability model was shaped by the system of conventions adopted under the auspices of the IMO (international compensation regime: CLC 1969/Fund Convention 1971[25]).[26]

[24] Nanda (1967), pp. 400–425, https://digitalcommons.du.edu/cgi/viewcontent.cgi?article=3788&context=dlr.

[25] Brodecki (1986), pp. 99–118, https://doi.org/10.1007/978-94-017-3707-4_4.

[26] Brodecki and Pyć (2009).

The international liability and compensation regime for persistent oil pollution damage from tankers was developed under the auspices of the International Maritime Organization (IMO). The International Convention on Civil Liability for Oil Pollution Damage (CLC) was adopted in 1969 to ensure that adequate compensation is available to persons who suffer oil pollution damage resulting from maritime casualties involving oil-carrying ships. During the work on the changes to the CLC 1969/Fund Convention 1971 compensation regime, in 1984 and 1992, the issues of the Amoco-Cadiz[27] accident were considered, which resulted in a change in the definition of damage. The changed definition of damage was based on the theory of the recovery of the costs of preventive measures or costs of reinstatement.

The international liability regime was established by the 1992 International Convention on Civil Liability for Oil Pollution Damage (CLC 1992), complemented by the 1992 Convention establishing the International Oil Pollution Fund (IOPC Fund) and the 2003 Protocol creating a Supplementary Fund with the same objective. After the Erika[28] disaster, and in particular the Prestige[29] oil tanker incident, the focus was on the 1992 Protocols to the CLC/Fund Convention system. The need to reform the regime was recognized, which aims at the acceptance of damage to the environment per se as "substitute" restitution; at changes in the concept of liability risk (balance of responsibilities); and at a significant increase in the amount of liability limits. The CLC-IOPC system covers damages caused by pollution resulting from the loss or dumping at sea of hydrocarbons transported by a ship. Marine pollution damages may also result from precautionary measures (preventive measures) taken to avoid pollution in the marine environment.

Payable damages are conceived broadly as (1) damages to goods, (2) the loss of revenue suffered by pollution, (3) environmental damages, and (4) pure economic losses resulting from the impossibility for the owners of nonpolluted goods to derive the usual revenues from their goods (the only applicable limitation to this type of damages pertains to the lack of a direct causal link between the economic loss and the pollution).

The International Convention on Civil Liability for Bunker Oil Pollution Damage (Bunker Oil Convention)[30] entered into force in 2008. It establishes a liability regime for the damages caused by bunker oil, which include damages resulting from both pollution and the impairment of the environment, as well as costs of preventive measures and further loss or damage caused by preventive measures (see Table 2.). According to the Bunker Oil Convention, liability for compensation is

[27] Gundlach (1989), pp. 503–508, https://www.oil-spill-info.com/Publications/1989_IOSC_Amoco_Cadiz_Litigation.pdf.

[28] Nolan and Foley (2008), pp. 41–78, https://www.hklaw.com/-/media/files/insights/publications/2008/12/the-ierikai-judgment%2D%2Denvironmental-liability-and/files/the-erika-judgment%2D%2Denvironmental-liability-and-pl/fileattachment/53490.pdf.

[29] London Steam-Ship Owners' Mutual Insurance Association Ltd v The Kingdom of Spain (M/T "PRESTIGE" No 5), https://www.bailii.org/ew/cases/EWCA/Civ/2022/238.html.

[30] International Convention on Civil Liability for Bunker Oil Pollution Damage, 2001 (the Bunkers Convention), OJ L 256, 25.9.2002, p. 9–16.

Table 2 Types of pollution damage costs

	International regime	Types of pollution damage costs (covered by international regimes)
1.	CLC/IOPC	- Cost of cleanup operations at sea and onshore - Cost of the reinstatement of the environment - Property damage - Economic losses by fishermen or those engaged in mariculture - Economic losses in the tourism sector - Costs of preventive measures to prevent or minimize such damage
2.	Bunker Oil Convention	- Cost of preventive measures and further loss or damage caused by preventive measures - Cost of cleanup operations at sea and onshore - Cost of the reinstatement of the environment - Property damage - Economic losses such as those engaged in mariculture, economic losses by fishermen, economic losses in the tourism sector, costs and losses for a harbor/harbor master
3.	HNS Convention	- Loss of life or personal injury on board or outside the ship carrying the hazardous and noxious substances caused by those substances - Loss of or damage to property outside the ship carrying the hazardous and noxious substances caused by those substances - Loss or damage by contamination of the environment caused by hazardous and noxious substances, provided that compensation for the impairment of the environment other than the loss of profit from such impairment shall be limited to the costs of reasonable measures of reinstatement actually undertaken or to be undertaken; and - The costs of preventive measures and further loss or damage caused by preventive measures

Created by author

exclusively assigned to the shipowner; it is automatic—with the same applicable exceptions as in the CLC-IOPC system, and it is guaranteed by compulsory insurance cover for vessels over 1000 tons. However, liability is also limited by the restrictions established in the Convention on Limitation of Liability for Maritime Claims (LLMC Convention). These limits should, in principle, cover any compensation claim for damages resulting from ship operations, in view also of current accident statistics, which show that pollution damages where LLMC limits proved to be insufficient have been relatively rare.

The 1996 International Convention on Liability and Compensation for Damage in Connection with the Carriage of Hazardous and Noxious Substances by Sea (HNS Convention)[31] covers damages caused by hazardous and noxious substances transported by sea other than hydrocarbons. It was amended by a Protocol in 2010. Based on the CLC-IOPC system, the HNS Convention also establishes two levels of compensation for victims: (1) on the first level, compensation relies on the

[31] International Convention on Liability and Compensation for Damage in Connection with the Carriage of Hazardous and Noxious Substances by Sea, 2010 (2010 HNS Convention) https://www.hnsconvention.org/wp-content/uploads/2019/05/2010-HNS-Convention-English.pdf.

liability of the shipowner, which is automatic and has a threshold of approximately 137 million euros that are covered by compulsory insurance taken by the registered shipowner; (2) if the latter is not responsible (i.e. Article 7(2)) or is in default or in case the liability threshold for the shipowner is surpassed, a special fund covers compensation up to approximately 300 million euros.

6.2 Preventive Measures

CLC Convention covers pollution damage resulting from spills of persistent oils suffered in the territory, including the territorial sea of a State Party to the CLC. It applies to ships that actually carry oil in bulk as cargo. Spills from tankers in ballast or bunker spills from ships other than tankers are not covered, nor is it possible to recover costs when preventive measures are so successful that no actual spill occurs.[32] The shipowner cannot limit liability if the incident occurred as a result of the owner's personal fault.

The 1992 Protocol also widened the scope of the CLC to cover pollution damage caused in the exclusive economic zone (EEZ) or equivalent area of a State Party. The Protocol covers pollution damage as before, but environmental damage compensation is limited to costs incurred for reasonable measures to reinstate the contaminated environment. It also allows expenses incurred for preventive measures to be recovered even when no spill of oil occurs, provided there is a grave and imminent threat of pollution damage.

The International Oil Pollution Compensation (IOPC) Fund, which governs the payment of compensation for pollution damage, relies on a common definition of preventive measures. "Preventive measures" means any reasonable measures taken by any person after an incident has occurred to prevent or minimize pollution damage. In practice, the term "preventive measures" means any reasonable actions taken with the aim of preventing or minimizing pollution damage in a Member State. The term usually applies to measures taken in response to spill and cleanup operations but may include salvage operations undertaken with the specific purpose of preventing or minimizing the loss of oil from a damaged tanker. The costs of repairing damage caused by cleanup operations may also be eligible for compensation, for example, roads or other access points damaged by traffic engaged in cleanup operations. Expenses for preventive measures may be recoverable even if no spill occurs, provided that there was a grave and imminent threat of pollution damage.[33]

[32] In the initial CLC liability regime, "preventive measures" means measures taken after the incident to prevent the occurrence of a new one (CLC 1969).

[33] Guidelines for presenting claims for clean-up and preventive measures, 2018 Edition, As approved by the 1992 Fund Administrative Council, acting on behalf of the Assembly, in April 2015, p. 4, https://iopcfunds.org/wp-content/uploads/2015/08/Clean-up-Guidelines_e.pdf.

6.3 Shipowner's Liability

A shipowner is entitled to limit his liability in respect of claims arising from pollution damage caused by his vessel. In this case, the convention regime becomes of significant importance. Some international conventions combine two legal regimes: (1) strict liability and (2) limited liability. The strict liability regime means that the shipowner is required to pay compensation without the need for the claimant to prove recklessness, negligence, or intention on the part of the shipowner. The limited liability concept means that liability is limited to a determined level. Relevant provisions provide for the mandatory insurance of the shipowner to cover his liabilities and for direct action against the shipowner's insurer. Liability limits in IMO conventions are expressed in Special Drawing Rights (SDR).

Under the 1992 CLC Protocol, strict liability applies to the shipowner, who is covered by compulsory insurance in accordance with the LLMC[34] provisions. The shipowner cannot be exonerated from liability, with the exception of cases of damages resulting from an act of war, a natural disaster taking the form of force majeure, or a third-party act committed with the intention to cause specific damages or of cases where the damage was caused exclusively through the negligence of the competent authority in charge of providing navigation assistance to the vessel during the exercise of that function. Under the 1992 CLC Protocol, a shipowner cannot limit liability if it is proved that the pollution damage resulted from the shipowner's personal act or omission and was committed with the intent to cause such damage or recklessly and with the knowledge that such damage would probably result.

6.4 Compulsory Insurance

The CLC requires ships covered by it to maintain insurance or other financial security in sums equivalent to the owner's total liability for one incident. The CLC applies to all seagoing vessels actually carrying oil in bulk as cargo, but only ships carrying more than 2000 tons of oil are required to maintain insurance in respect of oil pollution damage. For damages beyond the limits of the CLC or in the case of the nonresponsibility or the default of the shipowner, the IOPC Fund and Supplementary Fund will pay compensation to the victims. Under these regimes, liability exemptions are even narrower and apply only to circumstances of pollution resulting from an act of war or caused by a warship or a ship operated by a State for noncommercial purposes or in the case of a lack of evidence of causality between

[34]Convention on limitation of liability for maritime claims, 1976 (with final act). Concluded in London on 19 November 1976, https://treaties.un.org/doc/Publication/UNTS/Volume%201456/volume-1456-I-24635-English.pdf.

the ship and the damage caused or between the damage and the intentional act or negligence of the victim.[35]

7 Marine Pollution Insurance

Marine insurance is a financial instrument that guarantees the insured the minimization of negative financial effects through monetary compensation for damages resulting from various perils related primarily to maritime shipping and international maritime trade. Marine insurance belongs to the category of commercial property insurance but differs from them in terms of autonomous legal regulations. Marine insurance includes (1) property insurance and (2) civil liability. Marine insurance can be divided into (1) shipowner insurance (covering hull and machinery insurance, casco, liability insurance, and freight insurance); (2) cargo insurance; (3) builders' risk insurance (e.g., ships under construction); (4) fishery risk insurance (e.g., fishing equipment or planned catches); and (5) offshore insurance.

Currently, the 13 largest P&I clubs are associated with the International Group of P&I Clubs and insure about 90% of the world's fleet tonnage and 50% of all ships. As insurers, P&I clubs provide a very wide range of civil liability insurance related to shipping, cargo, collisions, and environmental and personal damages. Moreover, the P&I clubs conduct claim settlement proceedings around the world.

8 Protection and Indemnity Clubs

P&I clubs are shipowners' mutual insurance companies. Their name P&I comes from the abbreviation of the English words "protection and indemnity." P&I clubs provide insurance coverage for risks related to the civil liability of shipowners and other entities involved in the operation of ships. The rules of P&I club insurance differ from classic marine insurance: clubs as mutual insurance organizations are economic self-help organizations and do not aim to achieve profit (nonprofit organizations); the main purpose of the clubs is to provide insurance cover to shipowners (charterers), i.e., club members; the insurance is mutual, which means that each insured person is a member (shareholder) of the club, i.e., its co-owner and thus is the insurer; there is no fixed premium, and surcharges may apply; the club's liability is basically unlimited; and in the event of damage, the clubs themselves conduct negotiations with persons submitting claims against shipowners (charterers).[36]

P&I insurance is related to civil liability (protects against damages caused to third-party property by the traffic or in connection with the operation of the ship, not

[35] Sperdokli (2014), pp. 611–643.

[36] Anderson and de la Rue (2011), pp. 1257–1303.

covered by casco insurance), the consequences of accidents or diseases (provides compensation as a result of personal injury, illness, or loss of life to crew members or passengers), and risks of a different nature, such as the costs of keeping illegal passengers on board (stowaways) or fines for the violation of administrative or customs regulations.

P&I clubs are most often organized as legal persons in the form of companies, which are managed by committees composed of representatives of shipowners (charterers)—members of the club. The competencies of the committees include the day-to-day management of the club, the settlement and liquidation of damages, compensation payments, and making decisions on possible additional payments. In terms of marine pollution, insurance provided by P&I may cover costs and expenses incurred as a result of: (1) liability for loss, damage, contamination, costs and expenses; (2) any loss, damage or expense which the Member (P&I Club) incurs, or for which he is liable, as a party to any agreement in respect of pollution approved by the Committee (P&I Club), including the costs and expenses incurred by the Member in performing his obligations under such agreements; (3) The costs of any measures reasonably taken for the purpose of avoiding or minimizing pollution or any resulting loss or damage together with any liability for loss of or damage to property caused by measures so taken; (4) the costs of any measures reasonably taken to prevent an imminent danger of the discharge or escape from the insured vessel of oil or any hazardous substance; (5) the costs or liabilities incurred as a result of compliance with any order or direction given by any government or authority for the purpose of preventing or reducing pollution or the risk of pollution, provided always that such costs or liabilities are not recoverable under the Hull Policies of the insured vessel.[37]

9 Conclusions

The law of the sea regime for the global ocean and its resources (i.e., the marine environment) is based on the categorization and normatively established legal status of maritime areas, including the rules of their use as well as preventive responsibility. The contemporary law of the sea responds to changing global conditions, in particular with regard to the protection of the marine environment against pollution damage. The requirement for the rational use of the marine environment and its resources, technological progress, and the need to efficiently solve global problems in connection with the growing concern of the international community for the health of the global ocean,[38] as well as the need for the sustainable management of

[37] Rules of Classes 1&2, 2022, The West of England Ship Owners Mutual. Insurance Association, Luxembourg; https://www.westpandi.com/getattachment/9d902f6a-4592-4dd3-9a99-012399d90717/rules-of-classes-2022.pdf.

[38] Pyć (2023), p. 105328.

the sea, set the directions for the development of the law of the sea and the liability for damage regimes. Despite nearly three decades since the entry into force of UNCLOS, the obligation of States to further develop international law not only on international responsibility but also on civil liability and, if necessary, to develop criteria and procedures for adequate compensation, such as compulsory insurance or compensation fund, resulting from Article 235(3) UNCLOS, is still extremely valid.

References

Anderson CB, de la Rue C (2011) The role of the P&I clubs in Marine pollution incidents. Tulane Law Rev 85:1257–1303

Argüello G (2020) Marine pollution, shipping waste and international law. Routledge

Attard DJ (ed) (2016) The IMLI Manual on International Maritime Law, Volume III: Marine Environmental Law and Maritime Security Law., Oxford

Birnie P (1993) Protection of the Marine environment: the public international law approach. In: de la Rue CM (ed) Liability for damage to the marine environment. London, pp 1–22

Braverman J (ed) (2023) Laws of the sea. Interdisciplinary currents. Routledge

Brodecki Z (1983) Responsibility for Marine pollution, Gdańsk, *passim*

Brodecki Z (1986) Compensation in the Light of the 1984 Protocols to Revise the 1969 CLC and the 1971 Fund Conventions. In: Arroyo I (ed) Yearbook Maritime law. Springer, Dordrecht, pp 99–118

Brodecki Z, Pyć D (2009) Odpowiedzialność prewencyjna w prawie morza. In: Kozłowski A, Mielnik B (eds) Odpowiedzialność międzynarodowa jako element międzynarodowego porządku prawnego, Wrocław

Charney JI (1994) The Marine Environment and the 1982 United Nations Conventions on the law of the sea. Int Lawyer 28:883

Dow K (1999) Caught in the currents: pollution, risk, and environmental change in Marine space. Professional Geographer 51(2):414–424

Faule M, Hui W (2003) The international regimes for the compensation of oil-pollution damage: are they effective? RECIEL 12(3):242–253

Gundlach ER (1989) Amoco Cadiz Litigation: Summary of the 1988 Court Decision. Proceedings of the 1989 Oil Spill Conference. American Petroleum Institute, Washington DC, pp 503–508

Harrison J (2017) Saving the oceans through law. The international legal framework for the protection of the Marine environment. Oxford University Press

Jackson H (2005) Who is liable for Marine pollution? Personal liability for ship-sourced oil spills in four Australian jurisdictions. MLAANZ J 19:74–95

Laine V, Goerlandt F, Valdez BO, Baldauf M, Koldenhof Y, Rytkönen J (2021) A risk management framework for maritime pollution preparedness and response: concepts, processes and tools. Marine Pollut Bull 171:112724

Liability and Compensation for Ship-Source Oil Pollution: An Overview of the International Legal Framework for Oil Pollution Damage from Tankers Studies in Transport Law and Policy - 2012 No. 1, UNCTAD, New York-Geneva, 2012, pp 1–76

Nanda VP (1967) The Torrey Canyon Disaster: some legal aspects. Denv Law J 44:400

Nolan CR, Foley VJ (2008) The ERIKA Judgment - environmental liability and places of Refuge: a sea change in civil and criminal responsibility that the maritime community must heed. Tulane Maritime Law J 33:41–78

Pyć D (2023) Global ocean governance: towards protecting the ocean's rights to health and resilience. Marine Policy 147:105328

Roland Holst RJ (2022) Change in the law of the sea. Context, mechanisms and practice. Brill, pp 250–252

Schütte B (2019) Marine Pollution in the Arctic Region: What Future for Civil liability? - The need for a Comprehensive liability scheme, Patrick Chaumette, Transforming the Ocean Law by Requirement of the Marine Environment Conservation - Le Droit de l'Océan transformé par l'exigence de conservation de l'environnement marin, Marcial Pons, pp 449–465

Sperdokli E (2014) Marine insurance for Oli pollution. Tort Trial Insur Pract Law J 49(2):611–643

www.ingramcontent.com/pod-product-compliance
Ingram Content Group UK Ltd.
Pitfield, Milton Keynes, MK11 3LW, UK
UKHW020231290926
15470UKWH00002B/466
* 9 7 8 3 0 3 1 4 7 6 0 1 3 *